The Linguistic Atlas of the Upper Midwest, Volume 3

To Albert H. Marckwardt
In Memoriam, 1903–1975

THE LINGUISTIC ATLAS

OF THE

UPPER MIDWEST

In Three Volumes

by

HAROLD B. ALLEN

Volume 3 ● University of Minnesota Press 1976

Library of Congress Catalog Card Number: 72-96716

ISBN 0-8166-0789-3

CONTENTS

Preface

BACKGROUND

This book is about how people in five American states talk, the states known as the Upper Midwest—Minnesota, Iowa, North and South Dakota, and Nebraska. Specifically, it is about their pronunciation, and how different matters of pronunciation differ in different parts of the Upper Midwest or in different social groups. In this respect it rests upon a basic truth, that no language exists in a vacuum. When people use language to communicate, it is affected by a great many influences outside of language itself. Here the concern is how pronunciation is affected by where people live and where their parents came from and also by their social position in the community, a position which in turn is related to their education and their occupation. All these influences and others are behind the various differences described in this book.

Unless you are familiar with the phonetic alphabet, a first glance at some of the pages in this book might turn you off. There are some odd-looking phonetic symbols enclosed in [ ] or / / and there are some rather unusual technical terms. They have to be used, however, because unhappily there is no satisfactory way to write about pronunciation without the symbols or without the terms. The English alphabet, even when dictionary diacritics are used with letters, simply does not represent the minute variations in English speech, variations that often turn out to be significant differences between one region and another. Yet it is not difficult to understand the use of the symbols, and Chapter 1 gives you all the help you will need. The technical terms are usually defined or explained when they are first used, so they too will not block your learning about the speech of Upper Midwest residents.

This third volume completes *The Lin-guistic Atlas of the Upper Midwest*, a publication presenting the social and regional distribution of various features of the native English of 208 representative lifelong residents of the five states.

Volume 1 (1973) is in two parts. The first part treats the background of the project itself and the settlement history, the physiography of the area, the methodology of the investigation, the two questionnaires (worksheets for field interviews and checklists for the postal survey), descriptions of informants and their communities, and the patterns of speech distribution within the Upper Midwest. The second part deals with the vocabulary, that is, with those lexical and semantic items having regional or social significance within the Upper Midwest. Volume 2 is concerned with grammatical features. Volume 3 now offers an analysis of those features of pronunciation that are socially or regionally distinctive or may prove to be when further data emerge from research in neighboring areas.

The research project culminating in the publication of *The Linguistic Atlas of the Upper Midwest* began in 1947, with most of the fieldwork undertaken between then and 1954. It has continued, despite several protracted interruptions, up to the time of publication, with such assistance, financial and editorial, as is described in Volume 1. The Atlas project is independent financially and administratively, but it is closely associated with several similar investigations having their common origin in the never realized concept of a Linguistic Atlas of the United States and Canada. Although this huge enterprise never came into existence, its first phase was undertaken and completed under the direction of Professor Hans Kurath as the *Linguistic Atlas of New England*. It was published between 1939 and 1943 in three folio volumes (considered as six), with an accompanying explanatory volume, the *Handbook of the Linguistic Geography of New England*. Originally published by the American Council of Learned Societies, both the *Atlas* proper and the *Handbook* have recently been reprinted by the University of Chicago Press. The *Handbook* is invaluable as a background aid for using the Upper Midwest *Atlas*.

Also carried out under Kurath's direction was the fieldwork in the Middle and South Atlantic states, the data from which are now being prepared for publication by Professor Raven I. McDavid, Jr., of the University of Chicago. The first correlated but independent project was that for the North Central states. Fieldwork for the North Central area was planned and directed by the late Professor Albert H. Marckwardt of the University of Michigan and Princeton University. McDavid, who was to have been the associate editor of the North Central Atlas, has now accepted responsibility for seeing this project through to ultimate publication.

An early agreement among American linguistic geographers has led to the planning of related projects so as to make the ultimate publications easily comparable. Although only the New England survey has attained final publication, three derived books with data from the Middle and South Atlantic states have been accepted as guides for the selection and arrangement of most of the material in the Upper Midwest *Atlas*. For Volume 1 the guide was Kurath's *A Word Geography of the Eastern United States* (Ann Arbor, 1949). For Volume 2 the guide was E. Bagby Atwood's *A Survey of Verb Forms in the Eastern United States* (Ann Arbor, 1953). For the present volume the guide has been Kurath and McDavid's *The Pronunciation of English in the Atlantic States* (Ann Arbor, 1961). Unhappily, there is as yet no corresponding publication for the North Central States. An occasional reference to North Central data is directed either to the field records for Wisconsin, copies of which are in the Atlas office, or to Chapter 4, "Pronunciation," of Roger W. Shuy's doctoral dissertation ("The Boundary between the Northern and Midland Dialects in Illinois," Western Reserve University, 1962).

THE ORGANIZATION

In adhering to the general outline of the Kurath and McDavid work, henceforth identified as PEAS, I have found it desirable to make certain changes. The first two chapters of PEAS treat what here appears in Chapter 1: the system of phonetic representation, the theoretical base, and the general regional contrasts within the Upper Midwest (UM).

Then, because retention of post-vocalic /r/ in the UM reduces dialect variety and hence the space needed to describe it, there seemed to be no strong reason to devote a full chapter to the treatment of vowels before /r/. This treatment, Chapter 4 in PEAS, accordingly has here been incorporated with the preceding Chapter 3, on the diaphones of stressed vowels, as Chapter 2 in this volume. The favorable reception accorded Kurath's synopses, innovating full-page charts of the vowel systems of each cultured informant, has led to the extension of that feature here so as to include the vowel system of each of the 208 informants. The Synopses constitute, in fact, the major portion of Chapter 2, which describes the diaphones of the stressed vowels. In some small measure, the inclusion of all informants, rather than only the cultured ones, compensates for the absence of such large maps as those in the New England Atlas, maps bearing the full phonetic transcription of every item.

Chapter 3 in the present volume proceeds, like Chapter 5 in PEAS, to discuss the difference in the incidence of stressed vowels. But the small portion of PEAS's Chapter 5 devoted to consonant features is matched by an entire additional chapter here. A small hint provided by Kurath's one-paragraph notice of an excrescent /t/ on once and twice aroused my curiosity about other secondary phonetic details. The result is an elaborate and original expansion of the concern with social and regional variation in the behavior of consonants. Although such an extended presentation is not typically considered the function of a linguistic atlas, I justify its inclusion on the ground that the user of the volume will not otherwise have this information that adds its meaningful component to the fuller understanding of the dialect picture in the Upper Midwest. Furthermore, I should like to think, these data are of some significance to the sociolinguist who is willing to examine the whole American scene.

Chapter 5 offers additional findings not readily assigned to the preceding chapters.

The appendix gives the full transcription of the names of the communities in which the informants reside, the state and city names listed in the worksheets

for investigation, and those volunteered
local stream names that are of more than
passing interest.

TREATMENT OF DATA

The unfeasibility of trying to provide
the list manuscripts, that is, the full
phonetic transcription for every response
of the 208 informants, has compelled the
exercise of some discretion in selecting
and presenting details. In Volume 1 I was
able to indicate, through the use of the
assigned informant numbers, just who uses
a given lexical item without having to
give the word in full for each informant.
A similar practice took care of most of
the grammatical items in Volume 2. With
pronunciation, however, there may be not
three or four but twenty-three or twenty-
four variants for a given item, thanks to
the fieldworkers' finely discriminating
use of diacritics in their phonetic transcription. For example, consider the vowel in year. It actually turns up in the
field records with the following thirty
transcriptions: $+^<$, $+$, $\breve{+}$, $+$, $+^v$, $+^{\wedge}_<$, $+^<$,
$+^v_>$, $+^{\iota}$, $+^{<\iota}_>$, $\iota^{\wedge}$, ι^v, ι, ι, ι, ι^v, $\iota^v_>$,
$\iota^>$, $\iota^>$, $\iota^{\wedge\iota}_>$, $\iota^{\iota}_>$, $\iota^{\wedge\partial}$, $\iota\ddagger$, $\iota^{+<}$, $\iota\dagger$, i,
i^v, $\partial^{\wedge}_<$, $\varepsilon^{\wedge}$, ∂^{ι}.

Furthermore, in many other words, especially those with more than one syllable, the range of variation so expands
that to list each fully transcribed response is simply not possible within the
space available. The solution accepted is
bound to be less than satisfactory to
those few scholars who want to have before them such a complete record as appears in Harold Orton's *Survey of English
Dialects*, but the expedient resorted to
still yields a great amount of data for
further analysis. The expedient is,
first, to give only the phonetic feature
in question, say, the stressed vowel, instead of the entire word in which the
vowel appears. Second, the expedient requires "editorializing" in the form of a
meaningful grouping of the responses. A
first glance at the responses for year,
for example, reveals that such groupings
may be based upon vowel height, centralization, presence of retroflexion, and
length. A determination of which groupings are socially or regionally significant selects those in need of explicit
treatment. A subsequent decision answers
the question whether it is better to list
all the informants whose responses have
the specific feature, or only those with

unusual variants, or, with recourse only
to a general statement, none at all.
These decisions are so many that a re-
viewer of this volume will have a rich
field for the exercise of his craft, with
plenty of opportunity to single out those
decisions he considers unacceptable.

The listing of informants is by serial
numbers, not by name. They follow the
chronological order of the progress of
the survey in the five states: Minnesota,
1-65; Iowa, 101-152; North Dakota, 201-
226; South Dakota, 301-328; Nebraska,
401-437. At an early stage in the editing
reasons seemed sufficient for including
the five Canadian informants in the state
serial numbers, so that Canadian 1, 2,
and 3 are counted with the Minnesota informants, and Canadian 201 and 202 are
counted with those in North Dakota. More
recently, too late to change the system,
those reasons lost some validity. But no
great harm is done by the retained arrangement, for it does not materially
modify the percentages in those two
states and Canadian uses are always identified as such.

In order to render the *Atlas* more immediately useful to a wider circle of users
the listing of informants and the general
statements about social or spatial variation may be accompanied by simple frequency tables. But their usefulness will
be impaired if they are not used with
caution. A percentage figure indicates
the proportion of users of a given form
or pronunciation within the total number
of informants who respond with a particular item. For example, 49 of the 52 informants in Iowa may provide the word
tomato. If 21 informants pronounce the
word with a weak final vowel instead of
/o/, then the proportion is 21/49 or 43%.
Clearly, because of the inevitable subjective element in field recording, a
given percentage is hardly to be taken as
an absolute, nor does such a difference
as that between, say, 43% and 57% necessarily bear statistical significance. But
if similar percentages for similar forms
or pronunciations produce a cumulative
effect, then a reasonable inference can
be drawn and comparisons made with aver-
ages in other states. Such comparisons
can yield conclusions about both social
and regional distribution of variants.

Social comparisons are possible because, as explained more fully in Volume
1, the informants in American atlas surveys represent a social range. Type I informants are lifelong residents of the
community, native speakers of English belonging to the oldest generation and having no more than 8th grade schooling. Of

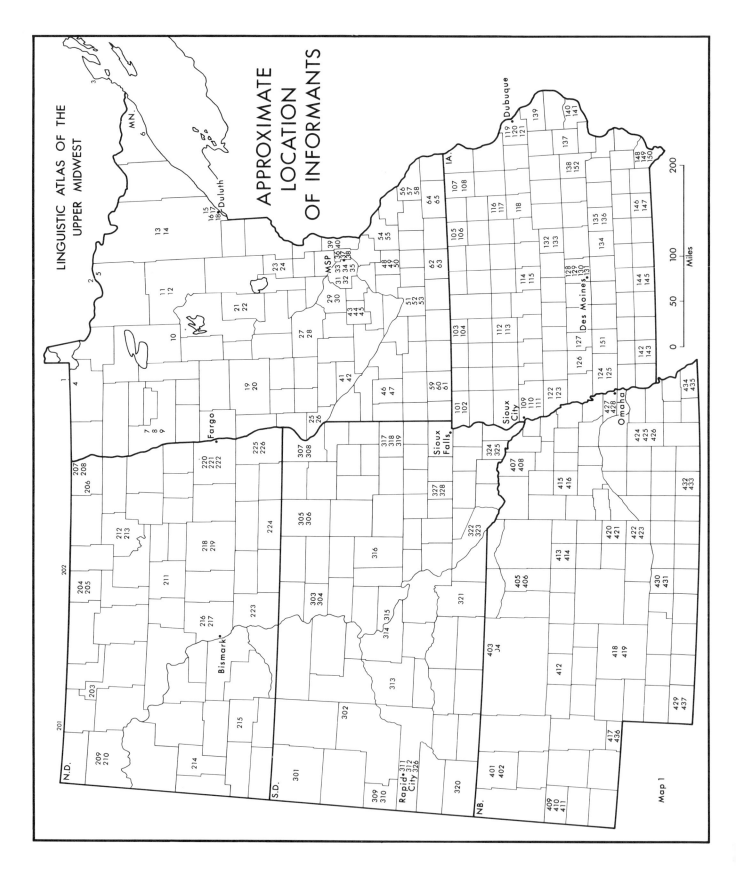

LINGUISTIC ATLAS OF THE
UPPER MIDWEST

APPROXIMATE
LOCATION
OF INFORMANTS

Map 1

the 208 informants in the Upper Midwest 103, or 48%, are best categorized in Type I. Type II informants are lifelong residents who have a high school education or the equivalent and who are generally between 50 and 60 years old. In the Upper Midwest survey 89 of the informants, 43%, are in Type II. Then in order to obtain evidence for what might be designated as regional Standard English, additional informants are interviewed who have graduated from an Upper Midwest college or university. There are 16 such informants in Type III, or 8%. They are usually about 40 years old. For each informant the year of the interview is given in Volume 1; the type classification of the informants is found in this volume on the pages of the Synopses.

The data from the three types of informants are found in the field records. For any one informant the field record consists of 76 pages of responses to about 800 questions, responses which are transcribed with a very narrow phonetic alphabet. The interviewer is a person with special training who seeks out the informant and conducts the one-to-one interview himself, usually in the informant's home. About one-half of the Upper Midwest interviews are accompanied by tape recordings of supplementary conversation in which the informant talks about such subjects as his childhood, his occupation, and the community. Further information about the field procedures and the interviewers appears in Volume 1.

USE OF MAPS

Although Volume 1 must also be consulted for a description of the informants and their communities, their location is shown on the adjacent map. The remaining maps in this volume, unlike those in PEAS, where they are grouped as a special final section, are distributed throughout the text so as to be with the relevant descriptions. Also unlike the maps in PEAS, the Upper Midwest maps arrange the symbols so that the horizontal line indicates various responses by the same informant, and the vertical row indicates different informants, usually with the Type I informant above the Type II and both above the Type III.

ABBREVIATIONS

A	Harold B. Allen (fieldworker)
F	figure (= map)
fw.	fieldworker
G	Virginia Glenn McDavid (fieldworker)
H	Frank Hanlin (fieldworker)
inf.	informant
M	Raven I. McDavid, Jr. (fieldworker)
NE	*Linguistic Atlas of New England*
NR	not recorded
P	Virgil Peterson (fieldworker)
PEAS	*Pronunciation of English in the Atlantic States*
UM	Upper Midwest
WG	*A Word Geography of the Eastern United States*
Wn	H. Rex Wilson (fieldworker)
Wr	Robert H. Weber (fieldworker)

RESPONSE LABELS

For a given pronunciation the informants using it are identified by their serial numbers, separated by commas except when a semicolon indicates a state division.

One or several of the following symbols, nearly all of them identical with those used in the *Linguistic Atlas of New England* and described in the *Handbook of the Linguistic Geography of New England*, may precede an informant's number, with meaning as indicated below. A symbol preceding a series, e.g., †135-39, is relevant to all the numbers in the series, 135, 136, 137, 138, and 139.

c	spoken during conversation
cr	correction by informant
cvr	recorded conversational response
f	response forced by fieldworker
n	normal for informant
r	form repeated at fieldworker's request
s	suggested and normal for informant
vr	recorded on tape
:	hesitation on part of informant
!	amusement shown by informant
?	uncertainty on part of informant
ɪ	heard in the community
†	archaic; old-fashioned
→	recently introduced; innovation
*	auxiliary informant
~	unchanged portion of repeated term

SUPPLEMENTARY BIBLIOGRAPHY

Since the initial listing in Volume 1 of publications based upon the files of the Atlas, only the following articles by me have appeared:

"Some problems in editing the Linguistic Atlas of the Upper Midwest," in Lorraine H. Burghardt, ed., *Dialectology: Problems and Perspectives*. Knoxville, TN:

U. of Tennessee, 1971. Pp. 54-78.

"Semantic implications of dialect research," in Don L. F. Nilsen, ed., *Meaning: A Common Ground of Linguistics and Literature*. Cedar Falls, IA: U. of Northern Iowa, 1973. Pp. 9-14.

"The use of Atlas informants of foreign parentage," in Harald Schaller, ed., *Lexicography and Dialect Geography: Festgabe für Hans Kurath*. Weisbaden: Franz Steiner Verlag, 1973. Pp. 17-24. [This corrects an item listed in Volume 1.]

"Principles of informant selection," *American Speech* 46.47-51 (1974 for 1971).

"Two dialects in contact," *American Speech* 48.54-66 (1975 for 1973).

APPRECIATION

The completion of this final volume has been effected with funds remaining from a welcome grant by the Graduate School of the University of Minnesota. I gratefully extend appreciation also to the College of Liberal Arts for the provision of office space since my retirement in 1971, to the department of geography for the excellent maps made by its cartography laboratory, and to the University of Minnesota Press for the personal and meticulous constant cooperation in preparing the manuscript for photo offset printing. And, as in Volume 2, I must thank Roberta Franklin for editorial help and for typing the entire difficult manuscript except the Synopses, which had been typed earlier by M. Joy Simpkins.

Harold B. Allen
Minneapolis, Minnesota
March 1, 1976

The Linguistic Atlas of the Upper Midwest, Volume 3

CHAPTER 1

Introduction

PHONETIC SYMBOLIZATION

The representation of the pronunciations treated in Volume 3 is in the International Phonetic Alphabet symbols with certain additions and modifications for use in American fieldwork. A full description of the phonetic apparatus appears in the *Handbook of the Linguistic Geography of New England* and should be consulted for more than immediate utility. But the selected descriptive details below, keyed chiefly to the *Handbook*, are adequate for practical understanding of the significant pronunciation differences treated in this volume. They may be skipped by readers with phonetic training.

A phonetic symbol stands for a feature of human speech interpreted by the hearer as resulting from specific articulatory circumstances. Although the physical articulation is not always observable, the correlation with the heard sound is so high that a trained fieldworker can easily translate the sound into a written symbol representing, say, what the tongue and vocal cords are doing at that instant. Of course, no speaker of English needs to peer into someone else's mouth in order to recognize the difference between bat and back or between bat and bad, even though he may be unable to describe that difference in terms of movements of the speech organs. But much finer differences turn out to be socially or regionally significant, and to record what he hears the trained fieldworker must understand the movements of the lips, tongue, and vocal cords and be able to symbolize them accurately with precise phonetic symbols. Such a symbol, standing for a specific kind of speech sound, is always enclosed within [ ].

Although some speech sounds are in a middle area, it is convenient to classify them all into two groups—consonants and vowels, the former in terms of points of articulatory contact or near-contact, and the latter in terms of the shape of the oral resonance chamber, the mouth, as determined by tongue-position, high or low, or front or back, or by lip-position.

Consonants

Consonants themselves fit into several overlapping categories, as shown on the accompanying chart. This chart is slightly modified from the basic consonant chart of the International Phonetic Association, with only those symbols included that are found in the Upper Midwest field records.

	Bilabial	Labiodental	Dental	Alveolar	Retroflex	Alveolo-palatal	Palatal	Velar	Glottal
Stops	p			t			c	k	ʔ
	b			d			ɟ	g	
Nasals	m	ɱ		n			ɲ	ŋ	
Laterals				l			ʎ		
				ɫ					
Flaps				ɾ	ʈ				
				ɺ					
Fricatives	Φ	f	θ	s			ʃ	χ	h
	β	v	ð	z			ʒ	ɣ	ɦ
				ɹ					
Frictionless continuants		ꜰ							
		ʋ							
Glides	(w)				r		j	w	
Affricates				tʃ					
				dʒ					

3

Each vertical row of symbols in the chart represents consonants in several categories based chiefly upon how the stream of air is completely or partly obstructed. Each horizontal row from left to right represents consonants in terms of the point of contact or near-contact from the lips back to the glottis, which is the space between the vocal cords in the larynx or voice-box.

Within two of the horizontal rows are subdivisions according to whether the consonant is voiceless or voiced. Voiceless consonants are produced without accompanying vibration of the vocal cords, and voiced consonants are those produced with such vibration.

Consonants can be broadly classified as either stops or continuants. Stops are made with complete blockage of the stream of air from the lungs. Continuants are sounds not marked by complete blockage even though they cannot always be continued.

Stops. The familiar stop consonants in English are made (1) with the lips closed, [p, b] as in [pɪl] pill and [bɪl] bill, (2) with the tip of the tongue against the upper or, less frequently, the lower gums or alveolar ridge, [t, d] as in [tɪl] till and [dɪl] dill, or (3) with the back of the tongue raised tightly against the hard palate or velum, [k, g] as in [kost] coast and [gost] ghost. A variant stop is made with the front (not the tip) of the tongue raised against the roof of the mouth, the mid part of the palate, [c, ɟ] as in the possible pronunciations [clæs, ɟlæs] of class and glass. An additional stop consonant is produced by bringing the vocal cords together with a snap, the sound heard between the two parts of "Oh, oh!" when used to reprimand a child. It is represented by [ʔ]. Popularly, it is not recognized as a consonant in English, but in the Upper Midwest it sometimes replaces [t] and [k].

Nasals. One subclass of continuants is the nasals, all of which are marked by complete blockage of the oral passage but with air released through the nose. In recent phonological theory nasals are assigned to the stops because of the oral obstruction, but from an articulatory point of view they are continuants, since the stream of air is not blocked but only diverted. With the velum lowered so as to allow air to escape through the nasal passage complete closure of the two lips produces [m] as in met, tight contact between the lower lip and the upper teeth produces [ɱ] as in one pronunciation of comfort as [kʌɱfɚt], blocking by the tongue against the alveolar ridge yields

[n] as in no, blocking by the front of the tongue against the mid-palate produces [ɲ] as in Spanish [kaɲon] cañon, and blocking by the raised back of the tongue against the velum yields [ŋ] as in [sɪŋ] sing. In English this velar nasal always is preceded by a vowel.

Laterals. A lateral consonant is one made with the sides of the tongue contracted while the tip of the tongue is in tight contact with the alveolar ridge, producing the [l] of [lɛt] let. If also the tongue-back is raised toward the velum, the result is the "dark l" [ɫ], as in [fɔɫ] fall. But if the front of the tongue is raised against the hard palate, the result is the palatal [ʎ], as in French bouillon [buʎɔ̃].

Flaps and Taps. A tapped consonant is made by a single instantaneous tap of the tip of the tongue against the alveolar ridge. The tapped [ɾ] often occurs as the middle consonant in [dɔɾɚ] daughter. A similar instantaneous movement of the tongue yields the flapped l [ɺ], often found after a labial as in [pɺaʊ] plow. A rare retroflex flap [ɽ] has been recorded in [kwɔɽɚ] quarter.

Fricatives. A large subdivision of continuants known as fricatives is marked by sufficient obstruction of the air-stream to cause more or less audible friction at the point of restriction. Each is a member of a voiceless-voiced pair.

Bilabial fricatives [ɸ, β] are made when the air is forced out between nearly closed lips. They are regular consonants in some languages. Spanish, for example, has [β] in [kuβɑ] Cuba. In English they occur only as variants of the labiodental fricatives [f, v] made by the forcing of air through a narrow aperture between the lower lip and the teeth as in [fil] feel and [vil] veal.

With the interdental fricatives [θ, ð] as in [θɪsl] thistle and [ðɪs] this the friction is that of air forcibly expelled between the tip of the tongue and the edge of the upper teeth.

If the tip of the tongue is pulled back to the alveolar ridge but the tip is slightly depressed so as to allow the stream of air to be directed toward the edge of the lower teeth, the result is the alveolar [s, z] as in [sɪp] sip and [zɪp] zip. But if the tip of the tongue is somewhat farther back and turned up, the result is [ɹ], for some speakers the sound of r after [t, d] as in [dɹen] drain and [dɹɪp] drip.

With the tongue still farther back, slightly arched between the alveolar ridge and the hard palate and with the entire tip depressed slightly, the resulting air friction yields the alveolo-palatal [ʃ, ʒ] as in [fɪʃən] fission and [vɪʒən] vision.

Another pair of fricatives is produced when air is forced through a tiny gap between the raised back of the tongue and soft palate [χ, ɣ]. These two sounds are not regarded as Modern English consonants but they are sometimes heard in [bʌχɪt] bucket and [wæɣən] wagon.

Finally, a fricative results from expelling the air through the glottis when the vocal cords are not very close together, [h] as in [haʊs] house and, murmured, [ɦ] as sometimes in [bɪɦaɪnd] behind.

Frictionless continuants. Two variants of the labiodentals [f] and [v] are recognized as [ꜰ, ʋ] when the articulation and the airstream pressure are quite weak. They might occur in [nɛꜰju] nephew and [glʌʋz] gloves.

Glides. Glides are essentially dynamic in that their quality changes while the tongue is in motion. A bilabial glide [w] as in [wet] wait is produced by two simultaneous motions, the progressive unrounding of the lips at the same time as the raised back of the tongue is lowered to the position for the following vowel. Phonetically, the reverse motion also yields [ʍ], that is, the rounding of the lips and the raising of the tongue-back toward the velum. This reverse [ʍ] occurs only after a vowel, as in the emphatic final pronunciation [goʍ] go.

When the tongue moves from a strongly retroflex or laterally constricted position to that of a following vowel, the result is the consonant [r], as in [raɪnd] rind and [rʌn] run. Other types of the consonant r, such as the trilled and the uvular varieties, are not found in the UM records. The reverse glide can follow a vowel, as in [pʊr] poor.

When the tongue is raised toward the hard palate and moves from that position to the position of a following vowel, the result is the y glide [j] as in [jɛlo] yellow and [ju] ewe. The reverse glide can occur in the Upper Midwest after a vowel in strongly articulated final position as in [tuˈdej] "Today?." In most recent American publications this palatal glide is represented by [y], but in narrow transcription that symbol is needed for the high-front rounded vowel.

Affricates. An affricate is a consonant that combines the characteristics of a stop and a glide. It begins with the tongue-contact of a stop consonant, but its identifying characteristic is a dynamic relatively slow withdrawal from that position so that the air is released

under pressure. English recognizes only one such position, that just behind the alveolar ridge, release from which yields the voiceless [tʃ] and the voiced [dʒ]. Considered phonemically these two consonants are transcribed /č/ and /ǰ/. Phonetically, affricates occur in other stop positions as well, as in one pronunciation of bucket [bʌkχɪt], but they are not considered English consonants.

[̥] The subscript small circle denotes complete or partial voicelessness of a sound that is usually voiced.

[ˬ] This symbol below a symbol for a voiceless consonant denotes a voiced sound uttered with rather strong and perhaps even abrupt articulation (fortis, not lenis).

[̣] The subscript dot denotes that a consonant is pronounced with marked tongue retroflexion.

[͟] This symbol for dentalization denotes tongue-tip contact with the upper teeth rather than with the alveolar ridge.

[͜] Occasionally a fieldworker uses this subscript symbol for labialization to indicate a degree of greater lip-rounding than is normal for a particular sound in the Upper Midwest.

[ˎ] The rarely used subscript tick denotes that a consonant, usually a sonorant [l, m, n, ŋ], is itself a syllable, but the symbol is omitted as unnecessary with such a transcription as [æpl] apple, where [l] can be understood as taking the syllabic peak in the absence of a vowel.

[ˑ, ː] These symbols denote length somewhat or considerably greater than is usual.

[̆] Conversely, an unusually short consonant may be marked with the breve. If the consonant is also weakly articulated, it may be transcribed with a superior letter, as in [pˡaʊ] plow and [fɚsᵗ] first.

[ˌ] A usually alveolar consonant with a tongue position somewhat retracted toward the palate is marked with this subscript for palatalization, as in [ʈun] tune.

[ˀ ˀ] Lateral arrows denote advanced or retracted position, as in [kˮɪp], keep.

[ʼ] This symbol, used because of its availability instead of the regular IPA [ˈ], denotes somewhat stronger aspiration of a stop than is expected. Still stronger aspiration is shown by the superior letter [ʰ].

[ˌ] Used as a subscript on [l] thus,

5

[ḷ], this symbol denotes a lateral that is advanced or "clear," as before a high front vowel, e.g., [ḷip] leap.

Stress and Intonation Marks

[ˈ, ˌ] These symbols denote primary and secondary stress respectively as in the phrase [ˌtʃɛri ˈpaɪ] cherry pie. Note, however, that by itself cherry contains a primary stress [ˈtʃɛri]. Tertiary stress is unmarked. Since English stress is generally predictable, stress is not usually indicated in the transcriptions.

[˥ ˩] Intonation, shown chiefly with calls to animals and the colloquial nasals, is indicated by lines below, level with, and above the transcription to represent the three pitch levels, (1) low, (2) normal, and (3) high, usually also with a line for the pitch glide from one level to another.

Vowels

The vowel symbols used in UM fieldwork appear in the accompanying accepted quadrilateral diagram. From left to right it schematically represents the range from the front to the back of the mouth; from top to bottom, the range from high or close tongue position to low or open tongue position. Symbols enclosed in parentheses denote rounded vowels that occur with lip-rounding or, occasionally, with the acoustic effect of lip-rounding.

In this volume, as in PEAS, vowels are treated as either free or checked. Free vowels are those that may end a stressed final syllable, that is, before a word boundary, as in [go] go or [dɪˈle] delay. Checked vowels are those that cannot end such a syllable but under stress must be checked, that is, followed by a consonant. A free vowel is usually produced with greater tension of the tongue and cheek muscles and hence is also denominated a tense vowel. A checked vowel is marked by laxness of those muscles and hence is also called a lax vowel. In addition, vowels are sometimes identified in purely articulatory terms as high or lower high in the upper sector of the diagram, mid or lower mid in the middle sector and higher low or low in the bottom sector. The three vertical sectors from front to back are known as front, central, and back.

Individual vowels. The vowel symbols are explained here in general terms for immediate identification with, for example, variations described in the text.

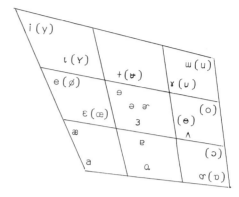

[i] The high-front tense vowel of [si] see.
[ɪ] The lower high-front lax vowel of [sɪt] sit.
[e] The mid-front tense vowel of [sem] same.
[ɛ] The lower mid-front tense vowel of [sɛt] set.
[æ] The higher low-front lax vowel of [fæt] fat.
[a] A low-front lax vowel found in eastern New England in cart and barn [ka·t, ba·n] but rarely in the UM except as the first element of diphthongs.
[y, ʏ, ø, œ] In American English the front rounded vowels occur only as rare variants when a front vowel undergoes rounding as an effect of an adjacent labial consonant.
[ɨ] The lower high-central lax vowel occasionally heard in [sɨstɚ] sister and frequently in the unstressed syllable of waited and horses [wetɨd, hɔrsɨz]. The high central [ɨ] does not occur in the UM records. [ʉ] is the rounded variety.
[ə, ɜ] The mid-central tense vowels without constriction or retroflexion, the first somewhat higher and advanced, both common in the "r-less" dialects of eastern New England and the South but found only two or three times as aberrant deviants in the UM.
[ɚ] The mid-central tense and lax constricted or retroflex vowel, "the vowel r," of [θɚd, sɚmən] third and sermon and, both with and without stress, of [ˈfɚðɚ] further. When it is weak after a vowel, the result may be a diphthong as in [puɚ] poor instead of a vowel followed by a consonantal glide. Phonemically, this retroflex vowel is considered as consisting of an underlying /ə/ plus /r/, so that further would be /ˈfərðər/.
[ɐ] The higher low-central lax vowel, usually occurring instead of [ɑ] or [ʌ].

[ɑ] The low-central lax vowel of [fɑðɚ] father. Exceptionally in the UM it is a free vowel in the pronunciations [mɑ·, pɑ·] ma and pa.

[u] The high-back rounded tense vowel of [tu, mus] two and moose.

[ɯ] The high-back unrounded vowel that may be heard instead of [ɪ] in [mɪ̵ʊk] milk, a pronunciation heard in southern Iowa from speakers with a South Midland background.

[ʊ] The lower high-back rounded lax vowel in [pʊt, bʊk] put and book.

[ɤ] The corresponding lower high-back unrounded vowel, sometimes found in an Upper Midwest pronunciation of good as [gɤd].

[o] The mid-back rounded tense vowel of [go, ots] go and oats as typically pronounced in the Upper Midwest.

[ɵ] The New England "short o," an advanced mid-back vowel with partial rounding. It is not found as such in the UM, although fw. M uses this symbol for some deviant Duluth pronunciations with a partly centralized [o].

[ɔ] The higher low-back rounded tense vowel, usually present before /r/ as in corn even if otherwise missing in an idiolect.

[ɒ] The low-back lax partly rounded vowel.

[ɑ̦] The low-back lax unrounded vowel. The three low-back vowels are problem children. Fieldworkers do not easily agree upon their identification and transcription, and their position in a systematic analysis of the vowel structure of the region is controversial. See the additional comment in Chapters 1 and 3.

Diphthongs

Phonetically, a diphthong is a dynamic vocalic sound, that is, one characterized by a tongue or lip glide from one vowel position to another in the same syllable. It cannot be continued as can a pure vowel.

If the syllabic stress is borne by the first vowel, the diphthong is called "falling"; if it is on the vowel that ends the glide, the diphthong is called "rising." In the UM all diphthongs are of the falling type except for instances of [ɪu] resulting from a weakening of the usual consonantal glide [j] as in [fju] few so as to yield [fɪu].

Under primary stress English tense vowels tend to have more or less appreciable offglides, that is, to be diphthongal. In some dialects lax vowels also may have offglides, as in the speech of those UM

informants with South Midland background.

Nearly all fieldworkers in the Upper Midwest usually transcribe a diphthong so as to show by the second element the position they consider reached by the tongue at the end of the glide, as in specific instances of [aɪ] in fight [faɛ^ɪt], [eɪ] in wait [weɪ̭t], [aʊ] in cow [kaʊ̆], or [ɔɪ] in boil [bɔ̌ɪ̌ɪ]. Fieldworker Wn, however, and occasionally Wr tend to indicate only the direction of the glide by using a covering symbol without indication of precise position, as in [aɪ, aʊ].

To indicate weakness and brevity the nonsyllabic portion of a diphthongal vowel may be shown by a superior letter, as in [a^ɪ̆, ɪ^u].

Two contiguous vowels that are in separate syllables may be so distinguished by an intervening hyphen, as [se-ɪŋ] saying.

Considered phonemically or generically, diphthongs are transcribed thus: /aɪ/, /eɪ/, /au/, and /ɔɪ/.

Signs and Diacritics for Vowel Symbols

That portion of the upper surface of the tongue closest to the palate is the critical portion, since that position determines the quality of the vowel. Because the critical part can be anywhere in the mouth on a continuum from high to low and also on a continuum from front to back the use of the accepted letter symbols to indicate points on a continuum is inadequate for recording the often significant finer distinctions a fieldworker is trained to recognize. Additional letter symbols could theoretically be used but would be confusing; a degree scale like that on a thermometer would be somewhat impractical for an Atlas publication. The solution accepted in American fieldwork is the use of small vertical or lateral arrowheads to denote the tongue position that is not quite that considered usual for a given vowel.

Thus, [i˃] is a high-front vowel with the tongue slightly retracted, and [u˂] is a high-back vowel with the tongue slightly advanced. It is clearly possible in this way to designate seven points along the horizontal range: [i, i˃, ɨ˂, ɨ, ɨ˃, u˂, u]. The vertical arrows sometimes need to be used along with the horizontal signs. A glance at the vowel quadrilateral diagram will reveal that technically a down-shifted high-front vowel is impossible, since normally the jaw is slightly retracted as it is lowered. A shifted high-front vowel would have to be transcribed [ɪ˩]. Hence there are 13 points that can be indicated on the vertical continuum: [i, i˩, ɪ^, ɪ, ɪ˩, e^, e, e˩, æ^, æ, æ˩, a^, a].

Further differentiation is effected through the use of one or more of five diacritics.

[˳] Lip-rounding, either unexpected or greater than expected, is indicated by this mark below the vowel symbol. Thus [bʊ̞m] boom with the strong labialization that is common in German or Russian; and [wɪ̞ʃ] is wish with some lip-rounding induced by the adjacent consonants.

[˲] Unrounding or spreading, either unexpected or greater than expected, is denoted by [˲] below the vowel symbol. Could may, for example, have very little rounding in much Upper Midwest speech, as shown by [kʊ̠d].

[˜] This diacritic for nasalization indicates that the vowel is pronounced while air is leaking through the nasal passage because the velum is only partly raised. Fieldworkers do not ordinarily indicate the moderate nasality nearly always present in a vowel preceding a nasal consonant.

[.] The subscript dot, as with consonants, denotes "r-coloring," produced by either retroflexion of the tip of the tongue or, less often in UM speech, by lateral contraction of the tongue.

[˳] The subscript small circle, as with consonants, stands for devoicing.

[·, :, ˘] The diacritics for vowel length appear only when it is considered of special significance. Vowels normally vary in length because of the phonetic context, on a range from brevity to appreciable length as they occur before voiceless stops, voiced stops, voiceless fricatives, voiced fricatives, nasals, and phrase boundary. Furthermore, the tense vowels are generally slightly longer than lax vowels. All such predictable variation need not be marked. Length is usually indicated, however, with calls to animals, often with colloquial nasals, and elsewhere when it is unpredictable but significant. Somewhat greater length than normal is shown by [·], much greater length by [:] or even [::]. Brevity is indicated by the breve [˘] or, if of the nonsyllabic element of a diphthong, by elevation to superior position, as [ºʊ̆˞, ºuˑ].

THE THEORETICAL BASE

Like the preceding European atlases the *Linguistic Atlas of New England* presented in the maps of its great folio volumes (1939-1943) the raw data of the narrow phonetic transcriptions by the several interviewers in the field. To the linguistic scholar such phonetic data provide evidence for support or rejection of theories in both synchronic and diachronic linguistics.

The Demand for a Structural Dialectology

In 1954 two adjoining articles in *Word* (Vol. 10) pointed out important past theoretical use of data and called for specific further application. The late Gino Bottiglioni, in his article, "Linguistic geography and achievements, methods, and orientations" (pp. 375-87), described, for example, the significant areal comparisons made by scholars using the raw phonetic materials of the French and Italian atlases and referred as well to the value of these materials in understanding different aspects of lexical semantics. The late Uriel Weinreich, in "Is a structural dialectology possible?" (pp. 388-400), was motivated by his own research for a proposed Yiddish dialect survey of Europe to raise questions that needed answering in any attempt to create what he called a phonological "diasystem" as a foundation for dialect comparison, particularly in America.

Following his *Word Geography of the Eastern United States* in 1949, Hans Kurath, with the collaboration of McDavid, produced in 1961 their *Pronunciation of English in the Atlantic States* (PEAS), in which the phonetic data from the eastern surveys are systematically treated in the framework of the dialect divisions of Northern, Midland, South Midland, and Southern as already determined upon a lexical basis. In PEAS the individual speech sounds are classified into the meaningful sound-classes identified in structural linguistics as phonemes, now referred to as "taxonomic phonemes" in contrast with the "systematic phonemes" of current phonological theory. In some measure, therefore, PEAS was a response to Weinreich's general question.

In this volume the general use of the virgules / / to indicate phonemic status is somewhat extended past that limitation. The context will reveal that sometimes, when a decision as to phonemic status is impracticable or irrelevant, the virgules simply indicate a larger sound-class in contrast to a specific subclass or phone shown by [ ].

In attempting to systematize the treatment of the phonetic data Kurath had already made a deliberate choice of one of the two currently available phonemic analyses. The older analysis accepted in the earlier days of English phonemic studies provides for thirteen or fourteen vowel phonemes. The phonetic fact that tense vowels usually have offglides and hence are actually diphthongal is considered within the framework of a single phoneme and its allophones. The high front pure /i/, for instance, commonly occurs as a phonetic diphthong, such as [ɪ^i̥]. Because the diphthongal variant is concealed within representation by a single phonemic symbol, this system became known as unitary.

Readers seeking a fuller exposition of Kurath's rationale for unitary analysis will find it in his *A Phonology and Prosody of Modern English* (Ann Arbor: University of Michigan Press, 1964).

The second system, with roots extending back at least as far as suggestions by Henry Sweet, the English phonetician, more than half a century earlier, treats an offglide as a distinct phonemic unit, a semivowel. In this analysis the tense /i/ of the unitary system is considered a true diphthong or "complex nucleus," written /iy/. The simple symbol /i/ then represents the lax vowel that in the unitary system is designated by /ɪ/. The full presentation of this analysis is that of George L. Trager and the late Henry Lee Smith in their *An Outline of English Structure, Occasional Papers* 3, Norman, Oklahoma, 1951. The Trager-Smith system postulates nine vowel phonemes in American English, consisting of the lax vowels /i, e, æ, ɨ, ə, ɑ, u, o, ɔ/ in addition to three semivowels /y, w, h/. Since theoretically each semivowel can follow each vowel, it follows that the system actually allows for the existence of 36 complex nuclei or diphthongs, although not necessarily in any one idiolect or any one dialect. This overall system became known as binary, naturally enough, because of the postulation of two phonemic units instead of one in each of the phonetic tense vowels.

Although the Trager-Smith binary system found wide favor among American structural linguists almost at once, several of its features provoked considerable controversy, such as its limitation to nine simple vowel nuclei and the provision of /h/ as a semivowel. Kurath himself adversely criticized this /h/ in "The binary interpretation of English vowels: a critique," *Language* 33.111-23 (1957); and in PEAS in 1961 he extended his attack while defending his choice of

the unitary system as more advantageous for dialect analysis. This choice itself turned out to be controversial. Samuel J. Keyser, in a review article in *Language* 39.303-16 (1963), took Kurath to task on several counts and argued in turn for the superiority of the use of the binary system in dialect analysis, although not so convincingly as to persuade practicing dialectologists at the time.

Further pressure upon dialectologists to discard the unitary system came from Robert P. Stockwell in "Structural dialectology: A proposal," *American Speech* 34.258-68 (1959). Stockwell held, like Weinreich, that an objective of dialectology must be the establishment of a diaphonemic inventory, one that will allow all contrasts in all dialects of the language. To arrive at this inventory there is needed, he wrote, at least a partial phonemicization of idiolects, tape recordings of which could be assembled in a central repository for study by linguists. The phonemicization presumably would follow Stockwell's own version of a binary phonemic system, with fifteen simple vowels and the three Trager-Smith semivowels.

The Case for a Generative Approach

The cogency of Stockwell's article would have had a greater immediate effect upon the editorial preparation of this Atlas had it not appeared during a period when diversionary activity nearly stifled editorial work. In the meantime the impact of the new generative linguistics was beginning to affect the thinking of scholars who, though not field collectors of dialect data, found a growing interest in their interpretation. Charles-James Bailey, for instance, drew upon generative phonology in his sparsely documented paper (ERIC document: ED 021 240) criticizing Kurath's term "South Midland" as the designation for an area that Bailey considered more desirably classified as Inland Southern. But particularly did Rudolph Troike present the case for the generative approach in his article "Overall pattern and generative phonology," in Harold B. Allen and Gary N. Underwood, eds., *Readings in American Dialectology* (New York: Appleton-Century-Crofts, 1971, pp. 324-42). The article was available to the Atlas project several years before publication.

A full explication of generative phonology is given in Noam Chomsky and Morris Halle's *The Sound Pattern of English* (New York: Harper and Row, 1968), and it is described with varying detail in most current introductory textbooks in linguistics. In generative theory the focus is not on surface phonetic details, not even on the synthetic generalization of the phoneme fundamental in structural linguistic theory, but rather on highly abstract underlying phonological units which function within a basic system. These units, which may be, but usually are not, designated as "systematic phonemes," really are composed of bundles of phonetic features listed as consonantal, vocalic, sonorant, nasal, and coronal, and the like. These features are set forth in binary opposition through the use of + and - signs to denote the presence or absence of a given feature. Thus /i/, for example, is identified as +vocalic, +high, -back, +tense, and -round. A series of rules then accounts for the particular phonetic realization in actual speech. Formerly, these rules were thought to be sequentially ordered, but now this view is in dispute.

In his article Troike explicitly demonstrates how a generative model more effectively solves the problem that Kurath and McDavid sought to take care of in PEAS—the puzzling systemic relationships of the low-back, mid-back, and low-central vowels in western Pennsylvania and eastern New England. For western Pennsylvania they had resolved low-back vowel relationships by positing the existence of another phonemic entity, a low-back weakly rounded /ɒ/, into which /ɑ/ and /ɔ/ had presumably merged, though with [ɔ] remaining as an overt sound before /r/. But this solution, Troike avers, is inconsistent with their analysis for other dialects since /ɒ/ is "incommensurable" with /ɑ/ and /ɔ/. With the generative approach Troike was able to establish diaphonemic units underlying all the investigated dialects and, by a few phonetic rules, accounting for the varying situations in other dialects. The rules account for the dialect in western Pennsylvania, where hoarse and horse constitute a homophonous pair, as do caller and collar, and also, for example, for the dialect of eastern New England, where they do not.

With the use of verticals | | to distinguish the overall diaphonemic symbols, Troike offers these simple rules for western Pennsylvania:

1. |o| $\longrightarrow$ $\{\begin{bmatrix} \mathrm{ɔ^{\wedge}} \\ \mathrm{o} \end{bmatrix}$ / ___ |r|$\}$

2. |ɔ| $\longrightarrow$ $\{\begin{bmatrix} \mathrm{ɔ^{\wedge}} \\ \mathrm{ɒ} \end{bmatrix}$ / ___ |r|$\}$

Diaphonemic underlying |o|, in other

words, is lowered to [ɔ^] before /r/ but remains [o] elsewhere. Diaphonemic underlying |ɔ| also becomes [ɔ^] before /r/ but is lowered to [ɒ] elsewhere.

It is clear that the surface homophones in this dialect may be diaphonemically quite different:

hoarse	|hors|	$\longrightarrow$	[hɔ^rs]
horse	|hɔrs|	$\longrightarrow$	[hɔ^rs]
caller	|kɔlər|	$\longrightarrow$	[kɒlɚ]
collar	|kalər|	$\longrightarrow$	[kɒlɚ]

For eastern New England, Troike continues, only these rules are needed:

3. |o| $\longrightarrow$ [o]

4. |ɔ| $\longrightarrow$ [ɒ]

5. |a| $\longrightarrow$ $\{\begin{bmatrix} \mathrm{a} \\ \mathrm{ɒ} \end{bmatrix}$ / ___ |r|$\}$

Their application yields these overt pronunciations:

hoarse	|o|	$\longrightarrow$	[hoə̯s]
horse	|ɔ|	$\longrightarrow$	[hɒs]
caller	|ɔ|	$\longrightarrow$	[kɒlə]
collar	|a|	$\longrightarrow$	[kɒlə]
car	|a|	$\longrightarrow$	[ka:]

Here the same diaphonemic substratum yields quite different phonetic data when the specific surface rules for New England are applied, for now hoarse and horse are not pronounced alike.

Troike extends his treatment to consider Southern and South Midland speech as well, and then goes on to deal with the larger questions raised by the attempt to construct a uniform phonological system for all the dialects of a language, an attempt not immediately relevant to the problems of the Upper Midwest Atlas. But his original treatment of the curious problem of the vowels of western Pennsylvania and of eastern New England was so persuasive, especially in view of the known western Pennsylvania background of migration into the southern part of the Upper Midwest, that the preliminary editing for this volume was oriented to his generative approach.

Frustration in the Upper Midwest

For three years the analysis of the hundreds of thousands of significant phonetic data from the 208 informants was directed toward such ultimate dialectal and idiolectal rules as the consistent application of the generative model required. This endeavor turned out to be much more frustrating than had been expected.

As the settlement history in Volume 1 indicates, the direct westward movement of Midland speakers and their descendants from the Pennsylvania area became diffused when it reached the Mississippi River. Although the bulk of the settlers continued to move westward, many at this point were diverted northward into northern Iowa and southern Minnesota and others in the next generation moved into eastern South Dakota. At the same time many pioneer settlers went to Nebraska from such Northern speech territory as New York State. With infusion, usually by families rather than by little groups or colonies, even a small farming community could be a mixture of persons with both Northern and Midland speech antecedents.

Decorah, in northeastern Iowa, for example, is represented by one informant with a Pennsylvania parent and by another both of whose parents have a Northern speech background. Burwell, in eastern Nebraska, is represented by one informant with a New York State background and by another with a Pennsylvania background. Such community mixture is not general, but the few instances suffice to create a serious problem.

But this problem of establishing the underlying rules, particularly for the low and back vowels, is seen as even more serious when the speech of the second local generation is considered. An informant of this generation may be influenced not only by contrasting speech patterns in the speech of parents from different regions but also by similar contrasts in the speech of his peers in school and social life. For such an informant, then, a likely result is a certain inconsistency, in an idiolect marked by regional features of both Northern and Midland, and possibly even of South Midland.

As is observed in Volume 1 (p. 124), Charles Houck found in this idiolectal mixture the basis for the claim in his Iowa doctoral dissertation that lexically Iowa cannot be said to have a clear Northern/Midland regional pattern. Although this claim can be rejected in terms of the usual basis for ascertaining the lexical heteroglosses of a dialect boundary, an idiolectal mixture of sound patterns is another matter indeed—and much more unresolvable.

An additional reason for the regional complexity lies in the frequency of a low-back unround vowel that Kurath had earlier posited only in r-less dialect areas in such words as c̄a̅r and hearth /kɒː/ and /hɒːːθ/. In the Upper Midwest this sound appears in other contexts, where some speakers have the round /ɒ/ or /ɔ/ or the unround central /ɑ/. Its existence makes more difficult the problem of relating the variety of overt vowels to the underlying idiolectal or regional structure.

It became increasingly clear that to arrive at valid phonological rules each idiolect in more than one-half of the Upper Midwest would require painstaking analysis and that subsequent laborious comparison would be needed to determine the web of underlying relationships. And in this clarity it also appeared that to engage in the analysis and the comparison was to exceed the reasonable scope of the 30-year extent of the project.

Another circumstance entering into this conclusion is the complex picture of vowels under weak stress, vowels that receive specific attention both in PEAS and in this volume. It is difficult to see how full description of the relationship between the substructure and the surface structure of a vowel system can ignore that picture. Yet of the application of generative theory to this situation Chomsky and Halle admit: "It is an open question to what extent vowel reduction is a matter of phonological rule . . . . In actual speech the reduction of vowels is determined not only by the functioning of the underlying grammatical rules but also by a variety of other factors (casualness, frequency of use of the item, predictability in a particular context, etc.)" (*The Sound Pattern of English*, p. 110).

Then, after noting that, perhaps idiosyncratically, the output of their surface phonological rules for reduction vowels does not always agree with the transcriptions in the Kenyon and Knott *Pronouncing Dictionary of American English*, they add significantly (p. 111): "Various modifications of these rules would be needed to accommodate dialects differing in a systematic way from what we have here assumed. It should be expected that low-level phonetic rules such as these we are now considering will differ in detail across dialects." They would have to differ in tremendous detail, of course, for the complexity in the Upper Midwest.

Chomsky and Halle themselves finally give up in dealing with the complexity of the actual speech situation by dismissing the problem as having little relevance. They say (p. 113): "Precise specification of the appropriate contexts for [application of the vowel reduction rule] is a complicated and, so it appears, relatively uninteresting matter." The dismissing term "uninteresting" is explained in a footnote: "In the sense that there are many details and special cases that do not seem to fall under any large-scale generalizations and that shed little light on general questions of phonological theory or on the structure of English."

But the overt phenomena that are "relatively uninteresting" to the theoretical linguist may be extremely interesting to the linguist whose concern is with language as an instrument of communication used in actual places on describable occasions by people with different social and educational backgrounds. "Interestingness" is a term that always has at least an implied point of reference.

Comparability with PEAS

A linguistic atlas is not a treatise on either phonological theory or sociolinguistic theory. By definition a linguistic atlas is and must be data-oriented. Even if the phonological component of generative theory remained stable (as it has not done during the period of editing this volume), the organization of Upper Midwest phonetic data within that framework would not now seem to be a feasible enterprise. Such a theoretical approach is not hereby discounted. It is simply left for the future. With some reluctance, therefore, but with conviction in the rightness of the decision, an original editing plan calling for such an organization and treatment has been replaced by a plan that retains comparability with PEAS.

In this volume, then, the phonetic materials are presented essentially in terms of taxonomic phonemics. I say "essentially" because I often have preferred—for reasons indicated above—not to attempt a phonemic classification without prolonged examination of individual field records. Here, the virgules / / accepted generally as a signal of phonemic status are not to be taken as dogmatic assertion of that status. On the contrary, they may indicate simply a major sound-class, the allophones or variants within which are then indicated by the traditional allophonic brackets [ ]. An incidental further distinction is that for phonetic [tʃ] and [dʒ] the usual phonemic symbols /č/ and /ǰ/ are used.

Further comparability with PEAS resides

in the decision to keep also the unitary system. In other contexts I have found the Trager-Smith binary system advantageous, but I cannot easily adapt it to the exigencies of dealing with the minute phonetic gradations described in the narrow transcription of the field records. Despite the arguments raised against it, Kurath's own arguments, for me at least, retain their cogency in the context of *The Linguistic Atlas of the Upper Midwest*.

UPPER MIDWEST SPEECH PATTERNS

Northern and Midland Influx

Two westward migration movements in the nineteenth century account for most of the regional speech contrasts within the Upper Midwest. One is that of Northern dialect speakers from western New England and New York State across northern Ohio and northern Indiana and Illinois to the Mississippi River. The other is that of Midland speakers from New Jersey and Pennsylvania and northern West Virginia across Ohio and Indiana and central Illinois. A minor population thrust is that of those emigrants from the Carolinas, Virginia, and Tennessee who pushed across Kentucky into southern Indiana and southern Illinois. Not necessarily described here is the westward movement in Canada that brought to Ontario, Manitoba, and Saskatchewan the five informants interviewed for the Atlas.

Chapter 2 of the first volume describes in some detail the complex patterns of settlement by these native speakers of English with eastern antecedents. Those with South Midland speech were pioneers who first homesteaded in southeastern Iowa. Midland speakers crossed the Mississippi and, with the opening of Indian lands, fairly rapidly extended their settlement in the southern two-thirds of Iowa as far as the Missouri River and then into Nebraska.

In the meantime an original Northern speech foothold by Vermont and Maine lumbermen along the St. Croix River in eastern Minnesota was followed in the 1850s by rapid land development in the southeastern quadrant of the state, with the Minnesota River valley a spearhead for western expansion. Settlers from New England, New York, Michigan, and Ohio provided a Northern speech basis in all of southern Minnesota as well as in the upper third of Iowa. But the Mississippi steamboats that unloaded the thousands of newcomers on the St. Paul levees before the Civil War affected in some measure what otherwise would in all probability have been a fairly consistent Northern dialect area. They brought up the river to Winona and Red Wing and St. Paul not only the Northern speakers who had reached the Mississippi in northern Illinois but also a sizable number of Midland speakers who had reached it at St. Louis.

Further mingling of some Midland speakers with a dominant Northern speech group occurred also in southern and southwestern Minnesota, where settlers moved in from Iowa, and, for the same reason, in southeastern South Dakota.

A substantial grasp of the complexity of the population mixture, without considering the great numbers of immigrants from Europe, can be quickly obtained by a study of the diverse backgrounds, even within a single family, succinctly outlined in the biographical data for respondents providing the postal survey data. (See Volume 1, pp. 98-119.)

Some Major Characteristics

In contrast to the manifold and often extreme diversity of speech in other areas of the United States, especially along the Atlantic Coast and in the Deep South, the speech of the lifelong residents of the Upper Midwest appears quite uniform. Indeed, some writers both popular and not so popular have been beguiled by this appearance into accepting a mythical homogeneous entity, Midwest English.

But if the first two volumes of this Atlas have not yet dispelled that myth, this volume should dispel it, for both in general speech characteristics and in specific pronunciations the Upper Midwest is far from homogeneous.

Upper Midwest variety in pronunciation is, as a matter of fact, closely linked to the regional variations in vocabulary and grammar treated in Volume 1 and Volume 2. To make comparison easier four maps from Volume 1 are here reprinted. Map 2 illustrates one of the two main distribution patterns, evidenced by heteroglosses of Northern features that do not overspread South Dakota and of Midland features that do. Map 3 illustrates the other main pattern, with Northern features restricted by the South Dakota border. Although it is convenient to denominate these as two distinct distribution patterns, it must be recognized that other heteroglosses can be drawn between

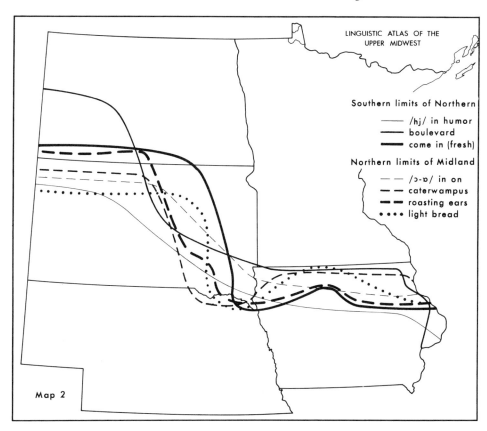

LINGUISTIC ATLAS OF THE
UPPER MIDWEST

Southern limits of Northern

——— /hj/ in humor
——— boulevard
——— come in (fresh)

Northern limits of Midland

— — /ɔ‑ɒ/ in on
– – caterwampus
– – roasting ears
•••• light bread

Map 2

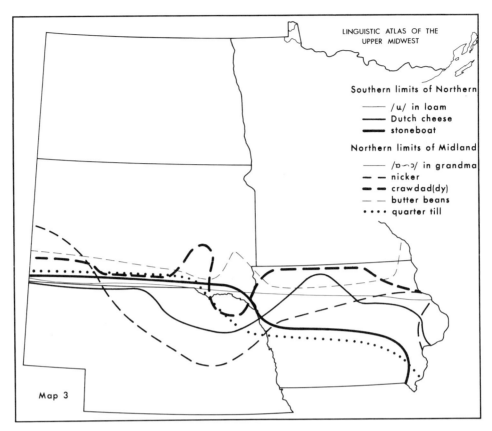

Map 3

LINGUISTIC ATLAS OF THE
UPPER MIDWEST

Southern limits of Northern

——— /u/ in loam
——— Dutch cheese
——— stoneboat

Northern limits of Midland

——— /ɒ~ɔ/ in grandma
— — nicker
— — crawdad(dy)
— — butter beans
• • • • quarter till

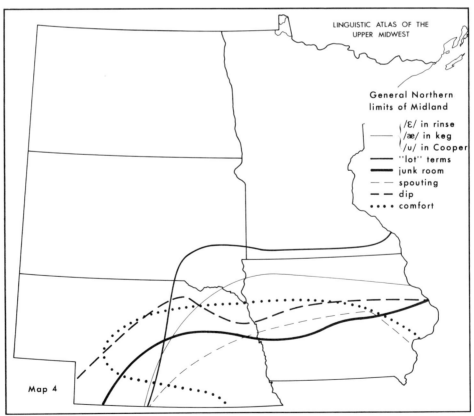

Map 4

LINGUISTIC ATLAS OF THE
UPPER MIDWEST

General Northern
limits of Midland

——— /ɛ/ in rinse
——— /æ/ in keg
——— /u/ in Cooper
——— "lot" terms
——— junk room
— — spouting
— — dip
• • • • comfort

14

these two bundles, so that actually all of South Dakota but the eastern fringe can be considered a transition zone between Midland and Northern.

One appreciable speech feature in most of the Upper Midwest is the relative purity of tense vowels. The vowels /i, e, u, o/ are not infrequently as purely monophthongal as if they were French or German vowels; and even when they are diphthongal the offglide is generally short and weak. The lax vowels, however, sometimes exhibit a regional contrast, for in Midland Iowa and Nebraska they tend to develop a weak offglide so that <u>wood</u>, for example, may be heard as [wʊ ᵻd].

The unstressed reduction vowel in the -<u>es</u> and -<u>ed</u> syllabic plural and preterit morphemes tends to be /ᵻ/ for Northern speakers and plain /ə/ in the Midland area. Thus, Northern /wetᵻd/ contrasts with Midland /wetəd/. This contrast, as a matter of fact, often appears in other situations as well, as in the middle syllable of <u>appendicitis</u>.

Upper Midwest diphthongs also manifest Northern/Midland differentiation. They tend in Midland speech to produce the acoustic effect of lengthening, either through actual lengthening of the first element or through shortening of the second element—or, in final position,

through both devices. Thus /aɪ/ may surface as [a·ᵻ] in <u>rind</u> and <u>side</u> or as [aᵗ] in <u>wire</u>. Before /r/, indeed, /aʊr/ is not only [aᵁɚ] or [aᵊɚ] for many Midland speakers but possibly even [aɚ] as in <u>flower</u> or <u>ours</u>. Elsewhere /au/ varies between the Northern allophones [ɑʊ, aʊ, ao] and the Midland [æʊ, æo] found in Iowa south of the Des Moines parallel as well as throughout Nebraska. Although there are two main subtypes of the /ɔɪ/ diphthong, that with a mid-beginning [oɪ] is clearly a minor variant vis-à-vis the dominant [ɔɪ].

The often controversial "long u" of the schools is almost universally /u/, not a diphthongal [ɪu] or [ju], after the alveolars in <u>dues</u> and <u>Tuesday</u>.

Although a survey of the present younger generation might indicate a different situation, the Upper Midwest informants interviewed at mid-century favored the aspirated /hw/ rather than /w/ in such words as <u>wheel</u> and <u>whip</u>. The incidence of minority /w/ in the records gives it a slight Northern orientation.

Specific Word Contrasts

The regional dialect contrasts indicat-

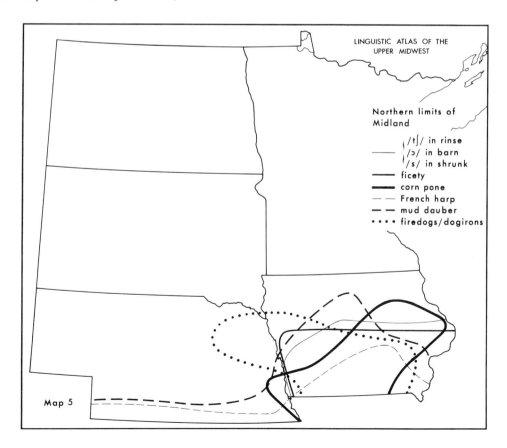

Map 5

ed lexically on the four accompanying maps conform to additional contrasts in the pronunciation of specific words. The basic pattern of Map 2, for example, is that not only of Northern [hjumɚ] humor and Midland [ɔn, ɒn] on, as shown there-on, but also of /u/ in goal and /ɑ/ in aunt in the Northern sector and of the excrescent t in /əkrɔst/ across in the Midland half.

To Map 3, besides the [ɔ - ɒ] contrast in the final syllable of grandma, there can be added such other Midland features as [ʌ+] in mush, the voiced plural /šævz/ shafts, the voiceless preterit /lɚnt/ learnt instead of learned, and—though not recorded in northern Nebraska—the voiced pronunciation of greasy with /z/ instead of Northern /s/.

Besides the /ɪ/ of rinse, the /æ/ of keg, and the /ʊ/ of Cooper additions can be made to Maps 4 and 5 as well. The pattern of receding Midland features shown on Map 4 is also that of /ɑ/ in rather and the infrequent /u/ in dues. In the South Midland speech area set off by the heteroglosses on Map 5 the /č/ of rinse, the /ɔ/ of barn, and the /s/ of shrunk can be supplemented by /ʊ/ in bulge and by the 1-less pronunciation of help as [hɛʊp] or [hɛɹp]. Also in this area, but apparently of South Midland provenience, is the pronunciation /blɪt/ for bleat, a variant in PEAS McDavid describes as "exceedingly rare." It may be increasing as a spelling pronunciation among persons unfamiliar with rural terminology.

But, like many vocabulary items described in Volume 1, a number of pronunciation features in the UM also reflect such dialect intermingling that only percentages or a graded scale can adequately represent the relative decrease of Northern forms and the relative increase of Midland forms on a continuum from the Canadian border to Missouri and Kansas.

Northern /kup/ coop, for example, gradually yields dominance to Midland /kʊp/ as one goes southward in the Upper Midwest. Northern /rʊf/ roof gives way to Midland /ruf/; and Northern /rut/ root, although still dominant throughout all the Upper Midwest, meets the growing competition of /rʊt/ in Midland territory. Such relative strength distinguishes also Northern /yok/ yolk, /dɔtɚ/ daughter, and /wɔtɚ/ water in contrast with the variants /yɛlk/, /dɑtɚ/, and /wɑtɚ/, all of which are strongest in Iowa. The intrusive r in wash as /wɔrš/ is likewise a Midland feature whose frequency increases gradually on the north to south scale.

Of course, much of the relative strength of Midland and Northern features is subject to a variety of influences conducive to further change, determination of which would be less tentative if the existing body of data could be supplemented by a survey of the present younger generation. The 83% dominance of Northern /krɪk/ creek, for instance, may be threatened by non-linguistic forces favoring the variant /krik/. The form /fɑg/ fog still persists but probably is declining, in favor of the rapidly spreading [ɒ], a West Midland replacement of /ɔ/ and /ɑ/ in certain words.

Evidence of past change appears in the occurrence of relic forms, comparable to the relic terms described in Volume 1. Barely surviving in the Upper Midwest are the following pronunciations: /pɒm/ palm, the South Midland /čɪr/ chair, /dɪpθɛrjə/ diphtheria, /deri/ dairy, /ʌ/ in worry and furrow, and /ɑ/ in rather.

Social, rather than regional, contrast in pronunciation is restricted to specific words, and generally to pronunciations that also can be classed as relics. All of the following pronunciations, for example, are found only in the speech of Type I informants: /tæsəl/ tassel, /šumek/ sumac (a Midland form), /kætrɪǰ/ cartridge, /hɚθ/ hearth, and /gumz/ gums. The excrescent t infrequently found with orphan, skiff, trough, and cliff is a minor social marker, too, and so is the occasional anaptyxis occurring in the pronunciation of castrate and umbrella as /ˈkæstəˌret/ and /ˈʌmbəˌrɛlə/.

CHAPTER 2

The Diaphones of Stressed Vowels
and Vowels before /r/

Several different ways of organizing the vowel data in the UM Atlas files were explored. Each attempt led to the conclusion that, however advantageous might be the features of some other system, their advantages were outweighed by the values of adhering to the system used by Kurath in PEAS. Although the projected Linguistic Atlas of the United States and Canada did not become a reality, it is good for the independent projects inspired by that dream to adhere with reasonable closeness to a format that facilitates the kind of comparison that would have been inherent in a national atlas. This chapter, accordingly, treats the diaphones of the checked and free stressed vowels as Kurath treated them. It also includes the treatment of vowels before /r/, a topic which, because postvocalic /r/ is retained in the UM and hence does not yield the variety of allophones that its absence produces, does not here call for a full chapter as it did in PEAS.

The favorable reception accorded Kurath's innovating synoptic presentation of the vowel systems of individual infs. has led to the inclusion of similar synopses here. In PEAS, however, only the cultured infs. were thus represented; here all infs. are included. Their synopses, arranged sequentially by inf. number, follow the description of diaphones of stressed vowels, which are then illustrated in the exemplary transcriptions of key terms from the field worksheets.

THE CHECKED VOWELS

Although for the majority of UM infs. the checked high and mid vowels are the monophthongal [ɪ, ʊ, ɛ, ʌ], ingliding

varieties are common in Midland speech territory, i.e., Iowa, Nebraska, and part of South Dakota. Since Kurath's study of their frequency in the East reveals only scattered incidence in North Midland and northeastern New England, it seems that they may be an expanding feature in the UM.

Low-front /æ/ and low-central /ɑ/ do not fit into the preceding generalization, as /æ/ has a strongly diphthongal upgliding variant throughout the UM and /ɑ/ is often accompanied by rounding and backing in its own unique distribution pattern.

The Vowel in whip, crib, chimney

/hwɪp, krɪb, čɪmni/

The lower high-front /ɪ/ is strongly monophthongal for nearly all UM speakers in nearly all situations. In chimney, for

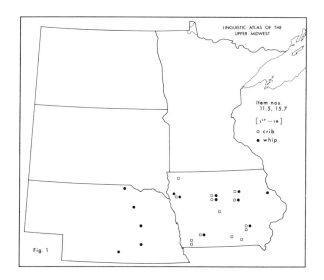

example, the vowel is uniformly [ι] throughout the five states. Before a stop consonant in a monosyllable, however, the western Pennsylvania diphthongal [ιᵊ] or [ι⁺] with an inglide persists in the focal Midland speech areas of Iowa and Nebraska. (See map for its distribution in whip and crib.) A centralized variation of the monophthong, /+/, occurs in whip, but not in crib, in the speech of infs. 49; 125, 131; 204, 211, 214-15, 217, 219; 320, 323, 329; 435, for whom it may be induced by the preceding /w/. (See Synopses for crib.)

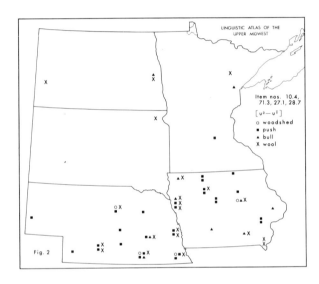

Item nos. 10.4, 71.3, 27.1, 28.7
[uᵊ — uᶥ]
o woodshed
■ push
▲ bull
X wool

Fig. 2

The Vowel in wood, wool, pull, push

/wud, wul, pul, puš/

The lower high-back /u/ is typically· a monophthong for UM speakers, as is suggested by the responses for wood and pull transcribed in the Synopses. Wood was recorded during field interviews as the first element of woodshed or woodhouse, in which position any tendency toward diphthongization is likely to be blocked. But an ingliding diphthongal variation, ranging from [uᵊ] to [u⁺], does occur in many words in the UM as a reflection of its sporadic appearance in New England and New York State and Pennsylvania. As with the ingliding variant of /ι/, the ingliding variant of /u/ is found chiefly in Iowa and Nebraska. The accompanying map indicates the distribution of this diphthong in bull and wool. The infs. thus mapped are as follows: bull—16; 101, 109, 118, 136, 139, 151; 220; 422, 424, 433. wool—14; 101, 109-12, 118, 136, 149-

50; 214, 221; 307; 413, 424, 427-28, 430-32, 434.

A similar regional pattern in the UM is found for the generally upgliding diphthong [u+ — uᶥ˘] induced by the following palatal [ʃ] in push. Infs. with this variant are 35; 103-5, 110-16, 137-38; 410, 414, 416, 420, 423-24, 427-35. (See map.)

The Vowel in vest, sled, ten, egg

/vεst, slεd, tεn, εg/

Although fw. A tends to recognize a weak upglide, as in transcriptions [εεˆ] and [εε˘], essentially the lower mid-front /ε/ is monophthongal in the UM. An exception is the inconsistent retention of an ingliding diphthongal [ε⁺ — εᵊ] in stressed monosyllables.. This feature, which is a reflex of its irregular occurrence in New England and New York State and its high frequency in western Pennsylvania, is only sparsely found in the UM outside the Midland speech area in Iowa and Nebraska. For the distribution of [tεᵊn], with its 37% frequency in Iowa and 31% in Nebraska, the Synopses provide the details. Two additional exemplary words are vest and sled. In them the diphthong occurs as follows: vest—101-5, 109-16, 118, 132-33, 138, 151; 405, 413, 415, 423-25; sled—101-5, 109-16, 130, 132-34, 137, cvr138; 304, 315, 326-27; 401, 410, 413-14, 416-18, 423, 426-27, 430, 434-35. Its frequency in Iowa is 33% for vest and 37% for ten; in Nebraska, 11% for vest and 31% for ten.

Egg presents a special situation. See p. 271.

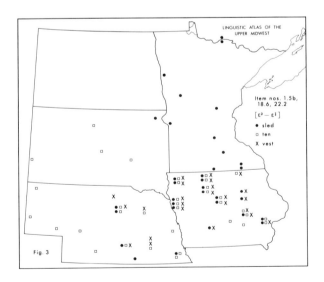

Item nos. 1.5b, 18.6, 22.2
[εᵊ — εᶥ]
● sled
□ ten
X vest

Fig. 3

The Vowel in <u>sun</u>, <u>judge</u>, <u>brush</u>, <u>mush</u>

/sʌn, ĵʌĵ, brʌš, mʌš/

In the UM, as in the Northern and Midland sectors of the eastern states, [ʌ] is typically the monophthongal vowel exemplified in <u>sun</u>. (See Synopses.) Before the fricative /š/ and the affricate /ĵ/, however, this vowel develops a regional variant with a centering offglide sometimes extending in a high-front direction, e.g., [ʌᵊ, ʌᵻ, ʌᶥ]. Although such a variant outside the South is reported in PEAS as found only in the South Midland and along the lower Susquehanna River in Pennsylvania, its distribution in the UM reaches past the southern Iowa region of South Midland influence. In <u>judge</u> it is found in northern Iowa and eastern Nebraska; in <u>mush</u> and <u>brush</u> it occurs there and also, though rarely, in South Dakota and Minnesota. (See map.) One variant of <u>brush</u>, [brɛš] and [brɛᶦš], is used by Iowa infs. cvr139 and cvr142 but is not recorded in the Synopses.

A slight social contrast may exist in the acceptability of the diphthongal pronunciation, since in <u>mush</u> it is used by 21% of Type I infs., 9% of Type II's, and 7% of Type III's, and in <u>brush</u> it is used by 33% of the Type I's and only 25% of the Type II's and Type III's.

Some minor and regionally nonsignificant variants occur in terms with adjacent /š/, as is indicated by responses for <u>brush</u> in the Synopses and for <u>mush</u> by the following instances of rounding: [ʌ̞] 225; 407-8, 417. [ʊ̈] 222; 429. [ʊ] 4, 14-15, 21, 26, 41-42, 45, 55; 126, 134; 221; 301; 411, 427, 432. Four infs., 14, 40; 403-4, reportedly have in <u>judge</u> a mid-central [ɜ] which, though common in the South in this word, apparently here is without Southern ties. Infs. 146 and 220 have a fronted vowel in [ʤɛˀʤ].

Unfortunately, the UM worksheets contain no word beginning with the negative prefix <u>un-</u>, which for many speakers in the UM is noticeably pronounced with so low a tongue position that to other speakers it is heard as /ɑ/. Without specific returns no regional ascription can be ventured with assurance, although informal observation suggests that this pronunciation is largely found in the Northern speech area and that it is more likely to occur in the speech of persons subject in the home or elsewhere to a Scandinavian influence. The only recorded instance of the prefix is in the pronunciation [ɑˀnjuzĵʊəl], by inf. 436, both of whose parents were Swedish, but analogous examples are probably in the pronun-

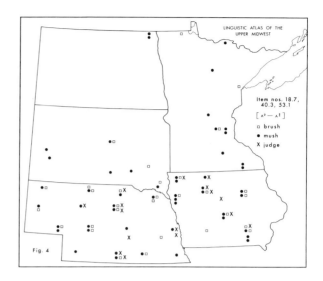

ciation of <u>tongue</u> with the [eᵛ] vowel by infs. 13, 17, and 206. Infs. 17 and 206 are of Scandinavian extraction.

The Vowel in <u>sack</u>, <u>bag</u>, <u>ashes</u>, <u>half</u>, <u>aunt</u>, <u>ram</u>, <u>glass</u>

/sæk, bæg, æš+z, hæf, ænt, ræm, glæs/

Although on the whole the short raised low-front vowel /æ/ is fully forward and is monophthongal in the UM, it tends to be lengthened in monosyllables and to develop an offglide in certain phonetic environments. The Synopses give the details for <u>ashes</u>, <u>bag</u>, <u>half</u>, <u>glass</u>, and <u>aunt</u>, and a treatment of <u>aunt</u> appears in Chapter 3. A problem in analyzing the field data is occasioned by fw. variation. Fieldworkers P and Wn tend to ignore [æ] offglides. Fieldworker H tends to write as an offglide the onset of a following continuant.

Before the voiceless velar stop in <u>sack</u>, the pure monophthong described in PEAS as typical in the North and Midland seems, in the speech of two-thirds of the UM infs., to have given way to a weak upgliding diphthong that, while common in southern New Hampshire, is rare elsewhere in the North and absent in the Midland. In the Midland speech areas of Iowa and Nebraska the offglide tends to be centralized as [+]: 101-4, 106; 109-14, 116, 122-36, 138, 142-50, 152; 220; 413. There are two instances of [ə] as the offglide, 414 and 431. Distribution of the diphthong is as follows: Minnesota 55%, Iowa 79%, North Dakota 69%, South Dakota 36%, and Nebraska 76%.

As in the Northern speech areas of the eastern states, the voiced velar stop in bag has induced greater than normal diphthongization of [æ] in bag. Nearly three-fourths of the UM infs. have a rising offglide as in [bæᵊ'g], again found in somewhat higher frequency among Midland-oriented speakers. Only once, on the Iron Range in northern Minnesota, does a centered [ə] appear, to fw. M, as the off-glide.

After both /æ/ and /æ┼/, the velar stop tends to be fronted as [kᶜ] or [gᶜ].

The voiceless fricatives /f/, /s/, and /š/ also tend to induce offglides from a preceding /æ/, but in varying degree and with some regional differentiation. In half (or calf) a distinctive diphthongal [æᶜ] or [æ┼] occurs in only 10 instances scattered in all the states but Minnesota. In ashes the diphthongal version is somewhat more frequent but with most of the examples in Iowa and Nebraska. In glass it is still more frequent but not throughout the area. Such variants as /glæ┼s/ are not recorded at all in the Dakotas, but they are in the speech of 20% of the Minnesota infs., 70% of the Iowa infs., and 13% of those in Nebraska. Only three infs. have a centering diphthong [æᵊ], 118; 414, 430. The lower vowel, [a], is used by one Canadian (201), by two female infs. (39; 213) with some awareness that this pronunciation has carried prestige, and by one North Dakotan Type I speaker of Norwegian parentage (216), the only inf., incidentally, with [a] in hammer.

Before the nasals /n/ in aunt and /m/ in ram an offglide from [æ] appears in different degrees. In aunt the offglide is described as rising, [æᶜ], in the speech of 41 infs., most of whom are split evenly between Minnesota and Iowa, and as central, [æᵊ], for seven infs., six of whom are in Nebraska. In addition one Minnesotan, 58, has a glide after a central vowel, in [aᵊnt]. With ram the offglides are much more frequent, appearing in the speech of 90 infs. with marked Midland weighting: Minnesota 31%, Iowa 76%, Nebraska 41%, but none in the Dakotas. The offglide is centering, as in [æᵊ], for three Iowans (118, 139, 151) and for six Nebraskans (423-26, 431, 435).

The Vowel in father, palm, crop, oxen, on, college

/faðɚ, pam, krap, aksɨn,
an, kalɨǰ/

The binary analysis of current phono-logical theory classifies /ɑ/ as a low-back vowel. Although this classification simplifies the analysis, a phonetic description, as Halle and Chomsky recognize in *The Sound Pattern of English* (New York, 1968, p. 247), must be based upon a physical scale. According to this scale /ɑ/ is a low-central vowel with a rather wide phonic range that for most UM speakers includes [aˀ, ɑᶜ, ɑ, ɐ, ɑˀ, ɚᶜ, ɚ]. The variety of phonic types that may be subsumed under the rubric /ɑ/ and then of /ɔ/ probably provides opportunity for more controversy than does any other part of the American phonetic inventory.

For the eastern states the descriptive statement in PEAS is amply supplemented by the thorough doctoral study of Thomas H. Wetmore, published as *The Low-Central and Low-Back Vowels in the English of the Eastern United States. Publication of the American Dialect Society*, No. 32 (1959).

In the UM the universal presence of postvocalic /r/ makes possible here the omission of the free /ɑ/ category described by Kurath as needed to classify the vowel in /r/-less barn and similar contexts. Here /ɑ/ is considered a checked vowel class, with the recognized existence of exceptional final /ɑ/ in ma and pa and of occasional greater length in palm and calm as simple anomalies.

In father /ɑ/ is the normal vowel for all but two UM infs. Only 126 and 149, in Iowa, have a low-back rounded [ɔ] or [ɒˀ]. In certain contexts, however, /ɑ/ exhibits some regional restrictions. It is generally found before stops as in crop and stopper, lot, rock and oxen, except for a few sporadic occurrences of a backed [ɚ] and a rounded [ɒ] or [ɔ] in Minnesota and North Dakota and a slightly higher incidence in South Dakota, Iowa, and Nebraska. A similar situation prevails before /l/ in college. Noticeably, three Canadian infs. have a rounded vowel and another has a backed variant.

A preserved pronunciation, described in PEAS as "Appalachian," appears in the conversationally recorded [dræp] for drop in the speech of inf. 132, who almost certainly acquired it from his father, born in Kentucky.

Before the /n/ of stressed on as in "Put it on," however, the proportion of rounded variants rises sharply. The single instance of rounded [ɒ] in Minnesota contrasts with the 61 instances of [ɒ] and [ɔ] in Iowa, South Dakota, and Nebraska. (See the treatment of on in Chapter 3.)

In the stressed final syllable in the queried expression, [ɑ] often undergoes lengthening and sometimes undergoes atypical diphthongization, usually transcribed as a slight upglide [ɑᵉ]. For some speakers in the Midland speech area of Iowa and Nebraska the offglide is likely to be a higher centralized version, written by various fws. as [ɨ], [ə], [ʊ], and [ɤ]. Also in this situation [ɑ] is subject to rather strong nasalization.

In palm, aside from instances of old-fashioned /pæm/, for which see the treatment in Chapter 3, /ɑ/ is usual in the UM. It often undergoes lengthening, especially by infs. who do not pronounce /l/. For a small minority of speakers, mostly in Midland territory, the vowel is backed and often rounded, yielding [ɒ] and [ɒ].

THE FREE VOWELS

The high and mid free vowels in the UM are either monophthongs or diphthongs with short and weak rising offglides. Low-back vowels appear in several variations that are mingled in their regional distribution, but with some indication of an increasing loss of rounding. Certain diphthong allophones exhibit regional correlation, e.g., the comparable [əi] and [ɜu] in Canada and the "slow" varieties of [au] and [ai] in Midland and South Midland speech areas.

The Vowel in three, grease, bean

/θri, gris, bin/

In the UM only two phonic types of /i/ occur: a pure monophthong [i, i·] and an upgliding diphthong. The latter has two varieties, one with a fairly open beginning, as in [ɪi], more likely to be found in Iowa, Nebraska, and the Midland sector of South Dakota, and another, with a high beginning, as in [iˇi], more likely to be found elsewhere. The Southern ingliding diphthong is not present.

Actually, the monophthongal incidence is stronger than the Synopses suggest. One reason is that fw. A tends to record as [ɪˇi] or [iˇi] an allophone with such a barely discernible offglide that other fws. would be inclined to transcribe it as [i]. Another is that the three words, three, grease, and bean, do not exemplify the contexts in which the monophthong is most frequent. When it does occur, the context may induce lengthening, but on the whole it is generally rather short.

In checked position, of 201 infs. only 3%, all in Minnesota, are recorded with the monophthong [i] in beans; of 208 infs. only 5%—all in Minnesota, Iowa, and Nebraska—have it before the voiceless /s/ in grease. In three, usually uttered by the speaker in a counting sequence, 25% of 204 infs. have the pure vowel.

But a wider variation is revealed by an analysis of instances of other terms offered by infs. Before voiceless final stops the monophthong is not very common— 15% of 185 infs. in wheat, 21% of 153 infs. in sweet corn, and 18% of 55 infs. in creek (/krik/ not /krɪk/). Before the voiceless slow-release stop, or affricate, in peach pit or peach seed, 28% of 39 infs. have the monophthong.

When the voiced /d/ is in word-final position, as in peach seed and cherry seed, 17% of 40 infs. have a pure preceding [i]; when it ends the shorter first element of feedyard and feedlot, then 31% of 27 infs. have [i].

The frequency of the monophthong is highest when it occurs as a free vowel before a consonant that begins a following syllable. Thus in screech owl, which syllabically is often /ˈskriˌčaul/, 48% of 88 infs. have it. In eaten, which phonetically has /i/ as the first syllable, the frequency of [i] among 158 infs. is 40%. Similarly in needle the proportion among 100 infs. is 46%; in depot among 192 infs. it is 50%; and in Negro among 178 infs. it is actually 52%.

The Vowel in two, shoes, tooth

/tu, šuz, tuθ/

In the UM /u/ is either a pure vowel or

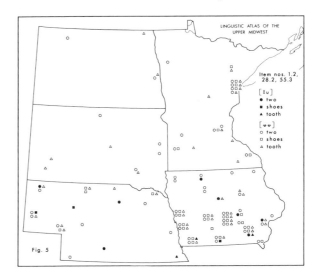

Fig. 5

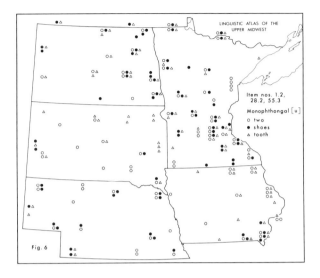

an upgliding diphthong, with a distribution similar to that of the diaphones of /ɪ/. There are no instances of an ingliding diphthong.

Some individual fw. variation necessitates careful interpretation of the statistical summaries. Fieldworkers Wn and H tend to write only /u/ and fw. Wr tends to generalize all responses as /ʊᵘ/, while fw. M transcribes as centralized a vowel perhaps better written as [uˁ]. With allowance for these differences it is clear that the pure vowel is stronger in Northern speech territory. For <u>two</u> the data are as follows: Minnesota 42% and North Dakota 39%, but Iowa 20% and Nebraska 22%. For <u>shoes</u>: Minnesota 66% and North Dakota 72%, but Iowa 35% and Nebraska 31%. For <u>tooth</u>: Minnesota 46% and North Dakota 23%, but Iowa 33% and Nebraska 11%.

It is clear also that a centralized diphthong is much more likely to occur in Midland speech territory. (See map.) Phonic variations of [ʊᵘ] are distributed as follows:

	Mn.	Ia.	N.D.	S.D.	Nb.	Ave.
two	15%	54%	6%	16%	25%	25%
shoes	13%	33%	0	0	9%	14%
tooth	16%	39%	4%	14%	17%	21%

A rare centralized diphthong with unrounded beginning, /ɨu/, is sharply Midland. There are five instances of [tɨᵘ] in Iowa and two in Nebraska, and one each of [tɨᵘθ] in these states. It does not appear in <u>shoes</u>.

As with /ɪ/, it may be that a lower beginning of the diphthong, as in fw. Wr's [ʊᵘ], is more likely in the speech of Midland-oriented infs. Such a beginning is more frequent in Iowa than in Minneso-

ta, but Wr's consistent use of this transcription probably suggests a higher frequency in Nebraska than actually exists.

The Vowel in <u>April</u>, <u>eight</u>, <u>bracelet</u>

/epr+l, et, bresl+t/

In the UM the mid-front vowel occurs either as a pure monophthong or as an upgliding diphthong. Monophthongal [e] is widespread before the voiceless stop in the short stressed initial syllable of <u>April</u>, although not so transcribed by fws. H and P. It is much less frequent in other phonetic contexts, as in <u>eight</u>, <u>bracelet</u>, and <u>shades</u>; and it does not occur at all in <u>pail</u>.

In the UM Northern speech region, however, the upgliding diphthong [eᵉ^] and [e⁺ᵛ] generally has such a slight and brief upglide that the resulting diphthong may easily be apprehended as a pure vowel. A lower beginning of the diphthong, as in [ɛ⁺] and [eᵛ⁺], is found principally in Iowa and Nebraska, where its occurrence probably reflects similar incidence in western Pennsylvania. (See map.) The instances in northeastern Minnesota, recorded by fw. M, may be due to fw. variation or may be further evidence of Midland influence in Duluth and on the Iron Range.

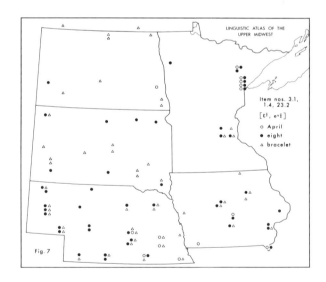

The Vowel in <u>ago</u>, <u>coat</u>, <u>road</u>

/əgo, kot, rod/

Except for a few scattered occurrences

22

of a centralized diphthong, only two of
the four eastern varieties of /o/ are
found in the UM—a monophthongal [o] and
an upgliding diphthongal [oᵁ]. The ingliding subtypes of eastern New England
and Pennsylvania are not recorded.

According to Kurath, monophthongal [o]
is essentially limited to the South Atlantic coast and the Pennsylvania German
settlement area. In the UM, however,
there appears to be a trend to the pure
[o] as a result of progressive weakening
of the upglide in [oᵁ] to the point where
the most commonly used transcription,
[o°ᶺ], indicates only the briefest and
slightest tongue movement. This trend toward monophthongization seems stronger in
Northern speech territory.

Several factors render analysis somewhat difficult. Fieldworkers A, G, and Wr
tend to use [o°ᶺ] rather broadly, to cov-
er a possible lengthened [o·] as well as
a possible [oᵁ] with a quite short glide.
On the other hand, reference to later
voice recordings suggests that the [oᵁ]
of fws. P and H in Iowa would better be
written as [o°ᶺ]. In South Dakota likewise, comparison with voice recordings
leads to considering fw. Wn's pure [o] to
be better transcribed as [o°ᶺ] or [oᵁ].
Further, an expected lengthening or diphthongization of /o/ as a phrase terminal
in the response "a year ago" may be
blocked when the response is "a year ago
today."

The diaphonic subtype [o] appears in
the field records as [o], [oˋ], [oˇ], and
[oᶺ]. In the words found in the Synopses
it is regionally distributed as follows:

	Mn.	Ia.	N.D.	S.D.	Nb.
ago	16%	2%	34%	52%	0
road	19%	2%	36%	35%	15%
coat	47%	6%	58%	47%	14%

The diaphonic subtype [oᴜ] appears in
the field records in several narrow transcriptions as shown in the Synopses. Its
regional distribution is as follows:

	Mn.	Ia.	N.D.	S.D.	Nb.
ago	51%	44%	0	11%	53%
road	15%	68%	0	19%	33%
coat	18%	59%	0	18%	54%

The diaphonic subtype [o°ᶺ], most instances of which may best be assigned to
[oᴜ], is distributed as follows:

	Mn.	Ia.	N.D.	S.D.	Nb.
ago	33%	54%	66%	37%	49%
road	66%	30%	64%	46%	52%
coat	35%	35%	42%	35%	32%

There are 18 instances of a centralized
diphthong. As the Synopses show, one is
in ago (434), nine in road (11, 25, 30,

56; 220; 401, 409, 411, 429), and eight
in coat (25, 30, 56; 220; 401, 409, 411,
429). Since they are scattered without a
clear pattern and since all but two are
recorded by fw. A, it is conjecturable
that other actual instances may be concealed under a generalized transcription.

The Vowel in law, dog, strawberries

/lɔ, dɔg, strɔbɛrɪz/

In the New England survey, according to
PEAS, three main types of low-back vowels
emerged—a fully rounded raised variety
[ɔ], a slightly rounded lower variety
[ɒ], and an upgliding diphthong [ɒɔ].

Not in New England but in later fieldwork in the Middle Atlantic states there
was recognized also a completely unrounded low-back vowel for which a new American symbol, [ɑ̶], was devised.

An exhaustive analysis and interpretation of the distribution of these varieties is the previously cited monograph by
Thomas H. Wetmore. Wetmore's treatment
does not attempt to make definitive phonemic judgments but rather provides in
full detail the involved incidence of the
several types and the additional complication caused by their overlapping even
in relatively homogeneous areas.

Such complication as appears in the
East is compounded in the UM by two factors—(1) the partial mingling of the
Northern and Midland population streams
as described in Volume 1, and (2) fw.
variation in recording the gradation from
[ɔ] to [ɑ].

In the Dakotas fw. A, for example,
tends to use [ɒ] for both the unrounded
and the weakly rounded vowels, according
to the practice of the New England inves-
tigators. Fieldworkers Wn, H, and P tend
to use a broad transcription [ɔ] for a
low-back vowel and hence to overlook significant phonic contrasts. Some correction has been effected, however, by a
cross-check of the voice recordings and,
for each of two surviving Iowa infs., 115
and 131, originally interviewed by fws. H
and P, by a second tape-recorded interview by Gary Underwood in 1969.

The fully rounded [ɔ], which dominates
western New England, northern New York,
southeastern Pennsylvania, and western
Maryland, expectedly dominates the UM as
well, although in varying proportions in
different phonetic contexts. In final position in law, for example—as the Synopses indicate—[ɔ] or [ɔ·] is strong in all
the states but Iowa: Minnesota 73%, Iowa
45%, North Dakota 72%, South Dakota 92%,

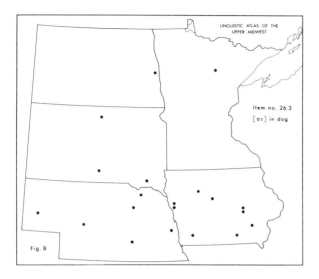

LINGUISTIC ATLAS OF THE
UPPER MIDWEST

Item no. 26.3
[ɒɔ] in dog

Fig. 8

Nebraska 71%. Before velar /g/ it is somewhat less frequent: Minnesota 50%, Iowa 50%, North Dakota 62%, South Dakota 61%, Nebraska 70%. In syllable final position before a consonant, as in strawberries, [ɔ] occurs as follows: Minnesota 46%, Iowa 69%, North Dakota 38%, South Dakota 68%, Nebraska 73%. The geographical picture is a bit puzzling, however, since with law and dog [ɔ] has strong Northern orientation but in strawberries its orientation appears to be toward Midland and South Midland.

The weakly rounded low-back [ɒ], which is common in central New York and in much of Pennsylvania, consistently appears also in both Northern and Midland speech areas of the UM. With law the distribution is as follows: Minnesota 24%, Iowa 45%, North Dakota 24%, South Dakota 8%, Nebraska 29%. With dog the over-all proportion is somewhat higher: Minnesota 42%, Iowa 31%, North Dakota 38%, South Dakota 36%, Nebraska 27%. With strawberries it is about the same: Minnesota 34%, Iowa 25%, North Dakota 46%, South Dakota 29%, Nebraska 22%. Both dog and strawberries reveal a Northern orientation for [ɒ].

Although this regional weighting in the widespread distribution of both [ɔ] and [ɒ] reflects the general situation in the eastern states, the fact that both vowels often appear in the same locality reflects the intermingling of settlers with antecedents in distinct [ɔ] and [ɒ] areas in the East.

At the same time, the tendency toward unrounding historic [ɔ] in such words as law, the tendency that then yields the unrounded [ɑ], may actually be strengthened in the UM. Returns are somewhat in-

consistent. In law [ɑ] is reported with a frequency of 10% in Iowa and 4% in North Dakota, but in dog the frequency in Minnesota is 17%, with 10% in North Dakota and 3% in Nebraska. In strawberries [ɑ] has a 12% frequency in Minnesota, 4% in Iowa, and 15% in North Dakota. Even low-central [ɑ] has a 3% frequency in law in Minnesota, and in dog Minnesota has 1%, Iowa 4%, South Dakota 3%, and Nebraska 3%, while in strawberries the proportion is 8% in Minnesota, 2% in Iowa, 4% in South Dakota, and 5% in Nebraska. On the whole, there seems to be a slightly stronger tendency in Northern speech toward unrounding the low-back vowel and even accepting [ɑ] as its replacement.

Actually, the limitation of Atlas data to the midcentury and to older speakers ignores an apparently rather rapid and highly noticeable development in the UM since the time of the field investigation. During the past 30 years I have observed in my classes at the University of Minnesota a steadily increasing proportion of students who have no low-back rounded vowel except before /r/. Annually, more and more students have only [ɑ] or even [ɑ] in law, jaw, fall, and the like, and hence lack any distinction between, for example, caller and collar, tot and taught, and don and dawn. The rapid extension of this development among younger speakers for whom it is not an inherited pattern clearly calls for rather intensive research. The culmination of this tendency might well be the reduction of the regional phonemic inventory by eliminating an /ɔ/ - /ɑ/ contrast through the general merging into /ɒ/ or /ɑ/.

The Vowel in thirty, Thursday, sermon, girl

/θɚti, θɚzdi, sɚmən, gɚl/

The extreme variability of this mid-central vowel in the states of the East and South contrasts sharply with the uniform occurrence of one type in the UM. This type is the constricted /r/, with the blade of the tongue bulging upward and often with some retroflexion of the tip of the tongue. This vowel is here represented by [ɚ], a symbol which covers such allophonic subtypes transcribed as [ɝ] and [ɹ].

As PEAS points out, a traveler from Boston to Charleston can encounter a variety of mid-central phones ranging from nonconstriction to full constriction, with the possibility of lip-rounding as

well. This range contrasts sharply with
the uniformity in the UM, where all infs.
have the historical constricted vowel
formerly derided by some teachers and
orthoepists who may well have thus de-
fended an inability to produce [ɚ] with
facility and grace.

In the UM only one Black speaker, Minnesota inf. 35, and one Canadian inf.,
201, have less than full constriction
with their [ɜ] in thirty and girl, for
the latter of which other allophonic constricted variations are recorded as well,
e.g., [ʌɚ], [ɜɚ], and [ɜˠ].

A solitary instance of a preserved pronunciation reflecting the situation before the coalescence of the vowel and /r/
appears in [ˈsɑɚvɨs ˌbɛriˠ] used by inf.
309 for service berry.

The Vowel in five, nine, twice

/faiv, nain, twais/

Despite the considerable extent of
phonic variation in the complex nucleus
of nine, and also despite some obvious
biases on the part of fws., a fairly
clear over-all picture can be drawn of
UM diaphonic distribution.

In the East the situation as described
in PEAS is quite complex. The low-front
beginning [a⁺, aɪ] is widespread and common, but a low-central beginning, as in
[ɑ⁺], prevails in New Jersey and southward along the Atlantic coast. A mid-
central beginning, as in [ɐ⁺, ə⁺, ʌ⁺], is
declining in popularity in northeastern
New England and parts of Upstate New
York, where it is chiefly rural and old-
fashioned. In eastern Virginia and in
coastal South Carolina and Georgia this
mid-central beginning is subject to contextual variation, for there it occurs
only before voiceless consonants, as in
twice and white. A similar feature in
Canada has received such attention as in
Martin Joos's "A phonological dilemma in
Canadian English," *Language* 18(1942),
141-44, and J. K. Chambers's "Canadian
raising," *Canadian Journal of Linguistics*
18(1973), 113-35. A so-called "slow" variety with either a lengthened first element [a·⁺, ɑ·⁺] or a very brief offglide
[a⁺, ɑ⁺] is found in New Jersey, the New
York and Philadelphia metropolitan areas,
and, before voiced consonants, in much of
the South and South Midland.

In the UM [a⁺, aɪ] is likewise widespread and most common. With the recognition that fw. Wn's and most of the Iowa
transcriptions of five and twice (see the
Synopses) and also of nine with [ɑ⁺]

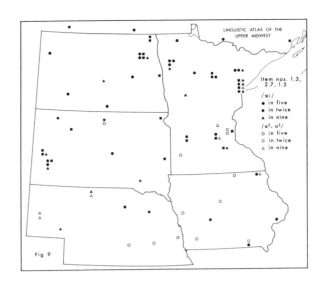

Fig. 9

should be corrected to [a⁺], it is clear
that roughly two-thirds of the UM infs.
have this low-central diphthong. There
seems to be a consistent, though slight
and perhaps insignificant, Northern
weighting in the distribution of [a⁺].

A much stronger regional pattern is
evident in the distribution of other UM
regional varieties. That with a centralized first element, [ɐ⁺], possibly a
reflex of Upstate New York origins, is
preponderantly Northern (see map), and
apparently is on the increase. It was recorded only three times in the Wisconsin
segment of the North Central survey.
Since, even in the speech of the Canadian
infs., it occurs before both voiced and
voiceless consonants, it lacks the contextual contrast observed in Virginia.

The slow diphthong, however, with a
conspicuously short offglide [a⁺, ɑ⁺] or
with a long first element, appears chiefly in those parts of Nebraska and Iowa
subject to some South Midland influence.
(See map.)

The Vowel in house, out, down, mountain

/haus, aut, daun, maunt+n/

Although with /au/ the same problems of
interpretation arise as with /ai/, some
quite definite statements can be made
about diaphonic distribution. This diphthong varies in three principal respects:
in the tongue position for the first element, the syllabic peak; in the relative
length of that element and the offglide;
and in the extent of the offglide.

As in the North and North Midland areas
of the eastern states, the dominant vari-

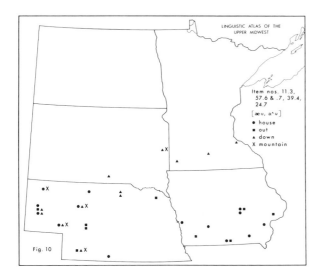

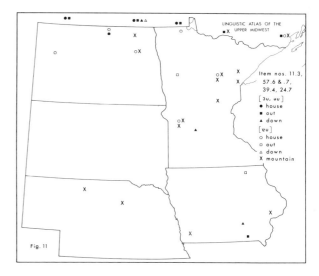

ety is a diphthong with an onset ranging from [a] to [ɑ], that is, from low-front to low-central. Within this range an indeterminate situation due to fw. variation and inconsistency makes undesirable any attempt to assign regional frequencies to distinct [aʊ] and [ɑʊ] types. This is true even though the problem in variation has been partly resolved by careful checking of the voice recordings. The check reveals that, for example, fw. A's [ɑˤʊ] should often be interpreted as [aˀʊ], that in the transcription of fws. H, P, Wn, and Wr the symbol [ɑʊ] frequently covers also a pronunciation shown better as [aʊ], and that, correspondingly, [aˆʊ] should be taken as an allophone of [æʊ]. Further, it reveals that to some of fw. A's South Dakota and Nebraska transcriptions there should be added an indication of the relative length of the peak and offglide, e.g., [a·ʊ] or [aʊ], the "slow" diphthongs. In the Synopses [ɑˤ] has generally been retained, but the length indication has been added when called for by a particular voice recording.

If, somewhat cavalierly, there is constructed a frequency chart of the common distribution of [aʊ] and [ɑˤʊ], a picture emerges that is rather consistent except for the situation in Nebraska. The chart, for which too much must not be claimed, is as follows:

	Mn.	Ia.	N.D.	S.D.	Nb.
house	75%	23%	46%	26%	51%
out	81%	35%	48%	40%	67%
down	67%	21%	40%	40%	68%
mountain	87%	18%	43%	55%	36%

With a much greater assurance it is possible to identify areas where other subtypes of /au/ occur. PEAS reports that the raised low-front [aˆʊ] and [æʊ] persist in rural northern New England and Upstate New York and are found also in sections of Pennsylvania as well as in Delaware and Maryland. In the UM they are, except for three instances in southern Minnesota, chiefly limited to the Midland speech derived from the Pennsylvania background. (See map.) Their absence in most of eastern Nebraska is less likely attributable to fw. variability than to the fact that most of the infs. in this area lack the language background that includes them. This phonological feature of front raising is probably not so readily acquired as are other phonological features or the lexical items that join eastern Nebraska to the southern two-thirds of Iowa. (See Volume 1.)

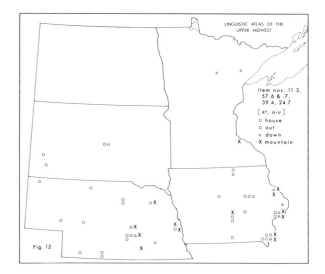

Tongue-raising in the central portion of the mouth yields a second subtype. A slight raising produces [ɐʊ]; a more extended raising, the mid-central [ɜʊ] or [əʊ]. Such raising, according to PEAS, had become old-fashioned where found in coastal Maine, southern New Hampshire, Upstate New York, and eastern Maryland. In the UM it is likewise a minority feature, recorded particularly in Minnesota and northern North Dakota. The higher variety, mid-central [ɜʊ], is especially characteristic of Canadian speech, where it yields to a phonological rule restricting its occurrence to a position before a voiceless consonant. (See map.)

A third subtype, overlapping the first in distribution, is marked by the acoustic effect of lengthening, produced either by a greater duration of the peak of the diphthong, e.g., [a·ʊ], or by a decreased duration of the offglide, e.g., [aᵁ]. Distribution of this feature in the eastern states correlates roughly with that in the UM. Besides being found in the South and the South Midland areas, it appears in part of the Midland, i.e., in New Jersey and eastern Pennsylvania and along the upper Ohio. It seems to be an expanding feature, since in the UM it is spread, though thinly, in one or more of the key words throughout the Midland area.

A possible fourth subtype might be that with only a slight tongue movement for the offglide, as in [ao] rather than [aʊ]. But although such pronunciations appear, they seem to be idiosyncratic with either the inf. or the fw. and lack social or regional correlation.

The Vowel in oil, boiled, poison, joint

/ɔil, bɔild, pɔizɫn, ǰoint/

The complex nucleus /ɔi/ offers less conspicuous variation in the UM than in the eastern states. For nearly all UM infs. this diphthong begins with a rounded low-back vowel ranging from [ɒ] to [ɔ], very much as does the free vowel /ɔ/.

A minority subtype with a mid-back beginning, [oɩ], described in PEAS as occurring around Chesapeake Bay and in New England, is recorded in the UM chiefly by fw. M in the Duluth and Iron Range area, by fw. P in southern Iowa, and, in joint, by fw. Wr in eastern Nebraska. The incidence of occurrence of a higher beginning is perhaps significantly increased by the inclusion of the raised variant [ɔ^]. See map for the comparative distribution in

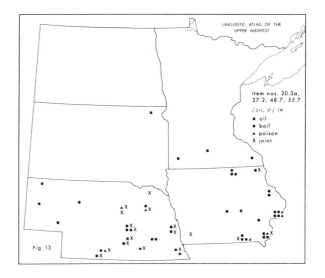

the listed key words. Since the speech of northeastern Minnesota already has been observed as having some Midland characteristics, it would seem that the UM distribution of [oɩ] and [ɔ^ɩ] correlates with that in the mid-Atlantic region, although not with that in New England.

A more sparsely distributed minority subtype is that with an unround beginning, ranging from [aɩ] to [ʌɩ]. In the East it is regionally restricted, according to PEAS, to northeastern New England and the South and South Midland, and socially restricted to the less educated. In the UM it persists in 21 instances in the last three key terms, but not at all in oil. All but one of the instances appear in the first settled eastern portion of the five states, in the speech of 19 infs.—11 Type I's, seven Type II's, and

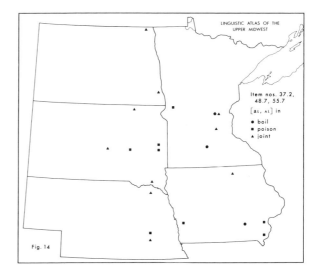

one Type III. They are as follows: 25, 29, 52; 106, 125, 135, 148, 152; 207, 226; 305, 315-16, 318-19, 325; 408, 424, 426. (See map.)

A clearer regional pattern emerges in the distribution of the diphthong that in either of two ways indicates greater proportionate length of the beginning element, the nuclear peak. The variations are represented by [ɔ·ɩ] and [ɔᶫ]. Such a diphthong is found in the South and South Midland areas of the East, but it has spread in the UM beyond the South Midland base in southeastern Iowa. (See map.)

The character of this diphthong exhibits a contextual variation as well. Before /l/ in the monosyllables oil and boil(ed) it may be so protracted before the onset of /l/ that there is produced a two-syllable word with a weak intervening /j/ glide, e.g., [ɔjəl] and [ɒᶫjəl]. This disyllabic form for either or both oil and boil is recorded in the speech of the following infs. in Iowa and eastern Nebraska: 101-4, 108-13, 116, 124, 126-33, 137-38, 145, 150; 413, 424, and 435.

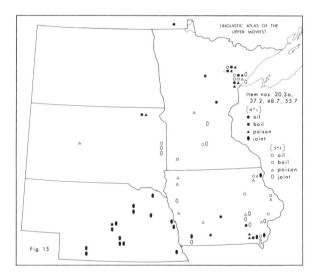

Fig. 15

The Vowel in music, dues, Tuesday, new

/mɪuzɩk, dɪuz, tɪuzde, nɪu/

Instead of the usual /ju/ and, after alveolars, /u/, a minority variant with stress on the initial element, /ˈɪu/, is described in PEAS as found in northern New England and, less frequently, in the New England settlement areas of New York and northern Pennsylvania. That this falling diphthong precariously survives

in the UM is suggested by its being recorded in one or more of the key words in the speech of 17 scattered infs., 10 of them with at least one parent who probably had inherited the New England pronunciation. These 10 are 31, 50, 57 (in three words); 122, 144 (in three words), 146 (in three words); 201; 410 (in two words), 413, 426. The seven others are 48; 129, 131; 210; 302; 418, 429.

THE VOWELS BEFORE /r/

As an area not significantly influenced by the speech of eastern New England and of the South, the UM lacks the complexity found in the eastern distribution of the several variations manifested by vowels before /r/ as well as by /r/ itself. Upper Midwest speakers uniformly maintain postvocalic /r/ as [ɚ] and display only moderate variation in the preceding vowel. No infs. exhibit the eastern and southern loss of postvocalic /r/. Yet, although there is hence no need for such a detailed phonetic description as Kurath provides in PEAS, there seems to be no strong reason to make comparison difficult by not following Kurath's basic outline in his Chapter 4. This section, then, will reflect that outline in its treatment of, first, the vowels before tautosyllabic /r/, that is, before /r/ in the same syllable, and, second, the vowels before intersyllabic /r/.

Postvocalic /r/ is essentially a nonsyllabic offglide from the preceding vowel. During the glide the tongue becomes laterally constricted. Either the body of the tongue is arched toward the roof of the mouth and the tip approaches the alveolar ridge (constricted /r/) or, with only slight such arching, the tip of the tongue is turned upward toward the hard palate (retroflex /r/).

The tongue position for retroflex /r/ in particular is so readily assimilated with that for the preceding vowel that it is not uncommon for that vowel to be "r-colored" and even, especially with [ɑ], for the result to be a single strongly retroflex vowel, as in my own usual pronunciation of barn as [bɑɹn].

A more significant and probably more noticeable assimilatory effect of /r/ upon the preceding vowel is centralization. This effect, manifested by many speakers, sometimes with regional distribution, is generally that of lowering and centralizing high and mid vowels and raising and centralizing low vowels. Thus, for example, the vowel of year, which historically should be the high-front /i/ of mean and meat, is either lowered slightly as in [ji˙ɚ] or lowered considerably as in [jɪɚ]; and the low-front /æ/ in marry appears as the slightly raised allophone [æˆ] or even as a mid-front vowel [ɛ].

For several reasons any effort to infer diaphonemes from the existing phonic data for vowels before /r/ in the UM is likely to be inadequate. Fieldworkers differ in their attention to subphonemic detail. A single inf. is likely to exhibit a fairly wide vocalic range in a given word, depending upon phrasal stress and other contextual factors. Furthermore, he may have a fairly consistent variation between words expectedly similar, e.g., beard as [biˈɚd] and year as [jɪɚ]. Finally, the population mix in much of the UM renders less than certain whether the source of individual allophonic variation is idiosyncratic or regional.

In PEAS a rule of thumb basis interpreted a raised tongue position for one vowel as equivalent to that of the next higher vowel. Thus [ɛˆ] is phonemicized as /e/, [ɪˆ] as /i/, [ʊˆ] as /u/, and [ɔˆ] as /o/. If the vowel in care is more like that in bat than the [ɛ] of bet, it is taken as /æ/. For the reasons stated above this rule has not been generally applied in the Synopses, although any user of this volume can easily make that application if he so desires.

How high a degree of uniformity is reached by the application of that rule to the UM data appears in the contrast between the following tables of responses for certain key words from selected infs., who, unlike the cultured infs. of the comparable tables in PEAS (p. 117), represent the full range from Type I to Type III. A few minor differences, such as greater vowel length in some Midland speech, are revealed in the phonic data of Table 1 and described fully in the subsequent detailed treatment. But Table 2 shows that the UM as a whole lacks conspicuous regional patterns in the distribution of the simple vowel phonemes before /r/. In Table 2 ascription to the /ɔ/ phoneme is actually tentative, in light of the probable coalescence of /ɑ/ and /ɔ/ into /ɒ/ for some speakers, such as 131.

<table>
<tr><td colspan="3"></td><td colspan="6" align="center">Table 1
Phonic Data</td><td colspan="6" align="center">Table 2
Phonemic Interpretation</td></tr>
<tr><td>Inf.</td><td>Type</td><td>Place</td><td>ear</td><td>care</td><td>barn</td><td>corn</td><td>door</td><td>poor</td><td>ear</td><td>care</td><td>barn</td><td>corn</td><td>door</td><td>poor</td></tr>
<tr><td>2</td><td>II</td><td>Ft. Frances, Ont.</td><td>ɪ⁺ɚ</td><td>ɛɚ</td><td>ǫɚ</td><td>ɔˇɚ</td><td>oˇoˊɚ</td><td>ʊɚ</td><td>ɪr</td><td>ɛr</td><td>ɑr</td><td>ɔr</td><td>or</td><td>ʊr</td></tr>
<tr><td>202</td><td>II</td><td>Killarney, Man.</td><td>ɪɚ</td><td>ɛɚ</td><td>ɑɚ</td><td>ɔˇɚ</td><td>oˇɚ</td><td>ʊˇɚ</td><td>ɪr</td><td>ɛr</td><td>ɑr</td><td>ɔr</td><td>or</td><td>ʊr</td></tr>
<tr><td>15</td><td>I</td><td>Duluth, Mn.</td><td>iˇ˒ə̣</td><td>ɛˇ˒ɚ</td><td>ɑ˙ə̣</td><td>ǫˇɚ</td><td>oˊɚ</td><td>y̦ɚ</td><td>ir</td><td>ɛr</td><td>ɑr</td><td>or</td><td>or</td><td>ʊr</td></tr>
<tr><td>18</td><td>III</td><td>Duluth, Mn.</td><td>iˇ˒ɚ</td><td>æˆɚ</td><td>ɑˆɚ</td><td>ǫˇɚ</td><td>o̦ˊɚ</td><td>ɔˆ˙ə̣</td><td>ir</td><td>ær</td><td>ɑr</td><td>or</td><td>or</td><td>ʊr</td></tr>
<tr><td>31</td><td>I</td><td>Minneapolis, Mn.</td><td>ɪˊ˒ɚ</td><td>ɛɚ</td><td>ǫˊɚ</td><td>ɔˊ˒ɚ</td><td>oˊ˒˙ɚ</td><td>uˊ˒ɚ</td><td>ɪr</td><td>ɛr</td><td>ɑr</td><td>ɔr</td><td>or</td><td>ʊr</td></tr>
<tr><td>34</td><td>III</td><td>Minneapolis, Mn.</td><td>ɪˊ˒ɚ</td><td>ɛɚ</td><td>ǫɚ</td><td>ɔˊ˒ɚ</td><td>oˇɚ</td><td>ʊɚ</td><td>ɪr</td><td>ɛr</td><td>ɑr</td><td>ɔr</td><td>or</td><td>ʊr</td></tr>
<tr><td>220</td><td>I</td><td>Fargo, N.D.</td><td>ɪɚ</td><td>ɛɚ</td><td>ɑɚ</td><td>ɔɚ</td><td>oˊɚ</td><td>oˆɚ</td><td>ɪr</td><td>ɛr</td><td>ɑr</td><td>ɔr</td><td>or</td><td>or</td></tr>
<tr><td>222</td><td>III</td><td>Fargo, N.D.</td><td>ɪɚ</td><td>ɛɚ</td><td>ɑɚ</td><td>ɔˇɚ</td><td>oˇɚ</td><td>uˊ˒ɚ</td><td>ɪr</td><td>ɛr</td><td>ɑr</td><td>ɔr</td><td>or</td><td>ʊr</td></tr>
<tr><td>115</td><td>II</td><td>Jewell, Ia.</td><td>ɪɚ</td><td>ɛɚ</td><td>ɑ̃ˊə̃ɚ</td><td>ɑˊɚ</td><td>ɔɚ</td><td>ʊɚ</td><td>ɪr</td><td>ɛr</td><td>ɑr</td><td>ɔr</td><td>ɔr</td><td>ʊr</td></tr>
<tr><td>131</td><td>III</td><td>Des Moines, Ia.</td><td>ɪˆiˇɚ</td><td>ɛɚ</td><td>ǫˊɚ</td><td>ɒɚ</td><td>ɔɚ</td><td>ʊɚ</td><td>ir</td><td>ɛr</td><td>ɑr</td><td>ɔr</td><td>ɔr</td><td>ʊr</td></tr>
<tr><td>311</td><td>I</td><td>Rapid City, S.D.</td><td>ɪˊ˒ɚ</td><td></td><td>ɑɚ</td><td>ɔɚ</td><td>oˊ˒˙ɚ</td><td>ʊɚ</td><td>ɪr</td><td></td><td>ɑr</td><td>ɔr</td><td>or</td><td>ʊr</td></tr>
<tr><td>326</td><td>III</td><td>Rapid City, S.D.</td><td>ɪɚ</td><td>ɛɚ</td><td>ǫɚ</td><td>ɔɚ</td><td>oˊ˒˙ɚ</td><td>uˊ˒ɚ</td><td>ɪr</td><td>ɛr</td><td>ɑr</td><td>ɔr</td><td>or</td><td>ʊr</td></tr>
<tr><td>148</td><td>I</td><td>Keokuk, Ia.</td><td>ɪɚ</td><td>ɛɚ</td><td>ɔɚ</td><td>ɔɚ</td><td>ɔˆɚ</td><td>ɔɚ</td><td>ɪr</td><td>ɛr</td><td>ɔr</td><td>ɔr</td><td>ɔr</td><td>ɔr</td></tr>
<tr><td>150</td><td>III</td><td>Keokuk, Ia.</td><td>ɪˆə̣</td><td>ɛɚ</td><td>ǫˊ˙ɚ</td><td>ɔˊɚ</td><td>oˇˊɚ</td><td>u˙ɚ</td><td>ir</td><td>ɛr</td><td>ɑr</td><td>ɔr</td><td>or</td><td>ʊr</td></tr>
<tr><td>409</td><td>I</td><td>Scottsbluff, Nb.</td><td>ɪˊ˒ɚ</td><td>ɛɚ</td><td>ɐ˙ɚ</td><td>ɔɚ</td><td>ɔˊ˒ɔˊɚ</td><td>ʊɚ</td><td>ɪr</td><td>ɛr</td><td>ɑr</td><td>ɔr</td><td>ɔr</td><td>ʊr</td></tr>
<tr><td>411</td><td>III</td><td>Scottsbluff, Nb.</td><td>ɪˊ˒ɚ</td><td>ɛɚ</td><td>ɑ˙ɚ</td><td>ɒˊˆ˙ɚ</td><td>ɔˊˆɚ</td><td>ʊɚ</td><td>ɪr</td><td>ɛr</td><td>ɑr</td><td>ɔr</td><td>ɔr</td><td>ʊr</td></tr>
<tr><td>429</td><td>I</td><td>Scottsbluff, Nb.</td><td>ɪˊ˒ɚ</td><td>ɛɚ</td><td>ǫˊ˒ɚ</td><td>ɒˊˆɚ</td><td>ɔˊˆ˙ɚ</td><td>oˊˆɚ</td><td>ɪr</td><td>ɛr</td><td>ɑr̩</td><td>ɔr</td><td>ɔr</td><td>or</td></tr>
</table>

29

The Vowels before Tautosyllabic /r/

The Vowels in ear, year, beard, here, queer

/ir - ɪr/

In ear and the other key words historic /i/ appears only along the range from [i] to [ɪ] in the UM. South Atlantic [e] and [ɜ] do not occur. As in the North and North Midland areas in general, nearly all UM speakers have the simple short [ɪ] before /r/. If [ɪ^] is to be considered an allophone of /i/, there is, of course, a greater incidence of /i/, which otherwise would be relatively infrequent; but in either case there seems to be some Midland weighting of /i/. Its incidence is greatest in southern Iowa, where 10 infs. have [i] or [ɪ^] in three or more of the key terms, as follows: 17-18, 26, 29-30, 36, 40, 46, 49-50. One inf., 147, has [jɚ] for year.

The Vowels in theirs, care, chair

/er - ɛr - ær/

In the three key words UM usage is remarkably uniform. The common /ɛ/ of New England, Upstate New York, and North Midland speech is even more dominant in the UM, where there appear only a few surviving instances of the receding /æ/ and the occasional /e/ of New England. The accompanying map includes as evidence for /e/ several instances of [ɛ^], noted especially by fw. P in Iowa, where they may perhaps better be interpreted as /e/. One

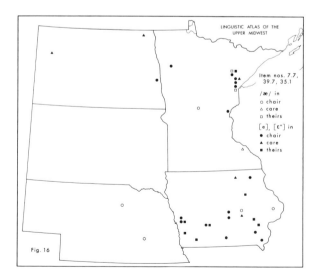

Fig. 16

Iowa inf., of Kentucky and Tennessee parentage, has /čɪr/, a South Midland pronunciation. Some variation in the length of the /ɛ/ vowel is recorded, with most of such instances in Midland speech territory.

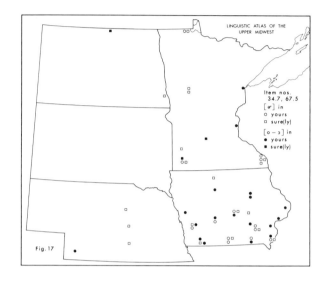

Fig. 17

The Vowels in sure, yours

/ur/

The lower high-front [ʊ] reported in PEAS as dominating the North and North Midland pronunciation of sure and, in the *Linguistic Atlas of New England*, as similarly dominant in yours, is equally common in all the UM except southern Iowa. Only six scattered infs. have a higher variety in yours—[ʊ^] 6, 17, 65; 123, [ʊˇ] 58; 123—and only four have it in sure—[ʊ^] 65; 120, [ʊˇ] 13; 129.

In the East /u/ competes with /o/ and even /ɔ/ in eastern New England and in the South and South Midland regions, with some relic occurrences of these lower vowels in Upstate New York. The UM distribution of these mid- and low-back vowels reflects the eastern situation, for there are only a few instances in Minnesota but a number in southern Iowa. (See map.) This minority form, not favored by educated speakers, may have become recessive, as it has not spread into the more recently settled portions of the UM. Infs. with /o/ or /ɔ/ are as follows: sure—45, c59; 204; yours—18, 40; 113, c117, 118, 122, 124, 126, 129, 131, 134, 138-39, 141-43, 147-48; 429. (Study of the taped recordings has resulted in correcting fw. Wn's [ɔɚ] and [oɚ] to [ʊɚ].)

It may be observed that in conversation inf. 13 has [pɔɚ] in the expression "poor ground."

But totally assimilated variants with only the retroflex vowel, [ʃɚ] and [jɚz], turn up in the UM without having background occurrences in neighboring Wisconsin or in the East, except for possibly the lone [jɝz] in Vermont. Recorded by four different fws., the UM instances are chiefly in the two eastern states. (See map.) Infs. manifesting this assimilation are as follows: sure—c4, c19-20, c47, c57-58; 104; 124, 128, c133, 136, 143, 149; 226; 420, c423, c428; yours—4, 56-57, c60; 125, 127-28, 135-36, 144-46, 149.

The Vowels in four, door, hoarse

/or - ɔr/

The eastern dialect research revealed sharply outlined areas dominated by the /o/ and /ɔ/ variants of the key words as well as of other investigated terms—boar, mourning, courting, and core. In PEAS the /o/ vowel is described as universal in the South and South Midland, and common in New England and its western settlement areas. In metropolitan New York, however, and in all the Midland region extending west from New Jersey and Maryland through Pennsylvania the usual vowel is [ɔ], which is phonemic as such except in western Pennsylvania, where for many speakers it functions as /o/ in contrast with /ɒ/.

Although in the UM the boundaries are not so sharp, the chief contrast between these Northern and Midland variants has generally been retained. Iowa and much of Nebraska clearly keep the Midland /ɔ/, and perhaps Midland influence via the Great Lakes accounts for fw. M's recording it at the lakehead of Duluth.

The contrast is not, however, a conspicuous one for all Northern speakers who can be considered as having /o/, since many of them have, for example, a raised [ɔ^] in four as opposed to a lowered [ɔˇ] in forty. This fairly close similarity between the contrasting vowels is like the situation Kurath notes as found in western New England and Upstate New York. Apparently also some Midland speakers can contrast what otherwise for them would be the homophonic pairs four-for, hoarse-horse, and mourning-morning by utilizing the Midland tendency to lengthen stressed free vowels. Thus several Iowa infs. have the contrast between /ho·rs/ hoarse and /hɔrs/ horse.

The Vowels in forty, morning, horse

/ɔr/

In the key words exists a vocalic range from a lowered [ɔˇ] to [ɒ] and even an occasional unrounded [ɤ], but most commonly found in [ɔ] or [ɔ^]. As is noted in PEAS, the eastern instances are generally to be phonemicized as /ɔ/, except that when in Pennsylvania and New Jersey the vowel position is higher than in law and loss it is probably assignable to the /o/ phoneme.

As has been previously explained, the settlement mixture in the UM makes it impossible within the scope of this work to attempt to make specific phonemic ascriptions for each occurrence of [ɔ] and [ɒ]. The Synopses treat them as instances of /ɔ/, despite the strong likelihood that for some Iowa speakers, at least, this phoneme does not exist after the coalescence of /ɔ/ and /ɑ/ as /ɒ/.

In the UM some northern speakers and many Midland speakers have so coalesced /o/ and /ɔ/ before /r/ that they are unable to distinguish in their own speech such pairs as hoarse and horse, for one, and mourning and morning, for another. Nearly one-third fail to contrast the members of these pairs, and about one-sixth lack contrasting vowels in four and forty. There is no social distribution pattern, but there is a regional one, as is clearly indicated in the accompanying map. The typical pattern appears also in the percentage of infs. who do not differentiate between mourning and morning: Minnesota 12%, Iowa 54%, North Dakota 8%, South Dakota 15%, Nebraska 38%, with an over-all average of 27%.

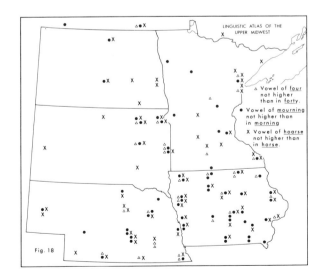

LINGUISTIC ATLAS OF THE UPPER MIDWEST

△ Vowel of four not higher than in forty.

● Vowel of mourning not higher than in morning

X Vowel of hoarse not higher than in horse.

Fig. 18

The minor Midland variation that is the reverse of the rounding of /ɑ/ before /r/ is the unrounding of /ɔ/ in that context, especially before the /rn/ or /rm/ cluster. As [ɒ] or [ɑ] this unrounding appears in the pronunciation of morning by the following infs.: 131-32, 147; 207, 213; 301; 413, 433; and in mourning in the speech of inf. 146. Perhaps related is the pronunciation of sorghum as [sɑɚgɨm] by Iowa inf. 109.

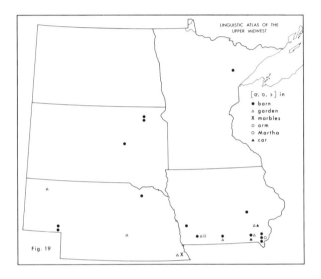

Fig. 19

The Vowels in barn, car, garden

/ɑr - ɒr - ɒr - ɔr/

Almost without exception the UM pronunciation of the key words is primarily with the low-central /ɑ/ before /r/ and secondarily with a low-back vowel ranging from unrounded [ɒ] through [ɒ] to fully rounded [ɔ]. Low-central /ɑ/ in the UM reflects its domination of Northern speech in the East by being the general pronunciation for nearly all UM speakers but those few in southern Iowa and Nebraska who have the low-back variants. (See map.) It is not possible, without specific study of the speech backgrounds of individual infs., to assign its occurrences to the putative disparate origins described in PEAS as existing in Maryland, eastern Pennsylvania, and western Pennsylvania.

Only rarely is the vowel fronted to the [a] position in such words, and not, apparently, in any distribution pattern. Infs. 36 and 118 are so recorded for garden and infs. 17, 29, 32, 40; 114, 118; and cvr305 for barn. A peculiarity of

barn is that, more than any other of the "ar" words in the worksheets, it lends itself to intensive retroflexion of the vowel. Forty-seven infs. are recorded with [bɑɚn] in contrast with only nine, for example, who have [ə] in garden.

A minor but distinctive regional variation is the rather complete rounding of /ɑ/ before /r/, especially when /r/ precedes a nasal consonant, so that to non-users barn sounds like born. Speakers with this dialect feature are likely to have the converse as well, so that to non-users their born sounds like barn. Informants with [ɒ] or [ɔ] are as follows: barn—125, 133, 143-44, *146, 148-49; 307-8, 316; car—135, 147. This vowel is used also by inf. 435 in marbles.

The Vowels in wire, tired

[a⁺ɚ - a⁺ɚ - ɑɚ - ɔ⁺ɚ]

Although throughout the UM there occur before /r/ the same monosyllabic allophones of /aɪ/ described earlier in this chapter, for some speakers in southern Iowa and Nebraska with a Midland speech heritage additional variations exist.

One noticeable characteristic is a shorter upglide, as indicated by the frequent field transcription [a⁺] and verified by a check of the voice recordings. Another, pointed to by Kurath in PEAS as typically Midland, is the complete loss of the glide, so that tired, for instance, becomes homophonous with tarred as /tɑrd/. A third is a combined backing and rounding of the vowel, as in western Pennsylvania—with the rounding likely greater after the /w/ of wire—so as to

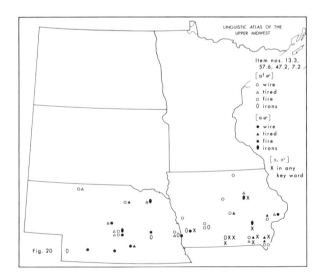

Fig. 20

yield either [ɒ⁺ɚ] or [ɔ⁺ɚ] or even the
simple vowel of [ɒɚ] or [ɔɚ], as in New
Jersey and Delaware. The distribution of
these features appears on the accompanying map. Informants with at least one example in their speech are as follows:
[a⁺ɚ] 105, 115-16, 123-24, 126-28, 138,
140, 144, 146-47, 150; 404, 413, 421-23,
425, 427-29; [aɚ] 117, 124, 128, 135,
cvr137, 140, 146, 149; 413, 416, 421-24,
428, 430, 432; [ɔ⁺ɚ, ɒ⁺ɚ] 117, 125, 136,
145, 147; [ɔɚ, ɒɚ] 144, 146, 148. Besides
these instances fw. Wr records in Nebraska several pronunciations which apparently are disyllabic, a feature that Kurath
ascribes, however, only to South Carolina
and Georgia. The following infs. are recorded with [ajɚ] for wire, andirons, or
fire: 413-14, 420, 425, 427, 431, 433,
435; and fw. P, in addition, records Iowa
inf. 117 as having [tɔ^ɪjɚd] for tired.

The Vowels in flower, ours

[æʊɚ - aʊɚ - ɑʊɚ - ɑɚ]

Although as the complement of the lexical item pick/pluck flowers (73.4) the
term flowers is not generally recorded by
the fws., enough instances are transcribed to demonstrate that variation in
its complex nucleus parallels that of the
diphthong in wire and tired. The treatment of /aʊ/ earlier in this chapter is
relevant.
But, as with /aɪ/, the following /r/
induces variants in Midland speech that
have persisted in the western migration
to Iowa and Nebraska. The weakening of
the offglide to yield [ɑᵁɚ, ɑᵊɚ] appears
in the speech of infs. 103; 416, 422-23,
427, 430. The eastern and western Pennsylvania phenomenon of complete loss of
the glide appears in the form [flɑɚ] used
by infs. 144; 415, 420-21, 428, and 431,
and in the rounded variants [flɔɚ, flɒɚ]
used by infs. 141, 143, 148, and 149.
(See map.)
Supplementary data for generally recorded ours suggest that the tendency to
simplify the /aʊ/ diphthong before /r/ is
affecting speakers outside the Midland
speech area. Loss of rounding, as in
[ɑɚz], occurs with infs. 20; 114; 220-23;
402, 409, 411. Weakening of the offglide
as in [ɑᵁɚz, ɑᵊɚz], is evinced in the
pronunciation of infs. 24, 33, 37; 148;
202; 305, 327; 414, 416, 421, 423-24.
Complete loss, yielding [ɑɚz], appears in
the field records of the following infs.:
c47, 60-61; 105, 107-8, 113, 115, c121,
125, cvr126, 127, 129-30, 136, 140, 142-
44, 147, 149; 305, 307; 413, 427, 431.

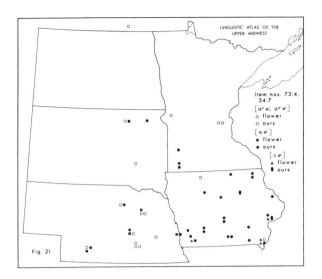

Fig. 21

But it is my opinion that a current survey would reveal this pronunciation to be
spreading rapidly, as it is now fairly
common in the Twin Cities and among students at the University of Minnesota. Two
infs. have a single rounded vowel in
[ɔɚz], 116 and 141; and one inf. has a
rounded diphthong [ɒʊɚz], 57.

The Vowels before Intersyllabic /r/

In PEAS Kurath described a variety of
dialectal differences found in the eastern states when the /r/ following a vowel
is itself followed by a vowel. Although
the situation is less distinctive in the
UM, where the uniform existence of tautosyllabic /r/ reduces the possibility of
vowel variation between, say, beer and
diphtheria, it still demands some attention here.

The Vowels in diphtheria

[i - iᵛ - ɪ^ - ɪ]

Because of its predominance in the
speech of the North Midland and the
North, the expected transmitted vowel in
the UM before /r/ in diphtheria is the
checked /ɪ/ in six and fit, often centralized as [ɪ'] or, for infs. 31, 36;
303; 402, 405, even [ɨ].
However, a high free vowel [i, iᵛ],
such as PEAS reports for eastern New England and the South, is offered by two
Minnesotans (13 and 16) and five Iowans
(117, 140, 146-47, and 149), the parents

33

of none of whom were born in either of those areas. If the transcription [ɩ^] is to be assigned to the free vowel /i/, as Kurath assigns it, then these additional infs. are to be listed: 2, 14, 23-24, 29, 37-38, 59; 103-4, 113, 141; 224; 328. Only two of them, 23 and 103, have immediate parental ties with eastern New England (Maine), but several others, with Wisconsin or Ohio parents, may have that particular speech legacy. Certainly it is not a principal feature of UM speech.

A lowered mid-front vowel /ɛ/, found in eastern New England and West Virginia as well as along the South Atlantic coast, is used before the /r/ in diphtheria by three scattered infs., 143; 209; and 415, none of whom has a relevant family background.

One inf., 114, has only the retroflex [ɚ], not reported as such in the eastern states.

The Vowels in cherry, merry

[ɛ - ɚ]

With even greater uniformity than in the eastern states UM speakers have the mid-front /ɛ/ before /r/ in cherry and merry. The principal modification is simply that of appreciable retroflexion of the vowel as indicated by [ɚ] and occurring sporadically without patterned distribution in the area. The centralizing effect observed in Pennsylvania has reached into the UM in the variant form [tʃ ɜˤ ri ̌] used in conversation by Iowa inf. vr115 and in the fully retroflex [ɚ] in the cherry of infs. 117, c138-39, 140, 144, and in the merry of infs. 148; 422. (See map.)

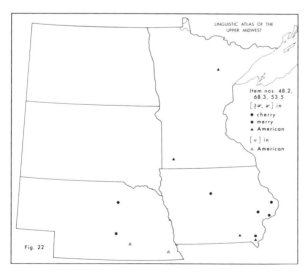

The lower high-front [ɩ] of Upstate New York appears in the pronunciation of Iowa inf. 114, [tʃ ɩˀri ̌], whose mother was born there; and an unexplained [æ] occurs in cherry as spoken by inf. 56. Midland backing may also be the cause of the pronunciation of American as [əmuɹɩˀkɨn] by Nebraskans 432 and 435. For this word slighter backing of the vowel appears as [ɜ] in the speech of infs. 14, 59; 147, 149. Otherwise American has only [ɛ].

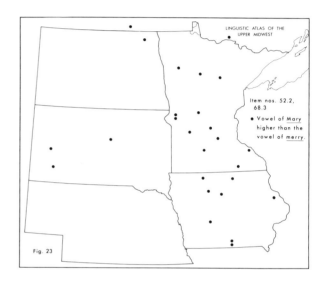

The Vowels in Mary, dairy

/e - ɛ/

The distinction created by a higher vowel, [e, eˇ, ɛ^], in Mary than in merry has been preserved in the first settled parts of the UM by some speakers directly related to the eastern areas where it occurs, but generally the distinction appears to be headed for obsolescence as more and more younger speakers adopt the [ɛ] vowel in Mary.

In the eastern states the distinction is described by Kurath as common in most of New England, western New York, northern Pennsylvania, and the South. In the UM it appears chiefly in Minnesota and northern Iowa. (See map.) Of the 26 UM infs. retaining this distinction five are from foreign-language family background but all the others have at least one parent directly in the stream of language flow from eastern origins in the Northern speech area, or, with infs. 144 and 320, from Maryland and Kentucky, or, with infs. 2, 25, 44, 52, and 202, from the British Isles, where the distinction is common. Sixteen of the 26 are the older speakers of Type I, only 10 are in Type II, and none in Type III. The 26 are as follows: 2, 7, 10-11, 25-26, 28, 41, 44, 49, 52, 56, 65; 104, 106, 113-14, 121, 126, 144-45; 202, 207; 312, 314; 320.

Dairy, which has a similar eastern distribution of the /deri/ variant, has moved faster than Mary toward a common UM pronunciation with [ɛ]. Only three speakers have [e] and 14 have [ɛ^]. These are 6, 32, 34, 40, 62, 65; 104, 107-8, 136, 139; 141, 151; 214; 310, 314; 401. Two infs., 114 and 129, are recorded with the unusual high-front [ɪ^].

The Vowels in married, wheelbarrow, harrow, barrel, lariat

/ɛ - æ - ɑ/

Presumptively, the first four key words would today have the low-front [æ] as the stressed vowel. But this is not true in England or in America. Both in the eastern states and in the UM an older pronunciation with [ɑ] retains vitality, and a newer one, with [ɛ], caused by the following /r/, seems to be gaining ground. Lariat, found in the southwestern sector of the UM as a loan from American Spanish to the cattle industry, fits into the complex patterns of the other terms, which are by no means consistent in their proportion of the several vowel variants.

Although the specific details may be somewhat skewed because of the tendency of the Iowa fws. to record as [ɛ] instances that other fws. record as [æ^], the general picture is probably not significantly distorted.

Of the four words brought from England, married is most successful in keeping historic [æ]. Widespread in the East, this vowel, lower than the [ɛ] of cherry, is favored by 62% of the UM infs., rather unevenly distributed as follows: Minnesota 67%, Iowa 14%, North Dakota 96%, South Dakota 84%, Nebraska 47%. The converse percentages would indicate the distribution of the [ɛ] vowel, since no other variant occurs, a minority form with [ɑ], common in western Pennsylvania, having not survived among Midland speakers in the UM.

In wheelbarrow, however, [ɑ] competes on even terms with [æ]. Kurath observes in PEAS that [ɑ] is generally found in the folk speech of the East, excepting southwestern New England, a section with a strong influence upon Northern speech in the UM. This may be the reason why [ɑ] is stronger in Iowa and Nebraska. In the

UM one-half of the infs. with the [ɑ] variant are in Type I. The proportions are as follows:

	Mn.	Ia.	N.D.	S.D.	Nb.	Ave.
[æ]	42%	8%	53%	67%	30%	40%
[ɛ]	20%	37%	4%	4%	27%	14%
[ɑ]	33%	50%	35%	30%	43%	39%

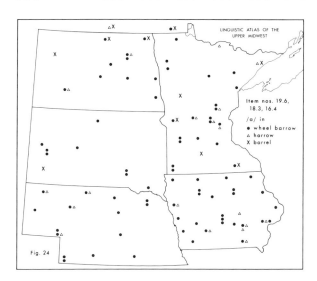

Fig. 24

As is true in the East, neither harrow, a farm term, nor widely known barrel has the high incidence of [ɑ] found in wheelbarrow. In both words the low-front [æ] seems to have a Northern weighting, in contrast with Midland strength in [ɛ]. The proportions follow:

	Mn.	Ia.	N.D.	S.D.	Nb.	Ave.
harrow						
[æ]	52%	24%	62%	94%	44%	55%
[ɛ]	37%	66%	24%	6%	42%	35%
[ɑ]	12%	13%	14%	0	14%	11%
barrel						
[æ]	45%	16%	38%	61%	24%	37%
[ɛ]	40%	84%	42%	35%	76%	44%
[ɑ]	5%	0	20%	3%	0	6%

A footnote to the pronunciation of /æ/ and /ɛ/ before intersyllabic /r/ is provided by the deviant form /kwɛri/ observed in the speech of infs. 105 and 139 for the word quarry. Lariat was added to the worksheets when the investigation reached the cattle country of South Dakota and Nebraska. Seventeen infs. are recorded with a pronunciation interpreted as /æ/: 310-12, 320, 326, 328; 403-4, 408, 410-12, 418-20, 429, 436. Twelve infs. have /ɛ/: 402, 413-14, 417, 421, 423-24, 426-27, 431, 434-35. One, 409, has [a], perhaps here

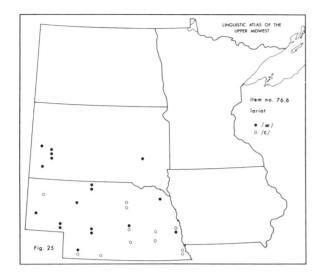

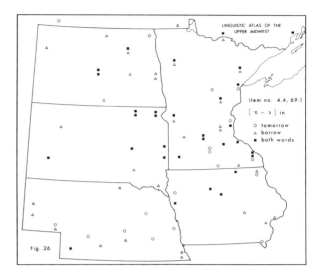

to be taken as an instance of /ɑ/, since the same inf. has /ɑ/ in wheelbarrow. (See map.)

The Vowels in tomorrow, borrow, orange

[ɑ - ɒ - ɒ - ɔ]

Although in the eastern states an un-round vowel ranging from [a] through [ɑ] to [ɒ] occurs almost everywhere in tomorrow and borrow, the wide though uneven distribution of a rounded vowel [ɒ] or [ɔ] as well is predictive of both diversity and overlapping in the UM. Indeed, the overlapping is such that even more difficult than in the East would be an attempt to assign each instance of [ɒ] to the /ɑ/ phoneme or each instance of [ɒ] to the /ɔ/ phoneme, especially because of some fw. uncertainty in selecting either [ɒ] or [ɒ] as an impressionistic decision.

The unround vowel [a] or [ɒ] likewise dominates the UM in both tomorrow and borrow, more strongly so in the former. In harmony with the [ɒ] and [ɔ] of New England, the rounded vowel clearly has Northern orientation in the UM, but the concurrent existence of a rounded vowel in western and central Pennsylvania makes only tentative any ascription of its UM use to specific eastern source areas. (See map.)

The regional distribution of the un-round [ɑ - ɒ] in contrasting tomorrow and borrow is as follows:

	Mn.	Ia.	N.D.	S.D.	Nb.	Ave.
tomorrow	34%	12%	19%	28%	19%	23%
borrow	38%	18%	38%	39%	24%	31%

A quite different situation obtains with orange. The stronger position of a rounded vowel in this word in the East is the basis for its strength in the UM, where only nine infs. have /ɑr+nǰ/, six of them in Minnesota. They are as follows: 2, 12, 18, 22, 29, 31, 35; 303; 403.

The Vowels in furrow, worry

/ɚ - 3r - ʌr/

In both furrow and worry two main pronunciations appear in the UM without distinctive regional or social distribution differences. They reflect two variants found in the eastern states.

By far the dominant type, used by about one-sixth of the UM infs., is exemplified by /fɚo, wɚi/, that is, by a pronunciation marked by a strongly retroflex or constricted syllabic vowel followed, without conspicuous glide, by a final weak syllable. It reflects the variety generally recorded in New England, Upstate New York, and the Midland.

A much less common, though widely scattered, variety is that which is also found in eastern New England, eastern Pennsylvania, and the South. It is marked by a mid-central syllabic /3/, often "r-colored" and sometimes transcribed as [ʊ] or [œ], which is followed by a noticeable consonantal /r/ glide to the next vowel, as in /f3ro, w3ri/. These two varieties were not distinguished in Nebraska, however, by fw. Wr.

A third and rare variety, such as is found in metropolitan New York and eastern New England, is marked by [ʌ] or [ə] with a conspicuous consonantal /r/ glide to the final vowel. Aside from the fact that in South Dakota fw. Wn used this symbolization apparently for the second variety, this pronunciation is limited in worry to Canadian inf. 1, and in furrow to the following infs.: 27, 41-42, 54; 137; 305, 308, 316; 422.

Three curious examples of /ɛ/ turn up in furrow, used by infs. 1, 20, 44, perhaps as a result of extreme fronting of the second variety.

The Vowels in squirrel, stirrup, syrup

/ɪr - ɛr - ɚ/

The fairly high incidence of /ɪ/ in the key words as pronounced in New England, New York State, and eastern Pennsylvania is reflected in its occurrence in syrup in the UM, less so in stirrup, but not at all in squirrel. An alternate /ɛ/, also widespread in the East, has barely sur-

vived in the UM with three instances of syrup and four of stirrup in Iowa and one of syrup and two of stirrup in Minnesota. As the following table shows, /ɛ/ does not turn up at all in the speech of the last generation to settle in the western half of the UM.

	Mn.	Ia.	N.D.	S.D.	Nb.	Ave.
/ɪ/						
stirrup	6%	9%	4%	11%	9%	8%
syrup	20%	18%	27%	32%	10%	20%
/ɛ/						
stirrup	3%	9%	0	0	0	6%
syrup	3%	6%	0	0	0	3%

Informants with /ɪ/ are as follows: stirrup—14, 38, 40, 48; 128-29, 149-50; 226; 308, 310, 317-19; 425, 431, 433; syrup—7, 18-19, 24, 26, 38, 41, c43, 52, 57-58, 60, 62; 112, 123-24, 126, 128-29, 131, 143, 149; c202, 205, 208-9, 211-13; 306, 308, 310, 315, 317, 326, 328; 407, 410, 431.

Those with /ɛ/ are stirrup—12, 39; 126, 136, 144; syrup—c9, 14, 43, 50; 118, 144, 147; c216, c218.

The dominant UM pronunciation of both stirrup and syrup is disyllabic, with the vowel /ɚ/, e.g., [stɚəp] and [sɚəp], although in the speech of the following infs. both words have become monosyllabic: [stɚp] 5-6, 9, 21, 24, 49-50, 57, 65; 208-9, 213, 216, 222; 301, 305, 321; 407, 430; [sɚp] 12, 20, 22-23, 57; 137; 203, 216, 224; 421. Other monosyllabic variants recorded are [sɪrp] 141; [sɛrp] 147.

Squirrel, recorded in "gray squirrel" as a lexical item competing with gopher, contrasts with the two preceding terms in its nearly complete acceptance of the pronunciation with [ɚ] or, occasionally, [əɚ]. No UM inf. has the eastern New England [skwɛrəl], and only one has the form [skwɪrəl]—Minnesota inf. 52, who surely has derived this British variant directly from his Welsh parents.

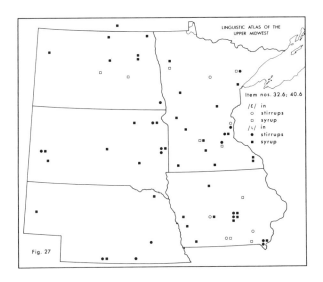

LINGUISTIC ATLAS OF THE
UPPER MIDWEST

Item nos. 32.6; 40.6

/ɛ/ in
○ stirrups
□ syrup
/ɪ/ in
■ stirrups
■ syrup

Fig. 27

Synopses

The following Synopses present analyses of the vowel systems of the 208 Upper Midwest informants in the form of schematic tables of the transcribed stressed vowels of certain selected key terms, essentially the same terms used in similar tables in PEAS. The assignment of a given vowel transcription to a particular column is in large measure consistent with the principles of traditional taxonomic phonemics. As was observed in Chapter 1, however, the intermingling of Northern and West Midland features in much of the region, not only with respect to different informants in the same community but even in the speech of a single informant living in the transition zone, sometimes makes uncertain such an assignment of the low-back vowels.

The assignment then needs to be interpreted as equivalent to the use of virgules / / to denote large sound-classes without specific intent to phonemic status.

Not every field record contains transcribed responses for every key term. To complete the individual informant's chart the vowels from words with approximately similar phonetic environments have been substituted. The nature of the approximation needs consideration when generalizations are made, of course. The final /o/ of know, for example, is not in every respect analogous to the /o/ of the replacement term froze, where the vowel is followed by a voiced continuant.

The key terms thus replaced are listed below, together with the substitute words and the relevant informant numbers:

APRIL: apron—206; 327-28; 405.

BAG: drag—13; jag—24, 27, 34, 42; 113-18, 129; 213-14, 220, 225; 301, 313-15; 402-3, 405, 407, 413, 415, 429, 433-34, 436.

BOIL: spoil—305.

CARE: careless—25, 36, 44, 46, 48, 51, 55, 59-60; 201, 223; 305, 309, 311-12, 327; 429; carry—14, 18; 131; scared—316.

CROP: slop—214.

DOWN: pounds—413.

EAR: cleared—56; year—327.

FLOWER: hours—2, 44; 101-16, 118-21, 125-27, 129-33, 136-44, 147-50, 152; 202-3, 205-12, 214-17, 219-22; 301-8, 311-13, 320, 323-28; 407-10, 412, 417-19, 429, 436.

GLASS: class—56; 105, 135.

HALF: calf—1, 4, 9, 20-21, 24, 28, 37, 48, 61; 103, 108, 111-12, 119, 133, 141; 213-14, 219, 221-22; 303-4, 308, 325; 408, 411, 416, 425, 427-28, 430, 432-35.

HEAD: bedspread—213; sled—57, 65; 317.

JOINT: joined—327.

KNOW: froze—115-16, 118, 128, 132, 134; 405, 410, 417, 424, 428-29.

LAW: saw—3, 11; 317; 407.

MARRIED: carried—314.

MERRY: cherry—32, 40, 48, 56-58, 62-65; 317, 328; 427, 436.

OUT: drouth—316.

PULL: bull—436.

ROAD: toad—204, 216.

SIX: sixth—56; 108; 408.

TEN: fence—436; genuine—206; Pennsylvania—328; twenty—408.

THIRTY: purpose—327.

THREE: tree—328.

TWICE: white—118; 327-28.

TWO: new—118.

YOURS: pure—21, 58; yourself—315.

	i	ɪ	e	ɛ	ɜ	æ	ɑ	ai	ɔi	au		ɔ	ʌ	o	ʊ	u	
three	iᵛi																
																u˂	two
grease	ɪ˃̂iᵛ																
																u˂	tooth
six		ɪ															
															---		wood
crib		ɪ															
															ʊ		pull
ear	ɪɚ																
															ʊɚ		yours
beard	ɪ^·ɚ													oᵒ^			ago
eight			eɪᵛ											o˃			coat
April			e											oᵒ^			road
ten				ɛ										oᵒ^			home
egg				ɛeᵛ										oᵘ			know
head				ɛ										oɚ			four
Mary						æ^ɚ								oᵒ^ɚ			door
chair				ɛᵛɚ								ɔ^·ɚ					hoarse
care				ɛɚ										oᵛ·ɚ			mourning
merry				ɛɚ													
thirty					ɜᵛ˃ɚ								ʌ				sun
sermon					ɚ								ʌ				brush
furrow				ɛᵛɚ													
ashes						æ·						ɔᵛ					frost
bag						æɛ˃̂						---					log
married						æ^ɚ						ɔᵛ					dog
half						æɛ^						ɔᵛ·					fog
glass						ææ̃^	ɚ˂										water
aunt						æ̃æ̃^						ɔᵛ					daughter
father							ɑ					ɔᵛ					law
palm						æ						ɒ^ɚ					warm
barn							ɑɚ										
garden							ɑɚ					ɔɚ					forty
crop							ɑᵉ					ɔɚ					morning
on							ɑə					ɒ^ɚ					corn
college												ɒ˂ɑᵛɚ					horse
borrow												ɒ^ɑ					
five								a˃ɪ^		ɑ˂u˂̂							down
twice								a˃ɫ˂		3˂ᵛu							out
wire								e˂ɪ˃̂ə		ɑ˂u˂̂ɚ							flower
joint									ɒ^ɪ˃								
boil									ɔᵛɫ								
	i	ɪ	e	ɛ	ɜ	æ	ɑ	ai	ɔi	au		ɔ	ʌ	o	ʊ	u	

39

	ɪ	ι	e	ε	з	æ	ɑ		aι	ɔι	au		ɔ	ʌ	o	ʊ	u	
three	i ˅ i																ʉ ˃ u	two
grease	i ˅ i																u ˂	tooth
six		ι														ʊ		wood
crib		---														ʊ		pull
ear		ι ᵗ ɚ														ʊɚ		yours
beard		ι ˆ • ɚ													o ŏ ˆ			ago
eight			e e ˆ												o •			coat
April			e												o			road
ten				ε ε ˆ											o o ˆ			home
egg				ε ˆ e ˅											o			know
head				ε ε̆ ξ										o ˅ o ɚ				four
Mary				ε ˆ ĕ ɚ										o ˅ o ɚ				door
chair				ε ɚ									ɔ ˅ • ɚ					hoarse
care				ε ɚ									ɔ ˆ • ɚ					mourning
merry				ε r														
thirty					ɚ									ʌ				sun
sermon					ɚ									ʌ ˂ ʌ				brush
furrow					ɚ													
ashes						æ							ɒ ˆ					frost
bag						æ ι ˃							---					log
married						æ ˆ ɚ							ɒ ˆ					dog
half						æ •							ɒ					fog
glass						æ ε̆ ˃ ˄							ɒ ˆ					water
aunt						æ ε̆ ξ ˆ ˃							ɒ					daughter
father							ɑ						ɔ ˅					law
palm													ɒ • ɔ ˅ ɚ					warm
barn							ɑ • ɚ											
garden							ɑ ɚ						ɔ ɚ					forty
crop							ɑ e						ɔ ˅ ɚ					morning
on							ɑ e						ɔ ˅ ɚ					corn
college													ɔ ˅ • ɚ					horse
borrow																		
five									e ˂ ι ξ		ɑ ˆ ˂ ʋ							down
twice									ə ι ˃		з ˂ ʋ							out
wire									ə ˂ ᵗ ˂					ɚ				flower
										ɒ ˆ ι ˃								joint
										ɔ ˅ ᵗ								boil
	ɪ	ι	e	ε	з	æ	ɑ		aι	ɔι	au		ɔ	ʌ	o	ʊ	u	

	i	ɪ	e	ɛ	ɜ	æ	ɑ	aɪ	ɔɪ	au	ɔ	ʌ	o	ʊ	u	
three	iᵛi														uᵛ	two
grease	ɪↃi														u‹u	tooth
six		ɪ												ʊ		wood
crib		ɪ•												ʊ		pull
ear		ɪɚ												ʊɚ		yours
beard		ɪ^ɚ											o o^			ago
eight			e e^										o‹o			coat
April			e										o‹o^			road
ten				ɛɛ̆^									o o^			home
egg			eᵛe^										oʊᵛ			know
head				---									o•ɚ			four
Mary				ɛɚ									oᵛo‹ɚ			door
chair				ɛɚ							ɔ•ɚ					hoarse
care				ɛɚ							ɔ^•ɚ					mourning
merry				ɛɚ												
thirty					ɚ							ʌ				sun
sermon					ɚ							---				brush
furrow					ɚ											
ashes						æ	'ɑ									frost
bag						æɛ^>	ɑ>									log
married						æ^ɚ					ɒ^					dog
half						æ					ɒˠ					fog
glass						ææ^					---					water
aunt						ææ̆^					ɔᵛ					daughter
father							ɑ				ɔᵛ					law
palm						æᵛˠ					ɒ^ɚ					warm
barn							ɑɚ									
garden							ɑɚ				ɔɚ					forty
crop							ɑ>				ɔ‹ᵛɚ					morning
on							ɑe				---					corn
college							ɑ‹				ɔᵛɚ					horse
borrow																
five								ɑ‹^•ɪ>		ɑ‹^u						down
twice								e‹ɪ>		3ᵛu						out
wire								ɑ>ɪ>ɚ		ɑˠɚ						flower
joint									ɔᵛɪ>							joint
boil									ɔᵛ+							boil
	i	ɪ	e	ɛ	ɜ	æ	ɑ	aɪ	ɔɪ	au	ɔ	ʌ	o	ʊ	u	

41

	i	ɪ	e	ɛ	ɜ	æ	ɑ		aɪ	ɔɪ	au		ɔ	ʌ	o	ʊ	u	
three	i˅i																u<	two
grease	i˅>i																u	tooth
six		ɪ>														ʊ		wood
crib		---														ʊ		pull
ear		ɪ>ɚ														ʊ˅•ɚ		yours
beard		ɪɚ													oo^			ago
eight			ee^												o<o^			coat
April			e												o•			road
ten				ɛɛ˘^											oo<			home
egg				ɛ^e˅											oo^			know
head				ɛɛ^											o<˅ɚ			four
Mary				ɛɚ											oo<^ɚ			door
chair				ɛɚ										ɔo˅ɚ				hoarse
care				---										ɔɚ				mourning
merry				ɛɚ														
thirty					ɚ										ʌ				sun
sermon					ɚ									ʌ<ɤ				brush
furrow							e^r											
ashes						æ							ɒ<^					frost
bag						æɛ^>							---					log
married						æ^ɚ							ɔ˅					dog
half						æɛ^							ɒ<ɑ					fog
glass						æɛ^							ɔ˅					water
aunt							ɑ						ɒ^					daughter
father							ɑ						ɔ˅					law
palm							ɑ						ɔ˅ɚ					warm
barn							ɑ•ɚ											
garden							ɑɚ						ɔɚ					forty
crop							ɑɑ˘^						ɔ˅ɚ					morning
on							ɑe˅						ɔ˅ɚ					corn
college							ɑ>						ɔ˅ɚ					horse
borrow							ɑɚ											
five									e<ɪ^		ɑ<^ʊ^							down
twice									a˘>ɪ˞		ɑ<ʊ^							out
wire									a>ɪ^ɚ		ɑ<ʊɚ							flower
joint										ɔ˅ɪ>								joint
boil										ɔ˅ɪ>								boil
	i	ɪ	e	ɛ	ɜ	æ	ɑ		aɪ	ɔɪ	au		ɔ	ʌ	o	ʊ	u	

word	i	ɪ	e	ɛ	ɜ	æ	ɑ	ai	ɔi	au	ɔ	ʌ	o	ʊ	u	word
three	i˅														u˂	two
grease	i˅i														u•	tooth
six		ɪ													---	wood
crib		ɪ												ʊ		pull
ear		ɪɚ												ʊɚ		yours
beard		ɪɚ											o^			ago
eight			e e^										o˂			coat
April			e										o˂ o^			road
ten				ɛ ɛ^									o o^			home
egg				ɛ^ e˅									o o^			know
head				ɛ									o˅ɚ			four
Mary				ɛɚ									o˅ o˂ɚ			door
chair				ɛ˅ɚ									ɔ^ oɚ			hoarse
care				ɛɚ									o•ɚ			mourning
merry				ɛɚ												
thirty					ɚ							ʌ				sun
sermon					ɚ							ʌ ʌ•				brush
furrow					ɚ^											
ashes						æ					ɒ^					frost
bag						æ æ^					ɒ^					log
married						æ^ɚ					ɔ˅					dog
half						æ					ɒ					fog
glass						æ æ^					ɒ^					water
aunt						æ̃ æ̃					ɒ^					daughter
father							ɑ				ɔ˅•					law
palm							ɑ•				ɔ˅ɚ					warm
barn							ɑɚ									
garden							ɑɚ				ɔ˅ɚ					forty
crop							ɑ˃				ɒɑ^ɚ					morning
on							ɒ				ɒ^ɑɚ					corn
college											ɔ˅ɚ					horse
borrow																
five								a˃ɪ^		ɑ˂ʊ^						down
twice								a^˃ɪ^		3˂ʊ^						out
wire								e˂ɪ˃ɚ		a˃ʊɚ						flower
joint									ɒ^ɪɑ˃							joint
boil									ɔ˅ɪɔ˃˂							boil

| | i | ɪ | e | ɛ | ɜ | æ | ɑ | ai | ɔi | au | ɔ | ʌ | o | ʊ | u | |

43

	i	ɪ	e	ɛ	ɜ	æ	ɑ		aɪ	ɔɪ	au		ɔ	ʌ	o	ʊ	u	
three	i ̌ i																u ̌ u	two
grease	ɪ ̂ i																u	tooth
six		ɪ														---		wood
crib		ɪ														ʊ		pull
ear		ɪɚ														ʊ ̂ ɚ		yours
beard		ɪ ̣ ̂ ɚ													oʊ			ago
eight			eɪ ̂												o ̆ ʊ			coat
April			e												oʊ			road
ten				ɛ ɛ ̂											o·			home
egg				ɛ ̂ ɛ ̌											o ̥ ʊ			know
head				ɛ ̆ ̂											oɚ			four
Mary				ɛ ̌ ɚ											o ̌ ɚ			door
chair				ɛɚ								ɔ ̌ ɔ ̂ ɚ						hoarse
care				ɛɚ								ɔ ̂ ɚ						mourning
merry				---														
thirty					ɚ									ʌ ̂				sun
sermon					ɚ									ʌ				brush
furrow					ɚ													
ashes						---						ɒ ̂ ə ̛						frost
bag						æ ɛ						ɒ ɑ ̂						log
married				ɛ ̌ ɚ								ɔ ̌						dog
half						æ·	ɑ ̛ ɑ ̆ ̂ ̛											fog
glass						æ ɪ ̆ ̌ ̛						ɔ ̌						water
aunt						æ ɛ						ɔ						daughter
father							ɑ					ɔ						law
palm							ɑ					ɔ ̌ ɚ						warm
barn							ɑɚ											
garden							ɑɚ					ɔɚ						forty
crop							ɑ ̆ e					ɒ ɑ ̂ ɚ						morning
on							ɑ e					ɒɑ						corn
college							ɑ					ɔ ̌ ɚ						horse
borrow							ɑɚ											
five									a ̛ ɪ		ɑ ̥ u							down
twice									a ̂ ɪ ̂		ɑ ̥ ʊ							out
wire									aɪɚ		ɑ ̥ ʊ ɚ							flower
joint										ɒ ̂ ɪ ̛ ɑ								joint
boil										ɔ ̌ ɪ								boil
	i	ɪ	e	ɛ	ɜ	æ	ɑ		aɪ	ɔɪ	au		ɔ	ʌ	o	ʊ	u	

44

	i	ɪ	e	ɛ	ɜ	æ	ɑ	aɪ	ɔɪ	au	ɔ	ʌ	o	ʊ	u	
three	i̯ˇ>i															two															u
three	i̯ˇ>i														u	two
grease	i̯>i														u<u	tooth
six		ɪ												ʊ		wood
crib		ɪɪ>												ʊ^		pull
ear		ɪ^ɚ												ʊɚ		yours
beard		ɪ>ɚ											o ŏ^			ago
eight			ɛ^e										o<			coat
April			e										o<			road
ten				ɛ									o<^			home
egg				---									o o^			know
head				---									oɚ			four
Mary				ɛ^ɚ									o•ɚ			door
chair				ɛɚ							ɔ^•ɚ					hoarse
care				ɛɚ							ɔ•ɚ					mourning
merry				ɛɚ												
thirty					ɚ							ʌ				sun
sermon					ɚ							ʌʌ^				brush
furrow					ɚˇr											
ashes						æˇ					ɔˇ					frost
bag						æɛ^					---					log
married						æ^ɚ					ɒ^					dog
half						æ					ɔˇ					fog
glass						æɛ^>					ɔˇ					water
aunt							ɑ				ɒ					daughter
father							ɑ				ɔ					law
palm							ɑ				ɔɚ					warm
barn							ɑɚ									
garden							ɑɚ				ɔɚ					forty
crop							ɑ>e				ɔˇɚ					morning
on							ɑe				ɔ<ˇ					corn
college							ɑɚ				ɔɚ					horse
borrow							ɑɚ									
five								ɐ<ɪ^>		ɑ<u						down
twice								ɐɪ^>		ɑɣ						out
wire								ɐ<ɪ>ɚ		ɑu<^ɚ						flower
joint									ɔˇɪ>							joint
boil									ɔˇɪ^>							boil

| | i | ɪ | e | ɛ | ɜ | æ | ɑ | aɪ | ɔɪ | au | ɔ | ʌ | o | ʊ | u | |

	i	ɪ	e	ɛ	ɜ	æ	ɑ	aɪ	ɔɪ	au	ɔ	ʌ	o	ʊ	u	
three	ɪˇi														ʉ˃u	two
grease	ɪˇi														u˂	tooth
six		ɪ												ʊ		wood
crib		ɪ˃												ʊˆ		pull
ear	ɪˆɪˇ ɚ													ʊɚ		yours
beard	ɪɚ												oOˆ			ago
eight			e										oOˆ			coat
April			e										o˂Oˆ			road
ten				ɛɛ̆ˆ˃									oŎˆ			home
egg				---									oOˆ			know
head				ɛɛ̆ˆ˃									oɚ			four
Mary				ɛɚ									oO˂ɚ			door
chair				ɛɚ									o•ɚ			hoarse
care				ɛˇɚ									oOɚ			mourning
merry				ɛɚ												
thirty					ɚ							ʌ				sun
sermon					ɚ							ʌ				brush
furrow					ɚ											
ashes						æ					ɔˇ					frost
bag						æɛˆ					---					log
married				ɛˇɚ							ɔˇ					dog
half						æ	ɑ̆									fog
glass						æɛ˃					ɒˆ					water
aunt						æɛˇ˃	ɑ				ɒ					daughter
father							ɑ				ɔ					law
palm							ɑ̆				ɔˇɚ					warm
barn							eˇɑ̆ɚ									
garden							ɑɚ				ɔɚ					forty
crop							ɑeˇ				ɔˇɚ					morning
on							ɑe				ɒˆɚ					corn
college							ɑ˃				ɔˇɚ					horse
borrow																
five								eˇˆɪ˃		ɑ˂ʊ						down
twice								eˇɪˆ˃		ɑ˂ʊ˂						out
wire								aɪ˃ɚ		ɑʊ˂ɚ						flower
									ɔˇɪ˃							joint
									ɔˇɪ˃							boil
	i	ɪ	e	ɛ	ɜ	æ	ɑ	aɪ	ɔɪ	au	ɔ	ʌ	o	ʊ	u	

	i	ɪ	e	ɛ	ɜ	æ	ɑ	ai	ɔi	au	ɔ	ʌ	o	ʊ	u	
three	i˅i															u˂u	two
grease	i˅i															u	tooth
six		ɪ													ʊ		wood
crib		---													ʊ		pull
ear		ɪ•ɚ													ʊɚ		yours
beard		ɪɚ											o				ago
eight			ee^										o˂				coat
April			e										o˂				road
ten				ɛ•									oo^				home
egg				---									oo^				know
head				ɛɛ̆^									o•ɚ				four
Mary				ɛɚ									o˅ɚ				door
chair				ɛɛ̆˃ɚ									ɔ•ɚ				hoarse
care				ɛɚ									---				mourning
merry				ɛɚ													
thirty					ɚ							ʌ					sun
sermon					ɚ							ʌʌ̆˂					brush
furrow					ɚ˅r												
ashes						æ	ɑ										frost
bag						ææ̆^					---						log
married						æ^					ɔ˅						dog
half						æ•ɛ^					ɒ^						fog
glass						æɛ^					ɔ˅						water
aunt							ɑ•				ɔ˅						daughter
father							ɑ				ɔ						law
palm							ɑ				ɔ˅ɚ						warm
barn							ɑɚ										
garden							ɑɚ				ɔ˅ɚ						forty
crop							ɑ•				ɒ˅˂ɚ						morning
on							ɑᵉ				ɔ˅ɚ						corn
college							ɑ				ɔ˅ɚ						horse
borrow											ɒ˂ɚ						
five								a˅ɪ˃		ɑ˂˅ʊ^							down
twice								a˅ɪ^		ɑ˂ʊ							out
wire								a˅ɪ˃ɚ		ɑʊ˂ɚ							flower
joint									ɒɔ˅ɪ˃								joint
boil									ɔ˅ɪ˃								boil

i	ɪ	e	ɛ	ɜ	æ	ɑ	ai	ɔi	au	ɔ	ʌ	o	ʊ	u

	i	ɪ	e	ɛ	ɜ	æ	ɑ	ai	ɔi	au	ɔ	ʌ	o	ʊ	u	
three	i˅															
															u˂ u	two
grease	i˅>i															
															u˂ ŭ	tooth
six		ɪ>														
														ʊ		wood
crib		ɪ														
														ʊ		pull
ear		ɪɚ														
														ʊɚ		yours
beard		ɪ^ɚ											o o^			ago
eight			e e^										o˂ o^			coat
April			e										o˂ o^			road
ten				ɛ ɛ>									o ŏ^			home
egg			e˅e^										o o^			know
head				---								ɔ^ɚ				four
Mary			e˅ɚ										o o˂^ɚ			door
chair				ɛ˅ɚ								ɔ•^ɚ				hoarse
care				ɛɚ							ɔ˅•ɚ					mourning
merry				ɛɚ												
thirty					ɚ							^				sun
sermon					ɚ							ʌ^^				brush
furrow					ɚ											
ashes						æ	ɑe									frost
bag						æɛ^>					ɔ˅					log
married						æ^ɚ					ɒ^					dog
half						æ•					ɒɔ˂					fog
glass						ææ^					ɒ^					water
aunt							ɑ•				ɒ˂^					daughter
father							ɑ				ɒ^					law
palm							ɑ•				ɒ^ɚ					warm
barn							ɑɚ									
garden							ɑɚ				ɔ˅ɚ					forty
crop							ɑ>				ɔ˅ɚ					morning
on							ɑe				ɒ˂ɚ					corn
college							ɑ				ɔ˅ɚ					horse
borrow							ɑ>ɚ									
five								e˂ɪ>		ɑ˂^ʊ^						down
twice								aɪ>		ɑ˂ʊ^						out
wire								a^ɪ>ɚ		ɑ˂ʊ˂ɚ						flower
									ɒ˂ɪ>							joint
									ɒ^+							boil
	i	ɪ	e	ɛ	ɜ	æ	ɑ	ai	ɔi	au	ɔ	ʌ	o	ʊ	u	

	i	ɪ	e	ɛ	ɜ	æ	ɑ	aɪ	ɔɪ	aυ	ɔ	ʌ	o	υ	u	
three	ɪ˅>i˅														u<u	two
grease	ɪ>i														u<u	tooth
six		ɪ												υ		wood
crib		ɪ·												υ		pull
ear		ɪ^>ɚ												υɚ		yours
beard		ɪ>ɚ											o<o^			ago
eight			e e^										ɜ>o^			coat
April			e										o<o^			road
ten				ɛ ɜ^									oo^			home
egg				ɛ^e									ʌo^			know
head				ɛ									oɚ			four
Mary				ɛ^ɚ									o˅o<ɚ			door
chair				ɛɚ							ɔ·ɚ					hoarse
care				ɛɚ							ɔ·ɚ					mourning
merry				– – –												
thirty					ɝ							ʌ				sun
sermon					ɚ							ʌʌ^				brush
furrow					ɜ<ɚ											
ashes						æ˅					ɒ<					frost
bag						æɛ^					– – –					log
married						æ>ɚ					ɒ^					dog
half						æ·					ɒ˞					fog
glass						æ æ^	ɑ>									water
aunt						æ˅					ɒ^					daughter
father							ɑ				ɒ					law
palm							ɑ·				ɔ˅ɚ					warm
barn							ɑ<ɚ									
garden							ɑɚ				ɔᵊ<					forty
crop							ɑ ɚɚ									morning
on							ɑe				ɔ˅ɚ					corn
college							ɒ<				ɔ˅ɚ					horse
borrow							ɚɚ									
five								a˅ɪ^		ɑ<υ˅						down
twice								e<ᵊ		a>υ˅						out
wire								e<ɪ>ɚ		ɑ˞ɚ						flower
									ɔɪ<							joint
									ɔ˅+							boil
	i	ɪ	e	ɛ	ɜ	æ	ɑ	aɪ	ɔɪ	aυ	ɔ	ʌ	o	υ	u	

	i	ɪ	e	ɛ	ɜ	æ	ɑ	aɪ	ɔɪ	au	ɔ	ʌ	o	ʊ	u	
three	iᵛi															two
grease	ɪᵛ>i														u·	tooth
six		ɪ>												ʊ		wood
crib		ɪ>												ʊ		pull
ear		ɪ^>ɚ												ʊᵛɚ		yours
beard		ɪ>ɚ											oo^			ago
eight			ee^										o·			coat
April			e										ʌ>o			road
ten				ɛɛ^									oo^			home
egg				ɛ^eᵛ									o<o^			know
head				ɛɛ^									o·ɚ			four
Mary				ɛɚ									oo^ɚ			door
chair				ɛᵛɚ							ɔ·ɚ					hoarse
care				ɛɚ							ɔ·ɚ					mourning
merry				ɛɚ												
thirty					ɚ							ʌ				sun
sermon					ɚ							ʌ<ʌʌ				brush
furrow					ɜɚ											
ashes						æ	ɑ<e									frost
bag						æɛ>					---					log
married				ɛᵛɚ							ɔᵛc					dog
half						æ					ɑuᵛ<					fog
glass						ææ^	ɚ									water
aunt						æɛᵛ					ɑ					daughter
father							ɑ				ɑ^					law
palm							ɑ·				ɔɚ					warm
barn							ɐɚ									
garden							ɑɚ				ɔɚ					forty
crop							ɑ				ɔ<ɚ					morning
on							ɑ>e				ɔᵛɚ					corn
college							ɑ				ɔᵛɚ					horse
borrow							ɑɚ									
five								e<ɪɜ		ɑ<u<						down
twice								e<ɪ>		ɑ<u<						out
wire								aɪ>ɚ		eᵛuᵛɚ						flower
									ɑ^ɪ>							joint
									cᵛɪ							boil

| i | ɪ | e | ɛ | ɜ | æ | ɑ | aɪ | ɔɪ | au | ɔ | ʌ | o | ʊ | u |

	i	ɪ	e	ɛ	ɜ	æ	ɑ	aɪ	ɔɪ	au	ɔ	ʌ	o	ʊ	u	
three	i˅i														u˅u<	two
grease	ɪ^i														u<˅u<	tooth
six		ɪ												u<		wood
crib		---												u<˅		pull
ear		ɪɚ												ʊ˅ɚ		yours
beard		ɪɚ											o<u<			ago
eight			e˅+										o^u			coat
April			e˅+										o<u<			road
ten				ɛ^•									o^u			home
egg			ɛ^+										o<u<			know
head				ɛ^									o̥˅ɚ			four
Mary				ɛɚ									o̥<ɚ			door
chair				ɛɚ									o̥˅ɚ			hoarse
care				---									o̥˅ɚ			mourning
merry				ɛɚ												
thirty					ɜ>ɚ							ʌ̃				sun
sermon					ɚ>							ʌ<				brush
furrow					ɜ^ɚ											
ashes						æ					ɒ•ə					frost
bag						æ^•					---					log
married			ɛɚ								ɒ•ə					dog
half						æ					ɒ					fog
glass						æ					ɒ<					water
aunt						æ•					ɔ˅					daughter
father							ɑ				ɒ•					law
palm							ɑə						æ^ɚ			warm
barn							ɑ^ɚ									
garden							ɑ̣ɚ				ɔ̣ɚ					forty
crop							ɑ						ɔ^ɚ			morning
on											ɒ˅		o̥˅ɚ			corn
college							ɑ				ɔ̣ə					horse
borrow							ɑ<ɚ									
five								əɪ		ɑ^•o<						down
twice								e^ɪ		ɐo<						out
wire								aɪɚ		ɑoɚ						flower
									o˅ɪ							joint
									o<˅ɪ							boil

| i | ɪ | e | ɛ | ɜ | æ | ɑ | aɪ | ɔɪ | au | ɔ | ʌ | o | ʊ | u |

51

	i	ɪ	e	ɛ	ɜ	æ	ɑ		ai	ɔi	au		ɔ	ʌ	o	ʊ	u	
three	i·i^																u˅< u<	two
grease	i˅i																ʉ·ʉ^	tooth
six		ɪ^														ʊ<		wood
crib		---														ʊ·ə		pull
ear		ɪ˞														ʊ<˞		yours
beard	i˅˞												ɔ^ʊ					ago
eight			e·ɪ										o<·ʊ<					coat
April			e˅ɪ										o< ʊ<					road
ten				ɛ^									o< ʊ<					home
egg				ɛ^									o<·ʊ<					know
head				---									o<˞					four
Mary				ɛ˞									ɔ˅^˞					door
chair				ɛ^˞									o˅˞					hoarse
care				ɛ˞									o<·˞					mourning
merry				ɛ˞														
thirty					ɜ^˞									ʌ				sun
sermon					ɜ<^˞									ʌ				brush
furrow					ɜ^˞													
ashes						æ							ɛ·ə					frost
bag				ɛ˅·ə									ɛ<˅ə					log
married				ɛ˞									ɛ·ə					dog
half						æ							ɛ·ə					fog
glass						æ	ɑ>											water
aunt						æ							ɒ					daughter
father							ɑ·						ɒ·					law
palm							ɑ·ə						ɒ^ɑ					warm
barn							ɑ˞											
garden							ɑ·						ɔ·˞					forty
crop													ɒ		o˅˞			morning
on							ɑ·								o˅˞			corn
college							ɑ								o˅˞			horse
borrow													ɔ˅˞					
five									ɑ<^ɪ		ɑ>·o<							down
twice									ɑ>^ɪ		ɐo<							out
wire									ɑ<^ɪ˞		ɐo<˞							flower
										ɛ˅ɪ								joint
										o<˅ɪ								boil
	i	ɪ	e	ɛ	ɜ	æ	ɑ		ai	ɔi	au		ɔ	ʌ	o	ʊ	u	

	i	ι	e	ε	ɜ	æ	ɑ		ai	ɔi	au		ɔ	ʌ	o	ʊ	u	
three	ᵢᵛⁱ																uᶜu	two
grease	ᵢᵛⁱ																---	tooth
six		ι^														ʊᶜ		wood
crib		---														ʊᵛ		pull
ear	iᵛə															ʊɚ		yours
beard		ιᵊɚ													oᶜʊᶜ			ago
eight			eᵛɨ												ɔ^ʊᶜ			coat
April			eᵛɨ												oᶜʊᶜ			road
ten				ε^											ɔ^ʊᶜ			home
egg				ε^ɨ											oᶜʊᶜ			know
head				ε^											ɔ^ə			four
Mary			eᵛɨ												oᶜɚ			door
chair				εᵛɚ											ɔ^ɚ			hoarse
care			eᵛɚ												ɔᶜɚ			mourning
merry				εɚ														
thirty					ɜ^ɚ									ʌᶜ				sun
sermon					ɜ>ᐧə 3<													brush
furrow					ɜᵛɚ													
ashes						æ							ɒ^ə					frost
bag				εᐧ									ɒ^ɔ					log
married						æ^ɚ							ɔᐧə					dog
half						æ^							ɒ					fog
glass						æ^							ɔᵛ					water
aunt						æ^ᐧ							ɒ^					daughter
father							ɑᐧ						ɒ^ə					law
palm							ɒᐧ						ɒᐧɚ					warm
barn							ɑᐧ											
garden							ɑᶜɚ								oᵛɚ			forty
crop							ɚ								ɔᶜ^ɚ			morning
on							ɒ								oᵛɚ			corn
college							ɚ								ɔᶜɚ			horse
borrow													ɒ^ɚ					
five									a^ɨ		ã^õᶜ							down
twice									e^ɨ		a^oᶜ							out
wire									eᶜɨɚ		ɑ^oᶜɚ							flower
joint										ɔᶜɨ								
boil										oᵛɨ								

| | i | ι | e | ε | ɜ | æ | ɑ | | ai | ɔi | au | | ɔ | ʌ | o | ʊ | u | |

	i	ɪ	e	ɛ	ɜ	æ	ɑ	aɪ	ɔɪ	aʊ	ɔ	ʌ	o	ʊ	u	
three	ɪ· i^														ʊ< u	two
grease	ɪ i														ʉ·	tooth
six		ɪ·												ʉ^>		wood
crib		– – –												ʊ		pull
ear	i ˇ ɚ													ʊ·ɚ		yours
beard		ɪ̣ɚ											o< ʊ<			ago
eight			e ˇ ɬ										o< ʊ<^			coat
April			e ˇ ɬ										o< ʊ<			road
ten				ɛ ^									o< ʊ<			home
egg			ɛ ^ ɬ										o< ʊ<			know
head				ɛ ^									ə̣ >ɚ			four
Mary				ɛ̣ ^ ɚ									ọ< ɚ			door
chair				ɛ ^ ɚ									o ˇ ɚ			hoarse
care				ɛ̣ɛɚ									ɔ̣ ^ ɚ			mourning
merry				ɛ̣ ^ ɚ												
thirty					ɚ >						ʌ ^				sun
sermon					ɚ ^						ʌ<				brush
furrow					ɜ ^ ɚ										furrow
ashes						æ ^					ɒ ˇ ə				frost
bag						æ̂·ɛ					ɔ̣ ˇ ə				log
married				ɛ̣ ˇ >ɚ							ɔ̣ ˇ ə				dog
half						æ ^ ·					ɔ̣ < ə				fog
glass						æ					ɒ				water
aunt						æ ^					ɔ ˇ				daughter
father							ɑ								law
palm							ɑ̣·>ə				ɒɚ·				warm
barn							ɑ·ə̣								barn
garden							ɑ̣^ɚ						ɔ̣<^ɚ		forty
crop							ɑ						ɔ̣ ˇ ɚ		morning
on							ɑ̣>·						ɔ̣ ˇ ɚ		corn
college							ɑ<						ɔ̣ ˇ ɚ		horse
borrow							ɑ̣ɚ								borrow
five								ɑ^ɬ	ɑ̣<^o<					down
twice								ə^ɬ	ɑ^o<					out
wire								əɬ əɬ	ɑ̣^>o<ɚ					flower
joint									o ˇ ɬ< ˇ					joint
boil									ɔ ^ ɬ<					boil
	i	ɪ	e	ɛ	ɜ	æ	ɑ	aɪ	ɔɪ	aʊ	ɔ	ʌ	o	ʊ	u	

	i	ɪ	e	ɛ	ɜ	æ	ɑ		ai	ɔi	au		ɔ	ʌ	o	ʊ	u	
three	i ˯ᵛ i																u˂ u	two
grease	i ˯ᵛ i																ʉ·	tooth
six		ɪ														ʊ˂		wood
crib		---														ʊ		pull
ear	i˯ᵛ ɚ															ʊ˂ᶺɚ	yours
beard		ɪ ˃ɚ											ɔᶺʊ˂					ago
eight			eᵛ ɫ ᵛ										oˈ˂ ʊ˂					coat
April			eᵛ ɫ										o˂ ʊ˂					road
ten				ɛ ᶺ									o˂ ʊ˂					home
egg				ɛ ᶺ·									θ ʊ˂					know
head				ɛ ᶺ									ǫᵛ ɚ					four
Mary				ɛɜɚ									ǫ˯ᶺ ɚ					door
chair			e˯·ᵛ ɚ										oᵛ ɚ					hoarse
care				ɛ ˃ɚ									o˯·ᵛ ə					mourning
merry				---														
thirty					ɚ									ʌ˂				sun
sermon					ɜɚ									ʌ ᶺ				brush
furrow					ɜ˯ᶺ ɚ													
ashes						æ ᵛ							ɔ˯ᵛ·ə					frost
bag						æ ᶺ·							ɔ·ə					log
married				ɛɜɚ									ɔ·ə					dog
half						æᶺ·ɚ							ɔ·ə					fog
glass						æ·							ɔᵛ					water
aunt						æ·							ɔᵛ					daughter
father							ɑ·						ɒ˯ᶺ·					law
palm													ɔ̣ə					warm
barn													ɔ·ɚ					
garden							ə̣ɚ						ɔ·ɚ					forty
crop							ɑ								ɔᶺɚ				morning
on							ɑ·								ǫᵛɚ			corn
college							ɑ˃								ǫᵛɚ			horse
borrow													ɔ·ə̣ə					
five									a˯ᶺ·ɫ	a˃ᶺ·ɛ̃								down
twice									a ɫ	aᶺo˂								out
wire									e˯ᵛ ɫɚ	aᶺo˂ ɚ								flower
joint										ɔᶺ ɫ								
boil										ɒ˂ᶺ ɫɑ								
	i	ɪ	e	ɛ	ɜ	æ	ɑ		ai	ɔi	au		ɔ	ʌ	o	ʊ	u	

	i	ɪ	e	ɛ	ɜ	æ	ɑ		ai	ɔi	au		ɔ	ʌ	o	ʊ	u	
three	i˅ⁱ																	
																	u˂u	two
grease	ɪ˄ⁱ																	
																	ʉ·	tooth
six		ɪ														ʊ·		wood
crib		ɪ˄·														ʊ		pull
ear	i˅ɚ												ɔ̂·ə					yours
beard		ɪ̣˄ɚ													ɔ˄ʊ			ago
eight			e˅ⱡ												o˂ʊ˂			coat
April			e˅ⱡ												o˂ʊ˂·			road
ten				ɛ˄·											o˂ʊ˂			home
egg				ɛ˄											o˂ʊ˂			know
head				ɛ˄											ɔ˄ɚ			four
Mary				ɛ·ɚ											ǫ˂ɚ			door
chair				ɛ̣ɚ									ɔ˂·ə					hoarse
care						æ˄ɚ									o˅ə̣			mourning
merry				ɛɚ̣˃														
thirty					ɚ									ʌ˄				sun
sermon				ɝ˄ɚ										ʌ˂				brush
furrow				ɝ˄ɚ														
ashes						æ												frost
bag						æ˄·							ɒ˄·ə					log
married			ɛɚ̣										ɔ˂·ə					dog
half						æ˄							ɒ·ə					fog
glass						æ˃̂							ɒ˂					water
aunt						æ·							ɔ˅					daughter
father							ɑ ɑ˂·											law
palm							ɑ·ə						ɔ˅ə̣					warm
barn							ɑ̣˄ɚ											
garden							ɒ̣·ɚ								ɔ˄ɚ			forty
crop							ɑ˂						ɔ̣˜˄ɚ					morning
on							ɒ·						ǫ˅ɚ					corn
college							ɒ·						ǫ̣˅ɚ					horse
borrow							ɒ˂ɚ											
five									a˃ⱡ				a˃·o˂					down
twice									a˅ⱡ˂				a˄o˂					out
wire									ɐ˅ⱡɚ				ɑ˄ʊ˂ᵂɚ					flower
										ɒ˂̂ⱡ								joint
										ɵⱡ								boil

	i	ɪ	e	ɛ	ɜ	æ	ɑ		ai	ɔi	au		ɔ	ʌ	o	ʊ	u	

	i	ɪ	e	ɛ	ɜ	æ	ɑ	aɪ	ɔɪ	au	ɔ	ʌ	o	ʊ	u	
three	i⌄i															two
grease	i⌄i														u<⌄u	tooth
six		ɪ												ʊ^		wood
crib		ɪ>												ʊ		pull
ear		ɪɚ												ʊɚ		yours
beard		ɪɚ											o^u⌄			ago
eight			e^e^										o·			coat
April			e										o o^			road
ten				ɛ									o·			home
egg				ɛ^e⌄									o			know
head				ɛɛ^>									o<ɚ			four
Mary						æ^ɚ							o⌄ɚ			door
chair				ɛ^ɚ							ɔ·ɚ					hoarse
care				---							ɔ·ɚ					mourning
merry				ɛr												
thirty					ɝ							ʌ				sun
sermon					ɝ							ʌ				brush
furrow					ɜ>r											
ashes						æ					ɔ⌄					frost
bag						æ·æ^>					---					log
married						æ^ɚ					ɔ⌄					dog
half						æ·					ɒ^					fog
glass						ææ^					ɔ⌄					water
aunt						æ⌄					ɔ⌄					daughter
father							ɑ				ɔ⌄					law
palm							ɑ·				ɔ⌄ɚ					warm
barn							ɑɚ									
garden							ɑɚ				ɔ⌄ɚ					forty
crop							ɑ>				ɒɚ					morning
on							ɑe				ɒ^ɚ					corn
college							ɑ				ɔ⌄ɚ					horse
borrow							ɑr									
five								e<ɪ^		ɑ<u						down
twice								a>ɪ>		ɑ<^u						out
wire								e<ɪ>ɚ		au>ɚ						flower
									ɔ⌄ɪ<							joint
									ɑ˘ɪ<							boil
	i	ɪ	e	ɛ	ɜ	æ	ɑ	aɪ	ɔɪ	au	ɔ	ʌ	o	ʊ	u	

	i	ɪ	e	ɛ	ɜ	æ	ɑ		aɪ	ɔɪ	au		ɔ	ʌ	o	ʊ	u	
three	i ᵛi																u	two
grease	i ᵛ>i																u<ũ	tooth
six		ɪ														---		wood
crib		ɪ>														ʊ		pull
ear		ɪɚ														ʊɚ		yours
beard		ɪ^•ɚ													o			ago
eight			e eᵉ^												o<o			coat
April			e												oᵒ^			road
ten				ɛ											o< õ			home
egg				---											oᵘᵛ			know
head				ɛ ɛ^>											oᵛoɚ			four
Mary				ɛɚ											oᵛɚ			door
chair				ɛ ɛ^>ɚ											ɔ^oɚ			hoarse
care				ɛɚ											ɔ^•ɚ			mourning
merry				ɛr														
thirty					ɚ^>									ʌ				sun
sermon					ɚ								ʌ	ʌ+ᵛ>ɪ				brush
furrow				ɛɚ														
ashes						æ							ɒ<^					frost
bag						æ ɛ̆ᵛ>												log
married						ær						ɒ^						dog
half						æ ɛ̆ᵛ>							ɒ^					fog
glass						æ ɛ^						ɔᵛ					water
aunt						æ ɛ̆^						ɒᵛ					daughter
father							ɑ						ɔ					law
palm							ɑ•						ɔᵛɚ					warm
barn							ɑɚ											
garden							ɑɚ						ɔɚ					forty
crop							ɑ						ɔɚ					morning
on							ɑᵉ						ɔᵛɚ					corn
college							ɑ						ɔᵛɚ					horse
borrow							ɑɚ											
five									aᵛ>		ɑ<u							down
twice									a>ɪ^>		ɑ<ʊ<^							out
wire									e<ɪ^>ɚ		ɑʊ<ᵛɚ							flower
joint										ɒ^ɪ>								joint
boil										ɔᵛɪ>								boil

| i | ɪ | e | ɛ | ɜ | æ | ɑ | | aɪ | ɔɪ | au | | ɔ | ʌ | o | ʊ | u |

	i	ɪ	e	ɛ	ɜ	æ	ɑ		aɪ	ɔɪ	au	ɔ	ʌ	o	ʊ	u	
three	iˇ															uˇ	two
grease	ɪˆ>ⁱ															u<ˇu	tooth
six		ɪ													---		wood
crib		ɪ>													ʊ		pull
ear		ɪ>ɚ													ʊɚ		yours
beard		ɪˑɚ												oᵒˆ			ago
eight			eᵉˆ>											oˑ			coat
April			e											oᵒ<ˆ			road
ten				ɛ										oᵒˆ			home
egg			eˇɪ											oᵘˇ			know
head				ɛᵋˆ>										o<ŏˆɚ			four
Mary				ɛɚ										oˇo<ˆɚ			door
chair				ɛɚ										oˇˑɚ			hoarse
care				ɛɚ									ɔˆɔ ˑɚ				mourning
merry				ɛɚ													
thirty					ɚ								ʌ				sun
sermon					ɚ								ʌʌˆ				brush
furrow					ɚ												
ashes						æ						ɔ					frost
bag						æɪˇ>						---					log
married						ær						ɒˆ					dog
half						æˑ						ɔˇɤɔ					fog
glass						ææˆ						ɒˆ					water
aunt						æ̃æ̃ˆ						ɔ					daughter
father							ɑ					ɔˇɔ					law
palm							ɑˆ					ɔˇɔɚ					warm
barn							ɑˑɚ										
garden							ɑ<ɚ					ɔɚ					forty
crop							ɑ					ɒ<ˆˑɚ					morning
on							ɑᵉ					ɔɚ					corn
college							ɑ					ɔɚ					horse
borrow							ɑɚɚ										
five									aˇ>ɪ>		ɑ<ʊ						down
twice									aˇ>ɪˆ>		ɑ<ʊ						out
wire									aˇ>+<ɚ		aˇɤɚ						flower
joint										ɔˇ+ᶜ<							
boil										ɔˇ+ᶜˆ							

| i | ɪ | e | ɛ | ɜ | æ | ɑ | aɪ | ɔɪ | au | ɔ | ʌ | o | ʊ | u |

	i	ɪ	e	ɛ	ɜ	æ	ɑ	ai	ɔi	au	ɔ	ʌ	o	ʊ	u	
three	i ˅i															two
grease	i ˅> i														ʉ ˄ u	tooth
six		ɪ												---		wood
crib		ɪ												ʊ˂		pull
ear	ɪ ˃ɚ													ʊɚ		yours
beard	ɬ ˅< ɚ												o ŏ ˄			ago
eight			e ˃•										o˂ ŏ			coat
April			e										o ŏ ˄			road
ten				ɛ ɛ̆ ˄>									o o ˄			home
egg				---									o o ˄			know
head				ɛ ɛ ˄>							ɔ ˅ɚ					four
Mary				ɛɚ									o ˅ɚ			door
chair				ɛ ˃ɚ									o˂ oɚ			hoarse
care				ɛɚ							ɔ ˄ɚ					mourning
merry				ɛɚ												
thirty					ɚ							ʌ				sun
sermon					ɚ							ʌ ˄				brush
furrow					ɚ											
ashes						æ	ɑ˂									frost
bag						æ ɛ ˄					---					log
married				ɛ ˅ɚ							ɒ ˄					dog
half						æ					ɒ ˄<					fog
glass						æ æ ˄>	ɑ									water
aunt						a •>	ɑ˂									daughter
father							ɑ				ɔ ˅					law
palm							ɑ •				ɒ ˄ɚ					warm
barn							ɑɚ •									
garden							ɑɚ				ɔ ˅ɚ					forty
crop							ɑ				ɔ ˅c					morning
on							ɑ ᵉ˅				ɒ ˄ɚ					corn
college							ᵉ ˅				ɔ ˅•ɚ					horse
borrow							ɑ ˃ɚ									
five								a ˀɪ ˃		a ˃ʊ ˄						down
twice								a ˀɪ ˃˄		ɑ˂ ˄ ʊ ˄						out
wire								ᵉ˂ ɬ ˃ɚ		ɑ˂ ʊ˂ ˅ ɚ						flower
joint									ɒ ɪ ˄>							
boil									˂ ɔ ˅ɪ ˃c							

| | i | ɪ | e | ɛ | ɜ | æ | ɑ | ai | ɔi | au | ɔ | ʌ | o | ʊ | u | |

60

	i	ɪ	e	ɛ	ɜ	æ	ɑ	ai	ɔi	au	ɔ	ʌ	o	ʊ	u	
three	i														u<	two
grease	iˇⁱ														u	tooth
six		ɪ⟩													---	wood
crib		ɪ												ʊ		pull
ear		ɪɚ												ʊɚ		yours
beard		ɪɚ											oᵁ			ago
eight			eᵉ^⟩										oᵒ^			coat
April			e										oᵒ^			road
ten				ɛᵋ^									oᵒ^			home
egg													o			know
head				ɛᵋ̆^									o·ɚ			four
Mary				ɛɚ									oɚ			door
chair				ɛɚ									oᵛŏ<ɚ			hoarse
care				ɛɚ									oᵛoɚ			mourning
merry				ɛɚ												
thirty					ɚ							ʌ				sun
sermon					ɚ							ɐᵛ				brush
furrow					ɜ·³r											
ashes						æ					ɒ^					frost
bag						æᵋ^					ɒ^					log
married						æ^ɚ					ɒ^					dog
half						æ					ɒ^·					fog
glass						ææ^					ɔᵛ					water
aunt						æᵌᵋ^					ɒ<					daughter
father							ɑ				ɒ					law
palm							ɑᵉ̆ᵛ				ɔᵛɚ					warm
barn							ɑ·ɚ									
garden							ɑɚ				ɔɚ					forty
crop							ɑᵉ⟩				ɒ<^ɚ					morning
on							ɑ⟩ᵉ				ɔᵛɚ					corn
college							ɑ⟩				ɔᵛɚ					horse
borrow																
five								a⟩ɪ		ɑ<u						down
twice								aɪˆ⟩		ɑ<u						out
wire								aɪ⟩ɚ		---						flower
joint									ɔᵛɪ⟩							joint
boil									ɔᵛ+<							boil

| | i | ɪ | e | ɛ | ɜ | æ | ɑ | ai | ɔi | au | ɔ | ʌ | o | ʊ | u | |

61

	i	ɪ	e	ɛ	ɜ	æ	ɑ		ai	ɔi	au	ɔ	ʌ	o	ʊ	u	
three	i ˇ															uˇᵁ	two
grease	i															uˇᵁ	tooth
six		ɪ													ʊ		wood
crib		+ɪ													ʊ		pull
ear		ɪɚ													ʊɚ		yours
beard		ɪɚ												oᵁ			ago
eight			eᵉˆ											o			coat
April			e											o			road
ten				ɛᵋˆ										oᵁˇ			home
egg				- - -										oᵁ			know
head				ɛᵋˆ										oɚ			four
Mary						æˆɚ								o o<ˆɚ			door
chair				ɛ.ᵋˀ ɚ								ɔˆɚ					hoarse
care				ɛɚ								ɔˆɚ					mourning
merry				ɛɚ													
thirty					ɚ								ʌ				sun
sermon					ɚ								ʌ				brush
furrow					ɚ												
ashes						æ						ɒ					frost
bag						æᵋˆ						ɔˇ					log
married						æˆɚ						ɒˆ					dog
half						æᵆˆ	ɚˀɑ										fog
glass						æᵋˆ						ɔˇ					water
aunt						æᵆˆ						ɒ					daughter
father							ɑ					ɔˇ					law
palm							ɑ					ɔ ɚ					warm
barn							ɑ.ɚ										
garden							ɑɚ					ɔ ɚ					forty
crop							ɑˀ					ɔˇɚ					morning
on							ɑ					ɔˇɚ					corn
college							ɑ					ɔˇɚ					horse
borrow																	
five									aɪ		ɑˀʊ						down
twice									aɪˆˀ		ɑˀˆʊ						out
wire									aˀɪˀɚ		ɑˀʊɚ						flower
joint										ɒˆˀ							
boil										ɔˇ+ˀ							

| | i | ɪ | e | ɛ | ɜ | æ | ɑ | | ai | ɔi | au | ɔ | ʌ | o | ʊ | u | |

	i	ɪ	e	ɛ	ɜ	æ	ɑ	aɪ	ɔɪ	au		ɔ	ʌ	o	ʊ	ʉ	
three	iᵛⁱ															uᵛ	two
grease	iᵛⁱ															u·	tooth
six		ɪˀ													ʊ		wood
crib		ɪ													ʊ		pull
ear		ɪɚ													ʊɚ		yours
beard		ɪ˖ɚ												oᴼ^			ago
eight			eᵉ^											oᐟᴼ^			coat
April			e											oᴼ˂^			road
ten				ɛ^										oᴼ^			home
egg				– – –										o			know
head				ɛ										o·ɚ			four
Mary				ɛ^ɚ										oᴼ˂ɚ			door
chair				ɛ ɛ˃ɚ										oᵛoɚ			hoarse
care				ɛɜɚ										ɔ·^ɚ			mourning
merry				ɛɚ													
thirty					ɝ								ʌ				sun
sermon					ɝ								ʌ				brush
furrow					ɝ												
ashes						æ						ɔᵛ					frost
bag						æᵆ^											log
married				ɛ^ɚ								ɔᵛ					dog
half						æ^˃						ɑ					fog
glass						æᵆ^						ɑ^					water
aunt						æᵆ^						ɑ					daughter
father							ɑ					ɔᵛ					law
palm							ɑ·					ɔᵛɚ					warm
barn							ɑ˂ɚ										
garden							ɑɚ					ɔɚ					forty
crop							ɑ˃					ɔᵛɚ					morning
on							ɑ					ɔᵛɚ					corn
college							ɑ					ɔᵛɚ					horse
borrow																	
five								a^˃˖		ɑ˂ʊ˂^							down
twice								a˃˖˂		ɑ˂ʊ							out
wire								a˃˖˂ɚ		ɑʊɚ							flower
joint									ɔᵛɪ˂˃								
boil									ɔᵛ˖˖								
	i	ɪ	e	ɛ	ɜ	æ	ɑ	aɪ	ɔɪ	au		ɔ	ʌ	o	ʊ	u	

63

	i	ɪ	e	ɛ	ɜ	æ	ɑ	ai	ɔi	au	ɔ	ʌ	o	ʊ	u	
three	iᵛi														u<ᵛu	two
grease	iᵛ														u·	tooth
six		ɪ												ʊ		wood
crib		ɪ												ʊ		pull
ear		ɪ·ɚ												ʊᵛɚ		yours
beard		ɪ>ɚ											oŏ<^			ago
eight			e·e^										o<o			coat
April			e										o<o			road
ten				ɛɛ̆^									o·			home
egg				ɛ^e^									oo^			know
head				ɛɛ̆^									o<ɚ			four
Mary				ɛ^ɚ									oo<ɚ			door
chair				ɛɚ							ɔ^o^ɚ					hoarse
care				ɛɚ							oᵛo^ɚ					mourning
merry				ɛɚ												
thirty·					ɝ							ʌ				sun
sermon					ɝ							ʌ				brush
furrow					ɚʳ											
ashes						æ					ɔᵛ					frost
bag						æɛ^>					---					log
married						æ^ɚ					ɔᵛ					dog
half						æ					ɒ					fog
glass						æ̆æ^					ɒ					water
aunt						æ	ɒ									daughter
father							ɑ				ɔᵛ					law
palm							ɑ				ɒ^ɑ					warm
barn							ɑɚ									
garden							ɑɚ				ɔᵛɚ					forty
crop							ɑ ɑɚ									morning
on							ɑɑ^				ɒ<ɑɚ					corn
college							ɑ				ɔɔ<ɚ					horse
borrow																
five								aɪ>		ɑ<ʊ						down
twice								ə>+>		ɑ<ʊ						out
wire								aɪ>ɚ		ɑ^ʊɚ						flower
joint									ɔɪ>							joint
boil									ɔ+<							boil
	i	ɪ	e	ɛ	ɜ	æ	ɑ	ai	ɔi	au	ɔ	ʌ	o	ʊ	u	

	i	ɪ	e	ɛ	ɜ	æ	ɑ		ai	ɔi	au		ɔ	ʌ	o	ʊ	u	
three	i˅																u˂ ᵘ	two
grease	i˅ⁱ˃																u˂˅	tooth
six		ɪ															---	wood
crib		ɪ˃ɪ														ʊ		pull
ear		ɪ·ɚ														ʊɚ		yours
beard		ɪ̣ɚ													o°˄			ago
eight			e˃												o˂°˄			coat
April			e												o°˄			road
ten				ɛ											o°˂˄			home
egg				---										ʌ˅	ʌ˄°			know
head				ɛ ɛ̆˃											o˂ ɚ			four
Mary				ɛɚ											o˅ɚ			door
chair						æ˄ɛɚ								ɔ˄o˅ɚ				hoarse
care				ɛɚ										ɔ˄ɚ				mourning
merry				ɛɚ														
thirty					ɚ									ʌ				sun
sermon					ɚ									ʌ˄ʌ˄				brush
furrow					ʌ˂̂ɚ													
ashes						æ							ɒ˄˂					frost
bag						æ							---					log
married				ɛ˅ɚ									ɔ˅					dog
half						æ æ̆˄	ɑᵉ˅											fog
glass						æ̃ æ̆˄							ɔ˅					water
aunt						æ̃ æ̆˄							ɒ					daughter
father							ɑ						ɔ˅					law
palm							ɑ˃						ɔ˄ɚ					warm
barn							ɑ̣·ɚ											
garden							ɑɚ						ɔɚ					forty
crop							ɑ ɑ̆˄						ɒ˄ɚ					morning
on							ɑ ɑ˄						ɒ˄ɚ					corn
college							ɑ						ɔ˅ɚ					horse
borrow							ɑ˃ɚ											
five									a˃⁺˂ⁱ		ɑ˂ʊ							down
twice									aɪ˂̂		ɑ˂ʊ							out
wire									a˃⁺˂ɚ		ɑ˂ʊ˂˅ɚ							flower
joint										ɔ˅ɪ˂̂ⁱ								joint
boil										ɔ˅⁺˄								boil

| | i | ɪ | e | ɛ | ɜ | æ | ɑ | | ai | ɔi | au | | ɔ | ʌ | o | ʊ | u | |

65

	i	ɪ	e	ɛ	ɜ	æ	ɑ		aɪ	ɔɪ	au		ɔ	ʌ	o	ʊ	u	
three	i ˇi																uˇ	two
grease	i ˇ> i																u< ˇu	tooth
six		ɪ														ʊ		wood
crib		ɪ >ɪ														ʊ		pull
ear		ɪɚ															ʊɚ	yours
beard		ɪɚ													o õˆ			ago
eight			e eˆ												o< oˆ			coat
April			e												o oˆ			road
ten				ɛ											o oˆ			home
egg				ɛˆeˇ ɜ											o oˆ			know
head				ɛ ɛ̃ˆ ɜ											oɚ			four
Mary			eˇɚ												oˇɚ			door
chair				ɛ ɛ>ɚ										ɔ ɔ<ˆɚ				hoarse
care				ɛɜ ɚ										ɔˆɚ				mourning
merry				ɛɜ														
thirty					ɚ									ʌ				sun
sermon					ɚ									ʌ				brush
furrow					ɚ													
ashes						æ							ɒˆ					frost
bag						æ æˆ							ɔˇ					log
married						æ ˆɚ							ɒ					dog
half						æ							ɒ					fog
glass						æ æ̃ˆ							ɒ<					water
aunt						æ æˆ							ɔˇ					daughter
father							ɑ						ɔˇ					law
palm							ɑ·						ɒˆɚ					warm
barn							ɑɚ											
garden							ɑɚ						ɔɚ					forty
crop							ɑ>						ɒ<ˆɚ					morning
on													ɒˆ•ɒɚ					corn
college							ɑ						ɔ<ˆɚ					horse
borrow							ɑɚ											
five									ɑ<ɪ >		ɑ<ˆu							down
twice									a >ɪ >		a >u							out
wire									a>+ɚ		a ʊɚ							flower
joint										ɒ̃<ˆɪ̃>									joint
boil										ɔˇ+								boil

| | i | ɪ | e | ɛ | ɜ | æ | ɑ | | aɪ | ɔɪ | au | | ɔ | ʌ | o | ʊ | u | |

66

	i	ɪ	e	ɛ	ɜ	æ	ɑ	aɪ	ɔɪ	au	ɔ	ʌ	o	ʊ	u	
three	ɪ^i															two (u<ˇ)
grease	i<ˇi															tooth (u•)
six		ɪ												ʊ		wood
crib		ɪ												ʊ		pull
ear		ɪˇɚ												ʊ<ɚ		yours
beard		ɪ^ɚ											oᵁ			ago
eight			eᵉ^										o<ŏ			coat
April			e										o<o^			road
ten				ɛ									o<ˇo			home
egg			ɛᵉ^										oᵘˇ			know
head				---									o<ˇɚ			four
Mary				ɛˇr									oᶜ^ɚ			door
chair				ɛ•ɚ							ɒ<ˆ•ɚ					hoarse
care				ɛɚ							ɔ<•ɚ					mourning
merry				ɛr												
thirty					ɚ							ʌ				sun
sermon					ɚ							ʌ				brush
furrow					ɜˇ>•											
ashes						---					ɔˇ					frost
bag						æᵃ^					ɒ<^					log
married						æ^r					ɒ<					dog
half						æ	ɑᵃ^									fog
glass						æ					ɔˇ					water
aunt						æ̃•	ɚ									daughter
father							ɑ ɚ<•									law
palm							ɑ<•				ɒ^ɚ					warm
barn							ɑ<•ɚ									
garden							---				ɔˇɚ					forty
crop							ɑ				ɔ>ˇɚ					morning
on							ɑ>ᵉ>				ɒ^ɚ					corn
college							ɑ				ɔˇɚ					horse
borrow							ɑ>ɚ									
five								aˆ>+		ɑᵁˇ						down
twice								aˆ>+<ˆ		a>ᵁ^						out
wire								a+<ɚ		---						flower
joint									ɐɪ^							
boil									ɔ<ˇ+							

| | i | ɪ | e | ɛ | ɜ | æ | ɑ | aɪ | ɔɪ | au | ɔ | ʌ | o | ʊ | u | |

	i	ɪ	e	ɛ	ɜ	æ	ɑ		aɪ	ɔɪ	au		ɔ	ʌ	o	ʊ	u	
three	i ᵛ˃ i																u	two
grease	ɪ i																ʉ ᵛ˃ u	tooth
six		ɪ														ʊ		wood
crib		ɪ														ʊ		pull
ear		ɪ ˃ɚ															ʊɚ	yours
beard		ɪ̣ ˃ɚ													o˂ o^			ago
eight			e e^												ʌ^˃o^			coat
April			e												o˂ o			road
ten				ɛ											o˂ o^			home
egg				ɛ ɛ^˂											o˂ o^			know
head				ɛ^											o˂ᵛ ɚ			four
Mary				ɛr											o ᵛ•ɚ			door
chair				ɛɚ									ɔ•ɚ					hoarse
care				ɛɚ									ɔ•ɚ					mourning
merry				ɛr														
thirty					ɝ									ʌ				sun
sermon					ɝ									ʌ				brush
furrow					ɝ													
ashes						æ^•							ɒ˂^					frost
bag						æ æ^							---					log
married						æ˂^ɚ							ɔ ᵛ•					dog
half						æ							ɒ					fog
glass						æ æ˂^	ɑ											water
aunt						æ ɛ˂^							ɒ					daughter
father							ɑ						ɒ˂					law
palm							ɑ						ɒ˂ɔ ᵛ ɚ					warm
barn							ɑɚ											
garden							ɑɚ						ɔɚ					forty
crop							ɑ e						ɒ˂^ɚ					morning
on							---						ɒ˂^ɚ					corn
college							ɑ˃						ɔ ᵛ˂ɚ					horse
borrow							ɑ˃r											
five									a^˃ɪ		ɑ˂ o˂^							down
twice									a^˃ɪ		ɑ˂ o˂ᵛ							out
wire									a^˃ɪɚ		---							flower
joint										ɔ˂ᵛ ɪ˂								joint
boil										ɔ˃ᵛ ɪ˂								boil

| | i | ɪ | e | ɛ | ɜ | æ | ɑ | | aɪ | ɔɪ | au | | ɔ | ʌ | o | ʊ | u | |

	i	ɪ	e	ɛ	ɜ	æ	ɑ		aɪ	ɔɪ	au		ɔ	ʌ	o	ʊ	u	
three	i˅>i																	two
grease	ɪ<ˆi																u	
six		ɪ>														ʊ		tooth
crib		ɪ														ʊ		wood
ear		ɪ>ɚ														ʊ<˅ɚ		pull
beard		ɪ>ɚ											o o<ˆ				yours
eight			e˅ɪ˅										o<˅ oˆ				ago
April			e										o o<ˆ				coat
ten				ɛ ɛ̆ˆ									o•				road
egg				ɛ ɪ˅									o o<ˆ				home
head				ɛ									o<•ɚ				know
Mary				ɛɜ ɚ									o>•˅ɚ				four
chair				ɛɚ							ɔ•ɚ					door	
care				ɛɜ ɚ							ɔ•ɚ					hoarse	
merry				ɛr													mourning
thirty					ɚ							ʌ					sun
sermon					ɚ							ɜ<					brush
furrow				ɜ˅•													
ashes						æ ɑ•e											frost
bag						æ æˆ						ɒ>˅ɤ˅					log
married						æ<ɚ						ɔ˅>					dog
half						æ						ʋ•					fog
glass						æ ɛ>						ɔ˅<					water
aunt						æ ɛ<ˆ						ʋ<ˆ					daughter
father							ɑ					ʋ<ˆ•					law
palm						ɑ˅						ʋ<ˆ ɚ					warm
barn						ɑ< ɚ											
garden						ɑɚ						ɔɚ					forty
crop						ɑ						ʋ ˆɚ					morning
on						ɑe						ɔ<˅ ɚ					corn
college						ɑ						ʋ ˆɚ					horse
borrow										ʋ< r							
five								e<˅ɪ>	ɑ<ʊ							down
twice								aˆ>ɪˆ	ɑʊˆ							out
wire								aˆ>ɪ ɚ	ɑ ˆʊ ɚ							flower
joint									ʋ<ɪ ˆɑ							joint
boil									ɔ<˅ ɪ<							boil
	i	ɪ	e	ɛ	ɜ	æ	ɑ		aɪ	ɔɪ	au		ɔ	ʌ	o	ʊ	u	

69

	i	ɪ	e	ɛ	ɜ	æ	ɑ	aɪ	ɔɪ	au	ɔ	ʌ	o	ʊ	u	
three	iᵛi															two
grease	iᵛi															tooth
six		ɪ													---	wood
crib		ɪ												ʊ		pull
ear		ɪᐱɚ												ʊɚ		yours
beard		ɪɚ											oᵁ			ago
eight			eᶫ										oᵒᐱ			coat
April			e										oᵒᐱ			road
ten				ɛ									oᵁ			home
egg			eᶫ										oᵁ			know
head				ɛ									oɚ			four
Mary				ɛɚ									oᵛɚ			door
chair				ɛᐱɚ									oɚ			hoarse
care				ɛɚ									oɚ			mourning
merry				ɛᵛɚᴵᐟ												
thirty					ɚ							ʌ				sun
sermon					ɚ							ʌ				brush
furrow					ɚ											
ashes						æ					ɔˑᶜɔ					frost
bag						æɛᐱ					ɔᵛ					log
married				ɛᵛə•			ɚ									dog
half						æ	ɑɑᐱ									fog
glass						æ	ɚ									water
aunt						æ̈					ɔᵛ					daughter
father							ɑɑᐳɑᐠ									law
palm							ɑᵉ				ɔᵛɚˑ					warm
barn							ɑᶜɚ•									
garden							ɑɚ				ɔɚ					forty
crop							ɑᶜɚ									morning
on							ɑˑ				ɔᵛɚ					corn
college							ɑ				ɔɚ					horse
borrow											ɔɚ					
five								aᐳɪ		aᐳu						down
twice								aɪ		ɑᶜu						out
wire								æᵛɪɚ		aᐳuɚ						flower
joint									ɔᶜɪ							
boil									ɔɪ							
	i	ɪ	e	ɛ	ɜ	æ	ɑ	aɪ	ɔɪ	au	ɔ	ʌ	o	ʊ	u	

	i	ɪ	e	ɛ	ɜ	æ	ɑ	ai	ɔi	au	ɔ	ʌ	o	ʊ	u	
three	ĭ>i															two (uᵛ)
grease	ɪ>î̌															tooth (u<ᵛu)
six		ɪ												ʊ		wood
crib		ɪ>												ʊ		pull
ear		ɪ>ɚ												ʊ<ɚ		yours
beard		ɪ̣ɚ											oᴼ^			ago
eight			eᵉ^										o<ŏ			coat
April			e										oᴼ<^			road
ten				ɛᴱ^									oᵁᵛ			home
egg				ɛ•									oᴼ^			know
head				---									o•ᵛɚ			four
Mary				ɛɚ									oᵛoᴬɚ			door
chair				ɛɛ>ɚ							ɔ•ɚ					hoarse
care				ɛɚ							ɔ^ɚ					mourning
merry				ɛɚ												
thirty					ɚ							ʌ				sun
sermon					ɚ							ʌʌ^				brush
furrow					ɚ>r											
ashes						æ>					ɒ•					frost
bag						ææ^>					ɒ^ŭ<					log
married						æ^r					ɔᵛ					dog
half						æ•					ɒŭ<					fog
glass						ææ^					ɒ^					water
aunt							a				ɒ^					daughter
father							ɑ				ɔᵛ					law
palm							ɑ<•				ɔᵛɚ					warm
barn							ɑᵃ•ɚ									
garden							ɑ•ɚ				ɔᵛɚ					forty
crop							ɑ>				ɒɚ					morning
on							ɑᵉ				ɔᵛɚ					corn
college							ɑ>				ɔᵛɚ					horse
borrow							ɑ>ɚ									
five								eᶜɪ<^		ɑ<ᴬʊ^						down
twice								a>ɪ^		ɑ<^ʊ						out
wire								a<ɪ>ɚ		ɑ<^ʊɚ						flower
									ɒ<ᴬɪ<							joint
									ɒ^ɪ							boil

| | i | ɪ | e | ɛ | ɜ | æ | ɑ | ai | ɔi | au | ɔ | ʌ | o | ʊ | u | |

	i	ɪ	e	ɛ	ɜ	æ	ɑ	ai	ɔi	au	ɔ	ʌ	o	ʊ	u	
three	iᵛi														u·	two
grease	iᵛi														u·	tooth
six		ɪ												ʊ		wood
crib		ɪ>ɪ												ʊ		pull
ear		ɪ>ɚ												ʊᵛɚ		yours
beard		ɪɚ											oᵒ^			ago
eight			e·										oᶜoᶜ			coat
April			e										oᶜo^			road
ten				ɛᵉ>									ooᵒ^			home
egg				ɛᵉeᵛ									ooᵒ^			know
head				ɛ									oᶜoᵛɚ			four
Mary				ɛᵛɚ									oᵛɚ			door
chair				ɛᵉɛᵛɚ									ɔᶜoᵛɚ			hoarse
care				ɛɚ							ɔᵛɔ̃ɚ					mourning
merry				ɛr												
thirty					ɚ							ʌ				sun
sermon					ɚ							ʌ·				brush
furrow					ɚ·											
ashes						æ	ɚ									frost
bag						ææ̃^					ɒ					log
married				ɛ>r							ɒ					dog
half						æ					ɒᶜ					fog
glass						æɛ̃ᵛ	ɚ									water
aunt						æ̃ɛ̃>					ɒ					daughter
father							ɑ				ɔᶜ					law
palm							ɚ				ɔᵛɚ					warm
barn							ɑɚ									
garden							ɑɚ				ɔᵛɚ					forty
crop							ɑ>eᵉ>				ɔᵛɚ					morning
on							ɑᵉ				ɔᶜɚ					corn
college							ɑ				ɔᵛɚ					horse
borrow							ɑ>ɚ									
five								eɪ>		ɑu						down
twice								aᶜɪᶜ		ɑ^u						out
wire								a>+ɚ		ɑᶜʊɚ						flower
joint									ɚ^+ᶜ							
boil									ɔᵛ+ᶜ							

| | i | ɪ | e | ɛ | ɜ | æ | ɑ | | ai | ɔi | au | | ɔ | ʌ | o | ʊ | u |

	i	ɪ	e	ɛ	ɝ	æ	ɑ		ai	ɔi	au		ɔ	ʌ	o	ʊ	u	
three	ɪi˅ˑ																ʉu	two
grease	ɪ˃˅i																u˂u˅	tooth
six		ɪ														ʊ		wood
crib		ɪ														ʊ		pull
ear		ɪˆɚ														---		yours
beard		ɪˑɚ											oʊˆ					ago
eight			ɛ˂ˆeˆ										oˆo˂ˆ					coat
April			e										oʊ˂ˆ					road
ten				ɛ									oˆo˂ˆ					home
egg			ɛ˂ˆɪ˅˃										o˂ˆoˆ					know
head				ɛ									oˆo˂ˆɚ					four
Mary				ɛr									ɔ˂ˆˑɚ					door
chair				ɛˑɚ								ɔˑɚ						hoarse
care				ɛɚ									oˑɚ					mourning
merry				ɛr														
thirty					ɝɚ									ʌ				sun
sermon					ɛ˃ˆɚ									ʌ˅				brush
furrow					ɚ													
ashes						æ						ɔˑˆ˃						frost
bag						æˆɛ˂						ʊ˂ˑ						log
married						æ˂ˆr						ɔˑ˃ˑ						dog
half						æ						ʊˑ						fog
glass						æˆæ˂						ʊ˂ˆ						water
aunt						---						ɔˑ˃						daughter
father							ɑ					ɔˑ˃						law
palm							ɑ					ɔɚ						warm
barn							ɑˑɚ											
garden							ɑɚ					ɔɚ						forty
crop							ɑˆe					ɔɚ						morning
on							---					ɔˑˆɚ						corn
college							ɑ					ɔ˂ˆɚ						horse
borrow							ɑɚ											
five									aɪˑˆ˃		ɑˆoˆ˂							down
twice									aˆ˃ɪ		aˑ˃o							out
wire									aɪˑˆ˃æɚ		---							flower
										ɔɪˑˆ˃								joint
										ɫɔ								boil

i	ɪ	e	ɛ	ɝ	æ	ɑ		ai	ɔi	au		ɔ	ʌ	o	ʊ	u

	i	ɪ	e	ɛ	ɜ	æ	ɑ	aɪ	ɔɪ	au	ɔ	ʌ	o	ʊ	u	
three	i̯ˇi														ʉ̶ˀu	two
grease	ɪˆi														u·	tooth
six		ɪˀ												ʊ		wood
crib		ɪ												ʊ		pull
ear		ɪˆˀɚ												---		yours
beard		ɪˆ·ɚ									o<ˇʊˆˀ					ago
eight			eɪˆ								o̮<ˆ					coat
April			eˇˀ								oo<ˆ					road
ten				ɛ·							o<ˇo<ˆ					home
egg				ɛ·							o<ˀʊ					know
head				ɛ							ɔ<ˆɚ					four
Mary				ɛˀˀˇr							oˇ>ɚ					door
chair				ɛ>ˀˇɚ							ɔ·ɚ					hoarse
care						æˆɚ					o<ˇɚ					mourning
merry			ɛr													
thirty					ɚ							ʌ				sun
sermon					ɚ							ʌ				brush
furrow					ɚʳ											
ashes						æ					ɒ<ˀ					frost
bag						æɛˆ	ɑ<·ˠ									log
married						æˇ>r					ɒ<ˆ·					dog
half						æ	ɑ>ˀˠ									fog
glass						ææˆ					ɔˀˇ>					water
aunt						æɜˆˇ>					ɒ<ˆ					daughter
father						---					---					law
palm						ɑ·					ɒ<ˆɚˀ					warm
barn						ɑ<ˀ·ɚ										
garden						aɚ					ɔɚ					forty
crop						ɑ·					ɒ<ˆɚ					morning
on						ɑ·					ɒ<ˆɚ					corn
college						ɑ					ɔˀ>ɚ					horse
borrow						ɑˀr										
five								aˆ>ɪˆ>		ɑ<ˆo<ˆ						down
twice								eˀɪ<ˆ		ao<ˆ						out
wire								aˆ>ɪˀˀˇɚ		ɑ<ˆo<ɚ						flower
									ɔˀɪˀˀ							joint
									ɒɪ							boil

i	ɪ	e	ɛ	ɜ	æ	ɑ	aɪ	ɔɪ	au	ɔ	ʌ	o	ʊ	u

	i	ɪ	e	ɛ	ɜ	æ	ɑ	aɪ	ɔɪ	au	ɔ	ʌ	o	ʊ	u	
three	i ᵛ i															two (u< ŭ)
grease	i ᵛ> i															tooth (ʉ >ʊ)
six		ɪ													---	wood
crib		ɪ >												ʊ		pull
ear		ɪ·ɚ												ʊ< ɚ		yours
beard		ɪ·ɚ											oᵁ			ago
eight			e eᵛ										o<ᵛ oᵛ			coat
April			e										o< oᵛ			road
ten				ɛ ɛᵛ>									o oᵛ			home
egg			eᵛeᵛ>										oᵁ >			know
head				ɛ									oᵛʊ<ɚ			four
Mary				ɛɚ									o< oᵛɚ			door
chair				ɛᵛ ɛᵛ>ɚ									oᵛ·ɚ			hoarse
care				ɛɚ							ɔ·ᵛ					mourning
merry				ɛɹ												
thirty					ɚ							ʌ				sun
sermon					ɚ							ʌ				brush
furrow					ɚ											
ashes						æ					ɒ ᵛ					frost
bag						æ æᵛ>					ɔ·ᵛʊᵛ<					log
married						æ ᵛɚ					ɔᵛ					dog
half						æ æᵛ					ɒᵛ·					fog
glass						æ ɛᵛ>					ɔᵛ					water
aunt						æ æᵛ>					ɒ					daughter
father							ɑ				ɔᵂ					law
palm							ɑᵛ^				ɒᵛɑɚ					warm
barn							ɑɚ									
garden							ɑɚ				ɔɚ					forty
crop							ɑ				ɔᵛɚ					morning
on							ɑ> ɒ>				ɔᵛɚ					corn
college							ɑ				ɔᵛɚ					horse
borrow							ɑɚ									
five								a>ɪ>		ɑ<ʊᵛ<						down
twice								ɐ<ɪ>		ɑᵛʊ						out
wire								ă>ɨɚ		ɑ<ʊɚ						flower
									ɒɪ>							joint
									ɔ<ᵛɪ>							boil

i	ɪ	e	ɛ	ɜ	æ	ɑ	aɪ	ɔɪ	au	ɔ	ʌ	o	ʊ	u

38 (III) RAMSEY, MN. (A)

	i	ɩ	e	ɛ	ɜ	æ	ɑ		aɪ	ɔɪ	au		ɔ	ʌ	o	ʊ	u	
three	ǐ>i																u·	two
grease	ɩ^i																u·	tooth
six		ɩ														---		wood
crib		ɩ														ʊ		pull
ear		ɩ̂>ɚ														ʊ̠ɚ		yours
beard		ɩ·ɚ													oŏ<^			ago
eight			e>ɩ̌>												oo<^			coat
April			e												o<ǒ			road
ten				ɛ											oo<^			home
egg			ɛɩ												oʊ̠<			know
head				ɛ											ǒ>·r			four
Mary				ɛr											---			door
chair				ɛɚ									ɔ·ɚ					hoarse
care				ɛɚ									ɔɚ					mourning
merry				ɛr														
thirty					ɚ									ʌ				sun
sermon					ɚ									---				brush
furrow					ɚ													
ashes						æ							ɒ·					frost
bag						æɩ̆̌>							ɔ̂<·					log
married						ær							ɒ̂<·					dog
half						æ							ɒ̂<ǒ					fog
glass						æ							ɒ					water
aunt						æ̃·							ɔ˅					daughter
father							ɑ						---					law
palm							ɑ·						ɔ̌>ɚ					warm
barn							ɑ̆·ɚ											
garden							ɑɚ						ɔɚ					forty
crop							ɑ						ɔɚ					morning
on							ɑ·						ɔ˅ɚ					corn
college							ɑ						ɔ·ɚ					horse
borrow							ɑr											
five									aɨ<		a>ô<							down
twice									â>ɨ̂<		ɑ<ô<							out
wire									ɑ̂<ɨ<ɚ		ɑ<ʊ̠̌>ɚ							flower
										ɔ̌>ɨ								joint
										ɔ̌>ɨ								boil
	i	ɩ	e	ɛ	ɜ	æ	ɑ		aɪ	ɔɪ	au		ɔ	ʌ	o	ʊ	u	

	i	ɪ	e	ɛ	ɜ	æ	ɑ	ai	ɔi	au	ɔ	ʌ	o	ʊ	u	
three	i ˅ i															two
grease	i														u ˅ u	tooth
six		ɪ ˅ >												∟--		wood
crib		ɪ												ʊ ˄		pull
ear		ɪ ˄ ɪ > ɚ												ʊ ɚ		yours
beard		ɪ > ɚ											oᵁ			ago
eight			e e ˄										oᵒ< ˄			coat
April			e										o			road
ten				ɛ ɪ									o			home
egg			e ˅ e ˄										o			know
head				ɛ									o ˅ ɚ			four
Mary				ɛ ˅ ɚ									o ˅ ɚ			door
chair				ɛ ˅ ɚ									o ɚ			hoarse
care				ɛ ɚ									o ɚ			mourning
merry				---												
thirty					ɚ							ʌ				sun
sermon					ɚ							ʌ				brush
furrow					ɚ r̆	æ										frost
ashes						æ	ɚ									frost
bag						æ ɛ					ɒᵉ					log
married				ɛ ˅ ɚ							ɒ< ˄					dog
half						æ					ɒ< ˄					fog
glass						a ˄					ɒ ˄					water
aunt						æ ɛ					ɔ ˅					daughter
father							ɑ ˄				ŏ< ɔ					law
palm							ɑ >ɯ				ɒ ˄ ɚ					warm
barn							ɑ ɑ ˄ ɚ									
garden							ɑ ˄ ə				ɔ ˅ ɚ					forty
crop							ɑ >				ɔ ɚ					morning
on							ɑ ·				ɔ ɚ ˅					corn
college							ɑ				ɔ ɚ ˅					horse
borrow							ɑ > ɚ									
five								ɑ< ˄ ɪ		a >ᵁ ˅						down
twice								a > ɪ		a >ᵁ ˄						out
wire								a > ɪ ɚ		a >ᵁ ɚ ˄						flower
joint									ɔ ˅ ɪ ˅							joint
boil									ɔ ˅ ɪ< >							boil
	i	ɪ	e	ɛ	ɜ	æ	ɑ	ai	ɔi	au	ɔ	ʌ	o	ʊ	u	

77

	i	ɪ	e	ɛ	з	æ	ɑ		ai	ɔi	au		ɔ	ʌ	o	ʊ	u	
three	ɪᵛi																uᶜu	two
grease	iᵛi																ŭ	tooth
six		ɪ														---		wood
crib		ɪ														ʊ		pull
ear		ɪɚ													oɚ			yours
beard		ɪɚ													oᵁ			ago
eight			eᵉ^												oᴼ˂^			coat
April			e												oᴼ^			road
ten				ɛᵋ^											oᴼ^			home
egg				ɛ^e											oᴼ^			know
head				ɛ											oᵛɚ			four
Mary						æ^ɚ									oᵛɚ			door
chair				ɛᵛɚ											oɚ			hoarse
care				ɛɚ											oɚ			mourning
merry				ɛ^ɚ														
thirty					ɚ									ʌ				sun
sermon					ɚ									ʌ^ ^				brush
furrow					ɚ·													
ashes						æ	ɑ˂											frost
bag						æɪ							ɒ˂					log
married				ɛᵛɚ			ɑ˂^											dog
half						æ							ɒᴰ^					fog
glass						æᵋ							ɒ^					water
aunt						æ							ɒ^					daughter
father							ɑ·						ɒᵊ^					law
palm							ɑ˃						ɔᵛɚ					warm
barn							ɑɚ·											
garden							ɑɚ						ɔᵊ					forty
crop							ɒᵊ						ɔᵊ					morning
on							ɑ˃						ɔᵊ					corn
college							ɑ˃						ɔ^ᵊ					horse
borrow													ɔᵊ					
five									e˂ᵛɪ		a˃ʊ^							down
twice									ɑ˂^ɪ		a˃ʊ							out
wire									ɑ˂^ɪᵛɚ		a˃ʊɚ							flower
joint										ɔᵛɪ								
boil										ɔᵛɪ								
	i	ɪ	e	ɛ	з	æ	ɑ		ai	ɔi	au		ɔ	ʌ	o	ʊ	u	

	i	ɪ	e	ɛ	ɜ	æ	ɑ	aɪ	ɔɪ	au	ɔ	ʌ	o	ʊ	u	
three	i˅i														u<u	two
grease	i˅i														u	tooth
six		ɪ												ʊ		wood
crib		ɪ>												ʊ		pull
ear		ɪ^ɚ												ʊɚ		yours
beard		ɪ^ɚ											o^ʊ			ago
eight			e ĕ^										oᵒ<^			coat
April			e										o< ᵒ<^			road
ten				ɛ ɛ̆^>									oᵒ^			home
egg				--- |									oᵁ			know
head				ɛ									o˅ɚ			four
Mary				ɛ^ɚ									o˅ᵒ<ɚ			door
chair				ɛᵋ>ɚ									ɔ^o˅ɚ			hoarse
care				ɛɚ									ɔ^oᵛɚ			mourning
merry				ɛr												
thirty					ɚ˅							ʌ^				sun
sermon					ɚ							ʌʌ^				brush
furrow					ʌ<ɚ r											
ashes						æ					ɔ					frost
bag						æ					---					log
married						æ^ɚ					ɔ˅					dog
half						æ					ɔ˅					fog
glass						æᵆ^					ɔ					water
aunt						æ					ɒɑ<					daughter
father							ɑ				ɔ˅					law
palm											ɒɔ˅ɚ					warm
barn							ɑɚ									
garden							ɑɚ				ɔ˅ɚ					forty
crop							ɑɑ^				ɒ^ɚ					morning
on							ɑ3^				ɔ˅ɚ					corn
college							ɑ				ɔɚ					horse
borrow							ɑɚ									
five								a>ɪ>		ɑ<u						down
twice								e<ɪ>		ɑ<u						out
wire								ɑ<^ɪ>ɚ		a>ʊɚ						flower
joint									ɒ^+<							joint
boil									ɔ˅+							boil

| | i | ɪ | e | ɛ | ɜ | æ | ɑ | aɪ | ɔɪ | au | ɔ | ʌ | o | ʊ | u | |

	i	ɪ	e	ɛ	ɜ	æ	ɑ		aɪ	ɔɪ	aʊ		ɔ	ʌ	o	ʊ	u	
three	i ᵛ ɪ̆																ʉ ᵛ ᵘ	two
grease	i ᵛ i																u	tooth
six		ɪ															---	wood
crib		ɪ															ʊ	pull
ear		ɪ ^ ɚ															ʊɚ	yours
beard		ɪ̣ɚ													o			ago
eight			e ĕ ^												o˂ o ^			coat
April			e ˃												o o˂̂			road
ten				ɛ											o ŏ ^			home
egg				ɛ										ʌ ˃ o				know
head				ɛ ɛ̆ ^											oɚ			four
Mary						æ ^ r									oɚ			door
chair				ɛ ᵛ ɚ											o ᵛ oɚ			hoarse
care				ɛɚ											o ᵛ ɚ			mourning
merry				ɛɚ														
thirty					ɚ									ʌ				sun
sermon					ɚ								---					brush
furrow					ʌ̣ ^ r													
ashes						æ							ɒ ^					frost
bag						æ							ɒ ^					log
married						æ ^ ɚ							ɔ ᵛ					dog
half						æ	ɑ ɑ ^											fog
glass						æ							ɒ ^					water
aunt						æ ᵛ æ ^							ɒ					daughter
father							ɑ ·						ɔ					law
palm							ɑ						ɔ ᵛ ɚ̣					warm
barn							ɑ̣ɚ											
garden							ɑɚ						ɔɚ					forty
crop							ɑ						ɒɚ					morning
on							ɑ ᵉ ᵛ						ɒɚ					corn
college							ɑ						ɔɚ					horse
borrow													ɒ ^ ɚ					down
five									a ˃ ɪ ˃		ɑ˂ ʊ							down
twice									ɐ˂ ɪ ^		ɑ˂ ʊ							out
wire									ˌa ˃ ɪ ɚ		a ˃ ʊ ɚ							flower
										ɔ ᵛ ɪ ˃								joint
										ɔ ᵛ ɪ								boil
	i	ɪ	e	ɛ	ɜ	æ	ɑ		aɪ	ɔɪ	aʊ		ɔ	ʌ	o	ʊ	u	

	i	ɪ	e	ɛ	ɜ	æ	ɑ	ai	ɔi	au	ɔ	ʌ	o	ʊ	u	
three	i															
															u˅u	two
grease	ɪ^i															
															u	tooth
six		ɪ														
														ʊ		wood
crib		ɪ														
														ʊ		pull
ear	ɪɚ															
														ʊɚ		yours
beard	ɪ̆ɪ:ɚ															
													o^<ʊ			ago
eight			e e^													
													o			coat
April			e													
													o o^			road
ten				ɛ												
													o ʊ			home
egg				ɛ ɛ^												
													o^<ʊ			know
head				ɛ												
													o^vɚ			four
Mary				ɛɚ												
													oɚ			door
chair				ɛɚ							ɔɚ					
																hoarse
care				ɛɚ									oɚ			
																mourning
merry				ɛɚ												
thirty					ɚ							ʌ				
																sun
sermon					ɚ							ʌ				
																brush
furrow					ɚ̆r											
ashes						æ	ɑ^									
																frost
bag						æ æ^					---					log
married				ɛɚ			ɚ									
																dog
half						æ	ɑ^>									
																fog
glass						æ ɛ					---					water
aunt						æ					ɒ					
																daughter
father							ɑ				ɔ^vɔ					
																law
palm							ɑ				ɔɚ					
																warm
barn							ɑ̆:ɑɚ									
garden							ɑɚ				ɔɚ					
																forty
crop							ɑ				ɔɚ					
																morning
on							ɑ^				ɔɚ					
																corn
college							ɑ				ɔɚ					
																horse
borrow							ɑɚ									
five								aɪ>		aʊ˅						
																down
twice								a>ɪ˅		aʊ˅						
																out
wire								aɪɚ								
																flower
joint									ɔɪ^>							
boil									ɔɪ							

| | i | ɪ | e | ɛ | ɜ | æ | ɑ | ai | ɔi | au | ɔ | ʌ | o | ʊ | u | |

	i	ɪ	e	ɛ	ɜ	æ	ɑ	ai	ɔi	au	ɔ	ʌ	o	ʊ	u	
three	i˅i														u˅u	two
grease	i˅i														uʊ˅	tooth
six		ɪ												---		wood
crib		ɪ												ʊ		pull
ear		ɪɚ												---		yours
beard	ĭ!ĭɚ												oo^			ago
eight			ee^										ŏ<			coat
April			e										oo^			road
ten				ɛ									o^ʊ			home
egg				ɛ									o^ʊ			know
head				ɛ									o^ʊɚ			four
Mary				ɛ^ɚ									o˅ɚ			door
chair				ɛɚ									o˅ɚ			hoarse
care				ɛ˅ɚ									oɚ			mourning
merry				ɛɚ												
thirty					ɝ							ʌ				sun
sermon					ɝ							ʌ				brush
furrow					ɛ·ə											
ashes						æ˅					ɔ					frost
bag						æ^	ɑ									log
married				ɛ˅ɚ							ɒ<^					dog
half						æ˅	ɑ									fog
glass						æ˅					ɑ					water
aunt							a				ɔ˅					daughter
father							ɑ				ɔɘ<					law
palm							ɑ				ɔɚ					warm
barn							ɑ̆>ɑ̆>ɚ									
garden							ɑɚ				ɔɚ					forty
crop							ɑ				ɔɚ					morning
on							ɑ>				ɔɚ					corn
college							ɑ				ɔ˅ɚ					horse
borrow																
five								aɨ		au˅>						down
twice								aɪ>		au˅						out
wire								ɑ<ĭ˅ɚ		au^						flower
joint									ɔɪ>							joint
boil									ɔɨ							boil
	i	ɪ	e	ɛ	ɜ	æ	ɑ	ai	ɔi	au	ɔ	ʌ	o	ʊ	u	

82

	i	ι	e	ɛ	ɜ	æ	ɑ		ai	ɔi	au		ɔ	ʌ	o	ʊ	u	
three	¡ᵛⁱ																uᵛu	two
grease	¡ᵛⁱ																uᵛ	tooth
six		ι															---	wood
crib		ι															ʊ̞	pull
ear		ιᵛɚ															ʊɚ	yours
beard		ιɚ													oᵘ			ago
eight			eeᵉ^												o			coat
April			e												ooᵒ^			road
ten				ɛ											ooᵒ^			home
egg				ɛᵋ^											oᵘ			know
head				ɛ											oɚ			four
Mary				ɛɚ											oᵛə			door
chair				ɛɚ											oɚ			hoarse
care				ɛɚ											oɚ			mourning
merry				ɛɚ														
thirty					ɚ									ʌ				sun
sermon					ɚ̆ɚ·									ʌ				brush
furrow					ɚ·													
ashes						æ							ɔ					frost
bag						æɛ							ɒ^					log
married				ɛᵛə									ɒ					dog
half						æᵛ							ɒ					fog
glass						æ							ɔᵛ					water
aunt						æ							ɔᵛ					daughter
father							ɑ						ɔɔ̰<					law
palm							ɑ·						ɔᵛɚ					warm
barn							ɑ̆ɑ̆ɚ											
garden							ɑɚ						ɔɚ					forty
crop													ɒ/ɔɚ					morning
on													ɒ·ɔɚ					corn
college							ɑ						ɔɚ					horse
borrow													ɔɚ					
five							ɑ<ι>		aᵛʊᵛ									down
twice									aι>		aᵛʊᵛ							out
wire									aι>ɚ		aʊᵛɚ							flower
										ɔ^ι>								joint
										ɔι>								boil
	i	ι	e	ɛ	ɜ	æ	ɑ		ai	ɔi	au		ɔ	ʌ	o	ʊ	u	

	i	ɪ	e	ɛ	ɜ	æ	ɑ		aɪ	ɔɪ	au		ɔ	ʌ	o	ʊ	u	
three	iᵛi																	two
grease	ɪᶺi																uᶺᵁ	tooth
six		ɪ														ʊ		wood
crib		ɪ														ʊ		pull
ear		ɪɚ														ʊɚ		yours
beard		ɪ̆ɪ̆ɚ													oᵁ			ago
eight			e·eᶺ												o			coat
April			e												oᵒᶺ			road
ten				ɛ											oᵁ			home
egg			eᵉᶺ												oᵁ			know
head				ɛ											oɚ			four
Mary				ɛ·ɚ											oᵛə			door
chair				ɛɚ											oᵛɚ			hoarse
care				ɛᵛ>ɚ											oɚ			mourning
merry				ɛɚ														
thirty					ɚ									ʌ				sun
sermon					ɚ									ʌ				brush
furrow					ɚ													
ashes						æᵋ							ɔᵛ·ɒ					frost
bag						æ							ɒᵉ>					log
married				ɛɚ									ɒᶺ					dog
half						æ	ɑᵉ											fog
glass						æ							ɔᵛ					water
aunt						æ							ɔ					daughter
father							ɑ						ɔᵛɔᵛ					law
palm							ɑᵉ						ɔɚ					warm
barn							ɑɚ											
garden							ɑᶺɚ						ɔᵛɚ					forty
crop							ɑ						ɔᵛ					morning
on							ɑ						ɒᶺɚ					corn
college							ɑ						ɔᵛɚ					horse
borrow							ɑɚ											
five									aɪᵛ>		aᵛ>ʊᵛ							down
twice									aɪ>		aʊᵛ							out
wire									aɪᵛ>ɚ		aᵛ>ŏɚ							flower
										ɔᵛɪᵛ>c								joint
										cᵛɪᵛ>								boil
	i	ɪ	e	ɛ	ɜ	æ	ɑ		aɪ	ɔɪ	au		ɔ	ʌ	o	ʊ	u	

84

	i	ɩ	e	ɛ	ɜ	æ	ɑ		ai	ɔi	au		ɔ	ʌ	o	ʊ	u	
three	i																ju<	two
grease	$i^{\vee i}$																u<	tooth
six		ɩ														ʊ		wood
crib		ɩ														ʊ		pull
ear		ɩɚ														ʊɚ		yours
beard		ɩɚ													$o^{ʊ}$			ago
eight			e												o			coat
April			e												$o^{o\wedge}$			road
ten				ɛ											$o^{ʊ}$			home
egg			$e^{\vee e}$	$ɛ^{ɛ\wedge}$											$o^{ʊ<}$			know
head				ɛ											oɚ			four
Mary				ɛɚ											$o^{\vee}$ɚ			door
chair				ɛɚ											$o^{\vee}$ɚ			hoarse
care				---											oɚ			mourning
merry				ɛɚ														
thirty					ɚ									ʌ				sun
sermon					ɚ									ʌ				brush
furrow					ɚ													
ashes						æ							ɔ					frost
bag						$æ^{ɛ}$							ɒ					log
married				$ɛ^{\vee}$ɚ									ɒ̯					dog
half						æ	$ɑ^{e}$											fog
glass						$æ^{\vee}$							$ɔ^{\vee}$					water
aunt							ɑ						$ɔ^{\vee}$					daughter
father							ɑ						$ɒɔ̠^{\vee}<$					law
palm							ɑ<						$ɔ^{\vee}$ɚ					warm
barn							ɑ̣ɚ											
garden							ɑɚ						ɔɚ					forty
crop							ɑ<						ɔɚ					morning
on							$ɑ<^{e}$						ɔɚ					corn
college							ɑ						ɔɚ					horse
borrow							ɑɚ											
five									aɩ>		$\hat{a}$>$ʊ^{\vee}$							down
twice									a·ɩ̣>		$aʊ^{\vee}$							out
wire									aɩ>$^{\vee}$ɚ		a>ŏɚ							flower
										ɒ̱ɩ>								joint
										$ɔ^{\vee}$ɩ>								boil
	i	ɩ	e	ɛ	ɜ	æ	ɑ		ai	ɔi	au		ɔ	ʌ	o	ʊ	u	

word	i	ɪ	e	ɛ	ɜ	æ	ɑ	aɪ	ɔɪ	au	ɔ	ʌ	o	ʊ	u	word
three	i ᵛ i														ʊʊ	two
grease	i̩														u·	tooth
six		ɪ												---		wood
crib		ɪ												ʊ		pull
ear		ɪ·ɚ												ʊɚ		yours
beard		ɪ^ɪɚ											oᵁ			ago
eight			e·ɪ										oo^			coat
April			e										oo^			road
ten				ɛ									oo^			home
egg			e										o			know
head				ɛ									oɚ			four
Mary					ər						ɔᵛɚ					door
chair				ɛ^·ɚ							ɔɚ					hoarse
care				ɛɚ									oᵛɚ			mourning
merry				ɛɚ												
thirty					ɚ							ʌ				sun
sermon					ɚ							ʌ				brush
furrow					ɚ											
ashes						æ					ɔ					frost
bag						æᶦ	ɑ>									log
married				ɛɚ			ɑ>									dog
half						æ					ɔᵛ					fog
glass						ɐ										water
aunt						æᵋ	ɐ·									daughter
father							ɑ				ɔᵛ					law
palm							a				ɒɚ·					warm
barn							ɑ·ɚ									
garden							ɑɚ				ɔɚ					forty
crop							ɑ				ɔɚ					morning
on							ɑ				ɔ^ɚ					corn
college							ɑ>				ɔɚ					horse
borrow											ɒɚ					
five								ɑ^ɪ		ɑˤu						down
twice								eɪ		ɑˤu						out
wire								ɑ^ɪɚ		ɑˤuɚ						flower
joint									ɔɪ							
boil									ɔɪ							

| | i | ɪ | e | ɛ | ɜ | æ | ɑ | | aɪ | ɔɪ | au | | ɔ | ʌ | o | ʊ | u |

	ɪ	ɪ	e	ɛ	ɜ	æ	ɑ		aɪ	ɔɪ	au		ɔ	ʌ	o	ʊ	u	
three	i ˅ i																u	two
grease	i ˅ i																u·	tooth
six		ɪ														ʊ		wood
crib		ɪ ˃ ɪ														ʊ		pull
ear		ɪɚ															ʊɚ	yours
beard		ɪ·ɚ													oʊ			ago
eight			e e ˂˃												o ˂ ^			coat
April			e												o ˂			road
ten				ɛ ɛ̆ ˃											oʊ			home
egg															oʊ			know
head				ɛ ɛ̆ ^											oʊɚ			four
Mary				ɛ ^ ɚ											o ˅ ɚ			door
chair				ɛɚ									ɔɚ					hoarse
care				ɛɚ											o ˅ ɚ			mourning
merry				ɛɚ														
thirty					ɚ									ʌ				sun
sermon					ɚ									ʌ ^				brush
furrow					ɚ ˅													
ashes						æ	ɚ											frost
bag						æ ɛ ˃							ɒ ^					log
married						æ ^ r							ɒ ^					dog
half						æ ɛ ˃							ɔ ˅ ɔ					fog
glass						æ æ ^							ɒ					water
aunt							ɑ ˂						ɒ ^					daughter
father							ɑ						ɔ ˅					law
palm							ɑɯ						ɔ ˅ ɚ					warm
barn							ɑɚ											
garden							ɑɚ						ɔɚ					forty
crop							ɑ ĕ						ɒ ˂ ɚ					morning
on							ɑ						ɔ ˅ ɚ					corn
college							ɑ						ɔ ˅ ɚ					horse
borrow							ɑr											
five									a ˃ ɪ ^		ɑ ˂ u							down
twice									a ˃ ɪ ^		a ˃ u							out
wire									ɑ ˂ ^ ɪ ˃ ɚ		a ˃ ʊɚ							flower
										ɔ ˅ ɪ ˂ ^								joint
										ɔ ˅ ɪ ˂								boil
	i	ɪ	e	ɛ	ɜ	æ	ɑ		aɪ	ɔɪ	au		ɔ	ʌ	o	ʊ	u	

87

	i	ɪ	e	ɛ	ɜ	æ	ɑ	aɪ	ɔɪ	au	ɔ	ʌ	o	ʊ	u	
three	iˇi														uˇu<	two
grease	iˇi														ʉˇu	tooth
six		ɪ												ʊ		wood
crib		ɪ												ʊ		pull
ear		ɪˆɚ												ʊɚ		yours
beard		ɪɚ											oᵁ			ago
eight			eᵉˆ										o·			coat
April			e										oᵒˆ			road
ten				ɛᵉˆ									oᵁ			home
egg				---									o·ᵁ			know
head				ɛᵉˆ									oᵁɚ			four
Mary				ɛɚ									oᵁɚ			door
chair				ɛˇɚ							ɔ·ɔˏɚ					hoarse
care				ɛɚ									oˇoɚ			mourning
merry				ɛr												
thirty					ɚ							ʌ				sun
sermon					ɚ							ʌˏ				brush
furrow					ɚˇɚ											
ashes						æ	ɚ									frost
bag						æɛˆˏ										log
married						æˆr					ɔˇ					dog
half						æ					ɒ					fog
glass						æɛˆ					ɔˇ					water
aunt						æɛˆ					ɒ					daughter
father							ɑ				ɔˇ					law
palm							ɑ·ᵉ				ɒˏɚ					warm
barn							ɑɚ									
garden							ɑɚ				ɔɚ					forty
crop							ɑ				ɔɚ					morning
on							ɑᵉ				ɔˇɚ					corn
college							ɑ				ɔˇɚ					horse
borrow							ɑɚ									
five								aˏɪ		aˏʊ						down
twice								aɪˏ		ɑˏʊ						out
wire								aˏɪˆɚ		ɑˏʊɚ						flower
									ɔˇɪˏ							joint
									ɔˇɪˏ							boil
	i	ɪ	e	ɛ	ɜ	æ	ɑ	aɪ	ɔɪ	au	ɔ	ʌ	o	ʊ	u	

88

	i	ɪ	e	ɛ	ɜ	æ	ɑ	aɪ	ɔɪ	au	ɔ	ʌ	o	ʊ	u	
three	i^v i															two
grease	i^v i														u^v u	tooth
six		ɪ													u^v u	wood
crib		ɪ													---	pull
ear		ɪɚ													ʊ	yours
beard		ɪɚ												ʊɚ		ago
eight			e eᵉ^										oᵁ			coat
April			e										oᵒ<			road
ten				ɛ									oᵒ<			home
egg			e eᵉ^>										oᵒ^			know
head				ɛ									oᵒ^			four
Mary			ɛ^v ɚ										oɚ			door
chair				ɛɚ							ɔɚ		o^v ɚ			hoarse
care				ɛɚ									o^v ɚ			mourning
merry				ɛɚ												
thirty					ɚ							ʌ				sun
sermon					ɜ^ɚ							ʌ				brush
furrow					ɚ											
ashes						æ	ɑ									frost
bag						æ					ɒ					log
married				ɛɚ							ɔ^v					dog
half						æ					ɐ>					fog
glass						æ ɛ					ɒ^					water
aunt						æ					ɒ^					daughter
father							ɑ				ɔᵒ<					law
palm							ɑ				ɔɚ					warm
barn							ɑɚ									
garden							ɑɚ				ɔɚ					forty
crop							ɑ˞				ɔɚ					morning
on							ɑ^				ɔɚ					corn
college							ɑ>				ɔɚ					horse
borrow							ɑ>ɚ									
five								a>ɪ		a>ʊ<^v						down
twice								aɪ		aʊ<						out
wire								ɑ<ɪɚ		aʊᵂɚ						flower
joint									ɔɪ							joint
boil									ɔ^ɪ<>							boil
	i	ɪ	e	ɛ	ɜ	æ	ɑ	aɪ	ɔɪ	au	ɔ	ʌ	o	ʊ	u	

	i	ɪ	e	ɛ	ɜ	æ	ɑ		aɪ	ɔɪ	au	ɔ	ʌ	o	ʊ	u	
three		ɪ ^ i														ʊ̥ ^ u	two
grease	i ˅ i															ʊ ^ u	tooth
six		ɪ ˅													---		wood
crib		ɪ													ʊ ˅		pull
ear		ɪɚ													ʊ ˅ ɚ		yours
beard		ɪ ! ˑ ˃ ɚ												o ʊ			ago
eight			e e ^											o o ˂ ^			coat
April			e											o o ˂ ^			road
ten				ɛ										o ˞			home
egg			e e ^ ˃											o o ˂ ^			know
head				ɛ										oɚ			four
Mary				ɛ ^ ɚ								ɔ ^ ɚ					door
chair				ɛ ˅ ɚ								ŏ ˂ oɚ					hoarse
care				ɛɝ								oɚ					mourning
merry				ɛɝ													
thirty					ɝ								^				sun
sermon					ɝ								ʌ ^ ^				brush
furrow					ɝ)												
ashes						æ ˅ æ						ɔ ˂					frost
bag						æ ɛ						ɔ ˅ ɔ ˂					log
married			ɛ ˅ ɝ									ɔ ˅					dog
half						æ						ɒ ^					fog
glass						æ						ɒ					water
aunt						æ						ɒ ^					daughter
father							ɑ					ɒ ɔ ˂ ˅					law
palm							ɑ ˃					ɔ ˅ ɝ					warm
barn							ɑ ɑˑ ɚ										
garden							ɑɝ					ɔɚ					forty
crop							ɑ ^					ɔɚ					morning
on							ɒ					ɔɚ					corn
college							ɒ					ɔɚ					horse
borrow							ɑ ˃ ɚ										
five									ə ˃ a ˃ ɪ		a ˃ ʊ ˅ ˂						down
twice									aɪ ˃		a ˃ ʊ						out
wire									ɑ ˂ ɪ ə		au ˅ ɚ						flower
joint										ɔ ˂ ɪ ˃							joint
boil										ɪc							boil

| | i | ɪ | e | ɛ | ɜ | æ | ɑ | | aɪ | ɔɪ | au | ɔ | ʌ | o | ʊ | u | |

90

	i	ɪ	e	ɛ	ɜ	æ	ɑ	ai	ɔi	au	ɔ	ʌ	o	ʊ	u	
three	iᵛi														ʊᵛ ᵘ	two
grease	iᵛi														ʊᵛ ᵘ	tooth
six		ɪ												ʊ		wood
crib		ɪ												ʊ̆		pull
ear	ɪɚ														ʊɚ	yours
beard	ɪᵛ ɪɚ												oᵁ			ago
eight			eᵉ ^										oˢ oˆ₍			coat
April			e										oᵒˆ₍			road
ten				ɛ									oᵁˢ			home
egg			eᵉ ^										oᵁ			know
head				ɛ									ɔ^ɚ			four
Mary				ɛɚ									ɔ^ɚ			door
chair				ɛɚ									oˢ ɚ			hoarse
care				ɛɚ									ɔ^ɚ			mourning
merry				ɛɚ												
thirty					ɚ							ʌ				sun
sermon					ɚ							ʌ				brush
furrow					ɚ											
ashes						æ					ɔ					frost
bag						æᵌ					ɒ^ɔˢ					log
married				ɛɚ							ɔᵛɞˢ					dog
half						æ					ɔᵛɞˢ					fog
glass						---	ɒ									water
aunt						æᵌ						ɒ				daughter
father							ɑɑ·ɐ									law
palm							ɑ·				ɔɚ					warm
barn							ɑ̆ɑ̆ɚ									
garden							ɑɚ				ɔɚ					forty
crop							ɑ				ɔɚ					morning
on							ɑɑ^				ɔɚ					corn
college							ɑ				ɔɚ					horse
borrow							ɑɚ									
five								aɨ		a^ʊˢ						down
twice								aɪ^		a⟩ʊ						out
wire								ɑˢɨ		aʊɚ						flower
joint									ɔɪ⟩							
boil									ɔ^ɨ							

| | i | ɪ | e | ɛ | ɜ | æ | ɑ | ai | ɔi | au | ɔ | ʌ | o | ʊ | u | |

	i	ɪ	e	ɛ	ɜ	æ	ɑ	aɪ	ɔɪ	au	ɔ	ʌ	o	ʊ	u	
three	i˅i															
two															u<	
grease	i˅i															
tooth															ʉ<˅u	
six		ɪ														
wood														ʊ		
crib		ɪɪ^>														
pull														ʊ		
ear		ɪɚ														
yours														ʊɚ		
beard		ɪ·ɚ											o·ʊ			
ago																
eight			ẽẽ^										o·			
coat																
April			e													
road																
ten				ɛ̃ɛ̃^									oʊ			
home																
egg				ɛ^e									oʊ			
know																
head				ɛɛ^									o·ə>ɚ^			
four																
Mary				ɛɚ									o·ɚ			
door																
chair				ɛ·ɚ							ɔ^oɚ					
hoarse																
care				ɛɚ							ɔ^ɚ					
mourning																
merry				ɛɚ												
thirty					ɚ							ʌ				
sun																
sermon					ɚ							ʌʌ^				
brush																
furrow					ʌ<^ɚr											
ashes						æ	ɑ>									
frost																
bag						æ·ɛ					ɔ˅					
log																
married						æ̃^ɚ					ɔ˅·					
dog																
half						æ·					ɒ					
fog																
glass						æɛ˅					ɒ<					
water																
aunt						æ̃	ɚ									
daughter																
father							ɑ				ɔ˅					
law																
palm							ɑ·e˅				ɒ^r					
warm																
barn							ɑ̃ɚ									
garden							ɑɚ				ɔ˅ɚ					
forty																
crop							ɑe˅				ɒɚ					
morning																
on							ɑe˅				ɒ^ɚ					
corn																
college							ɑ>				ɔ˅ɚ					
horse																
borrow											ɒɚ					
five								a>ɪ>		a^u						
down																
twice								a>ɪ^		a>u						
out																
wire								at<^ɚ		a>uɚ						
flower																
joint									ɔ˅ɪ							
boil									ɒ<^t							

	i	ɪ	e	ɛ	ɜ	æ	ɑ	aɪ	ɔɪ	au	ɔ	ʌ	o	ʊ	u

word	i	ɪ	e	ɛ	ɜ	æ	ɑ	ai	ɔi	au	ɔ	ʌ	o	ʊ	u	word
three	ɪ^i														u˅	two
grease	i^i														u<u	tooth
six		ɪ ɪ^												ʊ		wood
crib		ɪ												ʊ		pull
ear		ɪ†ɚ												ʊɚ		yours
beard		ɪɚ											o ʊ			ago
eight			e ɪ˅										o			coat
April			e										o			road
ten				ɛ									o ʊ			home
egg				---									o ʊ			know
head				ɛ ɛ̆^									o ʊɚ			four
Mary				ɛ˅ɚ									oɚ			door
chair				ɛ˅ɚ									o·ɚ			hoarse
care				ɛ˅ɚ									o·ɚ			mourning
merry				ɛɚ												
thirty					ɚ˅>							ʌ				sun
sermon					ɚ							ʌ·				brush
furrow					ɚ˅>											
ashes						æ					ɒ˅<					frost
bag						æ ɜ̆^					ɒ^<					log
married						æ^ɚ					ɒ^					dog
half						æ	ɑ<									fog
glass						æ æ^					ɔ˅					water
aunt						æ̃ ɜ̆^					ɔ˅					daughter
father							ɑ				ɔ˅					law
palm							ɑ·ẽ				ɔ˅ɚ					warm
barn							ɑɚ									
garden							ɑɚ				ɔɚ					forty
crop							ɑ>				ɔ˅ɚ					morning
on							ɑ				ɔ˅ɚ					corn
college							ɑ				ɔ˅ɚ					horse
borrow							ɑɚ									
five								a>ɪ>		ɑ<u						down
twice								a>ɪ>̂		ɑ<u						out
wire								ɑ<ɪ>ɚ̂								flower
joint									ɔ˅†<							joint
boil									ɒ<†							boil

i	ɪ	e	ɛ	ɜ	æ	ɑ	ai	ɔi	au	ɔ	ʌ	o	ʊ	u

	i	ɪ	e	ɛ	ɜ	æ	ɑ	ai	ɔi	au	ɔ	ʌ	o	ʊ	u	
three	i															two (u ᵛᵁ)
grease	ɪᵛi															tooth (u)
six		ɪ												ʊ		wood
crib		ɪ												ʊ		pull
ear		ɪɚ														yours (---)
beard		ɪ̣ɚ											oᵁ			ago
eight			e eˆ										ŏᵒ			coat
April			e eˆ										oᵁ			road
ten				ɛ									oᵿ			home
egg				---									o̲˂ᵁ			know
head				ɛ									oɚ			four
Mary				ɛˆɚ									ɔˆ˙ɚ			door
chair				ɛɚ							ɔᵛɚ					hoarse
care						æɚ					ɒɐɚ					mourning
merry						æˆɚ										
thirty					ɝ							ʌ				sun
sermon					ɝ							ʌ˂				brush
furrow					ɝ											
ashes						æ˃					ɒˆ					frost
bag						æɪ										log
married						æɚ					ɒ					dog
half						æ					ɒᵒˆ					fog
glass						æ					ɒ					water
aunt						æ̃					ɒ˙					daughter
father							ɑ˙				ɒ					law
palm							ɑ˂˙				ɒɚ					warm
barn							ɑɚ									
garden							ɑ˃ɚ				ɔɚ					forty
crop							ɑ				ɒɑˆɚ					morning
on							ɑᵉ				ɔᵛɚ					corn
college											ɒ̣ɐɚ					horse
borrow											ɒɚ					
five								ɑ˂ɪ		ɑ˂ʊ						down
twice								ɑɪ		ɑʊ						out
wire								ɑɪɚ		ɑ˂ʊɚ						flower
joint									ɔᵛɪ							
boil									ɔɪ							

| i | ɪ | e | ɛ | ɜ | æ | ɑ | | ai | ɔi | au | | ɔ | ʌ | o | ʊ | u |

	i̇	ɪ	e	ɛ	ɜ	æ	ɑ	aɪ	ɔɪ	au	ɔ	ʌ	o	ʊ	u	
three	i̇ˇ															two ʉu
grease	i̇ˇi̇														u	tooth
six		ɪ												---		wood
crib		ɪ												ʊ		pull
ear		ɪ·ɚ												---		yours
beard		ɪˇɪɚ											oŭ			ago
eight			eᶦ										oˆ			coat
April			e										oоˆ			road
ten				ɛᵋˆ									oоˆ			home
egg				ɛ									oᵁ			know
head				ɛˆ							ɔɚ					four
Mary				ɛɚ							ɔˇɚ					door
chair				ɛˀɚ							ɔˇɚ					hoarse
care				ɛɚ							ɔˇɚ					mourning
merry				ɛɚ												
thirty					ɝ							ʌ				sun
sermon					ɝ							ʌ				brush
furrow					ɝ											
ashes						æ					ɒ·ɔ					frost
bag						æ					---					log
married				ɛ·ɚ							ɒɔ					dog
half						æ					ɒɔ					fog
glass						æɛ					ɒ					water
aunt						æ	ɑ·									daughter
father							ɑ				ɒ·					law
palm							ɑ·				ɔɚ					warm
barn							ɑɚ									
garden							ɑˆɚ				ɔɚ					forty
crop							ɑ				ɔɚ					morning
on							ɑ				ɔɚ					corn
college							ɑˀ				ɔɚ					horse
borrow							ɑ·									
five								ɑˆɪ		au						down
twice								ɑɪ		au						out
wire								ɑ·ɪɚ		auɚ						flower
joint									ɔˀɪ							
boil									ɔˇɪ							
	i̇	ɪ	e	ɛ	ɜ	æ	ɑ	aɪ	ɔɪ	au	ɔ	ʌ	o	ʊ	u	

95

	i	ɪ	e	ɛ	ɜ	æ	ɑ		aɪ	ɔɪ	au		ɔ	ʌ	o	ʊ	u	
three	iˇi																ŭu	two
grease	iˇi																uˇu	tooth
six		ɪ														---		wood
crib		ɪ														ʊ		pull
ear	ɪ^ɚ																uɚ	yours
beard	ɪ ɪ^ɚ														o^ʊ			ago
eight			e e^												oʊ			coat
April			e												o o^			road
ten				ɛ											o o^			home
egg			e ɪ												o			know
head				ɛ ɛˇ^											oɚ			four
Mary				ɛ ˇɚ									ɔɚ					door
chair				ɛɚ									ɔˇɚ					hoarse
care				ɛ ˇɚ											ɔ^ɚ			mourning
merry				ɚɛ														
thirty					ɚ									ʌ				sun
sermon					ɚ·									ʌ				brush
furrow					ɚ													
ashes						æ							ɒ					frost
bag						æ ɪ							ɒ					log
married				ɛˇɚ									---					dog
half						æ							ɒ·ɔ					fog.
glass						æ æ^							ɒ					water
aunt							ɑ^e						ɒ·					daughter
father							ɑ						ɒ ɒ^					law
palm							ɑ e						ɒɚ					warm
barn							ɑɚ											
garden							ɑɚ						ɔɚ					forty
crop							ɑ						ɔɚ					morning
on							---						ɔɚ					corn
college							ɑ						ɔɚ					horse
borrow							ɑɚ											
five									ɑ^ɪ		ɑ^ʊ							down
twice									ɑɪ		ɑʊ							out
wire									ɑɪɚ		ɑ^ʊɚ							flower
joint										ɒ								
boil										ɔ								

| | i | ɪ | e | ɛ | ɜ | æ | ɑ | | aɪ | ɔɪ | au | | ɔ | ʌ | o | ʊ | u | |

	i	ɪ	e	ɛ	ɜ	æ	ɑ		ai	ɔi	au		ɔ	ʌ	o	ʊ	u	
three	ɪ^i																uˇu	two
grease	ɪ^i																uˇu	tooth
six		ɪ															---	wood
crib		ɪ														ʊ		pull
ear	ɪɚ															ʊɚ		yours
beard	ɪ̆ɪ̆ɚ														oᵁ			ago
eight			eᵉ^												oŏ^			coat
April			e												oᵁ			road
ten				ɛ											oᵁ			home
egg				ɛ^ᵉ											oᵒ^			know
head				ɛ											oɚ			four
Mary				ɛɝ	ɚ										ŏ<ᵒ ɔɚ			door
chair				ɛɚ											ɔ^oˇɚ			hoarse
care				ɛˇɚ											oɚ			mourning
merry				ɛɝ														
thirty					ɚ									ʌ				sun
sermon					ɚ									ʌ^				brush
furrow					ɚ													
ashes						æᵆ^							ɔ					frost
bag						æ							---					log
married				ɛə̣									ɔ<ˇ					dog
half						æ							ɒɔ<					fog
glass						æɛ							ɔˇ					water
aunt						æ							ɔ<ˇ					daughter
father							ɑ						ɔɔˇ<					law
palm							ɑ·						ɔɚ					warm
barn							ɑ̣ɚ											
garden							ɑ^ɚ						ŏ<ˇ ɚ					forty
crop							ɑ^						ɔɚ					morning
on							ɑ						ɔɚ					corn
college							ɑɹ						ɔɚ					horse
borrow													ɔ<ˇ ɚ					
five									aɨ		a>ᵘˇ^							down
twice									aɪˇ>		a^ʊˇ							out
wire									aɪɚ		---							flower
										ɔɪˇ								joint
										ɔ^ɨ								boil
	i	ɪ	e	ɛ	ɜ	æ	ɑ		ai	ɔi	au		ɔ	ʌ	o	ʊ	u	

	i	ɪ	e	ɛ	ɜ	æ	ɑ	aɪ	ɔɪ	au	ɔ	ʌ	o	ʊ	u	
three	i˅i														u˅u	two
grease	ɪˆi														u˅	tooth
six		ɪ												---		wood
crib		ɪ												ʊ<		pull
ear		ɪɚ		ɚ												yours
beard		ɪɚ											oᵁ			ago
eight			eeˆ										o			coat
April			e										o			road
ten				ɛ									oᵁ			home
egg				ɛ									oᵁ			know
head				ɛ									o·ɚ			four
Mary			ɛ˅ɚ										ɔˆɚ			door
chair			ɛɚ										ɔ<ˆɚ			hoarse
care			ɛə·										o˅ɚ			mourning
merry			ɛɚ													
thirty					ɚ							ʌ				sun
sermon					ɚ							ʌ				brush
furrow					ɚ											
ashes						æ	ɚ									frost
bag						æᵋ					---					log
married			ɛɚ								ɒˆ					dog
half						æ					ɔ˅ɔ<					fog
glass						æᵋ					ɒ					water
aunt						æ					ɔ					daughter
father							ɑ				ɔ<					law
palm							ɑ<				ɔ˅ɚ					warm
barn							ɑɚ									
garden							ɑɚ				ɔɚ					forty
crop							ɑ				ɔɚ					morning
on							ɑ>				ɔɚ					corn
college							ɑ				ɔɚ					horse
borrow							ɑɚ									
five								aˆ>ɬ		a>ʊ˅						down
twice								aɪ		ɑ<ʊ						out
wire								aɬɚ		a>ʊ˅ɚ						flower
									ɔɪ>							joint
									ɔ ɬ							boil
	i	ɪ	e	ɛ	ɜ	æ	ɑ	aɪ	ɔɪ	au	ɔ	ʌ	o	ʊ	u	

	i	ι	e	ɛ	ɜ	æ	ɑ		ai	ɔi	au		ɔ	ʌ	o	ʊ	u	
three	i˅i																u˅u	two
grease	ι˄i																u˅u	tooth
six		ι														ʊ		wood
crib		ι														ʊ		pull
ear		ιɚ														ʊɚ		yours
beard		ῐῐ̣ɚ													---			ago
eight			e^{e}˄												o^{ʊ}			coat
April			---												o^{o}˄			road
ten				ɛ											o^{ʊ}			home
egg			e˅^{e}												---			know
head				ɛ											---			four
Mary				ɛɚ									ɔɚ					door
chair				ɛɚ											o˅ɚ			hoarse
care				ɛɚ									ɔɚ					mourning
merry				ɛ̣ɚ														
thirty					ɚ									---				sun
sermon					ɚ									ʌ				brush
furrow					ɚ^{r}													
ashes						æ							---					frost
bag						æ˄ɛ							ɔ˅ɔ̠˂					log
married				ɛɚ									ɔ˅ɔ					dog
half						æ^{ɛ}							---					fog
glass						æ^{ɛ}							ɒ˄					water
aunt							ɑ̃						ɔ˅					daughter
father							ɑ						ɔɔ̠˂					law
palm							ɑ˂ ·						ɔɚ					warm
barn							ɑ̆ɑ̣̆ɚ											
garden							ɑɚ						ɔɚ					forty
crop							ɑ˃̂						---					morning
on							ɑ^{ɐ}						ɔɚ					corn
college							ɑ˃						ɔɚ					horse
borrow							ɑɚ											
five									a˃ι˃̌		ao							down
twice									a˃ι˃		aʊ							out
wire									ɑ˂ ɨɚ		a˃ʊ˅ɚ							flower
										ɔ˂ι˃								joint
										ɔι˃								boil
	i	ι	e	ɛ	ɜ	æ	ɑ		ai	ɔi	au		ɔ	ʌ	o	ʊ	u	

word	i	ɪ	e	ɛ	з	æ	ɑ	aɪ	ɔɪ	au	ɔ	ʌ	o	ʊ	u	word
three	i˅i														ʊ˄u	two
grease	ɪ˄i														ʊ˅u	tooth
six		ɪ												ʊ		wood
crib		ɪ												ʊ		pull
ear		ɪɚ													ʊɚ	yours
beard		ɪɚ											oᵁ			ago
eight			eᵉ˄										ŏ<			coat
April			e										oᵒ˄			road
ten				ɛᵋ˄									oᵁ			home
egg			eᵉ˄										oᵒ˄			know
head				ɛ									o˅ɚ			four
Mary		ɪ˅ɚ		ɛɝ									o˅ɚ			door
chair				ɛɚ									oɚ			hoarse
care				ɛɝ									oɚ			mourning
merry				ɛɝ												
thirty					ɚ							ʌ				sun
sermon					ɚ̥							ʌ				brush
furrow					ɚ											
ashes						æ					ɒ˄					frost
bag						æ					ɒ					log
married				ɛɚ							ɒ˄					dog
half						æ					ɒ˄ʌ˃					fog
glass						æᵃ˄					ɒ					water
aunt							a				ɒ					daughter
father							ɑ				ɔ˅					law
palm							ɑ				ɔɚ					warm
barn							ɑɚ									
garden							ɑᶜɚ				ɔɚ					forty
crop							ɑɾ				ɔɚ					morning
on							ɑ				ɔɚ					corn
college							ɑ˃				ɔɚ					horse
borrow							ɑɚ									
five								a˃ɪ		a˃ʊ						down
twice								aɪ		au						out
wire								ɑᶜ˄ɪɚ		a˃ʊɚ						flower
									ɔɪ							joint
									ɔ˅ɪ							boil

| | i | ɪ | e | ɛ | з | æ | ɑ | aɪ | ɔɪ | au | ɔ | ʌ | o | ʊ | u | |

	i	ɪ	e	ɛ	ɜ	æ	ɑ		aɪ	ɔɪ	au		ɔ	ʌ	o	ʊ	u	
three	ɪˆⁱ																ʊuˇ	two
grease	iˇ																ʊˇu	tooth
six		ɪ														ʊ		wood
crib		ɪ														ʊ̲		pull
ear		ɪ·ɚ														ʊɚ		yours
beard		ɪɚ													oʊ			ago
eight			eeˆ												o			coat
April			e												oʊ			road
ten				ɛ											oʊˇ			home
egg				ɛˆ											oʊ			know
head				ɛ											oˇɚ			four
Mary				ɛˇɚ											ɔˆɚ			door
chair				ɛɚ											oɚ			hoarse
care				ɛˇɚ									ɔɚ					mourning
merry				ɛɚ														
thirty					ɚ									ʌ				sun
sermon					ɚ									ʌ				brush
furrow					ɚ													
ashes						æ							ɒˇ ɒˆ					frost
bag						æɛ							---					log
married				ɛɚ									ɒ					dog
half						æ	ɑˊ											fog
glass						---	ɚ											water
aunt							ɑ ɚ											daughter
father							ɑ						ɔ·					law
palm							ɑˊ						ɔɚ					warm
barn							ɑɚ											
garden							ɑˋɚ						ɔɚ					forty
crop							ɑˊ						ɔɚ					morning
on							ɑ						ɔɚ					corn
college							---						ɔɚ					horse
borrow							ɑɚ											
five									aɪ		aˊu							down
twice									aˊɪ		aˊu							out
wire									aˊɪɚ		aˊuˇɚ							flower
										ɔɪ								joint
										ɔˇɪ								boil

| | i | ɪ | e | ɛ | ɜ | æ | ɑ | | aɪ | ɔɪ | au | | ɔ | ʌ | o | ʊ | u | |

	i	ɪ	e	ɛ	ɜ	æ	ɑ	aɪ	ɔɪ	au	ɔ	ʌ	o	ʊ	u	
three	i˅i															u˅u	two
grease	ɪˆ˃i˅															ʉ˂u	tooth
six		ɪ													ʊ		wood
crib		ɪ˃													ʊ		pull
ear		ɪˆɚ													ʊɚ		yours
beard		ɪɚ											oŭ				ago
eight			eeˆ										oʊ˅˂				coat
April			e										o˂o				road
ten				ɛ									oʊ˅				home
egg				ɛe˃˅									oʊ˅				know
head				ɛɛ̆ˆ									oʊɚ				four
Mary				ɛ˅ɚ									oɚ				door
chair				ɛɛ˃ɚ									o˅oɚ				hoarse
care				ɛɚ									o˅ɚ				mourning
merry				ɛɚ													
thirty					ɚ˃˅							ʌ					sun
sermon					ɚ							ʌ					brush
furrow					ɚ												
ashes						æ					ɔ˅						frost
bag						æɛ					---						log
married						æ˅ɚ					ɔ˅						dog
half						æ					ɒɒ˂ˆ						fog
glass						æɛ					ɔ˂						water
aunt						æɛ̆˅					ɔ˅						daughter
father							ɑ				ɔ						law
palm											ɒˈ̆ᵐɑˆɚ						warm
barn							ɑ̣ɚ										
garden							ɑɚ				ɔɚ						forty
crop							ɑɑˆ				ɒˆɚ						morning
on							ɑ˃				ɔ˅ɚ						corn
college							ɑ				ɒˆɚ						horse
borrow							ɑɚ										
five								a˃ɪˆ		ɑ˂u							down
twice								aɪ		ɑ˃̆u							out
wire								ɑ˂ˆɪ˅ɚ		a˃ʊɚ							flower
									ɒ˂ɪ								joint
									ɔ˅ɪ˃								boil
	i	ɪ	e	ɛ	ɜ	æ	ɑ	aɪ	ɔɪ	au	ɔ	ʌ	o	ʊ	u	

	i	ɪ	e	ɛ	ɜ	æ	ɑ	ai	ɔi	au	ɔ	ʌ	o	ʊ	u	
three	ɪ>i														uˇːũ	two
grease	i														uˇu	tooth
six		ɪ												ʊ		wood
crib		ɪ												ʊ		pull
ear	ɪ>ɚ														uˆuˇɚ	yours
beard	ɪ˙ɚ												oᵁ			ago
eight			eɪˇ										oõˆ			coat
April			e										oºˆ			road
ten				ɛ									o•ᵁˇ			home
egg			eˇe										oᵁ			know
head				ɛɛ̆ˆd									oᵁɚ			four
Mary			eˇɚ										oᵁɚ			door
chair				ɛɛ̆ˆɚ									o•ˇɚ			hoarse
care				ɛɚ									oˇɚ			mourning
merry				ɛɚ												
thirty					ɚ							ʌˁʌˆ				sun
sermon					ɚˁɚ							ʌʌˆ				brush
furrow					ɜ>ˇr											
ashes						æɛ̆ˆ					ɔˇ					frost
bag						æɪˇ>					---					log
married						æ>ɚ					ɒˆ					dog
half						æ•	ɑɑˆ									fog
glass						æɛˇ					ɔˇ					water
aunt						æ̃ɪ̃ˇ					ɔˇ					daughter
father							ɑˁ				ɔˇ					law
palm							ɑɑˆ				ɔˇɚ					warm
barn							ɑˁɚ									
garden							ɑɚ				ɔˇɚ					forty
crop							ɑɑˆ				ɔˇɚ					morning
on							ɑᵉ				ɔˇɚ					corn
college							ɑ				ɔˇɚ					horse
borrow											ɒˆɚ					
five								aɪˆ		---						down
twice								aˆ>ɪˆ		ɑˁʊ						out
wire								aˁˆɬɚ		aˁˆʊɚ						flower
									ɔˇɪˁ>							joint
									ɒɬˁ							boil
	i	ɪ	e	ɛ	ɜ	æ	ɑ	ai	ɔi	au	ɔ	ʌ	o	ʊ	u	

	i	ɪ	e	ɛ	ɜ	æ	ɑ		ai	ɔi	au		ɔ	ʌ	o	ʊ	u	
three	i ˇ> i																ʉ ᵘˇ<	two
grease	ɪ >i																ʊ ^ᵘ	tooth
six		ɪ														ʊ		wood
crib		ɪ ɪ>														ʊ		pull
ear		ɪɚ														ʊɚ		yours
beard		ɪɚ													oʊ^			ago
eight			e e<^												oʊ^			coat
April			eɪ^												oʊ^			road
ten				ɛ†											oʊ^			home
egg				ɛ†<											oʊ^			know
head				ɛ†									ɔɚ					four
Mary				ɛɚ									ɔɚ					door
chair				ɛɚ									ɔɚ					hoarse
care				ɛɚ									ɔɚ					mourning
merry				ɛ^ɚ														
thirty					ɝ									ʌ				sun
sermon					ɝ									ʌ†				brush
furrow					ɝ													
ashes						æɪ^							ɒ†					frost
bag						æɪ^							---					log
married				ɛɚ			ɑᴅ											dog
half							ɑ						ɒɔ^					fog
glass						æ†	ɑ											water
aunt						æ†							ɒ					daughter
father							ɑ						ɔ					law
palm							ɑ						ɔɚ					warm
barn							ɑɚ											
garden							ɑɚ						ʊɚ					forty
crop							ɑ						ɔɚ					morning
on							ɑ						ɔɚ					corn
college							ɑ						ɔɚ					horse
borrow							ɑɚ											
five									a>·ɪ>		ɑʊ^							down
twice									ɑ^ɪ^		ɑʊ^							out
wire									ɑɪ^ɚ		ɑʊ^ɚ							flower
joint										ɔɪ^								
boil										ɔɪ·†^								

| | i | ɪ | e | ɛ | ɜ | æ | ɑ | | ai | ɔi | au | | ɔ | ʌ | o | ʊ | u | |

104

	i	ɪ	e	ɛ	ɜ	æ	ɑ	aɪ	ɔɪ	au	ɔ	ʌ	o	ʊ	u	
three	ɪ>i															two (ʉˇu)
grease	i															tooth (u<ˇu)
six		ɪ												ʊ		wood
crib		ɪ												ʊ		pull
ear		ɪɚ													ʊɚ	yours
beard		ɪɚ											oʊ^			ago
eight			eɪ^										oʊ^			coat
April			eɪ^										oʊ^			road
ten				ɛ†									oʊ^			home
egg				ɛ†<									oʊ^			know
head				ɛ†							ɔɚ					four
Mary				ɛɚ							ɔ<ɚ					door
chair				ɛɚ							ɔɚ					hoarse
care				ɛɚ							ɒɚ					mourning
merry				ɛɚ												
thirty					ɚ							^				sun
sermon					ɚ							ʌɪ<				brush
furrow					ɚ											
ashes						æɪ^					ɒ†					frost
bag						æɪ^					---					log
married				ɛɚ							ɒ					dog
half						æ					ɒ^†					fog
glass						æ	ɑ									water
aunt						æ†					ɒ					daughter
father							ɑ<ɚ									law
palm							ɑ				ɔɚ					warm
barn							ɑɚ									
garden							ɑɚ				ɔɚ					forty
crop							ɑ				ɒɚ					morning
on							ɑ†				ɔɚ					corn
college							ɑ				ɔɚ					horse
borrow							ɑɚ									
five								a^ɪ>		ɑu^						down
twice								ɑɪ^		ɑu<ˇ						out
wire								ɑɪ^ɚ		ɑuɚ						flower
joint									ɔɪ^							
boil									ɔɪ·^†							
	i	ɪ	e	ɛ	ɜ	æ	ɑ	aɪ	ɔɪ	au	ɔ	ʌ	o	ʊ	u	

	i	ɪ	e	ɛ	ɜ	æ	ɑ	ai	ɔi	au	ɔ	ʌ	o	ʊ	u	
three	ĭ̆˅>i															two (ʉ˅ᵘ)
grease	ɪ>i														u	tooth
six		ɪ												ʊ		wood
crib		---												ʊ		pull
ear		ɪɚ													ʊɚ	yours
beard		ɪɚ											oᵁ^			ago
eight			eᶦ^										oᵁ^			coat
April			eᶦ^										o Ŏ<			road
ten				ɛᵗ<									oᵁ^			home
egg				ɛ^ᵗ<									oᵁ^			know
head				ɛᵗ							ɔɚ					four
Mary				ɛɚ							ɔɚ					door
chair				ɛɚ							ɔ^ɚ					hoarse
care				ɛɚ							ɔɚ					mourning
merry				ɛɚ												
thirty					ɚ							ʌ				sun
sermon					ɚ							ʌᶦ<				brush
furrow					ɚ											
ashes						æ^ᶦ^					ɒᴰ^					frost
bag						æᶦ^					ɔ<ˠ					log
married			ɛ•ɚ								ɒ^					dog
half						æᵗ<					ɒ					fog
glass						æᶦ<	ɑ<									water
aunt						æ•					ɒ					daughter
father							ɑ				ɔ					law
palm							ɑ				ɔɚ˙					warm
barn							ɑ<ɚ									
garden							ɑɚ				ɔɚ					forty
crop							ɑ>ĕ				ɔɚ					morning
on							ɑ•ᵉ				ɔɚ					corn
college							ɑ				ɔ•ᵉɚ					horse
borrow							ɑɚ									
five								ɑ<ɪ^		ɑᵁ^						down
twice								ɑ^ɪ^		ɑᵁ^						out
wire								ɑᶦɚ		ɑ•ˠɚ						flower
									ɔɪ							joint
									ɔɪ•ɪ							boil
	i	ɪ	e	ɛ	ɜ	æ	ɑ	ai	ɔi	au	ɔ	ʌ	o	ʊ	u	

	i	ɩ	e	ɛ	ɜ	æ	ɑ		ai	ɔi	au		ɔ	ʌ	o	ʊ	u	
three	iˇi																ᵼuˆ	two
grease	iˇi																uᵗˁ	tooth
six		ɩ														ʊ		wood
crib		ɩ														ʊ		pull
ear		ɩɚ														ʊɚ		yours
beard		ɩɚ													oʊˆ			ago
eight			eɩˆ												oʊˆ			coat
April			eɩˆ												oʊˆ			road
ten				ɛᵗˁ											oʊˆ			home
egg			ɛˆɩˆ												oʊˆ			know
head				ɛᵗˁ											o•ɚ			four
Mary			ɛˆɚ										ʊɚ					door
chair				ɛɚ									ɔɚ					hoarse
care				ɛɚ									ɔɚ					mourning
merry				ɛɚ														
thirty					ɚ									ʌ				sun
sermon					ɚ									ʌ				brush
furrow					ɚ													
ashes						æɩˀ							ɔ					frost·
bag						æˆɩˆ							---					log
married			ɛˁɚ				ɒ											dog
half						æˁᵗˁ	ɑ						ɒ					fog
glass						æᵗ	ɑ•											water
aunt						æᵗ	ɒ											daughter
father							ɑ						ɔ					law
palm							ɑˁ						ɔɚ					warm
barn							ɑˁɚ											
garden							ɑˁɚ						ɔɚ					forty
crop							ɑ						ɔɚ					morning
on							ɑ•						ɒˁɚ					corn
college							ɑ						ɒˆɑɚ					horse
borrow							ɑɚ											
five									aˀɩˆ		ɑˁuˆ							down
twice									aˀɩˆ		aˀu							out
wire									ɑˁɩˆɚ		ɑuɚ							flower
										ɔˁɩˆ								joint
										ɔɩ•ᵗˁ								boil
	i	ɩ	e	ɛ	ɜ	æ	ɑ		ai	ɔi	au		ɔ	ʌ	o	ʊ	u	

	i	ɪ	e	ɛ	ɜ	æ	ɑ	aɪ	ɔɪ	aʊ	ɔ	ʌ	o	ʊ	u	
three	i														ʉu˂	two
grease	i														u·	tooth
six		ɪ												ʊ		wood
crib		ɪ												ʊ		pull
ear		ɪr												ʊr		yours
beard		ɪr											oᵁ˃			ago
eight			e˂ɪ^										oᵁ			coat
April			eɪ^										oᵁ^			road
ten				ɛ									oᵛᵁ			home
egg				ɛ^									oᵁ^			know
head				ɛ							ɔr					four
Mary				ɛr							ɔr					door
chair				ɛr							ɔr					hoarse
care				ɛr							ɔr					mourning
merry				ɛ˃r												
thirty					ɝ							ʌ				sun
sermon					ɝ							ʌ				brush
furrow					ɝ											
ashes						æɪ					ɔ					frost
bag						æɪ˂					ɔ					log
married				ɛr							ɔ·					dog
half						æ	ɑ									fog
glass						æ	ɑ˃									water
aunt						æ					ɒ					daughter
father							ɑ				ɔ					law
palm							ɑ				ɔr					warm
barn							ɑr									
garden							ɑr				ɔ					forty
crop							ɑ˃				ɔr					morning
on							ɑ				ɔ·ɚ					corn
college							ɑ˃				ɔ·ɚ					horse
borrow							ɑ˃r									
five								a^˃ɪ		ɑˠ						down
twice								ɑɪ˃		a˃o^						out
wire								ɑˡr		ɑɚ						flower
joint									ɔɨ							joint
boil									ɔɨ							boil
	i	ɪ	e	ɛ	ɜ	æ	ɑ	aɪ	ɔɪ	aʊ	ɔ	ʌ	o	ʊ	u	

108

	i	ɪ	e	ɛ	ɜ	æ	ɑ	ai	ɔi	au	ɔ	ʌ	o	ʊ	u	
three	i															two
grease	i														u	tooth
six		ɪ													u	wood
crib		ɪ												ʊˇ		pull
ear	ɪr													ʊr		yours
beard	ɪˆɚ												oˇuˇ			ago
eight			eɪˆ										oˇuˇ			coat
April			e>ɪˆ										oˇuˇ			road
ten				ɛ									oˇuˇ			home
egg				ɛˆ									ouˇ			know
head				ɛ							ɔr					four
Mary			eˆr								ɔˆr					door
chair				ɛˇɚ							ɔr					hoarse
care				ɛˇɚ							ɔr					mourning
merry				ɛr												
thirty					ɚ							ʌ				sun
sermon					ɚ							ʌ				brush
furrow					ɜr											
ashes						æɪ					ɒˇ					frost
bag						æɪˆ					---					log
married				ɛr							ɔˆʊ					dog
half						æ					ɔ					fog
glass						æ					ɑ>					water
aunt						æˇ					ɒ					daughter
father							ɑ				ɔ					law
palm							ɑ				ɔr					warm
barn							ɑr									
garden							ɑr				ɔr					forty
crop							ɑ				ɒˇr					morning
on							ɑ				ɔr					corn
college							ɑˆ				ɔˇr					horse
borrow							ɑr									
five								ɑˆɪˆ		aʊ>						down
twice								ɑˆɪˆ		ɑˆʊˇ						out
wire								ɑɬr		aʊˇɚ						flower
joint									ʌˇ>ɪˆ							
boil									ɔˆeˇɪ							
	i	ɪ	e	ɛ	ɜ	æ	ɑ	ai	ɔi	au	ɔ	ʌ	o	ʊ	u	

	i	ɪ	e	ɛ	ɜ	æ	ɑ	ai	ɔi	au	ɔ	ʌ	o	ʊ	u	
three	i̥														ᵾuˁ	two
grease	i˃														u	tooth
six		ɪ												ʊ		wood
crib		ɪ												ʊ		pull
ear		ɪ·ɚ												ʊr		yours
beard		ɪɚ											oᵁ			ago
eight			eɪ^										ou			coat
April			eɪ^										oᵁ			road
ten				ɛ									oᵁˇ			home
egg				ɛˇ^									oᵁ			know
head				ɛ									o·ɚ			four
Mary				ɛr							ɔ^r					door
chair				ɛr										ʊˇr		hoarse
care				ɛr										ʊˇ		mourning
merry				ɛr												
thirty					ɝ							ʌ				sun
sermon					ɝ							ʌ				brush
furrow					ɝ											
ashes						æɪ^					ɒˁ					frost
bag						æɪ^					---					log
married				ɛr							ɔ					dog
half						æ					ɔ					fog
glass						æ	ɑ									water
aunt						æ†					ɒˁ					daughter
father							ɑ				ɔ					law
palm							ɑ·				ɔr					warm
barn							ɑr									
garden							ɑr				ɔɚ					forty
crop							ɑ				ɔɚ					morning
on							ɑ·˃əˇ				ɔɚ					corn
college							ɑ				ɔr					horse
borrow											ɔr					
five								əɪ		ɑuˇ						down
twice								ɑɪ^		eˁʊˇ<						out
wire								ɑ†r		ɑɚ						flower
joint									ɔ·ɪ^							joint
boil									ɔɪ^ə							boil
	i	ɪ	e	ɛ	ɜ	æ	ɑ	ai	ɔi	au	ɔ	ʌ	o	ʊ	u	

	i	ɪ	e	ɛ	ɜ	æ	ɑ	ai	ɔi	au	ɔ	ʌ	o	ʊ	u	
three	i															two
grease	i															tooth
six		ɪ														wood
crib		ɪ												ʊ<		pull
ear		ɪr												ʊr		yours
beard		ɪr											o< ʊ			ago
eight			eᵗ										oᵘ			coat
April			eᵗ										oᵘ			road
ten				ɛ									o< ʊ			home
egg				ɛ									oᵘ			know
head				ɛ									ɔ^r			four
Mary				ɛr									---			door
chair				ɛ^r									ɔ^r			hoarse
care				ɛr							ɔ·r					mourning
merry				ɛr												
thirty					ɝ							ʌ				sun
sermon					ɝ							ʌ				brush
furrow					ɝ											
ashes						æ< ɪ^					ɒ					frost
bag						æɪ^					---					log
married				ɛˇr							ɔ					dog
half						æ					ɒ<					fog
glass						æ	ɑ				ɔ					water
aunt						æ<					ɒ					daughter
father							ɑ				ɔ					law
palm							ɑ·				ɔr					warm
barn							ɑr									
garden							ɑr						ɔ^r			forty
crop							ɑ				ɔr					morning
on							ɑ>				ɒr					corn
college							ɑ				ɔr					horse
borrow							ɑɝ									
five								ɑɪ^		au>^						down
twice								ɑɪ^		au						out
wire								ɑɨr		aɝ						flower
joint									ɔɪ^							
boil									ɔ^ɪ^ᵊ							
	i	ɪ	e	ɛ	ɜ	æ	ɑ	ai	ɔi	au	ɔ	ʌ	o	ʊ	u	

	i	ɪ	e	ɛ	ɝ	æ	ɑ	aɪ	ɔɪ	au		ɔ	ʌ	o	ʊ	u	
three	ɪ>i															u	two
grease	i															u<u	tooth
six		ɪ·													ʊ		wood
crib		ɪ													ʊ		pull
ear	ɪ^ɚ														ʊɚ		yours
beard		ɪɚ												oʊ^			ago
eight			eɪ^											o·ʊ^			coat
April			eɪ^											oʊ^			road
ten				ɛɪ<										oʊ^			home
egg				ɛ·ɪ										oʊ^			know
head				ɛɪ								ɔ^ɚ					four
Mary				ɛɚ								ɔɚ					door
chair				ɛɚ								ɔɚ					hoarse
care				ɛɚ								ɔɚ					mourning
merry				ɛɚ													
thirty					ɝ								ʌ				sun
sermon					ɝ								ʌ+				brush
furrow					ɚ>												
ashes						æɪ^						ɔə^<					frost
bag						æɪ^											log
married				ɛɚ								ɒɔ					dog
half						æ·	ɚ										fog
glass						æ	ɑ										water
aunt						æ+						ɒ					daughter
father							ɑ					ɔ					law
palm							ɑ					ɔr					warm
barn							ɑɚ										
garden							ɑɚ					ɔ^ɚ					forty
crop							ɑ					ɔɚ					morning
on							ɑ+					ɔɚ					corn
college							ɑ					ɔɚ					horse
borrow							ɑɚ										
five								ɑ<ɪ^		au^							down
twice								ɑɪ^		au^							out
wire								ɑɪ^ɚ		au^ɚ							flower
joint									ɔ^ɪ^								
boil									ɔɪ·ɪ								
	i	ɪ	e	ɛ	ɝ	æ	ɑ	aɪ	ɔɪ	au		ɔ	ʌ	o	ʊ	u	

	i	ɪ	e	ɛ	ɜ	æ	ɑ	ai	ɔi	au	ɔ	ʌ	o	ʊ	u	
three	ɪ>i															two ʊᵘ
grease	ɪ>i															tooth ʊʌᵘ
six		ɪ												ʊ		wood
crib		ɪᵗ												ʊ		pull
ear		ɪɚ													ʊɚ	yours
beard		ɪɚ											o<o			ago
eight			eɪ^										oᵘ^			coat
April			eɪ^										oᵘ^			road
ten				ɛᵗ<									oᵘ^			home
egg				ɛ									oᵘ^			know
head				ɛᵗ<							ɔɚ					four
Mary				ɛɚ							ɔɚ					door
chair				ɛɚ							ɔɚ					hoarse
care				ɛɚ							ɔɚ					mourning
merry				ɛɚ												
thirty					ɝ							ʌ				sun
sermon					ɝ							ʌᵗ<				brush
furrow					---											
ashes						æɪ^					ɒᵗ					frost
bag						æɪ^					---					log
married				ɛɚ							ɒ^ɑ					dog
half						æ					ɔ.					fog
glass						æᵗ	ɑ									water
aunt						æᵗ<					ɒ					daughter
father							ɑ				ɔ					law
palm							ɑ				ɔɚ					warm
barn							ɑɚ									
garden							ɑɚ				ɔɚ					forty
crop							---				ɔɚ					morning
on							ɑ				ɔɚ					corn
college							ɑ				ɔɚ					horse
borrow							ɑɚ									
five								ɑɪ^		ɑʊ^						down
twice								ɑ^ɪ^		ɑʊ^						out
wire								ɑɪ^ɚ		ɑʊɚ						flower
joint									ɔɪ^							
boil									ɔɪ^ᵗ							
	i	ɪ	e	ɛ	ɜ	æ	ɑ	ai	ɔi	au	ɔ	ʌ	o	ʊ	u	

	i	ɪ	e	ɛ	з	æ	ɑ	aɪ	ɔɪ	au	ɔ	ʌ	o	ʊ	u	
three	ɪ>i														ʉᵛᵘ	two
grease	ɪ>i														ʊ^ᵘ	tooth
six		ɪ												ʊ		wood
crib		ɪ												ʊ		pull
ear		ɪɚ												ʊɚ		yours
beard		ɪɚ											o^ᵘ^			ago
eight			eɪ^										o<o			coat
April			eɪ^										o^ᵘ^			road
ten				ɛ†<									o^ᵘ^			home
egg				ɛɪ^									o^ᵘ^			know
head				ɛ†									ɔ^ɚ			four
Mary				ɛɚ							ɔɚ					door
chair				ɛɚ							ɔɚ					hoarse
care				ɛɚ							ɔɚ					mourning
merry				ɛɚ												
thirty					ɚ							ʌ				sun
sermon					ɚ							ʌ†<				brush
furrow					ɚ											
ashes						æɪ^					ɒ^†ᵛ					frost
bag						æɪ^					ɒ^					log
married			ɛɚ								ɔ·					dog
half						æ†					ɔ†ᵛ>					fog
glass						æ	ɑ>									water
aunt						æ†					ɒ					daughter
father							ɑ				ɔ					law
palm							ɑ·				ɔɚ					warm
barn							ɑɚ									
garden							ɑɚ				ɔɚ					forty
crop							ɑ				ɔɚ					morning
on							ɑ				ɔɚ					corn
college							ɑ				ɔɚ					horse
borrow											ɔɚ					
five								ɑɪ^		aʊ^						down
twice								ɑɪ^		aʊ^						out
wire								ɑɪ^ɚ		aʊɚ						flower
joint									ɔɪ^							
boil									ɔɪ^							

	i	ɪ	e	ɛ	з	æ	ɑ	aɪ	ɔɪ	au	ɔ	ʌ	o	ʊ	u	

	i	ɪ	e	ɛ	ɜ	æ	ɑ	aɪ	ɔɪ	au	ɔ	ʌ	o	ʊ	u	
three	ɪ˂ˆi														ɐˀuˑ˂	two
grease	i														u˅˂u	tooth
six		ɪ												ʊ		wood
crib		ɪ												ʊ		pull
ear		ɪɚ													ʊɚ	yours
beard		ɪɚ											oʊˆ			ago
eight			eɪˆ										oʊˆ			coat
April			eɪˆ										o•oˆ˂			road
ten				ɛɾ˂									o•ʊ˂˅			home
egg				ɛɾ˂									oʊˆ			know
head				ɛɾ							oɚ					four
Mary				ɛɚ							ɔɚ					door
chair				ɛ˅ɚ							ɔɚ					hoarse
care				ɛɚ							ɔɚ					mourning
merry				ɛɚ												
thirty					ɚ							ʌ				sun
sermon					ɚ							ʌɾ				brush
furrow					ɚ											
ashes						æɪˆ					ɔɔ̣ˆ˂					frost
bag						æɪˆ					ˌ- - -ˌ					log
married				ɛɜ							ɔ					dog
half						æɾ					ɒ˅ʌˆɔ					fog
glass						æ	ɑ									water
aunt						æɾ					ɒ					daughter
father							ɑ				ɔ					law
palm							ɑ				ɔɚ					warm
barn							ɑ•ɚ									
garden							ɑ˃ɚ				ɔɚ					forty
crop							ɑ•ᵉˆ				ɔɚ					morning
on							ɑ				ɔ•ɚ					corn
college							ɑ				ɔɚ					horse
borrow							ɑɚ									
five								ɑɪˆ		ɑuˆ						down
twice								ɑɪˆ		a˃ʊ˅˂ˌ						out
wire								ɑɪˆɚ		ɑuˆɚ						flower
									ɔɪˆ							joint
									ɔɪˆɾ˅							boil
	i	ɪ	e	ɛ	ɜ	æ	ɑ	aɪ	ɔɪ	au	ɔ	ʌ	o	ʊ	u	

	i	ɪ	e	ɛ	ɜ	æ	ɑ	aɪ	ɔɪ	au	ɔ	ʌ	o	ʊ	u	
three	ɪ^i·														ŭ>u̬	two
grease	ɪ^i														---	tooth
six		ɪ												ʊ		wood
crib		ɪ												ʊ		pull
ear		ɪɚ									ɔɚ					yours
beard		ɪɚ											oʊ^			ago
eight			eɪ^										oʊ^			coat
April			eɪ^										o·ʊ̬			road
ten				ɛ†									oʊ^			home
egg				ɛ†<									oʊ^			know
head				ɛ†<							ɔɚ					four
Mary				ɛ^ɚ							ɔɚ					door
chair				ɛˇɚ							ɔɚ					hoarse
care				ɛɜ							ʊɚ					mourning
merry				ɛ												
thirty					ɚ							ʌ				sun
sermon					ɚ							ʌ				brush
furrow					ɚ											
ashes						æɪ>					ɔ†					frost
bag						æɪ^					---					log
married				ɛɜ							ɒɔ					dog
half						æ					ɒ<ɔ					fog
glass						æ†<	ɑ									water
aunt						æ†	ɑ˞									daughter
father							ɑ·				ɔ					law
palm						æ·t̃					·ɔɚ					warm
barn							ɑ·ɚ									
garden							ɑ<ɚ				ʊɚ					forty
crop							ɑ				ɔɚ					morning
on											ɔɒɑ^ ɔɚ					corn
college							ɑ				ɒ^ɑ ɔ^ɚ					horse
borrow											ɔɚ					
five								ɑɪ^		ɑʊ^						down
twice								ɑɪ^		ɑʊˇ						out
wire								ɑɪ^·ɚ		ɑɚ						flower
joint									ɔɪ^							joint
boil									ɔɪ·^†							boil
	i	ɪ	e	ɛ	ɜ	æ	ɑ	aɪ	ɔɪ	au	ɔ	ʌ	o	ʊ	u	

	i	ɪ	e	ɛ	ɜ	æ	ɑ	ai	ɔi	au		ɔ	ʌ	o	ʊ	u	
three	ɪ>ⁱ															ʉᵛᵘ	two
grease	ɪ>ⁱᵛ>															ʊuᵛ<	tooth
six		ɪ													ʊᵗ		wood
crib		ɪᵗ													ʊ		pull
ear		ɪɚ														ʊɚ	yours
beard		ɪɚ												oᵁ^			ago
eight			eɪ^											o<ᵁ^			coat
April			eɪ^											oᵁ^			road
ten				ɛᵗ<										o<o			home
egg				ɛᵗ<										oᵁ			know
head				ɛᵗ<										ɔ^ɚ			four
Mary				ɛ^ɚ								ɔɚ					door
chair				ɛᵛɚ								ɔɚ					hoarse
care				ɛɚ								ɔɚ					mourning
merry				ɛɚ													
thirty					ɚ								ʌ				sun
sermon					ɚ								ʌᵗ<				brush
furrow					– – –												
ashes						æᵗ						ɔᵗᵛ					frost
bag						æɪ^											log
married				ɛ̣								ɒᵒ^					dog
half												ɔᵁᵛ					fog
glass						æ^ᵗ<						ɒ>					water
aunt						æᵗᵛ						ɒ					daughter
father							ɑ					ɔ					law
palm							ɑ					ɔɚ					warm
barn							ɑ>ɚ										
garden							ɑɚ							ɔ^ɚ			forty
crop							ɑ					ɔɚ					morning
on							ɔ̱<					ɔ̃ɚ					corn
college							ɑ^					ɔɚ					horse
borrow												ɔɚ					borrow
five								ɑ^ɪ^		ɑ>ᵁ^							down
twice								ɑ˄>ɪ^		ɑᵁ^							out
wire								ɑ>ᵗɚ		ɑwɚ							flower
									ɔɪ>								joint
									ɔᵗ<ə								boil

| | i | ɪ | e | ɛ | ɜ | æ | ɑ | ai | ɔi | au | | ɔ | ʌ | o | ʊ | u | |

115 (II) HAMILTON, IA. (H)

	i	ι	e	ε	ɜ	æ	ɑ		aɪ	ɔɪ	au		ɔ	ʌ	o	ʊ	u	
three	i˃˅i·																ʉ̠u˂	two
grease	i˃˅i																ʉu·	tooth
six		ι														ʊ		wood
crib		ι+˂														ʊ˂·		pull
ear		ιɚ														ʉ˂ɚ		yours
beard		ι˃ɚ													oo˂^			ago
eight			e˅e^												oo˂^			coat
April			ε˂^ι												oo˂^			road
ten				ε̃											oo^			home
egg				ε											oʊ^			know
head				ε·ɚ									ɔ˂ɚ		ɔ^ɚ			four
Mary				εɚ									ɔ˂˅o˂^ɚ					door
chair				ε˅ɚ									ɔ̣˅ɚ					hoarse
care				εɚ									ɒ˂^ɔ̠˂˅ɚ					mourning
merry				εɚ														
thirty					ɚ									ʌ				sun
sermon					ɚ									ʌ				brush
furrow					ɚ													
ashes						æ·ε˅							ɒ·					frost
bag						æ·ε												log
married				εɚ									ɔ˅ɔ̠^					dog
half						æ							ɔ˅ɤ					fog
glass						ææ^˃	ɑ˃·											water
aunt						æ·ε˅˃	ɑ˃											daughter
father							ɑ						ɒɒ˂^					law
palm							ɑ˂·ɤ						ɔ̣˂ɚ					warm
barn							ɑ̃˂ɚ̃											
garden							ɑɚ						ɒ̠ɚ					forty
crop							ɑ·e						ɔ˅ɚ					morning
on							ɑ / ɑ˂·ɚ											corn
college							ɑ / ɑ˂ɚ											horse
borrow							ɑɚ											
five									a˃+		ɑo˂^							down
twice									a˃ι˂^		ɑ˂o˂^							out
wire									ɑ˂+̆˅ɚ		ɑo̠˂^ɚ							flower
										ɒ˂^ι								joint
										ɒ+˂+								boil
	i	ι	e	ε	ɜ	æ	ɑ		aɪ	ɔɪ	au		ɔ	ʌ	o	ʊ	u	

	i	ɪ	e	ɛ	ɜ	æ	ɑ	ai	ɔi	au	ɔ	ʌ	o	ʊ	u	
three	i̯ʌ̂i														ʊu̯ᵛ	two
grease		ɪɪ^												ɵu		tooth
six		ɪ												ʊ^ʊ		wood
crib		ɪ^ə												ʊᵛʊ		pull
ear	iɚ													ʊr		yours
beard		ɪ̣ɚ											oᵛʊ			ago
eight			ɛ+										oᵛʊ^			coat
April			eɪ^										oᵛʊ			road
ten				ɛɛ^									o.ᵛ			home
egg				ɛ+									ɔ^ʊ^			know
head				ɛɛ^>									oᵛɚ			four
Mary				ɛ^r									ɔᵛ<ɚ			door
chair				ɛɚ									ɔ^ɚ			hoarse
care				ɛᵛɚ										ʊ>ɚ		mourning
merry				ɛ^ɚ												
thirty					ɚ							ʌ				sun
sermon					ɚᵛ							ʌ^+				brush
furrow					ɚ											
ashes						æ^+					ɒ+ᵛ					frost
bag						æ^ɪ^					ɔ<					log
married				ɛ>ɚ			ɑ+>									dog
half						æɛᵛ>					ɔʊ					fog
glass						æ+	ɑ									water
aunt						æᵛ+	ɑ									daughter
father							ɑ<				ɔ					law
palm							ɑ				ɔr					warm
barn							ɑɚ									
garden							ɑ>ɚ				ɒɚ					forty
crop							ɑɑ^				ɒɚ					morning
on							ɑ				ɔɚ					corn
college							ɑ<				ɔɚ					horse
borrow							ɑɚr									
five								ɑ<ɪ^		au^						down
twice								ɑ^ɪ^		ɑ^ʊ<ᵛ						out
wire								ɑ+^ɚ		---						flower
joint									ɔɪ<^							
boil									ɔ+							
	i	ɪ	e	ɛ	ɜ	æ	ɑ	ai	ɔi	au	ɔ	ʌ	o	ʊ	u	

	i	ɪ	e	ɛ	ɜ	æ	ɑ		ai	ɔi	au		ɔ	ʌ	o	ʊ	u	
three	ɪˆi																ʉˇu	two
grease	i																ʉu	tooth
six		ɪ														ʊˍ		wood
crib		ɪˇ														ʊ		pull
ear	iˇˍɚ												ɔˆɚ					yours
beard	iˇˍɚ														o·oˆˍ			ago
eight			eɪˆ												oˍˇʊ̆			coat
April			eɪˆ												oʊˆ			road
ten				ɛ											oʊˆ			home
egg				ɛˆ											oʊ			know
head				ɛ									ɔˆɚ					four
Mary					ɚ										---			door
chair				ɛɚ									ɔ̆ɚ					hoarse
care				ɛɚ									ɔˇɚ					mourning
merry				ɛɚ														
thirty					ɚ									ʌ				sun
sermon					ɚ									ʌ				brush
furrow					ɚ													
ashes						æ							ɔ					frost
bag						æ							---					log
married				ɛˀɚ									ɒ					dog
half						æ	ɒˀ											fog
glass						æ	ɑ											water
aunt						æ	ɒˀ											daughter
father							ɑ						ɒɑˆ					law
palm							ɑ						ɔˇɚ					warm
barn							ɑˆɚ											
garden							ɑɚ						ɒˍɑ					forty
crop							ɒˆ						ɔɚ					morning
on													ɔ·ˍɔ·ɚ					corn
college							ɑ						ɔɚ					horse
borrow							ɑɚ											
five									ɑˆɪ		ɑˆʊˇ							down
twice									ɑiˇˋ		ɑˍoˆ							out
wire									ɑɚ		ɑˆʊˍ wɚ							flower
joint										ɔɪˆ								boil
boil										ɔ̇								

| | i | ɪ | e | ɛ | ɜ | æ | ɑ | | ai | ɔi | au | | ɔ | ʌ | o | ʊ | u | |

120

	i	ɪ	e	ɛ	ɜ	æ	ɑ	aɪ	ɔɪ	au	ɔ	ʌ	o	ʊ	u	
three	---														uˇᵁ<	two
grease	i.ʝ														uˇ< ·	tooth
six	---													ʊ< ə		wood
crib		ɪ ə												---		pull
ear	ˀiɚ·												oɚ			yours
beard	iɚ·												---ǀ			ago
eight			--- ǀ										oˇʊˇ			coat
April			---										oˇoˆ			road
ten				---									oˇʊˆ			home
egg				ɛ>									ooˆ			know
head				ɛ>									---			four
Mary				ɛɚ									oǫˆɚ			door
chair				ɛɚ·									oˇoɚ			hoarse
care				ɛɚ									---			mourning
merry				---												
thirty					---							---				sun
sermon					---							ʌ<ˆə				brush
furrow			ɚˆˇr													
ashes						æˑæˆ					ɔˑˇə					frost
bag						æ·					ɔˑˇɔ					log
married				---							ɔˑˇɔ					dog
half						---					---					fog
glass						æ·ə					ɔˇ<					water
aunt						æ·ə>					ɒˆ					daughter
father							ɑ				---					law
palm							ɑ<·				ɔˇ<ɚ					warm
barn							aˆ>ɚ·									
garden							aˆ>ɚ				---					forty
crop							ɑ<·				---					morning
on							---				ɔ<ˇɚ̃					corn
college							---				ɔˇ<ɚ·					horse
borrow							---									
five								---		auˇ						down
twice								aˆ>ʇˆ		a·ʊˇ						out
wire								aˆ>ʇˆ·		aˆʊɚ						flower
									ɔˇ<ʇˆ							joint
									ɔʇ							boil
	i	ɪ	e	ɛ	ɜ	æ	ɑ	aɪ	ɔɪ	au	ɔ	ʌ	o	ʊ	u	

	i	ɪ	e	ɛ	ɜ	æ	ɑ	aɪ	ɔɪ	au	ɔ	ʌ	o	ʊ	u	
three	i														uᵛᵁ	two
grease	i														u	tooth
six		ɪ^												ʊ		wood
crib		ɪ												ʊ		pull
ear		ɪr												ʊ⋗r		yours
beard		ɪr											oᵁ			ago
eight			eɪ^										oᵛᵁ			coat
April			eɪ										oᵁ			road
ten				ɛ									oᵛᵁ			home
egg				ɛ^									oᵛ			know
head				ɛ									ɔ^r			four
Mary				ɛr							ɔr					door
chair				ɛ^r									ɔ^r			hoarse
care				ɛr									ɔ^r			mourning
merry				ɛr												
thirty					ɜ˞							ʌ				sun
sermon					ɜ˞							ʌ				brush
furrow					ɜ˞											
ashes						æɪ^	ɑ⋗									frost
bag						æɪ^	ɑ									log
married				ɛr							ɒˢ					dog
half						æ·	ɑ⋗									fog
glass						æ	ɑ									water
aunt						æᵛ	ɑ⋗									daughter
father							ɑ				ɔ					law
palm							ɑ·/ɑ									warm
barn							ɑ·									
garden							ɑ˞						ɔ<^˞			forty
crop							ɑ				ɔr					morning
on							ɑ⋗						ɔ^r			corn
college							ɑ						ɔ^r			horse
borrow							ɑr									
five								aɪ^		aʁ						down
twice								aɪ^		au						out
wire								aɪr		auɚ						flower
joint									ɔɪ^							
boil									ɔ^ɪ^ə							
	i	ɪ	e	ɛ	ɜ	æ	ɑ	aɪ	ɔɪ	au	ɔ	ʌ	o	ʊ	u	

122

	i	ɪ	e	ɛ	ɜ	æ	ɑ	ai	ɔi	au	ɔ	ʌ	o	ʊ	u	
three	i														u<ᵛᵁ	two
grease	i														u	tooth
six		ɪ												ʊᵛ		wood
crib		ɪ												ʊᵛ		pull
ear		ɪr												ʊr		yours
beard		ɪr											oᵁ			ago
eight			eˡ^										oᵁ			coat
April			eˡ^										oᵁ			road
ten				ɛᵛ									oᵁ			home
egg				ɛ^									oᵁ			know
head				ɛ									oᵛr			four
Mary				ɛr									oᵛɚ			door
chair				ɛᵛr									ɔ^ɚ			hoarse
care				ɛr										ʊɚ		mourning
merry				ɛ>r												
thirty					ɜ							ʌ				sun
sermon					ɜ							ʌ				brush
furrow					ɚ^											
ashes						æˡ					ɒ					frost
bag						æ^ˡ					---					log
married			ɛɚ								ɔ					dog
half						æ					ɔ					fog
glass						æ	ɑ									water
aunt						æ					ɒ					daughter
father							ɑ>				ɔ					law
palm							ɑ·				ɔ^r					warm
barn							ɑr									
garden							ɑr						oᵛɚ			forty
crop							ɑ						ɔ^ɚ			morning
on							ɑ.						ɔ^r			corn
college							ɑ				ɔr					horse
borrow							ɑr									
five								ɑɨ		ɑʊ						down
twice								ɑ>ɨ		ɑʊ						out
wire								ɑɪr		ɑʊ						flower
joint									ɔɪ^							boil
boil									ɔɪ^							
	i	ɪ	e	ɛ	ɜ	æ	ɑ	ai	ɔi	au	ɔ	ʌ	o	ʊ	u	

123

	i	ɪ	e	ɛ	ɜ	æ	ɑ		ai	ɔi	au		ɔ	ʌ	o	ʊ	u	
three	i																u‿ᵛᵁ	two
grease	i																u	tooth
six		ɪ														ʊ		wood
crib		ɪ														ʊ		pull
ear		ɪr														ʊr		yours
beard		ɪr													oᵁ			ago
eight			eɪ^												oᵛᵁ			coat
April			eɪ^												oᵛᵁ			road
ten				ɛ											oᵛᵁ			home
egg				---											oᵁ			know
head				ɛ											ɔ^r̥			four
Mary				ɛ^r											ɔ^r			door
chair				ɛr											ɔ^r			hoarse
care				ɛr									ɔr					mourning
merry				ɛr														
thirty					ɝ									ʌ				sun
sermon					ɝ									ʌ				brush
furrow					ɝ													
ashes						æ							ɔᵉ					frost
bag						æ<ɪ^												log
married				ɛ^r									ɔ					dog
half						æ							ɒ					fog
glass						æ<	ɑ											water
aunt						æ							ɒ					daughter
father							ɑ						ɒ					law
palm							ɑ·						---					warm
barn							ɑr											
garden							ɑr								ɔ^			forty
crop							ɑ								ɔ^r			morning
on							ɑ›								ɔ^r			corn
college							ɑ								ɔ^r			horse
borrow							ɑr											
five									ɑ^ɪ^		ɑʊ							down
twice									ɑ^ɪ^		ɑʊ							out
wire									ɑɪr		ɑɝ							flower
										ɔɪ^								joint
										ɔ^ɪ^ᵉ								boil
	i	ɪ	e	ɛ	ɜ	æ	ɑ		ai	ɔi	au		ɔ	ʌ	o	ʊ	u	

	i	ɪ	e	ɛ	ɜ	æ	ɑ	ai	ɔi	au	ɔ	ʌ	o	ʊ	u	
three	₊i														ʊ̣ᵁ	two
grease	₊i														ʊ̣ᵁ	tooth
six		ɪ												---		wood
crib		ɪ												ʊˑ		pull
ear	ɪ˞										ɔˑ˞					yours
beard	ɪ^˞												oˑo̬^			ago
eight			e eᵉ<										oo^			coat
April			eɪ										oo^			road
ten				ɛ									oo^			home
egg				---									oo^			know
head				ɛ									oˇə̣			four
Mary				ɛ˞							ɔᵉ˞					door
chair			eˇɬ˞										ɔ^r			hoarse
care				ɛ˞									oˇ˞			mourning
merry				ɛ˞												
thirty					˞							ʌ				sun
sermon					˞							ʌ				brush
furrow					˞̮											
ashes						æ					ɔ					frost
bag						æ					ɒ					log
married				ɛ˞							ɔ^oˇ					dog
half						æ					ɔ					fog
glass						æ	ɑ˃									water
aunt						æ					ɔ					daughter
father							ɑ				ɔ					law
palm							ɒ				ɔ˞					warm
barn							ɑ^˞									
garden							ɑ˞				ɔ̲˞					forty
crop							ɑ				ɔ˞					morning
on											ɒˑ---					corn
college							ɑ				ɔ˞					horse
borrow							eˇ˞									
five								aˑɪ˃		ɑo^						down
twice								ɑɪ^		ɑo^						out
wire								ɑɬ˞								flower
joint									oˇɪ^							
boil									ɔɪ							
	i	ɪ	e	ɛ	ɜ	æ	ɑ	ai	ɔi	au	ɔ	ʌ	o	ʊ	u	

125

	i	ɪ	e	ɛ	ɜ	æ	ɑ	aɪ	ɔɪ	au	ɔ	ʌ	o	ʊ	u	
three	₊i														ʉu	two
grease	₊i														ʉu	tooth
six		ɪ												ʊ		wood
crib		ɪ												ʊ<		pull
ear	ɪiɚ														ʉuɚ	yours
beard	₊iɚ												oo^			ago
eight			eɪ										oo^			coat
April			eɪ										oo^			road
ten				ɛ									oo^			home
egg				---									oo^			know
head				ɛ									ɔ^ɚ			four
Mary				ɛɝ							ɔɚ					door
chair				ɛ^ɝ							ɔɚ					hoarse
care				ɛɝ							ɔɚ					mourning
merry				ɛɝ												
thirty					ɝ							ʌ				sun
sermon					ɝ							ʌ				brush
furrow					ɝ											
ashes						æ					ɔ					frost
bag						æ					---					log
married			ɛɝ								ɔ^ᵛ					dog
half						æ					ɔ					fog
glass						æ	ɑ									water
aunt						æ<					ɒ^					daughter
father							ɑ				ɒ^					law
palm							ɑ				ɔɚ					warm
barn							ã<ɚ									
garden							ɑɚ				ɔᵛɚ					forty
crop							ɑ				ɔɚ					morning
on							---				ɔɚ					corn
college							ɑ				ɔɚ					horse
borrow							ɑɚ									
five								aɪ		ao^						down
twice								ɐɪ		ao^						out
wire								aɪɚ		ao^ɚ						flower
joint									ɔɪ							boil
boil									o^ᵛɪə							
	i	ɪ	e	ɛ	ɜ	æ	ɑ	aɪ	ɔɪ	au	ɔ	ʌ	o	ʊ	u	

	i	ɪ	e	ɛ	ɜ	æ	ɑ	aɪ	ɔɪ	au	ɔ	ʌ	o	ʊ	u	
three	ᵼⁱ														ᵫᵘ	two
grease		ᵼⁱ													ᵫᵘ	tooth
six		ῐˆ												ʊ		wood
crib		ɪ												ʊˇ		pull
ear	ᵼ ɪˆ ɚ										ɔɚ					yours
beard		ɪɚ											ou			ago
eight			eɪ										ou<			coat
April			eɪˆ										ou			road
ten				ɛ									ʸou<			home
egg				ɛ									ou			know
head				ɛ							ɔɚ					four
Mary				ɛɚ									---			door
chair				ɛɚ							ɔɚ					hoarse
care				ɛɚ							ɔɚ					mourning
merry				ɛɚ												
thirty					ɚ							ʌ				sun
sermon					ɚ							ʌ				brush
furrow					ɚ											
ashes						æ					ɔ					frost
bag						æ					ɔ					log
married				ɛɚ							ɔˆ					dog
half						æ					ɔ					fog
glass						æ	ɑ									water
aunt						æ					ɒˇ					daughter
father							ɑˆ				ɒˆ					law
palm							ɑ˞				ɔɚ					warm
barn							ɑːɚ									
garden							ɑɚ				ɔɚ					forty
crop							ɑ				ɔɚ					morning
on							---				ɔᵉ					corn
college							ɑ				ɔɚ					horse
borrow							ɑɚ									
five								ɑˆɪ		auˆ						down
twice								ɑɪˆ		ɑu						out
wire							ɛə			---						flower
joint									ɔɪˆ							
boil									ɔɪə							
	i	ɪ	e	ɛ	ɜ	æ	ɑ	aɪ	ɔɪ	au	ɔ	ʌ	o	ʊ	u	

127

	i	ɪ	e	ɛ	ɜ	æ	ɑ		aɪ	ɔɪ	au		ɔ	ʌ	o	ʊ	u	
three	i ˅ i̥																ʉ ᵘ	two
grease	ᵢi̥																ʉ ᵘ	tooth
six		ɪ														- - -		wood
crib		ɪ														ʊ		pull
ear		ɪɚ		ɚ														yours
beard	iɚ														oo˄			ago
eight			eɪ												ˠou˂			coat
April			eɪ												ou			road
ten				ɛ											ˠou˂			home
egg				ɛ											ou˅			know
head				ɛ											o˅ə			four
Mary				ɛɚ											o˅ɚ			door
chair				ɛɚ											o˅ɚ			hoarse
care				ɛɚ								ɔɚ						mourning
merry				ɛɚ														
thirty					ɚ									ʌ				sun
sermon					ɚ									ʌ				brush
furrow					ɚ													
ashes						æ									o˂˅ə			frost
bag						æ						- - -						log
married				ɛɚ							ɑ˄o˂							dog
half						æ æ̂˃							ɒ					fog
glass						æ	ɑ											water
aunt						æ						ɔ						daughter
father							ɑ					ɒ						law
palm							ɑ					ɔɚ˙						warm
barn						ɑɑ̣												
garden							ɑɚ					ɒɚ						forty
crop							ɑ					ɔɚ						morning
on												ɔ˂						corn
college							ɑ					ɒɚ						horse
borrow							ɑɚ											
five									ɑ˄ɪ		ao˄							down
twice									e˅ɪ˄		ɑo˄							out
wire									ɑɪ		ɑɚ							flower
										ɔɪ								joint
										oɪo								boil

| | i | ɪ | e | ɛ | ɜ | æ | ɑ | | aɪ | ɔɪ | au | | ɔ | ʌ | o | ʊ | u | |

128

	i	ɪ	e	ɛ	ɜ	æ	ɑ	aɪ	ɔɪ	au	ɔ	ʌ	o	ʊ	u	
three	i˅>ⁱ														ʉ˅>u˅<	two
grease	ɪⁱ														ʉu	tooth
six		ɪ												ʊ		wood
crib		ɪ												ʊ		pull
ear	iɚ									ɔɚ						yours
beard	iɚ												ou˅<			ago
eight			eᵉ˂^										ou<			coat
April			eɪ										o˂o˂^			road
ten				ɛ									oo˂^			home
egg				ɛ									ou˅<			know
head				ɛ^							ɔ^ɚ					four
Mary			eɪɚ								ɔ^ɚ					door
chair				ɛɚ							ɔ^ɚ					hoarse
care				ɛɜ						ʊ˂ɚ						mourning
merry				ɛ>ɚ												
thirty					ɚ							ʌ.				sun
sermon					ɚ							ʌ				brush
furrow					ɚ											
ashes						æ					ɑ					frost
bag						æ										log
married				ɛɚ			ɑ>									dog
half						æ					ɒ					fog
glass						æ					ɔ˂					water
aunt							a^				---					daughter
father							ɚ				ɒ˂					law
palm							ɑ				ɔɚ					warm
barn							ɑ˙ɚ									
garden							ɑɚ				ɔɚ					forty
crop							ɑ				ɔɚ					morning
on							ɑ>ə				ɔɚ					corn
college							ɑ>				ɔɚ					horse
borrow							ɑ^ɚ									
five						eˇɪ		ɑ˂ʊ˅<								down
twice						əɪ		a>o˂^								out
wire						ɑɪɚ		ɑo^wɚ								flower
joint									ɔɪ^							
boil									eᵊɪ˅ɔə							

| | i | ɪ | e | ɛ | ɜ | æ | ɑ | | aɪ | ɔɪ | au | | ɔ | ʌ | o | ʊ | u | |

129

	i	ɪ	e	ɛ	ɜ	æ	ɑ	ai	ɔi	au	ɔ	ʌ	o	ʊ	u	
three	₊i														ʊ̆ᵁ	two
grease	ɪi														ʊ̆ᵁ	tooth
six		ɪ												ʊˆ		wood
crib		ɪ												ʊˆ		pull
ear		ɪɚ		ɚ												yours
beard	iˇɚ												oʊˇ			ago
eight			eɪ										ˠoʊ			coat
April			eɪ										oʊˇ			road
ten				ɛ									oʊˇ			home
egg				ɜ									oʊˇ			know
head				ɛ							ɔɚ					four
Mary				ɛɚ									oˆɚ			door
chair				ɛɚ									ɔˆɚ			hoarse
care				ɛɚ									oɚ			mourning
merry				ɛɚ												
thirty					ɚ							ʌ				sun
sermon					ɚ							ʌ				brush
furrow					ɜɾ											
ashes						æ	ɑ̆									frost
bag						æ					– – –					log
married				ɛɚ							ɑ					dog
half						æ					ɔˇ					fog
glass						æ	ɑ									water
aunt						æ	ɑˇ									daughter
father							ɑ				ɔ					law
palm							ɑ				ɔɚ					warm
barn							ɑɚ									
garden							ɑɚ				ɔɚ					forty
crop							ɑ				ɔɚ					morning
on											ɔˇə / ɔˇɚ					corn
college							ɑ				ɔɚ					horse
borrow							ɑˇɚ									
five								əɪ		ɑˆʊ						down
twice								əɪ		ɑʊ						out
wire								ɑɪɚ		ɑˀɚ						flower
joint									ɔɪˆ							
boil									ɔɪə							
	i	ɪ	e	ɛ	ɜ	æ	ɑ	ai	ɔi	au	ɔ	ʌ	o	ʊ	u	

130

	i	ɪ	e	ɛ	ɜ	æ	ɑ		aɪ	ɔɪ	au		ɔ	ʌ	o	ʊ	u	
three	ᵼi																	two: ʊu
grease	ᵼi																	tooth: ʊu
six		ɪ														ʊ		wood
crib		ɪ														ʊˑ		pull
ear		ɪɚ			ɚ													yours
beard	iɚ														oo^			ago
eight			eɪ												oo^			coat
April			eˇɪ												---			road
ten				ɛ											oo^			home
egg				---											oo<^			know
head				ɛ									ɔɚ					four
Mary				ɛɜɚ											ɔ<^ɚ			door
chair				ɛ^ɚ									ɔɚ					hoarse
care				ɛɜɚ									ɔɚ					mourning
merry				ɛɜɚ														
thirty					ɚ									ʌ				sun
sermon					ɚ									ʌ				brush
furrow					ɚ													
ashes						æ							ɔ					frost
bag						æ							ɔˇ					log
married				ɛɜɚ									ɒ					dog
half						æ							ɔ					fog
glass						æ	ɑ											water
aunt						æ	ɑˇ											daughter
father							ɑ ɑˇ											law
palm							ɑ						ɔɚ					warm
barn							ɑɚ											
garden							ɑɚ								ɔ^ɚ			forty
crop							ɑ								ɔ^ɚ			morning
on							ɑ						ɔɚ					corn
college							ɑ						ɔ<ɚ					horse
borrow							ɑɚ											
five									ɑɪ^		ɑ<o^							down
twice									ɑɪ		ɑo<^							out
wire									ɑˡɚ		---							flower
										ɔɪ								joint
										eɪə								boil
	i	ɪ	e	ɛ	ɜ	æ	ɑ		aɪ	ɔɪ	au		ɔ	ʌ	o	ʊ	u	

	i	ɪ	e	ɛ	ɜ	æ	ɑ	ai	ɔi	au	ɔ	ʌ	o	ʊ	u	
three	i̯ᵛ i															two
															ᵾu	
grease	ᵻi															tooth
															ᵾu	
six		ɪ														wood
														ʊ		
crib		ɪ														pull
														ʊ		
ear	ɪ^ɚ										ɔɚ					yours
beard	iɚ												o			ago
eight			ɛ<^ e<^										oo^			coat
April			eɪ										o<o<^			road
ten				ɛ									oo^			home
egg				---									ou^			know
head				ɛ							ɔ		o^ɚ			four
Mary				ɛɚ							ɔɚ					door
chair			eɚ										o:ɚ			hoarse
care				ɛɚ							ɔɚ					mourning
merry				ɛɚ												
thirty					ɝ							ʌ				sun
sermon					ɝ							ʌ<				brush
furrow					ɝ											
ashes						æ					ɔ					frost
bag						æ					---					log
married						æ^æ ɚ					ɒ<					dog
half						æ					ɔᵛ					fog
glass						æ	ɑ				ɔ					water
aunt						æ					ɔ					daughter
father							ɑ				ɒ<					law
palm							ɑ				ɔɚ					warm
barn							ɑɚ									
garden							ɐɚ				ɔɚ					forty
crop							ɑ				ɔɚ					morning
on											ɒ< ɔɚ					corn
college											ɒ<ɑ ɔɚ					horse
borrow							ɑɚ									
five								ɑ^ɪ		ɑ<o						down
twice								ɑ^ɪ		ɑo						out
wire								ɑɪɚ		ɑɚ						flower
joint									ɔɪ^							
boil									ɔ^ɪə							

	i	ɪ	e	ɛ	ɜ	æ	ɑ	ai	ɔi	au	ɔ	ʌ	o	ʊ	u	

	i	ɪ	e	ɛ	ɜ	æ	ɑ	ai	ɔi	au	ɔ	ʌ	o	ʊ	u	
three	i ̌>ⁱ															two (ʉᵘ)
grease	ɪⁱ															tooth (ʉᵘ)
six		ɪ														wood (ʊ)
crib		ɪ														pull (̆ʊ)
ear	ɪ^ɚ															yours (---)
beard		ɪɚ											o			ago
eight			eɪ										o< ᴏʊ			coat
April			eɪ										oo^			road
ten				ɛ									oo^			home
egg				---									oo^			know
head				ɛ									ɔ^ɚc			four
Mary				ɛɚ									ɔ^c^ɚ			door
chair				ɛ^ɚ									ɔ^c^ɚ			hoarse
care				ɛɚ							ɔɚ					mourning
merry				ɛ^ᵛɚ												
thirty					ɚ							ʌ				sun
sermon					ɚ							ʌ				brush.
furrow					ɚ											
ashes						æ					ɔ					frost
bag						æ					---					log
married				ɛɚ							ɔᵛ					dog
half						æ					ɒ^ɔ^					fog
glass						æ	ɑ									water
aunt						æ	ɐ									daughter
father							ɑ				ɑ					law
palm							ɑ				ɔ^ə<^ɚ^					warm
barn							ɑ^>ɚ									
garden							ɑɚ				ɔɚ					forty
crop							ɐ				ɔɚ					morning
on											ɒ^ᵛᶜ^ɒ^					corn
college							ɑ				ɑ^ɒ<^					horse
borrow							ɑɚ									
five								ɑɪ^		aᴏ^						down
twice								ɑɪ		aᴏ^						out
wire								ɑɪɚ		ɑɚ						flower
joint									ɔɪ							
boil									ɔɪə							
	i	ɪ	e	ɛ	ɜ	æ	ɑ	ai	ɔi	au	ɔ	ʌ	o	ʊ	u	

	i	ɪ	e	ɛ	ɜ	æ	ɑ		aɪ	ɔɪ	au		ɔ	ʌ	o	ʊ	u	
three	i ˇ ⁱ ˎ																ʉ ᵘ	two
grease	i ˇ i ˎ																ʉ ˎᵘ	tooth
six		ɪ															---	wood
crib		ɪ̆														ʊ		pull
ear		ɪˆ iˇ														ʊɚ		yours
beard		ɪ ˎ											o<o<ˆ					ago
eight			eˇeˆˎ										o<o<ˆ					coat
April			eˇe<ˆ										ʌˎo<ˆ					road
ten				ɛ									o<o<ˆ					home
egg				ɛ̃ɛˇˆˎ									oo ˆ					know
head				ɛ									ɔˆɚ					four
Mary				ɛɚ									ɔ<ˎ ɚ					door
chair				ɛɚ									ɔˇɚ					hoarse
care				ɛɚ									ɒ<ˆɚ.					mourning
merry				ɛɚ														
thirty					ɜˇ									ʌ				sun
sermon					ɚ									ʌ<				brush
furrow					ɚ													
ashes						æ							ɑˆoˇ					frost
bag						æɛˆˎ							ɔ					log
married						æ̃ˆɚ ɑ·												dog
half						æ ɑ·ᵉ												fog
glass						æˎ							ɒ					water
aunt						æ							ɒˇˆ ɑ					daughter
father							ɑ						ɒˇˆ ɑ					law
palm						ɑ̃·ᵉ̃							ɔɚ·					warm
barn						ɑ<ɚ												
garden						ɑɚ							ɔˇɚ					forty
crop						ɑ ɑˎɚ												morning
on						ɑˎ							ɔɚ					corn
college						ɑ							ɔˇɚ					horse
borrow						ɑ<ɚ												
five									aˎɪˆ		ɑˆʊˇˎ							down
twice									a·ɪ		aˎʊ							out
wire									aˆˎɪ<ˆ		aˎo<ˆɚ							flower
joint										ɒˆɪˇˎɑ								joint
boil										ɔɪə								boil
	i	ɪ	e	ɛ	ɜ	æ	ɑ		aɪ	ɔɪ	au		ɔ	ʌ	o	ʊ	u	

134

	i	ɩ	e	ɛ	ɜ	æ	ɑ		ai	ɔi	au		ɔ	ʌ	o	ʊ	u	
three	iˇ>i																ʊ^u	two
grease	ɩ^i																u<ˇu	tooth
six		ɩ														ʊ^		wood
crib		ɩᵊ														ʊᵘ^		pull
ear		jɩɚ														ʊɚ		yours
beard		ɩɚ													oˇo			ago
eight			eɩ^												oʊ^			coat
April			eˇ>												oʊˇ			road
ten				ɛɨˇ											o<·ʊ			home
egg				ɛ^											o			know
head				ɛɨˇ											oˇ·ɚ			four
Mary				ɛ̣											o·o<^ɚ			door
chair						æɚ							ɔɚ					hoarse
care				ɛɚ									ɔɚ					mourning
merry				ɛ̣														
thirty					ɚ									ʌ				sun
sermon					ɚ									ʌ^				brush
furrow					---													
ashes						æɨ							ɔ^ɨ					frost
bag						æɩ^												log
married				ɛ̣											o^ʊ			dog
half						æ							ɔɚ					fog
glass						æ	ɑ											water
aunt						æɨ							ɔ					daughter
father							ɑ>								ɔ̣^			law
palm							ɑ						ɔɚ					warm
barn							ɑ̣ɚ											
garden							ɑɚ						ɔɚ					forty
crop							ɑ						ɒɚ					morning
on													ɔ̃· ɔ:ɚ					corn
college							ɑ>								ɔ^ɚ			horse
borrow							ɑɚ											
five									ɑ<ɩ^		ɑ<ʊ^							down
twice									ɑɩ^		æ>·o<·							out
wire									a<·ɚ		ɑ<ʊɚ							flower
										ɔ^ɩ^								joint
										ɔ^ɨ<^ˇ								boil
	i	ɩ	e	ɛ	ɜ	æ	ɑ		ai	ɔi	au		ɔ	ʌ	o	ʊ	u	

	i	ɪ	e	ɛ	ɜ	æ	ɑ		aɪ	ɔɪ	au		ɔ	ʌ	o	ʊ	u	
three	i̯ᵛⁱ																˩ˢu˂·	two
grease	ɪ^i																u̯ᵛu	tooth
six		ɪ														ʊᵛ		wood
crib		ɪˀ														ʊᵛʊ		pull
ear		ɪɚ															ʊɚ	yours
beard		ɪɚ													^o˂			ago
eight			eɪ^												ŏu^			coat
April			eɪ^												oᵘ^			road
ten				ɛˀ˂											oᵘᵛ˂			home
egg				ɛɪ^											oᵘ˂			know
head				ɛˀ˂										ɚ^ᶜ				four
Mary				ɛɚ									ɔɚ					door
chair				ɛɚ										ɔ^ɚ				hoarse
care				ɛ^ɚ									ɔɚ					mourning
merry				ɛɚ														
thirty					ɚ									ʌ				sun
sermon					ɚ									ʌɪ				brush
furrow					ɚ													
ashes						æ·æ^˃							ɒᵉ					frost
bag						æɪ^							- - -					log
married				ɛɚ									ɔ^ᴜᶜ					dog
half						æ·							ɔɔ^ᶜ					fog
glass						æˀᵛ	ɑ						ɔ·ᵉᶜ					water
aunt						æˀ˂							ɔ^ᶜ					daughter
father							ɑ						ɔɔ^ᶜ					law
palm											aᴜ^		ɔɚ					warm
barn							ɑ˃ɚ											
garden							ɑ˂ɚ						ɔɚ					forty
crop							ɑ						ɔɚ					morning
on							ɑ˃ɚ						ɔɚ					corn
college							ɑ˃						ɔɚ					horse
borrow													ɒ˂ɚ					
five									a^˃ɪ^		ɑ˂ᴜ^							down
twice									aɪ˃		ɑ˂ᴜ^							out
wire									a˃ˀɚ		ɑ˂ᴜɚ							flower
joint										ɔ^ɪ^ᶜ								boil
boil										ɔˀ˂^								
	i	ɪ	e	ɛ	ɜ	æ	ɑ		aɪ	ɔɪ	au		ɔ	ʌ	o	ʊ	u	

	i	ɪ	e	ɛ	ɜ	æ	ɑ	ai	ɔi	au	ɔ	ʌ	o	ʊ	u	
three	ᵼi															two
grease	ᵼi													ʊ ˄		tooth
six		ɪ												---		wood
crib		ɪ												ʊ		pull
ear	iɚ										ɔɚ					yours
beard	ᵼiɚ												oʊ˂			ago
eight			eɪ										oʊ˂			coat
April			eɪ										oʊ˂			road
ten				ɛ									oʊ˂			home
egg				---									o˂ ʊ			know
head				ɛ									ɔ˄ɚ			four
Mary				ɛɚ							ɔɚ					door
chair				ɛɚ							ɔ˄ɚ					hoarse
care				ɛɚ							ɔɚ					mourning
merry				ɛ˃ɚ												
thirty					ɚ							ʌ				sun
sermon					ɚ							ʌ				brush
furrow					ɚ											
ashes						æ					---					frost
bag						æ					---					log
married				ɛɚ							ɒ˂					dog
half						æ					ɔ					fog
glass						æ	ɑ									water
aunt						æ˂æ˃					ɒ					daughter
father							ɑ˄				ɔ					law
palm							ɑ				ɔɚ					warm
barn							ɑɚ									
garden							ɑɚ				ɔɚ					forty
crop							ɑ				ɔɚ					morning
on							ɑ				ɔɚ					corn
college							ɑ				ɔɚ					horse
borrow							ɑɚ									
five								ɑɪ˃		ɑ˂ʊ˂						down
twice								ɑɪ		ɑʊ						out
wire								ɑ˂ɪɚ		---						flower
									ɔɪ							joint
									ɔɪ							boil
	i	ɪ	e	ɛ	ɜ	æ	ɑ	ai	ɔi	au	ɔ	ʌ	o	ʊ	u	

	i	ɪ	e	ɛ	ɜ	æ	ɑ	ɒ	ai	ɔi	au		ɔ	ʌ	o	ʊ	u	
three	ᵻi																ᵾ ᵛu	two
grease	ᵻi																ᵾ u	tooth
six		ɪ														ʊ		wood
crib		ɪ														ʊ		pull
ear	ᵻiɚ			ɚ														yours
beard	iᵛɚ														oo^			ago
eight			eᵻ												ŏ< o^			coat
April			e												oo^			road
ten				ɛ ɛ >											ou<ᵛ			home
egg				---											o< ʊ			know
head				ɛ									ɔ^ɚ					four
Mary				ɛɚ											oᵛɚ			door
chair		ɪᵛɚ													oᵛɚ			hoarse
care				ɛɚ									ɔɚ					mourning
merry				ɛɚ														
thirty					3ᵛ>									ʌ				sun
sermon					ɚ									ʌ^				brush
furrow					ɚ													
ashes						æ							ɒ<					frost
bag						æ							ɔ					log
married				ɛ>ɚ									ɔ					dog
half						æ							ɔ					fog
glass						æ	ɑ						ɔ					water
aunt						æ							ɔ					daughter
father							ɑ						ɔ					law
palm						æ												warm
barn							ɑɚ											
garden							ɑɚ						ɔɚ					forty
crop							ɑ^						ɔɚ					morning
on													ɔᵛc ɔᵛɚ					corn
college							ɑ						ɔɚ					horse
borrow							ɑɚ											
five									ɑɪ		ɑʊᵛ							down
twice									ɑɪ		ɑ<ʊ							out
wire									ɑɪɚ		---							flower
										ɔɪ								joint
										ɔɪə								boil

| | i | ɪ | e | ɛ | ɜ | æ | ɑ | | ai | ɔi | au | | ɔ | ʌ | o | ʊ | u | |

	i	ɪ	e	ɛ	ɝ	æ	ɑ	ai	ɔi	au	ɔ	ʌ	o	ʊ	u	
three	ɪ̯i															two → ʊ̯u
grease	ɪ̯i															tooth → ʊ̯u
six		ɪ												---		wood
crib		ɪ ɪ>												ʊ^		pull
ear	ɪ^ɚ			ɚ												yours
beard	iɚ												o<ʊ^			ago
eight			eɪ										ŏ<ʊ<^			coat
April			eɪ										oʊ<ˇ			road
ten				ɛɛ>									oʊ<^			home
egg				---									oʊ<ˇ			know
head				ɛ									ɔ^ɚ			four
Mary				ɛɚ									ɔ^ɚ			door
chair			eˇɪɚ								ɔɚ					hoarse
care				ɛɚ									ɔ^ɚ			mourning
merry				ɛɚ												
thirty					ɝ							ʌ				sun
sermon					ɝ							ʌ				brush
furrow					ɝ											
ashes						æ					ɔ^ɔ<					frost
bag						æ										log
married				ɛɚ			ɑ									dog
half						æ					ɒ					fog
glass						æ	ɑ									water
aunt						ææ>					ɒ					daughter
father							ɑ				ɒ					law
palm							ɑ>				ɔɚ					warm
barn							ɑ>ɚ									
garden											ɔɚ					forty
crop							ɑ				ɔɚ					morning
on							ɑ				ɔ		ɔ^ɚ			corn
college							ɑ>						ɔ^ɚ			horse
borrow							ɑɚ									
five								ɑ^ɪ		ɑ<ʊ						down
twice								ɑɪ		ɑ<ʊ						out
wire								ɔɪɚ·ɛɪ	æɒ ɑɚ							flower
joint									oˇɪ^							
boil																

	i	ɪ	e	ɛ	ɝ	æ	ɑ	ai	ɔi	au	ɔ	ʌ	o	ʊ	u	

	i	ɪ	e	ɛ	ɜ	æ	ɑ	aɪ	ɔɪ	au	ɔ	ʌ	o	ʊ	u	
three	iˇi														ɬuˑ	two
grease	ɬ<ⁱ														ʮu	tooth
six	ɪ	ɪ												ʊˆ		wood
crib		ɪɬ<												ʊˇ		pull
ear		ɪɚ												ʊɚ		yours
beard		ɪˆɚ											o<ˇʊˆ			ago
eight			eˇɪ													coat
April			e·ɪ										oˇuˇ			road
ten				ɛɬ<									o<ˇoˆ			home
egg				ɛɪ>									oˇuˇ<			know
head				ɛɬ<									o·ɚ			four
Mary				ɛɚ									o·ˇɚ			door
chair				ɛˇɚ										ʊ>ɚ		hoarse
care				ɛˇɚ								ɔ<ˆɚ					mourning
merry				ɛɚ												
thirty					ɚ							ʌ				sun
sermon					ɚ							ʌɬ				brush
furrow					ʌˆ											
ashes						æ·ɪˆ					ɑɒˆ					frost
bag						æɪ					ɒ<ɒˆ					log
married				ɛ·ɚ							ɔɔˆ					dog
half						æɬ	ɑ·				ɔ					fog
glass						æɬ	ɑ·									water
aunt						æɬ<					ɔ					daughter
father							ɑ				ɔ					law
palm							ɑ				ɔɚ					warm
barn							ɑɚ									
garden							ɑ>ɚ				ɔɚ					forty
crop							ɑ				ɔɚ					morning
on							ɑ>ɒ				ɔ<ˇæ̃					corn
college							ɑ>				ɔ<ɚ					horse
borrow							ɑɚ									
five								a>ɪ>	ɑu ˆ							down
twice								ɑɪ<	au ˆ							out
wire								ɑ>ɬɚ	ɑuˆɚ							flower
joint									ɔˆɪˆ							
boil									ɔɬ>							

| | i | ɪ | e | ɛ | ɜ | æ | ɑ | aɪ | ɔɪ | au | ɔ | ʌ | o | ʊ | u | |

	i	ɪ	e	ɛ	ɜ	æ	ɑ		ai	ɔi	au		ɔ	ʌ	o	ʊ	u	
three	ɪ^i																u‿u	two
grease	ɪ>i																uˇu	tooth
six		ɪ·														ʊ		wood
crib		ɪ†														ʊ		pull
ear		ɪɚ											ɔɚ					yours
beard		ɪɚ													oʊ^			ago
eight			eɪ^												oʊ^			coat
April			eɪ̆												oʊ^			road
ten				ɛ											oʊ^			home
egg				ɛ†<											oʊ^			know
head				ɛ†<											oᵒ<^ɚ			four
Mary				ɛɚ											ɔ^ɚ			door
chair				ɛɚ									ɔɚ					hoarse
care				ɛɚ									ɔɚ					mourning
merry				ɛɚ														
thirty					ɚ									ʌ				sun
sermon					ɚ									ʌ†				brush
furrow					ɚ													
ashes						æɪ^							ɑ^ɘ^					frost
bag						æɪ^							---					log
married			ɛɚ										ɔˇɔ					dog
half						æ							ɔˇɔ					fog
glass						æ†	ɑ						ɔ					water
aunt						æ†							ɔ					daughter
father							ɑ						ɔ					law
palm							ɑɘ^						ɔˤɚ					warm
barn							ɑ>ɚ											
garden							ɑɚ						ɔ·ɚ					forty
crop							ɑ						ɔɚ					morning
on													ɔˇɔɪ					corn
college							ɑ						ɔɚ					horse
borrow													ɔɚ					
five									aɪ>		ɑu^							down
twice									ɑ^ɪ^		ɑu^							out
wire									ɑɪɚ		ɑuɚ							flower
joint										ɔɪ^								joint
boil										ɔɪ·^†ˇ								boil
	i	ɪ	e	ɛ	ɜ	æ	ɑ		ai	ɔi	au		ɔ	ʌ	o	ʊ	u	

	i	ɪ	e	ɛ	ɜ	æ	ɑ	ai	ɔi	au	ɔ	ʌ	o	ʊ	u	
three	i˅ɪ>														u<ᵁ	two
grease	i														u·	tooth
six		ɪˆ												ʊ		wood
crib		ɪˆ												ʊˆ		pull
ear		ɪr									ɔˆr					yours
beard		ɪr											oᵁ			ago
eight			e˅ɪˆ										o˅ᵁ			coat
April			e†										oᵁ			road
ten				ɛ˅									oᵁ			home
egg			eɪˆ										o˅			know
head				ɛ˅									oᵒˆ<ɚ			four
Mary				ɛˆr									ɔˆɚ			door
chair						æˆɚ								ʊˆɚ>		hoarse
care				ɛr										ʊˆɚ>		mourning
merry				ɛˆ<r												
thirty					ɚ							ʌ				sun
sermon					ɚ							βˆɪ>				brush
furrow					ɜr											
ashes						æˆ†					ɔ					frost
bag						æɪˆ					---					log
married			ɛˆr								ɒ					dog
half						æ					ɔ					fog
glass						æ	ɑ									water
aunt						æ					ɒ					daughter
father							ɑ				ɔ					law
palm							ɑ·				ɔr					warm
barn							ɑ<r									
garden							ɑr						ɔˆ			forty
crop							ɑ				ɔr					morning
on											ɔ / ɔ<˅r					corn
college							ɑ				ɒr					horse
borrow							ɑ>r									
five								aɪˆ		au						down
twice								aˆɪˆ		e<ᵁ˅						out
wire								aɪr		auɚ						flower
joint									ɒɪˆ							
boil									ɒɪˆ							
	i	ɪ	e	ɛ	ɜ	æ	ɑ	ai	ɔi	au	ɔ	ʌ	o	ʊ	u	

	i	ɪ	e	ɛ	ɜ	æ	ɑ	ai	ɔi	au	ɔ	ʌ	o	ʊ	u	
three	ɪ^i															two (ɵu<)
grease	i															tooth (u)
six		ɪ												ʊ		wood
crib		ɪ												ʊ		pull
ear		ɪɚ												ʊɚ		yours
beard		ɪɚ											o<ʊˇ			ago
eight			eɪ										oʊ			coat
April			eɪ										oʊˇ			road
ten				ɛˇ									o ɔ<^			home
egg													oʊ			know
head				ɛ									oˇɚ			four
Mary				ɛˀr												door
chair				ɛɚ							ɔ^ɚ					hoarse
care				ɛ·ɚ									oˇɚ			mourning
merry				ɛr												
thirty				ɛr								ʌ				sun
sermon					ɚ									ʊ		brush
furrow					ɚ											
ashes						æ					ɔ					frost
bag						æɪ					---					log
married				ɛˀɚ							ɔ^					dog
half						æ·æ^>					ɒ					fog
glass						æ	ɑ									water
aunt						æ	ɑ									daughter
father							ɑ>				ɔ ɔ<^					law
palm											ɔ ---					warm
barn							ɑɚ									
garden							ɑɚ				ɔɚ					forty
crop							ɑ				ɔɚ					morning
on											ɔ·ɔ^ ɔ·ɚ					corn
college							ɑ				ɔ<ɚ					horse
borrow							ɑɚ									
five								aˀɪ>		ɑʊ						down
twice								aˆɪ>		aˆo<						out
wire								aɚ		ɑɚ						flower
									ɔɪ							joint
									ɔˀ^ɪ							boil
	i	ɪ	e	ɛ	ɜ	æ	ɑ	ai	ɔi	au	ɔ	ʌ	o	ʊ	u	

141 (I)   SCOTT, IA.   (P)

word	i	ɪ	e	ɛ	ɜ	æ	ɑ	ai	ɔi	au	ɔ	ʌ	o	ʊ	u	word
three	əi														u	two
grease	i̯														u	tooth
six		ɪ												ʊ		wood
crib		ɪ												ʊ		pull
ear	ɪ^ɚ										ɔɚ					yours
beard	i̯ɚ												oᵘ			ago
eight			eˡ										o̲ᶜᵘ			coat
April			eˡ										oᵘ			road
ten				ɛ^									oᵘ			home
egg				---									oᵘ			know
head				ɛ							ɔɚ					four
Mary				ɛr							ɔɚ					door
chair				ɛɚ									ɔ^ᶜɚ			hoarse
care				ɛɚ							ɔɚ					mourning
merry				ɛˀr												
thirty					ɚ							ʌ				sun
sermon					ɚ							ʌ				brush
furrow					ɚ											
ashes						æ					ɒ					frost
bag						æ					---					log
married				ɛr							ɒ					dog
half						æ					ɒ					fog
glass						æ	ɑ									water
aunt						æ					ɒ					daughter
father							ɑ				ɒ					law
palm							---				ɒ					warm
barn							ɑɚ									
garden							ɑɚ				ɔɚ					forty
crop							ɑ				---					morning
on											ɔᶜɚ					corn
college							ɑ				ɔɚ					horse
borrow							ɒ̲ᶜɚ									
five								ɐɪ		ɑᵘ						down
twice								ɑ^ˡ		---						out
wire								ɑɚ		ɔɚ						flower
									ɔɪ							joint
									ɔˡ							boil
	i	ɪ	e	ɛ	ɜ	æ	ɑ	ai	ɔi	au	ɔ	ʌ	o	ʊ	u	

144

	i	ι	e	ε	ɜ	æ	ɑ		ai	ɔi	au		ɔ	ʌ	o	ʊ	u	
three	i˃ˇ i																ʉ u˂	two
grease	ɨ i																ɨ ˃u	tooth
six		ι														ʊ		wood
crib		ι +ˇ˃														ʊ		pull
ear		ιɚ											ɔɚ					yours
beard	iˇɚ														oo^			ago
eight			eι												oo^			coat
April			eι												oo^			road
ten				ε											oʊ^			home
egg				---											---			know
head				εˇ											ɔ^ɚ			four
Mary				εɚ											ɔ^ɚ			door
chair				εɚ											oˇɚ			hoarse
care				εɚ											ɔ^ɚ			mourning
merry				εɚ														
thirty					ɚ									ʌ				sun
sermon					ɚ									ʌ				brush
furrow					ɚ													
ashes						æ							ɒ					frost
bag						æ							ɔˇ					log
married				εɚ			ɑ˃ɑ^											dog
half						æ^							ɔ					fog
glass						æ	ɑ˃											water
aunt						æ							ɒ					daughter
father							ɑ						ɔˇ					law
palm							ɑ						ɔɚ					warm
barn							ɑɚ											
garden							ɑɚ						ɔɚ					forty
crop							ɑ˃						ɔɚ					morning
on													ɔ ɔ·ɚ					corn
college							ɑ˃						ɔɚ					horse
borrow							ɑɚ											
five									a+˂		ɑo^							down
twice									ɑι		æ˃o^							out
wire									ɑιɚ		ɑɚ							flower
										ɔ.:ι^								joint
										ɔιə								boil
	i	ι	e	ε	ɜ	æ	ɑ		ai	ɔi	au		ɔ	ʌ	o	ʊ	u	

	i	ɪ	e	ɛ	ɜ	æ	ɑ	ai	ɔi	au	ɔ	ʌ	o	ʊ	u	
three	i ᵛⁱ >														ʉᵁ	two
grease	₊ⁱ														ʉᵁ	tooth
six		ɪ												ʊ		wood
crib			ɛ^ ə<												ʊ<	pull
ear		ɪɚ									ɔ<ɚ					yours
beard		ɪɚ											oo^			ago
eight			eɪ										oʊ^			coat
April			eᵛɪ										oo^			road
ten				ɛ									oo^			home
egg				---									oo^			know
head				ɛ									oᵛ•ɚ			four
Mary				ɛ>ɚ									ɔ^ɚ			door
chair				ɛɚ									ɔ^ɚ			hoarse
care				ɛɚ									ɔ^ɚ			mourning
merry				ɛ>ɚ												
thirty					ɚ							ʌ				sun
sermon					ɚ							ʌ				brush
furrow					ɚ•											
ashes						æ					ɔᵛ					frost
bag						æ					---					log
married				ɛ>ɚ							ɔᵛo^<					dog
half						æ					ɔ					fog
glass						æ	ɑ									water
aunt						æ	ɑ>									daughter
father							ɑ>				ɔ					law
palm											ɑ ɑɚ					warm
barn											ɑɚ					
garden											ɑɚ ɑɚ					forty
crop							ɑ				ɑɚ					morning
on											ɔ<ɔ< ɚ^					corn
college							ɑ						ɚ^ɔ<			horse
borrow							ɑɚ									
five								a^ɪᵛ>		ɑo^						down
twice								ɑɪ^		ɑ<o^						out
wire								ɔɚ		ɑɚ						flower
joint									ɔ^ɪ^							joint
boil									oᵛɪə							boil
	i	ɪ	e	ɛ	ɜ	æ	ɑ	ai	ɔi	au	ɔ	ʌ	o	ʊ	u	

146

	i	ɪ	e	ɛ	ɜ	æ	ɑ	aɪ	ɔɪ	au	ɔ	ʌ	o	ʊ	u	
three	₊i														ᵾu	two
grease	₊i														ᵾu<	tooth
six		ɪ												---		wood
crib		ɪ												ʊ		pull
ear	ɪɚ			ɚ												yours
beard	iˇɚ												ou<ˇ			ago
eight			eɪ										ɤou<ˇ			coat
April			eɪ										ou<ˇ			road
ten				ɛ									ou<ˇ			home
egg				---									ou<ˇ			know
head				ɛ									oˇɚ			four
Mary			eˇəˆr										ɔˆɚ			door
chair			eˇɪɚ								ɔɚ					hoarse
care				ɛɜ							ɔɚ					mourning
merry				ɛɜ												
thirty					ɚ							ʌ				sun
sermon					ɚ									ʊ		brush
furrow					ɚ<											
ashes						æ					ɒ					frost
bag						æ					---					log
married				ɛɜ							---					dog
half						æ	ɒ									fog
glass						æ					ɒ					water
aunt						æ	ɒ									daughter
father							ɑ				---					law
palm							ɑ				ɔɚ					warm
barn							ɑɚ									
garden							ɑɚ				ɔˇɚ					forty
crop							ɑ				ɔɚ					morning
on											ɒɑ ɔɚ					corn
college							ɑ				ɔɚ					horse
borrow							ɑɚ									
five								ɑɪˆ		ɑu<ˇ						down
twice								eɪ		ɑuˇ<						out
wire								ɒˈɑ	ɚˈɚ	ɑɚ						flower
joint									ɔɪˆ							
boil									oˇˈɑˇ							boil

| | i | ɪ | e | ɛ | ɜ | æ | ɑ | aɪ | ɔɪ | au | ɔ | ʌ | o | ʊ | u | |

	i	ɪ	e	ɛ	ɜ	æ	ɑ		ai	ɔi	au		ɔ	ʌ	o	ʊ	u	
three	ɪⁱ																ʊᵘ	two
grease	₊ⁱ																u<ˇ:	tooth
six		ɪ														---		wood
crib		ɪ															ʊ	pull
ear		ɪɚ		ɚ														yours
beard	iˇɚ														ʌoˆ<			ago
eight			e+												ouˇ<			coat
April			eɪ												ou<ˇ			road
ten				ɛ											oˆ<			home
egg				ɛ											---			know
head				ɛ											ɔˆɚ			four
Mary			ɛˆɚ												---			door
chair			ɛɝ												ɔˆɚ			hoarse
care			ɛɚ									ɔɚ						mourning
merry			ɛɚ															
thirty					ɝ									ʌ				sun
sermon					ɝ									ʌ				brush
furrow					ɝ													
ashes						æ						ɔˆ						frost
bag						æ						ɔo						log
married			ɛɚ												ooˇ<			dog
half						æ						ɔˇ						fog
glass						æ	ɑ											water
aunt						æ<						ɒ						daughter
father							ɑ·					ɒˆ						law
palm							ɒɚ					ɒɚ						warm
barn							ɑɚ											
garden												ɒɚ ɑˆɚ						forty
crop							ɑ					ɔɚ						morning
on												ɒ<ɚ						corn
college							ɑ					ɔɚ						horse
borrow							ɑɚ											
five									ɑɪˆ		ɑoˆ<							down
twice									ɑɪ		aˇʊ							out
wire									ɔˇɚ		---							flower
joint										ɔɪ								joint
boil										əɪ								boil
	i	ɪ	e	ɛ	ɜ	æ	ɑ		ai	ɔi	au		ɔ	ʌ	o	ʊ	u	

	i	ɪ	e	ɛ	ɜ	æ	ɑ		ai	ɔi	au		ɔ	ʌ	o	ʊ	u	
three	i˅>i																ᵗu	two
grease	i																ᵊu	tooth
six		ɪ														ʊ		wood
crib		ɪᵗ˅														ʊ<		pull
ear	iɚ			ɚ														yours
beard	i˅ɚ														oʊ			ago
eight			eɪ												o<˅u			coat
April			eɪ												o<˅ o<^			road
ten				ɛ^											oʊ			home
egg				---											oʊ			know
head				ɛ											o•ᵊ			four
Mary				ɛr											---			door
chair				ɛɚ											o˅ɚ			hoarse
care				ɛɚ		ɑɚ												mourning
merry				ɛ>ɚ														
thirty					ɚ									ʌ				sun
sermon					ɚ											ʊ<		brush
furrow					ɚ													
ashes						æ							ɔ̲^					frost
bag						æ							---					log
married				ɛ>ɚ		æ							ɔ					dog
half						æ							ɔ					fog
glass						æ	ɑ											water
aunt						æ							ɒ					daughter
father							ɑ<						ɔ					law
palm													ɔ	ɔ^ɚ				warm
barn													ɔ<ɚ					
garden													ɔ̯ɚ ɔɚ					forty
crop							ɑ>						ɔ̯ɚ					morning
on													ɔ<ɔ˅ɚ					corn
college							ɑ								oᵁɚ			horse
borrow							ɑɚ											
five									ɑ<•ᵗ		ɑ<u							down
twice									ɑɪ		aɔ<^							out
wire									ɑᵗr		---							flower
										ɔ̰^ɪ								joint
										ɔɚ								boil
	i	ɪ	e	ɛ	ɜ	æ	ɑ		ai	ɔi	au		ɔ	ʌ	o	ʊ	u	

149

	i	ɪ	e	ɛ	ɜ	æ	ɑ	ai	ɔi	au	ɔ	ʌ	o	ʊ	u	
three	ɪ̵i															
														u		two
grease	i															
															uˇ	tooth
six		ɪ>														
														ʊ		wood
crib		ɪ														
														ʊ		pull
ear	iˇɚ															
											ɔɚ					yours
beard	iˇɚ															
													ou			ago
eight			eɪ													
													o<ʊ			coat
April			eɪ													
													ou			road
ten				ɛ^												
													o<ʊ			home
egg				---												
													ou			know
head				ɛ												
													oˇɚ			four
Mary				ɛ̇ə												
													---			door
chair				ɛɚ												
													oɚ			hoarse
care				ɛɚ								ɔˇɚ				
																mourning
merry				ɛɚ												
thirty					ɚ							ʌ				
																sun
sermon				ɚ								ʌ				
																brush
furrow				ɛɚ												
ashes						æ					ɔ					
																frost
bag						æ					---					
																log
married				ɛɚ			ɒ									
																dog
half						æ					ɒ					
																fog
glass						æ^ɪ	ɑ									
																water
aunt						æ					ɒ^					
																daughter
father							ɑ				ɒ<					
																law
palm							ɑ						ɔ^ɚ			
																warm
barn							ɑ>ɚ									
garden							ɑ>ɚ				ɔɚ					
																forty
crop							ɑ				ɔˇɚ					
																morning
on											ɔɒɚ					
											ɔɒɚ					corn
college							ɑ				ɔ					
																horse
borrow							ɑɚ									
five								əɪ		ɑʊ						
																down
twice								ɑɪ		ɑ<ʊ						
																out
wire								ɔɪɚ		ɑɚ						
																flower
									oˇɪ^							joint
									ɒɪ							boil

| | i | ɪ | e | ɛ | ɜ | æ | ɑ | ai | ɔi | au | ɔ | ʌ | o | ʊ | u | |

	i	ɪ	e	ɛ	ɜ	æ	ɑ	aɪ	ɔɪ	au	ɔ	ʌ	o	ʊ	u	
three	i														u	two
grease	i														u	tooth
six		ɪ^												---		wood
crib		ɪ												ʊ		pull
ear		ɪɚ									ɔɚ					yours
beard		ɪɚ											oᵁ			ago
eight			eᴵ										oᵁ			coat
April			e										o̱ᵁ			road
ten				ɛ^									oᵁ			home
egg				ɛ									oᵁ			know
head				ɛ									o̱ᵁɚ			four
Mary				ɛɜ									ɔ^ɚ			door
chair				ɛ^ɜ									ɔ^ɚ			hoarse
care				ɛɜ									oɚ			mourning
merry					ɚ											
thirty					ɚ							ʌ				sun
sermon					ɚ							ʌ				brush
furrow					ɚ											
ashes						æ					ɔ					frost
bag						æ					---					log
married				ɛˁɜ							ɔ					dog
half						æ					ɔˇ					fog
glass						æ	ɑ									water
aunt						æ					ɔ					daughter
father							ɑ^				ɔ					law
palm							ɒ				ʊɚ					warm
barn											ɔɚ					
garden							ɑɚ				ɔ̱ɚ					forty
crop							ɑ				ɔɚ					morning
on											ɔ̓ɔɚ					corn
college							ɑ				ɔ̱ɚ					horse
borrow							ɑ^ɚ									
five								ɑˀɪ		ɑˁʊ						down
twice								eɪ		ɑʊ						out
wire								ɔɚ		ɑᵂɚ						flower
joint									ɑˀiˇ							joint
boil									ɔ^ə							boil
	i	ɪ	e	ɛ	ɜ	æ	ɑ	aɪ	ɔɪ	au	ɔ	ʌ	o	ʊ	u	

word	i	ɪ	e	ɛ	ɜ	æ	ɑ	aɪ	ɔɪ	au	ɔ	ʌ	o	ʊ	u	word
three	i															
															u	two
grease	i														u	tooth
six		ɪ												ʊ		wood
crib		ɪ^												ʊ		pull
ear	iɚ			ɚ												yours
beard	ɪ^ɚ												oᵁ			ago
eight			eᴵ										o<			coat
April			eɪ										oᵁ			road
ten				ɛ									oᵁ			home
egg				ɛ^									oᵁ			know
head				ɛ^									o˅ɚ			four
Mary				ɛɜ									---			door
chair				ɛɜ									o˅ɚ			hoarse
care				ɛɜ									ɔ^ɚ			mourning
merry				ɛr												
thirty					ɚ							ʌ				sun
sermon					ɚ							ʌ˅>				brush
furrow					ɚ											
ashes						æ					ɔ<					frost
bag						æ					---					log
married				ɛ^>ɚ							ɔ					dog
half						æ					ɔ					fog
glass						æ	ɑ^									water
aunt						æ					ɒ					daughter
father							ɑ>				ɒ^ɑ / ɔ					law
palm							ɑ>				ɔɚ					warm
barn							ɒɚ									
garden							ɑɚ				ɔɚ					forty
crop							ɑ^						o<˅ɚ			morning
on											ɔɚ					corn
college							ɑ				ɔɚ					horse
borrow											ɑ>ɚ					
five								ɑ>ɪ		ɑᵁ						down
twice								ɑᴵ		ɑᵁ						out
wire								ɒɚ		ɑ^ɚ						flower
joint									o˅i˅							joint
boil									ɔᴵ							boil

| i | ɪ | e | ɛ | ɜ | æ | ɑ | aɪ | ɔɪ | au | ɔ | ʌ | o | ʊ | u |

	i	ɪ	e	ɛ	ɜ	æ	ɑ	ai	ɔi	au	ɔ	ʌ	o	ʊ	u	
three	ɪ‹ˆi															ʊ̯u	two
grease	ɪ‹ˆi														ʊ›ˆu	tooth
six		ɪ												ʊ̯		wood
crib		ɪ›·ɪˆ												ʊ		pull
ear	ɪˆə̣													ʊ·ɚ	yours
beard	ɪ‹ˆ·ə											o‹ᵛo		ago
eight			e›ᵛe‹ˆ										o·		coat
April			e›ᵛe										oo‹ˆ		road
ten				ɛ˘ɛ‹ˆ									o‹ᵛo‹ˆ		home
egg			e›ᵛ·eˆ										ʌˆ›o		know
head				ɛ									o·ɚ		four
Mary				ɛr									o·ᵛɚ		door
chair				ɛ·əɚ									ɔ‹ˆ·ɚ		hoarse
care				ɛɚ									o·ɚ		mourning
merry				ɛr											merry
thirty					ɜ̣·							ᵛʌ·			sun
sermon				ɚˆ								ɜ‹‹			brush
furrow				ɚ											furrow
ashes						æˆ					ɔ›·ᵛ˞				frost
bag						æɪ›					ɔ›·ᵛ				log
married						æ·r					ɔᵛ·				dog
half						æ̣					ɒ‹ˆ·				fog
glass						æᵋ					---				water
aunt						æ̃æ̃‹ˆ					ɒ·				daughter
father							ɑ‹·				ɒ‹ˆ				law
palm							ɑ·ẽˆ				---				warm
barn							ɑ›·ɚ̣								barn
garden											æ̣ɔ̸				forty
crop							ɑ‹				ɒɚ				morning
on											æ̸ɔ‹›ᵛ				corn
college							ɑ›				ɔ›ɚ				horse
borrow							ɑ‹r								borrow
five								a‹ˆɪˆ		æ›ᵛo‹ˆ					down
twice								a›ɪ‹ˆ		aoˆ					out
wire								a·ɨᵛ˞		ɑ‹ʊɚ					flower
									ɔɪ›						joint
									ɔɪ‹						boil
	i	ɪ	e	ɛ	ɜ	æ	ɑ	ai	ɔi	au	ɔ	ʌ	o	ʊ	u	

	i	ɪ	e	ɛ	ɜ	æ	ɑ		ai	ɔi	au		ɔ	ʌ	o	ʊ	u	
three	‒‒‒																ɵ ˅u˂	two
grease	ı·																‒‒‒	tooth
six		‒‒‒														ʊ˂		wood
crib		ı ə															‒‒‒	pull
ear		‒‒‒															‒‒‒	yours
beard		‒‒‒													‒‒‒			ago
eight			‒‒‒												o·			coat
April			‒‒‒												o·ᵁ			road
ten				‒‒‒											o·ṽ			home
egg				‒‒‒											oˆ·			know
head				‒‒‒											‒‒‒			four
Mary				‒‒‒											oˆ·ɚ			door
chair				ɛˆɚ											‒‒‒			hoarse
care				‒‒‒											‒‒‒			mourning
merry				‒‒‒														
thirty					‒‒‒									‒‒‒				sun
sermon					‒‒‒									ʌ·˂ˆəˆ˂				brush
furrow					‒‒‒													
ashes						æ							ɒˆ·ə					frost
bag						æ·ɛ							ɔː					log
married						‒‒‒							ɔ·ᴄ̃					dog
half						‒‒‒							‒‒‒					fog
glass						‒‒‒							‒‒‒					water
aunt						‒‒‒							‒‒‒					daughter
father							‒‒‒						‒‒‒					law
palm							‒‒‒						‒‒ᴷ					warm
barn							ɑ˂ɚ											
garden							‒‒‒						‒‒‒					forty
crop							‒‒‒						‒‒‒					morning
on							‒‒‒						ɔ˂ɚ					corn
college							‒‒‒						ɔ˂ɚ					horse
borrow							‒‒‒											
five									‒‒‒	aˆ·ṽ								down
twice									aɛˆ	a·ʊ˅								out
wire									a˃ɛˆɚ	‒‒‒								flower
joint										‒‒‒								
boil										‒‒‒								
	i	ɪ	e	ɛ	ɜ	æ	ɑ		ai	ɔi	au		ɔ	ʌ	o	ʊ	u	

154

	i	ɪ	e	ɛ	ɜ	æ	ɑ		aɪ	ɔɪ	au		ɔ	ʌ	o	ʊ	u	
three	i̯>i																ʉ̯>u	two
grease	i̯>i															ʉ>̂		tooth
six		ɪ														ʊ		wood
crib		ɪ														ʊ		pull
ear		ɪ>ɚ̂														ʊɚ		yours
beard		ɪ·ɪ̯̂ɚ													o			ago
eight			ɛ̯̂ê̯												o·			coat
April			e												o<			road
ten				ɛ											o< ŏ<			home
egg				ɛ̂·.										ʌ >ô<			know
head				ɛ ɛ̃<										o >̌·ɚ			four
Mary				ɛ >ɚ										---			door
chair				ɛ·ɚ										---			hoarse
care				ɛɚ										---			mourning
merry				---														
thirty					ɜ̯>ɚ̌									ʌ			sun
sermon				---									ʌ ʌ̂ ʌ̂				brush
furrow					ɚᴦ													
ashes						æ							ɒɑ ̌̌				frost
bag						æ							ɒɑ·ᵁ				log
married				---									ɒɑ·				dog
half						æ							ɒ				fog
glass				---									---				water
aunt						æ̃æ̃<·̂							ɒ<				daughter
father							ɑ<						---				law
palm							ɑ·̌<										warm
barn							ɑ<·ɚ										
garden							---						ɒ<̂ɚ				forty
crop							ɑ						---				morning
on							ɑ>ᵞ						ɒɑ				corn
college							---						ɔ̌<>ɚ				horse
borrow							---										
five									a>ɪ̂		a>ʊ>̌						down
twice									aɪ̂		a>o<̂						out
wire									a>̂·ɨɚ		ɑ<ʊ>̌ɚ						flower
										ɒ<̂ɪ>							joint
										ɒ<̂ɨ							boil
	i	ɪ	e	ɛ	ɜ	æ	ɑ		aɪ	ɔɪ	au		ɔ	ʌ	o	ʊ	u	

	i	ɪ	e	ɛ	ɜ	æ	ɑ	ai	ɔi	au	ɔ	ʌ	o	ʊ	u	
three	i ᵛ ⁱ														uˤ ᵘ	two
grease	i ᵛ ⁱ														uˤ ᵘ	tooth
six		ɪ													ʊ	wood
crib		---													ʊ	pull
ear		ɪ ᷉ ᵊ												ʊᵊ		yours
beard		ɪ ^ ᵊ											o o^			ago
eight			e e^										oˤ ŏˤ^			coat
April			e										o o^			road
ten				ɛ									o o^			home
egg				ɛ ɛ^									ʘ ǯʘ			know
head				ɛ									o ᵊ			four
Mary				ɛᵊ									o ᵛ ᵊ			door
chair				ɛ ᵊ							ɔ ᵛ ᵊ					hoarse
care				ɛᵊ							ɔˤ ᵛ ᵊ					mourning
merry				ɛᵊ												
thirty					ɜ							ʌ				sun
sermon					ᵊ							ʌˤ^				brush
furrow					ᵊ											
ashes						æ					ɔ ᵛ					frost
bag						æ æ^					---					log
married						æ r					ɔ ᵛ					dog
half						æ æ^					ɔ					fog
glass						a ᐟ					ɒ					water
aunt						æ æ̆^	ɑˤ									daughter
father							ɑ				ɔ ᵛ					law
palm							ɑ				ɔ ᵛ ᵊ					warm
barn							ɑˤ ᵊ									
garden							ɑᵊ				ɔ ᵛ ᵊ					forty
crop							ɑ				ɔ ᵛ ᵊ					morning
on											ɒ ɔc					corn
college											ɒˤ ɑ ᵊ^ᵊ					horse
borrow						ɑˤ r										
five								a^ɪ ᐟ		ɑˤ ʊ						down
twice								ɐˤ ᵛ ɪ ᐟ		ɜ ᵛ ʊ						out
wire								a ᐟ ɪᵊ		ɑʊᵊ ɪ						flower
joint									ɔ ᵛ ɪ ᐟ							joint
boil									ɔ ᵛ ɪ ᐟ							boil
	i	ɪ	e	ɛ	ɜ	æ	ɑ	ai	ɔi	au	ɔ	ʌ	o	ʊ	u	

	i	ɪ	e	ɛ	ɝ	æ	ɑ	aɪ	ɔɪ	au	ɔ	ʌ	o	ʊ	u	
three	i>ĭ															
															u<ŭ	two
grease	ɪ>̂i															
															u<ŭ	tooth
six		ɪ														
														ʊ		wood
crib		---														
														ʊ		pull
ear		ɪɚ														
														ʊ˅ɚ		yours
beard		ɪɚ														
													o<̂			ago
eight			e eᵉ^													
													o			coat
April			e													
													o<o			road
ten				ɛ												
													o<o			home
egg				ɛ^												
													o<o			know
head				ɛ												
											ɔ^ɚ					four
Mary				ɛ^ɚ									o˅ɚ			
																door
chair				ɛɚ							ɔ˅ɚ					
																hoarse
care				ɛɚ							ɔ<˅ɚ					
																mourning
merry				ɛr												
thirty					ɚ							ʌ				
																sun
sermon					ɚ 3											
																brush
furrow					ɚ											
ashes						æ					ɒ<̂					
																frost
bag						æ æ^>					ɒ^					
																log
married						æ<r					ɒ^					
																dog
half						æ·					ɒ·					
																fog
glass						æ					ɔ˅					
																water
aunt						æ·					ɒ					
																daughter
father							ɑ				ɒ^					
																law
palm						æ·					ɔ˅ɚ					
																warm
barn							ɑɚ									
garden							ɑɚ				ɔ˅ɚ					
																forty
crop							ɑ>				ɔ˅ɚ					
																morning
on							ɑ>ᵉ				ɔ˅ɚ					
																corn
college							ɑ				ɔ˅ɚ					
																horse
borrow							ɑɚ									
five								ɐ<̂ɪ		ɐ<u						
																down
twice								a>ɪ>̂		3<˅u						
																out
wire								a>̂ɪɚ		ɐɪ^						
											ɑ<̂ə>̂ɚ					flower
joint									ɒ>ɪ>							
boil									ɔ˅ɪ							

	i	ɪ	e	ɛ	ɝ	æ	ɑ	aɪ	ɔɪ	au	ɔ	ʌ	o	ʊ	u

	i	ɪ	e	ɛ	ɜ	æ	ɑ	aɪ	ɔɪ	au	ɔ	ʌ	o	ʊ	u	
three	i˅															
															ʉ˅u	two
grease	ɪ^i															
															u<˅u	tooth
six		ɪ														
														---		wood
crib		---														
														ʊ		pull
ear		ɪ^ɚ														
														ʊ		yours
beard		ɪ<ɚ											o			ago
eight			e e^										o·			coat
April			e										o<			road
ten				ɛ									o ŏ^			home
egg				ɛ^e˅ɜ									o< o^			know
head				ɛ									oɚ			four
Mary				ɛr									o˅ɚ			door
chair				ɛɚ							ɔɚ					hoarse
care				ɛɚ							ɔ·^ɚ					mourning
merry				ɛɚ												
thirty					ɚ							ʌ				sun
sermon					ɚ							ʌ				brush
furrow					ɚ											
ashes						æ					ɔ˅					frost
bag						æ æ^										log
married						æɚ					ɔ˅					dog
half						æ					ɒ^					fog
glass						æ					ɒ^					water
aunt						æ̃	ɒ									daughter
father							ɑ				---					law
palm							ɑ				ɔɚ					warm
barn							ɑɚ									
garden							ɑɚ				ɔɚ					forty
crop							ɑ				ɔ˅ɚ					morning
on							ɑ>ɒ				ɒ^ɑɚ					corn
college							ɑ				ɔ˅ɚ					horse
borrow							ɑɚ									
five								aɪ								
										ɑ<^ʊ<˅						down
twice								a^ɪ>								
										ɑ<ʊ						out
wire								e<ɪ>ɚ								
										ɑʊɚ						flower
									ɔ˅ɪ>							joint
									ɒ^ɫ							boil
	i	ɪ	e	ɛ	ɜ	æ	ɑ	aɪ	ɔɪ	au	ɔ	ʌ	o	ʊ	u	

word	i	ɪ	e	ɛ	ɜ	æ	ɑ	aɪ	ɔɪ	au	ɔ	ʌ	o	ʊ	u	word
three	ɪ^i															two · u<ᵛu
grease	ɪ>i															tooth · u<
six		ɪ												ʊ		wood
crib		ɪ												ʊ		pull
ear		ɪ^ɚ												ʊ<ᵛɚ		yours
beard		ɪ>ᵛɚ											o<ᵒ^			ago
eight			e e^										o<ᵛo^			coat
April			e										o<ᵛo			road
ten				ɛ									o<ᵒ			home
egg				ɛ^^e								ʌ>^o^				know
head				ɛ									o<ᵛɚ			four
Mary				ɛr									oᵛɚ			door
chair				ɛɚ							ɔɚ					hoarse
care				ɛɚ									o·ᵛɚ			mourning
merry				ɛr												
thirty					ɚ							ʌ				sun
sermon					ɚ							ʌ^				brush
furrow					ɚ											
ashes						æ					ɔᵛ					frost
bag						æᵛ>					ɒ^					log
married			ɛᵛr								ɒ^					dog
half						æᵛ^					ɒ^·					fog
glass						æ					ɒ					water
aunt						æᵛ^					ɒɑ^					daughter
father							ɑ				ɔᵛ					law
palm							ɑ				ɔᵛɚ					warm
barn							ɑ<ɚ									
garden							ɑɚ				ɔɚ					forty
crop							ɑ				ɔᵛɚ					morning
on							ɑ>				ɒ^					corn
college							ɑ				ɔᵛɚ					horse
borrow							ɑ>ɚ									
five								e<ɪ>^		ɑ<^ʊ<ᵛ						down
twice								a^ɪ		ɑ<^ʊ<						out
wire								e<ɾ<^ɚ		---						flower
joint									ɔᵛɾ<							
boil									ɔɾ<							
	i	ɪ	e	ɛ	ɜ	æ	ɑ	aɪ	ɔɪ	au	ɔ	ʌ	o	ʊ	u	

	i	ɪ	e	ɛ	ɜ	æ	ɑ		ai	ɔi	au		ɔ	ʌ	o	ʊ	u	
three	i ᵛ ⁱ																u< ᵛ u	two
grease	ι >̂ ⁱ																u·ᵛ	tooth
six		ι														ʊ		wood
crib		- - -														ʊ		pull
ear		ι >ɚ															ʊɚ	yours
beard		ι̣ɚ													o< o ^			ago
eight			e e ^												o< o			coat
April			e												o< o ^			road
ten				ɛ											o< o			home
egg				ɛ ^ e ᵛ											o o ^			know
head				ɛ											o·ɚ			four
Mary				ɛ ᵛ ɚ											o ᵛ ɚ			door
chair				ɛ·ɚ									ɔ ᵛ ɚ					hoarse
care				ɛɚ									ɔ< ·ɚ					mourning
merry				ɛɚ														
thirty					ɚ									ʌ				sun
sermon					ɚ									ʌ ^ ʌ< ^				brush
furrow					ɚ ᵛ													
ashes						æ	ɚ											frost
bag						æ ɛ >̂							- - -					log
married						æɚ							ɔ ᵛ					dog
half						æ							ɔ ᵛ ·					fog
glass						æ							ɔ ᵛ					water
aunt							ɑ·						ɒ·					daughter
father							ɑ						ɒ ^					law
palm							ɑ >·						ɔ ᵛ ɚ					warm
barn							ɑ ᵃ >̂ ɚ											
garden							ɑɚ						ɔɚ					forty
crop							ɑ						ɔ ᵛ ɚ					morning
on							ɑ >·						ɔɚ					corn
college							ɑ						ɔ ᵛ ·ɚ					horse
borrow													ɒ ^ ɚ					
five									ɑ<̂ ɪ<		ɑo<̂							down
twice									a >̂ ι >		ɑ<̂ ʊ<ᵛ							out
wire									a >̂ ɪɚ		ɑʊ<ᵛ ɚ							flower
joint										ɒ ^ ɪ<								joint
boil										ɔ ᵛ ι >								boil
	i	ι	e	ɛ	ɜ	æ	ɑ		ai	ɔi	au		ɔ	ʌ	o	ʊ	u	

	i	ɪ	e	ɛ	ɜ	æ	ɑ	ai	ɔi	au	ɔ	ʌ	o	ʊ	u	
three	- - -														- - -	two
grease	i ᵛ ⁱ														ʊ< uᵛ	tooth
six		ɪ												ʊ		wood
crib		ɪ ^ɚ												ʊ		pull
ear		ɪ ^ɚ											o<^ɚ			yours
beard		ɪ ^ɚ											o o^			ago
eight			e e^										o<			coat
April			e										o<			road
ten				ɛ									o< o			home
egg				ɛ ᵛ e ᵛ									o o^			know
head				ɛ									- - -			four
Mary				ɛɚ									o ᵛ ɚ			door
chair				ɛɚ							ɔ•ɚ					hoarse
care				ɛ ᵛ ɚ							ʊ<^ɚ					mourning
merry				ɛɚ												
thirty					ɚ							ʌ				sun
sermon					ɚ							ʌ ʌ ^				brush
furrow					ɚ											
ashes						- - -	ɑ >									frost
bag						æ ɛ ^					- - -					log
married						æ ^ ɚ					ʊ ^					dog
half						æ					ʊ					fog
glass						æ					ʊ<					water
aunt						æ	ɚ									daughter
father							ɑ				ʊ ^					law
palm							ɑ•				- - -					warm
barn							ɑɚ									
garden							ɑɚ				ɔɚ					forty
crop							ɑ >				ɔ ᵛ ɚ					morning
on							ɑ / ɑɚ									corn
college							ɑ >				ʊɚ					horse
borrow							ɑɚ									
five								- - -		a >ʊ< ᵛ						down
twice								- - -		ɑ< o<^						out
wire								a >ɪ >ɚ ^		ɑʊ< ᵛ ɚ						flower
joint									ʊ ^ ʈ< ɑ							
boil									ɔ ᵛ ɪ >							

| | i | ɪ | e | ɛ | ɜ | æ | ɑ | ai | ɔi | au | ɔ | ʌ | o | ʊ | u | |

	i	ɪ	e	ɛ	ɜ	æ	ɑ	aɪ	ɔɪ	au	ɔ	ʌ	o	ʊ	u	
three	i̯ᵛi														uᵛ	two
grease	i̯ᵛi														ʉ̯˒ᵛu	tooth
six		ɪ												ʊ		wood
crib		---												ʊ		pull
ear		ɪ˒ɚ												ʊᵛɚ		yours
beard		ɪˆɚ											o			ago
eight			ɛˆe										o˂ᵛo			coat
April			e										o˂			road
ten				ɛ									o˂ oˆ			home
egg			eᵛeˆ										o oˆ			know
head				ɛ									oᵛɚ			four
Mary				ɛˆɚ									oᵛɚ			door
chair				ɛɚ									o·ᵛɚ			hoarse
care				ɛˆɚ									o˂ˆɚ			mourning
merry				ɛɚ												
thirty					ɝ							ʌ				sun
sermon					ɝ							ʌ				brush
furrow					ɝ											
ashes						æ					ɒˆ					frost
bag						æ æ˒					---					log
married			ɛᵛɚ								ɔᵛ					dog
half						æ					ɒ					fog
glass						æ					ɔᵛ					water
aunt						æ					ɒ					daughter
father							ɑ				ɔᵛ					law
palm							ɑ·ʷ				ɔᵛɚ					warm
barn							ɑ̣ɚ									
garden							ɑɚ				ɔᵛɚ					forty
crop							ɑ ɒˆɚ									morning
on							ɒ˂				ɔᵛɚ					corn
college							ɑ				ɒɑˆɚ					horse
borrow							ɑ˒ɚ									
five								a˒ɪ˒		ɑˆuᵛ˂						down
twice								e˂ɪˆ˒		ɑ˂uᵛ˂						out
wire								ɑˆɪ˒ɚ		æuᵛ˂ɚ						flower
									ɑ˂ɪˆ˒							joint
									ɔɪ˒							boil

i	ɪ	e	ɛ	ɜ	æ	ɑ	aɪ	ɔɪ	au	ɔ	ʌ	o	ʊ	u

	i	ɪ	e	ɛ	ɜ	æ	ɑ	ai	ɔi	au	ɔ	ʌ	o	ʊ	u	
three	i˅														ʊ<˅u	two
grease	i˅i														ʊ<˅u	tooth
six		ɪ												---		wood
crib		ɪ												ʊ		pull
ear		ɪ^ɚ												ʊ<˅ɚ		yours
beard		ɪ·^ɚ											o			ago
eight			e e^										o<			coat
April			e										o< o^			road
ten				ɛ									o< o			home
egg				ɛ^									o<˅ o^			know
head				ɛ									o<˅ ɚ			four
Mary				ɛ˅ɚ									o˅ɚ			door
chair				ɛɚ									ɔ·^ɚ			hoarse
care				ɛɚ								ʌ>ɚ				mourning
merry				ɛr												
thirty					ɚ							ʌ				sun
sermon					ɚ							ʌ ʌ̃^				brush
furrow					ɚ											
ashes						æ	ɑ									frost
bag						æ										log
married						æ^ɚ					ɔ˅					dog
half						æ					ɒ					fog
glass						æ	ɑ<									water
aunt						æ̃	ɑ>									daughter
father							ɑ				ɔ^					law
palm							ɑ·				ɔ˅ɚ					warm
barn							ɑɚ									
garden							ɑɚ				ɔɚ					forty
crop							ɑ				ɔ<˅ɚ					morning
on							ɑ>e>				ɔ˅ɚ					corn
college							ɒ				ɔ˅ɚ					horse
borrow							ɑ>ɚ									
five								a>ɪ<		ɑ<ʊ<^						down
twice								e<ɪ<		ɑ^ʊ<˅						out
wire								ɑ<^ɪ˅ɚ		ɑʊɚ						flower
									ɒ>ɪ^							joint
									ɔ˅ɪ							boil
	i	ɪ	e	ɛ	ɜ	æ	ɑ	ai	ɔi	au	ɔ	ʌ	o	ʊ	u	

	i	ɪ	e	ɛ	ɜ	æ	ɑ		aɪ	ɔɪ	au		ɔ	ʌ	o	ʊ	u	
three	i˅˃																u�< ˅u	two
grease	i˅˃ⁱ																u< ᵘ	tooth
six		ɪ														ʊ		wood
crib		---														ʊ		pull
ear		ɪ ˃ɚ														ʊ ˅ɚ		yours
beard		ɪ·ɚ													o ᵒ˄			ago
eight			e ᵉ˄												o ᵒ˄			coat
April			e												o			road
ten				ɛ											o ᵒ˄			home
egg				ɛ ᵉ˄											o ᵘ<˅			know
head				ɛ											o ˅ɚ			four
Mary				ɛr											o·˅ɚ			door
chair				ɛɚ									ɔ·ᶜ					hoarse
care				ɛɚ									ɔ·ᵉɚ					mourning
merry				ɛr														
thirty					ɜ˅ɚ									ʌ				sun
sermon					ɚ									ʌ				brush
furrow					ɜ˅˃													
ashes						æ							ɔ˅					frost
bag						æ ᵉ˄							---					log
married						æ ˅ɚ							ɔᶜ					dog
half						æ							ɔ˅·					fog
glass						æ˅							ɔᶜ					water
aunt						æ̃							ɒ˄					daughter
father							ɑ						ɔᶜ					law
palm							ɑ						ɔ˅ɚ					warm
barn							ɑɚ											
garden							ɑɚ						ɔɚ					forty
crop							ɑ						ɒ<˄ɚ					morning
on							ɑ˃ᵉ˃						ɒ˄ɚ					corn
college							ɑ						ɒ˄ɚ					horse
borrow													ɒɚ					
five									e<ᵉ ɪ		ɑ˃u							down
twice									a<˄ ɪ˃		ɑu˅							out
wire									a˃ɪ˃ɚ		ɑu̯ɚ							flower
joint										ɔ˅ɪ˃								
boil										ɒ<˄ɪ˃								
	i	ɪ	e	ɛ	ɜ	æ	ɑ		aɪ	ɔɪ	au		ɔ	ʌ	o	ʊ	u	

	i	ɪ	e	ɛ	ɜ	æ	ɑ		aɪ	ɔɪ	au		ɔ	ʌ	o	ʊ	u	
three	i̯ᵛᵢ																u̯ᵛᵘ	two
grease	i̯ᵛᵢ																u̯ᵛᵘ	tooth
six		ɪ															ʊ̲	wood
crib		ɪˀ															ʊ	pull
ear		ɪˀɚ															ŭ̯ᵛɚ	yours
beard		ɪɚ													o ^			ago
eight			e ĕ̯^												o			coat
April			e												o			road
ten				ɛ·											o o ^			home
egg			e ᵛɪᵛ												o ʊ̯ᵛ			know
head				ɛ											ɔ ^ɚ			four
Mary				ɛɜ ɚ											o·ᵛ ə			door
chair				ɛ·ɚ									ɔɚ					hoarse
care				ɛ^ɚ		·							ɔɚ					mourning
merry				ɛɜ														
thirty					ɚ									ʌ				sun
sermon					ɚ									ʌ< ^				brush
furrow					ɚᵛ ʳ													
ashes						æ	ɚ											frost
bag						æ ɛ^							ˡ---					log
married						æɚ							ɔᵛ					dog
half						æ							ɒ^					fog
glass						æ	ɒ̲											water
aunt							aˀ						ɒ					daughter
father							ɑ						ɒ<^					law
palm							ɑ·						ɔᵛɚ					warm
barn							ɑɚ											
garden							ɑɚ						ɔɚ					forty
crop							ɑ						ɒ^ɚ					morning
on							ɑ						ɔᵛɚ					corn
college							ɑ				·		ɔᵛɚ					horse
borrow							ɑɚ											
five									aɪˀ		au							down
twice									aɪ		ɑ<ʊ							out
wire									aˀɪˀɚ		auɚ							flower
joint										ɒ^ɪɑˀ								
boil										ɔᵛɪ								

| | i | ɪ | e | ɛ | ɜ | æ | ɑ | | aɪ | ɔɪ | au | | ɔ | ʌ | o | ʊ | u | |

	i	ɪ	e	ɛ	ɜ	æ	ɑ	aɪ	ɔɪ	au	ɔ	ʌ	o	ʊ	u	
three	i̯>ˇi														u	two
grease	ɪ^i														u·	tooth
six		ɪ												ʊ		wood
crib		---												ʊ		pull
ear		ɪ^ɚ												ʊ<ˇɚ		yours
beard		ɪ^ɚ											o^			ago
eight			e e^										o·			coat
April			e										o<ˇo			road
ten				ɛ ɛ̆^									o< o			home
egg			e ˇe										o o^			know
head				ɛ									o ˇɚ			four
Mary				ɛɚ								ʌ >oɚ				door
chair				ɛ >ɚ									ɔ·ᶜɚ			hoarse
care				ɛɚ							ɔ·ɚ					mourning
merry				ɛɚ												
thirty					ɚ							ʌ				sun
sermon					ɚ							ʌ				brush
furrow					ɚ											
ashes						æ	ɐ									frost
bag						æ ɛ<ˇ					ʊ·					log
married						æ^ɚ					ɔ ˇ					dog
half						æ·					ʊ^					fog
glass						æ	ɐ									water
aunt						æ	ɐ									daughter
father							ɑ				ɔ ˇ					law
palm							ɑl				ɔ ˇɚ					warm
barn							ɑ·ɚ									
garden							ɑɚ				ɔ ˇɚ					forty
crop							ɑ				ɔ ˇɚ					morning
on							ɑ>·				ʊ^ɚ					corn
college							ɑ>				ʊ·ᶜɚ					horse
borrow							ɑ>r									
five								a<^ɪ		au						down
twice								a^ɪ		au						out
wire								ɑ<^ɪɚ		ɑuɚ						flower
									ɔˇᶜɪ							joint
									ɔɪ<^							boil
	i	ɪ	e	ɛ	ɜ	æ	ɑ	aɪ	ɔɪ	au	ɔ	ʌ	o	ʊ	u	

	i	ɩ	e	ɛ	ɜ	æ	ɑ		ai	ɔi	au		ɔ	ʌ	o	ʊ	u	
three	ɩ˃^i																u	two
grease	i̧ᵛi																u<ᵛu	tooth
six		ɩ														ʊ		wood
crib		ɩ														ʊ		pull
ear		ɩɚ														ʊ<ᵛɚ		yours
beard		ɩ̣ɚ													o			ago
eight			eɩ>												o<o			coat
April			e												o<ᵛo			road
ten				ɛ											o<o			home
egg			eᵛe^												oŏ^			know
head				ɛ											oᵛɚ			four
Mary				ɛr											oᵛɚ			door
chair				ɛɚ									ɔ·ɚ					hoarse
care				ɛɚ											oᵛɚ			mourning
merry				ɛr														
thirty					ɚ									ʌ				sun
sermon					ɚ									ʌ̮^				brush
furrow					ɚ< r													
ashes						æ							ɔᵛ					frost
bag						ææ^							---					log
married						æ^ɚ							ɒ^ɣ					dog
half						æ	ɑ>·											fog
glass						æ	ɑ˞											water
aunt						æᵛ>							ɒ^					daughter
father							ɑ						ɔ					law
palm							ɐᵛɣ̆						ɔᵛɚ					warm
barn							ɑ̣ɚ											
garden							ɑɚ						ɔᵛɚ					forty
crop							ɑ						ɔᵛɚ					morning
on							ɑɐ>						ɔᵛɚ					corn
college							ɑ						ɒ^ɚ					horse
borrow													ɒr					
five									ɐ<ɩ̂>		ɑ̂<ʊ<ᵛ							down
twice									ɐɩ>		ɑ<ʊ<ᵛ							out
wire									a>ɩ>ɚ		ɑʊ<ᵛɚ							flower
										ɔᵛɨ								joint
										ɒɩ>								boil
	i	ɩ	e	ɛ	ɜ	æ	ɑ		ai	ɔi	au		ɔ	ʌ	o	ʊ	u	

	i	ɪ	e	ɛ	ɜ	æ	ɑ		ai	ɔi	au		ɔ	ʌ	o	ʊ	u	
three	i˅																u˂˅u	two
grease	i˅i																u˂˅u	tooth
six		ɪ˃														ʊ		wood
crib		---														ʊ		pull
ear		ɪ˄ɚ														ʊ˄ɚ		yours
beard		ɪ̇ɚ												o˂o˄				ago
eight			ee˄											o˂˅o				coat
April			e											o˂˅				road
ten				ɛ											o			home
egg				ɛ˄e˅										oo˄				know
head				ɛ										o˅ɚ				four
Mary				ɛɚ										o˅ɚ				door
chair				ɛɚ									ɔ˄·ɚ					hoarse
care				ɛɚ									ɔ˄·ɚ					mourning
merry				ɛr														
thirty					ɚ									ʌ				sun
sermon					ɚ									ʌ				brush
furrow					ɚ													
ashes						æ˄ɛ							ɔ˅					frost
bag						æ˄							ɔ˅					log
married						æ˄ɚ							ɔ˅					dog
half						æɪ˅							ɔ˅					fog
glass						æ	ɑ											water
aunt							ɑ·ɚ											daughter
father							ɑ̆						ɒ˄					law
palm							ɑ̆̃						ɔɚ					warm
barn							ɑ˂ɚ											
garden							ɑɚ						ɔ˅ɚ					forty
crop							ɑɔ·ɚ											morning
on							---						ɒ˄					corn
college							ɑ						ɔ˅·ɚ					horse
borrow													ɔ˅ɚ					
five									e˂ɪ˃		ɑ˂˄u˅							down
twice									e˂ɪ˄˃		ɑ˂o˂˄							out
wire									e˂˅ɪ˂ɚ		---							flower
joint										ɔ˅ɪ˃								boil
boil										ɔ˅ɪ˃								

	i	ɪ	e	ɛ	ɜ	æ	ɑ	ai	ɔi	au	ɔ	ʌ	o	ʊ	u	
three	i˅˃															
															u	two
grease	i˅˃i														u˂u	tooth
six		ɪ												ʊ		wood
crib		ɪˆ												ʊ		pull
ear		ɪ˃ɚ												ʊɚ		yours
beard		ɪ̣ɚ											o			ago
eight			ɛˆeˆ										o˂oˆ			coat
April			e										o˂			road
ten				ɛ									oŏˆ			home
egg				ɛe˅									ooˆ			know
head				ɛ									o˅ɚ			four
Mary				ɛɜ									o˅ɚ			door
chair				ɛ˃ɚ									ɔˆ˙ɚ			hoarse
care				ɛɜ									o˙ɚ			mourning
merry				ɛɚ												
thirty					ɚ							ʌ				sun
sermon					ɚ						ɜ˃					brush
furrow					ɚ˃ʴ											
ashes						æ					ɔ˅					frost
bag						æɜ̆ˆ					ɔ˅					log
married						æ˃ˆɚ					ɔ˅˙					dog
half						ææˆ					ɔ˅					fog
glass						ææˆ					ɒ˂					water
aunt						æ					ɒˆ					daughter
father							ɑ ɒ˂									law
palm							ɑ˙				ɔ˅ɚ					warm
barn							ɑɚ									
garden							ɑɚ				ɔ˅ɚ					forty
crop							ɑ				ɒˆɚ					morning
on							ɑ˂e˃				ɔɚ					corn
college							ɑ				ɔ˅ɚ					horse
borrow							ɑɚ									
five								aˆɪ˃	ɑoˆ˂							down
twice								a˃ɪ˃	ɑ˂ʊ˂˅							out
wire								a˃ɪ˃ɚ	ɑʊ							flower
								ɒˆɪ˃ɑ								joint
								ɒ˂ɪˆ˙								boil
	i	ɪ	e	ɛ	ɜ	æ	ɑ	ai	ɔi	au	ɔ	ʌ	o	ʊ	u	

	i	ɪ	e	ɛ	ɜ	æ	ɑ	ai	ɔi	au	ɔ	ʌ	o	ʊ	u	
three	ɪˆ>i														u<ˇu	two
grease	ɪˆi														u<ˆu	tooth
six		ɪ												---		wood
crib		ɪ>												ʊ		pull
ear		ɪˆɚ												ʊɚ		yours
beard		ɪˆɚ											o oˆ			ago
eight			e										o·			coat
April			e										o oˆ			road
ten				ɛ ɛˆ	ɜ								o oˆ			home
egg			eˇeˆ										o oˆ			know
head				ɛ							ɔˆɚ					four
Mary			eˇr										oˇɚ			door
chair				ɛɚ							ɔ·ɚ					hoarse
care				ɛɚ							ɔ·ɚ					mourning
merry				ɛɚ												
thirty					ɚ							ʌ				sun
sermon					ɚ							ʌ				brush
furrow					ɚ											
ashes						æ	ɑˁ									frost
bag						æɛˆ					---					log
married						æˆɚ					ɔˇ					dog
half						æ					ɒ·ˀ					fog
glass						æ	ɐ									water
aunt						ææ̃ˆ					ɒ					daughter
father							ɑ				ɒ					law
palm							ɑ˞·				ɔɚ					warm
barn							ɑɚ									
garden							ɑɚ				ɔɚ					forty
crop							ɑ>				ɔˇɚ					morning
on							ɑ˞·				ɔˇɚ					corn
college							ɑ				ɔˇɚ					horse
borrow							ɑ>ɚ									
five								eˁɪ		ɑoˁ						down
twice								a>ɪ		ɑuˇ						out
wire								a>ɪ>ɚ		ɑuɚ						flower
joint									ɔˇɪ							joint
boil									ɔɪʲ							boil
	i	ɪ	e	ɛ	ɜ	æ	ɑ	ai	ɔi	au	ɔ	ʌ	o	ʊ	u	

	i	ɪ	e	ɛ	ɜ	æ	ɑ		ai	ɔi	au		ɔ	ʌ	o	ʊ	u	
three	ɪ˅ˎ																u˂ ˅u	two
grease	ɪ ˆˎi															ʊ ˄	u˂ ˅	tooth
six		ɪ														ʊ		wood
crib		ɪ														ʊ		pull
ear		ɪ ˎɚ														ʊ˂ ˅ɚ		yours
beard		ɪ ˎɚ													o ᵒ˄			ago
eight			e·e˄												o˂			coat
April			e												o˂ o˄			road
ten				ɛ											o˂ o			home
egg			e˅e˄											ʌˎ˂o˄			know
head				ɛ											o·˅ɚ			four
Mary				ɛɚ											o·˅ɚ			door
chair				ɛ˅ɚ										ɔ·˄ɚ				hoarse
care				ɛɚ										ɔ·˄ɚ				mourning
merry				ɛɚ														
thirty					ɚ˅									ʌ				sun
sermon					ɚ									ʌ				brush
furrow					ɚ													
ashes						æ							ɔ˅˓					frost
bag				æɛ˄									- - -					log
married				ɛ˅ɚ									ɒ˄					dog
half						æ							ɒ·					fog
glass							ɑˎ											water
aunt							ɑ·											daughter
father							ɑ						ɔ˅					law
palm							ɑl						ɔ˅ɚ					warm
barn							ɑɚ											
garden							ɑɚ						ɔ˅ɚ					forty
crop							ɑ						ɔˎɒ˄ɚ					morning
on													ɔ˅ᵘ ɔ˅ɚ					corn
college							ɑ						ɔ˅ɚ					horse
borrow													ɒ˄ɚ					
five									aɪˆˎ		ɑʊ˅˂							down
twice									aˎɪ		ɑɒˆ˂							out
wire									e˂ɪ˅ˎɚ		ɑʊɚ							flower
										ɔ˅ɪˎ								joint
										ɔ˅ɪ˂								boil

| | i | ɪ | e | ɛ | ɜ | æ | ɑ | | ai | ɔi | au | | ɔ | ʌ | o | ʊ | u | |

171

	i	ɪ	e	ɛ	ɜ	æ	ɑ	a i	ɔ i	a u	ɔ	ʌ	o	ʊ	u	
three	i˅i															two
															u˂˅u	
grease	i˅i															tooth
															u·	
six		ɪ												ʊ		wood
crib		ɪ												ʊ		pull
ear		ɪ˃ɚ												ʊ˅ɚ		yours
beard		ɪ˃ɚ											oᵒ^			ago
eight			e										o˂o^			coat
April			e										oᵒ^			road
ten				ɛ									oŏ^			home
egg				ɛɪ˅									oᵁ˅			know
head				ɛɛ^									o·ɚ			four
Mary				ɛɝ									o·ɚ			door
chair				ɛ̆ɝ							ɔ·ɚ					hoarse
care				ɛɝ							ɔ·ɚ					mourning
merry				ɛr												
thirty					ɝ							^				sun
sermon					ɝ							ʌ^ ^				brush
furrow					ɝ˂r											
ashes						æ					ɒ					frost
bag						æ					---					log
married						æ^r					ɔ˅					dog
half						æ·					ɒ					fog
glass						æ					ɔ˅					water
aunt						æ̃˅					ɒ^					daughter
father							ɑ				ɔ˅					law
palm							ɑ·				ɔ˅ɚ					warm
barn							ɑɚ									
garden							ɑɚ				ɔ˅ɚ					forty
crop							ɑ				ɔ˅ɚ					morning
on							ɑ˃				ɔ˅ɚ					corn
college							ɑ				ɔ·ɚ					horse
borrow											ɒ^ɚ					
five								a˃ɪ		ɑʊ˅<						down
twice								a˃ɪ˃		ɑʊ˅<						out
wire								a˃ɪ˃ɚ		ɑʊɚ						flower
joint									ɔ˅ɨ							
boil									ɔ˅ɪ˃							
	i	ɪ	e	ɛ	ɜ	æ	ɑ	a i	ɔ i	a u	ɔ	ʌ	o	ʊ	u	

	i	ɪ	e	ɛ	ɜ	æ	ɑ	ai	ɔi	au	ɔ	ʌ	o	ʊ	u	
three	ɪ̯ᵛ>ɪ															two
															u	
grease	i̯ᵛ>i															tooth
															u<ᵛu	
six		ɪ														wood
														ʊ		
crib		ɪ														pull
														ʊᵛ		
ear		ɪɚ														yours
														ʊ<ᵛɚ		
beard		ɪˆɚ											o			ago
													oᵒˆ			
eight			e													coat
													ŏ			
April			e													road
													oŭᵛ>			
ten				ɛ									o			home
egg				ɛᵋˆ									oᵒˆ			know
head				ɛ									o·ɚ			four
Mary				ɛr									oᵛɚ			door
chair				ɛ̆ɝ									o<ᵛɚ			hoarse
care				ɛɚ									ɔˆ·ɚ			mourning
merry				ɛr												
thirty					ɚ							ʌ				sun
sermon					ɚ							ʌ				brush
furrow					ɜr											
ashes						æ					ɔᵛ					frost
bag						æᵋ					ɔᵛˠ					log
married						æˆr					ɒˆ					dog
half						æ	ɑ									fog
glass						æ					ɔᵛ					water
aunt						ææˆ	ɒ									daughter
father							ɑ				ɔ<					law
palm							ɑ				ɔᵛɚ					warm
barn							ɑɚ									
garden							ɑɚ				ɔɚ					forty
crop							ɑ				ɒˆɚ					morning
on							ɑᵉ				ɒˆɚ					corn
college							ɑ				ɔᵛɚ					horse
borrow							ɑɚ									
five								eᵛ<ɪ		ɑʊ						down
twice								aˆ>ɪ		ɑʊ						out
wire								eᵛɪ>ɚ		ɑʊɚ						flower
joint									ɔ<ɪˆ>							joint
boil									ɒɪ>							boil
	i	ɪ	e	ɛ	ɜ	æ	ɑ	ai	ɔi	au	ɔ	ʌ	o	ʊ	u	

	i	ɪ	e	ɛ	ɜ	æ	ɑ	ai	ɔi	au	ɔ	ʌ	o	ʊ	u	
three	ɩ˄ɪ														u˂ᵘ	two
grease	ɩ˄ɪ														u·	tooth
six		ɩ												ʊ		wood
crib		ɩ												ʊ		pull
ear		ɩ˃ɚ												ʊ˂ɚ		yours
beard		ɩ˄·ɚ											o			ago
eight			e										o			coat
April			e										o			road
ten				ɛɛ˄									o			home
egg				ɛ˄eᵛ									o˂o˄			know
head				ɛ									o˂ɚ			four
Mary				ɛr									ɔ˄ɚ			door
chair				ɛ˃ɚ							ɛɔ					hoarse
care				ɛɚ							ɔ·ɚ					mourning
merry				ɛɚ												
thirty					ɚ							ʌ				sun
sermon					ɚ							ʌ				brush
furrow					ɜ˃r											
ashes						æ					ɒ					frost
bag						æ̃ɪ										log
married				ɛ˄ɚ							ɔᵛ					dog
half						æɛ˄					ɒ˄ʊ					fog
glass						æ					ɒ˄					water
aunt							ᵃɒ˄									daughter
father							ɑ				ɔᵛ					law
palm							ɑ·				ɔᵛɚ					warm
barn							ɑ˂ɚ									
garden							ɑɚ				ɔᵛɚ					forty
crop							ɑ				ɔᵛɚ					morning
on							ɒ				ɔᵛɚ					corn
college							ɑ				ɔ˄ɚ					horse
borrow											ɒ˂r					
five								aɪ˃		ɑʊ						down
twice								a˃ɪ˃		ɑʊ						out
wire								aɪ˃ɚ		ɑʊɚ						flower
									ɒɪ˃							joint
									ɒ˄ɪ˃ɑ							boil
	i	ɪ	e	ɛ	ɜ	æ	ɑ	ai	ɔi	au	ɔ	ʌ	o	ʊ	u	

174

	i	ɪ	e	ɛ	ɜ	æ	ɑ		ai	ɔi	au		ɔ	ʌ	o	ʊ	u	
three	i̯ˇ>ⁱ																ᵤˇu	two
grease	iˇⁱ																ʉ>ˇu	tooth
six		ɪ														ʊ		wood
crib		ɪ														ʊ		pull
ear		ɪɚ													oˆɚ			yours
beard		ɪɬɚ													oᵒˆ			ago
eight			eeˆ												ɵ>ᵒˆ			coat
April			e												oˁoˆ			road
ten				ɛ											oᵒˆ			home
egg				ɛˆe										ʌˆ>ᵒ				know
head				ɛ											oˁˇɚ			four
Mary				ɛɚ											oˁɚ			door
chair				ɛɚ											oˇ•ɚ			hoarse
care				ɛɚ											ɔˆ•ɚ			mourning
merry				ɛɚ														
thirty					ɚ									ʌ				sun
sermon					ɚ									ʌˆ				brush
furrow					ɚʳ													
ashes						æ	ɑˁ											frost
bag						æ	ɑˀ•											log
married						æˆɚ							ɒˀˆ					dog
half						æ							ɒ•					fog
glass						æ							ɔˇ					water
aunt						æ̃ɛ̃ˆ	ɑˁ											daughter
father							ɑ						ɔˇ					law
palm							ɑ•						ɔˇɚ					warm
barn							ɑɚ											
garden							ɑɚ•						ɔˇɚ					forty
crop							ɑ						ɔˁˇɚ					morning
on							ɑˀ						ɜɚ					corn
college							ɑˀ						ɔˇɚ					horse
borrow							ɑˀɚ											
five									aˀɪˀ		æˀʊˇ							down
twice									eˁɪˀˆ		ɑˁˆʊ							out
wire									aˀɪˆɚ		ɑˀɹʊˁɚ							flower
										ɒˆɪɑˀˆ								joint
										ɒˁˆɪˀɑ								boil
	i	ɪ	e	ɛ	ɜ	æ	ɑ		ai	ɔi	au		ɔ	ʌ	o	ʊ	u	

	i	ɪ	e	ɛ	ɜ	æ	ɑ	aɪ	ɔɪ	au	ɔ	ʌ	o	ʊ	u	
three	i˅>														ʉ˅u	two
grease	i˅i														u<u	tooth
six		ɪ												---		wood
crib		ɪ>												ʊ		pull
ear		ɪ>ɚ												ʊ˅ɚ		yours
beard		ɪ<ɚ											o o^			ago
eight			e										o<			coat
April			e										o˅o			road
ten				ɛ ɛ^									o o^			home
egg				ɛ^e>									o o^			know
head				ɛ									o< ɚ			four
Mary				ɛɚ									o˅ɚ			door
chair				ɛɚ							ɔɚ					hoarse
care				ɛɚ							ɔɚ					mourning
merry				ɛɚ												
thirty					ɚ>							ʌ				sun
sermon					ɚ							ʌ^				brush
furrow					ɜ˅ɚ											
ashes						æ					ɔ˅					frost
bag						æ ɛ^>					ɔ˅					log
married						æ^ɚ					ɒ^ɑ					dog
half						æ ɛ^					ɒʊ<					fog
glass						æ					ɔ<					water
aunt						æ·	ɒ									daughter
father							ɑ				ɔ˅					law
palm							ɑ·				ɒ^r					warm
barn							ɑɚ									
garden							ɑɚ				ɔɚ					forty
crop							ɑ				---					morning
on							ɑ>				ɔ˅ɚ					corn
college							ɑ				ɔɚ					horse
borrow											ɒ^r					
five								a>ɪ>		a>ʊ<						down
twice								aɪ^		a>o^						out
wire								a>ɪ>ɚ		æɚ>ɚ						flower
									ɒ^ɫ^ɑ							joint
									ɔɪ^							boil
	i	ɪ	e	ɛ	ɜ	æ	ɑ	aɪ	ɔɪ	au	ɔ	ʌ	o	ʊ	u	

176

	i	ɪ	e	ɛ	ɜ	æ	ɑ	ai ɔi au	ɔ	ʌ	o	ʊ	u	
three	iᵛi												uᵛ	two
grease	iᵛi												u<ᵛu	tooth
six		ɪ										ʊ		wood
crib		ɪ										ʊ		pull
ear		ɪɚ										ʊ<ᵛɚ		yours
beard		ɪɚ									oᴼ^			ago
eight			eᵉ^								o·			coat
April			e								oᵛᴼ			road
ten				ɛ							oᴼ^			home
egg				ɛ^eᵛ							oᴼ^			know
head				ɛ>							o·ɚ			four
Mary				ɛɝ							oᵛɚ			door
chair				ɛ·ɚ					ɔᶜ·ɚ					hoarse
care				ɛɝ					ɔᶜ·ɚ					mourning
merry				ɛɝ										
thirty					ɝ					ʌ				sun
sermon					ɝ					ʌᴧ^				brush
furrow					ɝ̮									
ashes						æ	ɑ̇							frost
bag						æᵃ>			ɒ					log
married				ɛᵛɝ					ɒ					dog
half						æ			ɒᶜ					fog
glass						æ			ɒ<ᶜ^					water
aunt					æ̃ɜ̃				ɒ					daughter
father							ɑ		ɔᶜᵛ					law
palm							ɑ·		ɔɚ					warm
barn							ɑɚ							
garden							ɑɚ		ɔɚ					forty
crop							ɑ		ɔᶜᵛɚ					morning
on							ɑ·		ɔᶜᵛɚ					corn
college							ɑ>		ɔɚ					horse
borrow									ɒɚ					
five								ɑ<^ɪ>^ ɑ<^o<^						down
twice								a>ɪ> ɑ<ᶜʊ<ᵛ						out
wire								a>ɬɚ ɑʊɚ						flower
joint								ɒ<^ɪ>						joint
boil								ɔᵛɪ>j						boil
	i	ɪ	e	ɛ	ɜ	æ	ɑ	ai ɔi au	ɔ	ʌ	o	ʊ	u	

	i	ɪ	e	ɛ	ɜ	æ	ɑ	ai	ɔi	au	ɔ	ʌ	o	ʊ	u	
three	ɪ⁾iᵛ															uᵛu	two
grease	ɪ˄i															uᵛu	tooth
six		ɪ													---		wood
crib		ɪ													ʊ		pull
ear	ɪ⁾ɚ													ʊᵛɚ		yours
beard	ɪ˄ɚ												oo˄			ago
eight			ee˄										oo˄			coat
April			eᵛ										oo˄			road
ten				ɛ									o			home
egg				ɛ˄eᵛ									oo˄			know
head				ɛ									o·ᵛɚ			four
Mary				ɛɜɚ									oᵛɚ			door
chair				ɛ˄ɚ							ɔ·ɚ					hoarse
care				ɛɜ							ɔ·ɚ					mourning
merry				ɛɜ												
thirty					ɚ							ʌ				sun
sermon					ɚ							ʌ				brush
furrow					ɚ											
ashes						æ					ɒ					frost
bag						æɛ˄					ɔᵛ					log
married				ɛɚ							ɒɑ˄					dog
half						æ					ɒ˄					fog
glass						æ					ɔᵛ					water
aunt						æ̃æ̃˄					ɒ˄					daughter
father							ɑ				ɔᵛ					law
palm							ɑ·				ɔᵛɚ					warm
barn							ɑɚ									
garden							ɑɚ				ɔᵛɚ					forty
crop							ɑ				ɔᵛɚ					morning
on											ɒᶜ ɔᵛɚ					corn
college							ɑ				ɔᵛɚ					horse
borrow											ɔᵛɚ					
five								eᶜɪ⁾ ɑoᶜ˄								down
twice								a⁾ɪ˄⁾ ɑoᶜ˄								out
wire								eᶜ⁾ɪɚ ɑɤɚ								flower
joint								ɔᵛɪ⁾								joint
boil								ɒ˄ɪ⁾								boil
	i	ɪ	e	ɛ	ɜ	æ	ɑ	ai	ɔi	au	ɔ	ʌ	o	ʊ	u	

word	i	ɪ	e	ɛ	ɜ	æ	ɑ	aɪ	ɔi	au	ɔ	ʌ	o	ʊ	u	word
three	ɪ^i															two (u)
grease	ɪ^i														u<˅u	tooth
six		ɪ												---		wood
crib		ɪ												u		pull
ear	ɪ^>ɚ													u<˅ɚ		yours
beard	ɪ^>ɚ												oO^			ago
eight			eɪ										oO^			coat
April			e										oO^			road
ten				ɛ									oO^			home
egg				ɛ^e									oO^			know
head				ɛ									o•ɚ			four
Mary				ɛr									o•ɚ			door
chair				ɛɚ							ɔ•ɚ					hoarse
care				ɛɚ									ɔ^•ɚ			mourning
merry				ɛɚ												
thirty					ɚ							ʌ				sun
sermon					ɚ							ʌ^				brush
furrow					ɚ^r											
ashes						æ					ɔ˅					frost
bag						æ					---					log
married						æ^ɚ					ɔ˅					dog
half						æ					ɔ˅					fog
glass						æ					ɒ<^					water
aunt						æ					ɔ˅					daughter
father							ɑ				ɔ•					law
palm							ɑ•ᵚ				ɔ˅ɚ					warm
barn							ɑɚ									
garden							ɑɚ				ɔɚ					forty
crop							ɑ^>				ɔ˅ɚ					morning
on							ɑ^e				ɔ˅ɚ					corn
college							ɑ				ɔɚ					horse
borrow							ɑɚ									
five								aɪ>		ɑo<^						down
twice								a>ɪ•		ɑo<^						out
wire								aɪ>ɚ		---						flower
									ɔɪ							joint
									ɔɪ^							boil

i ɪ e ɛ ɜ æ ɑ aɪ ɔi au ɔ ʌ o ʊ u

	i	ɪ	e	ɛ	ɜ	æ	ɑ		ai	ɔi	au		ɔ	ʌ	o	ʊ	u	
three	ɪˇiˊ																u̯ˇu	two
grease	ɪˆi																u̯ˇŭ	tooth
six		ɪ															---	wood
crib		ɪ														ʊ		pull
ear		ɪˊɚ														u̯ˇɚ		yours
beard		ɪˆ·ɚ													oˊo			ago
eight			eeˆ												oˇˊo			coat
April			e												oˇˊo			road
ten				ɛ											ooˆ			home
egg			eeˆ												oˊoˆ			know
head				ɛ											oˇɚ			four
Mary				ɛr											oˇɚ			door
chair				ɛ·ɚ											ɔˆ·ɚ			hoarse
care				ɛɚ											o·ɚ			mourning
merry				ɛr														
thirty					ɚ									ʌ				sun
sermon					ɚ									ʌ				brush
furrow					ɚˇˊ													
ashes						æ							ɒˆ					frost
bag						æɛˇ̆ˇ							ɔˇ·u̯ˇ					log
married						æ							ɒˆ					dog
half						æɛˆˇ							ɒˆ					fog
glass						æ							ɒˆˇ					water
aunt							ɑˊ						ɒ					daughter
father							ɑ						ɔ					law
palm							ɑ·						ɔˇɚ					warm
barn							ɑˊ·ɚ											
garden							ɑɚ						ɔɚ					forty
crop							ɑ						ɔˇɚ					morning
on							---						ɔˇɚ					corn
college							ɑ						ɔˇɚ					horse
borrow							ɑr											
five									ɐˇˊɪˆ		ɑˆu̲							down
twice									aˆˊɪˆ		aˊu							out
wire									aˆˊɪˊɚ		ɑˊu̲ˇɚ							flower
joint										ʌˊɪˆ								
boil										ɔˇɪˆˇ								
	i	ɪ	e	ɛ	ɜ	æ	ɑ		ai	ɔi	au		ɔ	ʌ	o	ʊ	u	

180

	i	ɪ	e	ɛ	ɜ	æ	ɑ		ai	ɔi	au		ɔ	ʌ	o	ʊ	u	
three	i ˅> i																	two	u< ˅
grease	i ˅> i																u< u	tooth
six		ɪ														ʊ		wood
crib		ɪ >														ʊ ^		pull
ear		ɪ >ɚ														ʊ< ɚ		yours
beard		ɪ ^>ɚ													o o^			ago
eight			e e^												o ŏ^			coat
April			e												o< o^			road
ten				ɛ											o o^			home
egg				ɛ^ e˅											o ʸ			know
head				ɛ											o·ɚ			four
Mary				ɛr											o ˅ɚ			door
chair				ɛɚ									ɔ·c					hoarse
care				ɛɚ											ɔ^·ɚ			mourning
merry				ɛr														
thirty					ɜ									ʌ				sun
sermon					ɜ									ʌ				brush
furrow					ɜ													
ashes						æ							ɔ·					frost
bag						æ ɛ^							ɔ˅					log
married						æ^r							ɔ˅					dog
half						æ							ɒ·					fog
glass						æ							ɔ˅					water
aunt						æ							ɒ^					daughter
father							ɑ						ɔ					law
palm							ɑ·						ɔɚ					warm
barn							ɑɚ											
garden							ɑɚ						ɔɚ					forty
crop							ɑ						ɔɚ					morning
on							ɑ e						ɔɚ					corn
college							ɑ						ɒ^ɚ					horse
borrow							ɑr											
five									ai >		ɑu							down
twice									a>ɪ^		ɑ<ʊ							out
wire									a>ɪ^ɚ		ɑ^ʊɚ							flower
joint										ɔ˅t<								
boil										ɔ<˅t<								

| | i | ɪ | e | ɛ | ɜ | æ | ɑ | | ai | ɔi | au | | ɔ | ʌ | o | ʊ | u | |

181

	i	ɪ	e	ɛ	ɜ	æ	ɑ		ai	ɔi	au		ɔ	ʌ	o	ʊ	u	
three	ɪiˇ																u<ᵁ	two
grease	iˇɪ																u<ˇ	tooth
six		ɪ														- - -		wood
crib		ɪ>														ʊ		pull
ear		ɪ>ɚ														ʊɚ		yours
beard		ɪ<ɚ											oŏ<					ago
eight			e>e										o<o<					coat
April			e										o<					road
ten				ɛ										o				home
egg				ɛ									o<					know
head				ɛ									oɚ					four
Mary				ɛɚ									ɔ^ɚ					door
chair				ɛ·ɚ									ɔɚ					hoarse
care				ɛɚ									ɔ·ɚ					mourning
merry				ɛɚ														
thirty					ɚ									ʌ				sun
sermon					ɚ									ʌ				brush
furrow					ɚ													
ashes						æ·							ɒ^					frost
bag						æ							- - -					log
married						æɚ							ɒ^					dog
half						æ							ɒ					fog
glass						æ							ɒ					water
aunt						æ							ɔˇ					daughter
father							ɑ						ɔˇ					law
palm							ɑ·						ɔˇɚ					warm
barn							ɑ<ɚ											
garden							ɑɚ						ɔɚ					forty
crop							ɑ>						ɔ<^ɚ					morning
on							ɑ>						ɔˇɚ					corn
college							ɑ						ɔˇɚ					horse
borrow							ɑ>r											
five									a>ɪ^		ɑʊ<							down
twice									ɐ<ˇɪ^		a<ô<							out
wire									a>ɪ^>ɚ		ɑʊ<ɚ̂							flower
joint										ɔˇɪ>								joint
boil										ɔɪ>								boil
	i	ɪ	e	ɛ	ɜ	æ	ɑ		ai	ɔi	au		ɔ	ʌ	o	ʊ	u	

	i	ɪ	e	ɛ	ɜ	æ	ɑ	ai ɔi au	ɔ	ʌ	o	ʊ	u	
three	i ᵛ>i													two (uᵛ<)
grease	ɪ ^>i													tooth (u<)
six		ɪ										ʊ		wood
crib		ɪ>										ʊ		pull
ear		ɪ>ɚ										u<ᵛɚ		yours
beard		ɪ>ɚ									o			ago
eight			e eᵉ<^								o			coat
April			e								o			road
ten				ɛ							o			home
egg				ɛ^e>							o			know
head				ɛ							o<o^			four
Mary				ɛr							oᵛɚ			door
chair				ɛɚ					ɔ^·ɚ					hoarse
care				ɛɚ					ɔ^·ɚ					mourning
merry				ɛɚ										
thirty					ɚᵛ					ʌ				sun
sermon					ɚ					ʌ				brush
furrow					ɚ									
ashes						æ			ɔᵛ					frost
bag						æ æ^			---					log
married				ɛᵛɚ					ɔᵛ					dog
half						æ			ɔᵛ					fog
glass						æ			ɒ^					water
aunt						æ̃			ɔᵛ					daughter
father							ɑ		ɔᵛ					law
palm							ɑ·		ɔɚ					warm
barn							ɑɚ							
garden							ɑɚ		ɔ·ɚ					forty
crop							ɑ		ɔᵛɚ					morning
on							ɒ<		ɔᵛɚ					corn
college							ɑ		ɔᵛɚ					horse
borrow									ʊ<r					
five								a>ɪ^> ɑ^o<^						down
twice								ɐ<ɪ<^ ɑ<o<^						out
wire								ɐ<ɪ>ə ɑṵ<ɚ						flower
joint								ɔᵛ†<						
boil								ɔɪ>						

| i | ɪ | e | ɛ | ɜ | æ | ɑ | ai ɔi au | ɔ | ʌ | o | ʊ | u |

	i	ɪ	e	ɛ	ɜ	æ	ɑ	ai	ɔi	au	ɔ	ʌ	o	ʊ	u	
three	i˅ˈi														ʉ˅ˈu	two
grease	ɪˍˆi														u·	tooth
six		ɪ														wood
crib		ɪˎ												ʊ̠		pull
ear		ɪˎɚ												ʊɚ		yours
beard		ɪˎɚ									oˍ					ago
eight			eᵉ̆ˆ								o					coat
April			e								oˍ o					road
ten				ɛ̃							o					home
egg			e˅								oˍ oˆ					know
head				ɛ							o˅ɚ					four
Mary				ɛr							o˅ɚ					door
chair				ɛɚ							ɔ·ɚ					hoarse
care				ɛɚ							ɔɚ					mourning
merry				ɛɚ												
thirty					ɚˎ˅							ʌ				sun
sermon					ɚ							---				brush
furrow					ɚ											
ashes						æ					ɒˆ					frost
bag						æɛ˅										log
married						æˆr					ɔ˅					dog
half						æˆɛˆ					ɒ·					fog
glass						æ					ɔ˅					water
aunt						æ̃	ɒ									daughter
father							ɑ				ɔ˅					law
palm											ɒˍ˅ɒ˅ɚ					warm
barn							ɑɚ									
garden							ɑɚ				ɔɚ					forty
crop							ɑ				ɔ˅ɚ					morning
on											ɒɔɚ					corn
college							ɑˎ				ɔ˅ɚ					horse
borrow							ɑˎr									
five								aˎɪ		aˆoˆ						down
twice								eˍɪˆə		ɑˍoˆ						out
wire								ɑˆɪˎɚ		ɑˍoˆɚ						flower
									ɒˆɪˎɑ							joint
									ɔ˅ɪˎ							boil
	i	ɪ	e	ɛ	ɜ	æ	ɑ	ai	ɔi	au	ɔ	ʌ	o	ʊ	u	

	i	ɪ	e	ɛ	ɜ	æ	ɑ		ai	ɔi	au		ɔ	ʌ	o	ʊ	u	
three	i̯>ǐ																u	two
grease	i̯>ǐ																u·	tooth
six		ɪ														ʊ		wood
crib		ɪ>														ʊ		pull
ear		ɪ>ɚ														ʊ<ɚ		yours
beard		ɪɚ													o			ago
eight			e˅e<^												o			coat
April			e												o			road
ten				ɛ·											o			home
egg				ɛ											o			know
head				ɛ											o·ɚ			four
Mary				ɛr											oɚ			door
chair				ɛɚ									ɔ·^ɚ					hoarse
care				ɛɚ									ɔ·ɚ					mourning
merry				ɛr														
thirty					ɚ									ʌ				sun
sermon					ɚ									ʌ				brush
furrow					ɚ													
ashes						æ							ɒ^					frost
bag						æɛ^							ɔ˅					log
married						æ^r							ɒ^ɤ					dog
half						ææ^							ɔ˅					fog
glass						æ							ɔ˅					water
aunt						æ							ɒ^					daughter
father							ɑ						ɔ˅					law
palm							ɑ·						ɔɚ					warm
barn							ɑɚ											
garden							ɑɚ						ɔɚ					forty
crop							ɑ						ɔ˅ɚ					morning
on							ɑ(e)						ɔɚ					corn
college							ɑ						ɔɚ					horse
borrow													ɒ<r					
five									a^>ɪ		ɑo^							down
twice									aɪ>		ɑo^							out
wire									e<ɪ>ɚ		ɑʊɚ							flower
joint										ɔ˅ɪ>								joint
boil										ɔɪ>								boil
	i	ɪ	e	ɛ	ɜ	æ	ɑ		ai	ɔi	au		ɔ	ʌ	o	ʊ	u	

	i	ɪ	e	ɛ	ɜ	æ	ɑ	ai	ɔi	au	ɔ	ʌ	o	ʊ	u	
three	ɪ^ⁱ														u<˅ᵁ	two
grease	i														u	tooth
six		ɪ												ʊ		wood
crib		ɪ												ʊ<		pull
ear		ɪr												ʊɚ		yours
beard		ɪɚ											o			ago
eight			ɛ<^ e^										oᵁ			coat
April			eⁱ										oᵁ			road
ten				ɛ									oᵁ			home
egg			eⁱ										oᵁ			know
head				ɛ							ɔ^ɚ					four
Mary				ɛr							ɔɚ					door
chair				ɛɚ							ɔɚ					hoarse
care				ɛr							ɔᵉr					mourning
merry				ɛr												
thirty					ɚ							ʌ				sun
sermon					ɚ											brush
furrow					ʌr											
ashes						æ	a>									frost
bag						æ					ɔᵉ					log
married						ær					ɑᵉ					dog
half						æ					ɔᵉ					fog
glass						æ					ɑᵉ					water
aunt						æ	ɒ									daughter
father							ɑ				ɔᵉ					law
palm							ɑ				ɔ˙					warm
barn							ɑ<ɚ									
garden							ɑr				ɔr					forty
crop							ɒ<				ɔr					morning
on							ɑ>				ɔr					corn
college							ɑr				ɔr					horse
borrow											ɔr					
five								aɪ		aᵁ						down
twice								aɪ		aᵁ						out
wire								aɪr		aᵁr						flower
joint									oɪ							
boil									ɔɪ							
	i	ɪ	e	ɛ	ɜ	æ	ɑ	ai	ɔi	au	ɔ	ʌ	o	ʊ	u	

	i	ι	e	ε	ɜ	æ	ɑ	ai	ɔi	au	ɔ	ʌ	o	ʊ	u	
three	i·															two
															u·	
grease	i															tooth
															u·	
six		ι												ʊ		wood
crib		ι												ʊ<		pull
ear		ιɚ												ʊɚ		yours
beard		ιr											o			ago
eight			eⁱ										o			coat
April			eⁱ										oᵁ			road
ten				ε									oᵁ			home
egg			eⁱ										oᵁ			know
head				ε							ɔɚ					four
Mary				εr							ɔɚ					door
chair				εɚ							ɔᵊr					hoarse
care				εɚ							ɔᵊr					mourning
merry				εr												
thirty					ɚ							ʌ				sun
sermon					ɚ							ʌ				brush
furrow														ʊ<r		
ashes						æ					ɔ					frost
bag						æ					ɔᵁ					log
married						ær					ɒᵊ					dog
half						æ					ɔˀ					fog
glass						æ					ɔ					water
aunt						æ					ɔ					daughter
father							ɑ				ɔᵊ					law
palm							ɑ				ɔr					warm
barn							ɑˀr									
garden							ɑr				ɔr					forty
crop							ɑ				ɔr					morning
on											ᵓɔr					corn
college							ɑ				ɔr					horse
borrow											ɔr					
five								ɑι		ɑʊ						down
twice								ɑι		ɑʊ						out
wire								ɑιr		ɑʊɚ						flower
									ɔι							joint
									ɔι							boil
	i	ι	e	ε	ɜ	æ	ɑ	ai	ɔi	au	ɔ	ʌ	o	ʊ	u	

word	i	ɪ	e	ɛ	ɜ	æ	ɑ	ai	ɔi	au	ɔ	ʌ	o	ʊ	u	word
three	i·														u·	two
grease	i·														u·	tooth
six		ɪ												ʊ		wood
crib		ɪ												ʊˇ<		pull
ear		ɪɚ												ʊɚ		yours
beard		ɪᵊr											---			ago
eight			eⁱ										oᵁ			coat
April			eᶥ										oʊ			road
ten				ɛ									oᵁ			home
egg			eⁱ										oᵁ			know
head				ɛ							ɔᵊr					four
Mary			ɛr								ɔᵊr					door
chair			ɛᵊr								ɔɚ					hoarse
care			ɛᶥr								ɔr					mourning
merry			---													
thirty					ɚ							ʌ				sun
sermon					ɚ							ʌ				brush
furrow					ɚ											
ashes						æ					ɔᶠ					frost
bag						æ					---					log
married						ær					ɔᵉ					dog
half						æ·					ɔˠ					fog
glass						æ					ɔ					water
aunt						æ					ɔ					daughter
father							ɑ				ɔᵉ					law
palm							ɑ·				ɔr					warm
barn											ɒr					
garden							ɑᵊr				ɔr					forty
crop											ɔᵉc ɔr					morning
on											ɔ ɔr					corn
college							ɑ				ɔᵊr					horse
borrow											ɔr					
five								ɑɪ·		ɑu						down
twice								ʌvⁱ		ɑu						out
wire								ɑɪr		ɑɚ						flower
joint									ɔi							
boil									ɔᶥ							

| i | ɪ | e | ɛ | ɜ | æ | ɑ | ai | ɔi | au | ɔ | ʌ | o | ʊ | u |

	i	ɪ	e	ɛ	ɜ	æ	ɑ	ai	ɔi	au	ɔ	ʌ	o	ʊ	u	
three	i̯>i̯															two (u̯<ᵁ)
grease	i														u	tooth
six		ɪ												ʊ		wood
crib		---												ʊ		pull
ear	iɪr												ʊɚ			yours
beard		ɪr											oo^			ago
eight			ɛ‹e^										oᵁ			coat
April			eⁱ										o‹o^			road
ten				ɛ·									oᵁ			home
egg			eᶫ										oᵁ			know
head				ɛ							ɔᵊrᶜ					four
Mary				ɛr							ɔᵊrᶜ					door
chair				ɛr							ɔɚ					hoarse
care				---							ɔᵊr					mourning
merry				ɛr												
thirty					ɝ							ʌ				sun
sermon					ɝ											brush
furrow					ʌ‹r											
ashes						æ					ɔ					frost
bag						æᶫ					---					log
married				ɛᵛr									oᵁ			dog
half						æ					ɔˠ					fog
glass						æ					ɔ					water
aunt						æ					ɔ					daughter
father							ɑ̈				---					law
palm							ɑ·				ɔ					warm
barn							ɑr				ɔr					
garden							ɑr				ɔr					forty
crop											ɔrᶜ / ɔr					morning
on											ɔ̃^ᶜ / ɔᵊr					corn
college											ɔ‹ᶜ / ɔᵊrⱶ					horse
borrow											ɔr					
five								aɪⁱ		ɑu						down
twice								aɪ		ãuᵛ						out
wire								aɪr		ɑu						flower
joint									ɔɪ							
boil									ɔɪ							
	i	ɪ	e	ɛ	ɜ	æ	ɑ	ai	ɔi	au	ɔ	ʌ	o	ʊ	u	

189

	i	ɪ	e	ɛ	ɜ	æ	ɑ		ai	ɔi	au		ɔ	ʌ	o	ʊ	u	
three	i˅ˎ																u˅ˏ	two
grease	i˅i																u·	tooth
six		ɪ														ʊ		wood
crib		ɪ														ʊ		pull
ear		ɪˏɚ													oˆˏɚ			yours
beard		ɪˏɚ													o oˏ			ago
eight			eˏˏeˆˏ												oˏ oˆ			coat
April			eˏˏ												o oˏ			road
ten				ɛ											o·			home
egg				ɛ											o õˏ			know
head				ɛ											o˅ˏɚ			four
Mary				ɛɹ											o˅ˏɚ			door
chair				ɛˏˏ·ɚ									ɔ·ɚ					hoarse
care				ɛɚ									ɔˆ·ɚ					mourning
merry				ɛɹ														
thirty					ɚ									ʌ				sun
sermon					ɚ									ʌˏ				brush
furrow					ɚ													
ashes						æ							ɔ˅ˏ					frost
bag						æ æˆ							ɔ˅ˏ					log
married						æˆr							ɔˏ					dog
half						æ							ɒ·					fog
glass						æ ɚ												water
aunt						æ̃ æˆ							ɒˏ					daughter
father							ɑ						ɔ·					law
palm							ɑ·						ɔɚ					warm
barn							ɑɚ											
garden							ɑɚ						ɔɚ					forty
crop							ɑˏ						ɔˏˏɚ					morning
on							ɒˏ ə						ɔˏˏɚ					corn
college							ɑˏ						ɔ·ɚ					horse
borrow							ɑr											
five									aˏˆɪˏ		ɑˏʊˏ							down
twice									eˏɪˆ		aoˏ							out
wire									eˏɪˏɚ		---							flower
										ɔˏɪ								joint
										ɔˏɪˏ								boil
	i	ɪ	e	ɛ	ɜ	æ	ɑ		ai	ɔi	au		ɔ	ʌ	o	ʊ	u	

	i	ɪ	e	ɛ	ɜ	æ	ɑ		aɪ	ɔɪ	au		ɔ	ʌ	o	ʊ	u	
three	i˅>																u<˅u	two
grease	ɪ<ˆi																u	tooth
six		ɪ														---		wood
crib		ɪ														ʊ		pull
ear		ɪ>ɚ														u>ɚ		yours
beard		ɪ>ɚ													o			ago
eight			e·eˆ												o<˅o			coat
April			e												o<˅o			road
ten				ɛ											o			home
egg				ɛ<ˆe											o·oˆ			know
head				ɛ											o·ɚ			four
Mary				ɛɾ											ɔ<ˆɚ			door
chair				ɛɚ								ɔ·ɚ						hoarse
care				ɛɚ								ɔ<ˆ·ɚ						mourning
merry				ɛɾ														
thirty					ɚ									ʌ				sun
sermon					ɚ									ʌ				brush
furrow					ɝ˞													
ashes						æ						ɒ<ˆ						frost
bag						æ æˆ>	ɑ<											log
married						æ<ˆɾ						ɒ<ˆ						dog
half						æ						ɒ						fog
glass						æ						ɔ>˅						water
aunt						æ̃æˆ						ɒ<ˆ						daughter
father							ɑ					ɔ<>˅ˆ						law
palm												ɒ<·>˅ ɚ<ˆ						warm
barn							ɑɚ											
garden							ɑɚ					ɔ>˅ɚ						forty
crop							ɑ					ɔ<ˆɚ						morning
on						ɒ<						ɒ<ˆ ɚ						corn
college							ɑ					ɔ>˅ɚ						horse
borrow							ɑɾ											
five									aˆ>ɪ<ˆ		ɑ<oˆ<							down
twice									ɐ<ɪˆ		ɑ<ʊ>							out
wire									a>ɪ<ˆ ɚ<ˆ		---							flower
										ɒ<ˆɪˆ								joint
										ɔɪ<								boil
	i	ɪ	e	ɛ	ɜ	æ	ɑ		aɪ	ɔɪ	au		ɔ	ʌ	o	ʊ	u	

191

	i	ɪ	e	ɛ	ɜ	æ	ɑ		aɪ	ɔɪ	au		ɔ	ʌ	o	ʊ	u	
three	i̯ᵛi																u	two
grease	i̯ᵛi																u·	tooth
six		ɪ															---	wood
crib		ɪ															ʊ	pull
ear		ɪ>ɚ															ʊɚ	yours
beard		ɪ·ɚ													o°^			ago
eight			eᵗ<												o<			coat
April			e												o<ᵛo			road
ten				ɛ											o			home
egg				ɛ<^											o			know
head				ɛ											oᵛ>ɚ			four
Mary				ɛr											oᵛ>·ɚ			door
chair				ɛɚ											ɔ·<^ɚ			hoarse
care				ɛɚ									ɔ·ɚ					mourning
merry				ɛr														
thirty					ɝ									ʌ				sun
sermon					ɝ								ʌ^					brush
furrow					ɝ>ᵛ													
ashes						æ							ɔ					frost
bag						æ æ<^							ɔ					log
married						æ<^r							ɔᵛ<					dog
half						æ							ɔ·					fog
glass						æ							ɔ><					water
aunt						æ æ^							ɔᵛ>					daughter
father							ɑ						ɔ					law
palm							ɑ·ᵛ						ɔɚ					warm
barn							ɑɚ											
garden							ɑɚ						ɔɚ					forty
crop							ɑ<						ɔ>ᵛ<ɚ					morning
on							ɑ·ɑ^						ɔɚ					corn
college							ɑ						ɔɚ					horse
borrow							ɑr											
five									aᵛ<ɪ^		ɑ<u							down
twice									aᵛ<ɪ		a·o<^							out
wire									a^>ɪ>ɚ		ɑuɚ							flower
										ɔᵗ<								joint
										ɔᵗ								boil
	i	ɪ	e	ɛ	ɜ	æ	ɑ		aɪ	ɔɪ	au		ɔ	ʌ	o	ʊ	u	

	i	ɪ	e	ɛ	ɜ	æ	ɑ	ai	ɔi	au	ɔ	ʌ	o	ʊ	u	
three	ɪ˅˃i															
															u	two
grease	ɪ˅˃i															
															u	tooth
six		ɪ													ʊ̆	
																wood
crib		ɪ												ʊ̆		
																pull
ear		ɪ˃ɚ												ʊ̆˃ɚ		
																yours
beard		ɪ˂̂ɚ											o˂o			
																ago
eight			e˅˃e˂̂										o˂			
																coat
April			e										o˂			
																road
ten				ɛ									o			
																home
egg			e˅˃e˂̂										o˂o			
																know
head				ɛ									o˅˃ɚ			
																four
Mary				ɛ˂̂r									o˅˃ɚ			
																door
chair				ɛ˅˃ɚ							ɔ·ɚ					
																hoarse
care				ɛɜ							ɔ˂̂·ɚ					
																mourning
merry				ɛɹr												
thirty					ɚ							ʌ				
																sun
sermon					ɚ							ʌ				
																brush
furrow					ɚ											
ashes						æ					ɔ˅˂					
																frost
bag						æɛ˂̂					ɒ˂					
																log
married						æ˂̂r					ɔ˅˃					
																dog
half						æ					ɒ·					
																fog
glass						æ					ɒ					
																water
aunt						æ					ɒ˂̂					
																daughter
father							ɑ				ɔ					
																law
palm							ɑ·				ɔɚ					
																warm
barn							ɑ˂·ɚ									
garden							ɑɚ				ɔ˅˃ɚ					
																forty
crop							ɑ				---					
																morning
on							ɑᵊ				ɔɚ					
																corn
college							ɑ				ɔ˅˃ɚ					
																horse
borrow							ɑr									
five								e˂̂˅ɪ˂̂		a˃o˂̂						
																down
twice								aɪ˃		a˃o˂̂						
																out
wire								a˃ɪ˃ɚ		ɑ˂ʊ˂̂ɚ						
																flower
									ɔɪ˂̂							joint
									ɔ˃ᵼ							boil
	i	ɪ	e	ɛ	ɜ	æ	ɑ	ai	ɔi	au	ɔ	ʌ	o	ʊ	u	

	i	ɪ	e	ɛ	ɜ	æ	ɑ	aɪ	ɔɪ	au	ɔ	ʌ	o	ʊ	u	
three	i>ᵛi														u<	two
grease	i>ᵛi														u·	tooth
six		ɪ												ʊ		wood
crib		ɪ												ʊ		pull
ear		ɪ<ˆɚ												ʊ<ᵛɚ		yours
beard	i>ᵛɚ												o<o			ago
eight			e										o			coat
April			e										o			road
ten				ɛ									o			home
egg				ɛ·									o<ŏ			know
head				ɛ									o>ᵛɚ			four
Mary				ɛɚ									---			door
chair				ɛɚ							ɔ<ˆ·ɚ					hoarse
care				ɛɚ							ɔ<ˆ·ɚ					mourning
merry				ɛɚ												
thirty					ɚ							ʌ				sun
sermon					ɚ							ʌ				brush
furrow					ɚ											
ashes						æ					ɔᵛ					frost
bag						æ					ɔᵛ					log
married						æ<ˆɚ					ɒ<ˆ					dog
half						æ					ɔ<ᵛ>					fog
glass						æ·					ɔᵛ					water
aunt						æ					ɔ>ᵛ					daughter
father							ɑ				ɔ					law
palm							ɑɯ				ɔ<ᵛɚ					warm
barn							ɑɚ									
garden							ɑɚ				ɔɚ					forty
crop							ɑ				ɔᵛɚ / ɒ<ˆ					morning
on											ɒ< ɔɚ					corn
college							ɑ				ɔᵛɚ					horse
borrow							ɑɚ									
five								aɪ<ˆ		a>ʊ<						down
twice								aˆɪ<		ɑu<						out
wire								a>ˆɪ>ɚ		ɑ<uɚ						flower
joint									ɔɪ<ˆ							joint
boil									ɔɪ							boil
	i	ɪ	e	ɛ	ɜ	æ	ɑ	aɪ	ɔɪ	au	ɔ	ʌ	o	ʊ	u	

	i	ɪ	e	ɛ	ɜ	æ	ɑ	aɪ	ɔɪ	au	ɔ	ʌ	o	ʊ	u	
three	i̯ˇ>i															two
grease	ɪ<̂i															tooth
six		ɪ												ʊ		wood
crib		ɪ												ʊ		pull
ear		ɪ>ɚ												u̲ˇɚ		yours
beard		ɪ>ɚ											oo^			ago
eight			eɪ>ˇ										oo^			coat
April			e										o			road
ten				ɛ									oo^			home
egg			eˇe										oʊˇ			know
head				ɛ̆									oɚ			four
Mary				ɛ^r									oˇ·ɚ			door
chair				ɛ·ɚ									oˇ·ɚ			hoarse
care				ɛɚ									oˇ·ɚ			mourning
merry				ɛr												
thirty					ɚ							ʌ				sun
sermon					ɝ							ʌ̆				brush
furrow					ɚ>ˇ											
ashes						æ					ɔ·					frost
bag						æ					ɔˇ					log
married						æ^r					ɔˇ					dog
half						æ					ɔ>ˇ					fog
glass						æ					ɒ					water
aunt						ææ^>					ɔ>ˇ					daughter
father							ɑ				ɔˇ					law
palm							ɑˇ				ɔˇɚ					warm
barn							ɑ·ɚ									
garden							ɑɚ				ɔ>ˇɚ					forty
crop							ɑ				ɔˇɚ					morning
on							ɑ>				oɚ					corn
college							ɑ				ɔˇɚ					horse
borrow							ɑr									
five								a>̂ɪ^		a·o<̂^						down
twice								aɪ^		a<̂·o<̂						out
wire								aɪ^ɚ		ɑuˇɚ						flower
joint									ɔ<ɪ>^							
boil									ɔˇɫ							
	i	ɪ	e	ɛ	ɜ	æ	ɑ	aɪ	ɔɪ	au	ɔ	ʌ	o	ʊ	u	

	i	ɪ	e	ɛ	ɜ	æ	ɑ	ai	ɔi	au		ɔ	ʌ	o	ʊ	u	
three	i̯ˇ>i															uˇ<	two
grease	i̯ˇi															ṳˇ>u	tooth
six		ɪ													ʊ		wood
crib		ɪ>													ʊ̲		pull
ear		ɪ>ɚ												o<ˆɚ			yours
beard		ɪ>ˆɚ												o<ˆ			ago
eight			eeˆ											o<oˆ			coat
April			e											o<oˆ			road
ten				ɛɛ̆ˆ										oʊ			home
egg			eˇeˆ											ooˆ			know
head				ɛˆ										o<ɚ			four
Mary				ɛɹ										oˇ·ɚ			door
chair				ɛˇɚ								ɔ·ɚ					hoarse
care				ɛɚ								ɔ̂·ɚ					mourning
merry				ɛɹ													
thirty					ɚ								ʌ				sun
sermon					ɚ								ʌ				brush
furrow					ɚʳ												
ashes						æ						ɒˆ					frost
bag						æ						ɔˇ					log
married						æˆɹ						ɒ<ˆ					dog
half						æ						ɔˇ·					fog
glass						æ						ɔˇ					water
aunt						æ̃	ɑ>										daughter
father							ɑ					ɔ					law
palm							ɑ					ɔɚ·					warm
barn							ɑ̆<ˆɚ										
garden							ɑɚ					ɔɚ					forty
crop							ɑ					ɒˆɑ					morning
on												ɑ<ˆ ɔɚ					corn
college							ɑ					ɔˇɚ					horse
borrow							ɑɹ										
five								eˇ<ɪˆ		ɑoˆ<							down
twice								a̮>ɪ<ˆ		a>ʊˇ							out
wire								eˇ<ɪ>ɚ									flower
joint									ʌ>ɪˆ								
boil									ɔˇɬ<								

	i	ɪ	e	ɛ	ɜ	æ	ɑ	ai	ɔi	au		ɔ	ʌ	o	ʊ	u	

left	i	ɪ	e	ɛ	ɜ	æ	ɑ	aɪ	ɔɪ	au	ɔ	ʌ	o	ʊ	u	right
three	i·															two (u·)
grease	i															tooth (u·)
six		ɪ˅ˏ												ʊ		wood
crib		ɪ												ʊ		pull
ear		ɪr														yours (ʊɚ)
beard		ɪᵊ											o			ago
eight			eⁱ										oᵊ			coat
April			eⁱ										oᵁ			road
ten				ɛ									oᵁ			home
egg			eⁱ										oᵁ			know
head				ɛ							ɔɚ					four
Mary				ɛr							ɔᵊr					door
chair				ɛɚ							ɔɚ					hoarse
care				ɛr							ɔr					mourning
merry				ɛr												
thirty					ɚ							ʌ				sun
sermon					ɚ							ʌ				brush
furrow					ʌ˂r											
ashes						æ					ɔ					frost
bag						æ					---					log
married						æ					ɒᵊ					dog
half						æ	ɑᵊ									fog
glass						æ					ɔ					water
aunt						æ					ɔᵊ					daughter
father							ɑ				ɔᵊ					law
palm							ɑˀl				ɔr					warm
barn											ɒr					
garden							ɑr				ɔr					forty
crop							ɑ˂				ɔr					morning
on											ɒ˅ɔr					corn
college							ɑ˂				ɔr					horse
borrow											ɔr					
five								aɪ		au						down
twice								aɪ		au						out
wire								aɪr		---						flower
									ɔi							joint
									ɔɪ							boil

| | i | ɪ | e | ɛ | ɜ | æ | ɑ | aɪ | ɔɪ | au | ɔ | ʌ | o | ʊ | u | |

197

	i	ɪ	e	ɛ	ɜ	æ	ɑ		ai	ɔi	au		ɔ	ʌ	o	ʊ	u	
three	i ̌ᵢ̌																ʉ ˃ᵘ	two
grease	i																u	tooth
six		ɪ														ʊ		wood
crib		ɪ														ʊ		pull
ear		ɪr														ʊɚ		yours
beard		---													o ᵒ^			ago
eight			eᵛ ɪᵛ												o ᵊ			coat
April			eɪ												o<ᵛ ᵒ^			road
ten				ɛ											o ᵒ^			home
egg			eɪ												o ᵁ			know
head				ɛ											o ᵛɚ			four
Mary			ɛɹ												o ᵛɚ			door
chair			ɛɹ											ɔ^r				hoarse
care						æ ˄>ɚ								ɔ^r				mourning
merry			ɛɹ															
thirty					ɚ									ʌ				sun
sermon					ɚ									ʌ				brush
furrow					ɚ													
ashes						æ							ɔˋ					frost
bag						æ							ɔ ᵊ̱ᶜ˄					log
married						æ							ɔ ᵊ					dog
half						æ·							ɔˋ					fog
glass						æ ᵊ							ᵊ̱ᶜ					water
aunt						æ							ɔ ᵊ					daughter
father							ɑ^						ɔ					law
palm							ɑ·						ɔˋ·r					warm
barn							ɑˋ r											
garden							ɑr								o ᵛr			forty
crop													ɔ ᵊᶜ ɔɚ					morning
on							ɑ˃·.						ᵊ̱ᶜɚ					corn
college													ᶜɔ ɔr					horse
borrow													ᵊᶜɚ					
five									ɑɪ		ɑʊ							down
twice									ɑ^ɪ		a˃ɑ̓							out
wire									ɑɪr		--- .							flower
									ɔ^ɪᶜ									joint
									ᶜɔ^ɪ									boil
	i	ɪ	e	ɛ	ɜ	æ	ɑ		ai	ɔi	au		ɔ	ʌ	o	ʊ	u	

	i	ɪ	e	ɛ	ɜ	æ	ɑ	aɪ	ɔɪ	aʊ	ɔ	ʌ	o	ʊ	u	
three	i·															two (u·)
grease	i															tooth (u)
six		ɪ												ʊ		wood
crib		ɪ												ʊ		pull
ear		ɪr												ʊɚ		yours
beard		ɪr											o			ago
eight			eɪ										o			coat
April			eɪ										oʊ			road
ten				ɛ									oʊ			home
egg			eɪ										oʊ			know
head				ɛ							ɔr					four
Mary				ɛr							ɔɚ					door
chair				ɛr							ɔr					hoarse
care				ɛr							ɔr					mourning
merry				ɛr												
thirty					ɝ							ʌ				sun
sermon					ɝ							ʌ				brush
furrow					ɝ											
ashes						æ^ɛ	ɑ									frost
bag						æ										log
married						ær	ɑ									dog
half						æ					ɔˇ					fog
glass						æ					ɔˇ					water
aunt						æ					ɒ					daughter
father							ɑ				ɒ·					law
palm							ɑ				ɒɚ					warm
barn							ɑr									
garden							ɑr				ɔr					forty
crop							ɑ				ɔ^r					morning
on							ɑ				ɔ^r					corn
college							ɑ				ɔ^r					horse
borrow							ɑr									
five								aɪ		aʊ						down
twice								aɪ		aʊ						out
wire								aɪr		---						flower
joint									ɔ^ɪ							joint
boil									ɔɪ							boil

| | i | ɪ | e | ɛ | ɜ | æ | ɑ | aɪ | ɔɪ | aʊ | ɔ | ʌ | o | ʊ | u | |

	i	ɪ	e	ɛ	ɜ	æ	ɑ	ai	ɔi	au	ɔ	ʌ	o	ʊ	u	
three	i ˅ʲ >														ʉ uᶜ	two
grease	i														u	tooth
six		ɪ												ʊ		wood
crib		ɪ												ʊˆ		pull
ear		ɪr												ʊɚ		yours
beard		ɪr											oᵁ			ago
eight			e eˆ<										oᵁ			coat
April			e ʲ										ooˆ			road
ten				ɛ									ooˆ			home
egg				ɛ									oᵁ			know
head				ɛ							ɔɚ					four
Mary				ɛr							ɔɚ					door
chair				ɛr									o˅r			hoarse
care				ɛr							ɔɚ					mourning
merry				ɛr												
thirty					ɝ							ʌ				sun
sermon					ɝ							ʌ				brush
furrow					ɝ											
ashes						æ					ɔᵉ					frost
bag						æ					--- `					log
married						ær					ɔᶜ					dog
half						æ					ɔ					fog
glass						æ >					ɔ					water
aunt						æ					ɔ					daughter
father							ɑ				ɔ					law
palm							ɑ·				ɔr					warm
barn							ɑ< r									
garden							ɑr				ɔɚ					forty
crop							ɑ				ɔɚ					morning
on							ɑ				ɔr					corn
college							ɑ<				ɔr					horse
borrow											ɒr					
five								ɑɪ		ɑu						down
twice								ʌɪ		a>oˆ						out
wire								ɑɪr		---						flower
									ɔˆɪ							joint
									ɔɪ							boil
	i	ɪ	e	ɛ	ɜ	æ	ɑ	ai	ɔi	au	ɔ	ʌ	o	ʊ	u	

	i	ι	e	ɛ	ɜ	æ	ɑ	ai	ɔi	au	ɔ	ʌ	o	ʊ	u	
three	ι<ˆi															
															u<ˇu	two
grease	i>ˇi															
															ʉ>ˇu	tooth
six		ι												ʊ		wood
crib		- - -												ʊ		pull
ear	ι>˞												o<ˆ˞			yours
beard	ι>˞												o			ago
eight			e>ˇe										o<			coat
April			e										o			road
ten				ɛ									o oˆ<			home
egg				ɛ									o<ˇ oˆ			know
head				ɛ>									o>ˇ˞			four
Mary				ɛ<ˆr									o>ˇ·˞			door
chair				ɛ˞							ɔ·˞					hoarse
care				ɛ˞							˞·ɔ					mourning
merry				ɛr												
thirty					˞							ʌ				sun
sermon					˞							ʌ<ˆʌ				brush
furrow					˞											
ashes						æ					ɔ					frost
bag						æ ɛ>					ɒ					log
married						æ<ˆr					ɔ>ˇ					dog
half						æ>ˇ					ɒ<ˆ					fog
glass						æ					ɒ<ˆ					water
aunt						æ·˜					ɔ					daughter
father							ɑ				ɔ>ˇ					law
palm							ɑ				ɔ˞>ˇ					warm
barn							ɑ·>˞									
garden							ɑ˞				ɔ˞					forty
crop							ɑ>ɤ				ɔ˞>ˇ					morning
on											ɒ< ɔ>					corn
college							ɑ				ɔ˞>ˇ					horse
borrow							ɑr									
five								ɑ<ˆι>		ɑ<ʊ>ˇ						down
twice								a>ˆι		a>ɔ<ˆ						out
wire								e<ɪ<˞>		ɑu						flower
joint									ɔι<ˆ							
boil									ɔɪ							
	i	ι	e	ɛ	ɜ	æ	ɑ	ai	ɔi	au	ɔ	ʌ	o	ʊ	u	

201

	i	ɪ	e	ɛ	ɜ	æ	ɑ		ai	ɔi	au		ɔ	ʌ	o	ʊ	u	
three	i̯ᵛi																u	two
grease	ɪ<ˆi																u·	tooth
six		ɪ														ʊ		wood
crib		ɪ														ʊ		pull
ear	ɪ>ɚ														o̞ˆɚ			yours
beard	ɪᵛɚ														o			ago
eight			eᵛeˆ												o			coat
April			e												oo̞ˆ			road
ten				ɛ											oˈoˆ			home
egg			eᵛe												oˈoˆ<			know
head				ɛ											oᵛ·ɚ			four
Mary				ɛr											oᵛ·ɚ			door
chair				ɛɚ									ɔ·ɚ					hoarse
care				ɛɚ									ɔᵛ·ɚ					mourning
merry				ɛr														
thirty					ɚ									ʌ				sun
sermon					ˈɚ									ʌ				brush
furrow					ɚ													
ashes						æ							ɒ<ˆ					frost
bag						æˆ												log
married			ɛᵛr										ɔᵛ					dog
half						æ							ɔ<					fog
glass						æ							ɒˆ					water
aunt						æˆ							ɔᵛ					daughter
father							ɑ						ɔ					law
palm							ɑ						ɔᵛɚ					warm
barn							ɑ<ɚ											
garden							ɑɚ						ɔɚ					forty
crop							ɑ						ɒˆɑˆɚ					morning
on													ɒ<ɔɚ					corn
college							ɑ						ɒˆɚ					horse
borrow							ɑr											
five									a>ɪˆ	ɑoˆ<								down
twice									a>ɪˆ>	ɑ<ʊᵛ<								out
wire									a>ɪ>ɚ									flower
										ɒ<ɪ								joint
										ɔᵛɪ								boil
	i	ɪ	e	ɛ	ɜ	æ	ɑ		ai	ɔi	au		ɔ	ʌ	o	ʊ	u	

word	i	ɪ	e	ɛ	ɜ	æ	ɑ	ɒ	ai	ɔi	au	ɔ	ʌ	o	ʊ	u	word
three	i˅i															ʉ˃u	two
grease	ɪ<ᶺi															u	tooth
six		ɪ													ʊ		wood
crib		ɪ													ʊ		pull
ear		ɪ˃ɚ													ʊ<˅ɚ		yours
beard		ɪ˃ɚ												o			ago
eight			eeᶺ											o<˅o			coat
April			e											o<oᶺ			road
ten			ɛ											o<			home
egg				ɛᶺ										o<			know
head				ɛ										o˅ɚ			four
Mary				ɛr										o˅ɚ			door
chair				ɛɚ								ɔ·ɚ					hoarse
care				ɛɚ								ɔ·ɚ					mourning
merry				ɛr													
thirty					ɚ								ʌ				sun
sermon					‑‑‑								‑‑‑				brush
furrow					ɚ												
ashes						æ						ɔ˅					frost
bag						ææᶺ						‑‑‑					log
married						æᶺɚ						ɔ˅					dog
half						æ						ɔ˅					fog
glass						æ						ɔ					water
aunt						ææ̃						ɒ					daughter
father							ɑ					ɔ					law
palm							ɑɯ<˅					ɔ˅ɚ					warm
barn							ɑɚ										
garden							ɑɚ					ɔɚ					forty
crop							ɑ					ɔ˅ɚ					morning
on								ɒ				ɔɚ					corn
college							ɑ					ɔɚ					horse
borrow												ʊɑr					
five									aᶺ˃ɪ˃		ɑoᶺ						down
twice									a˃ɪᶺ		ɑ<oᶺ						out
wire									ɑ<ᶺɪ˃ɚ		‑‑‑						flower
joint										ɔ˅ɫ<							
boil										ɒ<ᶺɫ˃<							
	i	ɪ	e	ɛ	ɜ	æ	ɑ		ai	ɔi	au	ɔ	ʌ	o	ʊ	u	

	i	ɩ	e	ɛ	ɜ	æ	ɑ		ai	ɔi	au		ɔ	ʌ	o	ʊ	u	
three	i˅˃ĭ																u	two
grease	ɩ˄i																ʉ˂˅u	tooth
six		ɩ														ʊ		wood
crib		ɩ														ʊ		pull
ear		ɩ˃ɚ														ʊ˂˅ɚ		yours
beard		ɩɚ													oᵒ˄			ago
eight			e												o			coat
April			e												o			road
ten				ɛ											o·			home
egg				ɛ											o˅ᵒ			know
head				ɛ											oɚ			four
Mary				ɛr											o˅ɚ			door
chair				ɛr											ɔ˂˄·ɚ			hoarse
care				ɛɚ											ɔ̂·ɚ			mourning
merry				ɛr														
thirty					ɚ									ʌ				sun
sermon					ɚ									ʌ				brush
furrow					ɜ̣˅˃r													
ashes						æ							ɔ˅					frost
bag						æᵆ˃̂							---					log
married						æ˅r							ɔ·					dog
half						æ							ɔ·					fog
glass						æ	ɑ˂											water
aunt						æ							ɔ˅					daughter
father							ɑ						ɔ					law
palm							ɑ						ɔ˅ɚ					warm
barn							ɑ̣ɚ											
garden							ɑ̣ɚ						ɔ˅ɚ					forty
crop							ɑ						ɒɚ					morning
on							ɑ·						ɔ˅ɚ					corn
college							ɑ						ɒɚ					horse
borrow							ɑr											
five									a˃ɩ˄		ɑ˂o˄							down
twice									a˃̂ɩ		ɑ˂o˄							out
wire									a̯˃ɨ˂ɚ		ɑʊ˂˅							flower
										ɒ˄ɩ˃								joint
										ɔ˅ɨ								boil
	i	ɩ	e	ɛ	ɜ	æ	ɑ		ai	ɔi	au		ɔ	ʌ	o	ʊ	u	

	i	ɪ	e	ɛ	ɜ	æ	ɑ		ai	ɔi	au		ɔ	ʌ	o	ʊ	u	
three	i˅>i																	
																u˅u	two
grease	ɪi˅																u<˅u	tooth
six		ɪ														ʊ		wood
crib		ɪ˘>														ʊ		pull
ear		ɪ>ɚ														u<˅ɚ		yours
beard		ɪ<ɚ													o o^			ago
eight			e ĕ^												o·			coat
April			e												o<			road
ten				ɛ											o·			home
egg				ɛ ɛ̆^											o< ˅o			know
head				ɛ											o ɚ			four
Mary				ɛr											o ˅ɚ			door
chair				ɛr										ɔ·ɚ				hoarse
care				ɛɚ										ɔ^·ɚ				mourning
merry				ɛr														
thirty					ɚ									ʌ^				sun
sermon					ɚ									ʌ˅				brush
furrow					ɜr·													
ashes						æ							ɒ^					frost
bag						æɛ̆˅												log
married						- - -·							ɔ˅					dog
half						æ							ɒ^					fog
glass						æɛ̆							ɒ^					water
aunt						æ							ɔ˅					daughter
father							ɑ						ɒ^					law
palm							ɑ·						ɔɚ					warm
barn							ɑ<ɚ											
garden							ɑɚ						ɔ˅ɚ					forty
crop							ɑ						ɒ<ɚ					morning
on							ɑ>						ɔ˅ɚ					corn
college							ɑ						ɒ^ɚ					horse
borrow							ɑr											
five									a>ɪ^		ɑ<o^							down
twice									a^>ɪ>		ɑo^							out
wire									a>ɪ<ɚ		ɑu<ɚ							flower
										ɒ<ɪ^								joint
										ɔɪ>								boil
	i	ɪ	e	ɛ	ɜ	æ	ɑ		ai	ɔi	au		ɔ	ʌ	o	ʊ	u	

	i	ɪ	e	ɛ	ɜ	æ	ɑ	ai	ɔi	au	ɔ	ʌ	o	ʊ	u	
three	i̯ᵛi														u·	two
grease	i̯ˠi														u‹ᵛu	tooth
six		ɪ												ʊ		wood
crib		ɪ												ʊ		pull
ear		ɪ ˃ɚ												ʊ‹ᵛɚ		yours
beard		ɨ‹ɚ											o‹			ago
eight			eᵛĕ^										o			coat
April			e										oo^			road
ten				ɛ									o‹			home
egg				ɛ									oo^			know
head				ɛ˃									oᵛɚ			four
Mary				ɛɚ									ɔ^ɚ			door
chair				ɛɚ									ɔ^·ɚ			hoarse
care				ɛɚ									ɔ^ɚ			mourning
merry				ɛɚ												
thirty					ɚ							ʌ				sun
sermon					ɚ							ʌ				brush
furrow					ɚ											
ashes						æ					ɒ^					frost
bag						æɨ‹					ɒ^					log
married				ɛɚ							ɒ^ˠ					dog
half						æɛᵛ					ɒˠ					fog
glass						æ					ɒ^					water
aunt						æ·					ɔᵛ					daughter
father							ɑ				ɔᵛ					law
palm							ɑ·				ɔᵛɚ					warm
barn							ɑ‹ɚ									
garden							ɑɚ				ɔɚ					forty
crop							ɑɑ‹ɚ									morning
on							ɑ˃e^				ɔᵛɚ					corn
college							ɑ				ɔᵛɚ					horse
borrow											ɒ^r					
five								e‹ᵛɪ^		a˃o^						down
twice								a^˃ɪ^		ɑ‹o^						out
wire								a^˃ɨɚ		ɑʊ‹ᵛɚ						flower
									ʌ˃ɪ˃							joint
									ɔᵛɪ˃							boil

| | i | ɪ | e | ɛ | ɜ | æ | ɑ | ai | ɔi | au | ɔ | ʌ | o | ʊ | u | |

	i	ɪ	e	ɛ	ɜ	æ	ɑ	ai	ɔi	au	ɔ	ʌ	o	ʊ	u	
three	i̯>i														u<̆u	two
grease	i̯>i														ʉ>̆u	tooth
six		ɪ												ʊ		wood
crib		ɪ												ʊ		pull
ear		ɪɚ												ʊ>̆ɚ		yours
beard		ɪɚ											o			ago
eight			eɛ̆<̂										o<̆ᵛo			coat
April			e										o			road
ten				ɛɛ̆<̂									o			home
egg			e>̆ᵛe<̂										o<ŏ<̂			know
head				ɛ									oɚ			four
Mary				ɛ>̆ɚ									o>̆ɚ			door
chair				ɛɚ							ɔ·ᴄ					hoarse
care				ɛɚ							ɔ·ᴄ					mourning
merry				ɛr												
thirty					ɚ							ʌ				sun
sermon					ɚ							ʌ				brush
furrow					ɚ ͬ											
ashes						æ					ɔ					frost
bag						ææ̂					ᴄ>̆					log
married						æ<̂r					ɒ<̂					dog
half						æ					ᴄ>̆ᵛˠ					fog
glass						æ	ɑ>									water
aunt						ææ̆>̂					ɒ<					daughter
father							ɑ				ɔ					law
palm							ɑ·				ɔɚ					warm
barn							ɑɚ·									
garden							ɑɚ				ɔ>̆ɚ					forty
crop							ɑ				ɔ>̆ɚ					morning
on							ɑ				ɔɚ					corn
college							ɑ				ɒ<̂ɚ					horse
borrow											ɒr					
five								a>̂ɪ>̂	ɑ<u							down
twice								a>̂ɪ	ɑo<̂							out
wire								aɪ<ɚ	ɑ<u<ᵛɚ							flower
joint									ɒ<̂ɪ<̂							
boil									ɔɪ							

| | i | ɪ | e | ɛ | ɜ | æ | ɑ | ai | ɔi | au | ɔ | ʌ | o | ʊ | u | |

word	i	ɪ	e	ɛ	ɜ	æ	ɑ	ai	ɔi	au	ɔ	ʌ	o	ʊ	u	word
three	i̯>i															two
grease	i̯>i														u·	tooth
six		ɪ̯>ɪ												---		wood
crib		ɪ												ʊ		pull
ear		ɪ^·ɚ												---		yours
beard		ɪ·ɚ											oᵁ			ago
eight			e eᵉ^										oᵁ>			coat
April			ɵ													road
ten				ɛ·ɪ>									oᵒ^			home
egg				ɛ^e									ou<			know
head				ɛ									o·ɚ			four
Mary				ɛr									o>·ɚ			door
chair				ɛ·ɚ							ɔ·ɚ					hoarse
care					æ<^ɚ								o>·ɚ			mourning
merry				ɛɚ												
thirty					ɚ							ʌ				sun
sermon					---							ʌ				brush
furrow																
ashes						æ					ɔ·					frost
bag						æɪ>					ɒ·ˠ					log
married						æ^r					ɔ>					dog
half						æ	ɑ									fog
glass						æ					ɒ					water
aunt						ææ^					ɔ<					daughter
father							ɑ				---					law
palm							ɑ				ɔɚ					warm
barn							ɑ<·ɚ									
garden							ɑɚ				ɔɚ					forty
crop							ɑ / ɔɚ									morning
on							ɑ				ɒ<ɚ					corn
college							ɑ				ɔɚ					horse
borrow							ɑr									
five								ai>		a>oᶜ^						down
twice								aɪ^		ɑ<oᶜ·						out
wire								e<ɚ		ɑəɚ						flower
joint									ɔ<ɪ<							joint
boil									ɔɪ<							boil

| i | ɪ | e | ɛ | ɜ | æ | ɑ | ai | ɔi | au | ɔ | ʌ | o | ʊ | u |

	i	ɪ	e	ɛ	ɜ	æ	ɑ		ai	ɔi	au		ɔ	ʌ	o	ʊ	u	
three	i˅˃i																	two
grease	i˅i																u˂ǔ	tooth
six		ɪ														ʊ		wood
crib		ɪ														ʊ		pull
ear		ɪ˃ɚ														ʊɚ		yours
beard		ɪˑ˄ɚ													o			ago
eight			e e˂˄												o˂ǒ			coat
April			e												o o˂˄			road
ten				ɛ											o o˂˄			home
egg			ɛ˂e												o ʊ			know
head				ɛ											---			four
Mary				ɛr											o˂ǒɚ			door
chair				ɛɚ									ɔˑ˖ɚ					hoarse
care				ɛɚ									ɔɚ					mourning
merry				ɛr														
thirty														ʌ				sun
sermon				ɚ										ʌ ə˄				brush
furrow				ɚ														
ashes						æ							ɒˑẽ˃					frost
bag						æ˄ɛ							ɒˑ					log
married				ɛr									ɔˑ					dog
half						æ							ɒˑ					fog
glass						æ							ɒ˂					water
aunt						æ˄ɛ˄							ɔ					daughter
father							ɑ						ɔ					law
palm							ɑˑ						ɔɚ					warm
barn							ɑɚ̇											
garden							ɑɚ						---					forty
crop							ɑ						ɒɚ					morning
on							ɑ˄e						ɒˑɑɚ					corn
college							ɑ						ɒɚ					horse
borrow							ɑr											
five									---		ao˂˄							down
twice									a˃ɪ˃˄		ɑ˂o˂˄							out
wire									aɬɚ		ɑ˂ʊɚ							flower
joint										ɔ˂˅ɬ˂˄								joint
boil										ɔ˂ɪ˄								boil
	i	ɪ	e	ɛ	ɜ	æ	ɑ		ai	ɔi	au		ɔ	ʌ	o	ʊ	u	

	i	ɪ	e	ɛ	ɜ	æ	ɑ	ai	ɔi	au	ɔ	ʌ	o	ʊ	u	
three	ɪ̂<i>														ɨu	two
grease	ɪ̂>i														ɵ̆<u	tooth
six		ɪ												ʊ̲		wood
crib		ɪ>												ʊ		pull
ear		ɪ>ɚ												ʊɚ		yours
beard		ɪ·ɚ											oºo^			ago
eight			ɛ^e^										ʌ̲>o^			coat
April			e										o<ºo^			road
ten				ɛºɛ<^									oº^			home
egg				ɛ									oʊ̲<ᵛ			know
head				ɛ									oᵛ·ɚ			four
Mary				ɛr									ɔ<^ɚ			door
chair				ɛ>·ɚ							ɔ·ɚ					hoarse
care				ɛɚ									oᵛ·ɚ			mourning
merry				ɛr												
thirty					ɚ							ʌ̂				sun
sermon					ɚ							ʌ̂ɨ̆				brush
furrow					ɚ											
ashes						æ					---					frost
bag						æɛ^	ɑ<									log
married				ɛ>ɚ							ɔ<ᵛ					dog
half						æ					ɔ<ᵛ·					fog
glass						æ					ɔᵛ					water
aunt						æ̃æ					ɔ<>					daughter
father							ɑ				ɒ^					law
palm							ɑ·				ɔɚ					warm
barn							ɑ·ɚ									
garden							ɑɚ				ɔɚ					forty
crop							ɑ				ɔ>ɚ					morning
on							ɑĕ				ɔɚ					corn
college							ɑ				ɔᵛɚ					horse
borrow							ɑɚ									
five								a>ɨ<	ɑ<ºo<							down
twice								a>ɪ>	a>o<							out
wire								a>ɨɚ		---						flower
joint									ɒ<ɪ>							joint
boil									ɒ<·ɨ^							boil

| i | ɪ | e | ɛ | ɜ | æ | ɑ | ai | ɔi | au | ɔ | ʌ | o | ʊ | u |

	i	ɪ	e	ɛ	ɜ	æ	ɑ	ai	ɔi	au	ɔ	ʌ	o	ʊ	u	
three	ɪ<^i															two: ŭʊ
grease	ɪ>^i															tooth: u<̌u
six		ɪ														wood: ʊ
crib		ɪ>														pull: ʊ
ear		ɪ>ɚ														yours: ʊɚ
beard		ɪ·ɚ											o o<^			ago
eight			e>e^										o o<^			coat
April			e										o< o^			road
ten				ɛ									o o<^			home
egg			e>e<^										o o<			know
head				ɛ									o^·ɚ			four
Mary				ɛr									ɔ<^ɚ			door
chair				ɛ>ɚ									ɔ<^·ɚ			hoarse
care				ɛɚ							ɔ·ɚ					mourning
merry				ɛr												
thirty					ɚ							ʌ				sun
sermon					ɚ							ʌ				brush
furrow					ɚˇ											
ashes						æ					ɔ·					frost
bag						æ					ɔ>ˇ					log
married						æ^r					ɔ					dog
half						æ					ɔ>·ʊˇ					fog
glass						æ>					ɒ<					water
aunt						ææ̃					ɔ>·					daughter
father							ɑ				ɔ>					law
palm							ɑ				ɔˇɚ					warm
barn							ɑ·ɚ									
garden							ɑɚ				ɔɚ					forty
crop							ɑ				ɒ<^ɚ					morning
on							ɒ				ɒɔɚ					corn
college							ɑ				ɔɚ					horse
borrow							ɑr									
five								a^>ɪ>		ɑ<o<^						down
twice								a^>ɪ^		a>o<^						out
wire								ɑ<^tɚ								flower
joint									ɒ<^ɪ							
boil									ɔˇt<							

| | i | ɪ | e | ɛ | ɜ | æ | ɑ | ai | ɔi | au | ɔ | ʌ | o | ʊ | u | |

	i	ι	e	ε	3	æ	ɑ	ai	ɔi	au	ɔ	ʌ	o	ʊ	u	
three	i̯>ǐ														u<ᵘ	two
grease	i̯>ǐ														ᵫu	tooth
six		ι												ʊ		wood
crib		ι												ʊ<		pull
ear		ι>ɚ											o>ɚ̌			yours
beard		ι>ɚ											ô<			ago
eight			e̯>eˆ										o<			coat
April			e										o<			road
ten				ε									o			home
egg			e̯ve										o<̌o			know
head				ε									ǒɚ			four
Mary			ε>ˆr								ɔ<ˆɚ					door
chair			εɚ								ɔ<ˆ·ɚ					hoarse
care			εɚ								ɔ<ˆ·ɚ					mourning
merry			εr													
thirty					ɚ							ʌ				sun
sermon					ɚ							ʌ e>				brush
furrow					ɚ											
ashes						æ					ɒ<ˆ					frost
bag						æ					---					log
married						æ<ˆr					ɒ<ˆ					dog
half						æ					ɒ<ˆᵁ					fog
glass						æ					ɒ<ˆ					water
aunt						æ·					ɔˇ					daughter
father							ɑ				ɔˇ>					law
palm							ɑᵚ				ɔɚ					warm
barn							ɑɚ									
garden							ɑɚ				ɔ<ˇ>ɚ					forty
crop							ɒ<				ɒ<ˇ ɚ					morning
on											ɒ<ˆ ɤ /					corn
college							ɑ				ɔ>ɚ̌					horse
borrow							ɑr									
five								ɑ<ˆιˆ		ɑ<o<						down
twice								a>ˆιˆ		ɑ<o>ˇ						out
wire								a>ιˆ<ɚ								flower
									ɒ<ˆιˆ							joint
									ɔ>ɫ̌							boil
	i	ι	e	ε	3	æ	ɑ	ai	ɔi	au	ɔ	ʌ	o	ʊ	u	

212

	i	ɪ	e	ɛ	ɜ	æ	ɑ	ai	ɔi	au	ɔ	ʌ	o	ʊ	u	
three	ɩ^î>															two	u
grease	i̯>i														u<u	tooth
six		ɪ													ʊ		wood
crib		ɪ													ʊ		pull
ear		ɪ>ɚ													ʊɚ		yours
beard		ɪ<ɚ											o			ago
eight			eɩ>										oᵁ>			coat
April			e										oᵘ			road
ten				ɛ									ooᵒ<			home
egg		ɛ<ɩ>										oᵒ			know
head				ɛ								ɔ<ɚ				four
Mary				ɛr								ɔ^ɚ				door
chair				ɛɚ								ɔ<·ɚ				hoarse
care				ɛɚ							ɔ·ɚ					mourning
merry				ɛr												
thirty					ɚ							ʌ				sun
sermon					ɚ							ʌ				brush
furrow					ɜ>r											
ashes						æ					ɔᵁ					frost
bag						æ>					ɔ>					log
married			ɛ>r			ɑ·										dog
half						æ					ɒ<					fog
glass						æ					ɒ<					water
aunt						æ^					ɒ<					daughter
father							ɑ				ɔ					law
palm											ɒ<ɔ>ɚ					warm
barn							ɑ>ɚ									
garden							ɑ>ɚ				ɔ>ɚ					forty
crop							ɑ>ɣ				ɔ>ɚ					morning
on							ɑ<ɣ				ɔ>ɚ					corn
college							ɑ				ɔ>ɚ					horse
borrow							ɑr									
five								a^ɩ^		a<o^						down
twice								a>ɩ		a·ᵒ						out
wire								a>ɩɚ		---						flower
joint									ɔ>ɩ<							
boil									ɔɩ<							

| | i | ɪ | e | ɛ | ɜ | æ | ɑ | ai | ɔi | au | ɔ | ʌ | o | ʊ | u | |

word	i	ɪ	e	ɛ	3	æ	ɑ	ai	ɔi	au	ɔ	ʌ	o	ʊ	u	word
three	i˅ᵢ>														u˅	two
grease	ɪ<ˆi														ʉ>u	tooth
six		ɪ												ʊ		wood
crib		ɪ												ʊ		pull
ear	ɪ>ɚ														ʊɚ	yours
beard	ɪ>ɚ													o		ago
eight		e											o< o<ˆ			coat
April		e											o o<ˆ			road
ten				ɛ ɛ>									o o˘<ˆ			home
egg				ɛ<ˆe									o o<ˆ			know
head				ɛ ɛ<ˆ									o·ɚ			four
Mary				ɛr									o>·ɚ			door
chair				ɛɚ									o>·ɚ			hoarse
care				ɛɚ							ɔ>·ɚ					mourning
merry				ɛr												
thirty					ɚ							ʌ				sun
sermon					ɚ							ʌ ɨ>				brush
furrow					ɚ											
ashes						æ					ɒ<ˆ·ʏ					frost
bag						æ·æ>					ɒ<ˆ·					log
married				ɛr							ɒ<ˆ·					dog
half						æ·					ɒ<ˆ·					fog
glass						æ					ɒ<ˆ					water
aunt						æ̃æ̃<ˆ					ɒ					daughter
father							ɑ				ɒ					law
palm							ɑ·ɯ				ɔ>ɚ					warm
barn							ɑ>ɚ									
garden							ɑ>ɚ				ɔɚ					forty
crop							ɑ>				ɔ>ɚ					morning
on											ɒɑ/ ɔ>ɚ					corn
college							ɑ				ɔɚ					horse
borrow											ɒr					
five								a>ɪˆ	ɑ<ˆo<ˆ							down
twice								a>ɪˆ	ɑ<ˆo<ˆ							out
wire								ɑ<ˆɨɚ	– – –							flower
									ɒ<ˆɨ<							joint
									ɒ<ˆɨ							boil
	i	ɪ	e	ɛ	3	æ	ɑ	ai	ɔi	au	ɔ	ʌ	o	ʊ	u	

	i	ɪ	e	ɛ	ɜ	æ	ɑ		aɪ	ɔɪ	au		ɔ	ʌ	o	ʊ	u	
three	i̯ˇɪ																uˇᵘ	two
grease	i̯ˇɪ																u˂ˇu	tooth
six		ɪˀɪ														ʊ		wood
crib		ɪ														ʊ		pull
ear		ɪˀɚ														ʊɚ		yours
beard		ɪˀɚ												oo˂ˆ				ago
eight			eˇ˃e˂ˆ											oo˂ˆ				coat
April			e											oo˂ˆ				road
ten				ɛˆ										oo˂ˆ′				home
egg				ɛ˂ˆeˇ										o˂ o˂ˆ				know
head				ɛ ɛ˂										o˂ ɚ				four
Mary				ɛr										ɔ˂ˆ·ɚ				door
chair				ɛɚ									ɔ˃·ˇɚ					hoarse
care				ɛɚ										o˃·ˇɚ				mourning
merry				ɛr														
thirty					ɚ									ʌ				sun
sermon					ɚ								– – –					brush
furrow					ɚ													
ashes						æ							ɔ˂ˇ˅					frost
bag						æ ɛ˃							ɒ˂ˆˠ					log
married						æ˂ˆr							ɒ˂ˆ·					dog
half						æ æ˂ˆ							ɒ·					fog
glass						æ	ɒ											water
aunt						æ æ˂ˆ							ɒ˂ˆ					daughter
father							ɑ						ɔˇ˃					law
palm													ɑˇ˂ɚ					warm
barn							ɑ·ɚ											
garden							ɑˀɚ						ɔɚ					forty
crop							ɑ						ɔˇ˃ɚ					morning
on													ɒ˂ˠɑ					corn
college													ɒˇ˂ɑ					horse
borrow							ɑr											
five									aˀɪ˂ˆ	ɑ˂ o˂ˆ								down
twice									aɪˀˆ˃	ɑ˂ o˂ˆ								out
wire									aˀɪˀɚ	ɑ˂ʊ								flower
									ɒ˂ˆɪˀ˃									joint
									ɒˀɑ									boil

| | i | ɪ | e | ɛ | ɜ | æ | ɑ | | aɪ | ɔɪ | au | | ɔ | ʌ | o | ʊ | u | |

	i	ɪ	e	ɛ	ɜ	æ	ɑ	aɪ	ɔɪ	au	ɔ	ʌ	o	ʊ	u	
three	ɪ̌>i															
															u	two
grease	ɪ<̂i															
															ʉu<	tooth
six		ɪ												ʊ		wood
crib		ɪ												ʊ		pull
ear	ɪ>ɚ													ʊɚ		yours
beard	ɪ̌>ɚ												oᵁ			ago
eight			ě>e<										o·			coat
April			e										oo<̂			road
ten				ɛ									oo<̂			home
egg				ɛ^e<̂									oo<̂			know
head				ɛ									o·ɚ			four
Mary				ɛr							ɔ<̂·ɚ					door
chair				ɛ̌>·ɚ							ɔ·ɚ					hoarse
care				ɛɚ									o>̌·ɚ			mourning
merry				ɛr												
thirty					ɚ							ʌ				sun
sermon					ɚ							ʌˠ				brush
furrow					ɚ											
ashes						æ					ɒ·ˠ					frost
bag						æ					ɔ>̌·ˠ					log
married				ɛ̌>r							ɒ<̂·					dog
half						æ·æ<̂					ɒˠ					fog
glass						æ̰˅					ɒ<̂					water
aunt						æ̰ ɛ>					ɒ<					daughter
father							ɑ				ɒ<̂					law
palm							ɑ·				ɒ>̌ɚ					warm
barn							ɑ·ɚ									
garden							ɑɚ				ɔɚ					forty
crop							ɑ>ə>				ɒ<̂ɚ					morning
on											ɒ·ɒ<̌>ɚ					corn
college							ɑ				ɔ·ɚ					horse
borrow							ɑr									
five								a>̂ɪ^	ɑ<o<̂							down
twice								aɪ^	ɑ<o<̂							out
wire								a>̂ɫ<ɚ	---							flower
joint									ɔ·ɪ>							
boil									ɒ<̂ɫ<̂							
	i	ɪ	e	ɛ	ɜ	æ	ɑ	aɪ	ɔɪ	au	ɔ	ʌ	o	ʊ	u	

216

	i	ɪ	e	ɛ	ɜ	æ	ɑ	aɪ	ɔɪ	au	ɔ	ʌ	o	ʊ	u	
three	---															two
															u	
grease	i̯>i														u<ʊu	tooth
six		ɪ												ʊ		wood
crib		---												ʊ		pull
ear		ɪ>ɚ												ʊɚ		yours
beard		ɪ>·ɚ											o<^ʊ			ago
eight			e e<^										o ŏo<̂			coat
April			e										o<ᵛo			road
ten				ɛ									o o<^			home
egg			e>ᵛe<^										---			know
head				ɛ ɛ<^							ɔ·ɚ					four
Mary				ɛr									o<ᵛ·ɚ			door
chair				ɛ·ɚ									ɔ<^·o>ɚ			hoarse
care				ɛɚ							ɔ·ᵛ·ɚ					mourning
merry				ɛr												
thirty					ɚ							ʌ				sun
sermon					ɚ							ʌɬᵛ				brush
furrow					ɚ											
ashes						æ					ɒ<^ʊ					frost
bag						æɛ^					ɔ<ᵛʊ					log
married						æ<^r					ɒ<^ɤ					dog
half						ææ^					ɒʊ					fog
glass						æ					ɒ					water
aunt						ææ<^					ɒ					daughter
father							ɑ				ɒ<^					law
palm							ɑ>				ɔɚ					warm
barn							ɑ>ɚɚ									
garden							ɑ>ɚ				---					forty
crop							ɒ				ɔ<ᵛ>ɚ					morning
on							ɒ<e				ɔ<ᵛ>ɚ					corn
college							ɑ>				ɔɚ					horse
borrow							ɑ>r									
five								aɪ<		ao<^						down
twice								aɪ<^		a^o<^						out
wire								a>ɬ<ɚ		a>ʊ						flower
joint									ʌ>ɪ<							
boil									ɒ<^ɬ<							

| | i | ɪ | e | ɛ | ɜ | æ | ɑ | aɪ | ɔɪ | au | ɔ | ʌ | o | ʊ | u | |

	i	ɪ	e	ɛ	ɜ	æ	ɑ	ai	ɔi	au	ɔ	ʌ	o	ʊ	u	
three	ɪˆiˇ															two (uˈ<ᵘ)
grease	ɪˇ>iˆ>															tooth (u·)
six		ɪ														wood (ʊ)
crib		ɪˀ>														pull (ʊ)
ear		ɪˀ>ɚ														yours (ʊɚ)
beard		ɪˇ>ɚ														ago (o)
eight			eˇ>ɪˀ>													coat (ʌˀ>oˆ)
April			e													road (ooˆ<)
ten				ɛˀɛˆ												home (ooˆ<)
egg				ɛˆeˇ>												know (oõˆ<)
head				ɛˀɛˆ												four (o·ɚ)
Mary				ɛr												door (ɔˀ<oˆ<ɚ)
chair				ɛɚ												hoarse (ɔˆ<·ɚ)
care				ɛɚ												mourning (oˇ<·ɚ)
merry				ɛr												
thirty					ɚ							ʌ				sun
sermon					ɚ							ʌ				brush
furrow					ɜr											
ashes						æ					ɒˆ<					frost
bag						æɛˇ>					ɒˆ<					log
married						æˆ<r					ɔˇ>					dog
half						æ					ɒˆ<·					fog
glass						æ					ɒˆ<					water
aunt						æɛˆ	ɑˀ<									daughter
father							ɑ				ɔ					law
palm							ɑ				ɔɚ					warm
barn							ɐ·ɚ									
garden							ɑɚ				ɔɚ					forty
crop							ɑ				ɔˇ>ɚ					morning
on							ɑˆ<				ɔɚ					corn
college							ɑˀ>				ɔɚ					horse
borrow											ɔˇ>r					
five								aˀ>ɪˆ		auˆ<						down
twice								aˆ<ɪˀ>		aˆ>oˆ<						out
wire								aˀ<ɚ	eˀ+ɚ	ɑɤ+ɚ						flower
									ɔˀ>ɪˇ							joint
									ɔ+							boil
	i	ɪ	e	ɛ	ɜ	æ	ɑ	ai	ɔi	au	ɔ	ʌ	o	ʊ	u	

	i	ɪ	e	ɛ	ɜ	æ	ɑ		ai	ɔi	au		ɔ	ʌ	o	ʊ	u	
three	i˅˃·i																ʉ˃˅u	two
grease	i˅˃i																ʉu	tooth
six		ɪ														ʊ		wood
crib		ɪ														ʊ		pull
ear		ɪ˃ɚ															ʊ·ɚ	yours
beard		ɪɚ											oo˂ˆ					ago
eight			ɛ˂ˆe˂ˆ										o·ʊ˃˅					coat
April			e										o·o˂ˆ					road
ten				ɛ˘ɛ˂ˆ									oo˂ˆ					home
egg				ɛˆe									oo˂ˆ					know
head				ɛ									o˂˅·ɚ					four
Mary				ɛr									ɔ˂ˆɚ					door
chair				ɛɚ								ɔ·ᴄ˓						hoarse
care				ɛɚ								ɒ˂ˆ·ɚ						mourning
merry				ɛr														
thirty					ɚ˅˃									ʌˆ				sun
sermon					ɚ									ʌᴧˆʌ˅				brush
furrow					ɚ													
ashes						æɛ˃ˆ							ɔ					frost
bag						æɛˆ							- - -					log
married						ær							ɔ˅˃·					dog
half						æ							ɔᴄ˃o˅˘					fog
glass						æ	ɑ˂											water
aunt						ææ̃ˆ							ɒ˂ˆ					daughter
father							ɑ						ɔ˅˃					law
palm							ɑ·e						ɔᴄ˃ɚ˅					warm
barn							ɑɚ·											
garden							ɑɚ						ɔɚ					forty
crop							ɑ						ɔ˃ɚ˅					morning
on													ɔ˃ɤᴄɚ					corn
college							ɑ						ɔɚ					horse
borrow							ɑ˂r											
five									a˂˃·ɪˆ	a˂ˆo˂								down
twice									a˂˃ɪˆ	aˆo˂								out
wire									ɑ˂ˆ·ɬ˂·ɚ		aʊ							flower
										ɔ˅˃ɬ								joint
										ɔ·ɬ								boil
	i	ɪ	e	ɛ	ɜ	æ	ɑ		ai	ɔi	au		ɔ	ʌ	o	ʊ	u	

	i	ɪ	e	ɛ	ɜ	æ	ɑ		aɪ	ɔɪ	aʊ		ɔ	ʌ	o	ʊ	u	
three	i̯ˇ>i																ɐu	two
grease	i̯ˇ>i																u·	tooth
six		ɪ														ʊ		wood
crib		ɪ·														ʊ		pull
ear		ɪ>ɚ														ʊɚ		yours
beard	i̯ˇ>·ɚ														oᴼ<ˆ			ago
eight			e̯ˇ>ɪ												ʌ<ˆ o			coat
April			e												ooˆ<			road
ten				ɛˑɛ̆ˆ											oᴼ<ˆ			home
egg				ɛˆɪˇ											ou̲ˇ>			know
head				ɛɛ̆ˆ<											o·ɚ			four
Mary				ɛr											ɔ<ˆ ɚ			door
chair				ɛɚ											oˇ·ɚ			hoarse
care				ɛɚ											ɔ<ˆ ·ɚ			mourning
merry				ɛr														
thirty					ɚ									ʌ				sun
sermon					ɚ									ʌ<ˆ ‡̃				brush
furrow					ɜ̣ˇ>r													
ashes						æ	ɑ<ˆ e>											frost
bag						---							ɒ					log
married						ær							ɒ<ˆ ˇ					dog
half						æɛˇ>							ɒ·					fog
glass						æ	ɑ<											water
aunt						æˇ>æˆ							ɒ<ˆ					daughter
father							ɑ						ɔ·					law
palm							ɑ·						ɔɚ					warm
barn							ɑ̣·ɚ											
garden							ɑɚ						ɔɚ					forty
crop							ɑ e						ɒ<ˆ ɚ					morning
on							ɑ>e						ɒ<ˆ ·ɚ					corn
college							ɑ						ɔ<ˆ>ˇ ɚ					horse
borrow													ɒr					
five									ɑ<ɪˆ		aoˆ<							down
twice									aˆ>ɪˆ		a>ʊˇ>							out
wire									a>ɨˆ<ɚ		ɑ<ʊ>ˇɚ							flower
joint										ɔˇ>ɪˆ< >								joint
boil										ɔˇ>ɨˆ< >								boil

| | i | ɪ | e | ɛ | ɜ | æ | ɑ | | aɪ | ɔɪ | aʊ | | ɔ | ʌ | o | ʊ | u | |

220

	i	ɪ	e	ɛ	ɜ	æ	ɑ		ai	ɔi	au		ɔ	ʌ	o	ʊ	u	
three	i⌃>i																u˅<u	two
grease	i˅>i																u˅<u	tooth
six		ɪ														---		wood
crib		---														ʊ		pull
ear		ɪ>ɚ														ʊɚ		yours
beard		ɪ>ɚ													o·ʊ			ago
eight			e˅>e												oo<			coat
April			e												oo<			road
ten				ɛ ɛ̆⌃											oo<			home
egg				ɛ ɛ<⌃											oo<			know
head				ɛ											o>·ɚ			four
Mary				ɛɹ											o>o<ɚ			door
chair				ɛ>·ɚ											ɔ<⌃·ɚ			hoarse
care				ɛɚ									ɔ·ɚ					mourning
merry				ɛɹ														
thirty					ɚ									ʌ				sun
sermon					ɚ									ʌ				brush
furrow					ɚʳ													
ashes						æ ɛ< ⌃							ɒ̧ʸ					frost
bag						æ ɛ							ɔ>˅ʊ					log
married						æ<⌃ɹ							ɔ> ˅					dog
half						æ							ɒ·ʸ					fog
glass						æ æ< ⌃							ɒ					water
aunt						æ æ̃ ⌃							ɒɑ<⌃					daughter
father							ɑ						ɒɑ<⌃					law
palm							ɑ·ɯ̈						ɔɚ					warm
barn							ɑ·ɚ											
garden							ɑ>ɚ						ɔ>˅ɚ					forty
crop							ɑe⌃						ɔ>˅ɚ					morning
on													ɒɑ<ʊ̲					corn
college							ɑ						ɔ>˅ɚ					horse
borrow							ɒɹ											
five									a<⌃ɪ⌃	a>⌃o⌃								down
twice									aɪ⌃	a>⌃o<⌃								out
wire									aɪ>ɚ		ɑʊɚ							flower
joint										ɔ>˅ɪ<⌃								
boil										ɒ<⌃ɑ̵								

i	ɪ	e	ɛ	ɜ	æ	ɑ		ai	ɔi	au		ɔ	ʌ	o	ʊ	u

221

	i	ɪ	e	ɛ	ɜ	æ	ɑ	ai	ɔi	au	ɔ	ʌ	o	ʊ	u	
three	ɪ<ˆi														ʉ u<	two
grease	ɪⁱ														ʊu	tooth
six		ɪ												ɤ		wood
crib		ɪ												ʊ̲		pull
ear		ɪɚ												ʊ̲ɚ		yours
beard		ɪˇɚ											ou			ago
eight			eˇe<										oo^			coat
April			eˇe<										o<uˇ			road
ten				ɛə									oo^			home
egg				ɛə									ou			know
head				ɛə									o̥ᵂɚ			four
Mary				ɛɚr							ɔᵂɚ					door
chair						æˆɚ					ɔ̝ɚ					hoarse
care				ɛɚ							ɔɑ					mourning
merry				ɛɚr												
thirty					ɚ							ʌ				sun
sermon					ɚ							ʌˇə				brush
furrow					ɚr											
ashes						æɪ					ɔʊ					frost
bag						æ†					---					log
married				ɛɚ							ɔ					dog
half						æ	ɑ•									fog
glass						æ	ɑˆ									water
aunt						æə	ɑ>									daughter
father							ɑ•				ɔˇ					law
palm							ɑə				ɔɚ					warm
barn							ɑɚ									
garden							ɑɚ				ɔɚ					forty
crop							ɑ<				ɑɚ̬					morning
on							ɑ•				ɔɚ					corn
college							ɑ				ɔɚ					horse
borrow							ɑr									
five								e<ɪ		ɑo						down
twice								aɪˆ		ɑ̲o̲						out
wire								ɑ ʲ ɚ		---						flower
joint									ɔᵂɪ							
boil									ɔɪˆə							

| | i | ɪ | e | ɛ | ɜ | æ | ɑ | ai | ɔi | au | ɔ | ʌ | o | ʊ | u | |

222

	i	ɪ	e	ɛ	з	æ	ɑ	ai	ɔi	au	ɔ	ʌ	o	ʊ	u	
three	ɪⁱ															two
															ʊu	
grease	ɪi															tooth
															ʊᵁ	
six		ɪˇ														wood
														ʊᵊ		
crib		ɪˇ														pull
														ʊ		
ear		ɪɚ														yours
														ʊɚ		
beard		ɪɚ											oᵁ			ago
eight			eˇɪˆ										oᵁ			coat
April			eɪ										oᵁ			road
ten				ɛᵊ									ooˆ			home
egg				ɛɪ									o̲ᵁ			know
head				ɛɪ							ɔᵂɚ					four
Mary				ɛr							ɔɚ					door
chair				ɛɚ							ɔ̬ɚ					hoarse
care				ɛɚ									o̬ɚ			mourning
merry				ɛɚr												
thirty					ɚ							ʌ				sun
sermon					ɚ							ʌ†				brush
furrow					ɚr											
ashes						æɪ	ɑ̬									frost
bag						æ					ɔ					log
married				ɛr							ɔ̬					dog
half						æ					ɔᵁ					fog
glass						æᵊ	ɑ									water
aunt						æᵊ	aˋ									daughter
father							ɑ				ɔˇ					law
palm							ɑᵊ				ɔɚ					warm
barn							ɑɚ									
garden							ɑɚ				ɔɚ					forty
crop							ɑ				ɔɚ					morning
on							ɑ				ɔɚ					corn
college							ɑ				ɔɚ					horse
borrow							ɑr									
five								aɪ		ɑo						down
twice								aˋɪˆ		ɑo						out
wire							ɑ·ɚ			ɑoᵂɚ						flower
joint									ɔᵂɪˆ							joint
boil									ɔɪ							boil
	i	ɪ	e	ɛ	з	æ	ɑ	ai	ɔi	au	ɔ	ʌ	o	ʊ	u	

	i	ɪ	e	ɛ	ɜ	æ	ɑ	ai	ɔi	au	ɔ	ʌ	o	ʊ	u	
three	i˅ⁱ>	ɪ												ʊ	ɵ>ᵁ	two
grease	i˅>														ʊᵁ	tooth
six		ɪ												ʊ̲		wood
crib		ɪ												ʊ̭		pull
ear		ɪɚ												ʊɚ		yours
beard	i˅ɚ												oᵁ			ago
eight			e˅ɪ								ɒ·					coat
April			eɪ										oᵁ			road
ten				ɛ									oᵁ			home
egg				ɛ˅									o>ᵁ			know
head				ɛ˅									oɚ			four
Mary				ɛ·r							ɔɚ					door
chair				ɛɚ							ɔ̰ɚ					hoarse
care				ɛɚ							ɔɚ					mourning
merry				ɛr												
thirty					ɚ							ʌ				sun
sermon					ɚ							---				brush
furrow					ɚr											
ashes						æ^					ɔ					frost
bag						æ^					---					log
married				ɛ˅ɜr							ɔ·ᵁ					dog
half						æ^					ɔ̰·					fog
glass						æ					ɔ					water
aunt						æ					ɔ̰					daughter
father							ɑ				ɔ					law
palm							ɑ									warm
barn							ɑ<ɚ									
garden							ɑɚ				ɔɚ					forty
crop							ɑ				ɔ<r					morning
on											ɒ̰ɔ̰ ɒɚ					corn
college							ɑ·				ɔɚ					horse
borrow							ɑɚr									
five								aɪ		ɑʊ						down
twice								a<ɪ		ɑ˅						out
wire						ɑɚɑɚ										flower
									ɒ̲ɪ^							joint
									ɒ˄ɪ							boil
	i	ɪ	e	ɛ	ɜ	æ	ɑ	ai	ɔi	au	ɔ	ʌ	o	ʊ	u	

	i	ɪ	e	ɛ	ɜ	æ	ɑ	ai	ɔi	au	ɔ	ʌ	o	ʊ	u	
three	ɪi													ʊʊ^		two
grease	i														ʊu	tooth
six		ɪ												ʊ		wood
crib		ɪ												ʊ̆		pull
ear	ɪɚ													ʊɚ		yours
beard	ɪˇɚ												oˋʊ			ago
eight			eɪ^										oʊ			coat
April			eˇɪ										oʊ			road
ten				ɛᵊ									oʊˇ			home
egg				ɛ									oˇʊ			know
head				ɛ							ɔɚ					four
Mary				ɛɚr							ɔɚ					door
chair				ɛˇɚ							ɔɚ̆					hoarse
care				ɛɚ							ɔɚ					mourning
merry				ɛɚr												
thirty					ɚ							ʌˋ				sun
sermon					ɚ							ʌ				brush
furrow					ɚr											
ashes						æ					ɔ̌ᵂᵊ					frost
bag						æ					ɔ					log
married				ɛˀᵊɚ							ɔ̱					dog
half						æ					ɔ̆ᵘ					fog
glass						æᵗ					ɔ					water
aunt						æᵊ					ɔ					daughter
father							ɑ				ɔ					law
palm							ɑᵊ				ɔɚ					warm
barn							ɑɚ									
garden							ɑɚ				ɔɚ					forty
crop							ɑ				ɔɚ					morning
on											ɔˑᶜ ɔɚ					corn
college							ɑ				ɔɚ					horse
borrow							ɑr									
five								aˆ̧ɪ		ɑʊ						down
twice								eˋɪ		ɑʊ						out
wire								ɑ̧ˆᵗ		ɑᵁɚ						flower
joint									ɔᵂiˇ							joint
boil									ɔi							boil

| | i | ɪ | e | ɛ | ɜ | æ | ɑ | ai | ɔi | au | ɔ | ʌ | o | ʊ | u | |

	i	ɪ	e	ɛ	ɜ	æ	ɑ		aɪ	ɔɪ	au		ɔ	ʌ	o	ʊ	u	
three	ɪˇ<î																ʉˇ>uˇ<	two
grease	ɪˇ<ǐ>																ʉ<ˇu	tooth
six		ɪ														ʊ		wood
crib		ɪˇ>ɪ														ʊ		pull
ear		ɪ>ɚ															ʊɚ	yours
beard		ɪ·ɚ													ou<			ago
eight			eˇ>eˆ												o<ˇo			coat
April			e												o<ˇo			road
ten				ɛˆɛ<											oo<ˆ			home
egg				ɛˆeˇ>											oo<ˆ			know
head				ɛ											o>ɚˇ			four
Mary				− − −											ɔ<ˆ·ɚ			door
chair				ɛ·ɚ											ɔ<ˆ·ɚ			hoarse
care				ɛɚ									ɔ·ɚ					mourning
merry				ɛr														
thirty					ɚ									ʌ				sun
sermon					ɚ									ʌ>ɚˇ<				brush
furrow					ɚ>													
ashes						æ							ɔˇ>·					frost
bag						æɛ>							ɔˇ>ʊ					log
married						æ<ˆr							ɒ·ʌ					dog
half						æ							ɒ<ˆ·					fog
glass						æ	ɑ											water
aunt						æ·æ<ˆ							ɒ<ˆ					daughter
father							ɑ>						ɒ<ˆ					law
palm							ɑ>·ɫ						ɔɚ					warm
barn							ɑ<ɚ											
garden							ɑ>ɚ						ɒ<ˆɚ					forty
crop							ɑ						− − −					morning
on													ɒ<ʊˇ ɔɚ					corn
college							ɑ>						ɔɚ					horse
borrow							ɑ>r											
five									aˆ>ɪ>		a>ʊ>							down
twice									aˆɪ<ˆ		a·oˆ							out
wire									a>·ɪ>ɚˆ		ɑ<ʉɚ							flower
										ɔ>ɪ<ˆ								joint
										ɒ<ˆɫˇ								boil
	i	ɪ	e	ɛ	ɜ	æ	ɑ		aɪ	ɔɪ	au		ɔ	ʌ	o	ʊ	u	

226

	i	ɪ	e	ɛ	ɜ	æ	ɑ	ai	ɔi	au	ɔ	ʌ	o	ʊ	u	
three	i˅i														ʉ˃ᵘ	two
grease	i˅i														u˂u	tooth
six		ɪ												ʊ		wood
crib		ɪ												ʊ		pull
ear		ɪ˃ɚ													ʊɚ	yours
beard		ɪ˃ɚ											o o˂			ago
eight			e˅e˄										o˃o			coat
April			e										o o˂			road
ten				ɛ ɛ˂									o o˂			home
egg				ɛ˄e˅								ʌ˄˃o				know
head				ɛ ɛ˂									o˅·ɚ			four
Mary				ɛr									ɔ˂·ɚ			door
chair				ɛɚ									ɔ˂·ɚ			hoarse
care				ɛɚ									ɔ˂·ɚ			mourning
merry				ɛr												
thirty					ɚ							ʌ				sun
sermon					ɚ							ʌə˂				brush
furrow					ɜr											
ashes						æ					ɔ˅ɤ					frost
bag						æɛ					ɒ˂ʌ˅					log
married						æ˂r					ɒ˂·ɤ					dog
half						æ					ɒe					fog
glass						ææ˂	ɑ˃									water
aunt						ææ̃˂					ɒ˂					daughter
father							ɑ				ɒ˂					law
palm							ɑ·e˅				ɔ˃ɚ					warm
barn							ɑ˂·ɚ									
garden							ɑ˃ɚ				ɔɚ					forty
crop							ɑ				ɔ˃ɚ					morning
on							ɑe				ɔɚ					corn
college							ɑ				ɔ˅ɚ					horse
borrow							ɑr									
five								a˂ɪ˄		a˃o˂						down
twice								a˃ɪ˃		a·ɤ						out
wire								a˄ɪ˃ɚ		aʊɚ						flower
joint									ɔ˃ɪ˃							joint
boil									ɔ˃ɬ							boil
	i	ɪ	e	ɛ	ɜ	æ	ɑ	ai	ɔi	au	ɔ	ʌ	o	ʊ	u	

227

	i	ɪ	e	ɛ	ɜ	æ	ɑ	ai	ɔi	au	ɔ	ʌ	o	ʊ	u	
three	i̯>i															two
grease	i̯>i														u<̆u	tooth
six		ɪ												ʊ		wood
crib		ɪ												ʊ		pull
ear		ɪ>ɚ												ʊɚ		yours
beard		ɪ>ɚ											oɵ<^			ago
eight			e̯>e^										oɵ<^			coat
April			e										oɵ<^			road
ten				ɛ									oɵ<^			home
egg			e̯>.e<^										oɵ<^			know
head				ɛ									o>·ɚ			four
Mary				ɛ̆>r									ɔ<^ɚ			door
chair				ɛ̆>·ɚ							ɔ·ɚ					hoarse
care				ɛɚ							ɔ·ɚ					mourning
merry				ɛr												
thirty					ɚ							ʌ				sun
sermon					ɚ							ʌt̆>				brush
furrow					ɚ											
ashes						æ	ɑ<e>									frost
bag						---					ɒ·					log
married						æ<^r					ɒ<^·					dog
half						æ					ɒˇ					fog
glass						æ					ɒ					water
aunt						æ, æ<^					ɒ					daughter
father							ɑ				ɒ<^					law
palm							ɑ·				ɔɚ					warm
barn							ɑɚ									
garden							ɑɚ				ɔ>c̆					forty
crop							ɑ				ɔɚ					morning
on							ɒ·ɑ				ɔ>ɚ					corn
college							ɑ				ɔˇɚ					horse
borrow							ɑr									
five								aɪ>		a>^ɔ<^						down
twice								a^ɪ^		a<^ɔ<^						out
wire								a<^ɪ>ɚ		ɑu̲ɚ						flower
									ɒ<^t<							joint
									ɒt<^							boil
	i	ɪ	e	ɛ	ɜ	æ	ɑ	ai	ɔi	au	ɔ	ʌ	o	ʊ	u	

	i	ɪ	e	ɛ	ɜ	æ	ɑ	ai	ɔi	au	ɔ	ʌ	o	ʊ	u	
three		ɪ^													ʊu	two
grease	ᶥi														ʊᵁ	tooth
six		ɪ												ʊ		wood
crib		ɪᵛ													---	pull
ear	jᵛɚ														ʊᵂɚ	yours
beard		ɪɚ											oᵁ			ago
eight			eɪ^										oᵁ			coat
April			eɪ^										oʊ			road
ten				ɛᵛɪ									oʊ			home
egg			eɪ										oᵁ			know
head				ɛ							ɔ̠ɚ					four
Mary				ɛɚr							ɔɚ					door
chair				ɛɚ									oɚ			hoarse
care				ɛɚ							ɔɚ					mourning
merry				ɛr												
thirty					ɝ							ʌ				sun
sermon					ɝ							ʌ				brush
furrow					ɝr											
ashes						æɪ					ɔ̠ᵁ					frost
bag						æɪ					---					log
married				ɛɚr									ɔᵒ			dog
half						æ					ɔ					fog
glass						æ					ɔ					water
aunt						æ					ɔ					daughter
father							ɑ				ɔ					law
palm							ɑ·				ɔɚ					warm
barn							ɑɚ									
garden							ɑɚ				ɔᵛɚ					forty
crop							ɑᵛ				ɔɚ					morning
on							ɑ˃				ɔɚ					corn
college							ɑ				ɔɚ					horse
borrow							ɑɚr									
five								a˃ɪ^		ɑˤo						down
twice								ai		ɑo						out
wire								ɑʲɚ		ɑɚ						flower
joint									ɔᵂɪ^							joint
boil									ɔi							boil
	i	ɪ	e	ɛ	ɜ	æ	ɑ	ai	ɔi	au	ɔ	ʌ	o	ʊ	u	

229

word	i	ɪ	e	ɛ	ɜ	æ	ɑ	ai	ɔi	au	ɔ	ʌ	o	ʊ	u	word
three	ɪⁱ														ᵾ˃ᵘ˂	two
grease	ɪⁱ														ʊᵘ	tooth
six		ɪˇ												ʊ		wood
crib		ɪ												ᵞ		pull
ear		ɪɚ												ʊ̠ɚ		yours
beard		ɪɚ											o˔ˆ			ago
eight			eɪ										əᵒʊ			coat
April			eˇɪ										oʊ			road
ten				ɛ									oʊ			home
egg				ɛɪ									oʊ			know
head				ɛ									oˇɚ			four
Mary				ɛɚr							ɔɚ					door
chair				ɛɚ							ɔ̰ɚ					hoarse
care				ɛɚ							ɔɚ					mourning
merry				ɛɚr												
thirty					ɚ							ʌ				sun
sermon					ɚ							---				brush
furrow					ɚr											
ashes						æɪ	ɑ									frost
bag						æ·ɪ					---					log
married				ɛ̰˃ɚ							ɔˇ					dog
half						---					ɑ̰˃					fog
glass						æ	ɑ									water
aunt						æ·	ɑ									daughter
father							ɑ				ɔ					law
palm							ɑ·				ɔɚ					warm
barn							ɑɚ									
garden							ɑˇɚ				ɔɚ					forty
crop							ɑ				ɔɚ					morning
on											ɔ·ɚ					corn
college							ɑ				ɔɚ					horse
borrow							ɑr									
five								a˃ɪ		ɑo						down
twice								aɪ		ɑo						out
wire								ɑ˂ɚ		ɑɚ						flower
joint									ɔʷɪˆ							joint
boil									ɔɪ							boil

| | i | ɪ | e | ɛ | ɜ | æ | ɑ | ai | ɔi | au | ɔ | ʌ | o | ʊ | u | |

Vowel headers (left to right): i ɪ e ɛ ɜ æ ɑ | aɪ ɔɪ au | ɔ ʌ o ʊ u

Word (left)	Transcription	Word (right)	Transcription
three	i̯ˇi̯	two	ʉu˂
grease	ɪⁱ	tooth	ʊu
six	ɪ	wood	ʊ
crib	ɪ	pull	ʊ
ear	ɪɚ	yours	ʊɚ
beard	ɪɚ	ago	oʊ
eight	ɛ˂ʌᵉ	coat	oʊ
April	eɪ	road	oᵁ
ten	ɛ	home	oᵁˇ˂
egg	ɛɪ	know	oʊ
head	ɛ	four	oˇɚ
Mary	ɛr	door	oˇɚ
chair	ɛˇɝ	hoarse	ɔɚ
care	ɛɚ	mourning	ɔ̥ɚ
merry	ɚr		
thirty	ɝ	sun	ʌ
sermon	ɝ	brush	ʌ
furrow	ʌˆr		
ashes	æ	frost	ɔᵁ
bag	æɪ	log	---
married	ɛɚr	dog	ɔoˆ
half	æ	fog	ɔ
glass	æ ɑ̈	water	
aunt	æ	daughter	ɔˇ
father	ɑ	law	ɔ˃
palm	ɑ	warm	ɔɚ
barn	ɑɚ		
garden	ɑɚ	forty	ɔɚ
crop	ɑ	morning	ɔ•ɚ
on	ɔ˂	corn	ọɚ
college	ɑ	horse	ɔɚ
borrow	ɔr		
five	aɪ ɑo	down	
twice	aɪˆ a˃o	out	
wire	aɪɚ ɑowɚ	flower	
joint	ɔʷiˇ		
boil	ɔɪ		

231

	i	ι	e	ε	ɜ	æ	ɑ	ai	ɔi	au	ɔ	ʌ	o	ʊ	u	
three	iˇ>i													ʊᵁ		two
grease	ιi													ʊu		tooth
six		ι												ʊ		wood
crib		ι												ʊ̲		pull
ear		ιɚ													ʊᵂɚ	yours
beard		ιɚ											oᵁ			ago
eight			eᵛe<^										oo^			coat
April			eι										oᵁ			road
ten				ε									oo^			home
egg				εˡ									oo^			know
head				εᵊ							ɔ^ɚ					four
Mary				εɚr							ɔɚ					door
chair				εɚ							ɔɚ					hoarse
care				ε^ɚ							ɔɚ					mourning
merry				εɚr												
thirty					ɚ							ʌ				sun
sermon					ɚ											brush
furrow					ɚr											
ashes						æˡ					ɔ					frost
bag						æˡ										log
married				ε̣>ɚ							ɔ̣·					dog
half						ææ^>					ɔ					fog
glass						æ	ɑ									water
aunt						æᵊ	ɑ·									daughter
father							ɑ				ɔ					law
palm							ɑɫ				ɔɚ					warm
barn							ɑ>ɚ									
garden							ɑɚ				ɔɚ					forty
crop							ɑ				ɔɚ					morning
on											ɔ< ɔɚ					corn
college							ɑ				ɔɚ					horse
borrow							ɑɚ									
five								ɑˡ		ɑo						down
twice								ɑ<i>		a>ɒ						out
wire								ɑɚ		ɑºɚ						flower
									ɔᵂι^							joint
									ɔi							boil

| | i | ι | e | ε | ɜ | æ | ɑ | ai | ɔi | au | ɔ | ʌ | o | ʊ | u | |

	i	ɪ	e	ɛ	ɜ	æ	ɑ	ai	ɔi	au	ɔ	ʌ	o	ʊ	u	
three	ɪi															two (ʊu)
grease	i															tooth (u)
six		ɪ														wood (ʊ)
crib		ɪ														pull (ʊ)
ear		ɪɚ												ʊɚ		yours
beard		ɪɚ											oᵁ			ago
eight			eɪ										oᵛᵁ			coat
April			eᵛɪ										oɤ			road
ten				ɛ									oʊ			home
egg				ɛᶺɪ						ɑˀᵁ						know
head				ɛ									oᵂɚ			four
Mary				ɛr							ɔɚ					door
chair				ɛɚ							ɔɚ					hoarse
care				ɛɚ							ɔɚ					mourning
merry				ɛɚ												
thirty					ɚ							ʌ				sun
sermon					ɚ							ʌ				brush
furrow					ɚˀr											
ashes						æ				ɑᵁ						frost
bag						æɪ					ɔ					log
married				ɛᵛr							ɔᵛ					dog
half						æ	ɑˀ									fog
glass						æ	ɑˀ									water
aunt						æ					ɔᵛ					daughter
father							ɑ·				ɔ					law
palm							ɑ				ɔˀɚ					warm
barn							ɑˀɚ									
garden							ɑr				ɔɚ					forty
crop							ɑˀ				ɔᵛr					morning
on											ɔɚ					corn (ɔɚ)
college							ɑ				ɔɚ					horse
borrow							ɒr									
five								ɑɪ		ɑu						down
twice								ɑˀɪ		ɑu						out
wire								ɑɪɚ		ɑˀʊɚ						flower
joint									ɒi							
boil									ɔɪə							
	i	ɪ	e	ɛ	ɜ	æ	ɑ	ai	ɔi	au	ɔ	ʌ	o	ʊ	u	

233

word	i	ι	e	ε	ɜ	æ	ɑ	ai	ɔi	au	ɔ	ʌ	o	ʊ	u	word
three	ι i													ʊᵤ		two
grease	i													ʊᵁ		tooth
six		ι												ʊ		wood
crib		ιˇ												ʊ		pull
ear		ιɚ												ʊr		yours
beard		ιɚ											oᵁ			ago
eight			ej										oᵁ			coat
April			eι										ou			road
ten				ε									ou			home
egg				εə									ou			know
head				---							ɔɚ					four
Mary				εr							ɔɚ					door
chair				εɚ							ɔʷɚ					hoarse
care				εɚ										ʊᵁɚ		mourning
merry				εɚ												
thirty					ɚ							ʌ				sun
sermon					ɚ							ʌə				brush
furrow					ɚr											
ashes						æə					ɔ					frost
bag						æ					ɔ					log
married				εˀr							ɔ					dog
half						æˀ					ɔ					fog
glass						æ					ɔ					water
aunt						æ					ɔ·					daughter
father							ɑ				ɔ					law
palm							aˀ				ɔɚ					warm
barn							ɑɚ									
garden							ɑɚ				ɔɚ					forty
crop							ɑ				ɔr					morning
on							ɔ				ɔɚ					corn
college							ɒ				ɔɚ					horse
borrow							ɑr									
five								ɑə		ɑu						down
twice								ɑι		ɑu						out
wire								aιɚ		ɑwɚ						flower
									ɔιˆ							joint
									ɔˇι							boil
	i	ι	e	ε	ɜ	æ	ɑ	ai	ɔi	au	ɔ	ʌ	o	ʊ	u	

	i	ɪ	e	ɛ	ɜ	æ	ɑ	ai	ɔi	au	ɔ	ʌ	o	ʊ	u	
three	i	ɪ														
two															ʊu	
grease	i															
tooth															ᵛu	
six		ɪ														
wood														ʊ		
crib		ɪ														
pull														ʊ		
ear		ɪɚ														
yours														ʊr		
beard		ɪˀɚ														
ago													---			
eight			ei													
coat													oᵛ			
April			ɛɪˆ													
road													o̞u			
ten				ɛᵊ												
home													ou			
egg				ɛ												
know													oᵛu			
head				ɛ												
four											ɔɚ					
Mary				ɛr												
door											ɔɚ					
chair						æˆɚ										
hoarse											ɔʷɚ					
care				ɛɚ												
mourning											ɔᵛɚ					
merry				ɛr												
thirty					ɚ							ʌ				
sun																
sermon					ɚ							ʌˁ				
brush																
furrow					ɚr											
ashes						æ·					ɑ̞ˀ					
frost																
bag						æ					ɔ					
log																
married				ɛɚr							ɔ					
dog																
half						æ					ɔᵛ					
fog																
glass						æ					ɔ					
water																
aunt							aˀ				ɔu					
daughter																
father							ɑ				ɔ					
law																
palm							ɑˁ·				ɔɚ					
warm																
barn							ɑɚ									
garden							ɑˁɚ				ɔɚ					
forty																
crop							ɑˀ				ɔᵛɚ					
morning																
on							ɑˀ				ɔˁᵛɚ					
corn																
college							ɑˀ				ɔɚ					
horse																
borrow							ɑr									
five								ɑɨ		ɑ·u						
down																
twice								ɑˁɪ		ɑu						
out																
wire								ɑɪr		ɑˁuɚ						
flower																
joint									ɑˁiᵛ							
boil									ɔɪ							

i	ɪ	e	ɛ	ɜ	æ	ɑ	ai	ɔi	au	ɔ	ʌ	o	ʊ	u

235

	i	ɪ	e	ɛ	ɜ	æ	ɑ		ai	ɔi	au		ɔ	ʌ	o	ʊ	u	
three	i˅ᶦ˲																u˅ᵁ˱	two
grease	ɪi																ʊu	tooth
six		ɪ														ʊ		wood
crib		ɪ˅														ʊə		pull
ear	ɪɚ															ʊɚ		yours
beard	ɪɚ												oᵒ˄					ago
eight			eɪ˄										əᵒᵁ					coat
April			eɪ										oᵒ˄					road
ten				ɛᵊ									oᵒ˄					home
egg			eᶦ										oᵁ					know
head				ɛ								ɔ˄ɚ						four
Mary				ɛɚr								ɔɚ						door
chair				ɛɚ											oɚ			hoarse
care				ɛɚ								ɔɚ						mourning
merry				ɛɚr														
thirty					ɜ̇									ʌ				sun
sermon				ɚ									ʌ˄					brush
furrow				ɚr														
ashes						æ˄ɪ						ɔ·						frost
bag						æ												log
married				ɛɚr								ɔ						dog
half						æ˄						ɔ						fog
glass						æ	ɑˀ					ɔ						water
aunt						æ						ɒˀ						daughter
father							ɑ					ɔ						law
palm							ɑ·ᵊ					ɔɚ						warm
barn							ɑɚ											
garden							ɑɚ					ɔɚ						forty
crop							ɑ					ɔɚ						morning
on												ɔ·ɔˀɔɚ						corn
college							ɑ					ɔɚ						horse
borrow							ɑr											
five								ɑɪ˄		ɑo								down
twice								ɑɪ˄		aˀo˄								out
wire								ɑᶦɚ		ɑᵁɚ								flower
joint									ɔʷi									joint
boil									ɔɪ									boil
	i	ɪ	e	ɛ	ɜ	æ	ɑ		ai	ɔi	au		ɔ	ʌ	o	ʊ	u	

	i	ɪ	e	ɛ	ɜ	æ	ɑ	ai	ɔi	au	ɔ	ʌ	o	ʊ	u	
three	i ᵛ i															two
grease	ɪ i															tooth
six		ɪ												ʊ		wood
crib		ɪ ᵛ												ʊ ʷ ə		pull
ear		ɪɚ												ʊɚ		yours
beard		ɪɚ											oᵁ			ago
eight			e ᵛ ᵉ										oᵉ			coat
April			eɪ								ʌ ^					road
ten				ɛ									oᶜ· ʊᵛ			home
egg				ɛ ɪ									oᵁ			know
head				ɛ									o oᶜ ^ ɚ			four
Mary				ɛɚr							ɔɚ					door
chair				ɛɚ							ɔɚ					hoarse
care				ɛɚ							ɔ ^ ɚ					mourning
merry				ɛɚ												
thirty					ɚ							ʌ				sun
sermon					ɚ							ʌ				brush
furrow					ɚr											
ashes						æ æ ^					ɑ ˃					frost
bag						æ æ ^					ɔ					log
married				ɛ ˃ r							ɔ oᵛ					dog
half						æ					ɔ					fog
glass						æ					ɔ					water
aunt						æ					ɔᶜ					daughter
father							ɑ				ɔ					law
palm							ɑ ɫ				ɔɚ					warm
barn							ɑɚ									
garden							ɑɚ				ɔɚ					forty
crop							ɑ				ɔᶜ ɚ					morning
on											ɔ ɔᶜ ᵛ ɚ					corn
college							ɑ				ɔ ᵛ ɚ					horse
borrow							ɑr									
five								a ˃ ɪ ᵛ ˃		ɑʊ						down
twice								a ɫ		ao ^						out
wire								ɑɚ		ɑɚ						flower
									ɔ ʷ i ᵛ							joint
									ɔɪ							boil
	i	ɪ	e	ɛ	ɜ	æ	ɑ	ai	ɔi	au	ɔ	ʌ	o	ʊ	u	

237

	i	ɪ	e	ɛ	ɜ	æ	ɑ	ai	ɔi	au	ɔ	ʌ	o	ʊ	u	
three	i̯>ǐ														uˇ	two
grease	ɪ<ˆi														u<u	tooth
six		ɪ												ʊ		wood
crib		ɪ												ʊ		pull
ear		ɪ>ɚ											o<ˆɚ			yours
beard		ɪ>ɚ											oʊ>			ago
eight			ɛ<ˆɪˇ>										ʌ<ˆo<ˆ			coat
April			e										oo<ˆ			road
ten				ɛ ɛ<ˆ									o<ˇʊ<ˇ			home
egg				ɛˆeˆ									oo<ˆ			know
head				ɛ									o·ɚ			four
Mary				ɛr									ɔ<ˆ·ɚ			door
chair				ɛ·ɚ							ɔɚ					hoarse
care				ɛɚ									ɔ<ˆ·ɚ			mourning
merry				ɛr												
thirty					ɚ							ʌ				sun
sermon					ɚ							ʌ				brush
furrow					ɚ											
ashes						æ					ɒˆ					frost
bag						æ					ɔ>ˇʊ					log
married						æ<ˆr					ɔ>ˇ·					dog
half						æ·					ɒ<ˆʊ					fog
glass						æ					ɔ>ˇ					water
aunt						æ̃ æ<ˆ					ɑ					daughter
father							ɑ				ɒ<ˆ					law
palm							ɑ				ɔ>ˇɚ					warm
barn							ɑ>ɚ									
garden							ɑ>ɚ				ɔ>ˇɚ					forty
crop							ɒ<				ɔ>ˇɚ					morning
on							ɑ				ɒ<ˆɚ					corn
college							ɑ				ɔɚ					horse
borrow											ɒr					
five								aɪ<ˆ		a>o<ˆ						down
twice								aˆɪ<ˆ		a>o<ˆ						out
wire								ɐ<ˇɪ̈ɚ		ɑ<ʊ						flower
joint									ɒ<ˆɪ>							joint
boil									ɒ<ˆɪˇ							boil
	i	ɪ	e	ɛ	ɜ	æ	ɑ	ai	ɔi	au	ɔ	ʌ	o	ʊ	u	

	i	ι	e	ɛ	ɜ	æ	ɑ		ai	ɔi	au		ɔ	ʌ	o	ʊ	u	
three	i˅ⁱ																u˅ᵘ	two
grease	ι ⁱ																ʊ u	tooth
six		ι˅														ʊ̲		wood
crib		ι														ʊ̲		pull
ear		ιɚ														ιʊɚ		yours
beard		ιɚ													oo^			ago
eight			e˅ι												oᵒ^			coat
April			ɛι												oᵒ^			road
ten				ɛ											oʊ			home
egg				ɛ											oʊ			know
head				ɛ											o·ɚ			four
Mary				ɛr											o˅ɚ			door
chair				ɛɚ											---			hoarse
care				ɛɚ											---			mourning
merry				ɛr														
thirty					ɚ									ʌ				sun
sermon					---									ʌ				brush
furrow					ɚr													
ashes						æ							ɔ̣					frost
bag						æˡ							ɔ					log
married						---							ɔᵉ					dog
half						æˡ							ɔ					fog
glass						æᵉ	ɑ˃											water
aunt						æᵉ							ɔ					daughter
father							ɑ						---					law
palm							ɑᵉ						ˈɔɚ					warm
barn							ɑɚ											
garden							ɑɚ						ɔɚ					forty
crop							ɑ						ɔɚ					morning
on													ɔ˅ɚ					corn
college							ɑɚ						ɔɚ					horse
borrow													ɔ˅r					
five									aι˃		ɑo							down
twice									a˄˅ι		a·ᵒ							out
wire									ɑɚ		ɑʷɚ							flower
joint										ɔʷι^								joint
boil										ɔᵉ								boil
	i	ι	e	ɛ	ɜ	æ	ɑ		ai	ɔi	au		ɔ	ʌ	o	ʊ	u	

word	i	ɪ	e	ɛ	ɜ	æ	ɑ	ai	ɔi	au	ɔ	ʌ	o	ʊ	u	word
three	ɪⁱ														ɪuˇ	two
grease	ɪi														ʊu	tooth
six		ɪ												ʊ		wood
crib		ɪ												ʊə		pull
ear	ɪɚ													ʊɚ		yours
beard	ɪɚ												oo^			ago
eight			eˇɪ										ʌ•o^			coat
April			ei										ʌ>o^			road
ten				ɛə									ʌ•o^			home
egg				ɛɪ									ou			know
head				ɛə							ɔɚ					four
Mary				ɛɚr							ɔ^wɚ					door
chair				ɛɚ							ɔɚ					hoarse
care				ɛɚ							ɔɚ					mourning
merry				ɛɚr												
thirty					ɚ							ʌ				sun
sermon					ɚ							ʌɪ				brush
furrow					ɚ^>r											
ashes						æ					ɔʊ					frost
bag						æ					---					log
married						ær	ɑ̮									dog
half						æ	ɑ									fog
glass						æɪ					ɔ					water
aunt						æ	ɑ̮>									daughter
father							ɑ				ɔ					law
palm							ɑ•ə				ɔˇɚ					warm
barn							ɑɚ									
garden							ɑɚ				ɔɚ					forty
crop							ɑ				ɔɚ					morning
on							ɑ•				ɔɚ|					corn
college							ɑ				ɔɚ					horse
borrow							ɑr									
five								ɑˇɪ^		ɑo						down
twice								ai		a>o^						out
wire								ajɚ		ɑɚ						flower
joint									ɔ^wi							joint
boil									ɔɪ^jə							boil

| | i | ɪ | e | ɛ | ɜ | æ | ɑ | ai | ɔi | au | ɔ | ʌ | o | ʊ | u | |

	i	ɪ	e	ɛ	ɜ	æ	ɑ	ai	ɔi	au	ɔ	ʌ	o	ʊ	u	
three	i															two: ʊu
grease	i															tooth: ʊu
six		ɪˇ												ʊ		wood
crib		ɪˇ												ʊˇ		pull
ear		ɪɚ												ʊɚ		yours
beard		ɪɚ											ou			ago
eight			ɛˇɪ										ou			coat
April			ɛɪ										ou			road
ten				ɛ									ou			home
egg			ɛɪ										oˇu			know
head			ɛɪ										---			four
Mary				ɛr							ɔɚ					door
chair				ɛɚ									oɚ			hoarse
care				ɛˇɚ									oᵁɚ			mourning
merry				ɛˀɚ												
thirty					ɜ̇							ʌ				sun
sermon					ɚ							ʌ ɫ				brush
furrow				ɚr												
ashes						æˆ					ɔ					frost
bag						æ					---					log
married				ɛɚ							ɔˀ·					dog
half						æˆ					ɔ·					fog
glass						æ					ɔˁ					water
aunt						æ	ɒˆ									daughter
father							ɑ·				---					law
palm							ɑ·ə				ɔˇɚ					warm
barn							ɑɚ									
garden							ɑɚ				ɔɚ					forty
crop							ɑ				ɔɚ					morning
on											ɔ̸ (on) ɔɚ (corn)					corn
college							ɑ				ɔɚ					horse
borrow							ɑˀr									
five								ɑˁɫ		ɑu						down
twice								aˀɪˀ		ɑˁu						out
wire								ɑˁɚ		ɑɤɚ						flower
joint									ɔʷi							
boil									ɔɪ							

| | i | ɪ | e | ɛ | ɜ | æ | ɑ | ai | ɔi | au | ɔ | ʌ | o | ʊ | u | |

	i	ɪ	e	ɛ	ɜ	æ	ɑ	ai	ɔi	au	ɔ	ʌ	o	ʊ	u	
three		ɪ ɪ^														two
grease	ɪi														ʊu	tooth
six		ɪˇ										ʌˆ>				wood
crib		ɪ												ʊᵁ		pull
ear		ɪɚ												ʊɚ		yours
beard		ɪɚ											oᵁ			ago
eight			eɪ^										oᵁ			coat
April			eɪ										oᵁ			road
ten				ɛ									oʊ			home
egg				ɛ									oᵁ			know
head				ɛə							ɔɚ					four
Mary				ɛɹ							ɔɚ					door
chair				ɛɚ							ɔˇwɚ					hoarse
care				ɛɚ							ɔˇɚ					mourning
merry				ɛɹ												
thirty					ɚ							ʌ				sun
sermon					ɚ							ʌ				brush
furrow					ɚr											
ashes						æ^					ɔˇwə					frost
bag						æ					---					log
married			ɛˇɹɹ								ɔˇ					dog
half						æˇ>					ɔ					fog
glass						æ					ɔ̲					water
aunt						æ̃					ɔ̲·					daughter
father							ɑ·				ɔ					law
palm							ɑə				ɔˇɚ					warm
barn							ɑɚ									
garden							ɑ>ɚ				ɔɚ>					forty
crop							ɑ>				ɔˆɚ					morning
on											ɔᵁɚ					corn
college							ɑ				ɔ<ɚ					horse
borrow							ɑ·r									
five								aɪ		ɑ<ʊ						down
twice								aɪ		ɑʊ^						out
wire								ɑ<jɚ		ɑˆʊɚ						flower
joint									ɔɪ							
boil									ɔˇɪ							
	i	ɪ	e	ɛ	ɜ	æ	ɑ	ai	ɔi	au	ɔ	ʌ	o	ʊ	u	

	i	ɪ	e	ɛ	ɜ	æ	ɑ	ai	ɔi	au	ɔ	ʌ	o	ʊ	u	
three	ɪˇ‡															two
grease	i·														ʊu	tooth
six		ɪˇ												ʊ̱		wood
crib		ɪˇ												ʊ		pull
ear	ɪjɚ													ʊɚ		yours
beard		ɪɚ											e·ʊ			ago
eight			eɪˆ										ou			coat
April			eɪ										ou			road
ten				ɛə									ou			home
egg				ɛɪ									---			know
head				ɛˇ·							ɔ(w)ɚ					four
Mary				ɛɚr							ɔɚ					door
chair				ɛˇɚ							ɔɚ					hoarse
care				ɛɚ										ʊɚ		mourning
merry				ɛr												
thirty					ɝ							ʌˇ				sun
sermon					ɝ							ʌˇ<				brush
furrow					ɚ>·r											
ashes						æˇ					ɔʊ					frost
bag						æˇ·					---					log
married				ɛɚ							ɔ·					dog
half						æˇ					ɔʊ					fog
glass						æ‡					ɔ					water
aunt						æˇ					ɒ<ˆ					daughter
father							ɑ>				ɔʊ					law
palm							ɑ>				ɔɚ					warm
barn							ɑ>ɚ>									
garden							ɑɚ				ɔɚ					forty
crop							ɑ>				ɔ̱ɚ					morning
on											ɔˇ ɔɚ					corn
college											ɔˇ ɔɚ					horse
borrow											ɔˇr					
five								a>‡ˇ		ɑʊ						down
twice								---		ɑʊ						out
wire								ɑ<ɪɚ		ɑ<ʊɚ						flower
									ɔ(w)ɪ							joint
									ɔ‡							boil
	i	ɪ	e	ɛ	ɜ	æ	ɑ	ai	ɔi	au	ɔ	ʌ	o	ʊ	u	

word	i	ɪ	e	ɛ	ɜ	æ	ɑ	ai	ɔi	au	ɔ	ʌ	o	ʊ	u	word
three	i̥														ʊᵘ	two
grease	ɪ i̥														ᵗu	tooth
six		ɪˇ									ə˃					wood
crib		ɪ˃												ʊ̠		pull
ear		ɪˇɚ												ʊɚ		yours
beard		ɪ˃ɚ											oᵁ			ago
eight			eɪ^										oʊ			coat
April			ɛɪ										oʊ			road
ten				ɛ˃									oʊ			home
egg				ɛˇ									o̠ʊ			know
head				ɛ							ɔ·ɚ					four
Mary				ɛˇr							ɔˇɚ					door
chair				ɛˇr							ɔɚ					hoarse
care				ɛɚ							ɔɚ					mourning
merry				ɛˇr												
thirty					ɚ											sun
sermon					ɚ							ʌˇ				brush
furrow					ɚr											
ashes						æ˃^	e˃									frost
bag						æ^					ɔ˃					log
married				ɛr							ɔ					dog
half						æˇ˃					ɔ̠·					fog
glass						æˇ	ɑ˃									water
aunt						æˇ					ɔˇ					daughter
father							ɑ˃				ɔ					law
palm							ɑ				ɔˇɚ					warm
barn							ɑ˃ɚ									
garden							ɑɚ				ɔɚ					forty
crop							ɑ				ɔɚ					morning
on											ɔˇ / ɔˇɚ					corn
college											ɒ / ɔˇɚ					horse
borrow											ɒr					
five								ɑɪ		ɑʊ						down
twice								a˃ɪ		ɑʊ						out
wire								ɑɚ^		ɑ˃ʊɚ						flower
joint									ɔɪ˃							
boil									ɔɪ							

| | i | ɪ | e | ɛ | ɜ | æ | ɑ | ai | ɔi | au | ɔ | ʌ | o | ʊ | u | |

244

	i	ɪ	e	ɛ	ɜ	æ	ɑ		ai	ɔi	au		ɔ	ʌ	o	ʊ	u	
three	i̥ˇi																u	two
grease	ɪˆiˇ																ʉˇ	tooth
six		ɪ														---		wood
crib		ɪ														ʊ		pull
ear		ɪˀɚ														ʊɚ		yours
beard		ɪˀɚ													ouˇ			ago
eight			eˇeˆ												oˇoˆ			coat
April			e												oˇo			road
ten				ɛ											ooˆ			home
egg				ɛeˇ											ooˆ			know
head				ɛɛˆ											oˇ·ɚ			four
Mary				ɛr											ɔˆɚ			door
chair				ɛɚ									ɚ·ɔ					hoarse
care				ɛɚ									ɔ·ɚ					mourning
merry				ɛr														
thirty					---									ʌ				sun
sermon					ɚ									---				brush
furrow					ɚ													
ashes						æ	ɑe											frost
bag						æɛˇ							ɒˆ·ʀ					log
married				ɛr									ɔˇ·					dog
half						æ							ɔ·					fog
glass						æˇ							ɒˀ					water
aunt						æɛ̃ˆ							ɒ					daughter
father							ɑ						---					law
palm							ɑ·						ɔɚ					warm
barn													ɔ·ɚ					
garden							ɑˀɚ						---					forty
crop							ɑ						ɔˇɚ					morning
on							ɒ·ɑ						ɔɚ					corn
college						---							ɔɚ					horse
borrow													ɒˀr					
five									aˆɪˆ		aˀoˆ							down
twice									---		aˀoˆ							out
wire									aˆɪˀɚ									flower
joint										ɒˆɪˆ								
boil										ɒˆɪ								

	i	ɪ	e	ɛ	ɜ	æ	ɑ		ai	ɔi	au		ɔ	ʌ	o	ʊ	u	

	i	ɪ	e	ɛ	ɜ	æ	ɑ	ai	ɔi	au	ɔ	ʌ	o	ʊ	u	
three	i̯ɪ̆>i															two (ʉ̆>u)
grease	i̯ɪ̆>i															tooth (u<)
six		ɪ													---	wood
crib		ɪ												ʊ		pull
ear		ɪɚ												ʊɚ		yours
beard		ɪ̦>ɚ											o<			ago
eight			eɪ^										o o<			coat
April			e										o o<			road
ten				ɛ									ou>			home
egg			eɪ									ʌ^>o<				know
head				ɛ ɛ^									o·ɚ			four
Mary				ɛ>r									ɔ<ɚ			door
chair				ɛɚ							ɔ>·ɚ					hoarse
care				ɛɚ									o>·ɚ			mourning
merry				ɛr												
thirty					ɚ							ʌ				sun
sermon					ɚ							ʌ				brush
furrow					ɚ											
ashes						æ					ɒ					frost
bag						æ·ɛ^					---					log
married				ɛ>r							ɒ<^·					dog
half						æ					ɒɤ					fog
glass						æ	ɑ>									water
aunt						æɛ̃					ɒ<					daughter
father							ɑ				ɔ>					law
palm							ɑ				ɔɚ					warm
barn							ɑɚ									
garden							ɑɚ				ɔɚ					forty
crop							ɑ									morning
on							ɒɤɑ				ɔɚ					corn
college							ɑ				ɔɚ					horse
borrow							ɑr									
five								aɪ^		a<o<						down
twice								a>ɪ^		a·o^						out
wire								a>ɪ<ɚ		ɑ<u>ɚ						flower
									ɒ<^ɪ^							joint
									ɒ<^ɪ							boil
	i	ɪ	e	ɛ	ɜ	æ	ɑ	ai	ɔi	au	ɔ	ʌ	o	ʊ	u	

CHAPTER 3

Variation in Particular Words: Vowels

In certain words idiosyncratic alternation occurs with social or geographical correlation. One contrast, between /goɪ/ and /guɪ/ for goal (71.1), is treated in Volume 1 because of a semantic distinction that for some users is attached to the phonetic distinction. Another, between diphthongal /au/ and monophthongal /ɔ/ or /u/ in drought or drouth (6.1), is treated in the preceding section on the free vowel diaphones.

Other contrasts found in the field records are considered below.

FREE VOWELS

/i/ and Variants

bleat   29.7. NE 195. PEAS 148.

Only one-sixth of the UM infs. respond

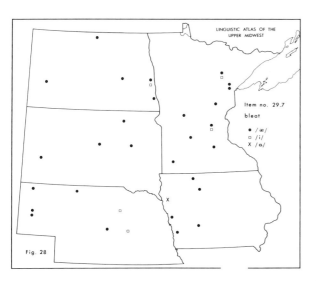

Fig. 28

with Northern bleat for the noise made by a hungry calf; the others have Midland bawl or beller. I straddle the fence over the question whether /blit/ and /blæt/ are two words or two pronunciations of one word, i.e., two morphemes or two allomorphs of one morpheme. In Volume 1 (q.v.) they are treated as distinct lexical forms; here they are treated as different pronunciations.

In the UM bleat has spread somewhat into Midland speech territory in southwestern Iowa and in western Nebraska. As in the East, the common form everywhere is /blæt/. Also as in the East, the variant /blit/ is peculiarly a book word or spelling pronunciation characteristic of speakers unfamiliar with farm life. Of the five UM infs. offering /blit/, four are women, one of whom ordinarily says "bawl"; the male inf. is an urban businessman.

A solitary western Iowa Type I farmer, of Illinois and Pennsylvania parentage, has the rare /ɑ/ in his [blɑ⁺ᶜt], a pronunciation reminiscent of the /blat/ found in parts of eastern New England.

Southern /blet/ does not occur in the UM.

/i/ 14, !33, ?42; 222; ¹404, ¹413, c420.
/ɑ/ 109.

Comment:
"Bleat is probably right, but we say blat"—401. "Sheep 'blat'; calves 'bawl'"—420.

depot   63.3. NE 544.

In the UM 189 infs. use railroad depot instead of or as well as station. (See Volume 1.) Well-nigh all of them have the pronunciation /dipo/, but two older variants survive, /depo/ and /dɛpo/. The former, with /e/, which NE records with 33 instances, chiefly in southern New England, appears in the speech of three infs.—one Minnesotan (3), one North Dakotan (218), and one Nebraskan (425). Two others (39; 117) report it as heard in their communities. The rarer pronunciation with /ɛ/, recorded in only five instances in New England, mostly in the eastern sector, is represented by a solitary UM inf., a Type I Minnesota housewife (65). No Type III inf. has either.

The field data, of course, do not provide evidence of the incidence of /ɛ/ among recent war veterans who brought it into civilian use from its occurrence in such expressions as military /dɛpo/ and naval /dɛpo/.

either, neither   54.5. NE 612. PEAS 149; F98.

Almost unanimous is the UM pronunciation of either and neither with the vowel /i/ of see. Midland /ʌ/ does not occur at all. The minor variant with /aɪ/, found in some eastern urban speech especially in New York City, is not characteristic of UM speech. Two Canadian infs. (c3; 201) offer /aɪðɚ/, but the second acknowledges that her use of this pronunciation is only "occasional." One St. Paul businessman admits that he has only recently adopted it. One Type II small-town Minnesota housewife says that she likes /aɪðɚ/ but would not use it. She and all other UM infs. regularly have /i/.

Negro   53.6. NE 452A. PEAS 149; F99, F100.

The recent wide replacement of Negro and its variants by the term Black makes evidence from mid-century surveys chiefly historical. The complex social and regional distribution of the two chief pronunciations of Negro, described by Kurath as found throughout the eastern part of the United States, is only weakly reflected in the UM, where no regional differences are obvious. Nearly all the infs. in the three types use the word Negro (see Volume 1 for lexical equivalents), some exclusively and others when deliberately trying not to give offense. Three-fourths of them have the pronunciation /nɪgro/, with the vowel of need. A contrasting variant with /ɪ/, the vowel of nit, appears in the speech of about one-sixth of the infs., but none in the cultivated group III. Three of these (16, 24; 311) have the form /nɪgrə/ and two (59; 116) have /nɪgru/; the others have /nɪgro/. About one-half of all infs., but only one-third of the Type III's, at least occasionally use also the pejora-

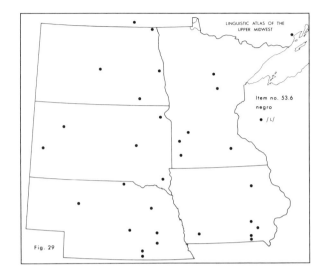

Fig. 29

LINGUISTIC ATLAS OF THE UPPER MIDWEST

Item no. 53.6
negro

• /ɪ/

tive term nigger, but some made the admission with obvious reluctance.

	Type I	Type II	Type III
/i/	72%	81%	94%
/ɪ/	15%	16%	0
[nɪgɚ]	55%	53%	37%

	Mn.	Ia.	N.D.	S.D.	Nb.	Ave.
/i/	75%	80%	80%	70%	73%	77%
/ɪ/	13%	14%	15%	15%	19%	14%
[nɪgɚ]	45%	40%	50%	70%	62%	52%

/i/ 1-2, 4-11, 14, 17-18, 20-23, 25-26, 28-34, 36-41, *43, 44-45, 47-48, 51-58, 60-65; 102-33, 137-38, 140-41, 143-45, 150, 152; 201, 203-6, 208-13, c214, 215, 217-19, 221-23, 225-26; 301, 304-5, 309, 311-20, c321, 322, 325-26, 328; 401-4, 406, 408-11, 413-14, 416, 418-20, 422, 425-31, 434-35, 437.
/ɪ/ 3, 12, c16, c21, 24, 42, 49, 59; 101, c116, 134, 136, 139, 142, 146-47; c202, 207, 224; 302, 308, c311, 324; 405, 415, 421, 424, 433, 436.
[nɪgɚ] 1-2, ¹3, ¹5, 6-8, ¹10, 13-15, 18, *19, ¹20, 23, 26-27, 29-30, c31, 37-39, †45, 46-47, c50-51, 52, !53, 55, 57, ¹58, 60-64; 101-5, 107-8, c109, ¹110-11, 112, 114-15, 123, 125, 128-29, 131-33, †135, 136, 138, 145, 148-49, ¹150, 152; c201-2, 203, c204, ¹208, 210, 213, !215, c216, 217-18, c220, ¹222, 225, ¹226; 301-10, 314, ¹315, 317-20, c321-23, †325, 328; 401, 403-5, c407, 408, 413, 415-17, s418, 419-22, ¹423, 424-27, 430, ¹431, 432-35, 437.

/e/ *and Variants*

tomato   43.3. NE 266. PEAS 151; F106.

Nearly all UM infs. agree upon the pro-

nunciation of tomato with the vowel /e/
of mate. Two competing eastern variants,
/æ/ and /ɑ/, get short shrift in the UM.
The Northern folk variant with /æ/ is
alive only in the speech of Minnesota
inf. 29, of New York parentage, although
one Canadian inf., 202, recalls having
heard it. Two Canadian infs., 3 and 201,
report that the other variant, /ɑ/, is
frequent in their communities, and one
Minnesotan, 57, and a South Dakotan, 308,
consider this pronunciation both old-
fashioned and amusing. A solitary occurrence of /ɛ/, not recorded elsewhere, is
probably here to be taken as an instance
of /e/ in rapid speech.

vase 14.7.

Not investigated in New England but
added to the Middle and South Atlantic
surveys, the word vase provides a study
in social attitudes toward pronunciations. Nearly all UM speakers have an /e/
vowel to rhyme the word with place. Canadian infs., however, typically have an
/ɑ/ vowel to rhyme it with ma's. Only one
American inf. regularly has this pronunciation, an elderly Iowa Type III speaker
with New York and Massachusetts parents.
A number of others admit to having once
discarded /vɑz/; some, aware of its continued use by others, with difficulty re-
strained their hilarious ridicule when
the question was asked during the interview. One Canadian, incidentally, was
equally amused by American /ves/. One
South Dakotan laughingly admitted saying
[vɒs] as well as her usual /ves/.

Apparently the past incidence of /vɑz/
was Northern-oriented, as only two of the
references or uses occur in Midland territory—in western Iowa.

/ves/ 3-15, 17-34, c35, 36-41, !42, 43-
58, :59, 60-65; 101-14, vr115, 116-30,
vr131, 132-34, 136-52; !¹202, 203-19,
221-26; 301-7, c308, 309-10, :311, 312-
28; 401-10, 412-25, !426, 427-31, sn432,
433-37.
/vɑz/ 1-2, ¹3, !¹26, !28, ¹31, ¹33,
!†37, ¹39, !44, !→46, !55, !¹61-62; 122,
!127; 201-2.
[vɒs] !308.

Comment:
/vɑz/ "A highfalutin pronunciation"—28.
"If it's a real nice one, it's a /vɑz/,
but I never heard that when I was young"—
46. "It's used to show off a bit"—55. "If
it costs over $5, it's a /vɑz/"—61. Inf.
strongly disclaims use—62. "If it costs
over $10"—122.
/vɒs/ "Highfalutin"—308.

/u/ and Variants

broom 9.2. NE 155. PEAS 152; F107.

Most UM infs. have a recognizable high
tense /u/, the vowel of tooth, in the
word broom. It is generally transcribed
by fws. as [uᵛu], [uᵛu], [u], [ʉu], or
[uᵛ]. A scattered one-sixth of the infs.
(see map) have a recognizable high lax
/ʊ/, the vowel of pull, in broom. This
second pronunciation is somewhat more
likely among the less educated: 19% of
·Type I, 6% of Type II, and 1% of Type
III; and it is found in those parts of
the UM settled before 1900. This distribution does not reflect its eastern occurrence, which PEAS describes as limited
to New England, eastern Virginia, and
southern Maryland.

But a clear picture of the distribution
of /brum/ and /brʊm/ does not readily
emerge from the data. Unlike the vowels
in tooth and pull, those in broom range
along a continuum without sharp contrast
along the range. Many infs. have a vowel
impressionistically midway between /ʊ/
and /u/, typically beginning in the /ʊ/
position and ending with a more or less
perceptible upglide of varying length.
Fieldworkers differ in their interpretation of the length and strength of the
glide. Fieldworker A typically records
[ʊᵛu], [ʊᶜuᵛ], [ʊuᵛ]; fw. H has [ʊᵛu];
fw. P has [ʉu]; fw. Wr has [ʊu]. A vowel
with an offglide transcribed as [u] is
not included in the preceding statistics
for the incidence of /ʊ/; indeed, without
detailed analysis of the individual
inf.'s phonemic system in comparison with
fw. practice it seems unwise to offer
here an arbitrary assignment of these intermediate vowels to either /u/ or /ʊ/
for this particular word.

A similar word, room, with a recognizable [ʊ] having a greater incidence in
the UM, presents a similar problem, but
one aggravated by two factors. One is
that it is likely to be phonetically affected by its regularly occurring under
secondary or even tertiary stress, as in
bedroom, front room, and living room, a
circumstance making for considerable variation. Another factor is that when an
inf. offers two or more of these com-
pounds he may have varying pronunciations
of room. The mechanical application of a
transcribed /u/-/ʊ/ contrast in either
the tonic vowel or the offglide can result in the conclusion that the inf. un-
consciously shifts back and forth from
one phoneme to another. Examples of such
ambiguous situations are provided by
infs. as follows: 63 [uᵛu], c[ʊ]; 115

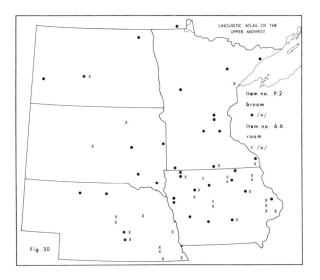

Fig. 30

	Type I	Type II	Type III
/u/	70%	72%	75%
/ʊ/	30%	28%	25%

	Mn.	Ia.	N.D.	S.D.	Nb.	Ave.
/u/	74%	59%	73%	83%	72%	72%
/ʊ/	26%	41%	27%	17%	18%	28%

/ʊ/ 8, 11-12, 15, c16, 19, 22, 29-30, 34, c35, 42-43, 54, 56, 64; 101-3, 105-6, 109-15, 121, 124, 126-27, 139, 144-45; 201, 206, 213, 216, 219-20, 226; 303, 320, 322, 327; 401, 404, 409, 411, 413, 416, 419, 425, 427, 435.
/u/ All others, excluding 118, 151-52, and 430, from whom no response is available.

coop 30.4. NE 112. PEAS 153; F108.

As a recorded lexical item coop competes with several other terms. (See Volume 1.) The two vowel types of coop, /u/ and /ʊ/, sharply contrast in the eastern states, where /u/ dominates the North and North Midland and /ʊ/ the South and South Midland. The southern Pennsylvania border is almost an isogloss separating the two.

Predictably, /ʊ/ has scarcely penetrated the UM. Of the six scattered instances all but one are from infs. with at least one parent as the likely source of that pronunciation. On the whole, /u/ is obviously dominant. It is transcribed variously by fws.: [ʊ], [ʊ·], [ʊˇ], [ʊˢᵘ], [ʊu], [ʊw], [ʊˤuˤ], [ɵu]. Three infs. are recorded by Wr with [ʊ·ᵘ]; perhaps they should be counted as speakers with /ʊ/ rather than /u/: 416, 420, 430.

/ʊ/ 6, 18; 108, 121, vr131; 311.
/u/ 1-2, 5, 7, 9, 11-17, 19-21, 23-24, 26-30, c31, 33-36, c39, 40-41, 43-44, 49-51, 56-58, 64-65; 103-7, 111-12, 114, vr115, 116, 118-21, 123-24, 132-33, 137, 139, 144-45, 150-52; c203, 204, 206, 208-10, 212-13, 216-21, 223, 225-26; 302, 304-7, 310, 312-15, 319-26; 401-2, 404-5, 407-9, 412, 414, c415, 416-20, 430, 433, 435-36.

Cooper 52.5. NE 436. PEAS 153; F109.

Some infs. offer Mrs. with a family name other than Cooper, the one sought. Of those replying with Cooper the great majority have the /u/ of tooth. Only 21, about one in 10, have the /ʊ/ of pull; all of these except one are in Midland and South Midland speech territory (see map), and that one, in Minnesota, has an Alabama father. This distribution accords with that in the East, where, as with coop, /u/ is distinctly Northern and North Midland and /ʊ/ is Southern and South Midland, except that /ʊ/ occurs

[ʊuˇ], [ʊˇu]; 118 [uˇu], [ʊˇu]; 203 [ʊˇu], [ʊˤᵘ]; 303 c[uˇu], [ʊᴧᵘ]; 405 [uˤᵘ], [ʊˤᵘ]; 421 [ʊ], [ʊu]; 425 [ʊ], [u]. As McDavid hinted in his remarks about room in PEAS, such a conclusion is clearly unacceptable. As with broom, there must be a single underlying vowel for each inf., but fw. variation and the need for a prior full phonemic analysis of the speaker block here the determination of that vowel for a given speaker and hence block also an acceptable detailed description of the regional distribution pattern.

At least 11 infs. have a recognizable /ʊ/ in both broom and room: 63; 101, 105, 110-12, 116, 121, 132; 421-22.

/ʊ/ in broom: 1, 6, 13, 19, 29-30, 35, 43, 58, 61, 63; 101-2, 105, 110-12, 116, 121, 127, 132; 206, 214; *316, 317, 322, 325; 404, 406, 421-22.
/ʊ/ in room: 18, 48, 57, 63; 101, 103, 105-8, 110-16, 119-21, 132, 139; 217; 305, 315; 407, 413-15, 421-22, 425-26, 428, 433, 435.

rheumatism 60.3. NE 506.

As in New England, the pronunciation of rheumatism with the lax /ʊ/ of bull is a scattered minority variant in the UM, contrasting with the more common tense /u/ of boom. About one-fourth of all infs. have /ʊ/, with no significant social or regional differentiation except for a slightly higher incidence in Iowa. That two of the four Type III users are also in Iowa may suggest that in general this pronunciation is less acceptable to the educated group.

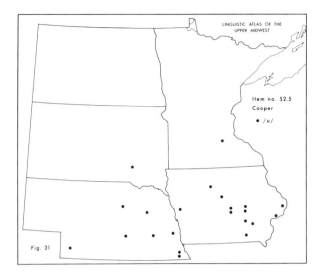

also in the urban concentration from southwestern Connecticut to Philadelphia.

/ʊ/ 35; 113, 115, 122, 128-29, 132-35, 139, 146; ⊥†312; 414, 416, 422, 425, 428-29, 434-35.

/u/ 1-3, 5-10, 15, c17, 18-20, 22, 26-34, 36-37, 39-42, *43, 44-46, c47, 48, 50-55, c56, 57-65; 101-12, 114, vr115, 116-27, 130, vr131, 136-38, 140, 142-45; 201-23, 225-26; 301-21, 323-28; 401-13, 417-21, 423, r424, 426, 430-33, 436-37.

/o/ 41.

hoop 17.1. NE 147. PEAS 153-54; F110.

The majority frequency of /u/ in hoop as reported by McDavid in central and western Massachusetts and Pennsylvania is not completely correlated with its distribution in the UM. All the Canadian

infs. have this pronunciation rhyming with soup as do nearly one-half of those in Minnesota and two-thirds of those in North Dakota, but the Pennsylvania Midland influence in Iowa yields less than a 1:3 ratio there.

An interesting discovery is that where /u/ and /ʊ/ compete the former seems to find slightly greater favor among the better educated. Two infs., indeed, 131 and 230, during the interview admitted saying /hʊp/ but wanted to correct it to /hup/, as more "proper" in their estimation.

	Type I	Type II	Type III
/u/	31%	44%	50%
/ʊ/	71%	56%	50%

	Mn.	Ia.	N.D.	S.D.	Nb.	Ave.
/u/	48%	27%	69%	39%	9%	37%
/ʊ/	52%	73%	31%	61%	91%	63%

/u/ 1-5, c7, 8-10, 12-14, 17-19, 25-26, c33, 36, 41, 43-44, 50, c52, 53-54, 56, 60, 63-64; 106, 112, vr113, 121-22, 124, 126, 129, vr.cr131, 133-34, 138, 140, 149; 201-8, cvr.cr209, 211, c212, 213, 215, c216, c221, 223, 226; 304-5, 309-10, 312-13, 318-19, 326-28; c406, 410, 421.

/ʌ/ 141; *316.

/ʊ/ All others except the following nonrespondents: 22; 110; 415, 431, 433, 437.

roof 10.2. NE 348. PEAS 154; F111.

In the eastern states the /ʊ/ vowel of good is common in roof in New England and upper New York State, around Delaware Bay, and in northern West Virginia. Elsewhere the competing /u/ of moon is more frequent, almost exclusively so in the metropolitan New York area, Pennsylvania,

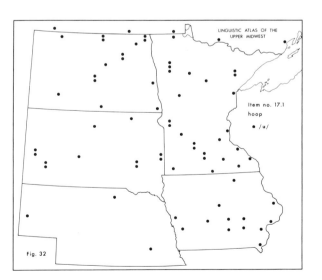

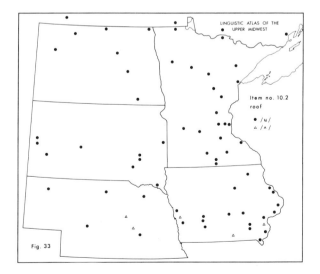

and the states south of Pennsylvania.

In the UM /ruf/ is also dominant as the choice of two-thirds of all infs., with its lowest incidence in Iowa. The form with the vowel /u/ of food is conversely most frequent in Iowa, with its low point in Nebraska. Although in PEAS McDavid reports that eastern urban educated speakers seem to consider /ruf/ more prestigious, no marked social contrast appears in the UM except that a very slight and probably insignificant preponderance of Type II and Type III speakers apparently favor /ruf/. Four uncertain speakers waver between the two pronunciations: 29, 36, 40; 211.

A northern New England and eastern Maryland nonstandard relic pronunciation, /rʌf/ rhyming with stuff, is barely preserved in Iowa and Nebraska.

	Type I	Type II	Type III
/u/	38%	27%	25%
/ʊ/	62%	72%	75%

	Mn.	Ia.	N.D.	S.D.	Nb.	Ave.
/u/	37%	53%	35%	32%	14%	47%
/ʊ/	68%	56%	70%	75%	81%	68%

/u/ 1-4, c5, 8, 10, 12, 14, 18, 21-23, c29, 32, c36, →40, 41, 45, 50, 53-54, 62-63; 107, 118-20, 122, 124, 126-27, 129, 133, 135-37, 139-40, 148, 150-51; 201, 203-4, 207, 210-11, 218, c224; 309-10, c312, 313, 317, c322, 325, 327-28; c401, 406-7, 418, 424.

/ʊ/ 6, c7, 9, 11, 13, 15-16, c17, 19, c20, ↓23, 24-28, c29, 30-31, 33-34, c35, 36-39, †40, 42, c43, 44, c46-48, 49, 51-52, 55-58, c59, 60-62, 64-65; 101-6, 108-17, 121, 123, 128, 130-32, 134, 138, 142-43, 147, 149, 152; 202, 205-6, 208-9, 211, c212, 214-17, 219, c220, 221-23, 225-26; 301-8, 311, c314-15, *316, 318-20, !321, 323-24, 326; 402, c403, 404, cvr405, 408-12, 415-17, 419, 421, c422-23, 425-27, c428-29, cvr430, 431-32, c433, 434, c435, 436-37.

/ʌ/ 125, 141, 146; 413, 420.

hoofs 28.4. PEAS 154; F112.

Although the plural hoofs or hooves has the same contrasting vowels as does roof, its incidence of /u/, which dominates the South Midland and South, is much lower in the North Midland and North than that of roof. Similar proportional contrast is revealed in the UM records, which show only one inf. in five using /u/, with the lowest frequency in the southwest sector, i.e., in South Dakota and Nebraska. No social contrast appears.

At least three infs. (18, 40; 131) use both vowels; and six more are recorded as having the lax /ʊ/ in the singular form

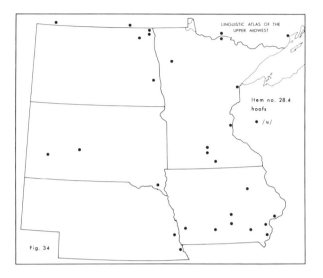

of the word but /u/ in the plural. They are 17, 62; 424, 426, 428, 434.

	Type I	Type II	Type III
/u/	15%	15%	25%
/ʊ/	88%	89%	88%

	Mn.	Ia.	N.D.	S.D.	Nb.	Ave.
/u/	15%	17%	27%	11%	8%	15%
/ʊ/	91%	85%	73%	89%	100%	86%

/u/ 2-3, c5, 8, 17-18, 40, 52-53, 62; 116, 125, 129, 131, 136-37, 141, 148, 151; 201-2, 206-8, 221-22; 312-13, 325; 424, 426, 428, 434.

/ʊ/ All others except one nonrespondent, 327.

root 47.7. NE 248. PEAS 155; F113.

In root the lax vowel /ʊ/, as in good, has major eastern distribution only in northern and western New England and upstate New York; elsewhere the tense /u/ of tooth predominates. This somewhat limited source area is not, however, matched by a corresponding limitation in the UM, where the /rut/ pronunciation has spread widely. It dominates not only the Northern speech area in Minnesota, North Dakota, and northern Iowa, but also southern Iowa and South Dakota and, by a slight majority, even Midland-speaking Nebraska. Nor is this wave of acceptance restricted to the less educated, for /rut/ is equally favored by Type I and Type II speakers and actually by all but two infs. in the college group.

The form /rut/ is the only one offered by the Canadian infs., and, expectedly, it is otherwise most frequent in southern Iowa and Nebraska.

Although an ingliding diphthong [ʊə] or [ʊ+] is a minor variant of root in New

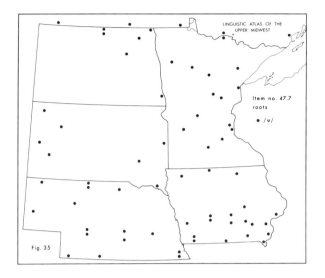

Fig. 35

England, where it is more frequent in the eastern half, such a diphthong in root is found in the UM only in Midland speech territory, where it often appears also in such words as coop, hoof, and roof. Infs. with this inglide are 104, 109-10, 113-14, 118; *316; 413-14, 423, 430.

	Type I	Type II	Type III
/u/	33%	35%	13%
/ʊ/	67%	66%	87%

	Mn.	Ia.	N.D.	S.D.	Nb.	Ave.
/u/	25%	33%	31%	39%	47%	32%
/ʊ/	75%	67%	69%	61%	54%	68%

/u/ c1, 2-3, 5, 8, c10, 12, c14, 18, 23, 28, ?34, 36, 40-41, 52; 102-3, 106, 124, 126-27, 129, 132, 134-35, 138, 140, 142-43, 145-46, 148, ?150; 201-2, c204, 205-7, 213, 225; 301-2, 309, 312, 317, 325, 328; 401, 403-4, 406, 411-12, 418-19, 421-22, 424, 431, 434-35, 437.

/ʊ/ 4, 6, c7, 9, 11, 13, 15-16, c17, 19-22, 24-27, 29-31, c32, 33, cr34, c35, 37-39, ⊥†40, 42-50, c51, 53-58, c59, 60, c61, 62-65; 101, 104-5, 107-23, 125, 128, 130-31, 133, 136-37, 139, 141, 144, *146, 147, 149, cr150, 152; 203, 208-11, cr212, 214-19, c220, 221-24, 226; 303-8, 310-11, 313-15, 318-24, 326-27; 402, 405, 407-10, 413, 415-17, 420, 423, 425-30, 432-33, 436.

/ʌ/ ?212; *316; †401, cvr414.

no response 151.

soot 7.5. NE 355. PEAS 155; F114, F115.

Three pronunciations of soot, rhyming with boot, foot, and mutt, occur in the eastern states in a rather complex social and geographical network. Of these three, the second, with lax /ʊ/, is clearly the most prevalent in the North in general as

well as in much of Pennsylvania. The first variant, /sut/, is widely scattered in the area, where at least for some speakers it seems to have an aura of prestige. The pronunciation with /ʌ/, on the contrary, though more frequent than /u/, is typically a folk form in the North. But in the South Midland and South /sʌt/ is a cherished pronunciation, even found by McDavid to be the choice of some cultivated speakers in South Carolina.

In the UM soot with tense /u/ seems to be old-fashioned and declining, perhaps kept alive because of a school tendency favoring spelling pronunciation. Only two Type III speakers have it, both in Minnesota, where expectedly most of the instances occur.

The form /sʊt/ is the majority form throughout the UM, with an even spread of two to one and with a distinctly higher level of social acceptability than /sut/ enjoys.

The third form, /sʌt/, is not chosen at all by cultivated speakers. It has a fairly obvious Midland speech orientation, although scattered instances occur elsewhere, even in Canada. Its strength among its users is perhaps attested by this incident. When inf. 322 replied "/sʊt/" to the fw.'s query, his wife correctively shouted from the kitchen, "It's /sʌt/!"

Allophones of /ʌ/ and /ʊ/ with a centering offglide [ə] or [+] occur with infs. 59, 61; 109, 112-13, 115, 118, 151; 324-25; 410, 413, 416, 424-26, 430, 435.

	Type I	Type II	Type III
/u/	18%	8%	13%
/ʊ/	51%	73%	88%
/ʌ/	34%	18%	0

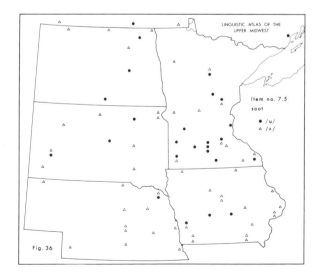

Fig. 36

	Mn.	Ia.	N.D.	S.D.	Nb.	Ave.
/u/	25%	8%	12%	14%	3%	13%
/ʊ/	63%	65%	70%	68%	68%	65%
/ʌ/	17%	32%	19%	25%	34%	20%

/u/ 3, 12, c22, 23, 34, 40-41, 44, 46, 51-53, 58-59, 62; 124, 126, 129; 202, 206, 218, c223; cr306, 312, 314; 408.

/ʊ/ 2, 4-7, 10, 14-22, ⚹†23, 26, 28-33, 38-40, 42-43, 45, †46, 47, 49-50, 54, c55, 57, 60-61, 63, 65; 102-4, 106-10, 112, 116-18, 120-23, 127-28, 130, vr131, 133, 136-38, 142-45, 148-52; 205-6, 208-11, 213-14, !215, 216-17, 219-22, 224-25; 301, 304-5, ?306, 308-10, 313, 315, 317-26; 402, c403, 404, 406, 409-12, 416, !417, 418-19, 422, 424-26, 428, 430-33, 435-37.

/ʌ/ cr1, 8, 11, 24, c25, 27, 35, 48, 56, 60, 64; c101, 105, 113-14, vr115, 119, 125, 132, 135, 139-40, cr141, 142-43, 146-47; !201, 203-4, 207, 212; 302-3, 307-8, 311, *316, 320, *322; 401, 405, 407, 414-15, 420-21, 423-24, c427, 429, 434.

[ɔə] 413.

no response 13; 134; 423, 432.

Comment:
Inf. doesn't know which is right—40, 60. "I used to say /sʊt/, but that's a provincialism"—46.

spook 67.1. NE 533. PEAS 156-57; F119.

The pronunciation of spook with the /u/ vowel of tooth is well-nigh universal both in the eastern states and in the UM. A regional Pennsylvania and West Virginia variant with lax /ʊ/, rhyming with cook, is attributed in PEAS to Pennsylvania German influence, but that cannot be the immediate source of the four UM instances found in Minnesota. The UM influences are probably directly the speech of the Scandinavian parents of inf. 17 and the German-born parents of infs. 30, 48, and 51.

wound 59.3. NE 514. PEAS 156; F117.

As in all the eastern regions except New England, wound and wounded universally have the vowel /u/ of tooth in the UM. Diphthongal /au/ as in sound, which is common in New England and rarely sporadic in New York and Pennsylvania, is preserved by nine scattered UM infs.—9, 45; 105, 116; 212, 218, 225; 314; 434—six of whom have at least one parent born in New York, Pennsylvania, or Ohio. Most are Type I speakers, but one, an inf. whose parents came from Quebec, is a physician. Inf. 137 reports /waund/ as heard in his community.

Much rarer in the UM is wound with the vowel of bull, /ʊ/, a pronunciation McDavid found in isolated instances in upper New York State and traced to two dialect areas in England. Two of the three UM users have a British background. The three are 19, 44; 220.

ewe 28.6. NE 201. PEAS 157; F120, F121.

Nearly all UM infs. offering this item have the common Northern and North Midland /ju/ pronunciation, transcribed usually as [ju], [jɪu], [jˡu], and [jɵu], that is, as a consonantal glide followed by [u] or by a rising diphthong with the stress upon [u]. The old-fashioned New England falling diphthong, with the stress upon the first element, [i], may survive in the UM, but the backgrounds of the infs. recorded as using it do not hint at a New England influence.

The rural pronunciation /jo/, less frequent in the North than in the Midland and South, is a minor variant in the UM, word, for 17 infs., mostly farmers, along the Canadian border and in the Midland speech territory of Iowa and Nebraska.

An unexplained [ju+n] is in the speech of a Minneapolis Type I inf., a Black with southern ancestry.

/jo/ 1, *5, 30; 107, 112, 135, 138, *145; 201, cr202, 206-8; 317, 322; 404, 434.

/jˡiu/ 4; 111, 114-15, 133.

/ˡiu/ 18; 318; *432.

/ju+n/ 35.

/ju/ All others except the following, who have no name for a female sheep: 9, 13, 15-16, 19, 25, 27, 36, 38, 41; 110, 134; 209; 308, 327; 415, 430, 433.

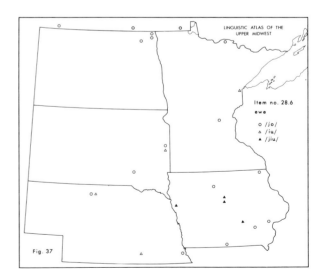

Fig. 37

Comment:
"The Norwegians here say /jujə/"—62.

/o/ and Variants

goal   71.7. NE 585. PEAS 157; F122.

The UM distribution of the two contrasting pronunciations of the children's
game term goal, with /o/ rhyming with
pole and /u/ rhyming with pool, closely
reflects that in the eastern states. The
former dominates the Midland and South
and is the cultivated form in New England
and upper New York State. But /gul/ is
common with all other speakers in New
England and is quite frequent among
lower- and middle-class speakers in upper
New York and northern Pennsylvania.

Although eight out of 10 UM infs. likewise have /gol/, many in Northern speech
territory, Minnesota and North Dakota,
use /gul/. Some speakers shift back and
forth between the two pronunciations,
treating /gul/ as an older child-used
form and /gol/ as a later acquisition. A
few of these admit not knowing "which is
correct." Others differentiate between
/gul/ in children's games and /gol/ in
football and other sports, apparently
considering them different and unrelated
words. A unique semantic distinction is
that of a Minnesota housewife whose parents came from Pennsylvania and England.
The conflict between her parents' usage
and that of her peers may have led her as
a child to construct her private semantic
paradigm, that /gul/ stands for the place
where one hides and that /gol/ stands for
the place to get to, the "home" or
"base."

Although several infs. in the college
group have /gul/ as an alternate childhood pronunciation, this form is more
likely to be the customary usage of the
less educated, in a 2:1 ratio.

	Type I	Type II	Type III
/u/	32%	18%	38%
/o/	71%	95%	84%

	Mn.	Ia.	N.D.	S.D.	Nb.	Ave.
/u/	42%	5%	54%	20%	0	26%
/o/	72%	95%	69%	80%	100%	83%

/u/ 4, 15-16, 21, †22, 23, ¹26, :27,
29, 31-32, †33-34, 35-36, †37, 39, ¹40,
¹42-43, sn44, 48, 50, †54, s†57, 58-60,
62, !63; †101, c†103, 117; 201, sn†203,
:204, †205, 206, †207-8, 210, 212, †215,
220, cr221, †222, 225; 303, 306, ¹308,
316-17; ¹433.
/o/ 1-3, 5-14, 17-20, 22, 24-26, 28,
30, 33, c34, 37-38, 40-47, 49, 51-53,
→54, 55-56, →57, 58, 61-62, 64-65; 101-

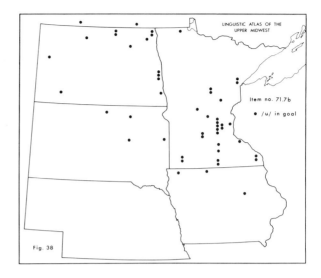

LINGUISTIC ATLAS OF THE
UPPER MIDWEST

Item no. 71.7b

• /u/ in goal

Fig. 38

16, 119-31, 133-38, 140-43, 145-49; 202-
3, →207-8, 209, 211, 213-19, 221, 223-24,
cr225, 226; 302, 304-5, 307-9, 311-12,
→313, 314-15, 318-19, sn320, s322, 323-
25, 327-28; 402-3, sn404, 412-14, 416,
420-28, 430-31, *432, 433-35.

Comment:
"/gul/ is in hide-and-go-seek"—22.
"/gul/ is the place to hide and /gol/ is
the place to get to"—39. "I think it was
/gul/ when I was young"—54, 57. As a
child inf. played a game in which an im-
aginary prison was a /gul/ or /gulǐ/—101.
"'Prison /gul/' was a children's game"—
103.

loam   24.1. NE 33. PEAS 158; F24.

As in the East, both geographical and
social contrast marks the distribution of
the pronunciations of loam in the UM.
The dominant eastern pronunciation is
/lom/, rhyming with dome. In northeastern
New England, however, there is a minor
variant with the lax vowel /ʊ/ of put.
Elsewhere in New England and in the North
and North Midland in general there is a
third variant with tense /u/, rhyming
with boom. This last is most common among
the rural least educated speakers, less
frequent within the middle group, and absent from the speech of the highly educated.
No instances of /lʊm/ appear at all in
the UM records, but /lum/ has persisted
with some strength. Predictably, it has
clear Northern orientation, nearly three-
fourths of the occurrences being in
Northern speech territory, especially
Minnesota and North Dakota. It also remains clearly nonstandard, in that 33 of
the 40 users are in Type I, only seven in

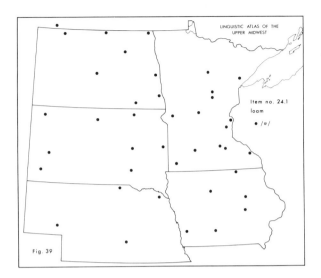

Type II, and none in Type III. The general pronunciation /lom/, however, dominates all five states.

/u/ 11, 15, 21-22, 25, 27, c35, 36, 39, 44, 48, 56, c60; 105, 113, 117, 125, 132, 151; 201, 203-4, 207, 212, 216, 220, 224-25; 301, 304-5, 311, 316-17, 320, 322; 405, 407, *417, 422.

/o/ All others (plus infs. 39 and 44, who have both pronunciations) except these nonrespondents: 42, 64; 103, 107, 121, 134, 138-39; 209, 211, 218; 303, 307, 313, 327; 415, 417, 432.

poached   37.3. NE 295.

The common pronunciation of poached in the East and in the UM is /počt/. Two rare variants survive in the UM, and two unusual variants appear.

The pronunciation /pauč̌t/, rhyming with crouched, is reported in NE from three infs., one each in New Brunswick, southwestern Connecticut, and Massachusetts (Martha's Vineyard). Likewise, three UM infs. have /pɑuč̌t/, but with no clear relationship to the eastern distribution. A pronunciation with intrusive /r/, either /porč̌t/ or /pɔrč̌t/, is reported in NE as used by two infs. in western Connecticut and three each in extreme western Massachusetts, Vermont, and southwestern New Hampshire. This pronunciation, carried west to yield six occurrences in the Wisconsin survey, persists in the UM with five examples—in each state but Nebraska.

One Type I North Dakotan has the unusual form /pɚč̌t/, and one Iowan has [ʊ̌], which in this instance may simply be a variant of /o/.

/o/ 1-5, c6, 7-20, 22-42, c43, 44, s¹48, 49-51, 53-55, 57-58, 60-65; 101-13, 115-31, 133-38, 140-42, 144-52; 201-8, 210-19, 221-26; 301-6, 308-16, 318-28; 401-17, c418, 419, s420, 421-29, 431-37.
/or/ 21; 220; /ɔr/ 114, 132; 317.
/au/ 52, 56; 143.
[ɚ] 209.
[ʊ̌] 139.

won't   45.6. NE 702. PEAS 158-59; F125.

Both in the East and in the UM stressed won't has several competing vowels.

In PEAS McDavid reports tense /o/ as dominant in the Midland and the South, with increasing frequency in the urban centers of southern New England. But generally in New England and its adjacent settlement areas in New York State and northern Pennsylvania the dominant vowel is the lax /ʌ/ of fun, perhaps along with some instances of the New England "short o," /ɵ/. A tense /u/ is found in the lower Hudson Valley and New York City and, rarely, elsewhere; a lax /ʊ/, scattered, in southern New England and New York and Pennsylvania and South Carolina; and a low /ɔ/ in North Carolina and, rarely, in Pennsylvania.

The UM is dominated throughout by /wont/. The vowel-type /o/ is here interpreted as any mid- or high-back onset with or without a rounded offglide, principally as follows: [ʌoˑ, ooˆ, oˑˇ, o·ᵁ, oˑ, ʌ̣ᵁˇ].

Twenty UM infs., however, mostly in Minnesota and northern Iowa, have Northern /wʌnt/. This vowel occurs with a centralized offglide [+] in the speech of four Iowa infs., 108, 113, 114, and 115, according to fw. H. No marked social contrast appears with the form /wʌnt/, although a slight preponderance of Type I

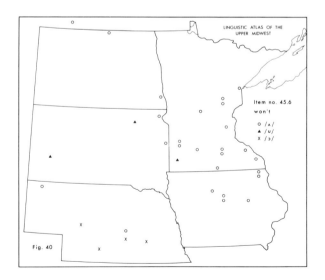

speakers use it.

The UM provides no instances of New
York City /u/, but the lax /ʊ/ is reflected in three isolated examples. The
low rounded /ɔ/ also occurs, but only in
Nebraska and there perhaps as a result of
foreign-language background. A single
[ɑˑ] is recorded in Nebraska by fw. Wr.

/ʌ/ [ʌ] 18, 24, 27, *47, 48, c55, 63;
107-8, 113-15, 118; 201, c204, c225; 307,
317; c401, 420. [ɵ] 23, 32, 43, 46, 50,
56.
  /ʊ/ 59; c306, 311.
  /ɑ/ 413.
  /ɔ/ 415, 418, 421, 426, 430.
  /o/ All others except the following who
did not respond: 20, 33-34; 101, 103,
134, 138, 144, 151-52; 214, 221; 305,
315, 322.

yolk   36.7. NE 209. PEAS 159; F125, F128.

Five pronunciations of yolk are found
in the UM, all of them probably reflexes
of variations reported in PEAS from the
eastern surveys.

One variant, /jok/ rhyming with poke,
occurs rather generally in the East,
though with frequency only in southwestern New England, New York City, and Pennsylvania. Where infrequent, it is likely
to appear chiefly in cultivated speech.
Another variant, /yolk/ with the /l/ pronounced, is strongly favored in New England and only slightly less so in the
derivative settlement area of New York
State. A third pronunciation, /jɛlk/, is
a widespread folk form. In parts of New
England, New Jersey, and West Virginia it
is heard even from middle-class speakers.
The minor variant /jʌlk/ occurs in New
England and New York State, and a still
less frequent variant with the low-back
vowel /ɒ/ is largely limited to Maine and
New Hampshire.

In the UM the pronunciation /jok/ has
become the expanding form, with dominance
in all states but Iowa, where it is evenly matched with /jolk/. The former, however, has a somewhat higher frequency
there and in other states, as more than
one-half of the users of /jok/ are in
Types II and III while more than one-half
of the users of /jolk/ are in Type I. The
folk pronunciation /jɛlk/ retains enough
vitality to be used among the lesser educated in the eastern half of the UM but
it seems unable to endure life on the
western prairies. The minor /jʌlk/ remains a minor variant in the UM, where
the background of most of its users hints
at its northeastern origin, even two of
the three Nebraskans having Ohio or New

York parentage. The single instance of
/jɔk/ in Iowa is possibly related to the
northeastern /ɒ/, but the connection with
the two Nebraska examples of /jɔlk/ is
uncertain.

	Type I	Type II	Type III
/jok/	57%	60%	75%
/jolk/	23%	17%	19%
/jɛlk/	22%	17%	6%
/jʌlk/	9%	2%	0

	Mn.	Ia.	N.D.	S.D.	Nb.	Ave.
/jok/	60%	40%	92%	64%	60%	55%
/jolk/	20%	40%	0	11%	10%	20%
/jɛlk/	17%	18%	8%	27%	22%	18%
/jʌlk/	6%	4%	0	7%	8%	5%

/jok/ 1-6, 8-9, 12-15, 17-19, 21-22,
24-26, 28, 35-36, 38, c39, 40-42, 44, 47,
50-51, 54-57, c61, 63-64; 101, 106, 108-
11, 119-20, 125-26, 130, 132-34, 138,
140, 149-50; 201-6, 208-19, 221-26; 302,
304-5, cr309, 310, →312, 313-15, 318-21,
323, cr325, 326-28; 402-4, 406-8, 410-11,
c416, 418, !419, 420-26, 431-32, 435-36.
  /jolk/ 23, 29, 32-33, 39, 43, 45-46,
49, 53, 58, 62, 65; 102-5, 112, 117, 122-
24, 128, vr131, 137, 139, 141-44, 146,
cr148, 152; 308, 311, 317; 413, 430, 433.
  /jɛlk/ 11, 27, 30-31, 34, *37, c46, 48,
52, 59-60, c61; 113-14, vr115, ¹117, 129,
135-36, 145, 147-48; 207, 220; 301, 303,
306-7, †312, !¹315, 316, 325; 405, 412-
14, 427, 429-30, ¹433, 437.
  /jʌlk/ 7, 10, 16, 20; 107, 121; 322,
324; 401, 409, 417.
  /jɔk/ 116. /jɔlk/ 415, 428.
  no response 151.

Comment:
  "[jɔˑˆˀˀlk] is the correct pronunciation"—115. /jolk/ is "more correct"—430.

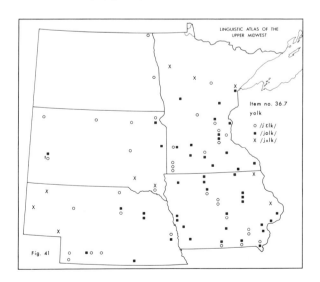

Fig. 41

LINGUISTIC ATLAS OF THE
UPPER MIDWEST

Item no. 36.7
yolk
○ /jɛlk/
■ /jolk/
x /jʌlk/

/ɔ/ and Variants

daughter 50.3. NE 376. PEAS 160-61; F129.

The problems presented by the recognition and transcription of back vowels, as indicated in the *Handbook of the Linguistic Geography of New England* and in the first chapter of this volume, are particularly acute in the interpretation of the data for the pronunciation of daughter.

Four vowel-types are recorded in the first syllable of daughter: rounded /ɔ/ and /ɒ/, and unrounded /ɑ/ and /a/, with an additional single instance of front [a] in Nebraska. But without detailed analysis of each individual field record, and perhaps additional evidence as well, it is not feasible to attempt a definition of the phonemic relationships among the vowel variants.

Transcription of the low-back vowels /ɒ/ and /ɑ/ cannot be accepted as consistently precise in an area of some dialect mixture, since the choice of one or the other is determined by a subjective impression of the presence or absence of the acoustic effect of slight lip-rounding. Considerable free variation is a complicating factor, several infs. being recorded as having either both /ɑ/ and /ɒ/, or both /ɒ/ and /ɔ/, or both /ɑ/ and /ɑ/.

If the fw.'s records are to be taken without correction, then the incidence of unrounded /ɑ/ and /ɑ/ is greatest in central Nebraska, i.e., in Midland speech territory, and in North Dakota in Northern speech territory. The former distribution might hint at an influence from western Pennsylvania and the latter at simply a continued decrease in the fea-

ture of rounding, although the incidence of the unrounded vowel in southern New England could be related to its appearance in the speech of infs. 11, 208, and 218.

The fully rounded /ɔ/, more easily determined, is common in daughter in the eastern states and is likewise common in Minnesota and North Dakota. Its occurrence in both southern Minnesota and southern Iowa suggests that possibly some examples recorded by fw. H in northern Iowa should have been transcribed as /ɔ/.

It would appear further that the rule calling for partial unrounding and the additional rule calling for complete unrounding and fronting of the vowel in daughter meet some resistance from the college group, as only one Type III inf. has either /ɑ/ or /ɑ/ in contrast with the 43 infs. in Types I and II who have an unrounded vowel. In this word at least the rounded vowel seems to connote some prestige.

	Type I	Type II	Type III
/ɑ/	4%	9%	0
/ɑ/	18%	15%	6%
/ɒ/	44%	48%	56%
/ɔ/	39%	26%	37%

	Mn.	Ia.	N.D.	S.D.	Nb.	Ave.
/ɑ/	0	12%	4%	4%	11%	6%
/ɑ/	14%	19%	40%	7%	3%	16%
/ɒ/	49%	54%	50%	25%	46%	47%
/ɔ/	42%	17%	4%	64%	38%	34%

[aˇ] c414.
/ɑ/ vr115, 116, 119, 140, 143-44; 208; 315; c413, 421, 423, 431.
/ɑ/ c11, c22, 26, c29-30, 48, 54, 57, 63; 104, 107, 113, 117, c124, 126-28, 130; c201, c203, 206-7, c211, 213, 216, c218-19, 220-21; 303-4; 432.
/ɒ/ c2, 4, c5, 7-8, c10, 11-12, c13-15, c20-23, 24-25, 27, 30, c31, c33, 34, 36-37, 40-41, c42, 43, 49, 51, c52, 53, 56, 58, 62; 101-3, 105-6, 109-12, 114, 118, 120-21, 123, c124, vr131, 134, 136, 139, 141-42, 145-47, 149-50, 152; 202, c203, 204-5, 209-10, f211-12, c214-15, 217, 222-23, 225-26; cvr305, 309-10, c312, 318, c322, 326; 404-8, c409-10, 411-12, 417, c418-19, 427, 429, 434, c436-37.
/ɔ/ 1, c3, 6, c9-10, 13, 16-18, c19, c21, 28, c31-32, 35, 38, 44-46, c47, 55, 59, 60-61, c65; 122, 125, 129, 132-33, 135, 137-38, 148; 224; 301-2, 306-8, c311, c313-14, *316, 317, 319-21, 323, c324-25, c327, 328; 401, c402-3, 415-16, 420, c422, 425-26, cvr428, 430, 433, 435.

faucet 15.5a-b. NE 143. PEAS 161; F130.

The dominant pronunciation of faucet in the eastern states and in the UM is with

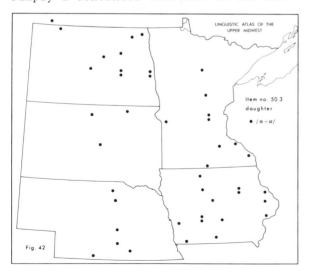

LINGUISTIC ATLAS OF THE
UPPER MIDWEST

Item no. 50.3
daughter
• /ɑ ~ ɑ/

Fig. 42

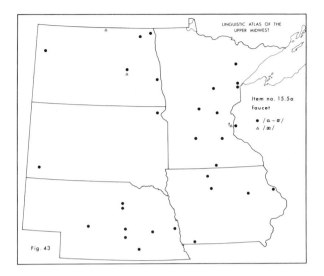

Fig. 43

a rounded vowel ranging from /ɔ/ to /ɒ/, often recorded as a vowel intermediate between the two, as either a lowered [ɔˇ] or a raised [ɒˆ].

Unrounded /ɚ/ and /ɑ/, as in the East, are minor sporadic variants. They are rare or absent in the western third of the UM. A concentration in eastern Nebraska is most likely due in part to the fw.'s preference for [ɚ] rather than [ɒ] for a pronunciation with less than full rounding.

A pronunciation with fronted /æ/, rhyming with basset, is a scattered nonstandard variant in New England and New York State. It survives weakly in the UM in two lonely instances in North Dakota, although one Minnesotan recalls /fæs+t/ as her parents' usual pronunciation. Otherwise no social differences appear in the UM.

/æ/ †40; 204, 219.
/ɑ/ 13, 27, 43; c108, 113, 117, 119, 143, c147; 206, 222; 307; 413-14, 418, 421-22, 427, 432.
/ɚ/ 17-18, 28-29, 40, 63; 104; 208, 210, 219; 424.
/ɒ/ 4, 9-10, 16, 19-22, 24, c25, 26, 30, 33-34, 36, 46, 48, 50, 52, 56-58; 101-2, 104-9, 115-16, 120, 127, 138-39, 142, 145, 151; 203, 205, 212, 216, 218, 220, 225; 301, 303, 309, 315, 322-24, 326; 401, 404, 408-9, 411-12, 417, 419, 429, 436.
/ɔ/ 3, 6-8, 11-12, 15, 23, 31, r32, 35, 37-39, 41-42, 44-45, 47, 49, 51, r52, 54, 59-62, 64-65; 102, 110-12, 114, 118, 121-26, 128-37, 140-41, 144-46, c147, 148-50, 152; 207, 209, 211, 213, 217, 219, 221, 223-24, 226; 302, 304-8, 310, 311-14, 316-19, 321, 325-26, 328; 402-3, 405-7,

410, 415-16, 420, 423, 425-26, 428, 430-31, 433-35.
Comment:
Inf. insists that a /fæs+t/ is on a barrel and that a /fɔs+t/ is on a water pipe—219.

sausage 37.4a. NE 304. PEAS 162; F132.

The dominant eastern and UM pronunciation of sausage is with a rounded vowel ranging from /ɔ/ to /ɒ/. In contrast is a scattered variant with an unrounded vowel ranging from /ɑ/ to /ɚ/. The eastern New England minority form with /æ/ is not recorded in the UM.

/ɑ - ɚ/ 1, 3-4, 6, 9, 12-16, 18-19, 31-32, 35, 53-54; 102, 104, 110, 119, 127, 131-32, 143, 152; 206, 210, 212, 214, 216, 220, 222, 225; 309, 318, 325; 401, 412, 427, 436.
[ə] 144.
/ɔ - ɒ/ All others except nonrespondents 41; 146, 150-51; 327.

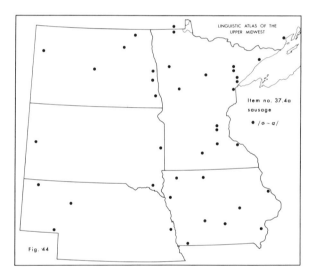

Fig. 44

because 65.7. NE 729. PEAS 162; F133.

As in the East, a back rounded vowel /ɔ - ɒ/ occurs in the stressed syllable of because throughout the UM. A corresponding unround vowel /ɑ - ɚ/ is less usual, with occurrences in western Iowa and Nebraska not quite consistent with its heavier frequency in New England and derivative western settlement areas.

Unlike other words in this class, because has also a pronunciation with /ʌ/ that lacks regional or social differentiation. It probably arose as [ə] in an unstressed pronunciation which later became the only pronunciation for many persons despite some efforts in the schools to castigate it as "slovenly." It has historical background in England and is common in the New England area and the eastern United States.

/ɔ/ 3, cv6, 7, c23, 24, 26, 36, c46, 49-50, 52, 55, 64-65; 117, 120-21, 128, 130-31, 135, 137, cvr140, 144; 201, 208, 210, 218, c224; 306, c311, 313, c324-25, 328; c401, cvr413, 415, c417, 420-22, 424, cr427, 431-34.

/ɒ/ 1-2, 5, 27-28, c40, 42, 54; 109, 112, 114, vrl15, 124, 127, 132-33, 138, 141, 146, 149; 202, 206-7, 212-13, c214, 215-17, 219, 221; 309, 314, cvr317, c320, c322, 323, c325, 326; 404, 435.

/ɚ/ c13, 18-19; 101, 104, 110, 139; 414, 426.

/ɑ/ 102-3, 119, 126, 150; cvr413, 416, 428.

[ɐ] 29-30, c31; 106-7; c222; 403, c409, 411, 418.

[ɤ] 15-16.

/ʌ/ 4, c8, 9, c10, 11, c12-13, 14, 17, c20-22, 25, 31-32, c33, 34, c35, c38, 39, 43, 45-46, c47, 48, c51, 52, c53, 56-65; c105, 108, 111, 114, cvr115, 116, 122-23, 125, 129, 131, 134, 136, 142-43, 145, 147-48; c203-4, 205, 211, c220, 223, 225-26; 301, 303, c304, 305, 307, c310, 312, 315-16, 318-19, 321, c325; c401, 402, 405-6, 408, c413, 423, 425, cvr429, 431, 437.

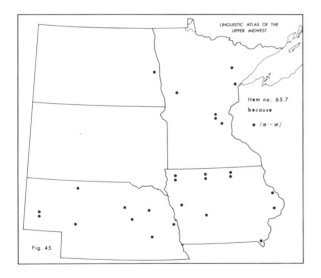

haunted 67.2. NE 534. PEAS 161; F131.

As in New England and the North Midland sector of the eastern states, haunted in the UM likewise commonly has a stressed rounded back vowel ranging from /ɔ/ to /ɒ/, without marked regional differentiation. As with daughter and faucet the selection of /ɔ/ rather than the more

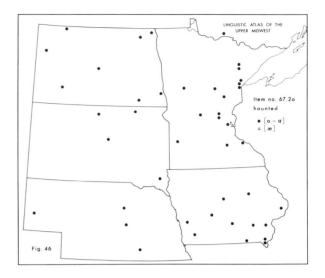

weakly rounded /ɒ/ is sometimes due simply to the word's being offered as a single stressed item, i.e., as a "citation form." An inf. may reply with /hɔnt‡d/ to the fw.'s query but a moment later remark, "There used to be a /hɒnt‡d/ house down the street."

An evenly distributed 20% of the UM infs. observe a rule that unrounds the vowel to /ɚ/ and may also front it to /ɑ/, pronunciations which in part, at least, reflect their relatively high frequency in New England as well as occasional occurrence in New York State and West Virginia. No social contrast is evident.

One Minnesota inf. recalls parental use of /hænt‡d/, rhyming with panted, an older minority form in New England and one common in the South Midland and the South. It seems to have disappeared as a living variant in the UM. One Minnesotan (19) has a clear diphthong /ɑʊ/, and several Nebraskans have a pronounced off-glide [ɔə].

/æ/ †40.

/ɑ/ 4, 14, 18, 29, c36, 46, *48; 135, 138-39, 147, 149; 206, 224; 305, c314; 414, 432.

/ɚ/ 2, 13, 16-17, 21, 23, 30, 54; 115, 126, 142, 150; 208, 210, 215-16, 225; 303; 411, 420.

/ɒ/ 3, 5, 10, 12, 15, 22, 24-25, 27, c28, 31, 33-34, 56-58, 65; 102, 104-5, 111-14, 116-18, 121, 124, 128, 130, 132-33, 136-37, 140-41, 143; 203-5, 209, 212, 220-21, 223, 226; 301-2, 304, 309-10, 312; 401, 403, 406, 412-13, 417-18, 429, 436-37.

/ɔ/ 1, 6-9, 11, 20, 26, 32, c35, 37-40, s41, 42-45, 47, 49-51, c52, 53, 55, 59-

64; 101, 103, 106-10, 120, 122-23, 125, 127, c129, 131, 134, 144-46, 148; 201-2, 207, 211, 213-14, 217-19, 222; 306-8, 311, 313; 402, 404, s407, 408-10, 415-16, 419, 421-28, 430-31, 433-35.
    no response 118; 405.

jaundice 60.5. NE 311.

As in the eastern states the two principal pronunciation types are that with a rounded vowel ranging from /ɔ/ to /ɒ/ and that with an unround vowel ranging from /ɑ/ to /ɚ/. The incidence of the unrounded type is higher in the UM than in the eastern states, where it is rare or infrequent except in North Carolina.

The great acceptance of an unrounding rule in the UM does not, however, characterize any particular section. Both varieties occur in roughly equal proportions in Minnesota, Iowa, and South Dakota, with even greater proportion of unrounding in North Dakota and Nebraska. As with other words in this group, the citation pronunciation tends to be somewhat more rounded than the one recorded from conversation or in a larger context. The occurrence of both varieties in the same area, and even sometimes in the speech of one inf., suggests that a surface phonemic analysis would overlook the possibility of an underlying common rounded /ɔ/.

Also in the East jaundice contrasts with haunted because of its greater retention of an earlier minority pronunciation with /æ/. Particularly, the slightly higher incidence of /æ/ in Pennsylvania than in New England is reflected in a higher incidence in the Midland speech territory of the UM. But it clearly is a dying form, as all but one of the users are in the oldest age group, and it is quite rare in the more recently settled northern and western portions of the UM.

A curious correlation is that between the pronunciation with /æ/ and a final syllable containing a retroflex or r-colored vowel, /ɚ/. This correlation is noticeable in New England, where most of the 47 instances are in the pronunciation /ʤændɚz/. More than one-half are in southwestern New England, i.e., in western Connecticut and the western fringe of Massachusetts, a seedbed area for forms in the Northern dialect range. But presumably this pronunciation is even more frequent in the Midland area, since most of the 19 UM examples are in Midland speech territory. They include 12 of the 16 responses that also have /æ/.

A sharp social distribution exists with this pronunciation as well. All of the UM instances with /ɚ/ in the second syllable

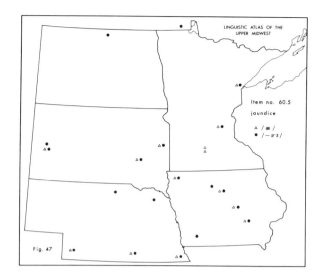

are from the least educated infs., those in Type I, and all but one (436) of the instances of /æ/ are from the same group.

This /ɚ/ of the final syllable is not parallel with the intrusive /r/ in wash. It first appeared, according to the *Oxford English Dictionary*, in the fifteenth century, apparently by analogy with the plural name of another disease, glanders.

/ɔ/ 1, 26, 40, 43, 45-46, c47, 53, 59, 61-63; 105-6, 110, 117, 119-20, 122-23, 136, 142-44, 146-49; 301, 305, 308, 313, 315-16, 319; 416, 420, 422, 425, 428, 433, 435.
    /ɒ/ 2, 4, 9, 11, 18, 21, 23, 25, 27, 29-30, 33, 37-38, 41-42, 54-58, 65; 107-8, 111-12, 129, 133, 137-38, 145; 201, 210-11, 219, 222, 226; 302, 304, 309-10, 314, 320-22, cv324, 325-26, 328; 405-6, 410, 437.
    /ɚ/ 6, 8, 13-14, 16-17, 19-20, 24, 31, 49; 141; 203, 208, 213; cr309, 312, 323; 402-3, 407-9, 412, 417-18, 421.
    /ɑ/ 3, 5, 7, 10, 12, 22, 28, 32, 34, 36, 39, 44, 48, 50, 60, 64; 102-4, 109, 113, 115-16, 121, 125-28, 130, vr131, 134, 139-40, 150; 202, 204-7, 209, 212, 214-18, 220, 224-25; 303, 306, 318; 401, 404, 411, 413-14, 419, 423-24, 426, 431.
    /æ/ 15, !ᴵ†29, 35, 51-52; 101, 114, 132, 135, !ᴵ†139; 306, 311, 317, *†328; 429, 432, 434, 436.
    /au/ 124.
    /-dɚz/ 1, 15, 35; 101, 113-14, 132, 135, !ᴵ†139, 143; 204; 309, 311, 317, 328; 405, 407, 429, 432, 434.

water 39.1. NE 311. PEAS 163; F134.

Most UM speakers have in water one or more varieties of a rounded back vowel /ɔ - ɒ/ that historically has its origin

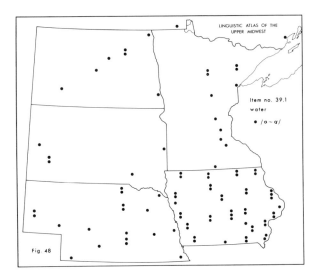

Fig. 48

in the lip-rounding effect of the initial /w/ upon an unround /æ/ or /ɑ/. No marked regional or social patterns appear among the varieties themselves, but the rounded vowel type, which prevails in most of the eastern states, is dominant in Minnesota, North Dakota, and South Dakota, and, somewhat less frequent, is still a majority form in Nebraska.

An unround vowel type ranging from central /ɑ/ to a backed /ɒ/ occurs as a minority variant in the three northern states, has a higher frequency in Nebraska, and dominates Iowa, even the northern third (where fw. practice may be a factor). These occurrences of the /ɑ - ɒ/ vowel in Midland speech territory are consistent with its high frequency reported in PEAS as found in eastern Pennsylvania, Ohio, and West Virginia.

/ɔ/ 4, 6-7, 9, 15, c17, 19, 23-24, 27, 29, 31, c36, 37, 41, 43, 45-46, 50, 55, c59, 64-65; 118, cvr126, cvr133; 202, 2 205, 207, 209, 217-18, 220-21, 223, 226; 303-4, 306-7, 310-11, 313, 315-16, cvr317, 319, 322; 401, 416, 420, 425-26, cvr427-28, 431-34.
/ɒ/ 2, 5, 8, 10, 12-13, c16, 18, 21-22, 25-26, 28, 33, 35, 38-40, 42, c44, 47, 49, 51-52, 54, 56-58, 60-62; vr131, 144; 201, 203-4, 206, 210, 214, 219, 222, 224; 301-2, 314, 321, 324-25, 327-28; 402-4, c405, 408-9, 412, 419, 429, 436.
/ɒ/ 1, 3, 22, 30, c32, 34, 48, 53, c63; 105, 111, 114, cvr115, 116, 122, 142; 208, 211-13, 215-16, 225; 309, 312, c320, 323; 407, 413, 417, cvr422. (All the Iowa instances except 114 are transcribed in the field records as [ɑˀ], which in view of the fws.' practice is here interpreted as /ɒ/.)

/ɑ/ 11, 14, 63; 101-4, 106-10, 112-13, 117, 119-21, 123-30, 132-36, cvr137, 138-41, 143, 145-49; 318, 326; 414-15, 418, 421, 423-24, 427, 430, 435, 437.

wash   15.1. NE 137. PEAS 163; F135.

Although in the UM a faint hint remains of the eastern distribution of the rounded and unrounded vowels in wash, on the whole the clear trend is toward a round vowel throughout the five states, without regional or social contrast.

In PEAS an unround vowel in the range /ɑ - ɒ/ is described as common in northern West Virginia and western New York State, but only sporadic elsewhere outside the South.

This pronunciation apparently was carried west as a minority variant. It is offered by almost exactly the same proportion of infs., 1:8, in Wisconsin and Minnesota, but it did not cross the Red River, as no instances are recorded in North Dakota. There are only two in South Dakota. Several of the few Iowa and Nebraska infs. with the unround vowel have parentage directly linked to a New York or West Virginia background. Three instances of the unround vowel are with a fronted [a] variety.

The rounded vowel, ranging from /ɔ/ to /ɒ/, not only is dominant in most of the East including the South Midland, but maintains and extends that dominance throughout the UM. There is no regional patterning of the /ɔ/ and /ɒ/ variants, however, as the same fw. generally finds both in the same region, often in the same community, and occasionally in the speech of a single inf. It seems that the greater the stress, as in a citation

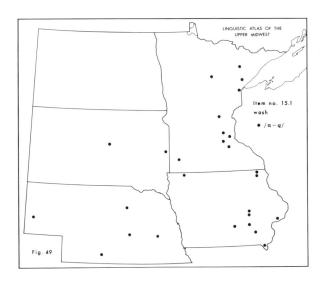

Fig. 49

262

form, the greater the likelihood of /ɔ/.

/ɔ/ 1, 3-5, c6, 7-8, c10, 11, 16, 19-25, 27-28, 30, 35-37, 39, 41-42, 45-47, 49-50, 53-55, 60-61, 64-65; 102-3, 109, 112, 114, 116, 118-20, 123-24, 126, 130-31, 135, 138-39, 142-48, 150; 201, 203, 206-11, 212-15, 217-19, 221, 224, c225, 226; 302-4, *306, 307-8, 311-13, 315, 317, 319-21, 324, 326, 328; 402, 405, 407-10, 412, c413, 414, 415-20, 422-23, 425-30, c431, 432, 434-37.

/ɒ/ 2, 17, 26, 31, 33, 40, 43-44, 51-52, 56-58, 63; 104-7, 110-11, 113, 115, 117, 121-22, 125, 127-29, 137, 141, 149; 202, 204-5, 211, 216, 220, 223; 306, 309-10, 323, 325; 401, 403-4.

/ɐ/ 12, 38, 48; 140; 314; 411, 413.

/ɑ/ 13, 18, 29, 32, 34, 59; 108, 132, 134, 136; 318; 421, 424, 431.

[a] 15; 101, 133.

<u>swamp</u> 24.3. NE 30. PEAS 163.

Because as a lexical item <u>swamp</u> competes with <u>bog</u>, <u>marsh</u>, and, especially in North Dakota, <u>slough</u>, it is offered as a response by only 131 of the 208 infs. Only six such responses are in North Dakota. (See Volume 1.)

In neither the East nor the UM has the rounding effect of the prevocalic /w/ universally yielded a rounded vowel in <u>swamp</u>. Actually, the vowel occurs on a continuum between unround /ɑ/ and higher low-back rounded /ɔ/, with an essential contrast between the low-central /ɑ/ and the low-back varieties /ɐ/, /ɒ/, and /ɔ/.

Kurath reports in PEAS that /ɑ/ occurs beside /ɔ/ in upstate New York and West Virginia, and that it dominates in New York and Philadelphia urban areas. Elsewhere /ɔ/ is predominant. Clearly the distinction is not in accord with the basic Northern/Midland division.

In the UM the Northern/Midland pattern is likewise irrelevant and the distribution is mixed, but the evidence does suggest some social and regional variation.

Low-central /ɑ/ seems to carry slightly more prestige, as it is favored by the high school and college groups, a situation that holds true if the occurrences of the low-back unround /ɐ/ are also included.

The geographical distribution, however, is less clearly defined. A Midland preference for an unround vowel, /ɑ - ɐ/, is indicated by its predominance in Iowa and its weakness in Minnesota, as well as by a higher incidence in Nebraska than in South Dakota. It is noticeably more frequent in the Midland southern two-thirds of Iowa than in the Northern third. An apparently inconsistent high proportion

of /ɑ/ in North Dakota can perhaps be discounted because of the inconclusive sampling in that state.

A rounded vowel, /ɒ - ɔ/, conversely, is the choice of three-fourths of the Minnesota and South Dakota infs. and almost three-fourths of those in Nebraska.

The presence of the four different pronunciations throughout the area, however, blocks any generalization about, say, a regional or even local adoption of a rule calling for backing and rounding of the vowel. The situation is describable as one in transition, conjecturally toward a low-back weakly rounded /ɒ/ despite the possible lingering presitge of /ɑ/.

	Type I	Type II	Type III
/ɑ/	24%	34%	33%
/ɐ/	6%	10%	16%
/ɒ/	26%	20%	25%
/ɔ/	45%	35%	25%

	Mn.	Ia.	N.D.	S.D.	Nb.	Ave.
/ɑ/	18%	55%	33%	6%	32%	29%
/ɐ/	6%	10%	17%	18%	7%	9%
/ɒ/	33%	16%	33%	12%	18%	23%
/ɔ/	43%	19%	17%	65%	43%	39%

/ɑ/ 1, 16-17, 34, 37, 39, 51, 57, 64; 107, 113-14, 117, 120, 123, 127-31, 134, 136-37, 139, 144, 151; 217, 221; 325; 414-16, 424-26, 430, 436-37.

/ɐ/ 24, 29, 63; 116, 125, c126; 221; 321, 326, 328; 418, 433.

/ɒ/ 2-3, 11, 13, 19, c23, 28, 31, 38, 40, 43, 45, 49, 56, 61; 105, 122, 124, 145-46; 207, c220, c222; 307, 309; 413, 421-22, 426, 428.

/ɔ/ 1, 4, 6-7, 10, 12, 14-15, 21-22, 30, 33, c35-36, 44, 50, 54-55, 59-60, 63; 113, 118, 135, 142, 147, 150; 301-2, 306, 308, 311-13, 316, 318-19, 325; 401, 403-6, 409, 417, 419, 423, 429, 431-32.

<u>watch</u> 4.5. NE 157.

The vowel in <u>watch</u>, like that in <u>water</u>, <u>wash</u>, and <u>swamp</u>, ranges in the East and in the UM from /ɑ/ to /ɔ/, but the degree of lip-rounding induced by the initial labial /w/ is much less in <u>watch</u>.

Low central unround /ɑ/ is actualized as [a], [aˁ], [ɑ], [ɐ], [ɐˇ], [ɑˀ], [ɑ·], and [ɑˢ] and, particularly in Iowa and Nebraska, with various offglides as [ɑə], [ɑˀɚ], [ɑˠ], [ɑˀᵉˆ], and [ɑˀⁱ]. Low-back unround /ɐ/ is actualized as [ɐˁ], [ɐ], [ɐ·], [ɐˆ], and [ɐˆᵉ].

Rounding occurs in instances of /ɒ/, realized as [ɒˁ], [ɒˬ], [ɒᵉˀ], and [ɒ] and of /ɔ/, realized as [ɔˇ], [ɔə], and [ɔ].

No social contrast is evident in the variation between round and unround vowels, for three-fourths or more of the infs. in each of the three types have an unround /ɑ/ or, rarely, /ɔ/. But regional preference appears in the greater frequency of rounding in Northern speech territory, i.e., Minnesota and the Dakotas, and in its sparse occurrence in Midland Iowa and Nebraska.

	Type I	Type II	Type III
/ɑ/	75%	77%	88%
/ɒ/	27%	22%	12%
/ɒ/	8%	9%	0
/ɔ/	14%	13%	12%

	Mn.	Ia.	N.D.	S.D.	Nb.	Ave.
/ɑ/	56%	98%	77%	65%	95%	75%
/ɒ/	16%	0	8%	14%	3%	8%
/ɒ/	27%	2%	15%	7%	3%	12%
/ɔ/	3%	0	0	14%	0	3%

/ɑ/ 1, 4, 6-7, 9, 13, 18-27, 29-32, 34-35, 38, 41-42, 48, 50-51, 53-57, 61, 63-64; 101-43, 145-52; 202-4, 206-7, 210-14, 217-26; 301-2, 304-5, 310, 314-15, 317-18, 320-26; 401-7, 409-18, 420-28, 430-37.
/ɒ/ 2-3, 5, 10, 17, 28, 33, 37, 52; 208, 216; 303, 309, 311-12.
/ɒ/ 8, 11-12, 15-16, 36, 39, 43-47, 49, 52, 58-60, 62; 144; 201, 205, 209, 215; 315, 319; 429.
/ɔ/ 14, 40; 306-8, 316.

fog 5.6. NE 96. PEAS 163; F136.

The fairly clear regional distribution of a rounded vowel /ɔ - ɒ/ and of an unround vowel /ɑ/ in fog in the eastern states is not well matched in the UM.

Unround /ɑ/ is common in western New England, New York State, eastern Pennsylvania, and the Tidewater regions of Maryland, Virginia, and North Carolina. Rounded vowels dominate elsewhere, particularly in eastern New England and western Pennsylvania. Kurath and McDavid in PEAS suggest that instances of weakly rounded [ɒ] in some areas may be variously phonemicized, as /ɑ/ in North Carolina and either /ɑ/ or /ɒ/ in western New England. In his doctoral dissertation on the low-back vowel Thomas Wetmore notes that /ɒ/ in western Pennsylvania may represent an unround [ɒ] as well as the more common slightly rounded [ɒ] or [ɒ^].

In the UM no equally clear pattern emerges. The field data do indicate, nevertheless, that fully rounded /ɔ/ is Midland-oriented, since it is used by more than one-half of the infs. in Iowa (52%), South Dakota (56%), and Nebraska (51%), in contrast to the smaller proportion in Minnesota (19%) and in North Dakota (23%). Fully unround /ɑ/, on the

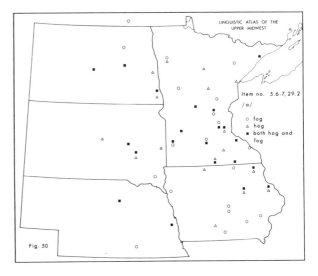

Fig. 50

contrary, is somewhat stronger in Minnesota (19%) and North Dakota (15%) than in the other states, Iowa (8%), South Dakota (7%), and Nebraska (11%).

An unresolved problem is raised, however, by the large number of infs. who have an intermediate low-back vowel between /ɑ/ and /ɔ/. Four percent of the infs. have an unround [ɒ] and 51% have the slightly rounded [ɒ]. Most of the few instances of [ɒ] are in Northern speech territory and nearly one-third of the many instances of [ɒ] are likewise in Northern territory. Probably those examples from southern Iowa, Nebraska, and southwestern South Dakota—Midland territory—are in large measure a reflex of the situation in western Pennsylvania, but this cannot be the origin of most of the occurrences in Minnesota and North Dakota.

A clue to the nature of the problem appears in the contrast between Minnesota and the neighboring North Central Atlas state of Wisconsin. In Wisconsin there are proportionately twice as many infs. with extreme /ɑ/ and extreme /ɔ/ as in Minnesota, but there are only one-half as many with intermediate [ɒ] and none with [ɒ]. (This latter symbol apparently was not used in the Wisconsin field survey.) A reasonable inference is that in the UM some speakers are now accepting a phonological rule that calls for slightly backing and rounding the [ɑ] vowel in fog that presumably was in their speech inheritance, and that others are similarly slightly unrounding and lowering the [ɔ] vowel in their inheritance. If this is true, it is not yet a general phenomenon in the region, for variation along the range exists within a community and even

264

within the speech of one informant. It is hence not feasible to attempt to classify an occurrence of [ɒ] as an allophone of either /ɒ/ or /ɑ/ except perhaps in a single idiolect, nor can it be assumed that as a sound-class /ɒ/ has phonemic status.

An unresolved problem appears also in the relationship of fog and its derivative adjective foggy, which likewise was recorded during the survey. Expectedly, the vowel in the citation form of the monosyllabic fog differs quantitatively from that in disyllabic foggy, either through simple lengthening or through a lengthening offglide, as with [ɔ⁺], [ɒᵒ], [aᵉ], and [ɔᵘ]. But for 45 infs. the difference is unsystematically qualitative, with no regional or social correlation. Twenty infs. have a slightly more rounded vowel in the simplex fog than in the derivative foggy: [ɔ - ɒ] 49, 60; 106, 114, 116, 138; 201, 205; 305; 410. [ɒ - ɤ] 19, 31; 202, 206, 226. [ɔ - ɑ] 107, 115, 129. [ɔ - ɒ] 1; 428. Twenty-four infs. have a slightly less rounded vowel in fog than in foggy: [ɤ - ɒ] 8; 109, 117, 136. [ɒ - ɔ] 20, 23, 34, 38, 59; 101, 112-13, 126, 130, 150; 203, 219; 314, 320; 401, 417. [ɐ - ɔ] 51. [ɑ - ɔ] 421. [ɑ - ɒ] 119. No trend or outline appears in this set of data.

As the accompanying map indicates, the distribution of /fɑg/ measurably overlaps that for the corresponding pronunciation of hog, i.e. /hɑg/. A number of speakers, in fact, consistently have /ɑ/ in both words.

/ɑ/ in fog: 6, c13, 27, 29, 32, 42-44, 46-47, c63, 65; 105, c109, 119, 131; 212, 218, 222, 225; 316, 327; c413, 421, 424.
/ɤ/ 8, 24, 36, c55; 117, 136, 144; 217.
/ɒ/ 2-5, 9-12, c13, 15, 18-20, 22-23, 25-26, 28, 30-31, 33-35, 37-40, 45, 50-52, 54-56, c57, 58-59, c62, 64; 101-4, 108, 112-13, 121, 125-26, 130-31, 136, 140-41, 147, 149, 152; 202-4, 206-8, 210-11, 215-16, 219-21, c222, 223, 226; 301, 303, 309-10, 312, c314, 320, 324-25, 328; c401, 403-9, 411-12, 417-19, 429, 437.
/ɔ/ 1, 7, 13-14, 16-17, 21, 41, 48-49, 53, 60; 106-7, 110-11, 114-16, 120, 122-24, 127-28, c129, 132-35, 138-39, 142-43, 145-46, 148-49; 201, 205, 209, 213-14, 224; 302, 304, c305, 306, 308, 311, 313, 315, 317-19, 321-23, 326; 401-2, 414-16, 420, 422-23, 425-28, 430, 432-36.

long, strong 33.2, 56.3. NE 51, 460. PEAS 164; F137.

The common Northern and North Midland /ɔ - ɒ/ vowel range in long and strong is paralleled by its universality in the UM.

Two distinctions appear, however. One is that, although fully rounded /ɔ/ occurs generally throughout the five states, weakly rounded /ɒ/ is less common. In strong it appears throughout, but less frequently in Minnesota. The second is that /ɒ/ in long has a rather obvious Midland orientation, with greatest frequency in Iowa and Nebraska. Of the 12 infs. with /ɒ/ in both words, 10 are in Midland speech territory.

Unround /ɑ/, sporadic in West Virginia, eastern Pennsylvania, northern New Jersey, Brooklyn, and western New England, survives in long and along with only two UM infs., and not at all in strong. But unround /ɤ/, not recognized in eastern field practice as distinct from /ɑ/, appears in the speech of nine widely scattered infs., few of whom have family ties with eastern /ɑ/ areas.

long
/ɑ/ 413; (along) cvr104.
/ɤ/ 207.
/ɒ/ c10, 14-15, 58, 64-65; cvr103, 109, 112-13, 116, 119, 121, 124, 128-29, 131, 136-39, 142.
/ɔ/ 1-5, c6, 7-9, c11, 12-13, 16-27, 29-33, 35-37, 39-47, 49-55, 57, 59-63; 102, 106-8, 110, 114-15, 118, 122-27, cvr130, vr132, 134-35, 141, 143, 145, 147, 152; 201, 203, 205, 208, c209, 210-12, 214-15, c216, 217-19, c220, 221-22, 224, 226; 301, 304-5, 307-8, 311-13, 315-16, 320, 322-26, c327, 328; 401-4, 409, c410, 416-17, 420-23, 425-28, 431, 436-37.

strong
/ɤ/ 29, 34; vr131; 206-8, 212; 321; 403.
/ɒ/ 7, 10, 30, 33, 38, 56-58; 107-9, 113, vr115, 118-19, 121, 123, 127, 133, 135, 138, cvr150; 201-5, 209-11, 215, 219, 222-23; 302, 310-11, 315, 319, 322, 325-26; 401, 406-8, 410-12, 417-19, 426, 429, 436-37.
/ɔ/ 3, 8, 11, 13, 16-17, 20-24, 27, 32, 36, 39-41, 43, c44, 46-54, c55, 59, 61-64; 101-2, 105-6, 111-12, 116, 120, 122, 128-29, 136-37, cvr140, 145-47, 149, 152; 213, 218, 220, 224; 304-8, 312-13, 316-18, 323, 328; 402, 409, 413-16, 421-23, 425, 427-28, 430-33, 435.

on   23.3. NE 708. PEAS 164; F138.

The sharply defined eastern distribution of the two principal variants of stressed on, as in Put it on!, is clearly reflected, though less sharply, in the UM.

An unround /ɑ/ uniformly appears in

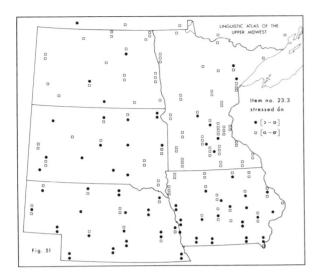

LINGUISTIC ATLAS OF THE UPPER MIDWEST

Item no. 23.3
stressed ón

□ [ɔ ~ ɒ]
• [ɑ ~ ɚ]

Fig. 51

southwestern New England, New York State, and the northern counties of Pennsylvania. Elsewhere in New England and in the Midland and South on has a rounded vowel ranging from /ɒ/ to fully rounded /ɔ/.

Despite the population intermixture in the UM, unround /ɑ/, with some instances of slightly backed /ɚ/, persists as a distinctive Northern dialect marker. It almost completely dominates Minnesota, North Dakota, and the northern third of Iowa. The rounded /ɔ - ɒ/, on the contrary, is strongest in southern Iowa, Nebraska, and, less so, South Dakota. Notably, the degree of rounding increases on the north to south and west to east range, as fully rounded /ɔ/ almost exclusively dominates southern Iowa and eastern Nebraska.

No instances of Southern /ɔn/ occur.

/ɑ/ 1-4, 6-10, 12, 14, 16-17, 19-27, 29, 31-34, 36-44, 46-51, c52, 53-56, 59-65; cvr101-4, 105, cvr107, 108-11, 114, cvr116, 119, 121, 126, 128, 131, 133-34, 136, 139, 150, 152; 202, c203-4, 205-6, 208-10, c211, 212, 217-21, c222, 224, 226; 304, cvr305, 312, 314, cvr317, 318, cvr319, 323-25, c326-27, 328; 401, 411, 413-14, 416, c420, 426, 428, cvr431.

/ɚ/ 5, 18, 52, 57; cvr107; 214-16, c219; 302, 310; 404, 408, c409, 418.

/ɒ/ 13, 15, 28, 30, 35, 45; 106, 113, vrl15, 120, 122, 144-45; 201, 207, 213, 223; 301, 303, *306, 309, c311, c313, 315, 320-22; 402, c403, c405-6, c407, 412, c417, 419, c429, c436, 437.

/ɔ/ 13; cvr115, 117, 123-24, cvr125, 127, cvr129-30, 132, 135, 137, cvr138, cvr140, 142, cvr143, 146-49; 307, cvr308, 316; 410, c414, cvr415-16, 421, cvr422-23, 424, c425, cvr427-28, 430-35.

postoffice   63.2. NE 545.

Although the first syllable in postoffice bears the primary stress, the second syllable usually carries a quite heavy secondary stress that preserves the quality of the vowel. Occurrences of this vowel fall into regional patterns contrasting round and unround varieties.

The New England distribution is quite clear. Most infs. have a low-back /ɒ/ or, occasionally, a higher /ɔ/, in office, but 76 have the unround /ɑ/. Nearly all of these latter are concentrated in central and northwestern New England—42 in Massachusetts and 21 in Vermont, with only 12 in Connecticut, one in Rhode Island, and none in either Maine or New Hampshire.

A predictable reflex of the frequency of the /ɑ/-type vowel in western New England is its persistence as a minority feature in the western secondary settlement areas. Hence it is the pronunciation favored by one-fourth of the infs. in the Wisconsin segment of the North Central survey, by at least one-fifth of those in Minnesota, and by several Nebraska infs. with a family background of Northern speech. But [ɑ] itself apparently is yielding to a backed [ɚ] or /ɔ/, since its frequency diminishes from 15% among UM Type I infs. to 11% among Type II's and to only 6% among Type III's, to say nothing of the decline to a single instance in each of the Dakotas. This apparent decline may be offset by further analysis that would assign some of the occurrences of [ɚ] to /ɑ/, since one-half of the North Dakota infs. are recorded as having [ɚ].

The extent of the West Midland /ɑ - ɔ/ merger in the UM is such, however, that even in Northern speech territory it is not possible to assign all instances of [ɚ], [ɒ], and [ɔ] in postoffice to phonemic categories without an analysis of the phonemic inventory of each individual speaker. It may be predicted, for example, that in Minnesota and North Dakota and northern Iowa there would be a fairly general two-way contrast between /ɑ/ and /ɔ/ described by Kurath (WG, p. 7) as characteristic of upstate New York. But the many instances of /ɚ/ and /ɒ/ do not independently lend themselves to this classification, even though in his early interviews in Minnesota fw. A may have transcribed as [ɚ] a vowel he later would have written as [ɑ]. Nor in southern Iowa and Nebraska is it readily possible to assign each [ɚ] or [ɔ] to the merged /ɒ/ of western Pennsylvania speech carried across the Mississippi by Midland speakers. The frequency of the fully rounded /ɔ/, for instance, is as great in Iowa as in Minnesota. The following data, hence, are provided without further interpretation.

	Type I	Type II	Type III
[ɑ]	15%	11%	6%
[ɝ]	17%	19%	31%
[ɒ]	34%	37%	25%
[ɔ]	34%	35%	37%

	Mn.	Ia.	N.D.	S.D.	Nb.	Ave.
[ɑ]	19%	6%	4%	4%	22%	12%
[ɝ]	22%	8%	50%	7%	17%	19%
[ɒ]	23%	44%	35%	50%	28%	34%
[ɔ]	37%	40%	12%	39%	25%	34%

[ɑ] 16, 32, 35, 43-44, 46-48, 52, 60-61, 63; 121, 132-33; 214; 303; 409, 415, 421, 424-26, 431-32.

[ɝ] 2-3, 11-12, 15, 21-22, 25, 29-31, 33, 59; 103-4, 110, 149; 201-3, 205, 208, 210-13, 215-17, 219-20, 223; 320, 326; 403, 406-7, 410-11, 419.

[ɒ] 1, 5, 7, 19, 23, 34, 36-38, 40, 42, 45, 54-56; 101-2, 105-6, 108-9, 111-14, vr115, 116, 119-20, 127, vr131, 135, 137-38, 144-45, 147; 204, 206-7, 215-17, 219-20, 223; 302, 304, 309-11, 313-15, 318-19, 321, 324-25, 328; 401, 405, 412, cvr413, 417-18, 420, 428-29, 436-37.

[ɔ] 6, 8-10, 13-14, 17-18, 20, 24, 26-28, 41, 49-51, 53, 55-59, 62, 64-65; 107, 117, 122-26, 128-30, 134, 136, 139-43, 146, 148, 150; 209, 225-26; 301, 303, 306-8, 312, 316-17, 322-23, 327; 402, v408, c414, cvr416, 420, 422-23, 427, c430, 433, 435.

grandma, grandpa   50.2-1. NE 383, 381. PEAS 5.12.

Expectedly, because of its being in a final syllable usually sustaining no more than secondary stress, the terminal vowel in grandma runs the gamut. The principal contrast is between an unround /ɑ/, occurring as a central [ɑ], a slightly raised [ɐ], or a backed [ɝ], and a round vowel occurring as [ɒ] or slightly lowered [ɔ]. Under zero stress, often accompanied by consonantal assimilation of /ndm/ to /m:/, the final vowel is simply schwa [ə]; i.e., /græm:ə/. Aberrant variants are the hypocoristic /i/ and the fronted /æ/.

In the eastern states the unround variants, including [ə], are typically Northern, as is [i] with a limited appearance in Maine and New Hampshire. Rounded /ɔ - ɒ/ is typically Midland and South Midland. The minor variant /æ/ is restricted to eastern Maryland, southern New Jersey, and western Pennsylvania.

The UM conspicuously preserves the Northern-Midland contrast. Unround /ɑ - ɒ/ is strongly Northern-oriented, with dominance in Minnesota, northern Iowa, North Dakota, and Iowa. Schwa [ə] is likewise Northern, with highest frequency in Minnesota and none at all in Midland Nebraska. Five examples of /i/ occur, three in Minnesota (two of them used by infs. having British parentage), one as a heard form in North Dakota, and one in South Dakota. There are no instances of final /æ/.

Consistently, the vowels found in the final syllable of grandpa have almost precisely the same distribution, regional and individual, as do those of grandma.

Nearly as close correlation exists with the various pronunciations of pa and ma. Since the rounded vowel pronunciation has led to a popular spelling differentiation, paw and maw, the variants were deemed to be lexical and hence are treated in Volume 1.

[ɑ] 1, 5-10, 19, 23-27, 32, 34, 38, 49-50, 57, 65; 103, 105, 111, 118; c203, 209, 213, 218, 221, ɪ†222; 317, 325; 402, 404, 413, 415, 419, 425-26, 431.

[ə] 2, 20, 30, 33, 42, 46, 56, 59, 64; 106-7, 120; 205, 210, c211, !ɪ†215, †216, 217, 219, 226; 302, 304, 315, 328; c406.

[ɝ] c16, 41, 54-55, 58, 62; 117, 131, 150; 224; 401, 408, c409, 410-11, 429, 437.

[ɒ] 17, 37; 101, 116, 119, 127-28, c133, 149; 314, 324; 403, 412, 417-18, 436.

[ɔ] 114, 124-26, 135, 137-39, 141, 147; 308; 416, 422, c423, 424, ɪ427, †428, 430.

[ə] 14-15, 18, 39-40, 43, 45, 47, 51-

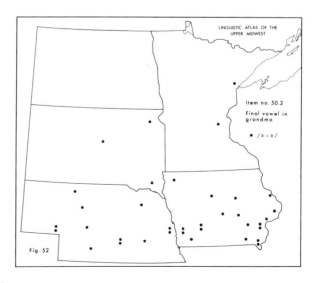

Fig. 52

53, 60-61, 63; 104, 108, 110, 112, 123;
201; 306, 318-19.
[ɪ] 3, 44, 48; [1]207; 311.

/ai/ *and Variants*

<u>appendicitis</u> 60.6. NE 509. PEAS 5.13;
F139.

The incidence of the archaic pronunciation of <u>appendicitis</u> with stressed /i/
instead of customary /ai/ is even lower
in the UM than in the eastern states. In
PEAS this variant is described as "a minority usage in New England, eastern Virginia, and South Carolina." In the UM
field records it appears only 11 times.
Of the five infs. with /i/ as presumably
their normal usage three are Canadian and
one admits also using /ai/. Five infs.
now consider the /i/ pronunciation old-
fashioned, and two simply report it as
heard in their communities. No cultivated
speaker has it. The Northern orientation
of /i/ suggests the derivative influence
of New England.

/i/ 1-2, [1]28, [†]40, 42; [†]201, 202, [1]213;
308, [1†]325; [†]409.

Comment:
"Perhaps just a wrong pronunciation"—
201. Her doctor's pronunciation—325.

<u>rind</u> 37.9. NE 202.

Although the common form of <u>rind</u> is
/raind/, in New England the variant
/rɪnd/, rhyming with <u>sinned</u>, is reported
in five widely scattered communities, besides one in New Brunswick. This variant
occurs once in the UM as well, either as
a survival or, more likely, as an auton-
omous spelling-pronunciation in the
speech of a North Dakota farmer of Ice-
landic extraction (206). Another single-
ton, unexplained, is /rɪnd/, also found
in North Dakota (213).

/au/ *and Variants*

<u>drought</u> 6.1. NE 97. PEAS 167; F142.

Because the variants <u>drought</u> (with final /t/) and <u>drouth</u> (with final /θ/) have
different common spellings, they are
treated as lexical variants in Volume 1.
But besides the usual vowel /au/ two
other vowels occur in the eastern states.
One, /u/, is an apparent Scotticism frequent in western Pennsylvania. The other,
/ɔ/, yields a rhyme with either <u>froth</u> or
<u>bought</u>. It is scattered in New England,
New York State, and the Pennsylvania German area.

Instances of the form with /ɔ/, all
with final /θ/ except for two (1, 9) with
final /t/, are sporadic in the UM, the
greatest frequency being in Minnesota.
There are two examples of /druθ/, both in
the speech of Canadian infs. in Manitoba
and Ontario. No social distinctions appear.

/ɔ/ 1, 7, 9, 11, 15-16, 29, 36, 58;
109, 139-40; 203; [1]312, 315, 323; 415,
430, 436.
/au/ All others except the following
nonrespondents: 5, 21, 31-32, 49, 52-53,
56, 61, 64; 119, 121, 134, 138, 151; 223;
307-8, 322; 409, 417, 432.

/ɔi/ *and Variants*

A number of words typically having the
/ɔi/ retain more or less viable traces of
social or regional variation. Several
feebly still retain an earlier /ai/;
others weaken or lose the offglide before
/i/.

<u>boil</u>, n. 59.1. NE 512. PEAS 167-68.
<u>boiled</u> 37.2. NE 284. PEAS 167-68; F144,
F145.

Although <u>boil</u>, a word for an infected
spot, and <u>boiled</u> as in <u>boiled eggs</u>, occasionally have /ai/ in the eastern states
where /jaint/ also occurs, this pronunciation is practically extinct in the UM.
One elderly Type I Iowan (135) with Kentucky and Tennessee parentage has /ai/ in
both words, although once corrected himself by adding /bɔil/, and another Iowan
(116) recalls having heard this form in
her community. No infs. in the UM have
/ai/ in <u>spoiled</u>.

<u>hoist</u> 34.3. NE 220. PEAS 168.

An eastern term said to a cow at milk-
ing time, usually to get it to lift its
leg, is <u>hoist</u>, which regularly is pronounced with /ai/. Only one instance
turns up in the UM, from a southern Minnesota Type I inf. (65) of New York background. But in conversation another
Minnesotan (29) has the same pronunciation with /ai/ as the name of a machine
for lifting hay.

<u>joint</u> 55.7. NE 491. PEAS 167; F143.

In the eastern states <u>joint</u>, referring
to the human elbow or knee, is often pronounced /jaint/ in the folk speech of the
Appalachians and of Maine and New Hampshire, and rarely in the Hudson Valley
and northeastern Pennsylvania. It has

weakly survived in the UM, with six scattered instances. But only three are from Type I speakers (39; 148; 207); one is from a Type II (152); two are from college graduates (34; 426). One of the latter is a physician who, however, acknowledges frequent deliberate adoption of nonstandard usages in order to be more acceptable to his patients. The evidence hardly warrants belief in the permanence of this pronunciation.

joined 66.1. NE 531. PEAS 167.

Six UM infs. also have /aɪ/ in joined, as in "They joined the church," but they are not the same six. Actualized as [ɔɪ], [aɪ], and [ɑɪ], the vowel is used in joined by four Type II infs. (208; 303, cvr305, 325) and two Type I's (6; cvr413) —all widely scattered in the UM.

Inf. 122 has [ʌ̆ɪ], which in light of his eastern New England background, may be accepted as an allophone of /aɪ/.

poison 48.7, 48.3. NE 251.

In poison ivy and poison(ous) /aɪ/ has a similarly feeble existence in the UM, and, except for inf. 29, with still different speakers. Its allophones appear as follows: [aɪ] 52; [ɑɪ] 125; [ɐɪ] 29; [ʌɪ] 316, 318-19; [ɜɪ] 424. Inf. 125 has the same vowel in poison and ivy.

oil 20.3a. NE 187. PEAS 167; F143.

Oil sometimes exhibits a different variation in the South and Midland, shared by boiled and spoiled, but to a lesser extent, in the UM. The high-front offglide /i/ is centralized to a weak [ə], [ᶦ], or [ᵻ] and for some speakers is so fused with the onset of the following velarized [ɫ] that the vowel becomes simply [ɔ]. For only one UM inf. (148) has fusion yielded the pure [ɔ] in his form /ɔl/, but several others have only a weak central offglide [ɔə] or a very weak raised offglide [ᶦ] or [ᵻ]. This development is limited to Midland speakers, except for two in North Dakota. Those with [ɔə] are 204, 216; 427. Those with [ɔᶦ] are 120-21, 139-40, 147, 149; 421. The single inf. with [ɔᵻ] is 105.

CHECKED VOWELS

/ɪ/ *and Variants*

bristle 29.4. NE 207. PEAS 130; F59.

As in the Atlantic states, the vowel in

bristles is commonly the vowel of sit, /ɪ/, which is slightly backed by some speakers, even to the centralized /ᵻ/ position by five Type I infs. (15, 25; 212, 216, 218) and by two Type II's (33; 215).

The New England variant with the vowel of sun, /ʌ/, persists only in the speech of eight old-fashioned and uneducated infs. in the first-settled areas of the UM: 56; 107, 113-14, 139, 151; 316, 322.

creek 24.5. NE 40-41. PEAS 148; F97.

For many persons in the North and North Midland speech regions the pronunciation /krik/, rhyming with meek, has become a shibboleth of "correctness." But even though it is bolstered by school insistence that the ee spelling must represent /i/, this form has won acceptance by only one out of five UM infs. as a whole and by only one-half of the Type III group. On the contrary, the dominance of the second form, /krɪk/, rhyming with pick, in the North and the North Midland excepting southern New England is reflected in similar dominance in the UM. No marked geographical pattern emerges.

The insecurity created by the notion of "correctness" is obvious in the replies of 16 scattered infs., who acknowledge using both pronunciations, at least sometimes with a rather self-conscious reaction to /krik/. They are 1, 22, 29, 44, 60, 65; 127, 129, 150, 152; 212, 222; 318; 401, 413-14.

	Type I	Type II	Type III
/ɪ/	89%	80%	56%
/i/	21%	27%	56%

	Mn.	Ia.	N.D.	S.D.	Nb.	Ave.
/ɪ/	86%	85%	72%	82%	81%	83%
/i/	23%	23%	36%	21%	32%	26%

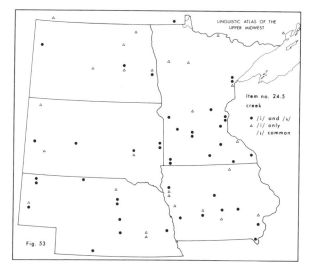

LINGUISTIC ATLAS OF THE UPPER MIDWEST

Item no. 24.5
creek
• /i/ and /ɪ/
△ /ɪ/ only
/ɪ/ common

Fig. 53

/ɪ/ c1, 2, 4, 6-8, 11-16, ?17, 19-22, c23, 24, c25-26, 27, c29, 30, c31, 32-37, c38, 39-41, c42, 44-45, c46, 47, c48, 49, c50-51, 52, c53, 54, 56-57, c58, 59, c60, c65; 101-5, c107, 108-9, 112-14, ?115, 116-21, 123, c124, 125, †126, 127-30, 132, 134-49, c150, 151, c152; 202-5, 207-9, ¹¹210, 211-12, c213, 214-16, c218, c220, 222-25; 302-9, cr310, c311, ¹313, 314-21, c322, 323-26, ¹328; 401, c402-3, 404-5, c409, †410, 411-12, cvr413, c414, 415-16, c417-18, 419, 421-22, c423, 427, ¹†428, c429, 430, ¹431, 432-37.

/i/ 1, 3, 5, 9, c10, cr17, 18, 22, cr?26, 28-29, cr?37, cr?39, c43, 44, 55, c60, 65; 106, 110-11, crl15, 122, ?124, 126-27, 129, 131, 133, 150, c152; 201, c206, 210, 212, 217-19, 221, c222; 301, ?310, c312-13, 318, c¹319, 327-28; c401-3, 406, 410, 413-14, 420, 425-26, 428, sn431.

no response 226.

Comment:

"/krik/ is more proper"—413. Inf. formerly used /krɪk/—126. Inf.'s normal pronunciation is /krɪk/, but she uses /krik/ to please her husband, who has made an issue of this—127.

milk 25.7. NE 297.

An early variant of milk with /ɛ/ rather than /ɪ/ is reported by 18 of the 416 New England infs. Eleven of these occurrences are in eastern Massachusetts and none in Maine or New Hampshire. Although in the UM no cultivated speakers have this form, it persists in the speech of four Type I infs., c214, c219; 413, and 432, and in the speech of four Type II infs., c30; c213; 308; and 428. All are in Northern speech territory or have parental Northern speech background. One Canadian inf., Type I c201, also has /mɛlk/.

rinse 15.2. NE 138. PEAS 130.

Throughout the UM the vowel of rinse is generally /ɪ/, but the vowel /ɛ/ of set is retained in the speech of 38 infs. Of them 29 are Type I speakers and 25 are in Iowa and Nebraska, evidence for the continued Midland orientation of what is clearly a declining and increasingly old-fashioned pronunciation. Only one Type III inf. has /ɛ/. One inf., 206, has /raɪnts/, a form not reported in the East.

/ɛ/ 6, c19, 21, 25, 31, †40, †44, 59; 105, 113, c116, 124-25, 129, 132, 139, 142-43, 145-49, 151; 203-4, ¹†222; 301, 303, 308, 317, ¹319, 327; 407, c413, 417, 420, 426-28, 432, 434.

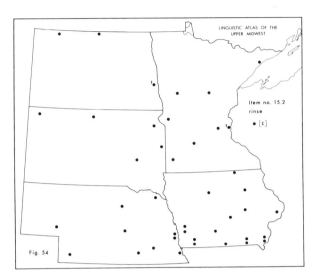

Fig. 54

Further suggestive evidence of an earlier alternative /ɛ/ for /ɪ/ appears in two stray pronunciations observed in conversation with inf. 139, who has /pɛθ/ for pith, and with inf. 212, who has /šɛfənɪr/ for chiffonier.

/ɛ/ *and Variants*

again 68.2. NE 428. PEAS 131; F60, F61.

In the UM the well-nigh universal pronunciation of again is with the vowel /ɛ/ of let. In the phrase Come again! the vowel is more likely to be followed by a diphthongal offglide in Midland speech territory, e.g., [ɛɛ̂].

The form /əgɪn/, widely used in the East among less-educated speakers, is recorded in the UM by only two fws., M in Duluth, Minnesota, and P in southern Iowa, where its Midland background is obvious. The infs. are 13-18; 117, 124, 126-27, 135-36, 138, 140, 142-43. If the diphthongal [ɛᶦ] or [ɛ⁺] is interpreted as /ɪ/, then its range is widened to include these infs. as well: 21, 25, 40, 58; 101, 103-6, 108, 110-11, 113-15, vr131, 132, 141, 149; 420-21, half of whom are likewise in Midland territory.

An ingliding diphthong, [eə] or [ɪə], appears in Midland speech territory in the speech of the following: 117, 121-22, 124-27, 129-31, 133-34, 139, 142, 144-45, 147; 413-14, 423-28, 430-32, 434.

deaf 58.6. NE 502. PEAS 131-32; F62.

Of the three pronunciations of deaf found in the eastern states, with the /ɛ/ of left, the /i/ of leaf, and the /ɪ/ of lift, only the first is general in the UM and the third occurs as a single instance.

Deaf with /ε/ is common in all five states, but nearly one-third of the infs. evince varying degrees of familiarity with the form /dif/. A number of them report only having heard its use by others; some admit having once used it themselves but describe it as old-fashioned. Of the 44 infs. still using /dif/, 14 declare that they also say /dεf/, although they do not always specify when and why they shift from one to the other. Only 30 infs., then, appear to be restricted to the /dif/ pronunciation, 19 in Type I and 11 in Type II. All but one of them live in either a rural or small-town community. The form appears to be rather rapidly receding and unlikely to survive.

/i/ 1, 5, ¹†6, 13, 16-17, 27, sn35, 37, ¹39, †40, 41, 45, !¹47, 48, 51, †54, 55, ¹58, ¹65; 106, 108-9, 114, 123, 125, 129-30, 136, 138, 140, 143, †145; ¹†202, †203, 204, ¹†205, !208, 212, ¹†213, ¹215, 216, †217-18, ¹†219, †220, ¹†221, 224; 302-3, 308, †309, 311, †320, 322-23, †325; †401, 405, 407, †409, ¹410, 416, !s417, 418, ¹420-21, 429, ¹431, 432, 434-36, †437.

/dɪf/ 56.

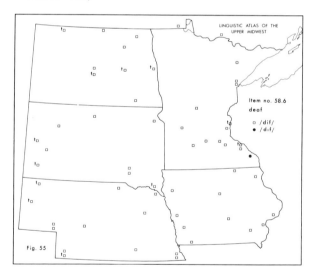

Fig. 55

egg   37.2. NE 294-95. PEAS 102, 132; F63.

For some speakers the velar /g/ in egg induces a raising of the vowel from /ε/ to /e/. This pronunciation is common in much of New England, especially in the northeast and in western Connecticut, and, as a minority variant more likely to be used by less-educated speakers, it competes with /ε/ elsewhere in the Northern and Midland areas.

For PEAS the problem of classifying as /ε/ or /e/ such intermediate pronunciations as [ε⁺] was usually solved by comparison with the inf.'s pronunciation of ague, a word included in the eastern worksheets.

Because the declining use of the term ague dictated its omission from the North Central and UM worksheets, no comparison can readily be made here in order to determine the phonemic category of the intermediate vowel in the various pronunciations of egg. The problem is acute with [ε⁺] in the speech of those infs., mostly in Iowa and Nebraska, who tend to diphthongize the checked vowels.

On a broadly inclusive basis /e/ can be interpreted as containing any diphthong such as [εᵉ], but not [εᵉᵛ], that is, with an offglide no lower than [e]. Such an interpretation yields the following social and regional distribution in the UM.

	Type I	Type II	Type III
/eg/	58%	38%	50%

	Mn.	Ia.	N.D.	S.D.	Nb.	Ave.
/eg/	50%	55%	31%	50%	53%	48%

If this interpretation is accepted, it is clear that the /eg/ variant has spread widely and may be gaining in frequency at the expense of /εg/.

On the other hand, a quite different picture emerges if, to avoid the ambiguity of [ε⁺] variants, only those pronunciations are counted that are transcribed as [e]. Then the distribution is as follows:

	Type I	Type II	Type III
/eg/	26%	12%	25%

	Mn.	Ia.	N.D.	S.D.	Nb.	Ave.
/eg/	31%	6%	15%	33%	11%	20%

A further complication is that fws. differ somewhat with respect to using the offglide symbol as indicative of the direction of the glide or, more exactly, of its terminus. Fieldworker variation is likely to be the reason for the sparse showing of /e/ in southern Iowa. Another complication is that population mixture in Iowa and eastern Nebraska prevents positive interpretation of diphthongs intermediate between /ε/ and /e/ without prior identification of each inf.'s own phonemic pattern. It may be noted, however, that it is even now clear that the pronunciation /eg/, often ridiculed by the spelling aig, is not without prestige in the UM, where it is heard from Type III speakers as well as those in Types I and II.

Without consideration of the diacritics

for length and for fronting or backing, the following analysis offers a relevant grouping of the responses shown in the Synopses.

[ε˅] 415-16.
[ε] 33, 35-36, 42-45, 47, 57, 60; 105, 108, 115, 148-49; 301-2, 304, 306, 313, 319, 323; 402, 413, 416. 421-22, 425, 428, 430, 433. [εᵋ^] 30; vr131; 201, 209, 218; 324; 401, 407, 409, 412. [εᵉ˅] 1, 24, 64; 214, 219; 436. [εᵉ^] 46, 52-53, 62; 225; 312. [εˡ˅] 31, 35; 217. [εˡ] 414, 423, 427, 431-32, 434. [εˡ^] 110-11. [ε⁺] 102, 113-16, 133, 138.
[ε^] 117, 119-21, 152; 202-3, 208. [ε^ᵉ] 220-21, 224. [ε^ˡ] 101; 420, 424. [ε^ˡ^] 104, 109, 112, 137. [ε^⁺] 103.
[e˅] 303. [e˅ᵉ] 37, 51, 61, 65; 211. [e˅ᵉ^] 3, 10, 39; 212; 315, 326; c402, 403, 408, 437. [e˅ˡ˅] 210. [e˅ˡ] 6, 21; 150; 405, 429.
[e] 48; 307, 318. [eᵉ^] 46, 52-53, 62; 225; 312. [eˡ] 32, 58. [eⁱ] 305, 317.

keg 16.7. NE 146. PEAS 133; F64.

All three of the eastern pronunciations of keg were carried into the UM, but the clear trend is toward the general adoption of standard /kεg/ and away from the popular eastern /kæg/, rhyming with bag, and from the New England and South Atlantic /keg/, rhyming with plague.

About eight out of 10 UM infs. have /kεg/. The form with /æ/, common in the South Midland and among less-educated speakers in rural New England and New York State, is represented in the UM by only 11% of the infs., 16 Type I and 5 Type II, most of whom are in the Midland territory in Iowa and Nebraska. The form /e/, found in New England and part of the

South Atlantic coastal region, is unmistakably used by only 17 UM infs., 8% of the total. The New England background is probably reflected in this distribution, since all but three are in Northern speech territory.

But an unresolved problem arises because of the tendency some speakers exhibit toward having an upglide before the velar consonant /g/. If the following instances of [εˡ] are interpreted as examples of /e/, then the incidence of /e/ rises sharply and its range is extended to include more of Iowa and Nebraska: 11, 14-17, 21, 48, 54-58; 102, 104, 107, 110-16, 133, 138; 315; 414, 416, 421, 423, 429-31, 434, 437.

More controversial would be the inclusion of the following instances of [εᵉ], which nevertheless has been proposed as a member of the /e/ sound-group because of the wide range of allophonic variation in this word for any one speaker: 6, 29, 37, 40, 44, 46; 131; 219; 312; 404, 410.

Fieldworkers L and W recorded three instances of a centering offglide [εə], all in Midland territory: 118, 150; 413.

/keg/ 2, 12, 15, 48, 52, 54, 56-58, 60; 148; 201, 215, 225; 305; 408-9.
/kæg/ 65; 109, 130, 132, 135, 137, 139-40, 142, 144, 151; 218; 307-8, 314; 405, 415, 417, 420, 427, 433.
/kεg/ All others except nonresponding 202.

kettle 14.5. NE 131. PEAS 133.

Both eastern pronunciations of kettle, that with cultivated /ε/ and that with popular /ɪ/, occur in the UM, but the second is clearly yielding to the former in the eastern half and barely surviving

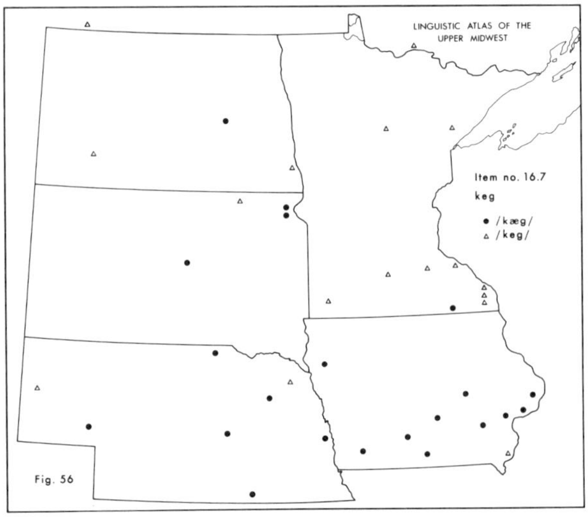

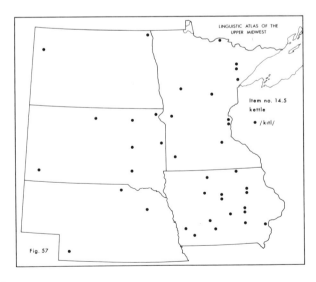

Fig. 56

Item no. 16.7
keg
• /kæg/
△ /keg/

Item no. 14.5
kettle
• /kɪtl/

Fig. 57

in the western half. Of the 157 infs. offering this term (see Volume 1 for the
equivalents), only 39, or 25%, have the
/ɩ/ pronunciation; and 30 of those are in
the oldest and least educated group. No
Type III speaker has it.

The higher frequency in Iowa may reflect a strong Midland background derived
from the common occurrence of /ɩ/ in central Pennsylvania.

One Nebraskan has a variant with a lowered vowel, /æ/.

/ɩ/ 5, 13-14, 16, 19, 22, 25, 35, 39-
40, 59; cvr104, 105, 113-14, cvr115,
c116, †117, 125, 127, 129, 132, c133,
134, c138, 142, 151; 208, c209; 303, 306,
c307, 316-17, 320, c322; 405, 415, 429.
/æ/ 435.
no response 2-3, 10, 12, 27, 38; 120,
147; 201, 204-5, 207, 213, 223; 302, 304,
308-9, 315, 321, 327.

muskmelon 44.5. NE 265. PEAS 134; F65.

All instances of this word have the
vowel /ε/ in melon, with no reported sur-
vivals of South Atlantic and South Midland /ɩ/. The variant mushmelon is
treated in Volume 1.

parents 49.7. NE 373. PEAS 150; F102,
F104.

Of the stressed vowels of parents in
the eastern surveys, one, southwestern
New England /e/, does not appear at all
in the UM investigation. Of the two others, the common Northern and universal
North Midland /ε/ is likewise dominant in
the UM, but with a slight but positive
Midland bias. In Minnesota and the Dakotas it meets the competition of the minor
variant form with /æ/, which is common in
New England and frequent in New York
State. Although in PEAS the form with /æ/
is linked with an American monosyllabic
pronunciation of parents, actually 40 of
the 41 monosyllabic occurrences in the UM
are with /ε/, /pɛɚnts/, and only one,
203, has /æ/. No strong social contrast
appears except a possible favoring of /æ/
by older and less-educated speakers.

	Type I	Type II	Type III
/æ/	16%	9%	6%
/ε/	84%	91%	94%

	Mn.	Ia.	N.D.	S.D.	Nb.	Ave.
/æ/	20%	0	27%	20%	5%	13%
/ε/	80%	100%	73%	80%	95%	87%

/æ/ 1, 6-7, 10-11, 22-24, 27, 39, 50,
56, 65; c201, 202-4, 206, 215, 219; 306,
310, 312-13, 321; 401, 412.
no response 119, 120-21, 151; 307, 327.
/ε/ All others.

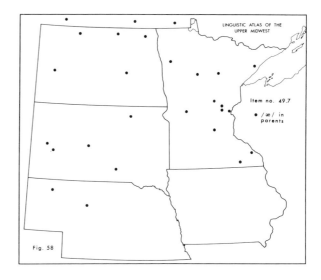

scarce 68.5. PEAS 150; F105.

Not sought in New England, this Middle
and South Atlantic survey item was added
to the UM worksheets to find whether the
South Midland pronunciation with /e/ had
penetrated the UM. No instances appear.
Of the two major eastern variants, that
with /ε/ strongly dominates all the UM.
That with /æ/ persists with 19 occurrences, Northern-oriented with distribution mostly in Minnesota and South
Dakota. It apparently is declining.

/æ/ 27, 36, 39, 45, 54-56, 58, 65; 107,
139; 213; 308-9, 312, 325-26; 402, 418.

yellow 37.1. NE 296. PEAS 134.

In the eastern states, particularly in
the South Atlantic and South Midland regions, there is a striking diversity in
the stressed vowel of yellow, ranging
from /æ/ and /ɩ/ to /ʌ/. In the UM, however, all instances of this word have
allophones of /ε/, except that fw. M recorded two Duluth infs., 15 and 16, as
having a more centralized vowel, /ɜ/.

A pronunciation with a lowered vowel,
/æ/, does, however, occur with bellow
(29.7). Three Type I infs., widely scattered, have the form /bælɚ/, rhyming with
valor: 41; 140; 224.

yesterday 4.3. NE 71. PEAS 134; F66.

Although commonly in the South Midland
and in many parts of New England the
first syllable of this word is yis-, with
the vowel /ɩ/, this pronunciation is rare
in the UM. It occurs only in the speech
of four scattered old-fashioned Type I
infs.: 41; 135; 204, 220. The pronunciation with /ε/ is predominant.

/æ/ and Variants

aunt 52.6. NE 384. PEAS 135; F167.

Most UM infs., eight out of 10, pronounce aunt as /ænt/, rhyming with pant, often with fairly strong nasality and sometimes with a distinct offglide, as [æᵋnt]. This dominant pronunciation is surely derived from western New England, where it is common, and the rest of the North and North Midland region, where it is universal.

But two out of 10 UM infs. have in aunt a vowel ranging in quality from [a] to [ɔ], a circumstance that only at first glance can be correlated with the occurrence of such vowels in eastern New England. In PEAS Kurath proposes that these "/ɑ - ɒ/" vowels of aunt in that area and also in Tidewater Virginia are attributable to the cultural influence of England in those sections during and even after the colonial period. But this reasonable inference cannot be applied to the situation farther west. Although the Minnesota and North Dakota distribution of this pronunciation clearly demonstrates Northern orientation, the generally weak effect of eastern New England speech upon the Middle West rather pointedly suggests that other causes may have operated to reinforce that effect. A clue appears in the fact that at least 15 of the 41 infs. with the /ɑ/ type of pronunciation also have /æ/, and that several of these acknowledge /ænt/ to be their customary form.

Two linked factors may have provided support for the weak carryover from eastern New England: the influence of the schools and the influence of spelling. The prestige of "Boston English" in the nineteenth century was reflected in the training of teachers and in prescriptions in textbooks. Many teachers were taught the social superiority or even absolute "correctness" of a backed vowel of some sort (sometimes labeled the "Italian a") in aunt, dance, chance, ask, laugh, and about 90 other words that in England in the eighteenth century had experienced the shift from an earlier front /æ/. But general enforcement of such a school-prescribed shift in normal pronunciation habits is so difficult that only partial or token enforcement seems to have resulted—and then only with a few students, not all.

That the token is aunt rather than any other of the possible shibboleths is presumptively due to its being the only word in the entire group with a spelling that in contrast with a homophone, ant, might

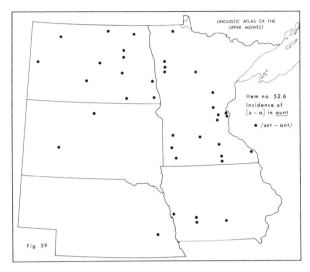

Fig. 59

suggest a phonetic as well as an orthographic difference. Several infs. recalled teachers who, ignoring normally present context, belabored students with the admonition "You don't want to call your aunt an insect, do you?" But dance, chance, example, and the like, which historically are parallel with aunt, are now spelled without the u and hence regularly have /æ/ in the UM. Relevant also is the fact that haunted, 67.2, always now spelled with u, typically has a back, even rounded, vowel [ɒ] or [ɔ].

A diverting effect of the prestigious imposition of the /ɑ/ pronunciation exists in the speech of several infs., whose native /æ/ form persists in the child-learned "Aunt Sue" and "Aunt Edie" and the hypocoristic aunty, but who carefully use /ɑnt/, perhaps especially when talking with a fw. For them and for many others this form seems to have become a learned status pronunciation symbolizing control of "correct English." But for younger infs. and others of a later generation, who have learned this pronunciation at home, with or without classroom reinforcement, /ɑnt/ is a natural form though acknowledged to be less frequent.

Field data do not suggest that /ɑnt/ is either increasing or decreasing in frequency in Northern speech, although the fact that in Wisconsin an earlier survey revealed only 12% frequency of /ɑ/ might hint at a possible increase. But recent informal surveys among University of Minnesota students indicate the persistence of the same general proportion, i.e., about three out of 10 state-born students have /ɑnt/.

The sound-type here symbolized as /ɑ/ represents phonetically recorded field

274

instances as follows: [aˤ] 121. [a] 33, 44, 61-62; 126; 219. [aˀ] 22, 26, 30; 203, 210. [ɑˤ] 34, 39, 49, 58; 208, 225; 312. [ɑ] 4, 7-10, 40, *41, 47, 63; 122, 127; 205, 211-13, 216; 304-5, 313; 426. [ɑˀ] 319. [ɒ] 224. [ɔə] 316. Of these the following were recorded with a noticeably long vowel: 9-10, 22, 30; 205, 211-13, 216, 219, 224; 313; 426.

Type	Mn.	Ia.	N.D.	S.D.	Nb.	Ave.
I	21%	8%	31%	14%	0	15%
II	40%	0	64%	16%	0	21%
III	50%	25%	50%	0	50%	32%
Ave.	31%	6%	46%	14%	3%	19%

[ɑnt] 4, 7, →8, 9, c10, 22, 26, 30, 33, c34, cr39-40, *41, 44, 47, 49, 59, 61-63; !122, 126, !127, vr131; 203, 205, 208, 210, c211, 212-13, 216, 219, *221, 224-25; 304-5, !¹312, 313, !*316, ¹319; c426. Of the infs. listed above the following also use /æ/: 8, 26, 30, 34, 39-40; 122, 127, 131; 203, 208, 211-12, 219, 224; 304-5, 312, 316, 319. All others have only /æ/, except unrecorded 35 and 151.

Comment:

"It's /ɑnt/ now." Says it's common here—40. Admits saying /æ/ sometimes. Thinks he learned /ɑnt/ in grade school—30. Apparently an acquired pronunciation; also uses /æ/—34. First offered /æ/; then corrected to /ɑ/—39, 40. But always /æ/ in aunty; admits changing from /ænt/ some years ago—*41. Always /ɑ/ because of her aunt Mary's insistence. "She was born a Yankee"—49. But /ænt/ in "Aunt Maren" and aunty is /ænti/—203. But then corrected to /æ/, conceded to be inf.'s usual pronunciation—208, 211; 304, 313. But /æ/ in "Aunt Edie"—212. But /æ/ in aunty as a vocative—224. Says /æ/ but thinks /ɑ/ is proper—226. But said /æ/ when form was repeated—305.

can't   45.3. NE 695. PEAS 53; F69.

In his article "Pronunciation of 'can't' in the Eastern States," *American Speech* 28(1953), 149-57, Sumner Ives describes the distribution of three principal variants of can't, one with the "broad a," [a] or [ɑ], in eastern New England, one with the "long a" /e/ in parts of New Jersey, Virginia, and North Carolina and the South Midland region, and one with the "short a" /æ/ elsewhere. Of these only one, /æ/, is typical in the UM. A single instance of [a] appears in the speech of one Type I Minnesotan, 44, but it is almost certainly due to his British parentage rather than to an eastern influence.

catch   72.1. NE 584. PEAS 139-40; F74.

The eastern variations of catch have been described by Raven I. McDavid, Jr., in "Notes on the pronunciation of *catch*," *College English* 14(1953), 290-91, where he observes that the maligned form /kɛč/ is actually the most frequent and that it so successfully competes with /kæč/ that nearly one-half the cultured speakers in New England, the Atlantic coast states, and the North Central region use it.

That the /ɛ/ pronunciation may be losing prestige or at least is less prestigious in the Upper Midwest is suggested by two circumstances. One is that only 1% of the cultured speakers use it, in contrast with 19% of the Type II infs. and 24% of the Type I infs. The second is that its frequency is less in the more recently settled western half of the region and hence may be declining in acceptability (Minnesota 16%, Iowa 10%, North Dakota 6%, South Dakota 7%, Nebraska 6%).

The preceding analysis relies upon an interpretation of [ɛˆ] and [ɛˇ] as allophones of /ɛ/ and of [æˆ] as an allophone of /æ/. Actually, the situation is not so clear-cut. Unlike such rhyme-words as batch, match, and scratch, catch is distinguished by a continuous range of vowel allophones from [ɪ] to [æ]. Much of this range, that from [ɛˆ] to [æ], may even be exemplified in the speech of one inf., a fact that renders doubtful the arbitrary assignment of all occurrences of [ɛˇ] to /ɛ/ and all occurrences of [æˆ] to /æ/, especially when the same speaker is recorded as having both [æ] and [ɛˇ], e.g., inf. 47. More examples might have been recorded had not fws. H, P, and Wi usual-

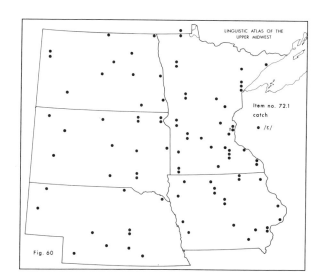

LINGUISTIC ATLAS OF THE UPPER MIDWEST

Item no. 72.1
catch

• /ɛ/

Fig. 60

275

ly contented themselves with a simple /æ/ - /ɛ/ contrast instead of indicating finer distinctions.

But the full /æ/ - /ɛ/ contrast is sometimes recognized as one between the acceptable and the unacceptable. Inf. 39, for example, after offering [kɛˇč] immediately corrected it to [kæč]; inf. 312 volunteered that /kɛč/ is "incorrect"; and inf. 40 acknowledged having discarded /kɛč/ as old-fashioned.

Besides the social preference for /æ/ in the UM, a geographical distribution appears in the occurrence of strong diphthongal offglides in the speech of 12 infs., all but one of whom are in Midland speech territory.

Only one Iowa inf. has the widespread eastern minority variant with /ɪ/; and one Minnesotan with Kentucky background has /ɑ/.

/ɪ/ 116.
[ɛˆ] 15; 113, 146.
[ɛ] 4, 8, 13, 16-17, 19, 25, 30, 35, †40, 43, c47, c61, 62; 102, 104-6, 108-9, 112, c121, 123-24, 138, 140; 210, 212, 220; 305, *306, 307-8, c311, c314; c401, 405, 407, 415, c418, 420-21, c429, 430.
[ɛˇ] 1, 6-7, 17, 20, 22, 24, 26, 37, 39, 41-42, c47, 48-51, 54, 56-57, 60, c61, 62; 130, 135; 204, 207, 209, 211, 215-16, 218, 224-25; 301-3; c409, 432.
[æˆ] 2, 5, 9-12, 14, 17-18, 21, 23, 27, 29, 31-34, 38, 52, c55, 59, 64; 117, 122, 128, 143; 201-3, 205-6, 208, 219, 221-23; 304, 309, 312-13; 404, 408, 412, 426, 433-34, 436.
[æ] 3, 22, 28, 36, cr39, 40, 44-46, c47, 53, c61, 65; 101, 103, 107, 110-11, 119-21, 124, 126-27, 129, 131, 134, 136-37, 139, 141-42, 144-45, 147-49; 213-14, 217, 226; 310; 403, 411, 413-14, 417, 422, 424-25, 427-28, 431, 435, 437.
[ɑ] 35.
[ɛɪ] 114-15.
[æᵋ] [æɪ] 58; 132-33; 402, 406, cvr416, c419, 423.

granary   11.6.   NE 105.

The two pronunciations of granary, with the /e/ of grain and with the /æ/ of ran, provide a significant case study. A spelling with grain-, attested by the *Oxford English Dictionary* as early as 1714, suggests strongly that the /e/ pronunciation, probably influenced by grain itself, has some historical standing. But the *Oxford English Dictionary* records only /æ/, and commercial dictionaries for more than two centuries ignored the ai spelling and either rejected the /e/ pronunciation or relegated it to inferior status by such a label as "popularly,"

found in the Webster's *New International Dictionary*, second edition, in 1934. The clearly preferred /æ/ is consistent with the Latin etymon *granarium*.

Then came the conclusive evidence of the New England Atlas materials. Of the 256 occurrences of the word in the field data, 241 were with the /e/ pronunciation and only 15 with /æ/. Seven of these latter were concentrated in eastern Massachusetts. In their *Pronouncing Dictionary of American English* in 1956 John S. Kenyon and Thomas A. Knott were constrained by this evidence to state that in the United States the /e/ pronunciation "appears to prevail," and they even unsuccessfully sought to revive the form grainery.

This evidence and this conclusion are slowly being accepted by commercial dictionaries. The arbitrary dictum of Margaret Nicholson in her *American English Usage* in 1957 that one must say "grānary, not granary" is reflected in the preferred status still given that pronunciation in Webster's *New World Dictionary*, *The World Book Encyclopedia Dictionary*, and *The American Heritage Dictionary*. But the G. & C. Merriam-Webster dictionaries and the Funk and Wagnall *New Standard Dictionary* now acknowledge that evidence by recording the /e/ pronunciation as prevalent.

Although the rarity of /ɡrænərɪ/ in western New England might suggest an even lower frequency in the UM, actually this form has slightly expanded, almost certainly through dictionary and school support. Its frequency in New England is only 6%; in the UM it is 12%, quite evenly distributed both socially and regionally. Six infs. (44; 124, 128, 131; 410, 414) use both pronunciations, and several others comment on their existence.

	Type I	Type II	Type III
/æ/	12%	12%	21%
/e/	88%	91%	79%

	Mn.	Ia.	N.D.	S.D.	Nb.	Ave.
/æ/	13%	10%	12%	15%	14%	13%
/e/	79%	92%	88%	89%	86%	88%

/æ/ 3, 11, 28, 33, 42, ?44, *46, 58, †62, 63, 65; 101, 107, 123, 126, 128, 130; 201, 214, 216; 313-14, 326-28; 404, ?410, 414, 418, s426, 434.
/e/ 1-2, 4-10, 12-27, 29-31, s?32, 34-41, 43, ?44, 45-47, c48, 49-57, 59, c60, 61-62, 64; 102-6, 108-22, *123, 125, 127-30, 133-50; 202-4, c205, 206-10, c211, 212-13, 215, 217-26; 301-3, c304, 305-12, †313, 316, c317, 318-21, c322, 323-25, †328; 401-3, 405-7, 409, ?410, 411, †412, 413, c414, 415, c416, 417, 419-21, c422,

423-24, 427, c428, 429, cvr430, 431-33, 435-37.
no response 408, 425.
Comment:
"We say /grɛnri/ but it's spelled /grænəri/"—47. "People not around one much call it /grænri/"—62. "/grɛnri/ is usual here"—328.

pasture 13.1. NE 114. PEAS 53.7; F70.

Pasture is generally pronounced with /æ/ in the UM. The eastern New England variant [a] is found in the speech of only four infs. (11, 50; 132; 220), three of whom have one parent each from Canada, Scotland, and Maine, areas in which that variant is frequent.

radish 43.2. NE 256. PEAS 140; F76.

Three-fourths of the UM infs. have /æ/ as the stressed vowel in radish. The variant /rɛdɪš/, with the vowel of red, has Southern and South Midland dominance in the East and infrequent occurrence in the North and North Midland. In the UM /rɛdɪš/ appears as a strong minority pronunciation in southern Minnesota and in the Midland speech territory of Iowa and Nebraska, where it is more common among the less educated than with Type II speakers. As is true in the East, the trend seems to be toward /æ/. The distribution of /ɛ/ is as follows:

Type I	Type II	Type III
33%	22%	6%

Mn.	Ia.	N.D.	S.D.	Nb.	Ave.
28%	35%	8%	25%	24%	23%

raspberry 48.6. NE 276. PEAS 5.3; F71.

The common pronunciation of raspberry in the UM is with [æ]. But 15 older infs., nearly all of whom are in Northern speech territory, offer a continuous range of backed and sometimes rounded vowels that probably reflects the more frequent occurrence of these variants in New England and the North Atlantic states. Aside from the common [æ], which is used by 109 below, the minor variants appear as follows:
[a] 14, 27; 223; 303.
[ɑ] 44, †¹47; 113, *116; *202, 219.
[ɒ˞] 45, 48.
[ɒ] 56, ¹58.
[ɔ] 42; 109; 422.
no response 151-52; 305, 317.

rather 67.3. NE 717. PEAS 5.3; F72, F73.

Of the several lexical variants for this item, rather is offered by two-

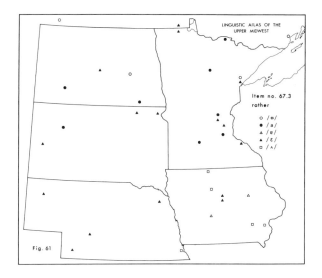

thirds of the infs., most of whom pronounce it with the vowel [æ]. But 35 infs. exhibit a phonetic range like that found with greater frequency in New England and the other eastern states. The minor variants occur as follows:
/ɛ/ ([ɛ] [ɛ̌]) 1, 4, 16, 30-31, 54; 114-15; 216; 305, 307, 309; 402, 408, 419, 429.
/a/ ([a] [aˆ] [aˀ]) 5, 11, 29; 215, 224; 302.
/ɑ/ 3, 15, 33; 201, 219.
/ʌ/ [ʌ] 103, 113, 135, 138; 434. [ɐˆ] 117, 126.

Of the infs. listed above, two, 219 and 402, also have [æ].
It is observable that the trend is clearly toward the uniform use of [æ]. Twenty-three of the infs. having other vowels are older and less-educated speakers; only 11 are high school graduates and not one is a college graduate. Even the variants with /a/ and /ɑ/, which are prestigious in the East, lack that prestige in the UM, where they are becoming old-fashioned if not nonstandard.
Some regional contrast in the UM appears in the fact that the higher central vowels [ʌ] and [ɐ] are more likely to be found in the speech of Midland-speaking infs. and that the /ɑ/ and [a] types are found only in the Northern speech area.
An analogous variation appears in the pronunciation /gɛð˞/ for gather, recorded in the free conversation of Type I Iowa infs. 101 and 107.

scallions 43.5. NE 258.

Although reported as common in New England at the time of the Atlas survey there, /skʌljɨnz/ is still unrecognized in commercial dictionaries as a variant of /skælj+nz/. Of the seven UM infs. who have this lexical variant (for others see Volume 1), only two have the accepted form with /æ/: 39 and 43. Since the five who have the variant with /ʌ/ are all in Type I, this form is clearly a minor social marker in the region. They are 27, 44; 103, 141; 212. One additional inf., 414, reports having heard this variant in the community.

sumac   48.4. NE 250. PEAS 5.3.

Although the several minor variants of the second vowel of sumac found in the East also occur in the UM, they are clearly giving way to the dominant pronunciation with /æ/.

Noted in PEAS as common among rural speakers in both the North and the North Midland, /e/ survives in the UM among uneducated speakers in Midland territory. The single exception is a college graduate in eastern North Dakota.

As an eastern variant reported from both sides of Chesapeake Bay, /ɛ/ appears singly in the UM as used by an inf. of Canadian parentage.

Considered by Kurath as an overrefinement, /ɑ/ may be that also in the UM, where seven scattered Type II infs. and two Type III's favor it, but only two Type I's.

Weakly stressed forms not reported in the eastern surveys, /ə/ and /ɩ/ occur once each in Iowa and Nebraska.

All infs., including 403 below, have /æ/ except the following:
  /e/ 132-33, 135, 146; 221; 401, 403, 429.
  /ɛ/ 8.

/ɑ/ 9, 12, 18, 44, 49, 57; 106, 121, 130; 205, 207; *¹316.
  /ɩ/ 413.
  /ə/ 148.
  no response 1, 4-5, 7, 17, 25; 101, 113, 140, 143, 151; 201, 203, 206, 209, 215-16, 223-24; 301-2, 305-8, 322; 415, 436.

tassel   44.3. NE 262. PEAS 5.3.

Nearly two-thirds of the UM infs. have the /æ/ of tack in tassel, but, as in much of the eastern part of the country, its frequency is higher among the cultivated speakers. In the UM the percentage drops from 79% for Type III to only 54% for Type I.

In PEAS Kurath reports that a rounded back vowel, [ɔ] or [ɒ], is common in the folk speech of western Pennsylvania, eastern New England, and parts of New York State. This social contrast is reflected in the UM, where nearly one-third of Type I infs. have a rounded vowel, but only one-tenth of those in Type II, and none of those in Type III.

Also like the eastern distribution is the pattern with another variant, the unrounded low central [ɑ]. Kurath finds it sporadic without social contrast; in the UM it likewise lacks social contrast, but it has slightly higher incidence in Midland speech territory.

Three infs. (51; 117; 415) who have the noun /tɑsəl/ reveal a contrast with the verb de-tassel, in which they have /æ/. Had this contrast been systematically investigated, other infs. with it may have been found. The circumstance suggests that for them the form with /ɑ/ has been consciously adopted.

As elsewhere in this volume, the following specifics are categorized by sound-type without suggesting rigid phonemic analysis, e.g., without questioning whether for a given speaker [ɒ], [ɔ], and [ɣ] belong to one, two, or three different phonemes.

	Type I	Type II	Type III
/æ/	54%	70%	79%
/ɑ/	23%	21%	21%
/ɔ/	27%	10%	0

	Mn.	Ia.	N.D.	S.D.	Nb.	Ave.
/æ/	64%	56%	69%	62%	65%	62%
/ɑ/	22%	28%	19%	8%	29%	23%
/ɔ/	16%	20%	12%	35%	14%	18%

/æ/ [æ] 1, 5-9, c10, 12-18, 20, 22, 27-30, 32, 34, 37-38, 43, 45, *46, 47, 49, 52-54, 57, cr60, 62-64, cr65; 101, 103-4, 107-8, 110-11, 114-16, 118, 120-24, 126, !127, 128, 131, 136-37, 139, 141, 143-45, 147-51; 201-3, 205-6, 210-12, 214-17, .

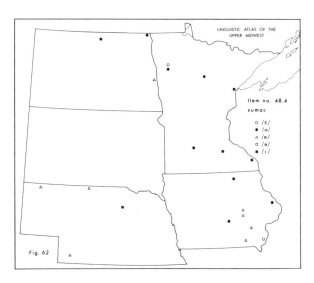

LINGUISTIC ATLAS OF THE
UPPER MIDWEST

Item no. 48.4
s u m a c
o /ɩ/
• /ɑ/
△ /e/
□ /ə/
▪ /ɩ/

Fig. 62

219, 223-24; 301, 304, 306-8, 312-16,
318, ¹323, 328; 401-3, 410, →411, 412-14,
418-19, 421, 423-26, cr427, 428, 430-31,
433-36. [æˇ] 325-26. [aˆ] 21, 33; 213;
302, 324. [a] 11.

/ɑ/ [ɑˁ] 130. [ɑ] 2, 44, 50-51, 58;
102, 106, 109, 112, 117, 119, 125, 134,
138, 142, 148; 207-9, 218, 225; 310, 321;
†411, 415, 422, 432. [ɑˀ] 24-25, 39-40,
59, 61; 404, 417. [ɒ] 2, 23, 35.

/ɔ/ [ɒ̣] 416. [ɑˀ] 420. [ɔ] 129, 135,
140, 146, 149; 316-17; 427. [ɔˇ] 226.
[ɔˇ] 31. [ɒˆ] 303, 322-23. [ɒ] 3, 19, 25-
26, 41-42, 55-56; 105, 113, †115, 127,
132-33; 204, 220; 305, 309, 311, 320;
409, 437.

/ɑ/ and Variants

<u>calm</u> 6.3, 57.5. NE 92, 478. PEAS 141;
<u>F77.</u>

<u>Calm</u> is recorded as the lexical variant
offered by 100 UM infs. in either of two
contexts, "Keep calm" and "The wind is
calming down." Nearly all of them have a
vowel like that in <u>father</u>, either /ɑ/,
usually slightly lengthened, or a slightly backed variant /ɒ/. This is the general pronunciation in New England and the
North and among cultivated and middle-
class speakers in Pennsylvania.

Folk speech in the Midland region, how-
ever, usually rhymes <u>calm</u> with <u>ham</u>. But
this /æ/ vowel apparently did not easily
survive the rigors of the western migration, since in the UM it appears singly
in the speech of a Type I Iowa housewife.
One other instance does occur, in southeastern Manitoba, but there its source is
palpably the speech of the inf.'s father,
who was born in southern England.

Five scattered UM speakers have rounded
/ɒ/ and one has /ɔ/, described by Kurath
as found in Pennsylvania with an origin
in northern England.

/æ/ 1; 135.
/ɑ/ 2, 4, 7-10, 18-22, 26, 28, 31, 33,
38-39, 43-47, 50-55, 57-58, 61-63, 65;
101-3, 106-8, 110, 118, 121, 123, 127,
130-31, 137, 142, 144, 150, 152; 201-2,
207, 211-13, 215, 219, 226; 302, 305-7,
310, 312-13, 315, 318-21, 326, 328; 401-
4, 421, 427-28, 433, 435, 437.
/ɒ/ 5, 13-14, 17; 126.
/ɒ/ 32, 34, 60; 119, 134.
/ɔ/ 145.

<u>palm</u> 55.5. NE 490. PEAS 142.

The eastern distribution of the /ɑ/ and
/æ/ variants of <u>palm</u> is like that of <u>calm</u>
except for a greater frequency of the /ɑ/

pronunciation on all social levels in the
Midland and South.

In the UM two Type I rural infs. in
Iowa, with Midland and South Midland ancestry, reflect the minority eastern
/pæm/, and three infs. in Canada reflect
the occurrence of that form in southern
England.

Although most other UM speakers have
/ɑ/ or its backed equivalent /ɒ/, a scattering of infs. have the rounded /ɒ/ or
/ɔ/. Some of these latter instances in
Iowa are clearly due to a South Midland
background.

/æ/ 1, 3; 113, 135; 202.
/ɒ/ 14, 34, 38, 57; 122, 124, 148; 215;
328; 407, 434.
/ɒ/ 13, 15, 17, 30, 64; 141, 143, 145;
303, 310; 404, 406.
/ɔ/ 140, 146.
/ɑ/ All other infs.

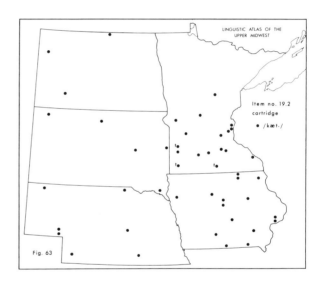

LINGUISTIC ATLAS OF THE
UPPER MIDWEST

Item no. 19.2
cartridge
• /kæt-/

Fig. 63

<u>cartridge</u> 19.2. NE 161. PEAS 142; F78.

<u>Cartridge</u> offers a conspicuous social
pattern. Although, as in the eastern
states, the stressed vowel is generally
/ɑ/, the eastern rural minority form with
/æ/ persists in the UM among rural and
less-educated speakers, particularly in
southern Minnesota and Iowa. Its reduced
frequency in the western half of the UM
hints at its decline. Several infs. note
that it is old-fashioned. No Type III
infs. have it.

Two infs. with the /æ/ variant (36;
436) retain the following /r/, perhaps
because of the spelling. Five others who
usually have the post-vocalic /r/ have
only /kɑt/ as the first syllable. They
are 4; 124; 308, 314; 407.

	Type I	Type II	Type III
/æ/	34%	19%	0
/ɑ/	69%	82%	100%

	Mn.	Ia.	N.D.	S.D.	Nb.	Ave.
/æ/	33%	31%	12%	23%	21%	25%
/ɑ/	63%	62%	81%	72%	78%	70%

/æ/ 21, 25, 27, 32, 35-36, 39-41, !45, †46, 47-48, ⊥51, 52, !⊥53, 56, †60, †62; 105-6, 108-9, 113-15, 117, 129, 135, 140-41, *145, 147, 151; *204, 209, 215; 301, 304, †⊥312, 316-17, 325; 401, 405, *417, 420, 429, 432, 436.

/ɑ/ All others except nonresponding 13-14, 16, 18; 121, 136, 139; 305-7, 318-19, 327; 402, 413-15, 421, 425.

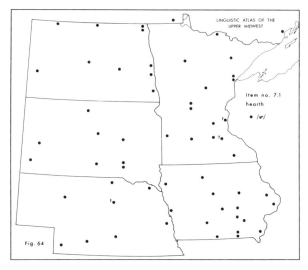

Fig. 64

hearth 7.1. NE 329. PEAS 142; F80.

The two recorded meanings of hearth (see Volume 1) and the two distinctive pronunciations exhibit no correlation.

Two-thirds of the UM infs. have /hɑrθ/; one-third have a retroflex vowel in [hɚθ]. As in the eastern states, a marked social contrast appears in the UM, where the former pronunciation is closely related to the degree of schooling. All but one of the college graduates have it, as do three-fourths of the Type II's, but only a few more than one-half of the least educated. The form [hɚθ], reported as common in the North and North Midland, is similarly distributed throughout the UM, with no decided regional pattern except a somewhat greater frequency in North Dakota. By several infs. it is considered old-fashioned, although one inf. (64), after changing her response to /hɑrθ/, then admitted that [hɚθ] is her customary pronunciation. An eastern and Southern variant with /æ/ does not occur, unless it is reflected in the form /hɛrθ/, used by two rural informants in the same southern Iowa community.

	Type I	Type II	Type III
/ɑ/	56%	77%	93%
[ɚ]	44%	26%	7%

	Mn.	Ia.	N.D.	S.D.	Nb.	Ave.
/ɑ/	75%	54%	57%	64%	71%	68%
[ɚ]	28%	35%	44%	36%	23%	33%

/ɑ/ 2, 6-8, 11-12, 14, 18, 20-21, 23-26, 29-31, 33-34, 36-40, 42-43, 45-47, 49, 50-51, f52, 53-55, s⊥56, 57-63, cr64, 65; 102-6, 108, 110-11, 113-14, 116-17, 119-20, 122, 124-28, 131-32, s136, 137, 141-44, 149, 152; 201-2, 204-5, 210-13, 215, 217-19, 221-22, †226; 301, 304, 307-10, 313, 319, 324-28; 401-4, 409-11, 413-14, 418, 420, s422, 424-26, 432, 434-35.

[ɚ] 1, 3, 5, 10, 13, 16-17, 22, 27-28, 32, 35, 40, 44, †48, 64; 109, 112, 115, 118, 121, 123, 129, 133-35, 139, ⊥†142,

145, 148, 150-51; 203-4, 207-8, 214, 216, 220, 223, 225; ⊥†302, 303, c311, 314, 316, 321-23; 405, 407, 412, †414, s⊥421, 423, 427, c429, 431.

/ɛ/ 146-47.

crop 33.6. NE 124. PEAS 143; F81.

As in the East, nearly all UM infs. have an /ɑ/-type vowel in crop. A minor backed variant /ɒ/ is scattered, and two fws., M and Wn, record rare instances of a rounded vowel. These backed forms may reflect the occurrence of /ɒ/ in eastern New England and western Pennsylvania. Atlantic coast /kræp/ does not occur in the UM.

/ɒ/ 2, 14-15, 24, 51, 62; cvr117; 311; 403, c405, 408, 429.

/ʊ/ 13.

/ɔ/ 307-8, 317.

God—in a religious context 66.2. God!—as an oath 66.3. NE 599.

These two items have the purpose of determining whether in their pronunciation infs. differentiate between God as in religious contexts and God as an expletive or oath, and, if they do, whether the difference is socially or geographically patterned. The records reveal that, as in New England although in a diminished proportion, some speakers do make the distinction but that there is no clear correlation with either social class or geographical area.

Sixty infs., more than one-fourth of those in the UM, apparently experience a psychological need to pronounce God in one way when they swear and in another when they pray. They fall into three groups.

For 19 of these infs. the difference lies in vowel quality alone. The contrast is between a low-central vowel /a/ and a low-back vowel /ɒ/ or /ɔ/ usually accompanied by lip-rounding. The first is manifested as [ɑˤ], [ɑ], [ɑˆ], [eˇ], [ɑˀ], and [ɒˤ]. The second appears as [ɒ], [ɒ], [ɒˬ], [ɔˀ], and [ɔ]. Sixteen of the 19 pronounce God! the oath with a low-central /a/ that contrasts with a back vowel in God as a religious term: 23, 25, 35, 39, 41, 50; 126, 133; 206, 208, 216, 224; 309-10; 403, 429. Three infs. reverse the contrast by having a back vowel /ɒ/ or /ɔ/ in the oath, the pronunciation sometimes mildly ridiculed in literature by the spelling "Gawd."

In the second group 22 UM infs. distinguish the two uses of God only by contrast in vowel length, realized either by extending the time duration of the pure vowel, i.e., from /gad/ or /gɒd/ to /gɑ·d/ or /gɒ·d/, or by extension through the addition of an offglide as in [gɑᵉd], [gɑˠd], [gɑᵗd], [gɒᵉˤd], and [gɒˬd]. Seventeen of the 22 pronounce the oath with a short vowel in contrast with a long vowel of similar quality in God the religious term: 13, 34, 37, 48, 53, 62; 117, 139; 207; 303-4, 322-23; 407, 418-19, 435. Five reverse the contrast, with the longer vowel in God! the expletive and a short one in the religious term: 106; 311, 328; 428, 437.

The 19 infs. constituting the third group are recorded as combining vowel length and vowel quality to differentiate the two uses of God. Perhaps some of these should be placed in the first category, however, since the feature of vowel length is not necessarily a contrast marker in English, where length is typically a function of primary stress position in a phonetic phrase. Thirteen of the 19 mark God! the oath with an unrounded vowel /a/ or [ɒˤ] shorter than the rounded long vowel /ɒ·/ in the God used in religious contexts: 1, 11, 18, 28, 54; 131; 204, 218-19; 405, 408-9, 412. Four make the contrast by having a long unround /a·/ in the oath but a short round vowel in the religious term: 27, 49; 202, 205. Two infs. completely reverse the situation by marking God! with a rounded short vowel in contrast with an unround longer vowel /a·/ in God as used in church: 58 and 404.

If by the ignoring of the length component the first and third groups are combined for a total of 38 infs. with vowel quality contrast, it appears that 33 of them, nearly 90%, distinguish the one God from the other by swearing with a low-central or unround vowel in /gad/ and praying with a low-back typically rounded vowel in /gɒd/.

Whether in the UM the contrasts described above are more than purely idiosyncratic is doubtful. Type I speakers constitute 48% of all the UM infs., 55% of those who have the contrast. Type II speakers constitute 43% of all UM infs. and only 37% of those with the contrast. But this apparent slight preference by the least educated speakers is contradicted by the fact that 8% of the college group also make the contrast, the same proportion as in the whole body of infs.

Nor is there any stronger evidence for conjecturing a geographical pattern in the UM. Infs. who contrast God! and God are somewhat more numerous in Minnesota and North Dakota, and of the eight infs. who have the rounded vowel /ɒ/ in the oath four are in Midland speech territory and four are in Northern. But much more intensive investigation is required before firm generalizations can be made about this particular problem.

God as a religious term:
/a/ 4, 6, 8-10, 12-13, 15, 19-22, 26, 29, 31, 34, 37-38, 42-44, 46-48, 51, 57-58, 60-61, 63-64; 101-17, 119-21, 123-25, 127-29, 131-32, 134-48, 150; 203, 207, 209-10, 212, 214, c220, 221-23, 225-26; 301-6, 308, 311-16, 318, 320-24, 328; 401-2, 404, 406, 410, 413-19, 422, 424-25, 427, 431-35, 437.
/ɒ/ 3, 17-18, 23-24, 39, 50, 52, 62; 122, 130; 205-6, 208, 211; c309, 325; 403, 405, 420-21, 423, 426, 429, 436.
/ɒ/ 1-2, 5, 7, 11, 16, 25, 27-28, 30, 32-33, 35-36, 40-41, 49, 54-56, 65; 126, 133; 201-2, 204, 213, 215-18, 224; 310, 326; 407-9, 411-12.
/ɔ/ 45, 53, c59; 149; 219; 307, 317, 319; 428.

God! as an oath:
/a/ 8, 10, 18, c23, 24, c25, 26-28, 30, 34, c35, c37-38, 39, 41, c44, 48, c50-51, 57, 62-64; 101-2, 104-15, 117, 119-21, 124-25, 131, 133, 137-39, 143, 146-50.
/ɒ/ 1-2, 11, 13, 49, 54; 126, 140; 310; 421, 428.
/ɒ/ 32, 39, 58; 132; 201, 204; 404, 407.
/ɔ/ 5, 53; 433.

harmonica 15.8. NE 413.

Forty-nine UM infs. are familiar with harmonica as a lexical equivalent of mouth organ. (For the other terms see Volume 1.) Three phonetic varieties occur.

Thirty-two infs. offer /har'manɪkə/, which is distributed without social or regional contrast. This pronunciation, with [ɑ] or, infrequently, [ɒ], is that usually recognized in commercial dictionaries. The UM users are as follows: 30-31, 35, 38; 101-2, 110-12, 116-17, 121, 141, 150; 206, 208, 212, 214; 319, 323; 401-2, 406, 411-12, c414, 421, 423-26, 428.

Five infs. have /hɑrˈmɒnɪkə/ or /hɑrˈmɒnɪkə/, with the rounded stress vowel. All are in Midland speech territory. They are 130; 305-6, 308, 318.

Eleven infs. have the minority form /hɑrˈmɒnɪkə/. Although this variant is recorded as widespread in the New England survey, its high frequency among Type I informants indicates why it lacks dictionary recognition. Similarly in the UM, where its acceptability seems to be decreasing, this form with stressed /o/ is a social marker. Ten Type I's (118, 126, 129; 204, 209, 220; 309, 316, 413, 415) and one Type II (144) use it.

Inf. 435, for whom the term may be an "eye-word," has the aberrant pronunciation /ˈhɑrməˌnɪtkə/.

yonder 41.3. NE 707. PEAS 143; F82.

Of the 54 infs. who use or have used the lexical variant yonder (see the section on adverbs in Volume 2) all but a handful have /ɑ/ as the stressed vowel.

A North Midland influence may have produced the single [ɜə] of inf. 303 with Ohio parents; and a South Midland influence may have yielded the /æ/ of inf. 132 with a Kentucky father. Two infs., 317 and 318, have a fully rounded /ɔ/.

/ʌ/ and Variants

brush 18.7. NE 155. PEAS 143; F83.

Nearly all UM infs. have the eastern dominant pronunciation with /ʌ/. The South Midland folk variant with /ɛ/, rhyming with mesh, turns up in South Midland speech territory in southern Iowa. A West Virginia and Virginia variant with /ɜ/ occurs six times, but some of the instances may be due simply to phonetic assimilation. They are chiefly in the speech of the least educated infs. A pronunciation with /ʊ/, found three times in southern Iowa, is probably to be associated with /ɜ/ and may well have a South Midland provenience. All the variant pronunciations seem to be on the way out.

/ɛ/ cvr139, 142; c422.
/ɜ/ 15, 31; 150; 202, 206, 214.
/ʊ/ 140, 144, 146.
no response 3, 38, 42; 303, 305, 308, 322; 406, 415, 423, 436.

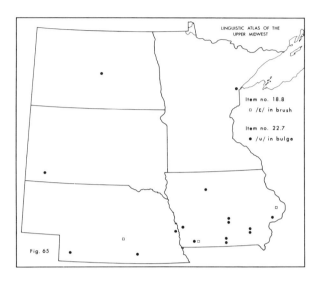

Fig. 65

bulge 22.7. NE 362. PEAS 144; F84.

The two contrasting variants of bulge are in sharp geographical contrast. That with /ʌ/ is distinctly Northern and North Midland. It is well-nigh universal in New England and nearly as dominant in the UM. The pronunciation with rounded /ʊ/ is distinctly South Midland. In all of New England there are only four instances, each of which is in south western Connecticut; it was reported on Nantucket Island as a remembered old-fashioned form. All the instances in the UM except three are in South Midland speech territory.

/ʊ/ 17; 113, 124, 129-30, 135-36, 141, 143, 146; 217, 320; 427, 429, 432.
/u/ 145.
/ʌ/ All other infs. except nonresponding 15, 31, 57; 137; 306-7, 322; 407, 409.

gums 55.4. NE 487. PEAS 144; F85.

Although /gʌmz/ dominates the UM, as it does the South Midland and, among educated speakers, the North Midland of Pennsylvania and New England and New York State, the persistence of the common Northern nonstandard pronunciations with the /u/ of boom and the /ʊ/ of good is conspicuous in the field data. Their status is threatened, though, by a growing awareness that by many they are considered old-fashioned and even humorous. Almost no other item in the worksheets so well illustrates the effect of negative social attitudes upon a once well-established pronunciation.

All but two of the college class have /ʌ/, as do eight out of 10 of the high school group but not quite six out of 10 of the Type I infs. By contrast one-half of the Type I's have either /u/ or /ʊ/, as do one-fourth of the middle group. This social distinction pervades the UM.

One Minnesota inf. of Welsh parentage (21) has /o/, not recorded elsewhere.

	Type I	Type II	Type III
/u/	32%	17%	6%
/ʊ/	18%	7%	6%
/ʌ/	58%	82%	88%

	Mn.	Ia.	N.D.	S.D.	Nb.	Ave.
/u/	20%	17%	35%	32%	22%	18%
/ʊ/	8%	21%	0	4%	19%	12%
/ʌ/	75%	67%	77%	71%	61%	63%

/u/ 4, ¹6-7, 8, !†11, 13-14, †20, †24, 26, ¹†33, ¹37, †40-41, 44, ¹47, ¹†49, 52, ¹53, 55-56, ¹†58, 60-61, ¹†62, 65; 101, 103, 112, 117-18, ¹128, 129, 139-40, 145, 148; cr201, ¹203, 204, †205, †208, 209, †210, 212, ¹†213, †215, 216-18, †219, †221, 223-24, †225, ¹†226; 304-5, 308, †312, ¹†313, c314, 315-16, 320, 323-24; 405, 407-8, 417, 423, 432, 436-37.

/ʊ/ 15-17, 41, 46; 109, 113, 117, †124, 127-28, 132, 137, 141; 321; 401, 403, 415-16, 420-22, 427.

/ʌ/ 1-3, 5-7, 9-14, 18, *19, 20, 22-25, 26-37, 39-40, 42-43, 45, 47-51, 53-54, 57-59, ¹60, 62-64; cr101, 102, 104-8, 110-11, 114-16, 118-21, 123-25, 130-31, 133-36, 138, 142-44, 146-50, 152; 201-3, →205, 206-8, 210-11, 213-15, →217, 219, 220-22, 224-26; 301-3, 305-7, ¹308, 309-11, →312, 316-19, 322, 325-28; 402, 404, 406, 409-14, 418-19, cr423, 424-26, 428-31, 433, 435, cr437.

no response 151.

Comment:
"Some say /gumz/"—6-7, 39. "I don't

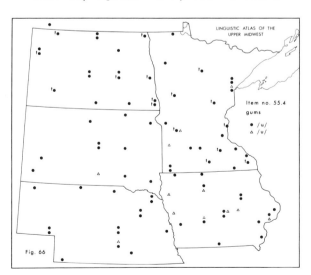

LINGUISTIC ATLAS OF THE UPPER MIDWEST

Item no. 55.4
gums
• /u/
△ /ʊ/

Fig. 66

know which is right"—7. "Some young people still say /gumz/"—39. "/gʌmz/ is correct. Most call 'em /gumz/"—53. "Elderly people say /gumz/—58. Inf. disapproves of /gʌmz/—60. Grandmother's term was /gumz/—62. /gumz/ is inf.'s usual term, although he corrected it to /gʌmz/—101. "Old people used to say /gʌm/"—145. Inf. says /gʌmz/ but considers /gumz/ "correct"—148. Her mother used /gumz/—213. Inf. admits /gumz/ is his usual term—224. "Some people say /gʌmz/"—308.

judge 53.1. NE 422. PEAS 144-45; F86.

Although a handful of instances of /ɛ/ and /ɪ/ occur in northern New England and northern New York, in general the North has the /ʌ/ of cut in judge. Several other vowels are reported by Kurath as appearing south of the Potomac, especially among infs. not in the cultivated group. The UM similarly reveals the predominance of /ʌ/ with only a scattering of variants used by 11 infs., none of whom is in Type III. Only two infs. have /ɛ/. Four have [ɝ], and three more are uniquely recorded by fw. M with [ɤ], both of which vowels are probably to be interpreted here as allophones of /ʌ/, especially since they are very close to the high allophone [ʌ^], frequently recorded in Minnesota and North Dakota. A rounded /ʊ/ turns up twice.

/ɛ/ 146; cvr220.
[ɝ] 14, 40; 403-4.
[ɤ] 14-16.
/ʊ/ 128; 415.
no response 151.

mush 40.3. NE 288. PEAS 145; F87.

As in the northern states of the eastern surveys, mush typically has /ʌ/ in the UM. About one-fourth of the UM infs., however, have allophones that reflect an eastern distribution sporadic in the North but somewhat more frequent in New Jersey, Maryland, and, to a lesser extent, West Virginia and adjacent parts of Ohio. An upgliding allophone [ʌɪ] found in those areas sharply sets off the Midland territory in the UM. Its apparent absence in southern Iowa is almost certainly due to the fact that the fw. there did not record the offglides.

A mid-central vowel type /ɜ/, nonphonemic in the UM, occurs three times—twice with r-like constriction—as a reflex of a variant found in western Pennsylvania and part of the South Midland. An instance in North Dakota is probably explained by the fact that the inf.'s father came from Tennessee. Three instances of high cen-

283

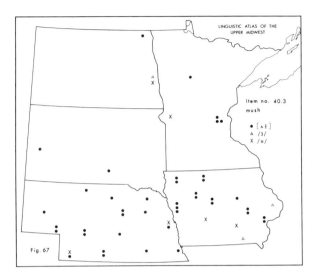

Fig. 67

tral [ɵ] are interpreted as examples of
/ɜ/. Rare are [ʊ] and [ɛ].

/ɛ/ 52.
/ɜ/ [ɜˆ] 139. [ɚˆ] 146. [ə] 220.
[ɵ] 25; c222; 429.
/ʊ/ 126, 134; 427.

nothing 74.5. NE 633. PEAS 145; F88.

Cultivated speakers in the North and
all speakers in the South and South Midland areas are reported by Kurath as having the /ʌ/ of nut in nothing. In New
England, New York State, and much of New
Jersey and Pennsylvania a variant pronunciation with /ɑ/ dominates the speech of
the middle and lowest groups. This regional and social orientation of the /ɑ/
form persists in the UM, although it is
clearly giving way to expanding /ʌ/. Only

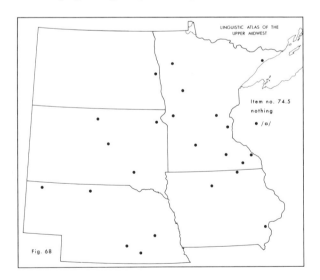

Fig. 68

11% of all UM infs. have /ɑ/; more than
one-half of them are in the oldest group,
Type I.

/ɑ/ [ɑ] c6, c8, c19, c25, c36, 56, 64;
138; c303, 308, c314, 322; 401, 404, 423-
24, 432. [ɐ] 50; 105, 112; 220, cvr225.

shut 9.7. NE 347. PEAS 146; F90.

About one-half the UM infs. chose shut
rather than close. Most of these have the
pronunciation /šʌt/. A spare few have the
northern New England and South Midland
variant /šɛt/, and two infs. of foreign
parentage have the vowel [ɜ], which for
them is more likely to be idiosyncratic
than attributable to any eastern influence.

/ɛ/ 6, 16, 35; 135; 202, 220; c322.
[ɜ] 36; 206.

Just (a minute!) 54.1. NE 6.

The adverb just has become a shibboleth
of pronunciation for many teachers, who,
because of the spelling, have insisted
that it should be pronounced like the adjective, i.e., /ǰʌst/, and have condemned
the alternate /ǰɨst/.

In the UM survey 167 infs. volunteered
for this item the temporal expression
"Just a minute!" (The others responded
with "Wait a minute!" or an equivalent.)
The various allophones in just can be
grouped into four general classes: widespread /ʌ/ and /ɨ/ and infrequent /ɛ/ and
/ɪ/.

The pedagogical assumption that the
pronunciation /ǰɨst/ is incorrect and
limited to the speech of the uneducated
is clearly not supported by the evidence.
It is actually the most common pronunciation in three of the five states and
among Type III as well as Type I and Type
II speakers. The variants in the /ʌ/
group run a close second on the whole,
and dominate in Iowa and North Dakota.
There seems to be no warrant for stigma-
tizing the pronunciation /ǰɨst/.

The two minor variants, on the other
hand, do exhibit a social correlation.
Jest /ǰɛst/ is strongest among the least
educated; no college-trained speaker has
it. The form /ǰɪst/ is likewise strongest
in Type I, with only one Type III inf.
using it.

/ʌ/ [ʌ] 19-20, 44, 52, c53, 56-57, s58,
63; 103, 106-7, 111, 113-14, vr115, 126-
27, 131, 133, 140-41, 144-45, 149; c413,
433. [ʌˆ] 1, 3, 5-6, 9-12, 24, 28, s33,
54-55, 65; 102, 118, 122, 139, s152; 202,
204, 206, 208, 210, 215-17, 219-20; 313,
315, 319, c326-27; 434. [ɜˆ] 17; c309;

c412. [ɜ˂] c55. [ɜ̂˃] c2, 3, 26; 320-21, 325; 406, 429.

/ɨ/ [ɨ] 16, 18, 38, 46, c61; 140, c150; 219, 223; 305, c310; c404, s421, 424-25, 428, s430, 431-32. [ɨˇ] 13-14, 23, s27, 39, 42; 303, c322, 327; 410, 414, c416-17, 423, 435. [ɨ̌˂] 37, 50; 201, c203, c205, c214, 224, s226; 304, 323; 402, c403, c409. [ɨ˂] 15, 35, c47; 108-9, 117, 125, 130, 142-43. [ɨ̌˃] 211; 426. [ʉ] 137. [ʉ+] 116. [ɘ] 4, c7-8, 21, c22, 35, c45; 221-22, c225; 302, s324, 326, 328. [ɘ˃] 36. [ə] 416. [ə̂˂] 31, 41, 49, 64; 212.

/ɛ/ [ɛ˃] c29, 34, c45-46, c59, c61.

/ι/ [ι˃] 43, 60; 123, 129, 135-36; 401, c405. [ι̌˃] 51; 124; 301.

<u>touch</u> 71.5. NE 689. PEAS 146; F91.

The New England and South Midland variant with /ɛ/ has not survived in the UM. All speakers have /ʌ/.

/ʊ/ *and Variants*

<u>butcher</u> 37.5. NE 553. PEAS 147; F93.

In <u>butcher</u> the predominant stressed vowel in the eastern states and in the UM is the /ʊ/ of <u>good</u>. Only three Type I infs. in Minnesota and Iowa retain the eastern folk variant /u/, clearly a declining pronunciation. Three fws. in Minnesota and Iowa also record six infs. as having an unround /ʌ/, a pronunciation found in southern England but, according to Kurath, not occurring in the eastern United States. It may well be a new development consistent with a tendency toward the unrounding of rounded vowels.

/u/ 32, 39; 143.
/ʌ/ 57-58; 119, 124, 127, 129.

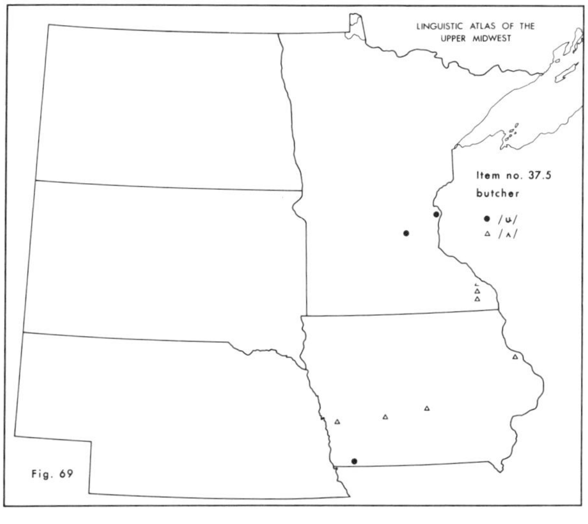

Fig. 69

<u>bushel</u> 34.3. NE 127. PEAS 147; F94.

No clear picture emerges from the sparse occurrence of two minority variant pronunciations of <u>bushel</u> in the UM. The nearly unanimous pronunciation with /ʊ/ is feebly countered by three instances of /u/ that only possibly may be directly related to the /u/ in West Virginia, and by six instances of /ʌ/, a pronunciation not reported at all in the eastern surveys. At least one such instance, however, may be the fw.'s version of the vowel /ɜ/, as both parents of the inf., 119, are from Pennsylvania, where /ɜ/ is found. Infs. with /u/ are c16, 21; 319. Those with /ʌ/ are 45, 47, 56, 63; 119; 307.

<u>boulevard</u> 63.8.

Although instances of regional <u>boulevard</u> were collected primarily as <u>lexical choice</u> (see Volume 1), several variant pronunciations turned up as well. Some instances in South Dakota and Nebraska were with a different lexical meaning.

Of the 104 examples of <u>boulevard</u> 79% are with the /ʊ/ vowel of <u>good</u> and 14% are with the /u/ vowel of <u>tooth</u>. No regional contrast exists, but a perhaps insignificant favoring of /u/ appears among the Type II infs.

Three infs. have the minor variant /ʌ/. Fw. Wr recorded three Nebraskans with [ɜ], a central vowel here best interpreted as /ʌ/ also. Wr also recorded one inf. with [o^], which may be taken as an instance of /ʊ/. Only two of the college group have minor variants (222; 319); the others prefer more prestigious /ʊ/.

/u/ 2, 7, 14, 24, 33, 36-37, 42; 203, 206, 211, 222; 318; 413.

/ʊ/ 1, 3-5, 9-11, 13, 15-23, 26-28, 30-32, 34-35, 38-39, c40, c43, 44-50, c51, 52-54, c55, 57-63, 65; 107-8, 140-41; c201, 202, 207, 209-10, 213, 216-21, 224-26; 303, c304, 308, 317; 422-27, 431, 433, c434, 435.

/ʌ/ c16; 307, 319.

[ɜ] c414, 416, 428. [o^] 420.

<u>put</u> 23.3. NE 708. PEAS 147; F95.

Although according to Kurath <u>put</u> is typically /pʊt/ north of the Potomac, a few occurrences of the relic pronunciation /pʌt/ are reported from southern Pennsylvania, northern West Virginia, and northeastern New England. In the UM the widespread dominance of the /ʊ/ vowel is broken by 14 instances of /ʌ/, some of which, particularly those in Minnesota, probably reflect an eastern origin.

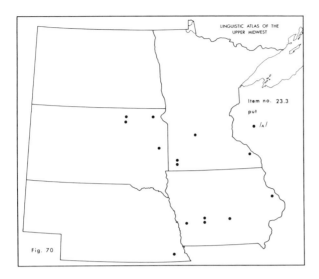

/ʌ/ 43, 56, 59-60; 120, 124, 126-27, 131; 305, *306, 307, 319; 435.

took 58.5. NE 492, 499. PEAS 147-48; F96.

Although the past tense of take was not regularly recorded in Minnesota and appeared elsewhere chiefly as a lexical variant, the data are enough to suggest the persistence—amid the general acceptance of /tʊk/—of a nonstandard pronunciation /tʌk/ found in the South Atlantic states, West Virginia, and New Hampshire. Most of the UM instances are in Midland speech territory, but one Canadian inf. has a clear occurrence.

The weakly rounded [ʊ̯] recorded in Nebraska seems best interpreted here as /ʌ/.

/ʌ/ [ʌ] cvr132-33; c201, 216; cvr320. [ɤˇ] 126; 209; c426, 435. [ʊ̯] c401-2, 408, 414, c428.

STRESS VARIANTS

Because stress variation affects vowel quality, some words of more than one syllable exhibit vowel variation that may be idiosyncratic but also is often clearly correlated with social or geographical distribution patterns. It appears in three sets of circumstances.

In one set the vowel varies because the stress itself varies in different pronunciations. In the second set there is variation within the allophonic range of a regularly unstressed vowel, the so-called

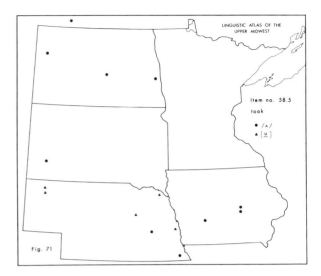

reduction vowel. In the third set variation reaches the point where reduction results in complete loss of the vowel.

Variable Stress

address, vb. 72.9.

Two principal classes of variants of the verb address occur, one with initial stress and one with final stress. The second is subdivided into instances preserving the quality of the initial vowel /æ/ and those with reduction to /ə/.

Because this item was added to the worksheets after the second year of fieldwork there are only six returns from Minnesota. Nevertheless, the contrast in frequency between the Dakotas, on the one hand, and Iowa and Nebraska, on the other, points to a Northern orientation for /əˈdrɛs/ and to a Midland orientation for /ˈæˌdrɛs/ and /ˌæˈdrɛs/. The variants with final stress are conspicuously preferred by the cultivated speakers.

	Type I	Type II	Type III
/ˈæˌdrɛs/	26%	25%	11%
/ˌæˈdrɛs/	38%	31%	44%
/əˈdrɛs/	36%	30%	44%

	Ia.	N.D.	S.D.	Nb.	Ave.
/ˈæˌdrɛs/	21%	12%	12%	56%	26%
/ˌæˈdrɛs/	27%	42%	64%	19%	37%
/əˈdrɛs/	50%	36%	24%	31%	38%

contrary 57.2. NE 471.

Because contrary is only one of several lexical responses for this item (see Volume 1), the evidence for its regional pronunciation is sparse. The 20 scattered instances, however, offer examples of two of the varieties found in New England; a third, with a two-syllable pronunciation, does not appear.

The usual pronunciation has stress on the antepenult, the first syllable, typically /ˈkɑnˌtrɛri/. The following UM infs. have it: 17, 20, 27, 40; 103, 105, 115, 132; 206-7, 214-15; 302, 316, c325; 405. All have /ɑ/ in the first syllable except 316 with /ɔ/ and 405 with /ɚ/.

But six infs. have stress on the penult, with consequent weakening of the vowel in the antepenult. One of them, 16, has /ɐ/; the others, 101, 129, 135, 145, and 201, have neutral schwa /ə/. Although four of the six American infs. with this variant (besides one Canadian) live in Midland speech territory and although the North Central survey of Wisconsin turned up only one instance of this stress pattern, there is not enough evidence to conclude that this form is Midland-oriented. It may, however, be significant that five of the seven with /ˌkənˈtrɛri/ are Type I speakers and that one of the two Type II infs. (325) first offered /ˈkɑnˌtrɛri/ as the presumably desired form but then lapsed conversationally into her usual /ˌkənˈtrɛri/. It does not appear as though the vitality of the nursery rhyme about "Mary, Mary, quite contrary" has been strong enough to make /ˌkənˈtrɛri/ the prestigious pronunciation.

forehead 54.6. NE 485.

Three distinct variants characterize the pronunciation of the second syllable of forehead. Two of them have secondary stress, one with and one without the prevocalic /h/. Each has a full /ɛ/ vowel. But the third variant, with only weak stress on the second syllable, has a correspondingly weakened vowel /ə/ ranging from a retracted [ɪ̌] and [+] to neutral [ə].

The first, /ˈfɔrˌhɛd/, occurs as a minor variant in New England. In the UM, on the contrary, it is easily predominant. Four out of five infs. of each type prefer it, probably because of the spelling. The second variant, /ˈfɔrˌɛd/, without /h/, is much less popular than in the East, since it is the choice of but one out of 10. The third variant, with only a weakly stressed vowel, is also the choice of one out of 10 infs.

	Type I	Type II	Type III
/ˈfɔrˌhɛd/	82%	77%	80%
/ˈfɔrˌɛd/	9%	15%	13%
/ˈfɔrəd/	9%	11%	6%

	Mn.	Ia.	N.D.	S.D.	Nb.	Ave.
/ˈfɔrˌhɛd/	87%	78%	72%	75%	65%	78%
/ˈfɔrˌɛd/	11%	16%	15%	4%	8%	11%
/ˈfɔrəd/	2%	6%	4%	21%	27%	10%

  -hɛd 1-2, 4-6, 8-9, 11-13, 15-22, 24-28, 30-32, 35, 37, 39-64; 101-17, 119, 121, 124, 126-28, 132-34, 136-41, 143-44, 146-50, 152; 201-4, 206-8, 210-12, 214-22, 224-25; 301-8, 310, 312, 314-16, 318-21, 323-25, 327; 401, 405-8, 411-12, 414-18, 422, 426, 429-37.
  -ɛd 3, 7, 10, 14, 33, 65; 122, 125, 129-30, 135, 142, 145; 205, 209, 213, 223; 328; 421, 428.
  -əd [ɪ̌] 29; 226; 311, 313, 322; 402, 404, 409, 419, 424. [+] 309, 326; 425. [ə] 115, 120; 413, 420. [ɚ] 123.

genuine 40.6. NE 308.

In the UM the two pronunciations of genuine, both of which are common in New England among the various groups of speakers, provide a fairly sharp social contrast and a bare hint of a geographical contrast.

The more common pronunciation is marked by a secondary stress on the final syllable and an accompanying retention of the free vowel—or diphthong—/aɪ/, as in /ˈɟɛnjuˌwaɪn/. Although two-thirds of the UM infs. have this, it is hardly a prestige form, being offered by more than eight of 10 Type I speakers, one-half of those in Type II, but only two in the college group. Contrasting /ˈɟɛnjuwɪn/, with weak stress on the final syllable, exhibits higher social acceptance.

	Type I	Type II	Type III
-waɪn	83%	54%	14%
-wɪn	17%	47%	86%

	Mn.	Ia.	N.D.	S.D.	Nb.	Ave.
-waɪn	66%	73%	56%	61%	62%	65%
-wɪn	34%	27%	44%	39%	40%	35%

  -wɪn 2, 9-11, s20, 22, 26, 28-29, 33-34, c38, 46-47, 52, ¹58, 61-62, 64; 102-3, 110-12, vr115, 120-23, 126, 130, vr131, 136; 203, 205-6, 208, 213-14, 217-18, c222, 223, 226; 304, 310, 312-13, c314, 319, 325-26, 328; 402, 406, 410-12, c414, 419, 424-26, 428, 431, 433, 437.

guardian 51.6. NE 391.

Although, as in the East, the cultivated pronunciation of guardian has three syllables with initial stress, as in /ˈgɑrˌdiən/, the two-syllable variant with even stress or, more commonly, primary stress on the second syllable, persists in the UM.

More than one-fifth of all UM infs. offer a pronunciation with a heavily stressed final syllable, as in /ˌgɑrˈdin/ or, more rarely—as with 46; 203; ˈ413, 416—/ˈgɑrˈdin/. One such speaker, 134, has /-din/ in the final syllable with rather heavy secondary stress.

A marked social contrast appears in the distribution of infs. who have the /ˈdin/ form. Three-fourths of them are the older and less well educated speakers in Type I, and the remaining one-fourth are in Type II. No college-trained speaker has it. Three infs. specifically characterize it as old-fashioned.

The high frequency in southern Iowa hints at a slight Midland orientation of /ˈdin/, but this inference is belied by the greater incidence in the Dakotas than in Nebraska. The distribution of /-ˈdin/ is as follows.

Type	Mn.	Ia.	N.D.	S.D.	Nb.	Ave.
I	26%	42%	37%	57%	27%	34%
II	4%	27%	18%	16%	10%	15%
III	0	0	0	0	0	

/-ˈdin/ 16, *19, 27, 35, cr39, †40, ˈ47, 48, 52, †53, 60, †62; 105, 107, 109, 112-15, 124, 132-33, 135-36, 138-39; 209, 212, 215, 220, 224-25; 303, 308, 311, 315-17, 320, 322, 327; ˈ†403, 407, 420, 424, 429, 432.

hotel 63.4. NE 543.

Three stress patterns mark the varied pronunciation of hotel, one with primary stress on the final syllable, one with the stress on the first syllable, and a rare pattern with even stress. The effect of this variation upon the vowels is minimal.

The prevalent pronunciation, with final stress, is that of 85% of the UM infs., with no distinct regional differentiation but with evidence of social contrast. It is the unanimous preference of the Type III college-trained group—although one inf. (222) also shifts to initial stress.

In this pattern the first syllable ho- almost invariably bears sufficiently strong secondary stress to maintain vowel quality. The /o/ is typically a monophthongal, slightly fronted, [oˁ], often specifically indicated as short [ŏ]; but a number of Iowa and Nebraska infs. are recorded with an offglide [oᵁ] or [oo^]: 101-10, 112-14, 116-19, 121-22, 124-28, 132, 134-41, 143-48; 423-25, 428, 431-32. Some speakers with weaker stress on the first syllable (often reflected also in weak aspiration) exhibit correspondingly less distinctive vowel quality. Five infs. have [ə]: 39, 44, 48, 56; 435. One, 223, has [ə̞ˁ].

Also in this first pattern the stressed

-tel sometimes has a centralizing off-glide in Midland speech territory, generally transcribed as [ɛ⁺] by fws. H and P and as [ɛᵊ] by fw. Wr. It occurs in the records of the following infs.: 101-4, 109-14, 116, 130, 132-33, 137-38, 150; 221; 407, 410-11, 413-14, 416-17, 419, 423, 427, c429, 431-32, c433, 434-35.

The second and less frequent pattern with stressed ho- is used by 19 of the Type I and Type II infs. (5, 15, 47; 120, 136, 142; 206, 208, c222; 306, 308, 315-17; 409, 418, 420-21, c422) and, as his unguarded form, by one Type III inf. (c222). The evidence is too scanty to infer that it has a Midland orientation. The lack of full stress on -tel apparently reduces the tendency to diphthongization, since 37% of the infs. with primary stress on -tel have an offglide but only 16% of those with secondary stress.

Three infs. are recorded as having even stress in hotel: 202, 204; 426. All have monophthongal [ɛ].

lasso 76.6.

This lexical item was sought only in Nebraska. Nineteen infs. responded with lasso instead of lariat or some other term. (See Volume 1.)

Three different stress patterns appear in lasso. Fourteen infs. have initial stress. Twelve of them have strong enough secondary stress on the second syllable so that the vowel quality is retained, either as /o/ (typically [oᵁ] or [ou]) by 414, 424 ,430, 433, and 435, or as /u/ by 405, 407, 409, 416, 418, 422, 432. For two infs., however, a weakened stress is indicated by their final vowels [ʊ˅] (401) and [ʌ] (405).

One inf. is recorded as having even stress in [ˈlæˈsu] (406).

Four infs. reflect the Spanish origin of the term with their stress on the second syllable. In that syllable three have /u/ (408, †410, and 429), and one has /o/ (425).

A social distinction likely resides in the fact that all but one of the infs. who have the spelling pronunciation with final /o/ are in Type II. The /u/ ending, conversely, seems favored in folk speech.

rodeo 76.7.

Added only when fieldwork was begun in the western cattle country, this item yielded 45 instances of rodeo. All are with the Anglicized pronunciation /ˈroˌdio/, none with the Spanish pronunciation /ˌroˈdeo/ common in the South-west. Infs. offering the term are 309-13, 320, 326, 328; 401-37.

shivaree   61.7. NE 409.

Although only a rare word in northeastern New England, shivaree is known to
nearly all the UM infs. It has two contrasting stress patterns. Three-fourths
of the UM infs. (151 of 201) keep the
original secondary stress on the first
syllable and primary on the last, as
/ˇɪvəˈri/, and one-fourth (49 of 201)
Anglicize the pronunciation by reversing
the pattern as /ˈˇɪvəˌri/. One inf. (428)
has even stress.

There may be both social and regional
significance in the UM contrast. A possible Northern weighting appears in the 40%
frequency of /ˈˇɪvəˌri/ in Minnesota and
the 17% in Iowa; a possible social differentiation appears in its range from
27% in Type I and 22% in Type II to 20%
in Type III. As with many other items,
the significance of such a slight difference can be affirmed or denied when the
materials of the North Central Atlas are
published.

Because the stress-shift in the speech
of the latter group left the final syllable with secondary stress, the final
vowel generally retains its diphthongal
quality, e.g., [iˇi].

Of the 49 infs. with initial stress, 12
have only a simple sound in the last
syllable—nine with [i] or [iː] (31, 56,
59; 107; 201; 307; 316-17; c403) and
three have [ɪ] or [ɨ] (33; 134; 425).

One inf., 425, remarked that [ˇɪvərɪˆ]
is "usual" but that [ˇəˌrɪvəˈri] is po-
lite.

strawberries   48.5. NE 274.

In New England the fairly common loss
of secondary stress on the second syllable of strawberries led to the reduction
of /ɛ/ to any of several centralized allophones and even to the disappearance of
the vowel, as in /ˈstrɔbriz/. In the UM,
however, secondary stress has generally
been preserved or reinstated, so that for
nearly all infs. /ɛ/ retains its full
front quality, usually as [ɛ] or [ɛˇ],
rarely as [æˆ] with inf. 56, [eˇ] with
inf. 18, or [ɪ] with infs. 15 and 16.

Centralizing of the vowel under weaker
stress is evident in the responses of
infs. 13-14, 306, and 428 with [bɚɨz],
infs. 317 and 422 with [bərɨz]; and infs.
c20, c211, 311-12, and 321 with [bɜrɨz].

theater   63.5. NE 542.

Although in New England this item was
used to elicit names for the building
where motion pictures are shown, the
North Central and UM surveys sought rather the varying pronunciations of theater.

The majority variant is /ˈθiətɚ/, with
/i/ as the stressed vowel and a neutral
vowel in the second syllable. This pronunciation is used by two-thirds of the
UM infs., with a slightly higher proportion among the Type II's. There is no
clear geographical pattern.

The two minor variants seem to exhibit
social contrast. The variant /ˈθɪətɚ/,
with /ɪ/ instead of /i/, is twice as frequent among the cultivated speakers as
among the others.

The reverse is true with respect to the
third variant, /ˈθiˌetɚ/, with a stressed
/e/ in the second syllable. Of the infs.
with this variant slightly more than one-
half have primary stress on the first
syllable /θi/ and secondary stress on
/e/; the others have secondary stress on
/θi/ and primary stress on /e/. This variant is a clear social marker. Three-
fourths of its users are in Type I, the
uneducated group; the only college graduate using it, a physician, acknowledged
that he sometimes used the forms of his
patients' folk speech as an accommoda-
tion.

	Type I	Type II	Type III
/ˈθɪətɚ/	13%	14%	31%
/ˈθiətɚ/	64%	78%	63%
/ˈθiˌetɚ/	23%	8%	6%

	Mn.	Ia.	N.D.	S.D.	Nb.	Ave.
/ˈθɪətɚ/	14%	13%	8%	15%	25%	15%
/ˈθiətɚ/	64%	76%	80%	77%	56%	69%
/ˈθiˌetɚ/	22%	11%	12%	8%	19%	16%

/ˈθɪətɚ/ 3, 6, 9-11, 14-15, 18, 22;
125-26, 128, 131, 143, 146; 216-17; 313,
320, 325-26; 404, 413-14, 416, 421-23,
426-27.
/ˈθiətɚ/ 1-2, 7, 12-13, 17, 19-21, 23-
24, 26-34, 36-37, 40, 42-43, 46-47, 49,
c50, 54-55, s56, 57-61, 63-65; 101-8,
110-17, 119-24, 127, 132-35, 137-39, 142,
145, cr147, 148-50; 201-6, c208, 210-11,
213-15, 218-23, 225-26; 303-4, 306-12,
314-19, 321-24, 327-28; c403, 405-12,
418-20, 425, 428, 431-35, 437.
/ˈθiˌetɚ/ 4-5, 8, 25, 35, 38, 52-53,
62; 109; 207, 209, 224; 302; 401-2, 436.
/θiˈetɚ/ cr39, 41, 44, 48, 51; 129-30,
136, 144; 301; 415, c417, 424, 429.
no response 16; 118, 140-41, 151-52;
212; 305; 430.

umbrella   23.4. NE 367.

A minor nonstandard variant of umbrella
has strong primary stress on the first
syllable, with or without secondary
stress on the second syllable. Under primary stress the initial vowel is necessarily an emphatic [ʌ] rather than a weak

[ʌ] or schwa [ə]. This variant, with only 11 instances in the New England survey, would appear to be a dying form but it persists in the speech of 11 scattered UM infs. Nine are Type I speakers: 35, 44, c56; 135; 204, 206; 306-7; 405. Two are in Type II, 12 and 405.

Alternation of Reduction Vowel

Regardless of whatever is postulated as the underlying vowel in a given unstressed syllable, it is a fact of English surface grammar that the overt vowel in a final unstressed syllable sometimes exhibits allophonic variation significantly correlated with social or geographical distribution. Not everyone pronounces that final syllable in the same way.

Examples collected during the UM survey include the endings -a, -ed and -es, -el, -ess, -et, -i, -day, -man, and -ow, as well as the final syllables of apron, stomach, and mountain.

-a /ə/ - /i/

Kurath reports in PEAS that several words ending in an unstressed syllable spelled -a have in that syllable not the expected vowel schwa /ə/ but a minor variant, /i/. It occurs in northern New England, West Virginia, and the Upper South. The New England effect upon the UM, however, is weak, as most of the occurrences of /i/ are in Midland speech territory. (See map.)

That this variant is declining is suggested by the fact that of the 38 infs. with final /i/, 28 are in the oldest and least educated group. Only three of the high school group have it at all, and only two college graduates, with one instance each.

Of the two words adduced by Kurath, one, sofa, has nearly lost this variant pronunciation with final /i/. It is offered by only two Midland speakers, 150 and 420. The other, china, occurs as /ˈčaini/ in the speech of the following: 48, 52, 56, †62; 135, 143, 151; 305-6, 308, 311, 316, 319, 325; 434.

A somewhat smaller number of UM infs., mostly in the Midland speech zone of Iowa and South Dakota, preserve the old pronunciation of diphtheria with final /i/, which in their speech usually accompanies a first syllable pronounced /dip/ rather than /dif/. They are c48, 56; 135, 140, 143, 146-47; 311-17; 432.

One Minnesota inf., 35, of Midland parentage, has the variant /harˈmɑniki/ for harmonica.

Five place names and one personal name exhibit the same variation and similar distribution. The final /i/ occurs with them as follows

Canada 59; 107, 113-14, 132, 146; cvr220; c301, 303, 311, c316, 317, 321; 429, c434.

Dakota 113-14, 135, 146-47; 225; 307, 317.

Minnesota 114, 135, 146; 225; 307, 317.

Nebraska c114, 135, 138, 146, 148; 311, c322; c417, c429, 432.

Pennsylvania 47, 59; 113-14, 135, 143, 146; 311, c322; c429, 434.

Martha c62; 114, 135, 140; 311, 316, 319, 322.

-ed and -es, -ess, -et, -is. PEAS 168; F148.

Before a final alveolar consonant, an underlying /ɛ/ appears overtly as an unstressed neutral /ə/ in regional contrast with some allophones of /ɪ/, such as [ɪˀ], [+ˁ], [+], or [+ᵛ].

Kurath notes that /ə/ is typically found in the lower Hudson Valley and all the Midland area, with /ɪ/ dominant elsewhere. The UM retains this division, which is marked by the rather sharp restriction of unmodified [ə] to the Midland speech areas of Iowa and Nebraska. Evidence for this distribution is in the plural ending of ashes, houses, and oranges, the preterit and participial endings of jilted and haunted, the final syllable of bracelet, bucket, and skillet, and the suffix of careless. Because several of these words are recorded only as less frequent lexical choices, the returns for them are incomplete, but the

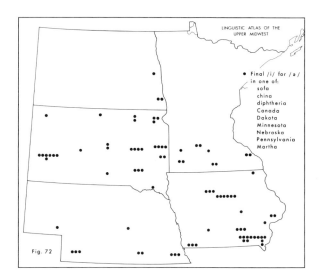

LINGUISTIC ATLAS OF THE UPPER MIDWEST

● Final /i/ for /ə/ in one of:
sofa
china
diphtheria
Canada
Dakota
Minnesota
Nebraska
Pennsylvania
Martha

Fig. 72

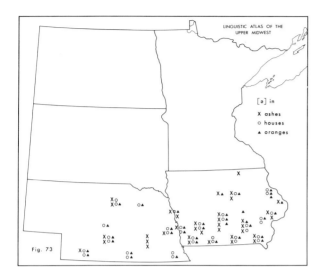

Fig. 73

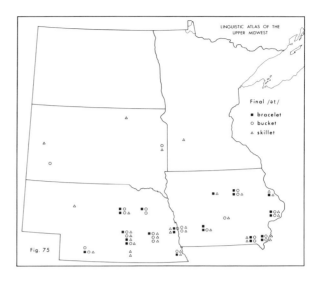

Fig. 75

distribution pattern discernible in the returns is similar for all. (See maps.)

A few instances of a raised central vowel [ə^] appear in the North Dakota and Minnesota records, especially in the transcription of fws. M and A. Comparison with tape recordings led to the reinterpretation of these as allophones of /ɨ/ in this context.

Distribution of unstressed [ə]:

ashes (7.6b; NE 331) 105, 114, 117-18, 122-24, 126-31, 134-36, 139-43, 145-49, 151; 413-14, 422-26, 428, 431.

houses (11.3) 117, 120-21, 124-30, 135-36, 139-41, 143-49, 151; 413-14, 416, 421-23, 425-26, 428, 430-35.

oranges (43.1; NE 273) 114, 117, 119-22, 124-30, 132, 134-35, 137, 139-40, 142-43, 145-46, 148-49; 414-15, 421-23, 427-28, 430-33, 435.

jilted (61.5; NE 407B) 107, 117, 121, 124-27, 130-31, 148-49; 422, 431.

haunted (67.2; NE 534) 117, 120-22, 124-25, 129-30, 135, 139-43, 146-49; 221; 414, 416, 421, 424-28, 430-31, 433-35.

bracelet (23.2; NE 369) 114, 116-17, 121, 127, 140-41, 146-49, 151; 413-14, 416, 421-24, 427-28, 431, 435.

bucket (14.1; NE 125) 116-17, 121, 124-25, 129, 140-41, 146-49, 151; 318, 320; 413-16, 420-21, 423-27, 430-31, 434.

skillet (14.4; NE 132) 47; 114, 117, 119-20, 124-25, 129, 140-41, 146-49, 151; 305, 310, 319; 412, 414, 420-28, 431-35.

careless (56.7; NE 467) 43-45; 105, 119-21, 124, 126, 137, 139-41, 146-49; 308; 413-14, 416, 420-28, 430-31.

The clear Midland propensity for neutral schwa [ə] for e in a final weak syllable is extended to i in a final weak

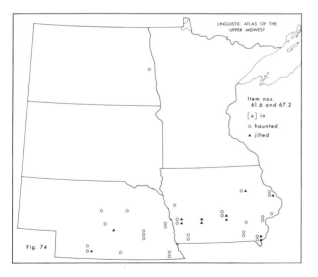

Fig. 74

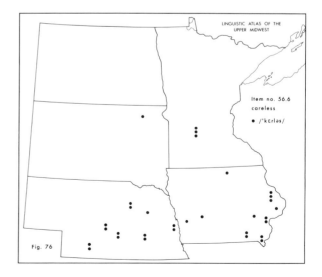

Fig. 76

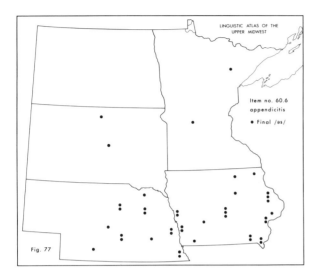

LINGUISTIC ATLAS OF THE UPPER MIDWEST

Item no. 60.6
appendicitis
• Final /əs/

Fig. 77

syllable in at least one word, appendicitis (60.6; NE 509), despite the presumed
influence of the spelling. The Iowa and
Nebraska concentration of [ə] rather
closely parallels that in the words noted
above. The infs. with [əs] in appendicitis are 13; 106-7, 117, 119-26, 128-30,
139-41, 143, 146-49; 304, 314; 407, 413-
16, 421-23, 426-28, 431, 434-35.

The Midland tendency to favor weak [ə]
in a final unstressed syllable where a
Northern speaker is more likely to have
[ɨ] may also exist in internal unstressed
syllables. This inference follows from
casually observed instances of any-. One
Iowan, 101, and one Nebraskan, 430, have
/ɛnəwe/ for anyway; and one South Dakotan, 305, and one Nebraskan, 427, have
/ɛnəθɪŋ/ for anything. The usual Northern
form is /ɛni/.

-el

In towel (15.3-4) the high central /ɨ/
of the weak syllable, reported by Kurath
as found in Atlantic coastal areas and
among older speakers in New England,
seems not to have retained any vitality
in the western migration. The North Central survey found only one in Wisconsin,
and only one inf., 39, is reported in
Minnesota as having this pronunciation.
Iowa fw. H has several examples which
comparison with the tape recording indicates are best interpreted as [ʊ] or [ɤ].
The general pronunciation has either /əl/
or /ɪ/.

In funnel (15.6; NE 140, 142, 145; PEAS
168, F148), however, the higher vowel before the sonorant /l/ has had a greater
survival rate. While only three instances
appear in the North Central data for Wisconsin, 21 each are recorded in Minnesota

and Iowa. Yet in this word, too, competing /əl/ and /ɪ/ apparently are increasing in acceptance, for the form with /ɨ/
turns up in the speech of only seven
North Dakotans and one South Dakotan,
with none in Nebraska. No social contrast
is evident.

/fʌnɨl/ 2-12, 19-22, 26-27, 29, 34, 36,
41; 101-5, 108, 110-15, 119, 122-23, 128,
132-34, 137-38; 210-11, 214-17, 224; 314.

-i /ə/ - /ɪ/.

Regional and social contrast appears in
the variation between /ə/ and /ɪ/ in the
unstressed final syllable of several
American place names ending in -i, e.g.,
Cincinnati, Ypsilanti, Paoli, and Missouri. For the origin of these pronunciations see George B. Pace, "Linguistic
geography and names ending in -i," *American Speech* 35(1960), 175-87.

Missouri (65.1; PEAS 169, F150) is the
only such name investigated in the UM.
The pronunciation with final /ə/, predominant in the state of Missouri itself,
suffers a decline in frequency roughly
proportionate to the distance from that
state. Awareness of a possible principle
with respect to this phenomenon is detailed in Harold B. Allen, "Distribution
patterns of place-name pronunciations,"
Names 6(1958), 74-79, where it is whimsi-
cally called "Allen's law." Unfortunately
for the law, the evidence in the eastern
states is not very helpful. Final /ə/ in
Missouri is found in western New England,
New Jersey, and Pennsylvania, and /ɪ/ in
eastern New England and metropolitan New
York and Philadelphia.

But in the UM the highest incidence of
/ə/ occurs in Iowa, fully contiguous with
Missouri, the next highest in Nebraska,
partly contiguous with Missouri, the next
in South Dakota, the closest noncontigu-
ous state, and the lowest frequencies in
Minnesota and North Dakota, the most dis-
tant UM states. (Data for Minnesota are
incomplete, since this item was included
after most of the fieldwork there had
been finished.)

The /ə - ɪ/ correlates also with the
three informant types. Perhaps because of
a school-engendered acceptance of spelling as a guide to pronunciation, the incidence of the /ɪ/ ending rises from Type
I to Type III. A college graduate living
in his birthplace some distance from Missouri is hardly likely to come out with
/məˈzurə/.

	Type I	Type II	Type III
/ə/	54%	48%	36%
/ɪ/	47%	54%	64%

	Mn.	Ia.	N.D.	S.D.	Nb.	Ave.
/ə/	17%	65%	21%	46%	58%	50%
/i/	83%	37%	79%	54%	45%	51%

/ə/ 35; 101, 103-4, 107, 111-12, 115-17, 119-20, 122-25, 127, 129-30, 132-33, 136-37, 139-42, 145, 147, 149-50; 212, 214, 216; 307, 312-14, 316, 318, 320-21, 323-25; 307, 312-14, 316, 318, 320-21, 323-25; 401-3, 405-6, 409, 413-14, 416, 420, 422-24, 426, 429, 431, 434-35, 437.

/i/ 29-30, 36-38; 102, 105-6, 108-9, 113-14, 121, 126, 128, 131, 134-35, 138, 140, 143-44, 146; 202-11, 215, 219-25; 301-6, 308-11, 315, 317, 319, 322, 326; 404, 407-8, 410-12, 415, 417-19, 421, 423, 425, 427-28.

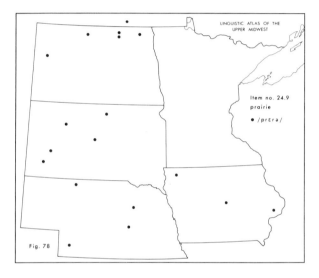

Fig. 78

LINGUISTIC ATLAS OF THE UPPER MIDWEST

Item no. 24.9
prairie
• /prɛrə/

Prairie (24.9), although not a place name, exhibits a similar contrast between final /i/ and /ə/. Of the 18 speakers with the variant /prɛrə/ only 11 are in the general Midland region where /mɪzurə/ is dominant, but eight of the 18 are recorded as having that pronunciation as well. See map.

/prɛrə/ 101, 132, *141; 202-6, 209; 302, 304, 311, 314, 320; 408, 413, 420, 429.

-day   /de/ - /di/

As a weakly stressed bound morpheme ending of yesterday and names of days of the week, -day early developed three regional variations in England, /di/, /dɪ/, and /də/, besides the full form /de/ perpetuated by the spelling. Predictably, British Northern English /də/ is not a New England pronunciation, but the three others occur in New England, with British Midland /dɪ/ dominant, and British South-

ern /di/ and general /de/ less frequent.

In the UM these three endings occur in almost equal proportions in the days of the week, but in yesterday, perhaps because of the analogy with today, the pronunciation /de/ is favored by two-thirds of the infs.

No marked variation among the three types of infs. appears, except a slight tendency of college speakers to use the full /de/. But, despite (or perhaps because of) some fw. inconsistencies in assigning an intermediate vowel to [ɪˆ] or [iˇ], both yesterday and, for example, Wednesday exhibit a definite Northern orientation of the /de/ form in Minnesota and North Dakota, and a corresponding Midland preference for /i/. (Comparison with the voice recordings suggests that some of fw. Wr's Nebraska infs. should be transcribed with /i/ rather than [ɪˆ].)

yesterday 4.3.

	Type I	Type II	Type III
/de/	66%	67%	87%
/dɪ/	18%	17%	13%
/di/	20%	17%	0

	Mn.	Ia.	N.D.	S.D.	Nb.	Ave.
/de/	84%	62%	81%	61%	46%	66%
/dɪ/	13%	6%	8%	18%	46%	25%
/di/	6%	32%	13%	25%	14%	25%

/de/ 1-11, c13, 14-17, c18, 19-22, 24-28, c31, 33-35, 37, c38, 39-42, 44-59, 63, 65; 106-7, 110-12, 114, cr115, 116-17, 119-24, 126-29, 131, 133-34, 137, 139, 141, 143-45, 148, 150, 152; 201-6, 208-13, 215-19, 222-26; 301-2, 304-5, 307-8, 310, 313-14, 317-19, 321, 323-25, 327; 401-2, 404, 406-8, c409, 410-11, c414, 417, 419, 424-26, 429, 436.

/dɪ/ c12, 18, 23, 29, c30, 31, 36, 64; 140, 142, 149; 207, 220; 309, 315, 320, 326, 328; 405, 413-16, 418, 420-23, 427-28, 430, 432, 434-35.

/di/ 43, 60, 62; 101-5, 108-9, 113, 125, 130, 132, 135-36, 138, 146-47; 214, 223, 225; 303, 306-7, 311-12, 316, 322; 403, 416, 431, 433, 437.

Wednesday 3.2.

	Type I	Type II	Type III
/de/	29%	26%	44%
/dɪ/	37%	35%	50%
/di/	37%	43%	6%

	Mn.	Ia.	N.D.	S.D.	Nb.	Ave
/de/	33%	26%	44%	11%	29%	29%
/dɪ/	30%	22%	36%	44%	62%	35%
/di/	39%	58%	20%	44%	9%	37%

/de/ 2, 4-5, 8-10, 13-14, 18-19, 27, 31, 34, 37, 49, 54-58, 64; 106, 111, 114, 119, cr131, 132-34, 138-39, 142; 201-3, 205, 210, 216-17, 219, 222, 224, 226;

303, 316, 322; 401, 403-4, 406-7, 410-11, 417, 424-25, 429.

/dɪ/ 1-3, 7, 11-12, c13, 15-16, 22, c23, 26, 29, 33, 36, 42, 46, 50, 52, 65; 107, 116, 120, 137, 140-41, 143, 152; 204, 208-9, 212, 214-15, 223, 225; 301, 304, 309, 311, 313, c315, 317, 320-21, 325; 402, 408-9, 412-16, 418, c419, 421-22, c423, 426-28, 431-37.

/di/ c6, 17, 20-21, 24-25, 28, 30-32, 35, 38-41, 43-45, 47-48, 51, 53, 59-60, 62-63; 101-5, 108-13, 115, 117, 121-30, 135-36, 144-50; 207, 211, 213, 218, 220-21; 302, 305-8, 310, 312, 314, 318-19, c323, 324, 326, c327; c405, 420, c423, 430.

-man /æ/ - /ə/

In such words as <u>chairman</u> and <u>gentleman</u> the bound morpheme <u>-man</u> universally seems to occur as /mən/ under zero stress. But in the investigated and relatively uncommon term <u>postman</u> the vowel has been reduced this much by only slightly more than two-thirds of the UM infs. who use it. Nearly one-third retain the older full vowel /æ/ in the <u>man</u> of <u>postman</u> under secondary stress. The newer and synonymous Americanism <u>mailman</u> has resisted the trend by generally keeping the /mæn/. Only a few infs., mostly in Minnesota, have /mən/. Otherwise, this contrast between <u>postman</u> and <u>mailman</u> yields no regional variation. A possible social difference may be adduced from the fact that /ˈpostˌmæn/ is preferred by eight of the Type I less-educated infs. but by only two of the Type II's and two of the college group.

In the tables below the sets of percentages are, first, of the infs. who respond with <u>mailman</u> and second, of those who respond with <u>postman</u>.

<u>mailman</u> 53.4.

	Type I	Type II	Type III
/mæn/	97%	94%	82%
/mən/	3%	6%	18%

	Mn.	Ia.	N.D.	S.D.	Nb.	Ave.
/mæn/	89%	97%	100%	100%	97%	95%
/mən/	11%	3%	0	0	3%	5%

<u>postman</u>

	Type I	Type II	Type III
/mæn/	38%	14%	29%
/mən/	62%	76%	71%

	Mn.	Ia.	N.D.	S.D.	Nb.	Ave.
/mæn/	33%	40%	33%	25%	30%	29%
/mən/	67%	60%	67%	75%	70%	71%

/melˈmæn/ 1, 3-5, 7-8, 10, 12-18, 20-28, 31-40, ¹42, 43, 47-57, 60, 63, 65; 101-4, 107-9, 111, 113-15, 117, 119-23, 126-28,

132-33, 136, 138-39, 141, 143, 145, 149-50, 152; 202, 203-6, 208-13, 215, 217-22, 224-26; 301-2, 305-7, 309-10, 314-19, 324-25, 328; 406-8, 410, 414, 416, 419, 421-23, 425, 427, 430-31, 433, 435-36.

/melˈmən/ 2, 6, 9, 58, 61, 64; 134; 401.

/pos(t)mæn/ 34, 43, 45-46, 59; s116, 127, 137, 152; 201; 319; 402.

/pos(t)mən/ 2, 11, 26, !¹29, 40, 42, 44, 55, c59, 61; 104, 110-12, 130, 144; 214, 222; 312, 316, 326; 403-4, 409, 411, 413, 417, 426, 428, 431.

no response 19, 30, 41, 62; 105-6, 118, 124-25, 129, 131.

-ow /o/ - /ə/

Six words in the worksheets end in a weakly stressed syllable spelled <u>ow</u> or <u>o</u>: <u>borrow</u>, <u>meadow</u>, <u>minnow</u>, <u>tomato</u>, <u>widow</u>, and <u>yellow</u>. Although an expected final /o/ dominates in the UM, it competes with several minor variants that occur with no clear over-all distribution pattern.

In PEAS Kurath describes <u>widow</u>, <u>meadow</u>, and <u>yellow</u> as having a similar distribution, with /o/ dominant in the North and among cultivated speakers in the North Midland, but with neutral schwa, /ə/, prevalent in western Pennsylvania and the South Midland. In the UM, however, these three terms are less closely coordinated.

<u>Yellow</u> does reflect the eastern distribution with the general dominance of /o/ and a stronger showing of /ə/ in the Midland region of Iowa and the Dakotas, particularly among Type I speakers. A third final vowel /u/ turns up in the speech of six Northern infs., four in Minnesota and two in North Dakota.

With <u>meadow</u> the /o/ dominance is greater than with <u>yellow</u> and the frequency of /ə/ is less, although still with some indication of Midland orientation. North Dakota has no instances of /ə/ at all. But the third variant /u/ is somewhat more frequent than it is in <u>yellow</u>, for instances appear in each state, though still with Northern orientation since nine of the 13 are in Minnesota and North Dakota.

<u>Widow</u> behaves quite differently. The few examples with final /ə/ give little hint of Northern/Midland contrast, and final /o/ is actually stronger in Midland Iowa and Nebraska. The shift is apparently occasioned by the strength of the /u/ variant in Northern speech. Manifested as [ʊˇ], [ʊ̞̂], [ʊ̌], and even [u], it is reported the choice of 20% of the infs. in the North Central state of Wisconsin, 31% of those in Minnesota, and 60% of those in North Dakota. As with [ə] in <u>meadow</u> and <u>yellow</u>, /u/ in <u>widow</u> is less favored

by educated speakers than is /o/.

As in the East, tomato offers a different picture. There, /ə/ is used by cultivated speakers not only in Pennsylvania but also in much of New York State, with /o/ common in New England. Correspondingly, /ə/ is much more popular in the UM, where nearly one-half of all infs. use it, even in Minnesota and North Dakota. There is, however, a clear indication of greater preference for /o/ among educated speakers.

Minnow has a variant not found with the preceding terms. As with them, /o/ is the majority preference, but the place of /ə/ as second choice is taken by /i/. Manifested as [ɨ], [ɨ·], and [ɪ·], this vowel apparently is a social marker as it is the choice of 25% of the Type I infs., only 12% of the Type II's, and none of the Type III's.

The weak schwa /ə/ is rare as a terminal vowel for minnow, examples being found in the speech of only eight infs., mostly in Midland territory.

For seven scattered Type I infs. in the UM borrow likewise has the high front /i/ variant. It is clearly a social marker. The variant with a centralized vowel [ə] or [əʊ] exhibits a certain social weighting toward the use of the less educated. Its use by Type III infs. is limited to two Minnesota speakers. The majority in the UM, however, strongly favor standard /o/. An irregular variant reported only for borrow appears in the speech of three Type I Iowans, 114, 135, 140, a monosyllabic /bɑr/, in which only a slight lengthening of the /r/ glide remains of the assimilated final vowel.

Except for a putative ghostly existence in monosyllabic /bɑr/ for borrow, the older folk pronunciation of unstressed final -ow as /ɚ/ seems to have survived but barely in the UM. One Iowa inf., 135, has not only /wɪdɚ/ for widow and /mɪnɚ/ for minnow but also /fɑlɚ/ for follow. Another Iowan also has /mɪnɚ/ and a South Dakotan has /jɛlɚ/ for yellow. This final /ɚ/ apparently is an extension of the more common final /ə/. Compare, for example, the form [ˈrutə͜bɛgɚz] offered for rutabagas by a South Dakota retired cattle rancher. The final /ɚ/ is clearly a social marker, as its occurrence is limited to Type I speakers.

borrow 69.1. NE 564. PEAS 169; F152, F153.

	Type I	Type II	Type III
/o/	70%	86%	88%
/i/	7%	0	0
/ə/	20%	14%	13%

	Mn.	Ia.	N.D.	S.D.	Nb.	Ave.
/o/	80%	72%	88%	64%	87%	78%
/i/	2%	6%	4%	7%	0	4%
/ə/	18%	14%	8%	29%	13%	17%

/o/ All but those listed below.
/i/ 25; c113, 132, cvr142; 204; 307, 316.
/ə/ 14-18, 21, 33-35, 37, 48, 56; 104-5, 107, 117; 204; 307, 316.
/bɑr/ 114, 135, 140.
no response 118, 151, 152.

meadow 24.2. NE 29. PEAS 170; F155.

	Type I	Type II	Type III
/o/	78%	93%	92%
/u/	9%	8%	8%
/ə/	14%	2%	0

	Mn.	Ia.	N.D.	S.D.	Nb.	Ave.
/o/	87%	95%	79%	73%	90%	86%
/u/	8%	4%	21%	9%	4%	8%
/ə/	7%	9%	0	18%	6%	7%

/o/ [oʊ, oˆ, o] 2-3, c4, 5, 8, 10-11, 19-20, 22-30, 33-38, 40, 42-45, c46, 47-65; 101-2, 104-6, 109, 111-13, 129-30, cvr131, 132-33, 137-38, 150, 152; 201-3, 205, 210-11, 213, 215-16, c217, 218, 221-24; 301-2, 309, 312, 323, 325-26, 328; 401-3, c404, 406-8, c409, 410-12, cvr414, 416-19, 421-26, 428, 430-32, 435, 437.
[ɵ] 6, 39, 41, 55; cvr115, 119-20.
/ə/ c21, 32, c62-63; c109, cvr115; c320, c322; c405, 429.
/u/ [u] c31; 405. [ʊ, ʊ, əʊ] 14, 16, 18, 44; 114; 206, 219, 225-26; 313; 433.

minnow 47.5. NE 29. PEAS 170.

	Type I	Type II	Type III
/o/	67%	82%	100%
/u/	10%	12%	6%
/i/	25%	12%	0

	Mn.	Ia.	N.D.	S.D.	Nb.	Ave.
/o/	84%	71%	62%	75%	87%	76%
/u/	11%	8%	27%	7%	3%	10%
/i/	9%	20%	15%	25%	16%	17%

/o/ 1-2, 9-21, 23-24 , 26-27, 29-34, 37-53, 55, 57-58, 60-65; 102-8, 110-11, 114, 116-28, 131, 133-34 , 136-37, 140-41, 143-45, 148-50; 201, 205-6, 208-11, cr212, 213-14, 217, 219, 221, 224-26; cr301, 302-5, 308-10, ⌐312, 315-19, 321-26, 328; 401-6, 408-9, 411-15, 418-23, 425-28, cr429, 430-31, *432, 433-37.
/u/ 8, 22, 28, 33, 36, 54, 56; 101, 112, 138-39; 202-4, 216, 218, 222-23; 313-14; 410.
/i/ 6, ¹21, ¹23, 25, ¹33, 35, ¹47, 59, 62; 109, 113, 115, 128-29, *134, 139, 141, 143, 146, 148-49, ¹150, 152; 207, 212, 215, 220; 301, 306, 311, ¹312, 316,

320, 327; :407, *410, 416-17, 429, 433,
s¹435.
  /ə/ 3-4; 130, 135, 142, 147; 307; c425.
  /ɚ/ 132, c135.
  no response 5; 151; 415.

tomato 43.3. NE 266. PEAS 170; F154.

	Type I	Type II	Type III
/o/	46%	62%	73%
/u/	1%	2%	0
/ə/	54%	38%	27%

	Mn.	Ia.	N.D.	S.D.	Nb.	Ave.
/o/	57%	57%	46%	46%	56%	54%
/u/	3%	0	4%	0	0	1%
/ə/	40%	43%	50%	54%	44%	45%

  /o/ 1-3, 7-12, 14, 16-18, 23-24, 28-29,
31, 33, 36-37, 40, 42, 44-46, c47, 48-49,
52-54, c55, 57-58, 60-61, 64-65; 104,
106-8, 110-11, 116, 118, 120, 122-37,
140-41, 143-45; 201-3, 209-11, 213, 215,
219, 221, 224; 303-4, 310, 313, c314,
317-18, 321, 324-28; c402, 406, 410-14,
416-22, 424, 426, 428-29, 431, 433.
  /u/ c28, 61; 225.
  /ə/ 4-6, 13, 15, 19-22, c25, 26-27, 30,
32, 34-35, 38-39, 41, 43, 50, c51, c56,
59, 62-63; 101-3, 105, 109, 112-15, 117,
119, 121, c128, c135, 138-39, 142, 146-
49; 204-8, 212, c214, 216-18, 220, 223,
226; 301-2, 305-9, 311-12, 315-16, 319-
20, c322-23; 401, 403, c404, 405, 408-9,
415, c416, 423, 425, 427, c430, 432, 434-
37.

widow 49.3. NE 389. PEAS 170; F155.

	Type I	Type II	Type III
/o/	55%	71%	82%
/u/	30%	25%	18%
/ə/	14%	4%	0

	Mn.	Ia.	N.D.	S.D.	Nb.	Ave.
/o/	62%	84%	36%	30%	85%	64%
/u/	31%	3%	60%	55%	10%	24%
/ə/	7%	12%	4%	15%	5%	11%

  /o/ 3, 5, 8, 12-19, 24-26, 31, 33-34,
37-40, 43-48, 50-54, 56-58, 60-61, 63-65;
101-12, 114-18, 120-23, 125-34, 136-38,
140-45, 148, 150, 152; 201, 205-7, 210,
217, 222-24; 304-5, 316, 318, 323, 325-
26, 328; 402-4, 406-12, 414-28, 430-31,
433-36.
  /u/ 1-2, 4, 6-7, 9-11, 20, 22-23, 27-
30, 36, 41-42, 49, 55; 113; 202-4, 208-9,
211-13, 215-16, 218-19, 221, 225-26; 301-
3, 306, 309-10, 312-13, 315, 317, 319-22,
324; 401, 405, 429, 437.
  /ə/ 21, 32, 35, 59, 62; vr115, 119,
124, 139, 146-47, 149; 220; 307-8, 311,
314; c405, 413, s429, 432.
  /ɚ/ 135.
  no response 151; 214; 327.

yellow 37.1. NE 240, 296, 511. PEAS 170.

	Type I	Type II	Type III
/o/	69%	81%	80%
/u/	2%	4%	0
/ə/	29%	15%	19%

	Mn.	Ia.	N.D.	S.D.	Nb.	Ave.
/o/	74%	74%	80%	69%	75%	75%
/u/	6%	0	4%	0	0	3%
/ə/	12%	26%	15%	30%	27%	21%

  /o/ 1-5, 7-8, c9, 10-11, 19-20, 23-33,
c35, 36, 39-50, c51-52, 53-61, c63, 64-
65; 101, c102, 103-6, 109-12, 116, 118-
31, 133-34, 136-38, 141-45, 150, 152;
201-2, 205-7, 209-12, 214-16, 218-19,
221-26; 302, 304, 308, 310, 312-13, 315-
21, c322, 323-24, 326, 328; 401-2, 406-
12, 414, c415, 416-26, 428, c430, 431,
433.
  /u/ 12-13, 17, 37; 213, 220.
  /ə/ 6, 14-16, 18, 21-22, 34, 38, 62;
107, 113-14, cvr115, 117, 132, 135 , 139-
40, 146, c147, 148-49; 203-4, 208, 217;
301, 305-7, 309, c310, 314, 325; 403-5,
413, 427, 429, 434-37.
  /ɚ/ 303.

/rən/ - /ɚn/

apron 21.7. NE 364.

  Although not all commercial dictionaries recognize the assimilated vowel /ɚ/
in the pronunciation /ˈeprən/, this form
is used by two-thirds of the UM infs.
Only one-third have /ˈeprən/. The latter
is historically older, but its persistence today is most likely due to the influence of spelling, especially among the
linguistically insecure.
  In the UM apron /ˈeprən/ is the choice
of only 26% of the Type I infs. but of
45%, almost twice as many, of the Type
II's. The majority in each of the three
groups have /ˈeprən/. The records also
suggest a possible regional weighting as
well, since /ˈeprən/ is more frequent in
the Northern speech areas.
  Both the social and regional import of
the evidence is curiously controverted,
however, by the records for the adjacent
North Central state of Wisconsin. Although both pronunciations occur throughout New England, /ˈeprən/ is recorded as
the well-nigh unanimous preference in
Wisconsin. Only two of the 50 infs. apparently have /ˈeprən/. Publication of the
North Central Atlas may resolve this
seeming paradox.

	Type I	Type II	Type III
/eprən/	74%	56%	63%
/eprən/	26%	45%	37%

	Mn.	Ia.	N.D.	S.D.	Nb.	Ave.
/epɚn/	74%	44%	73%	82%	61%	63%
/eprən/	36%	56%	27%	18%	42%	34%

/epɚn/ 1, 4-9, 12, 16-19, 21, 23-27, 29-31, 34-35, 39-48, 50-54, 56-63, 65; 101-3, 107, 112-14, cr115, 116-18, 120, 123, 126, 129, 135, 140-43, 146-47, 151; 201, 203-4, 206-9, 211-14, 216, 218, 220-25; 301-6, 308-13, 315, 317, 319-22, 324-28; c402, 403, 406-11, 414-16, 418-20, 423-24, 428-30, 433-34, 436.

/eprən/ 2-3, 10-11, 14-15, 20, 22, 28, 32-33, 36, 38, 49, 55, 64; 104-6, 108-11, 119, 121-22, 124-25, 127-28, 130-34, 136-39, 144-45, 148-50, 152; 202, 205, 210, 215, 217, 219, 226; 307, 314, 316, 318, 323; 401, 404-5, 413, 417, 421-22, 425-27, 431-33, 435, 437.

no response 412.

/ək/ - /ɪk/

stomach 61.1. NE 503.

Two variant pronunciations of the unstressed second syllable of stomach may be undergoing a change in relative frequency.

In New England the nearly universal pronunciation is with neutral /ə/. Only 18 of the 416 infs. manifest the second variant, a raised vowel /+/, sometimes as far front as /ɪ/, and 13 of them are in Maine and New Hampshire, a region without much influence upon UM speech.

Throughout the UM, however, the incidence of /'stʌm+k/ is much greater than in New England, both in Northern speech territory and in Midland speech territory. Only current data from the second survey in New England and the publication of the North Central materials will indicate whether this difference is regional as well as chronological. That it may be only the former can be inferred from the fact that the 1940 data from Wisconsin reveal the same frequency for /+/, 25%, as is shown by the 1947-48 data for Minnesota.

As the accompanying tables indicate, variation occurs within the UM, but no clear regional or social pattern emerges. It is conspicuous, however, that 10 of the 16 college graduates have /stʌm+k/, a pronunciation once considered nonstandard.

	Type I	Type II	Type III
/ə/	67%	73%	38%
/+/	37%	30%	63%

	Mn.	Ia.	N.D.	S.D.	Nb.	Ave.
/ə/	75%	62%	62%	41%	63%	65%
/+/	25%	38%	38%	63%	31%	36%

/ə/ 3, 7-8, 10-11, 13-20, 22-24, 26, 29-33, 35, 37, 39-40, 42-49, 52-57, 59-63, 65; 101-8, 111-17, 119-21, 124, 132-33, 136-37, 139, 141, 147-50; 201-4, 208-9, 211, 221, 224; 301, 304, 309, 312-13, 320-21, 325-26; 401-6, 408, 410-14, 416, 419-24, 426-27, 431, 433, 437.

/+/ 1-2, 4-5, 9, 12, 21, 25, 27-28, 34, 36, 38, 41, 50-51, 58, 64; 109-10, 122-23, 125-31, 134, 138, 143-46; 303, 305-8, 310-11, 314-19, 322-24; 407, 409, 415, 417-18, 425, 428-29, 434-36.

[ɪn] - [n̩]

mountain 24.7. NE 39. PEAS 168.

Except in northern Iowa, where fw. H may have stereotyped some responses, the low incidence of /tɪn/ or /t+n/ in the unstressed syllable of mountain reflects the situation in the East, where its occurrence is largely in coastal subareas. As a variant pronunciation it is apparently giving way to the common variant with simply a syllabic /n/, e.g. /maʊn?n̩/, for 15 of its 24 users are in the oldest group.

/-tɪn, -t+n/ 7, 49, 55-56, 62; 101-4, 109-15, 133, 137-38; 206, 219, 222; 313; 409.

Internal Vowel Loss

American 53.5. NE 451.

A perhaps questionable internal vowel loss is that of the medial weak vowel in American. The pronunciation /əmɛrkən/ is recorded by three fws., H, P, and Wr, in Midland speech territory in western Iowa and eastern Nebraska, though not in eastern Iowa. Whether this is actually a Mid-

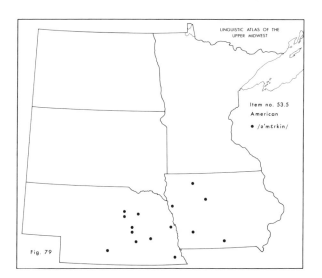

LINGUISTIC ATLAS OF THE UPPER MIDWEST

Item no. 53.5
American
• /ə'mɛrkin/

Fig. 79

297

land variant or a regionalism may be revealed in the forthcoming publication of the North Central materials. Infs. with this form are 104, 109, 112, 127, 145; 413-14, 416, 420-21, 423, 426-27, 430, 435. See map.

orange 43.1. NE 273.

In the UM the reduction of dissyllable orange /ɔr+nǰ/ to a monosyllabic /ɔrnǰ/ has been accepted by more than one-third of all infs., actually nearly one-half in Type II. A likely Midland orientation of the single syllabic form appears in its higher frequency in Iowa, particularly in the southern two-thirds, and also in Nebraska. In the North Central state of Wisconsin only 14% of the infs. have it.

	Type I	Type II	Type III
/ɔrnǰ/	33%	49%	36%
/ɔr+nǰ/	65%	51%	64%

	Mn.	Ia.	N.D.	S.D.	Nb.	Ave.
/ɔrnǰ/	43%	52%	23%	23%	49%	41%
/ɔr+nǰ/	57%	48%	77%	77%	51%	59%

/ɔrnǰ/ 8, 11, 13-16, 18, c20, 26, 28, 30, 32, 38, 40, 47-49, 51-53, 56-60, 62-64; 112, 115, 117, 122-31, 133-36, 140, 142-43, 145-49; 202, 208-9, 212, 217-18; 304-6, 312-13, 322; 404, c413, 414-16, 419, 421-23, 425, 427-28, 430-32, 435-36.
/ɔr+nǰ/ 1-7, 9-10, 12, 17, 21-25, 27, 29, 31, 33, 35-36, 39, 41-46, 50, 52, 54-55, 61, 65; 101-11, 113-14, 116, 118-21, 132, 137-39, 144; 201, 203-7, 210-11, 213-16, 219-26; 301-3, 307, 309-10, c311, 314-21, 323-26, 328; 401-3, 405-12, 417-18, 420, 429, 433-34, c437.

vegetables 40.4. NE 253.

Nearly all speakers of American English pronounce vegetables with three syllables, as, for example, /ˈvɛǰtabəlz/. Whether the presence of a weak vowel as a second syllable is due to retention of a historical form or to the spelling, the Northern distribution of the seven recorded instances in the UM hints at a possible regional pattern. Four have [ə]—c4; 202, 208; 314. Three have [+]—c3, 5; 204. No examples occur in Iowa and Nebraska. This circumstance parallels the presence of 16 instances in southern New England and 13 in Wisconsin. Whether there are Midland instances in the eastern surveys must await publication.

CHAPTER 4

Variation in Particular Words: Consonants

An extensive range of variables is evident in the production of consonants by native speakers of English in the Upper Midwest. Some of these variables exhibit regional or social contrast. Because of the impossibility of offering in this publication the full phonetic transcription of all the responses of all field informants, this volume is restricted to a broad selection of regional and social consonant feature markers.

AUGMENTATION

Intrusion or Consonantal Epenthesis

Liquids

/r/ An intrusive /r/ occurs both before a consonant in wash and Washington, tush, goad, and poached, and after a consonant in spigot and thills.

wash 15.1.
Washington 65.4b. NE 137. PEAS 137; F160.

As in the East, where only a few instances are recorded outside western Pennsylvania and West Virginia, an intrusive /r/ in wash and Washington is largely a Midland feature in the UM. Scattered examples appear in Minnesota and North Dakota, besides one in Manitoba, but most are in Iowa and Nebraska. (See map.)

Socially, it lacks sharp distinctiveness as it has even distribution between Types I and II, but, because only one college graduate offers an /r/ pronunciation, it apparently has come to be avoided by the more cultivated speakers. In conversation inf. 303 used /wɔrš boᵘɚd/.

/wɔrš/ 4, 16, 28, †¹33, 64; 103, 109, 111, 113, 115, 138, 151; 202-3, !211, !217, 226; *306, 309, 317, 319; 401-2,

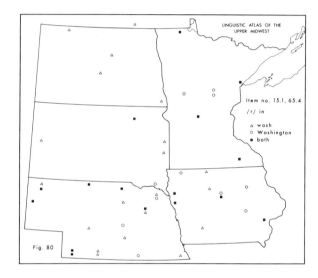

Fig. 80

c403, 405, 407, 409, c413, 415-16, *418, c423, c429, cvr430, c431, c435, 437.
no response 9, 14, 31, 35-36, 38; 222; 305, 316, 322, 327; 406.
/wɔrš+ŋtən/ 4, 16, 19-22, 28, 64; 101, 109, 111, 114-16, 133, 138; 306; 325; c402, 403, 405, 408-9, 415, 420, 429, c433, 437.
no response 3, 7; 151; 222; 430, 436.

With one exception, the few other instances of postconsonantal intrusive /r/ are noticeably limited to nonstandard speech. For tushes, itself a variant of tusks (29.3), an Iowan Type I inf., 146, has the unique form [tɚšəz], in which the intruded /r/ has become assimilated with the preceding vowel. One Type II speaker, c12, has the intrusive /r/ in goad, but the five others are all in Type I: 7, 15, 21; sn224; 306. Only six Type I speakers have it in poached (37.3): 21; 114, 132; 209, 220; 317. These have [porčt] or [pɔrčt] except inf. 209, who has an assimilated unique variant [pɚčt].
Preconsonantal intrusive /r/ is ex-

tremely rare. For spigot (15.5b) two Type
I speakers—132; 218—have sprigot and another—215—has sprocket. For thills an
Iowa farmer, 108, with one year of high
school, has the unique form thrills.

/l/   One instance of an intrusive /l/
appears in the term stone boat (18.4)
with the second element as /bolt/ in the
speech of a Type I Ontario inf., 3, and
of a Duluth, Minnesota, Type I inf., 15.
With the former, /bolt/ may be an instance of folk etymology, as she insisted
upon bolt as her spelling of the word.

Stops

With one exception, the recorded intrusive stop consonants result from a
homorganic occlusion following a continuant. The exception, the /t/ in attackted
for attacked, is more likely simply a
double preterit. It occurs in the speech
of 311, a Type I inf. Compare the remark
of inf. 414, "They would attackt."
Following /l/ an intrusive stop /d/ occurs in high holder for high holer, inf.
105's folk term for a woodpecker, and a
/t/ occurs in filts for fills (17.5), in
the speech of Type I inf. 41. Following
/n/ and before a vowel /ɚ/, /t/ also is
intrusive in whinter for whinner in the
speech of Type II inf. 123. A social contrast is implicit in the fact that none
of the preceding instances is found in
educated speech.
Following /n/ and before /s/, however,
an intrusive homorganic /t/ is general
throughout the UM, with possible geographical but no social contrasts. An
analysis of the pronunciation of answer,
dance, fence, once, rinse, and since reveals that only a small proportion (17%)
of all infs. are recorded with /ns/ in
even one of these words, and most of
these are in eastern Iowa and eastern
Minnesota. This distribution suggests
that the pronunciation without intrusive
/t/ is receding, but the suggestion is
weakened by the fact that in eastern
South Dakota and eastern Nebraska fws. Wr
and Wn recorded only /nts/. Fieldworker
variation may, then, exaggerate what is
probably a real contrast.
In the recorded instances of the following words only the indicated informants have the simple cluster /ns/. All
others have an intrusive /t/. The lower
frequency of intrusive /t/ in answer is
clearly a function of the word's dissyl-
labic structure, with /s/ belonging to
the unstressed second syllable rather
than to the first.
answer (73.1) 15, 17, 23, 32, 36, c38,

39, 50, 58, 65; 106-8, sn114, 115, 120,
123, 138-41; 206, sn220, 222.
dance (62.3) 13, 15, 17, 57. (For 13
and 15 the /n/ is actualized in the nasality of the vowel [æ̃].)
fence (13.2) 56.
once (2.7) 25; 429.
rinse (15.2) 6; 123, 125, 140-41.
(These infs. have /nš/: 129, 146-49.)
since (75.2) 13; 128, 140.
Like intrusive /t/ in the preceding
words, intrusive /p/ in something (74.6)
is found throughout the UM, with a somewhat similar distribution of the simple
/mθ/ cluster as an apparently receding
feature in the eastern portion of Minnesota and in Iowa. The more frequent lack
of the intrusive stop in Iowa, however,
suggests that in Midland speech there was
once a somewhat weaker articulation of
the stressed syllable. Such an inference
is supported by the absence from Iowa of
the assimilated variants [sʌmpən],
[sʌmpn̩], [sʌmpm̩], [sʌmpʔm̩], variants more
common in the speech of the less educated
when they do occur. /mpθ/ is widespread
except as follows:
/mθ/ c13, c15, 18, c31, 39, 48, c55,
c59; 103, c114, 117, 124, 126, 128, 130-
31, 134, 140-41, 144, 146-49; c327; 425,
c430.
/mp/ + nasal c13, c16-17, c24-25, c30-
32, c35, c38, c46, c50-51, c57, c59;
c117; c216, c225; c309, c311, c328; c404-
5, 415, c416, c419, 423, c429.

Excrescence

Excrescence typically occurs when vig-
orous articulation of a final continuant,
whether fricative, nasal, or liquid, pro-

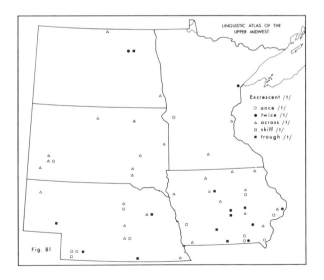

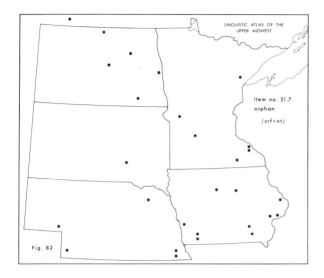

After homorganic /n/ in orphan (51.7) 26 infs. add /t/. Of them 21 are in Type I and 5 are in Type II. No cultivated speaker has this form. Although /ɔrfɨnt/ is a clear social marker there is no discernible geographical pattern except for its virtual absence in the westernmost portions of the UM, a circumstance implying that this is a recessive feature not strong enough to be carried west by the last settlement wave.

orphan(t) 16, 25, 48, 56-57, 65; 114, 117, 124, 135, 139-40, 147; 201, 204, 211-12, 220, 224; 322; 407, 417, 429, 434, c435.

After final /f/ 10 infs. add /t/ to skiff (6.5b) as /skɪft/, one to cliff as /klɪft/, one to sheaf (34.2) as /šift/, and 12 to trough (29.5) as /trɔft/. Of the total of 24 not one is a cultivated speaker, seven are in Type II, and 17, more than twice as many, are in Type I. After /f/, excrescent /t/ may be Midland-oriented, as all but one of the instances are in Iowa and Nebraska.

skiff(t) 117, 124, sn140, 146, sn149; 312; 414, 422, 429, 437.

cliff(t) 311.

sheaf(t) 129.

trough(t) 17; 113, 129, 132, 139, 145, 151; c212; 416-17, 429, 433.

After /θ/ one Minnesota Type I inf., 55, adds /t/ to drouth (6.1).

Homorganic /d/ appears uniquely after stubborn (57.2) in the speech of Type II inf. 60. It is a fairly frequent feature with drown as /draund/, the base form that retains the /d/ in the investigated preterit drowned (69.6) as /draundɨd/. Of the 36 infs. who use /draundɨd/ not one is a cultivated speaker and only seven are in Type II. Twenty-nine are in Type I. In addition four infs.—40, 42; 215; 418—report this form as heard in their communities. Since its distribution is quite uniform throughout the UM, the only contrast is along the social range.

/draundɨd/ c5, 19, c35, ¹40, ¹42, 48, 56, c57; c109, 112, c113-14, 117, 134-35, 138, c139, 140, 142-43, 147; ¹215, c218, 220, 224; 303, 305, 307, c311, 316-17, 320, c322; 401, 415-16, ¹418, 430, c437.

A single instance of homorganic /d/ after /l/ is found in the speech of Type I inf. 307, who pronounces goal as /gold/.

duces an occlusion that is heard as a homorganic stop. Thus if the tongue muscles are fairly tense in the pronunciation of the final /s/, especially if it also ends a phonetic phrase, the tension may lead to momentary complete contact with the teeth ridge. To a listener the result is the consonant /t/. Historically this phonetic process has yielded a number of now generally accepted forms in the language, such as sound from Middle English soun and against from Middle English ageyns. The process itself is still active, but the standardizing influence of writing and the schools has limited its effect in the UM to sporadic occurrences among uneducated speakers.

Two excrescent consonants, /t/ and /d/, are minor social markers. Homorganic /t/ occurs after /s/ and /n/ as well as after /f/ and /θ/; homorganic /d/ after /n/ and /l/ as well as after /r/. After /s/ four infs. add the /t/ to once (2.6) as /wʌnst/, four to twice (2.7) as /twaɪst/, and thirty to across (23.8) as /əkrɔst/. No cultivated speaker does this. Only 13 Type II infs. have excrescent /t/, but 25 uneducated speakers, nearly twice as many, have it. The regional distribution hints also at a Midland orientation, since North Dakota and Minnesota record only six infs. with /-t/. (See map.) Once and twice are treated also in PEAS 5.23, with a map on p. 179, where a Midland background is strongly indicated.

once(t) 25; 147; c225; 429.

twice(t) c128, 135, 147; c212.

across(t) 39, 53; 104-5, c107, 109, 113, 115, c116, c133, 138, c139; 204, c225; c304, 305-6, 311-12, c317, 320, c322, 323, 327; c402, c413, c416, c420, c422, sn435.

Linking or Hiatus-Filling

Akin to excrescence occurring before a vowel in a following word is the phenomenon of linking. The gap or hiatus between a final vowel and the initial vowel of a following word is likely to be filled either by a vocalic glide that may be heard as a consonantal /w/ as in go/w/at, /j/ as in see/j/it, or by a glottal stop, /?/.

China egg (13.7) was irregularly sought by fws. to ascertain whether the eastern china/r/egg was carried into the UM. No instances occur, but two infs. (314; 434) have /j/ and 21 (13-14, 35; 150, 152; 215, 225-26; 309, 315, 326; c403, 406-8, 410-11, 420, 426, 432, 437) with possible Midland orientation have the glottal stop /?/.

Law and order (64.4) was sought for the same reason. One example of linking /r/ occurs in the phrase law and justice used by inf. 16. Fourteen infs., most of whom are in Midland speech territory, have the glottal stop /?/, and six have a clear linking /w/ (20, 37, 49; 238; 414, 433).

How often (54.4) also is marked by a linking /w/ in the speech of 14 infs. (6, 21; 213, 218; 315, 322, 328; 408, 412-13, 423, 427-28, 431), and by a linking glottal stop in the speech of infs. 217 and 420.

Swallow it (45.1; PEAS 172, F159) is characterized by a greater frequency of linking than in any of the other phrases recorded. Eighty-eight infs., more than one-third of all UM infs., have linking /w/, apparently without social or regional contrast. Seven infs., all in Type I, retain the linking /r/ considered in PEAS as peculiar to eastern New England and the South Midland area. One has the glottal stop.

/-w-/ 2-4, 7-16, 18, c20, 21-23, 25, 28-31, 34-36, 38, 40-41, 43, 45-46, 49, 54, 57; 103-4, 109, 112, 115, 118, 123, 133, 137-38, 150; 208, 210, 215, c219, 221, c223-25, 226; 304, 306, 308, 314-15, 320, c322-23, 326, 328; 401, 403, 405-8, c410, 412-15, c416, 418, c419, 420, 422-24, 428-31, 436.

/-r-/ 55; c113, 114, c132, 143; 303, 311.

/-?-/ 404.

Cluster Separation by Anaptyxis

Although English belongs to a language type that allows internal two-, three-, and even four-consonant clusters, the presence of /l/, /r/, or a nasal in the cluster may lead to the development of an intrusive or epenthetic vowel that effectively breaks it up. The phenomenon is technically known as anaptyxis or, especially when /r/ or /l/ is the first consonant in the cluster, as svarabhakti (from its description in Sanskrit gram-

mar). Because in the UM anaptyxis is unusual in cultivated speech, it has some significance as a social marker.

castrate 29.6. NE 210.

Although no Type III speakers admit an intrusive vowel in this word, 14 Type II speakers have /ˈkæstəˌret/ and 26, nearly twice as many, Type I speakers have it. Perhaps to be included is the deviant /ˈkæsɚˌet/ of inf. 103, but not the curious form /ˈkæstɪˌnet/ offered by inf. 121. Infs. with an intrusive vowel are as follows:

Type I 4, *5, 10-11, 19, 23-24, 27, 35, 45, 48, 52; 118, 140, 143, 146, 151; 209, 212, 224, c225; 303, 314; 407, 417, 429.

Type II 22, 25; 147; 202, 211, 213, 217; 318, 321; 404, 408, 423, 431, 436.

umbrella 23.4. NE 367.

In umbrella as /ˌʌmbəˈrɛlə/ the anaptyctic or intrusive vowel seems to occur with both social and regional contrast. It is most strongly favored by uneducated speakers and it is nearly twice as likely to be found in Midland speech territory.

Type I	Type II	Type III
44%	24%	19%

Mn.	Ia.	N.D.	S.D.	Nb.	Ave.
25%	47%	27%	23%	41%	32%

1, 3, 10, 12, 15, 21-22, 31, 40, 44-45, 53, 60, c61, 64; 101, 104-5, 109-10, 113-18, 122, 124-25, 129, 132-33, 135, 137-38, 142, 146-47, 151; 201, 204-5, 212-13, 216-17; 307-8, 311, 314, 316, 320; 403-5, 407, c408, 413, 415-16, 422-24, 426-27, 429-30.

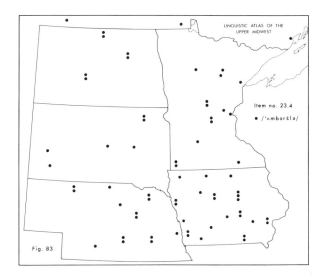

LINGUISTIC ATLAS OF THE UPPER MIDWEST

Item no. 23.4
• /ˈʌmbɚɛlə/

Fig. 83

mushroom 44.6. NE 279. PEAS 179; F177.

Strictly speaking, the medial schwa /ə/ in the minority pronunciation /ˈmʌšə͵rum/ is not intrusive but rather is historical. The three-syllable form, from Old French mousseron through Early Middle English musseroun, is the original. But the two-syllable form that first appeared in the sixteenth century has replaced it in Standard English, and that with medial schwa is often classed with nonstandard variants such as umberella and athaletics. According to Kurath, the trisyllabic form strongly persists in the folk speech of the South and South Midland, especially in the variant with final /-n/ (see p. 333), and it is not infrequent among rural speakers in upstate New York, Rhode Island, and the northern tier of counties in Pennsylvania.

The UM relative geographical distribution may reflect that in the eastern states, with most of the 11 occurrences in Iowa related to South Midland preponderance. But on the whole the intrusive /ə/ in the UM is not so Northern-oriented as the division in Pennsylvania might lead one to predict. There is an obvious Midland emphasis.

The social distribution remains the same, however, since the intrusive vowel, when it occurs, is clearly a social marker more likely to be used by Type I speakers. Only one Type III inf. has it, an old-fashioned retired Iowa lawyer.

Type I	Type II	Type III
23%	9%	6%

Mn.	Ia.	N.D.	S.D.	Nb.
8%	21%	8%	21%	19%

/-ə-/ 12, 16, 25, 35, 56; 105, 109, 115, c122, 130, 132, 134-35, 138-39; 217, 220; 301, 303, 307, 311, 316, 320; 401-2, 405, 407, 417, 429, 432.

pancake 36.4. NE 289.

Like the medial /ə/ in mushroom, an analogous vowel in pancake—actualized as /ɨ/—is probably historical rather than anaptyctic. Pannicake, a form not found in New England, may have been introduced into the western speech migration as an adaption of Dutch pannekak used in the colonial Dutch settlements in the Hudson Valley. It weakly survives in the UM only in Northern speech territory, with infs. as follows: *9, ¹47, 56-57, 64; ¹223.

Two words not sought in the field interviews also turn up with an anaptyctic vowel in incidental conversation. Elm appears as /ɛləm/ in the speech of four Dakotans (224; 307, 316-17); and film is /fɪləm/ in the speech of one Dakotan, 212.

chimney 6.7. NE 332.

Seven infs., all but one living in Midland speech territory, have an anaptyptic vowel in chimney, which they pronounce as /čɪmənɪ/. Three of them are in Type I, 140, 216, and 407; four are in Type II, 106, 134; 321; 421.

LOSS OR CLUSTER REDUCTION

Various phonetic processes, chiefly assimilation, have historically led to the simplification of consonant clusters in English by reducing a two- or three-consonant cluster to a single consonant. In the UM some of these changes revealed in the field data have social or regional correlations.

Aspiration + Glide

The historical tendency to simplify initial consonant clusters beginning with /h/ has been so successful over the centuries that /h/ remains in Modern English only before the glides /w/ and /j/, and then only in competition with the simple glide.

/hw/

When retained before /w/, the aspiration appears in the field records as [hw], [ʰw], or [ɦw]. In general, these

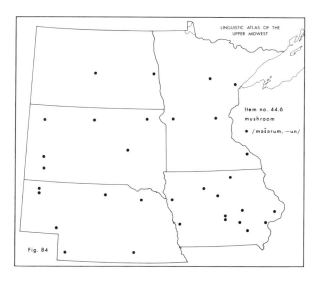

LINGUISTIC ATLAS OF THE UPPER MIDWEST

Item no. 44.6
mushroom
• /mašərum, —un/

Fig. 84

303

words preserve the /h/ in much of the East, except for the Middle Atlantic coast (including the megalopolis from Connecticut to Baltimore), most of eastern Pennsylvania, the Boston area, and a narrow coastal strip in Maine.

In the UM, although the proportion of loss varies slightly from word to word, the actual loss is no greater than in the East, where Kurath reports a tendency among cultivated speakers to restore the aspiration. More Minnesota speakers, on the whole, seem inclined to drop the /h/, as do more in Type III. The latter circumstance is interpretable as a countertendency of cultivated speakers, i.e., to accept the /h/-less form.

whip   15.7. NE 179. PEAS 178; F174.

About one of 10 UM infs. has /wɪp/ for whip, with a strong bias toward Type III speakers and Minnesota:

Type I	Type II	Type III
12%	11%	25%

Mn.	Ia.	N.D.	S.D.	Nb.	Ave.
24%	10%	4%	5%	8%	13%

/wɪp/ 1-2, 5-6, 12-13, 19, 33-34, 37-38, 48, 50, 54, 56; 124, 134, 148-49, 150; 201; 317, 321; 410, 415, 425.
/hwɪp/ All others except nonresponding 4; 140; 218.

wheelbarrow   19.6. NE 163. PEAS 178; F174.

The loss of /h/ in wheelbarrow is minimal, but again somewhat greater in Minnesota than elsewhere and perhaps slightly greater with the college infs.

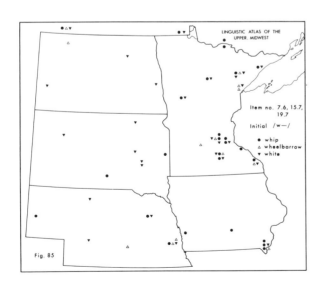

Fig. 85

Type I	Type II	Type III
7%	5%	13%

Mn.	Ia.	N.D.	S.D.	Nb.	Ave.
11%	2%	8%	0	8%	6%

/wɪl/ 13, 15-16, 34, 44, 48, 57; r150; 201, 203; 423-25.
/hwɪl/ All others except nonresponding 62; 313.

white   7.6. NE 98, 281, 341.

The presence of the /h/-less form of white in the speech of Minnesota Type III speakers may prevent recognition of a possible general trend toward /hw/ as suggested by the fact that, as with whip and wheelbarrow, /hw/ is slightly more frequent among Type II infs. than among the older and less-educated Type I's. Again there appears to be a slight Northern orientation:

Type I	Type II	Type III
15%	9%	20%

Mn.	Ia.	N.D.	S.D.	Nb.	Ave.
19%	2%	15%	18%	11%	13%

/waɪt/ 1, 6, 12, c13, 14-15, 19, 34-35, 48, 50, 57; 149; 201, 212, 214, 220; 302, 305, 316, 327-28; 404, sn415, c419, 425.
/hwaɪt/ All others except nonresponding 17; 106, 119, 122, 139-41, 143, 146-47.

whinner, -y, -ter   30.2. NE 198. PEAS 178; F174.

Except for a Minnesota Type III speaker, the loss of /h/ from whinny seems stronger among the less educated in Minnesota and the Dakotas, Northern speech territory:

Type I	Type II	Type III
13%	5%	9%

Mn.	Ia.	N.D.	S.D.	Nb.	Ave.
10%	3%	9%	18%	8%	9%

/w/ 1, 13, 15, 34, 41; 140; 201, 224; 304-5, 311, 318; 421, 424.
/hw/ All others except the following, who either did not respond or offered another word: 3-4, 7, 11, 14, 17, 19, 24, 33, 35-36, 38; 120-22, 128-29, 131, 133-36, 141-43, 146, 148-49; 202, 209, 211, 218; 308, 310, 314-15, 326-27; 412, 415, 417, 424-26, 430-33, 435.

whetstone   19.7. NE 159.

Except for a greater frequency of /w/ among Type II speakers than among Type I's and for a higher proportion in Nebraska, the general picture for the /w/-/hw/ contrast with whetstone is similar

to that with the words previously treated:

Type I	Type II	Type III
7%	15%	17%

Mn.	Ia.	N.D.	S.D.	Nb.	Ave.
11%	9%	12%	5%	12%	10%

/w/ 2, 17, 43-44, 57, 60; 121, 148-50;
201, 221, 224; 306; 415, s421, 425, 435.

/hw/ All others except the following,
who offered another term or did not respond: 1, 6, 13-14, 19, 21, 24, 30, 35-
36, 38; 101, 107, 110, 112, 119-20, 124-
25, 128; 208; 303, 307, 315, 319, 324,
326; 404-6.

wheat 33.6. NE 281.

Although a slightly smaller proportion
of infs. have /w/ in wheat, the greater
frequency in Minnesota again suggests its
Northern orientation:

Type I	Type II	Type III
9%	6%	7%

Mn.	Ia.	N.D.	S.D.	Nb.	Ave.
15%	2%	4%	10%	3%	8%

/w/ 2, 4, 6, c16, 19, 37, 48, 51, 57;
149; 201; 317, 319; 425.

/hw/ All others except the following,
who either did not respond or offered
another term, e.g., oats: 13, 15, 23-24,
56, 58, 64; 110, 118, 120-21, 140-41,
151; 214; 305-8, 316, 318, 327; 405, 428.

wharf 25.1. NE 183. PEAS 178; F175.

Although only 38 scattered UM infs. offer wharf as a lexical variant (see Volume I), it is clear that for them, as in
the East, this term is atypical with respect to the /w/-/hw/ alternation. Kurath
reports that the /w/ pronunciation of
wharf has spread into western Pennsylvania and thence down the Ohio Valley. This
spread is clearly reflected in the high
frequency of /wɔrf/ or /wɑrf/ in the Midland two-thirds of Iowa, where 10 infs.
have it in contrast to one with /hw/.

/w/ 11, 51, 54, 57; 101, 119-20, 122,
136-37, 140, 142, *145, s147, 148; 201-2,
208, 217, 221; s414, s424, 425.

/hw/ 3, 17, 46, 59, 61-62; s152; 217;
328; 411, 422, 426-28, 433.

Some measure of consistency in the individual's application of the /hw/ → /w/
rule appears in the fact that 27 infs.
apply it in at least two of the terms
treated above. One Canadian, 201, has /w/
in seven of the words. The 27 are as follows: 1-2, 6, 12-13, 15-16, 19, 34, 37,
44, 48, 50-51; 140, 148-50; 201, 221,

224; 305, 317; 415, 421, 424-25. This
consistency is proportionately greatest
in Minnesota and North Dakota.

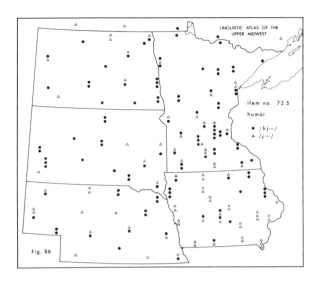

Fig. 86

/hj/

humor 72.5. NE 469. PEAS 178; F176.

According to Kurath most eastern speakers have accepted a deletion rule that
drops the initial aspiration from the
/hj/ cluster in humor. The full cluster
is retained only in New England and upstate New York.

Although apparently initial /h/ is a
declining feature, it persists in Minnesota and the Dakotas as the dominant form
and even has a bare majority in Nebraska.
But megalopolitan and Midland initial /j/
has pushed into Minnesota and North Dakota. The rate of its spread into Northern
speech territory may be decreasing, however, as the influence of the written
form seems to be maintaining /hjumɚ/ as a
more prestigious social marker. The cluster is actualized as [hj], [ʰj], [ɸⱼ],
[ɦj], and [h+].

Three infs. are reported as having the
unusual pronunciation /humɚ/.

	Type I	Type II	Type III
/j/	54%	29%	20%
/hj/	43%	70%	80%
/h/	2%	1%	0

	Mn.	Ia.	N.D.	S.D.	Nb.	Ave.
/j/	32%	61%	35%	23%	46%	40%
/hj/	67%	35%	65%	77%	54%	58%
/h/	1%	4%	0	0	0	2%

/j/ 3, 8, 15-16, 22, sn25, 28-29, 31,
39, 42, ?44, 45-46, 51-52, 59, 62-63;
101, 103-5, 112-15, 122, 124-25, 127,
129, 131-33, 135-43, 145-50, 152; 201-2,

204-5, 207, 210, 212, 215, 218; 316-17,
320, 324, 327; 401, 403-4, 409-10, †411,
412, 414, 418, 420, 425, 429, 433-34.
 /hj/ 1-2, 4, r5, 6-7, 9-14, 17-21, 23-
24, 26-27, 30, 32-35, 37-38, 41-43, cr44,
47, 49-50, 53-55, 57-58, 60-61, 64; 102,
106-11, 116, 119-21, 123, 126, 128, 130,
134, 144; 203, 206, 208-9, 211, 213-14,
216-17, 219-26; 302-4, 309-15, 319, 321-
23, 325-26, 328; 402, 405-8, 415-17, 419,
421, 424, 430, 435-36.
 /h/ 48; 117, 123.

Dental Obstruent + Glide

Greater ease in articulation led to the
development of a Modern English rule that
eliminates the palatal glide /j/ when it
is the second member of a cluster beginning with a dental obstruent. This rule
is, however, much more widely accepted if
that obstruent is an alveolar stop or
fricative than if it is an interdental
fricative. For support the UM survey provides data for five words containing the
alveolar sequence, new, due(s), Tuesday,
suit, and tube, and for one, Matthew,
containing the interdental fricative.

Although schematically it is possible
to suggest that the development after an
alveolar occurred in two stages, i.e.,
from [ju] to [iu] to [u], the historical
background actually seems to offer two
parallel developments. In one the earlier
[j] was weakened to an [i] that bore the
stress in a falling diphthong [íu]. This
pronunciation is widespread in New England and it survives, according to Kurath
and McDavid, as a nonstandard variant in
New York State and western secondary New
England settlements. No clear instances
of this falling diphthong are recorded in
the UM, although certain [iu] transcriptions should perhaps be so interpreted.

In the other development the [j] becomes simply a weak high front onglide
before [u], so weak that in certain areas
it is unable to survive. The older full
[ju], common in the South, is infrequent
in the North, though heard from some cultivated speakers in New York City.

The UM retention of /ju/ as either [ju]
or [ιu] is sporadic in Minnesota and
North Dakota, quite rare in South Dakota,
and more frequent and more consistent in
the Midland speech of Iowa and Nebraska,
as well as in the speech of two of the
five Canadian infs. (See map.)

Any attempt to relate the occurrence of
the alveolar + [j] cluster to its occurrence in the East must recognize the influence of the schools, where some infs.
had once been told to use [nju], [tju],

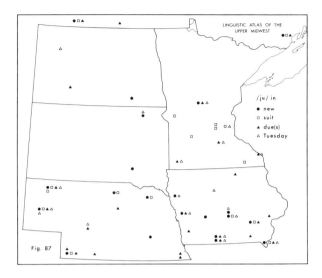

Fig. 87

and [dju] in preference to [nu], [tu],
and [du]. This interference with normal
area speech patterns is the likely source
of such hyper-correction as has been
noted in the formal speech of a Twin Cities radio announcer, who regularly said,
"And now for the noon [njun] news
[njuz]."

new 22.6. NE 361a. PEAS 174; F164.

For new the pronunciation /nu/ is well-
nigh universal in the UM. The rare full
variant /nju/ is recorded only by fw. M
in northeastern Minnesota, by fw. G in
the speech of inf. 59, who, however, also
has simple /nu/ in conversation, and by
fw. Wn in eastern South Dakota. But a
variant with a high mid vowel [+] occurs
much more frequently, though with fairly
sharp restriction to the Midland speech
area in Iowa and Nebraska. Where [nju]
and [n+u] appear, they may well have
value as an acquired prestige feature.
Only five Type I speakers have the diphthongal variant in contrast with 13 Type
II's and five Type III's.

 [nju] 14, 17-18, 59; 308.
 [nιu] 144; 426. [nˡu] 126; 145.
 [n+u^] 136. [n+u] 3, 28; 111, cvr122,
130; 224; 401. [n+u] 150; 201; 322; 406,
408, 437.
 /nu/ All others.

suit 22.6. NE 361A.

During an interview suit is usually obtained in the expression new suit in
order to provide immediate comparison of
the development after /n/ and that after
/s/. In the UM, simplification of the
cluster is greater after /s/. There are

no instances of full [sj]. All but two of its 19 putative occurrences are actualized as [s+], and eight of those 17 are recorded with a superior symbol, i.e., as [s⁺u], to indicate that for these speakers the historical /j/ has shrunk to only a faint onglide before the /u/.

What makes the situation rather difficult to interpret is that fws. A and P tended to record responses with a high central rounded vowel as in [sʉut]. If the rounding of the vowel is considered crucial as in the listing below, then most or all of such instances may be interpreted simply as /sut/, with an allophone of /u/. If the backward tongue movement is considered crucial, then at least some instances can be interpreted as variants of /s+ut/. In that case the range and frequency of the latter would be measurably extended.

Although no social contrasts are discernible among the instances of /sju/ and /sɪu/, there is a slight Midland preponderance.

[sɪut] 410-11.
[s⁺ut] 31, c35, 38, c65; 136, 150; 401-2.
[s+ut] 3, 25, 45, c65; vr131; 201; 406, 408, 437.
[sʉut] 1-2, 10.
[sʉᵘt] 27-28, 30, 33, 37, 42, 49, 64; 104, 122-25, 127-31, 133-35, 142-45, 152; 216-17, 219-22, 224, 226; 302, 314-15, 317; 404, 412, 418, 429.
[sʉut] 11, 13-15, 17, 26, 36, 50, 52, 57; vr115, 117; 203, 205-6, 208-11, 213-14.
[sʉut] 126, 152; 215; 403.
/sut/ All others.

due(s)   68.7. NE 563. PEAS 174; F163.

With due or dues the full /dj/ cluster is characteristic of the South and South Midland speech regions east of the Appalachians. It is infrequent in the North except as a prestige pronunciation in metropolitan centers. The weakened /di/ with the falling diphthong is found in New England and its western secondary settlement areas.

In the UM a full [dj] is recorded three times by fw. M in northeastern Minnesota and once in South Dakota in the speech of an inf., 317, who has a New England background. A diphthongal form, however, appears in the speech of 26 infs., most of whom are in the Midland speech territory of southern Iowa and Nebraska. Perhaps six of them retain the falling diphthong of New England.

[dju] 14, 16, 18; 317.

[dɪu] 48, 57; 144, 146; 410, 413. [dˡu] 3, 59; 150; 419, 429, 434, 437.
[d+u] 122, 136; 201-2, 215; 401. [d+ᵘ] 106, 125, 137.
/du/ All others.

Tuesday   3.2a. NE 67. PEAS 174; F165.

The distribution of the variants of Tuesday is much like that for suit in both the East and the UM, except that in the latter there are fewer occurrences in the Midland speech territory than with suit.

Again fw. M notes three examples of the full cluster as in /tju/ in northeastern Minnesota. An Iowan and a South Dakotan offer two more. That this is a receding form is suggested by inf. 62, whose comment is "Old-timers said /tjuzdi/." The variant /tiu/, typically realized as [t+u] or [t⁺u], seems predominantly Midland with a few instances in Minnesota. Two Canadians have the distinctive affricate /č/, actualized as [ǰʂ].

[ǰʂu] 201-2.
[tjuˇ] c18. [tjʉu] 14-15.
[tɪu] 57; 111, 144-45. [tɪˀu] 48.
[t+u] 40, 59; vr115, 122, 129, vr131; 210; 410, 418. [t⁺u] 28; 150; 401, 411.
[tu] All others.

tube   20.4. NE 186. PEAS 113, F33.

Of the five test words with the historical background of /ju/ or /iu/ it is tube that, in the UM, has most strongly resisted the trend toward simple /u/.

Besides the four infs. with the consonantal forms [ǰʂ], [tj], and [tç], there are 25 with reduced /t+ub/, including one instance of [ʉᵘ]. These 29 infs. consti-

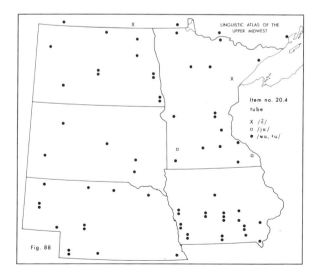

LINGUISTIC ATLAS OF THE UPPER MIDWEST

Item no. 20.4
tube
x /č/
□ /ju/
• /ʉu, +u/

Fig. 88

tute 14% of those pronouncing the word for the fw. In addition, 44 infs., 21% of the total, have a rounded diphthongal [tᵘu], [tʊᵘ], or [tʋᵘ] with a backward glide. Altogether, then, 73 infs., or nearly 36%, of the UM infs. have a pronunciation reflecting to some degree the original diphthong or consonant [j] plus [u].

Distribution of the two classes of variants lacks clear contrasts. A slight tendency of better educated speakers to consider the diphthongal varieties as more prestigious is inferable from the proportions: Type I, 33%; Type II, 45%; Type III, 44%. All the Canadian infs. have this kind of variant, which otherwise is scattered widely in the UM, with another area of concentration in the Midland speech sector of Iowa and with the lowest frequency in South Dakota.

/tʉub/ 1-2, 4-5, 10-11, 26, 29-30, 50, 52, 55, 64; 123-25, 127, 129-30, 133-35, 142, 144, 152; 204, 206, 213, 216-17, 223, 225-26; 302, 312, 315, 323; 406, 408, 418-19, 429, 436-37.
/tɨub/ 3, 6, 38, 59; vrl15, 122, 126, vrl31, 136, 143, 145-46, 150; 201, 210, 215-16, c222; 328; 401, 403, 410-11, 431, 435.
[tɕʉˇb] 15. [ʈʂub] 202. [tjub] 47, 57.
/tub/ All others but nonresponding 37, 118, and 151.

Comment:
"[tjub] is correct"—47.

Matthew 52.4. NE 434.

A cluster consisting of a labiodental and /j/ is quite rare in English. Only about half a dozen words exemplify it,

one of which, Matthew, is a key term in the UM survey. In NE the usual recorded pronunciation is /mæθju/ or /mæθiu/, but simple /mæθu/ is also frequent and widely distributed. But after the interdental /θ/ the /j/ glide is much more resistant to change than it is after alveolars. The variant /mæθu/ does persist in the UM, but only as a recessive old-fashioned form in Northern speech territory (see map). It is used by 10 Type I speakers (23, 27, 44, 59, 65; 103; 216, 218, 223; 409) and three Type II speakers (42, 63-64), all of whom are in Minnesota and North Dakota except inf. 409, both of whose parents were born in New York State.

Nasal + Homorganic Stop

In certain situations an optional rule may delete a homorganic stop in a cluster following a nasal consonant, with a resulting simplification exactly the reverse of that obtained by the rule of excrescence.

/ŋg/

Before /r/ and /l/ a rule reducing an internal cluster /ŋg/ to /ŋ/ has occasionally been accepted by a few UM infs.

Two Type I infs. (13; 216), one Type II (37), and one Type III (18) have only /ŋ/ in angleworm, 46.7; one Type II (37) has only the /ŋ/ in angry, 57.4; two Type I's (201; 316) and one Type II (202) have it in mongrel, 26.6; and three Type I's (15; 117, 143), one Type II (318), and one Type III (50) have it in singletree, 17.6.

Although the occurrences are too few to justify generalization, it is observable that seven of the 13 are from Type I speakers, four from Type II's, but only two from Type III's, and that all but two are in Northern speech territory.

An incidental observation is that with respect to mongrel four infs. (16; 105, 114; 316) have an r-less form /maŋgəl/ and one (138) has the unique /mogɨl/. Another unique variant is /mʌŋgɚ/, offered by inf. 427.

/nd/

No consistent social or regional contrast appears in the irregular acceptance of a rule reducing the /nd/ cluster to /n/, nor is the rule accepted to the same extent in different contexts.

grandpa 50.1. NE 381.

In grandpa the /nd/ cluster occurs in-

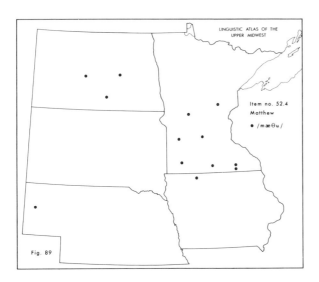

LINGUISTIC ATLAS OF THE UPPER MIDWEST

Item no. 52.4
Matthew
● /mæθu/

Fig. 89

ternally in a stressed syllable before a nonhomorganic consonant that could induce assimilation. Of the 128 infs. offering this lexical variant (see Volume 1), only six (5%) retain the full cluster, four in Type I and one each in Types II and III. One-third of the infs. (36%), evenly distributed by type, accept the reduction rule yielding simple /n/, as in /grænpɑ/. The remaining 59%, also evenly distributed by type, adopt a second rule replacing the alveolar feature by a bilabial feature to correspond with bilabial /p/, thus yielding /græmpɑ/. The pronunciation grampa appears to have Northern orientation, as it is less frequent in southern Iowa and Nebraska. This contrast may, however, be due to fw. variation as the zero zone in southern Iowa corresponds to the area covered by fw. P.

/grændpɑ/ 43, 45, 59; 150; 220; 415.
/grænpɑ/ 2, 5, 15-17, 20, 25-26, 28, 34, 49-50, 64-65; 103, 105, 110, 116-17, 124-28, 135, 137, 139, 141, 143, 147; 208, 220, 226; 308; c406, 410, c414, 419-20, 422, 424, 429, 431, 435.
/græmpɑ/ 1, 6, 8, 10-11, 14, 18-19, 23, 33, 37-40, 42, 46-48, 51, 53-54, 56, 58, 60, 62-63; 104-5, 107, 111, 114, 118, 120, *122, 123, c133; 201-2, 204-5, 207, 209-11, 215-17, 219, 221-25; 301-3, 306, 312-14, 316-17, 319, 324-25, 328; c401, 402, 404, 408, 413, 416-18, 426, 428, 436.

grindstone 19.8. NE 160.

In grindstone /nd/ occurs internally, at the end of a stressed syllable before a homorganic /st/ cluster. A reduction rule simplifying the cluster to /n/ has been accepted by exactly one-half of the Type III cultivated speakers, by a slightly higher proportion (59%) of the Type II infs., and by two-thirds (65%) of the least educated. A slight regional contrast also is suggested (Minnesota 57%, Iowa 69%, North Dakota 41%, South Dakota 87%, Nebraska 54%), but this apparent Midland orientation may be caused by fw. variation. In Minnesota and Iowa 8% of the infs. who have the full cluster are recorded with the released /d/ as [nd]; all other responses are transcribed as [nᵈ] with an unreleased stop. A North Dakota inf. (212) confirms the loss of [d] by using grining stone.

[nd] 10, 45-47, 60; 104-5, 111, 115.
[nᵈ] 2-4, 7-8, 21-24, 27, 29, 33-37, 50, 55, 58-59, 61, 64; 102, 106-7, 109, 113, 116, 121, 127, 139, 146, 150; 202, 205, 207, 209-11, 214, 216-17, 219, 223, 225-26; 312, 314, 319; 401-2, 406, 408,

411, 413, 416, 419, 427-29, 435-36.
/n/ *5, 6, 11-20, 25-26, 28, 30-32, 34, 38-44, 48-49, 51-54, 56-57, c62, 63, 65; 101, 103, 108, 112, 114, 117-20, 122-26, 128-38, 140-45, 147-49, 151; 203, 206, 208, 215-18, 220-22, 224; 301, 303, 305-8, 311, 313, 315-18, 321-25, 327; 403-5, 409-10, 412, 414, 417-18, 421-22, 431, 433, 437.

husband 49.1. NE 374.

In husband /nd/ occurs finally in an unstressed syllable. An even 50% of the responding infs. (see Volume 1) retain the full cluster, and nearly one-third, 31%, are recorded as having a final [nᵈ], a transcription indicating perception of an unreleased [d]. Because the two Iowa fws. may have been reluctant to make this distinction Iowa is reported as having a very high proportion of the full [nd] combination. Complete reduction to /n/ is perhaps a Midland characteristic, as Iowa and Nebraska records rather strongly suggest.

[nd] 1, c2-3, c10, 21, 23, 27, c28, 39, *41, 43-44, 46-47, 51, 53, 57, 62; 101-5, 107, 109, 110-11, 115, 118, 123, 126-28, 131-32, 134, 136-39, 141, 144-46, 148, 150, c152; c201, 202, 205, 209-10, c211-14, 215-19, 224; *301, 305, c313, c326; *408, 410, 413, c414, 415-16, 420-22, 424-27, 431, 433-35.
[nᵈ] *8, 11, 17-18, *19, 20, c22, 24-26, 30, 32, c33, c36, 40, c42, c49, 58, c59, 60-61, c63; 106, 108, 116, *122; c203-4, 206-8, 221; 302-4, c310, c311-12, 315, 321, c324-25, c328; c401, c403, 404, *405, 411, *412, c417, 418, 428, 430.
/n/ 4-5, 7, 12-15, c16, 34, 37, 48, 50, 54-55, c65; 112-13, *122, 140, 143; 222-23, 225; 306-8, 316, c317, 319-20, 322, 327; 423.

rind 37.9. NE 302.

In rind /nd/ occurs finally in a stressed syllable. The full cluster has been retained by only 22% of the infs. who offer this term (see Volume 1); reduction to simple /n/ is found in the speech of the 78% majority. One Minnesotan first responded with [raɪn] and then, after a pause, gave a correction as [raɪnd].

/nd/ 29, :30, cr31, 36; 127, 131, 136, 143-44, 147-48; 202, 206, 211, 213, 219, 223, 225; 305, 309-10, 315; 410-11, 419, 425-26, 433.
/n/ 30-31; 101-12, 114, 119, 121-25, 128-30, 132-35, 137-40, 142-49; 201, 203-4, 209-10, 214-18, 221-22, 224, 226; 301-2, 304, 306-8, 311-12, 314, 316-20, 322-

23, 325-26, 328; 401-9, 412-14, 416-18, 420, c421, 422-24, 428-32, 434, 436-37.

<u>hundred</u> 2.3b. NE 61.

Both social and regional contrast is indicated in the distribution of the three principal variants of <u>hundred</u>, /hʌndrɪd/, /hʌndɚd/, and /hʌnɚd/. The first variant, closest to the spelling but with an unstressed vowel range including [ɛ᾿] and [ə], is used by about one-third of all UM informants, with slightly heavier weighting among the better educated. It seems to be less frequent in the three western states than in Iowa and Minnesota.

Except in Iowa, the majority choice of UM speakers is the second variant, /hʌndɚd/. Although no marked social contrast is evident, the lower frequency in Nebraska as well as in Iowa suggests that this form has a slight Northern orientation.

The third variant, /hʌnɚd/, raises a question that can be answered only upon publication of the Middle Atlantic and North Central atlas evidence. Since no instances of the variant are reported in the New England survey and since it is found in Wisconsin (six examples) as well as in the UM, it may be inferred that /hʌnɚd/ is recent and expanding. It may be noted that this form is not listed in Kenyon and Knott's *A Pronouncing Dictionary of American English* of 1943. Further, since /hʌnɚd/ does not appear in New England but in the UM and clearly has its strength in Iowa and Nebraska, it may be inferred that the form is primarily Midland.

Finally, the social contrast is sharp. This variant, which would bear the schoolroom onus of being categorized as "slovenly," is used by no college graduates but by 18% of the Type I's.

Four infs. are reported by fws. A and M as having the strongly retroflex form /hʌndrɚd/.

	Type I	Type II	Type III
/hʌndrɪd/	30%	36%	50%
/hʌndɚd/	59%	53%	56%
/hʌnɚd/	18%	15%	0

	Mn.	Ia.	N.D.	S.D.	Nb.	Ave.
/hʌndrɪd/	41%	44%	36%	22%	22%	35%
/hʌndɚd/	64%	38%	64%	74%	54%	57%
/hʌnɚd/	5%	34%	4%	4%	35%	15%

/hʌndrɪd/ c1, 4, c6-7, 10-12, c14, 16, c18, c27, 28, c29, 31, 33, 35, c36, 37, 40, 45, c47, 53, c54, c59, c62, 65; 102-3, 106, 110-11, 113, 115-16, 119, 121, 127, 129, 131, 133, 136-37, 139, 144-45, 148, 150, 152; c201, c203, 205, 212-13,

c217, c219, c221, 226; 310, 313, c314, 318-19, 324; 401, 406, 410-11, 413, c415, 424-25.

/hʌndɚd/ c1, 2-3, 5, c7, 8-9, c15, c17, c19-21, 22, c23-25, 26, c29-30, 32, c34, c38, 39, 41, c42-44, c46-47, 48, c49-51, 52, c55, c57, c59, 60, c61, 63, c64; 101, 104-5, c107-9, 112, 114, 120, 122-24, 126, 130, 132, 138, 143, 146, 149; 202, c204, 207-8, c209, 210-11, c214, 215-16, c219-21, 222-24, c225; c302, 304-9, c311-12, c314, 316-17, c320, 321, c322, 323, c324, 325-26, c327; 402, c403-5, c407, c409, c412, c414, c416-17, c419, 420-21, c424-27, 429, 431, 433.

/hʌnɚd/ c6, c30, c56; 117, 125, 128, 134-35, 140-42, 147; c218; c301, 303; c407-8, c418, c422-23, c425, cvr427, c428, 430, 432, c434, 435, 437.

/hʌndrɚd/ 11, c12-13, c15.

Fricative Clusters

/ðz/

So complete is the acceptance of a rule reducing the /ðz/ cluster to /z/ that only four scattered and socially disparate infs. (33; 209; 310, 325) retain even a weakly articulated /ð/ in the pronunciation of <u>clothes</u> (16.6). For them this may be a <u>spelling</u> pronunciation. The common form is simple /kloz/.

It is pertinent that an analogous combination /ðs/ as part of the cluster /ðst/ is not generally affected by a reduction rule when a juncture intervenes between /ð/ and /s/. With only one exception <u>scythestone</u> (19.7), for example, retains the full cluster, although infs. 30, 117, and 125 devoice /z/ to /s/ before the voiceless /t/. The single exception, /saiston/, offered by inf. 112, is probably a reflex of the older variant /sai/ for /saið/.

/fθ/   f → ∅ / ___ θ#

θ → |t| / f ___ #
    |θ|

<u>fifth</u> 2.5a. NE 63.

Simplification of the unique /fθ/ cluster in <u>fifth</u> is effected in the speech of one-third of the UM infs. by the optional application of either of two reduction rules.

One rule affects the initial /f/ of the cluster by reducing it to zero. The resulting pronunciation, /fɪθ/, is that of about one-tenth of the infs. in Minnesota, South Dakota, and Nebraska. It was not observed by fws. in Iowa and North Dakota.

310

The other rule affects the final /θ/ of the cluster in either of two ways. After the /f/ this rule either replaces /θ/ by /t/ as in /fɪft/ or eliminates it altogether as in /fɪf/. Both pronunciations are social markers with their highest frequency among the least educated; and /fɪf/ may be Northern-oriented. Each pronunciation is used by only one college graduate.

Two-thirds of the infs. retain the full cluster, without strong regional contrast except for the lower frequency in Nebraska, only 47% as compared with 82% in Iowa. A few infs. alternate between one pronunciation and another.

	Type I	Type II	Type III
/fɪfθ/	57%	74%	69%
/fɪf/	15%	7%	6%
/fɪft/	18%	12%	6%
/fɪθ/	12%	7%	19%

/fɪfθ/ 1-2, 4-6, 8-10, 13-14, 16-18, 21-24, 26-29, 33-34, c35, 36, 39-40, 42, 44, 49-50, 52-55, 62-65; 101-6, 108-16, 119-36, 138, 140-41, 144-45, 148-50, 152; 202-3, 205, 208-13, 216, 219-23; 225-26; 304, 309-22, 325; 401-4, 406, 408, 418-19, 422, 424-25, 431-33, 435, 437.

/fɪf/ 3, 7, 11-12, 15, 25, 37-38; 117, 147; 204, 214-15, 217-18; 301, 303, 324; 411, 415, 417, 423, 429.

/fɪft/ c6, 19, 41, 43, 48, 51, 56, c57-58, 60; 107, 137, 139, 142-43, 146, 149; 201, 207, 224; 305, 307-8, 323; c407, 412, c421, 430.

/fɪθ/ 15, 30, c31, 32, 39, 45-47, c58, 59; 302, 306, 326; 409-10, 413, 416, 420, 426-27, 434.

Fricative + Stop

English has an optional surface reduction rule that operates upon a cluster consisting of a voiceless fricative and a voiceless stop, whether or not followed by another voiceless fricative. In the three-consonant cluster the rule operates in two stages, the first of which removes the second or the third consonant, and the second of which leaves only the first fricative. The rule is a formulaic description of the simplifying changes induced by the difficulty in articulating this particular succession of consonants.

/fts/

Sought as a lexical variant, shafts (17.5) reveals mixed acceptance of the rule simplifying the final plural cluster /fts/. One-fifth of the responding infs.

retain the full cluster, with no significant difference among the three types, but with a very low percentage in Iowa. One-fourth reduce the cluster to /fs/. More significant is the fact that more than one-half of the infs. accept a further voicing rule altering the cluster to /vz/ as in /šævz/ or, with inf. 426, /ševz/.

The significance lies in the fact that /šævz/ reveals both social and regional contrast. It clearly has Midland orientation and it is not favored by the more highly educated.

	Type I	Type II	Type III
/šæfts/	22%	18%	17%
/šæfs/	23%	27%	55%
/šævz/	56%	55%	18%

	Mn.	Ia.	N.D.	S.D.	Nb.	Ave.
/šæfts/	32%	4%	18%	14%	30%	20%
/šæfs/	30%	24%	22%	43%	14%	27%
/šævz/	39%	72%	50%	43%	56%	53%

/šæfts/ 5, 7, 14, 17-20, 26, 28-29, 40, 45-47; 126-49; 206, 220-21, 224; 309-10, 324; 408-10, 414-15, 417, 422, 424-26, 432.

/šæfs/ 1-4, 6, 11, 15, 34, 37, 51, 53, 57-58, 62; 108, 121, 123, 128-29, 131, 140-41, c143, 150-51; 201-3, 217, 219, 222, cr224; 308, 311-13, 316, 321, 323, 325-26; 402-3, 407, 412-13.

/šævz/ 8, 10, 12-13, 21, 25, 30-32, 35-36, 44, 49, 54, 60-61; 101-3, 109, 111-15, 117-20, 122, 124-25, 127, 130, 132-33, 135-39, cv141, 142, 145-48, 152; 204-5, 207-9, 211-15, 218; 301-3, 306, 315-18, 320, 322; 401, 404-5, 411, 416, 418-21, 423, 427-31, 433, 437-38.

/st/

A specific application of the rule recently described as characteristic of Black English reduces the cluster /st/ to simple /s/. This application has found little acceptance in the UM except in one context. It may be given thus:

    t → ∅ / s___#.

Worksheet items theoretically receptive to the rule are chest, vest, frost, and yeast, which usually occur during the interview singly as citation forms, and the phrasal contexts postoffice, first man, and first class.

Chest (56.1) appears with final /s/ twice in New England (NE 489)—in Vermont and in Connecticut—and only once in Minnesota, in the speech of inf. 35.

Vest (22.2), not sought for New England, is recorded as /vɛs/ only three times in the UM, with infs. 13, 16, and 17, all interviewed by fw. M.

Frost (6.4), occurs as /frɔs/ 10 times in all the New England states (NE 98) except Maine and New Hampshire, but in the speech of only one UM inf., South Dakotan 308.

Yeast (36.6 and NE 290) appears 15 times with final /s/ in all New England states except Maine, but only once in the UM, in the speech of inf. 16.

The preceding contrast between New England and the UM, slight as it is, may be inferred as due to greater insistence by the schools upon spelling as a guide to pronunciation, especially since no UM Type III inf., less concerned about such a relationship, has accepted this reduction rule in these words.

In two of the three collocations the reduction rule is similarly without marked acceptance. No New England informant has lost the /t/ in postoffice. In the UM field data the only instance is in the speech of a Canadian inf., 1.

When /st/ in first (2.4a) occurs before juncture followed by bilabial /m/ in man, only 10 scattered UM infs. have simple /s/: 37, 47, 50; 136; 323; 427-28, 430, 432, 439.

But the articulatory interference provided by the following velar stop as in typically recorded first class (62.6) or, in the records of fws. M, G, and Wn, first grade, yields a situation in which more than one-third of the infs. have /fɚs/ instead of /fɚst/. But no regional or social patterns emerge from the responses of the following infs.: 6, 11-13, 15, 17-19, 29-30, 35-38, 43-44, 47, 50-51, 63; 102, 105, 116, 132, 135, 138, 148; 201-3, 206-9, 211-15, 217-18, 220, 223-26; 302-4, 307-8, 311-12, 314, 316, 321, 323-28; 401-4, 408-9, 411, 413-14, 416-19, 421-22, 427-28, 436.

The precise and rapid tongue movements required to produce an /sts/ inflectional word-final cluster offer an acrobatic articulatory test that only one in three UM infs. seems able to meet. Most accept a rule that eliminates the plural or third-person singular /s/ morpheme and at the same time usually lengthens the first /s/; and most of those give up completely by accepting a further rule that eliminates the remaining /t/, thus leaving only a lengthened /s·/. Critical items in the worksheets are fists, ghosts, posts, and costs as single words and half past seven as a phonetic phrase.

fists   55.6.

Not sought in New England, fists is given its full form /fɪsts/ by 37% of the 207 recorded infs., with a clear prefer-

ence by the better educated. A small proportion, 12%, of those who do not meet this test of lingual dexterity manage to produce /fɪs·t/ as their plural form, but more than one-half, 52%, are content with simple /fɪs/, often with a noticeable prolonged [s:]. No geographical contrast is apparent.

	Type I	Type II	Type III
/sts/	28%	44%	56%
[s·t]	19%	5%	13%
[s·]	56%	13%	31%

/sts/ 2, 7-10, 13-17, 19-20, c21, 25-26, 29-30, 33-34, 36-37, 43, 46-47, 55-56; 106, 110-11, 115, 126, 131, 137, 144, 147, 149, 152; 202, 206-7, 211, 213-14, 216, 221-22; 303, 305, 308-11, 315, 319-21, 323, 325; 404, 408, 410-13, 417-20, 422, 425-27, 430-31, 433-36.
  [s·t] 3-4, 27, 58, 65; 127, 142, 146-47, 150; 203-4, 223-24, 226; 307, 314, 322; 403, 407, 409, 415, 424, 437.
  [s·] 1, 5-6, 11-12, 15, 18, 21, 24, 28, 31-32, 38-42, 44-45, 48-54, 57, 59-64; 101-5, 107-9, 112-14, 117-24, 128-30, 132-34, 136, 138-41, 143, 145, 148; 201, 205, 208-10, 212, 215, 217-20, 225; 301-2, 304, 306, 312-13, 316-18, 324, 326-28; 401-2, 405-6, 414, 416, 421, 423, 428-29, 432.

ghosts   67.1. NE 523.

This word, with the cluster following the back vowel /o/, offers a similar problem but one solved by all the Type III infs., who triumphantly produce /gosts/. Although 43% of the 95 infs. providing the plural form have the full cluster. Only one inf. has /st/ with lengthened /s·/. The remaining 57% retreat to simple /gos·/ as their plural.

	Type I	Type II	Type III
/sts/	37%	41%	100%
[s·t]	2%	0	0
[s·]	63%	59%	0

/sts/ 5, 7-8, 14-15, 17-18, 26, 39, 42, 45, 47, 51-52, 58; 103, 106, 110-11; 206, 208, 210-14, 222, 224; 301, 313, 319, 324-25; 417, 424, 426, 428, 431, 433-34.
  [s·t] 322.
  [s·] 6, 11, 13, 16, 27-28, 32-33, 36, 44, r45, 53, 59, 61-62, 64-65; 101-2, 107, 109, 113-14, 116-17, 121, 133, 137, 139; 202-3, 209, 216-17; 302, 304, 306, 318, 327; 413-14, 416, 421, 423, 425, 429-30, 432, 435.

posts   13.5. NE 118.

Posts varies slightly from ghosts in the proportions of infs. accepting the two stages of the reduction rule. Precisely one-third of the infs. retain the full cluster, 13% accept the step with the pronunciation [pos·t], and 60% offer the reduced plural [pos·]. In conversation inf. 62 has the unusual plural /pots/.

	Type I	Type II	Type III
/sts/	30%	37%	31%
[s·t]	17%	11%	13%
[s·]	62%	57%	63%

/sts/ 1-2, 5, 7, 9, 14, c15, 19-20, c21, 22, 26, 28, 35, 41-46, r47, c48; 118, 145, 152; c204, 207, 210-11, 213, 218, 220, 222, 224; 303-4, 309-10, c312, 314-15, 319-20, 328; 401, 404, 407-11, 413-14, c415, 417, 419-24, 426, c428, 430-31, 433, 435, 437.

[s·t] 4, 8, 13, 16-17, 30, 50, c52, 57, c58-59; 123, 135-36, 143, 151; 205, 212, 214, 223; 301, 305, 307, 321-23; 403, 429, 436.

[s·] 3, c6, 10-13, 15, 18, c19, c22, 23-25, 27, 29, 31-34, 36-40, c43-46, 47, 49, 51, 53-55, c56, c58-59, 60-61, c62, 63-65; 101-9, c110, 111-17, 119-22, 124-34, 137-42, 144, 146-50; 201-3, 206, c208, 209, 215-17, 219, 221, 225-26; 302, 306, 308, 311, c312, 313, 316-18, 324-27; 401-2, c405, 406, 412, 416, 418, 425, c427-28, 432, 434.

costs 68.4.

Queried in the context It costs too much, costs presents the /sts/ cluster before juncture and a following /t/. One-fifth of the UM infs. articulate the full cluster in the interview situation. One-tenth accept the first reduction rule that eliminates the third person /s/ but retains the /t/, the retention of its identity being indicated in transcription by /kɔst tu/ or [kɔst:u]. But three-fourths of the infs. solve the articulatory difficulty by reducing the cluster to simple /s/, sometimes lengthened. The context normally offers help in reducing the likelihood of ambiguity. No regional contrast appears.

One southeastern Iowa inf., 140, has the syllabic development in /kɔstəz/ that Atwood reports as a feature of Atlantic coast speech from Chesapeake Bay southward, and an auxiliary Iowa inf., *117, says that she has heard this in her community.

	Type I	Type II	Type III
/kɔsts/	19%	18%	25%
[kɔst:]	82%	75%	63%
[kɔs·]	11%	7%	13%

/kɔsts/ 5, 11-13, 17-19, 30-31, 33; 147, 149-50; 201, 206, 209, 212-14, 221;

301, 309-11, 313-15, 320-21, 326; 405-6, 408-9, 412, 419, 424, 436.

[kɔst:] 25-26, 38, 54-55, 58; 104, 113, 120, 127, 141, 144, 146, 148; 218, 223; 318; 423.

[kɔs·] 1-4, c6-7, 8-10, c13, 14-17, 20-24, 27-29, 34-37, 39-50, c51, 52-53, c56, 57, 59-61, c62, 63-65; 101-3, 105-12, 114-17, 119, 121-26, 128-39, 142-43, 145; 202-5, 207-8, c209, 210-11, 215-17, 219-20, 222, 224-26; 302-4, 308, 312, 319, 322-25, 327; 401-4, 407, 410-11, 413-14, 416-18, 420-22, 425-27, 429-32, 434-35, 437.

half past seven 4.6. NE 80.

This phrase contains an /sts/ cluster having a presumed juncture before the second /s/. Only 85% of infs. supply this response instead of an equivalent term (see Volume 1). Two-thirds of these reject a reduction rule by retaining the full /pæst sevən/, although more often than not with only a weakly released /t/ as indicated by the transcription [s^{t}s]. The remaining third accept a reduction rule that eliminates the /t/ but lengthens /s/ to accomodate the /s/ of seven. A presumption that the more carefully articulated /sts/ would be characteristic of the better educated infs. is not borne out by the data, nor is there any significant regional contrast.

/sts/ 2, 5, 7-8, 10-11, 19, 22-23, 26, 34, 36, 50, 55, 65; 102, 105, 109-10, 115, 117, 139; 201-3, 206-7, 210, 213, 224-26; 302, 306-7, 312-14, 317-19, 321-22, 324-26; c401, 402, 409, 413-14, 417, 419, 426, 431.

[s·] 13-14, 16, 18, c31, 32-33, 38, 41, 43, 45-47, 52-53, 59; 107, 113, 116, 120, 138, 150, 152; 208; 310-11, 316, 327-28; 420.

/sks/

Two UM worksheet items provide evidence of the acceptance of a reduction rule applying to the /sks/ cluster.

husks 44.1. NE 263.

Husks, with Northern orientation (see Volume 1), is pronounced with the full cluster by nearly two-thirds of the infs. who use this term, but one, 39, in conversation replaces /k/ by /t/ in /hʌsts/. About one-third, 37%, apparently drop the inflectional plural /s/, although this figure may be too large if some of the Iowa responses are taken to be collectives in reply to the question "What do you call the leaves on an ear of corn?"

One inf., 307, has a /t/ substitution in /hʌst/; another, 306, has a glottal stop in [hʌsʔ]. Several infs. are recorded as conspicuously lengthening the initial /s/ of the cluster as a kind of plural marker substitute for the /s/ morpheme. Only three infs. reduce the cluster to simple [s·], again with length as the plural sign. No marked social or regional differences appear.

/sks/ 1-2, 7-8, 10-11, 13-18, 20-23, 26, c30, 31, 34, 38, 40-44, c45, 46-47, 51-53, 59-65; 101-3, 106, 108, 110-12, 115-16, 119, 122, 129, 132, 138, 142, 149; 201-3, 205, 208, 210, 212-15, 217-24; 302, 304-5, 310, 314-15, 319, 323-28; 402, 406, 408, 414, 416-20, 422, 424-26, 428, 434.
/sk/ 3, 6, 24, 27-28, 32-33, 48, 50, 55-56, 58; 107, 118, 121-28, 130, 134-37, 139-41, 144-46; 308-9, 312-13, 316-18, 322; 407, c409, 416, 421-22, 430. [s·k] 4, 35-36, 54; 225-26; 311; 404, c436.
[s·] 102, c143; 427.

tusks 19.3.

Like husks, tusks is pronounced with the full cluster by a large majority (71%), with a slightly smaller proportion (66%) among Type I infs. than among the II's (87%) and the III's (85%). Seven percent reduce the cluster to /sk/, and 8%, mostly the least educated, reduce it to a simple /s/, sometimes clearly lengthened.

Twelve percent in the UM maintain an older cognate form, tushes /tʌš+z/, which is not derived from tusks. Tushes rather clearly has strong Midland orientation, (see map), and seems to be recessive. For the history of the two forms see the *Ox-*

ford English Dictionary. Two infs. apply a reduction rule to tushes, one, 135, having /tʌš/ and the other, 146, having an r-colored /təš/. An apparent blend appears in /tʌšks/, used by auxiliary inf. *134.

	Type I	Type II	Type III
/sks/	66%	87%	85%
[s·k]	8%	5%	15%
[s·]	12%	4%	0
/šəz/	15%	7%	0

/sks/ 1-11, 13-14, 16-25, 28-31, 33, 35, 37, 39-45, c46, 47-49, 51-61, c62, 63-65; 103-8, 110-12, 115-16, 118-21, 123-24, 127, 131, 133-34, 137-39, 142, 144-45, 150, 152; 201-3, 206, 208, 210-13, 215-18, 220-24, 226; 301-2, 308-10, 313-15, 320-21, 323-26, 328; 401-4, 406-11, 413-14, 416-26, 428-31, 433-34, 436-37.
[s·k] 12, 36, 50; 108, 122, 126, 136; 204, 207, 209; 303, 307, 311, 316; 412.
[s·] 15; 101-2, 113, 117, 130, 132, c141, 143, 148; 306, 317-18; 427.

Stop + Fricative

/ksθ/   θ → $\begin{vmatrix} t \\ θ \end{vmatrix}$ / ks___#

sixth 2.6b. NE 63.

For nearly one-third of the UM infs. a related cluster reduction affects the pronunciation of sixth by either substituting the obstruent /t/ for the final /θ/ or by reducing it to zero, that is, by eliminating it entirely. Either pronunciation is evidently a social marker avoided by the cultivated speakers. Most UM infs. have the full cluster in /sɪksθ/.

	Type I	Type II	Type III
/sɪksθ/	62%	80%	88%
/sɪkst/	18%	12%	6%
/sɪks/	20%	8%	12%

/sɪksθ/ 1-14, 17-18, 20-31, 33-34, 37-38, 41-42, 45, 47, 49, 53-55, c58, 60, 64-65; 101-6, 108, 110-12, 114-17, 120-21, 123-29, 131-34, 136, 138-39, 141-42, 144-45, 148-50; 202-5, 207-10, 212-14, 216-26; 301-4, 309-10, 313-15, 318-26; 402-4, 406, 408-11, 413-14, 416, 418-19, 422, 424-27, 429-31, 433, 437.
/sɪkst/ 4, 19, 43, 51, 56, c57, 58, 62; 107, 113, 119, 135, 137, 143, 147; 201, 211; 305-7, 312; 407, 412, 415, 417, 420, 423, 434.
/sɪks/ 15-16, 32, 35-36, 39-40, 44, 46, 48, 50, 52, 59, c62, 63; 109, c116, 122, 130, 146, 152; 215; 308, 310-11, 316-17; 401, 432, 435.

[dʒ]   d → ∅ / l___ʒ#

Whether [dʒ] following /l/ is inter-preted as a unit /ǰ/ consisting of an al-veolar obstruent with slow release or as an affricate cluster composed of an al-veolar obstruent and an alveolo-palatal fricative, certain UM infs. apply a rule that eliminates the obstruent. Although a great majority of both New England and UM infs. pronounce bulge (22.7; NE 362) with final /ǰ/, a few have only [ʒ]. Those in New England with only [ʒ] are concentrated in the southern sector, sev-en in Massachusetts, one in Rhode Island, and seven in Connecticut. Of the seven UM examples (21, 38; 122, 129-30, 135, 143) five are in Midland speech territory. This fact, conjoined with the lack of in-stances in Wisconsin, makes desirable a study of its incidence in the Atlantic and North Central materials when they are published.

Stop + Stop

/kt/   t → ∅ / k___#

Although no sought worksheet item ends in the cluster /kt/, two Type I infs. (220; 311) provide in conversation exam-ples of a surface reduction rule in their pronunciation of tract as /træk/ in "a track of land" and "They owned a big track." Other infs. with occasion to use the term always have tract.

Miscellaneous

/rd/   d → ∅ / r___#

UM field records contain three in-stances of a little-used optional rule reducing a final /rd/ cluster to simple /r/. For goad (15.7) an intrusive /r/ produced goard (q.v.). To this variant three Type I infs. (7, 15; 220) apply this reduction rule that yields /gor/ in their expressions gore stick (7, 15) and ox gore (220). A possible fourth applica-tion of the rule is the pronunciation /barnjar/ for barnyard, attested posi-tively by the fw. interviewing inf. 130.

/l/

A phonological rule accepted by many speakers in the Southern United States but rarely observed in North and Midland speech is that which calls for the vocal-ization or even loss of /l/ before a non-alveolar stop or spirant, particularly /p/ and /f/ and sometimes /k/. The re-sulting pronunciation is that often rec-

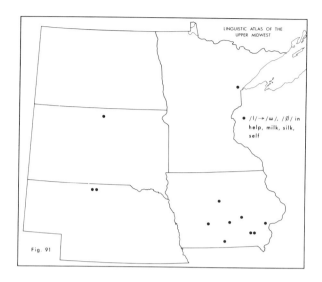

Fig. 91

ognized by dialog writers with such spellings as in "He'p yourse'f."

The decisive item help yourself (39.6) provides only a bare handful of recorded examples, all but one of which are in an area of possible South Midland influence. Help is [hɛwp] for infs. 18; 130; 303; 403; [hɛɤp] for vr115; [hɛʊˀp] for 127; and [hɛp] for c132, 135, 144. Self is [sɛwf] for inf. 403 and [sɛf] for 135. Inf. 403 analogically extends the rule to the plural with a voiced spirant, with [sɛwvz] for selves.

Before the /k/ in milk (25.7) /l/ be-comes [w] for inf. 137, and in silk (44.4) for inf. 133.

An unrelated loss of /l/ occurs in the pronunciation [ɔˈrɛdi] for already ob-served in the speech of Nebraska inf. 415 and in [ˈɔweˀz] or [ˈɔwɪˀz] for always, heard from Nebraska infs. 414, c415, 416, 420, c423, 428, 433, and 435.

/d/

Item 39.7, I don't care for any, is a specific for ascertaining the incidence of the loss of intervocalic /d/, a minor feature in Southern and South Midland speech. No response exhibited this phe-nomenon, but three Nebraska infs. in the area of South Midland influence revealed it in free conversation: "I [oʊnt] remem-ber"—423-24; "I [dɪənt] expect to see..." —423; "We [dɪənt] have no dishes"—430.

/w/

A loss of /w/ in always produces such a pronunciation as is exemplified with [ɔʊlʊˇz], [ɔɬəz], and [ɔɬˀz], heard chiefly in the conversation of 12 scat-tered Type I infs. but only one Type II and no Type III's. It is clearly a minor social marker. Its users are c23, c44, c46, c51; c101, c105, c109, 132; c311, c314; 405, c417-18.

/ər/

Of the 25 UM infs. offering the expression chest of drawers (see Volume 1, 8.9), four Type I's (151; 218, c225; 311), one Type II (328), and one Type III (426) have a monosyllabic r-less variant of drawer /drɔ/ instead of the more usual /drɔr/. This variant may have originated in the r-less region of eastern New England, but in other areas its origin is conjecturally otherwise. Several infs. in Michigan and the UM have explained their preference for this pronunciation as a way to avoid saying /drɔrz/, with its alternate meaning of men's underwear. For them, at least, it is a euphemism. This pronunciation has not been recognized in the commercial dictionaries.

ASSIMILATION

Assimilation is the phonetic process by which one or more of the distinctive features of one sound replace one or more of those of a neighboring sound. It is usually due to the tendency to simplify a difficult series of articulatory movements, a tendency sometimes more likely to be accepted by the less educated. A nasal consonant in a homorganic cluster is particularly susceptible to this process because the substitution of one nasal consonant for another does not necessarily lead to misunderstanding or ambiguity.

Nasal Clusters

/mf/

The /mf/ cluster in comfort/comfortable/comforter (23.6; NE 342) is retained as such by one-fourth (26%) of the UM infs. An equal percentage has accepted a rule replacing the bilabial feature of the consonant /m/ by a labiodental occlusion to coincide with this feature of /f/, thus producing a labiodental /ɱ/ in the cluster /ɱf/. The rule may be symbolized as m → ɱ / ___ f.

Nearly one-half of the UM infs., however, 45%, adopt a rule for progressive assimilation, according to which the bilabial feature of [m] replaces the labio-

dental feature of the fricative, thus yielding a bilabial fricative [ɸ] in the cluster [mɸ]. The rule is f → ɸ / m ___. A modification of the rule appears in the cluster /mp/ in the speech of inf. 59.

For five infs. an optional rule transfers the nasal feature of /m/ to the preceding vowel and deletes the labial closure, yielding [k̃fɚt].

A slightly higher proportion of Type II infs. prefer the [mɸ] cluster; and the [mf] cluster apparently has Midland orientation (Minnesota 22%, Iowa 40%, North Dakota 0, South Dakota 24%, Nebraska 32%). No other marked social or regional differences appear.

	Type I	Type II	Type III
[mf]	29%	21%	36%
[ɱf]	28%	23%	29%
[mɸ]	39%	55%	36%

[mf] 1, 4, 6-7, 14-17, 28, 38, 41, 50; 117-18, 120, 124-27, 136, 139-41, 144-51; 305, 311, 317, 319; 416, 420, 422, 424, 426-28, 432-33, 435.

[ɱf] 3, 29, 34, 43-48, c51, 52, 58, 60-61; 101-4, 124, 128, 134, 137, 143, 152; 216, 218, 221; 324, 326-27; 401-2, c403, 404-5, 410, 413-14, 421, 423, 430-31, 434.

[mɸ] 2, 8-11, 19-27, 30-31, 33-37, 42, 49, 53-56, 64; 105, 107-8, 115-16, 119, 121-23, 129-33, 135, 138, 142; 201, 204-6, 208, 210-15, 217, 220, 222-24; 301-2, 309-10, 312-15, 319, 325-26, 328; 408-9, 411, 417-18, 429, 437.

[V̨f] 111, 113-14; 225; c432.

/p-ŋ/

something 45.2.

Nine Type I infs. and three Type II's are recorded in free conversation with a presumably nonstandard variant of something that represents the final step in the application of several optional phonological rules. One rule allows the replacement of final /ŋ/ by /n/. (See p. 332.) Another permits the development of an intrusive /p/ after /m/. These two rules seem to be unordered. A third rule deletes /θ/ from the /mpθ/ cluster, leaving /ˈsʌmpən/ and then /ˈsʌmpm̩/. At this point an optional assimilative rule shifts the tongue-contact for the final alveolar nasal position to the bilabial position of preceding /m/ or /p/, yielding [ˈsʌmpm̩], a possible next stage with glottalization of /p/ as [ˈsʌmpʔm̩], and even an ultimate loss of /p/ in [ˈsʌmʔm̩]. This last stage seems to be a social marker. Its recorded users are Type I c1 c13, c16, c31; c117; c216, c225; c309, c311; c429; Type II c17; c328; c419.

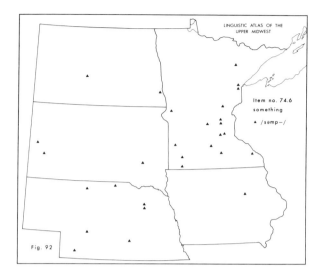

Fig. 92

LINGUISTIC ATLAS OF THE
UPPER MIDWEST

Item no. 74.6
something

△ /səmp‑/

/nk/

In the two relevant worksheet items, pancake and concrete, a few UM infs. accept an optional rule replacing the alveolar feature of a nasal by a velar feature in a context before syllabic juncture followed by the velar /k/. The rule is n → ŋ / ___ k.

For pancake (36.4) only 14 (15%) of the responding infs. (see Volume 1) have /pæŋkek/. The others, perhaps influenced by the semantic identity of pan, retain /pæŋkek/. One inf., 62, comments that /pæŋkek/ is his careful but not usual pronunciation.

With concrete (25.2a), however, the proportion accepting the rule is higher. This lexical form occurs as a variant offered by 43 infs., one-fourth of whom have /kaŋkrit/ instead of the more common /kankrit/. No clear social contrast is discernible, but the /ŋ/ variety is recorded more frequently in Minnesota and Iowa.

/pæŋkek/ 13, 17, 39, 61-63; 102, 108, 115-16, 138-39; 216; 416.
/kaŋkrit/ 2, 13, 18, 33, 40, 43, 48, 51, r56, 57, 59; 120; 421, 434-35.

/nt/

An optional surface reduction rule that by assimilation replaces the distinct intervocalic cluster /nt/ by an alveolar nasalized flap /r̃/ is accepted by some UM infs. to a varying degree in different contexts.

In twenty (2.1; NE 60) /nt/ occurs between a stressed vowel and a final unstressed vowel. A remarkably consistent proportion of UM speakers (56% of Type I,

54% of Type II, and 53% of Type III) accepts this assimilation rule in the pronunciation [twer̃i] in contrast with the [twɛnti] of the remaining infs. An apparent geographical pattern suggests that the nasal flap has a slight Northern orientation (Minnesota 47%, Iowa 42%, North Dakota 92%, South Dakota 64%, Nebraska 47%). Besides the instances of /r̃/ listed below there are nine examples of simple /n/ as in [twɛni]: 31; 117, 141; 316; c403, c422, 424, 431, 434. The two sets are counted as one in computing the proportion accepting assimilation.

[r̃] 1, c3, 5, 7-8, c12-13, c19, 21, c22, 24, c25, 26-28, c29, 31, 33, c34-35, 36, c38, c43, 44-45, c46-47, c55, c59, c62, 63; 108-9, 114, vr115, 116-17, 120-21, 123, 125, 128-29, 132, 134-36, 141-43, 145, 150; c201-2, 203, c204, 205, c207, 208, 210, c211, 212-15, c216, 217, c218-20, 221-22, c223-24, 226; 301-3, 305, 307, 310, c315, 316, 318-19, c320, 321-26, c327; 402, c403-5, 411, 417, c419, c422, cvr423, 424-25, c430, 431-35.
[n] All others except the following nonrespondents: 18; 118; 206; 328; 436.

Seventy (2.3; NE 57) contrasts sharply with twenty. Despite the frequent assimilation of [n] to a syllabic [m̩], the resulting freedom in tongue articulation does not yield an assimilated /r̃/ from the cluster /mt/. Seven such instances were found in New England, all recorded by fw. Bernard Bloch in Vermont and western Massachusetts. Only two instances appear in UM files, in the reply of South Dakota inf. 302 and in the conversation of Nebraska inf. 435.

In mantel (7.3; NE 328) the /nt/ cluster occurs between a stressed vowel and /l/, a combination often leading to a pronounced syllabic [l̩], sometimes velarized as [ɬ̩]. Most of the fws. record two or three instances of the nasal flap in all the five states, but whether fw. P's high frequency—with 12 of the total of 37—is due in part to a predilection for distinguishing the flap or whether there is a genuine regional weighting is not determinable until the corresponding North Central materials are published.

The /nt/ cluster itself appears in mantel in several allophonic variations.

[nt] 1-3, 5, 9, 11, 14-15, 17, 20-23, 28-29, 31-32, !35, 39-40, 42, 44-45, 47-48, 51-53, 55 *56, 57, sn58, *62, sn63, 64-65; 101, 103-4, 106, 109-12, 118-19, 124, 126-27, 133-34, 137, 141, 143-44, 146-47, *148, 150-51; 201, 204, 210, 212-13, 217, 219, 226; 304, 306, 310-12, 318-

19, 326; c401, 404, 408-9, 411, 413, 419, 422, 425-28. [nt] 26, 33; 108, c119, 120, 139, 152; 220; 323-24; 414. [ⁿt̪] 211. [nd̪] 136. [Ṽt] 416, 420, 423-24, 431, 433. [nt̪] 6, 10, c12, 24, 34, 37, 46; 116; 209, 214, 221-22; 309, 314, 321; 410, 412. [nᵥ] 30; 325. [ⁿt̪] 315.

[r̃] 8, 38, 54, 60-61; 102, 105, 113-15, 117, 121-23, 125, 128, 130-32, 135, 138, 142, *145; 203, 208, 215, 218, 223; 302, 308, *316, 320, 328; 402, 406, 417, 436.

[n] 18.

no response All others.

Haunted (67.2; NE 534) offers the /nt/ cluster between a stressed vowel and a weak vowel followed by a consonant. Here 17% of the UM infs. adopt the reduction rule yielding the assimilated /r̃/ in /hɔr̃+d/: 18% of Type I, 18% of Type II, and 13% of Type III. State frequencies are not as consistent, but they do not form a clear geographical pattern: Minnesota 18%, Iowa 28%, North Dakota 12%, South Dakota 15%, Nebraska 8%.

[nt] 3-9, 14, 18, 23, c28, 30, 32, 39-40, sn41, 42-44, 47, *48, 49, 51, c52, 53-58, 61-65; 101-12, 115-16, 119-21, 123-24, 126-27, 130-34, 137-39, 142-43, 146; 201, 203, 205-6, 210, 212-13, 217, 219; 301, 303-8, 312-13, 316-19, 325, 327-28; 408, 410-11, 413-16, 420-22, 424-28, 430-37. [nᵗ] 45-46, 59; 122, c129, 136, 140-41, 147, 149; 324; 423. [Ṽt] 113. [nt̪] 10-12, 19-22, 24-27, 29, 33-34, c36, 37, 50; 150; 202, 204, 207, 209, 211, 214-15, 218, 222-24, :225, 226; 302, 309-11, c314, 320, 322; 401-2, !403, 406, :sn407, 409, !417, 418-19, 429. [nt̪] 31; 220.

[r̃] 1-2, 13, 15-17, c35, 38; 114, 117, 125, 128, 135, 144-45; 208, 216, 221; 315, 321, 323; 404, 412.

[n] 60; 148.

no response 118, 151-52; 326; 405.

/vn/

The UM field records contain data about four words, seven, eleven, seventy, and davenport, in which the loss of the vowel in an unstressed syllable -en after v produces a cluster /vn/ that is susceptible to the effect of two ordered assimilation rules.

In the /vn/ cluster the nasal is usually syllabic [n̩] although in rapid speech the cluster as a whole may function within one syllable as in the pronunciation of seven as [sɛvn] and [sɛʋn]. In either case the labial feature of [v] is extended by a minority of the infs. to the nasal consonant, yielding rarely a labiodental [ɱ] but ordinarily the bilabial

[m], often syllabic as [m̩]. The final stage of the application of this rule replaces the labiodental feature in the fricative by the bilabial feature of /m/, hence producing either a bilabial fricative [β] or a bilabial obstruent [b]. The rules may be symbolized thus:

$$n \rightarrow m \; / \; v \underline{\quad}$$

$$v \rightarrow \left| \begin{matrix} b \\ \beta \end{matrix} \right| \; / \; \underline{\quad} m.$$

An apparent geographic pattern with a concentration of the /bm/ in eastern Nebraska is probably illusory. Either fws. A, P, and Wn generally did not recognize this cluster or fws. M and Wr tended to oversystematize. Probably the former is the better explanation. There is, however, some evidence for social differentiation, as in seven, eleven, and seventy 62% of the speakers with the /bm/ cluster are in Type I and only 38% in Type II, with none at all in Type III. This is not true of davenport, where the cluster is probably affected also by the following bilabial /p/. Thirteen of the infs. with /bm/ are in Type II and only eight in Type I.

With davenport a further difference lies in the retention of the vowel, as in /dæv+mport/. Here the /m/ is clearly the effect of the labial /p/ rather than of the /v/. The following infs. are recorded with this pronunciation: 112, 138; 327; 413-15, 421, 427-28, 430, 433.

The great majority of UM infs. have either [v+n] or [vn̩] in the following words. Listed here are only those who accept the ordered rules leading to the /bm/ cluster.

seven (1.4; NE 57) c15-16, c29, c35, c46; c207, 211, c220, c225; 314, c320; c403, c408, 416, c417, c422, cvr423, c425, c430, c435.

eleven (1.6; NE 58) c13, c15; 101, 105; 207, c220; c416, c421, cvr427, c435.

seventy (2.3; NE 57) 2, c13, c15-16, c31, 37; 101, 109, 113; 207, c225; cvr413, cvr416, 420, c422-23, 427-28, c430, c432, 435.

davenport (8.1; NE 326) 12, 31; 101-3, 108, 115, snl19, 132-33, 139, 152; 328; c414, c416, 422-23, 426, 431, sn434, 435.

Non-Nasal Clusters

Labialization

/fp/ In the /fp/ cluster of half past (4.6; NE 80) a surface assimilation rule accpeted by a number of UM infs. alters the labiodental feature of /f/ to the bilabial feature of the following /p/ with a resulting cluster of /ɸp/. The fricative may then undergo progressive weakening until it quite disappears except for an occasional compensatory lengthening of either the preceding vowel or, as perceived by fw. G, of the consonant. The rules may be given as Vf → VΦ / ___p and VΦ → V·∅ / ___p.

For the regional distribution of /Φ/ in half past no pattern can be determined, since fws. H, P, and Wr do not use this symbol in their transcription, and also since many infs. offer the lexical equivalent seven-thirty. There may, however, be a slight Northern orientation for the loss of /Φ/, because, while it was noted at least once by each fw., every occurrence of loss is in Northern speech territory.

But a measurable, though slight, social contrast does appear. The more precise articulation of /hæf pæst/ is preferred by the better educated; the loss of the fricative is accepted by a higher proportion of Type I speakers than of Type II, and by those in Type III not at all.

	Type I	Type II	Type III
Vfp	58%	64%	70%
VΦp	28%	25%	30%
V∅p	21%	13%	0

	Mn.	Ia.	N.D.	S.D.	Nb.	Ave.
Vfp	60%	71%	45%	48%	17%	61%
VΦp	23%	14%	41%	48%	9%	27%
V∅p	26%	14%	14%	8%	4%	16%

[Vfp] 7, 13-14, 29, 36, 40-41, 43-46, 51-53, 55, 57-58, c59, 60, 62-64; 102, 107, 109-10, 116, 132, 138-41; 203, 205, 225-26; 305-6, 310, 316, 318-20; c401, 402, 404-6, 418, 420, 426, 431, 436-37. [V^{f}p] 8, 23, 50, 54; 105, 120, 143; 201, 210, 212; 325, 327-28; 403, 410, 413-15. [Vꜰp] 5, 13-14, 17-18, c25, 26, 31; 215, 223-24; c309, 326; 405, 407, 409, 412, 419, 422.

[VΦp] 3, 32, 47; 150; c207; 301-2, 309, 313-14, 321-22. [V^{Φ}p] 12, 22, c29, 30, c31, 34, c35, 38, 42; 152; 206, 208-9, 213-14, 216, 218, 220; 311-12, 315, 323-24; 417, 429.

[V∅p] 44, 48, 56, c57, 59; 113, 115; c424. [V·∅p] 2, 6, 10-11, 16-19, 33, 65; 202, 211, 217; 307, 317. [V∅p·] 39, 44.

Fronting

/gl/ Before /l/, as in glass (39.1; NE 311), an initial velar [g] is likely to experience fronting as [g˂] or even to move to the palatal tongue position of /ɟ/ or alveolar /d/. In the UM this extreme fronting in glass shows a possible Northern orientation as well as some preference by the less-educated infs.

	Type I	Type II	Type III
[g]	82%	87%	93%
[ɟ, d]	18%	13%	7%

	Mn.	Ia.	N.D.	S.D.	Nb.	Ave.
[g]	89%	96%	73%	68%	87%	85%
[ɟ, d]	11%	4%	26%	32%	14%	15%

[g] 2-3, 6, 8, 13, 15-18, 20, 25-26, 31-32, 34, 38-41, 43, c44, 45-47, 51-52, 54-55, 57-62, 64-65; 101-4, 106-7, 108-16, 118-23, 125-32, c133, 134, 136-49; 212, 225; 302, 305-8, 316-17, c318, 319, 323, 325; 401, 404, 406, 409-10, 413-14, c415, 416, 420-28, 430-36. [g̊] 14. [g˂] 4, 7, 9-12, 19, 21-24, 27-28, 36-37, 42, 49; 201, 203-7, 209-11, 213-14, 219-22, 224, 226; 301, 304, 309, 311, 321, 324, 326, 328; 402, 408, 411-12, 417, 429, 437.

[ɟ] 1, 5, 30, 33, 35, 50; 215-17, 223; 303, 314-15, 322, 327; 403, 405, 407, 418-19.

[d͐] 29; 202, 208, 218; 310, 312-13, 320. [d] 117, 124.

no response 48, 53, 56, 63; 105, 135, 150-52.

/l/ Three words in the UM worksheets reveal the extent to which palatal [l] is affected by a front vowel environment. In broad terms about one-half of all UM infs. manifest such an assimilative effect by pronouncing a fronted consonant, the so-called clear l [l̡], in jelly, Nelly, and Billy.

A corresponding putative effect of a back vowel environment yielding the so-called dark l [ɫ] presumably would be determinable from the responses for the item bull (71.2). Unfortunately, however, only fws. A, G, and M distinguish [l] from [ɫ], so that returns are inadequate. In Minnesota, where these fws. interviewed, exactly 50% of the infs. have [l] and 50% have [ɫ], with an apparent preference for [ɫ] among Type I infs., 60% contrasting with 40% in Type II and 33% in Type III.

Although with respect to [l̡] no significant social contrasts appear, the data indicate that this particular assimilation is more likely to occur in Northern speech than in Midland, for in the three indicated words [l̡] has its highest frequency in Minnesota and North Dakota and its lowest in Iowa and Nebraska.

In at least part of the Midland area the lower incidence of clear [l̡] may be ascribed to the tendency to partly diphthongize a lax vowel. This tendency introduces a centralizing tongue movement that effectively blocks the fronting influence of the tonic vowel, i.e., [ɛ] or [ɩ]. Such transcriptions as [bɩəlɫ] and [nɛ^{ə}lɫ] from southern Iowa and [nɛəli] from eastern Nebraska evidence this blocking mechanism.

jelly 40.7.

The responses are fewest for jelly because some infs. offer instead the minor variant jell. A geographical weighting of this form, not noted in Volume 1, is revealed in the numbers of occurrences by state: Minnesota has five (12, 27, 31, 55, 58) and North Dakota two (218, 235) in contrast to three in South Dakota (301, 316, 320), nine in Nebraska (405-6, 409, 415, 418-19, 422, 429, 432), and 10 in Iowa (101, 106-7, 109, 114, 121, 125, 128, 130, 139).

Type I	Type II	Type III
42%	38%	43%

Mn.	Ia.	N.D.	S.D.	Nb.	Ave.
53%	40%	53%	22%	10%	40%

Nelly 52.3. NE 433.

Type I	Type II	Type III
50%	53%	63%

Mn.	Ia.	N.D.	S.D.	Nb.	Ave.
65%	39%	77%	43%	38%	53%

(Iowa inf. 118 has [ɬ].)

Billy 52.3. NE 433.

Type I	Type II	Type III
55%	56%	50%

Mn.	Ia.	N.D.	S.D.	Nb.	Ave.
62%	40%	85%	42%	43%	55%

(Iowa inf. 118 has [ɬ].)

Palatalization

/tj, dj/ When a prevocalic cluster composed of an alveolar stop and a palatal glide occurs in a stressed syllable, it is susceptible to the same articulatory demands underlying the assimilation rule commonly accepted in the final weak syllables of such words as nature [netʃɚ] and verdure [vɚdʒɚ]. Essentially, this rule requires a +strident feature characteristic of delayed release from the stop, hence yielding an affricate.

For [tj] the only evidence in the UM files is in the speech of two Canadian infs., 201 and 202, whose pronunciation [tʂuzdɪ] /čuzdɪ/ for Tuesday (3.2a; NE 67) is widespread in Canada and Great Britain.

For [dj], however, the evidence from nearly all UM infs. for the pronunciation of education (62.1; NE 535) amply displays the phonetic continuum only the end points of which appear in the abstract rule if it is stated thus:

$$j \rightarrow \left|\begin{matrix}\int\\3\end{matrix}\right| / \left|\begin{matrix}t\\d\end{matrix}\right| \underline{\quad} \acute{V}$$

No UM inf. offers the pronunciation /ed+kešən/, a New England recessive variant from which the palatal has quite disappeared, but a small and widely distributed number, 21 infs., retain the original /dj/ cluster, as appears in the proportions by type: Type I, 11 infs.; Type II, nine; Type III, one. These proportions are similar to those in the total population interviewed. The other infs. exhibit, according to fw. interpretation, the various stages on the continuum from [dj] to [dʒ], with the majority having the unmodified affricate. Although Iowa fws. usually record only a phonemic /dʒ/, the series is fully represented as follows:

[dj] 2-3, 19, c25, 27, 49, 54; 103, 130, 136; 208; 313, 320, 327; 401, 404, 406-7, 411, 417, 424.
[dʃ] c33, 41; 205. [gʃ] 403.
[dž] 9, 24, c25, 34, c50, 51; 321.
[gʒ] 36. [dž] 4-5, 12, 21-22, 58, 65; 203-4, 222, 225.
[dᶻʒ] c322. [dž] 29, 37, 42; 303, 324-25. [dž] c226. [dž] 59.
[dʒ] 1, 6, c7, 8, c10-11, 13-18, 20, 23, 26, 28, 30, c31, 32, 35, 38-40, 42-47, c51, 52-53, 56-57, 60-64; 101-2, 104-6, c107, 108-17, 119-29, 131-35, 137-50; c201-2, 206-7, 210, 212-14, 217-18, c220, 221; 301-2, 304-10, c311-12, 314-19, 323, 326, c327, 328; 402, 408, c409, 412-16, 419-21, c422, 423, 425, c426, 427-29, 431, c432, 433-35, c436, 437.
[dz] c209, 215-16, 219, 223-24.

/s/ Similar to the preceding relationship between [tj] and [tʃ] is that between [s] and [ʃ] as exemplified in the variations of the collocation this year and of the word horseshoe. Here, however, the assimilative influence is regressive rather than progressive, i.e., from the second consonant in the cluster to the first consonant.

this year 5.1. NE 82.

In this year the palatal glide [j] is usually retained and the preceding [s] is regressively palatalized to [ʃ], with a rather easily determined intermediate stage [ʂ]. Only 15% of the infs. (30 in the three types as follows: 17 in Type I, 10 in Type II, and three in Type III) retain the unaffected alveolar [s] in /ðɪs jɪr/. Thirty percent are recorded with the fully assimilated [ʃ]. The remaining 55% are recorded with sounds at various points along the continuum. No social or geographical patterns emerge that would not be suspect because of fw. variation.

[s] 2, 7, c13, 17-18, 23, 41, 43, 55; 112, 125, 131, 137, 139-41, 146-49, 152; 303; 406-7, 413-14, 424-28.
[sʂ] 433. [ʂ] 3-6, 8, 12, 14, 16, 21-22, c23, 25-28, 30-31, 34, 36-37, 48-49, 54, 56, 65; 109-10, 113, 115-17, 122-24, 126-27, 129-30, 132, 134-36, 138, 143-45; 201-2, 208, 210, 215-16, 218-20, 222; 301, 314, 323-25, 327-28; c403, 404, 411, 415-19, 421-22, 434-35.
[sʃ] 32; 105; 423.
[ʂʃ] 45-46, 53, c59; 101, 103-4, 133; c416, 420, 430-32, 435.
[ʃ<] 1, 9, 19-20, 24, 29, 33, 42, 53, c59; 204; 322; 409, 412, 429.
[ʃ] 10-11, c15, c35, 38-40, 44, 47, c50-52, 57-60, c62-63, 64; 102, 106-8, 111, 114, 119-21, 128, 142, 150; c203, 205, 207, 209, 211-13, c214, 217, 221, 223, 225-26; 302, 304, 310-11, 313, 315, 320-21; 401-2, c405, 410-17, 437.
[ɕ] 224; 309, 312, 326.

A curious further assimilation, this time progressive, is apparently manifested by some of the infs. whose underlying [s] has been modified to [ʃ] in [ðɩʃ]. For 33 of them this [ʃ] in turn affects the following [j] so strongly that the two merge in [ðɩʃɚ]: c59; 101-17, 119-21, 128, 133; c203, 206, 217, 221; c416, 420, 423, 430, 432, 435.

horseshoe 28.3. NE 199.

This word likewise is often influenced by a regressive assimilation rule by which the palatal feature of [ʃ] replaces the alveolar feature of the preceding [s], sometimes with length as a surface reminder in the actual pronunciation and sometimes with complete merger into a single short [ʃ]. Some speakers also have retroflexion of the fricative as a result of the preceding [ɚ].

Fieldworker transcription practice is not quite uniform, and fw. P, concerned with the vowel in horse, recognized no consonantal assimilation at all. Nevertheless, the field data amply evidence, as with the preceding varieties of assimilation, a continuum ranging from an unaffected [s] to the completely assimilated [ʃ]. Several infs. use two or more variants during the interview.

A hypothetically more frequent assimilation among the less educated is not supported. Indeed, by a rather remarkable coincidence, not only do the three types have quite similar proportions among the 95 infs. with [hɔɚs] (45% of Type I, 46% of Type II, and 9% of Type III) and 54

infs. with [hɔɚʃ] (50% of Type I, 43% of Type II, and 7% of Type III), but also these proportions are almost identical with the distribution of the three types in the total number of infs. (50% of Type I, 42.5% of Type II, and 7.5% of Type III). The continuum in horseshoe is represented as follows:

[sʃ] 2, 16-17, 24, 29-30, 36, 38, 41, 43-44, r45, c47, 48, 58, 60; 101-4, 108, 110, 116-18, 122-31, 133-38, 140-49, 151-52; 202-4, 206, 212, 214, 225-26; 302, 304, 312-13, 319, 323, 326, 328; 414, 422, 424, 426-27, 431, 434, 437. [sʃ] 106, c107, 119-21, 139; 207, 209, 211, 213, 217, 222; 303, 315, 321, 324; 423, 435. [sʃ] 424. [sʃ] 38.
[sʃ] 150; 309; 312; 403.
[ʂʃ] 23, 27-28, 42, 49-50; 105-6. [ʂʃ] 3, 7, 10, 25-26, 31, 33, 40, 46, 51, 57, 59, 61, 65; 112-15, 132; 201, 205, 210, 215-16, 218-19, 223-24; 301, 317-18, 320, 322, 325; 401-2, 408, 411, 415, 418. [ʂʃ] 34-35; 311; 404-5, 407, 409-10, 412, 417, 419, 429-30, 436-37.
[ʃ·] 4-5, 8-9, 19-22, 39, 55; 221; 401.
[ʃ] 6, 11, 13-15, 18, 32, 37, c51, 52-56, 62-64; 109, 111; 207-8, 220; 305-8, 310, 314, 316-17, 319; 413-14, 416, 420-21, 423, 425, 428, 432-33.

Voicing

A low-level voicing rule often affects an intervocalic voiceless consonant following a stressed vowel, with overt intermediate stages between voicelessness and full voice.

/t/

attic 8.5. NE 345.

Attic is a classic example of the application of this voicing rule to intervocalic [t], an application attracting considerable attention in American English. In 1943 Victor Oswald reported (*American Speech* 18, 19-25) an experiment demonstrating the homophony of latter and ladder. This position underlay the decision to use d for intervocalic t in the respelling to indicate pronunciation in the Merriam-Webster *Third New International Dictionary* in 1961. Adverse criticism led to reversing this decision, however, in *Webster's New Collegiate Dictionary* in 1973. Evidence from the UM responses supports that reversal.

Attic is a lexical item, contrasting with garret, obtained from 197 infs. in response to the query "What do you call an upper unfinished section of the house?" As a citation form offered in the interview situation attic is pronounced with [t] by 42 infs., only one of whom is in Type III. It has been observed earlier that some of the less-educated infs. tend to be precise in replying to the fw. Fifty-two infs. are recorded with a "voiced t" [t̬] and an even 100 with the "tapped t̄" [ɾ̌], but only three, all in Iowa, with [d]. Besides an apparent disinclination of the cultivated speakers to retain [t], there is no significant regional pattern except for a slightly higher frequency of [t] in Nebraska. Three of the five Canadian infs., however, have [t].

	Type I	Type II	Type III
[t]	24%	21%	7%
[t̬]	26%	26%	33%
[ɾ]	49%	51%	60%
[d]	1%	2%	0

	Mn.	Ia.	N.D.	S.D.	Nb.	Ave.
[t]	19%	16%	19%	19%	36%	21%
[t̬]	30%	38%	15%	15%	24%	26%
[ɾ]	52%	40%	69%	60%	39%	51%
[d]	0	6%	0	0	0	2%

[t] 2-5, 7, 23, 26-27, 31, 36, c52, 64; 104, 113, 119, 121, 128, 139, 141, 147; 201, 205-6, 219, 223; 304, 311, 320, 324-25; 401-2, 404, 411, 413, 415-16, 420-21, 423, 431, 435.

[t̬] 14, c15, 16, 18, 21, 29-30, 35, 37, 41, 43, 51, 53, 57-61, 63; 103, 109-12, 116-17, 122-23, 127, 129-30, 132, 134-35, 138, 144-45; 213, 220, 224; 309-10, 315, 323; 414, c422, 424-26, c427, 429-30.

[d] 110, 136, 149.

thirty 2.2. NE 59.

This word provides data supporting more strongly the persistence of intervocalic [t] in at least an isolated citation form. Actually, one-fourth of the 108 infs. offering [θɚti] are recorded as having this pronunciation in free conversation, with a very slight weighting toward Type I and away from Type III. About one-third of the UM infs. have [t̬] and only one-eighth the tapped [ɾ]. Two have [d]. The returns from forty (2.2; NE 54) are comparable.

	Type I	Type II	Type III
[t]	59%	49%	44%
[t̬]	31%	38%	38%
[ɾ]	11%	13%	19%
[d]	1%	1%	0

	Mn.	Ia.	N.D.	S.D.	Nb.	Ave
[t]	53%	42%	54%	42%	76%	54%
[t̬]	34%	34%	35%	46%	28%	35%
[ɾ]	14%	20%	12%	7%	3%	13%
[d]	0	1%	0	1%	0	1%

kettle 14.5. NE 131.

Kettle presents a situation different from the preceding, for here intervocalic /t/ is ordinarily followed by syllabic [ḷ], with the result—common allophonic variants [t] and [t̬]. Analysis of the records and the voice recordings has led to rewriting fw. H's [kɛtəl] as [kɛtḷ] and his [kɛtl] as [kɛt̬ḷ] and of fw. P's [kɛɾl] as [kɛt̬ḷ].

Eighty-eight, exactly 50% of the UM infs. using the word, have an unreleased [t] in kettle. Forty-six percent have [t̬]. Eight, the remaining 4%, apparently produce a vowel between /t/ and /l/.

[tḷ] 1, 5, 8, 20, 23, 26, 28, c31, 32, 34, c35, 39, 42, 48, 52, 54-55, c56, 58, 64-65; 101-3, c104, 106-8, c109, 110-13, 139, 140-41, 143-46, 148-49, 152; c202, 203, 206, 210-11, 215-20, 226; 301, 304, 306, 308, c311, 312, 320, 323, 326; 402-8, 410-13, c415, 416-17, 419-21, 423-24, c427, 428-29, 431, 433, 436.

[t̬] 4, c5, 6-7, 9, 11, c13, 14-19, 21-22, 24, c25, c29, 33, 36-37, 40, *41, 43-46, c47, 49-50, c51, 59, 60-62; cvr104, 114, cvr115, 116-18, 123-24, 128-34, c138, 142, 150-51; 208, c209, 212, 214, 221-22, 224-25; 303, *306, c307, 313-14, 316-19, c322, 324-25, 328; 401, 409, 414, 418, 422, 425-26, 430-32, 435, 437. [t̬əl] 434.

[ɾəl] c51, 53, 63; 105, 119, 121. [ʔəl] c415.

Tattle (73.3; NE 568) is not significantly different from kettle. in tattle 56% of the infs. have [t] and 40% have [t̬].

/f/

In the UM records only two words exhibit the intervocalic voicing of /f/. The single instance of /hwɪvəltri/ for whiffletree (17.6) in the speech of South Dakota inf. 317 is probably a valid example although arguably it could, on the other hand, be a confusing of whiffletree and the rare swiveltree, one occurrence of which is reported from Nebraska (see Volume 1). Nephew (51.5), however, clearly, though feebly, retains the earlier variant with /v/. In the New England survey in the early 1930's the form with the voiced /v/ was used by a scattered 14 of the 416 infs., only three of whom were in the southwestern sector most influential on UM Northern speech. But in the UM only four infs. have /v/ in nephew, a Type I Canadian inf. (1), two Type I Minnesotans (32, 48), and one Type III South Dakotan (319). All others have /f/. No instances were found in the North Central survey of neighboring Wisconsin.

/s/

The intervocalic voicing rule affects [s] in two UM lexical items, <u>Mrs.</u> and <u>greasy</u>.

<u>Mrs.</u> (52.5; NE 436; PEAS 177, F172), generally /mɪsɪz/ in the UM, becomes /mɪzɪz/ for six Iowa infs.: [ẓ] 130; [ṣ] 106, 112, c120, 133, 137. Fieldworkers irregularly recorded also a fast form, which is /mɪz/ for 12 infs., all but two of whom are Iowans (c35; 102-3, 105, 107, 113, 115, 130, 132, 139, 150; c207); and /mɪs/ for five others (135-36, 144, 148; c219).

<u>Greasy</u> (20.2; NE 188; PEAS 176, F171), typically /grisi/ in Northern speech, has a Midland voiced counterpart /grizi/ that is a well-known dialect criterion. (See George Hempl, "Grease and Greasy," *Dialect Notes* 1(1896), 438-44, and E. Bagby Atwood, "Grease and Greasy: A study of geographical variation," *University of Texas Studies in English* 29(1950), 249-60. Both articles are reprinted in H. B. Allen and G. M. Underwood, *Readings in American Dialectology* (New York, 1971).) In the UM, however, this voiced variant seems to be recessive, since it is not used by all Midland-type speakers. Except for three instances in Minnesota, most examples of [z] and [ṣ] are in southern Iowa and eastern Nebraska. (See map.) Users are 14, 35, 41; 106, 108, 119-20, 126, 130, 143, 146-48; c403, 418, 421, sn422, 425, 434.

The voiced variant /griz/ of the related verb <u>grease</u> is even less frequent than the form /grizi/. Only five Iowan Midland

speakers have it (c130, 131, 135, 146-47) and one Nebraskan (403).

DISSIMILATION OR LOSS OF /r/

An optional rule calling for the replacement or elimination of one of two /r/'s in a single word has occasionally affected certain words in the UM. The varying degrees in which this rule has been accepted result in wide differences among these words. One, <u>February</u> with prevocalic /r/, typically exhibits dissimilation; the others with postvocalic /r/ typically exhibit loss.

<u>February</u> 3.1b. NE 65.

In <u>February</u> the first retroflex glide /r/ is retained by slightly less than one-third of all UM infs. in the pronunciation /fɛbruɛrɪ/. Speakers with a Northern speech background seem more likely to retain it, as do Type III speakers in Midland speech territory, but the evidence is not very strong. Replacement of the retroflex glide /r/ by the palatal glide /j/, or by complete loss, is distributed as follows: Minnesota 55%, Iowa 86%, North Dakota 69%, South Dakota 69%, Nebraska 72%. In all states but North Dakota the majority form is /fɛbjuwɛri/. One North Dakotan inf., 218, has the idiosyncratic /fɛbjurɛri/, with dissimilation but also with an intrusive additional /r/ after /u/. Two other North Dakotans, 221 and 222, have lost /j/ but likewise have the intrusive /r/ to form /fɛbərɛri/. Loss of /j/ is more likely, however, to be accompanied by a distinct /w/ glide as in /fɛbuwɛri/ or /fɛbəwɛri/ (35, 48; 125, 128, 143; 208-9; 422, 434-35), three-syllabled /fɛbwɛri/ (105, 107), or the unique /fɛbəwi/ (135).

	Type I	Type II	Type III
/r/	33%	26%	50%
/j/	58%	66%	37%
/ʘ/	9%	8%	13%

	Mn.	Ia.	N.D.	S.D.	Nb.	Ave.
/r/	45%	14%	36%	31%	28%	31%
/j/	52%	74%	44%	65%	61%	60%
/ʘ/	3%	12%	20%	4%	11%	9%

/j/ 1, 3, 5, 8-11, 13, 17, c21, 22, 24-25, 28-34, 37, c42, 43-45, 50, 54, c55, 58-60, 64-65; 101, 103-5, 107-9, 111, 113, vrl15, 116-17, 119-24, 127, 129-30, 132-34, 136-37, c138, 139-42, 144-46, 148-49, 152; 203, 205, 214, 216-20, 224-26; 302-3, c304-5, 306, 308, 310-14, 316,

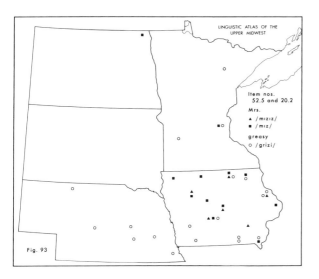

LINGUISTIC ATLAS OF THE
UPPER MIDWEST

Item nos.
52.5 and 20.2
<u>Mrs.</u>
▲ /mɪzɪz/
■ /mɪz/

<u>greasy</u>
○ /grizi/

Fig. 93

318, 321-22, 324, c325; 402, 404, 406-8, 410, 413-14, 316-18, 420-21, 424, 426-27, 429-31, 433, 436-37.

/Ø/ 35, 48; c105, 125, 128, 135, 143, 147; 208-9, 221-22; 307; 422, 432, 434-35.

/r/ All others except the following nonrespondents: 61; 118, 151; 327-28; 405.

secretary 53.3. NE 446.

With secretary the dissimilation rule results only rarely in replacement of the first /r/ by /j/ but frequently in complete loss, i.e., /Ø/. This loss of /r/ sharply accords with the scale of social differentiaion, as it occurs among more than one-half of the Type I speakers, only one-fourth of the Type II's, and in the speech of only one in the college group. Only two infs. (55; 142) have the /j/ replacement in /sɛkjətɛri/. Three infs. (13; 317; 415) have /sɛkətɛri/. There are no instances of the pronunciation /'sɛkrɪtri/.

	Type I	Type II	Type III
/sɛk+tɛri/	57%	27%	6%
/sɛkr+tɛri/	39%	74%	94%

	Mn.	Ia.	N.D.	S.D.	Nb.	Ave.
/sɛk+tɛri/	31%	37%	46%	63%	35%	49%
/sɛkr+tɛri/	66%	63%	54%	33%	62%	52%

/sɛk+tɛri/ 1, 5-6, 11, 16, 21, 23, 25-26, 29, 31, 37, c45, 51, 56-57, 59-60, 62; 101, 104-5, 113, vr115, 117-18, 122, 124, c127, 129, 134-36, 138, 140-41, 143, 147; 201-4, 207, 209, 212, 214, 216, 218, 220, 223; 301-3, 305-6, 308-9, 311, 316, 320-25, 328; 401, 405, 407, c409, 416-18, 421, 429-30, 432, 434, 436.

library 63.1. NE 540. PEAS 173; F161, F162.

Kurath and McDavid report that in the East library has two main pronunciation variants, a trisyllabic one, widespread, with a strong secondary stress on the second syllable, and another, extending from upper New York State and Manhattan, with a range from trisyllabic to disyllabic but always with only a weak stress on the second syllable.

Both types of pronunciation are found in the UM, where the first is increasingly dominant and the second is only very sparsely represented.

The first, ['laɪˌbrɛri], is the choice of nearly three-fourths of the UM infs. Most of the remaining one-fourth have so completely accepted the dissimilation rule that Ø has replaced the first /r/ in their variant ['laɪˌbɛri]. This form,

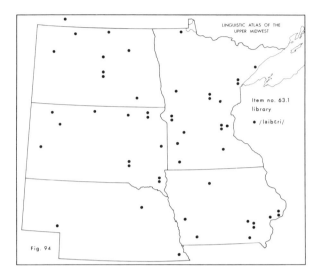

Fig. 94

most frequent in Minnesota and the Dakotas, appears to have Northern orientation. (See map.) It is furthermore also a social marker. More than two-thirds of its speakers are in Type I, slightly less than one-third in Type II, and only one, a Minnesota farmer, in Type III.

The second pronunciation variety, with only weak stress on the second syllable, is in its full form [laɪbrəri] offered by two Canadian infs. (3; 202) and, according to fw. Wn, by two South Dakotans (316, 318). A variant, [laɪbrɚɪ], with retroflexion extended to the vowel, is used by infs. 14; 101, 107, 116. A third variant, exhibiting loss of the first /r/, appears as [laɪbərɪ] (318) and [laɪbɚɪ] (217). Reduction to disyllabic [laɪbrɪ], a form reported in northeastern New England and the Philadelphia area, as well as in Virginia and North Carolina, is exemplified in the speech of only two UM infs. (141; 307).

Besides these two pronunciation types, a third and rare reverse development adds a syllable. Three similar minor four-syllable variants are recorded as follows: [laɪbərɛri] 305; [laɪbɚrɛri] 413, 423, 428; and [laɪbrərɛri] c51.

	Type I	Type II	Type III
/laɪbrɛri/	70%	75%	94%
/laɪbɛri/	28%	21%	12%

	Mn.	Ia.	N.D.	S.D.	Nb.	Ave.
/laɪbrɛri/	72%	80%	58%	54%	95%	74%
/laɪbɛri/	28%	18%	34%	36%	5%	23%

/laɪbɛri/ 4, 6, 15, 19, 21-22, 24-26, 31, 35-36, 41, c46, 50, 60; 113, 125, 134-36, 138, 140-41, 143, 147; 201, 203-4, c209, 211-12, 216-17, 224; 301-3, 306-8, 310, 318, 322-25; 416, c417, 435.

comforter   23.6. NE 342.

Comforter in the UM is generally pronounced [kʌmfətɚ], but sometimes is affected by this rule so as to yield the variant [kʌmfɨtɚ] or [kʌmfətɚ]. Because 29 of these are in Type I and 19 in Type II, but only one in Type III, it may be conjectured that among /r/-using speakers this variant is a social marker.

[kʌmfɨ(ə)tɚ] 29-31, 44-48, c51, 53, 59-61, 64; 113, 120, 139, 152; 201, 205-6, 208, 210, 212, 215, 217-18, 220, 224-25; 301-2, 309, 312, 314-15, 324, 326-27; 401, c403, 404, 409, 417, 424, 427-28, c432.

quarter   4.7. NE 81.

Generally /kwɔrtər/, [kwɔrtɚ], this word is pronounced [kwɔtɚ] by 20 UM widely scattered infs. Thirteen of these are Type I speakers, four are in Type II, but three in Type III, as follows: 11, 21, 29; 113, 121, 150; 214, 220-21; 314; 413, 418, 421-22, 424-29. Stray additional examples are [nɔðɚn] northern, inf. 21; [ɔdɚ] order, inf. 21; and [ɔɚtʃɨd] orchard, inf. 416.

ALTERNATION AND REPLACEMENT

For various historical reasons several words exist with alternate consonants having some correlation with either regional or social factors in the UM.

Lisping

Lisping is the use of one fricative for another. It often appears in the speech of children with such a pronunciation as /θιθtɚ/ for sister and /mʌvɚ/ for mother, deviations which their elders sooner or later help them to replace with the standard forms. But sometimes lisped variants, learned by ear rather then by eye, persist and become viable.

/θ/

thills   17.5. NE 171.

Historical thill /θιl/ (see Volume 1), from Middle English thylle, developed a lisped variant with initial /f/ as early as the late 17th century. The first instance cited in the *Oxford English Dictionary* is from Shakespeare's *Merchant of Venice* in 1596. Since then both forms have persisted with the same meaning. In the eastern United States they coexist principally in New England and the Hudson Valley, a circumstance accounting for the UM distribution in northern Iowa and southern Minnesota, with scattered instances in North Dakota and eastern South Dakota. In the UM the original thills, with only 13 instances, is used by eight Type I infs. and five Type II's: :33, 42, 52-53, 55, c59; :103, 107-8, :144; 314, 327; s424. Two infs. report having heard it in their communities: 29 and 51. The lisped fills is offered by more than twice as many infs., 19 Type I's, nine Type II's, and one college graduate, a Minnesota stock raiser: 16, 23, 27, 29-30, :41, 50, 54, 56, 61-65; 103, 105-7, 116-17, 139; 204, 210, 216, 223, 225; 307, 317; 420. In addition North Dakota inf. *219 acknowledges earlier use of fills; and seven others attest its occurrence in their communities: 42, 45, 60; 109, 118, 151; 224.

drouth   6.1. NE 97.

Two Type I infs., 35 in Minnesota and 140 in southern Iowa, have the lisped form /drauf/ for the usual /drauθ/.

hearth   7.1. NE 329.

One UM Type I inf., 401, has the lisped variant /hɚf/, apparently a nonce form, for the usual /hɚθ/ or /harθ/.

Matthew   52.4. NE 434.

One Type I inf., 303, has the lisped variant /mæfju/.

/f/

trough   10.3; 29.5. NE 208, 349.

Although the *Oxford English Dictionary* records the appearance of a variant trouthe in the 16th century, the common Modern English reflex of Old English trog is trough with final /f/. A lisped form with final /θ/ seems to be a recent development.

The lisped variant actually is the more common form in New England, with plurals /trɔθs/ or /trɔðz/. (See Volume 2.) The New England provenience of /trɔθ/ is probably reflected in the fact that, as reported by McDavid, it occurs in the speech of eight infs. in northern Illinois, and that 12, nearly one-fourth, of the Wisconsin infs. have this pronunciation. This origin is presumptive also in the UM distribution, since all but three of the 33 instances are in Northern speech territory. (See map.) But this form seems to be losing popularity and

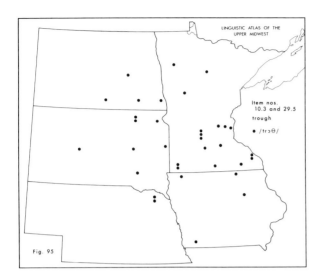

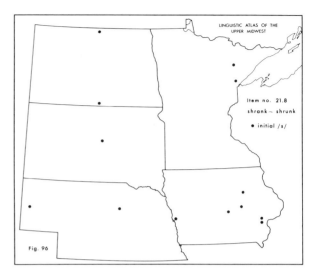

social status, as it is found in the speech of twice as many old-fashioned Type I infs. as Type II's, and is used by only one Type III.

I 19, 31, c36, 44-45, 48, 51, 56-57, 65; 101, 117, 143; 218, 223, c224; 305-6, 316-17; 407.
II 40, 43, 60-61, 63; 105; 226; 308, 313, 323; 408.
III 9.

sheaf   34.2. NE 126.

Of the 38 scattered infs. pronouncing the lexical variant sheaf (see Volume 1), five have a lisped variety with interdental /θ/ (3, c45; 133; 218) or, in the plural, the voiced interdental /ð/ (404). All are in Type I except 404, who is in Type II. Like other lisped forms, it is surely a nonstandard variation. Although this variant is reported nine times in the *Linguistic Atlas of New England*, the few occurrences in the UM warrant no statement about regional distribution.

funnel   15.6. NE 145.

One Type I Nebraska inf., 418, himself a user of funnel, reports frequently hearing a variant with initial /θ/, thunnel. Perhaps there is confusion with the disappearing variant tunnel. (See Volume 1.)

/š/

shrank/shrunk   21.8. NE 660.

With respect to the initial cluster /šr/ as in shrimp, a characteristic South Atlantic feature is the replacement of /š/ by /s/. The only UM item attesting

the incidence of this cluster is shrank. Although 12 UM infs. have either [š] or [s] in this context, the influence of Southern or South Midland speech cannot be the only cause. There are but five infs. in southern Iowa (125, 130, 132, 137-38) who have family backgrounds suggesting that for them it is an inherited pronunciation. The others are 13, 16; c117; 204, 223; 314; 409. Nine of the 12 are in Type I: 13, 16; 117, 132, 137; 204, 223; 314; 409. Three are in Type II: 125, 130, 138. None are in Type III. In the UM it is clearly a nonstandard variant.

/s/

rinse   15.2. NE 138.

According to the *Oxford English Dictionary*, a variant of rinse ending in /š/ rather than /s/ developed as early as the 15th century. It persists today in northeastern England. (See Harold Orton and Nathalia Wright, *A Word Geography of England*, London and New York, 1974.)

For some speakers an intrusive [t] follows the [n] so that both /rɪnš/ and [rɪntʃ] (/rɪnč/) occur.

In the United States rinch occurs as a minor variant in New England and the western extension of its speech. Only half a dozen infs. use it in the New England survey, but in Wisconsin 20% of the North Central infs. have this form. The forthcoming Middle and South Atlantic States Atlas may well reveal an even higher proportion, since the distribution in the UM suggests a strong South Midland background. (See map.)

Although scattered instances occur in Minnesota and the Dakotas, most of the

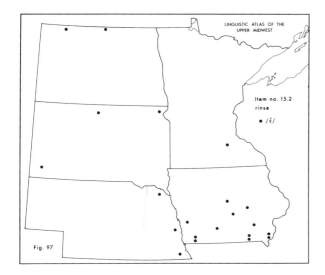

Fig. 97

examples are in Midland speech territory, with concentration in southern Iowa. This variant with final /š/ also exhibits sharp social cleavage, for 21 of the 26 current examples are in the speech of Type I infs. and only five in that of Type II's. One cultured inf. acknowledges having used it when he was a boy, and a Type II inf. recalls it as her mother's pronunciation.

A secondary correlation is that with the /ɛ/ vowel rather than with the usual /ɪ/. Nineteen infs. have the pronunciation rench /rɛnš/. For them the slightly backed tongue position for the alveolopalatal /š/ is articulatorily consistent with the slightly backed tongue position for /ɛ/; and, although fws. did not so indicate, for them the tongue contact for /n/ would then also be slightly behind that in the /ɪ__š/ context.

    I 16, 19, 21, 36, 48; 114, 124, 129, 132, 135, 142-43, 146, 148, 151; 204; 303, 307, 311; 427, 434.
    II ¹†40; 147, 149; 203; 407, 421.
    III †222.

Two stray additional instances appear. One is in the form cornish /kɔrnɪš/ for cornice, as pronounced by a Type I inf. in Nebraska, 434. The other is in the form shingletree /šɪŋgltri/ for singletree, offered by Iowa Type II inf. 134.

Voiced/Voiceless Alternation

Alternation between voice and voicelessness occasionally exhibits social and regional correlation. Although such al-

ternation may result from assimilation, the possibility of other factors justifies treating the following types here rather than in the section on assimilative changes.

/ð/ - /θ/

with   25.7b. NE 725.
without 25.7a. NE 725. PEAS 176; F170.

Both with and without typically have /ð/ in the United States, but variants with /θ/ have high regional frequency. These variants, described by Kurath as of northern British and Scotch-Irish origin, are extremely rare in New England but common in western Pennsylvania, West Virginia, and the Shenandoah Valley. With perhaps a somewhat different provenience they occur also in Tidewater Virginia and the lower South.

The eastern distribution pattern of /wɪθ/ is only weakly reflected in the UM, where it seems to be spreading actively into Northern speech territory. Tested in a context before a voiced consonant, such as with milk, /wɪθ/ is only slightly more common in Midland Iowa than in Minnesota, and in the Dakotas and Nebraska it is almost as frequent as /wɪð/. No marked social contrasts appear, although only among Type II infs. as a class does the incidence of /wɪθ/ rise above 50%.

Without, however, presents a different picture. The strength of the variant with voiceless /θ/ characterizes the Midland speech areas of Iowa and Nebraska. Only eight infs. in Minnesota have it, with three in North Dakota and one in South Dakota, besides two Canadian infs. in Manitoba and Saskatchewan. This clear regional pattern is supplemented by a so-

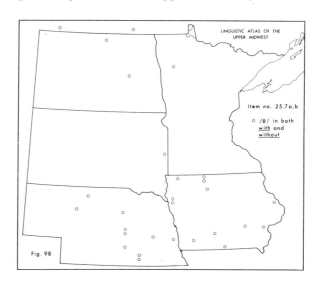

Fig. 98

cial contrast as well, since, except for Iowan inf. 110, the incidence of /wɪθaut/ is restricted to Type I and Type II infs.

The regional weighting looms more clearly when the infs. who have /θ/ in both with and without are considered together. The accompanying map reveals sharply the Midland orientation, with the original Scottish and Irish source of the five infs. shown in North Dakota, Minnesota, and Canada, all of whom have Irish or Scottish forebears.

	Mn.	Ia.	N.D.	S.D.	Nb.	Ave.
/wɪθ/	42%	62%	42%	45%	46%	49%
/wɪð/	62%	38%	58%	55%	54%	53%
/wɪθaut/	13%	33%	19%	5%	27%	21%
/wɪðaut/	87%	67%	81%	95%	73%	78%

/wɪθ/ 1, 7-12, c14, c16, 20, 22, 24-26, 28-29, 31, 34-36, c37, 39, 42, 50, 58, 62; 101-6, 108-10, 112, 114, 116-17, 119, 121-23, 125, 127-28, 134, 136-38, 140, 142-43, 145, 147, 149, 151-52; 201-3, 205, 208, 211, 213-14, 216, 219, c221; 302-3, 306, 310-11, 314, 318, 321-23; 402-4, 410, 412, 414-15, 418, 420-25, 428, 432-33.

/wɪð/ 2-6, c13, 14, c15-16, 17, c18, 19, 21, 23, 27, 30, 32-33, 37-38, 40-41, c43-45, 46, c47, 49, c52, 53-57, c59, 60-64, c65; 107, 111, 113, 115, 118, 120, 124, 126, 129-33, 135, 139, 141, 144, 146, 148, 150; 204, 206-7, 209-10, 212, 215, 217-18, 220, 222-26; 301, 304, c305, 309, 312, 315, 319-20, 324-26, 328; 401, 405-9, 411, 413, 416-17, 419, 426-27, 429-31, 434-37.

/wɪt/ 48, c51.

/wɪθaut/ 4, 6, 8, 12, c13, 56-57, 60; 101, 103-4, 107, 109-10, 112-13, 115, 121, 132, 134, 138, 142, 145, 148, 151; 201-2, 205, 217, 219; 318; 404, 412, 414, 420-21, 423-24, 428, 432-33.

/wɪðaut/ 1-3, 5, 7, 10-11, c13, 14, c15, 16-17, c18, 19-42, c43-45, 46, c47, 49-50, c52, 53-55, 58-59, 61-63, sn64, 65; 102, 105-6, 108, 111, 114, 116-20, 122-28, 130-31, 133, 135-37, 139-41, 143-44, 146-47, 149-50, 152; 203-4, 206-16, 218, 220-26; 301-4, 308-12, 314-15, 320-21, 323-26, 328; 401-3, 405-11, 415-19, 422, 425-27, 429-31, 434-37.

/wɪtaut/ 9, 51.

/wɪdaut/ 48.

moth 29.5.

trough 47.1b.

The alternation between the historical voiced plural of moth /mɔðz/ and the analogical plural /mɔθs/, treated in Volume 2 (p. 48), is paralleled by a similar contrast in the plurals of trough, whether original as /trɔvz/ or lisped as

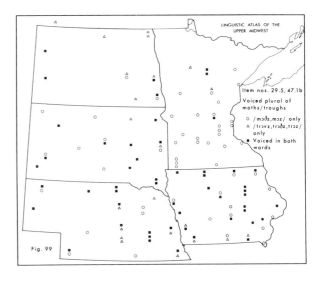

Fig. 99

/trɔðz/. Most of the infs. with voiced plurals are in Midland speech territory. (See map.)

/z/ - /s/

vase 14.7. PEAS 177.

In the UM the minor variant of vase with /ɑ/ instead of usual /e/ is invariably accompanied by a voiced /z/ instead of usual /s/. (See Chapter 2.) There are no instances of the uncommon eastern /vez/, but one inf., 308, offers, besides her normal /ves/, the form /vɒs/, which she considers humorously "hifalutin." Remarkably, only four Canadian infs. and one Iowan admit the use of /vɑz/ without some indication of amusement. It is clearly an acceptable Canadian pronunciation but one viewed in the UM as self-consciously pretentious.

/vɑz/ 1-2, ¹3, !¹26, !28, ¹31, !†37, ¹39, !44, !→46, !55, !¹61-62; 122, !127; 201-2.

sink NE 344.

Free conversation of three infs., Type I 138 and Type II 120 and 212, reveals an unusual voiced variant zink /zɪŋk/, a form perhaps suggested by an early use of zinc in the manufacture of kitchen sinks.

house 11.3.

An alternation between /s/ and /z/ due to the development of an analogical plural of house is treated as a grammatical feature in Volume 2 (p. 48). The distribution of the infs. with non-historical pronunciation /haus+z/ appears in the accompanying map.

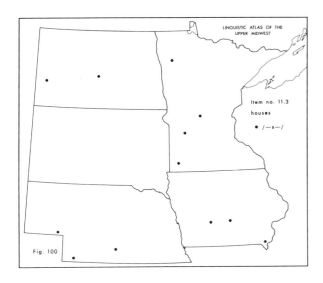

Fig. 100

/g/ - /k/

spigot 15.2a-b. NE 143.

As a lexical variant competing with
faucet and tap (see Volume 1), spigot occurs in two regionally weighted forms,
one with voiced /g/ and another, sometimes with its own spelling spicket, with
voiceless /k/. The word itself is a minor
variant in the North; only 29 of the 416
infs. in New England have it.

Of the two forms of spigot, that with
/g/ is more frequent in the northern part
of its range and that with /k/ in the
southern. Only nine of the New England
infs. have /k/. The North Central survey
of Wisconsin found seven of the 50 infs.
pronouncing spigot with /g/ and only one
with /k/. But the forthcoming Middle and
South Atlantic States Atlas is expected

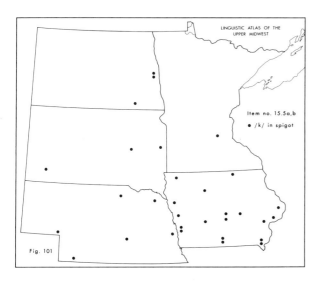

Fig. 101

to verify the increasing dominance of
/spɪk+t/ along an axis from north to
south.

The UM distribution of /spɪk+t/ strongly supports this expectation. Although
faucet dominates the area, 101 infs. offer their pronunciation of spigot, either
as their usual word or as a heard term.
The variant with /g/ is found in all five
states, though more frequently in Minnesota and North Dakota. The variant with
/k/, as is indicated on the accompanying
map, is more frequent in the southern
portion, especially in the South Midland
zone of southern Iowa.

No social contrasts appear in the use
of /spɪk+t/.

/k/ 35, ¹61; 101, 105, 111-12, 122-26,
128, 130, cr133, ¹137, 138, *139, 140,
¹143, 144, *145, 148, s149; 220-21, 224;
316-17, 320; 405, 408, ¹414, †421, 422,
427, ¹*432, 436-37.

/g/ 18, s29, 30-31, 38, †46; 102-3,
109-10, 116, *123, 127, 131, 150, 152;
208, 210, 212, 214, 217, ¹218, *219, 222,
225, :226; 301-2, 304, †306, 308-9, 311,
cr312, 313-14, ¹323, 324-28; 401-4, 406,
409-10, 412-13, s416, *417, 418-20,
s¹423, 424-26, 428, 431, 433-35.

hogshead 16.4.

One inf., 220, a North Dakota Type I,
has a voiceless variant for hogshead,
which for him has medial /ks/ rather than
the usual /gz/.

/d/ - /t/

Three participial adjectives exhibit a
historic alternation between final /d/
and final /t/—boiled, scared, and
spoiled. Although /bɔɪlt/ is rare in the
UM, the relative frequency of /spɔɪlt/
and /skɛrt/ is high enough to ascertain a
social and regional pattern. Final /t/ is
Midland-oriented and more likely to be
heard in the speech of Type I speakers.
For the details see Volume 2.

Glottal Stop Replacement

[t] - [?]

Ninety, nearly one-half, of the UM
infs. are recorded as having a glottal
stop [?] instead of [t] in mountain.
Probably the proportion of users is much
higher, since fws. H, Wn, and Wr rarely
observed the distinction and also since a
few infs. were prone to be somewhat over-
careful when speaking to the fw.

Nevertheless, it is clear that the incidence of [?] is related neither to re-

gion nor to informant type. Thirty-nine
of its users are in Type I, 41 in Type
II, and eight in Type III; and the examples are found proportionately in the
five states. Use apparently is idiosyncratic, dependent upon the personality of
the inf. Those with [?] are as follows:

I 4-6, c10, 11, 13, 21, 23, 25, 27, 31,
41, 48, c62; 117, 126-27, 140-41, 146,
148, 151; 201, 204, 212, c214, 216, 218,
220, 224; 307, 314, 322, 324; 403, 407,
418, 429, 434.
    II 2, 12, 20, 22, 24, 26, 28, 33, 54,
57, 60-61, 63; vr115, 128, 134, 136, 145,
147, 149, 152; 203, c205, 208, 210-11,
213, c215; 302, 304, 310, 315, 323, 325,
328; 404, 408, 410, 412, 419, 435.
    III 9, 34, 50, 58; 131; 221; 326; 411.

Nasal/Liquid Alternation

/n/ - /l/

chimney 6.7. NE 332.

The *Oxford English Dictionary* records
the development of a variant with /l/ for
/n/ as early as the 16th century; the research of Harold Orton for the English
Dialect Survey reveals the general occurrence of this variant today, along with a
subvariety having an intrusive /b/.
    Both /čɪmlɪ/ and /čɪmblɪ/ were carried
to New England, where the *Linguistic Atlas of New England* reports their high
frequency and wide distribution, at least
in the early 1930's. It is likely, however, that they are declining forms today.
    Certainly in the UM these two variants
are yielding to the influences of the

press and the schools. Only 14 bona fide
instances occur, all in the eastern half
except for a curiously persisting few in
northern North Dakota. No cultivated
speaker uses either of these forms. Only
three users are in Type II; the rest are
in Type I. One inf., 40, reported having
heard an /l/ pronunciation but considered
it "improper." A Canadian inf., 3, first
offered chimley but immediately corrected
it to chimney. A college graduate, 222,
laughed at it as being old-fashioned.
(See also Volume 1.)

    /čɪmblɪ/ c35, ¹40, ¹45; !†222.
    /čɪmlɪ/ ?3, c21, ¹40, !¹47; 113, c*117,
128, 135, 151; 201, 204, †205, 207, 209,
212; 307, c308.

Nasal/Nasal Alternation

/ŋ/ - /n/

For several generations many American
teachers, especially in the North, have
told students, "Don't drop your g's." Although put in terms of spelling, what
this injunction actually does is to deny
the acceptability of an optional phonological rule calling for the replacement
of a word-final velar nasal /ŋ/ by the
alveolar nasal /n/. No loss or "dropping"
is involved. But whether put as a spelling rule or as a pronunciation rule, no
simple generalization, positive or negative, can describe adequately the complex
conditions for exercising or denying that
option.
    For historical reasons a treatment of
this /ŋ/ - /n/ alternation appeared in
Volume 2. But, since the alternation today is clearly only phonetic rather than
grammatical, it seems appropriate here to
supplement that treatment with additional
material taken from the field data.
    A millennium ago Old English had one
suffix, -ung, for a verbal noun or ger-
und, functioning thus like the later
Latinate borrowed suffix -ation, and another ending, -enne, actually the dative
case of the inflected infinitive, which
likewise signaled a noun function. Besides these, Old English had also the
suffix -ende to denote the present participle. The *Oxford English Dictionary*'s
citations under -ing[1] and -ing[2] illus-
trate the confusing history of these
three forms, a confusion compounded by
the ultimate adoption of a single spelling -ing for noun and participle and the
inconsiderate persistence of two pronunciations, /ɪŋ/ and /ɪn/, for that spelling.
    The influence of spelling has undoubt-

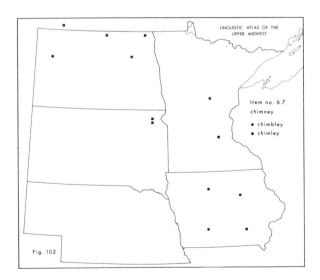

LINGUISTIC ATLAS OF THE
UPPER MIDWEST

Item no. 6.7
chimney
■ chimbley
● chimley

Fig. 102

edly affected the pronunciation, as well as attitudes toward the pronunciation, in both England and the United States. In the former, the /ɪn/ ending of the participle, common in the speech of educated and uneducated alike, is now apparently meeting stronger competition from spelling-induced /-ɪŋ/ within the ranks of educated speakers. In the United States, with its stronger devotion to correct spelling as a shibboleth, the /-ɪŋ/ form has traditionally been the only one accepted by teachers and textbook writers, authorities that have consistently stigmatized /ɪn/ as an overt marker of near-illiteracy.

At the same time it must be recognized that a counterinfluence apparently operates upon the speech of those people in public life, particularly elected officials, who wish to gain favor through an appearance of "folksiness," created by the free use of terminal /ɪn/. Such use by persons with some prestige probably serves then as a force counteracting for at least some impressionable hearers the prescriptive impact of the schools.

It has remained for dialect fieldwork to provide data for a more accurate description of the status of /ɪn/ in the United States. As Volume 2 reports, the New England survey revealed the widespread use of this form, even by some cultivated speakers. The forthcoming Middle and South Atlantic publication is likely to reveal even higher frequency, especially in the Southern states. What the North Central Atlas will show may be suggested by the fact that 41 of the 50 Wisconsin infs. use /ɪn/, some occasionally but others habitually.

The treatment in Volume 2 includes the analysis of responses to 45.2 and of incidental instances of /ɪn/. It indicates a rather high proportion of all infs. with at least occasional use of this ending. It will be helpful here to supplement that analysis with figures for specific items, since such evidence bears out the assumption that no easy generalization can be reached. The degree of formality, the rate of speech, the presence of competing noise, the apprehended social status of the person(s) addressed—these and similar factors conspire to affect the choice of one ending or the other. The phonetic context is equally important. Apparently few infs. do not at least once in a while have /ɪŋ/. But clearly the frequency of /ɪŋ/ increases from Type I to Type III.

Several present participles appear frequently enough to warrant these conclusions.

clearing (5.3; NE 89). Of the 149 infs. offering this term, 91% have /ɪŋ/, 9% /ɪn/. The latter is the form for 14% of the Type I infs. and 5% of the Type II's, as follows: 1, 6, :26, 32, 63; 114, 135, 143; c207; 317; 405, c422, 423.

coming (up) (6.2; NE 91). Of the 63 infs. offering this term, 78% have /ɪŋ/, 22% /ɪn/. Of the 14 having the latter, 12 are in Type I and two in Type II, as follows: 5, 19; 115, 148; 201, 207, 224; 302, 307, 309, 322; 409, 417, 429.

courting (61.5; NE 405). Despite the putative influence of alveolar /t/, of the 125 infs. pronouncing this term only 17, or 14%, have the /ɪn/ ending. Fourteen of them are in Type I and three in Type II as follows: 5-6, !15, !27, 32, !35; 105, 132, 135, 142, 147; 204-5, 209, 225; 307; 405.

dying (down) (6.3; NE 92). Only 41 infs. offer this term. Three have /ɪn/, two in Type I, 225 and 311, and one in Type II, 14.

hauling (18.1; NE 180). Of the 189 infs. who choose hauling, 95% have /ɪŋ/ and 6% have /ɪn/. Eleven percent of the latter are in Type I and 4% in Type II, thus: 6, 13, c25, 56; 140, 151; 302-3, c322; :417, 429.

keeping (company) (61.5; NE 405). Of the 25 infs. using this expression, eight have the /ɪn/ ending, as follows: 5, ¹25, 32, 54; 109-10, 141; 302.

rising/raising (6.2; NE 91). Seventy-six infs. with either of these two equivalents are divided with only 9% having /ɪn/, thus: 15, 25, 62; 114; c306, 311—all Type I.

sparking (61.5; NE 404). Six of the 23 infs. with this response use the /ɪn/ form. They are evenly split between Type I and Type II: 16; 105, 142, 147; 407, 423.

thinking (11.2; NE 682). Of the 86 infs. with this term, 63% have /ɪŋ/ and 37% have /ɪn/. Forty-nine percent of the Type I speakers have the latter form, 38% of the Type II's, and 18% of the Type III's. Those with /ɪn/ are 6, 15, 18-19, 27, 49-50; 113-15, c117, 123-25, 127-29, 132, 135, 138, 141-44, 146, 148; c216, c224; 305-7; c412.

One participial adjective occurs:

setting hen (30.3; NE 214). Two hundred infs. responded with this term. Seventy-eight percent have /ɪŋ/ and 22% /ɪn/. Of the Type I infs. 26% have the latter ending, of the Type II's 18%, and of the Type III's 12%.

Six gerunds occur:

(second) cutting (34.1; NE 125). Of the 115 infs. with this expression, only six have /ɪn/. Five are in Type I and one in Type II: 6; 114, 143; c302, 303; 429.

darning needle (45.8). Seventy-one infs. use this expression. Of the seven with /ɪn/, five are Type I and two Type II: 35; 101, c105, sn115; ¹225; 309, ¹314.

frying pan (14.4; NE 132). Of the 158 infs. with this term, 43, or 27%, have /ɪn/. Forty-eight percent of them are in Type I, 12% in Type II, and 6% in Type III. They are 3, 5-6, 13, 15, 21, 25, 31, 35, 39, 46, cvr47, 56-57, c62; 101, sn107, 117, 129, 135, 140, 146-47; 204, 207, 212, c220; 302, 306-8, 311, 314-17, 319, 322; 409, 417-19, 428-29.

living room (6.6; NE 423). Only 10 of the 151 infs. replying with this term use the /ɪn/ ending in living. Nine are in Type I and one is in Type II: 25, 32, 57, 62; 225; c303, 306, 316; 405, 413.

sewing needle (45.8). Of the nine infs. with this variant, only one Type I inf. has the /ɪn/ ending: 16.

sitting room (6.6; NE 423). Seventy-seven infs. use this term. Two Type I's have /ɪn/, and two Type II's: 6, 25; 105; ¹423.

Three nouns have an -ing ending no longer thought of as a suffix:

evening (3.6; NE 76). Of the 185 infs. cited, only eight have /ɪn/, seven of whom are in Type I and one in Type II: c15, 25, c30, 56, 62; c225; c409, c429.

morning (3.4; NE 77). Of the 189 infs. cited, only nine have /ɪn/, seven in Type I and two in Type II: c3, c15, 35, 57; c105; 225; c311, 322; c429. It may be suspected, however, that the number would be higher had more conversational responses been recorded in "Good morning."

mourning (60.1; NE 523). Only three of the 205 responses are with /ɪn/, all in Type I: 15; 140; 212.

The status of unstressed final -ing as a phonological rather than a grammatical matter is amply indicated not just by such words as evening and morning but especially by words like nothing and something, in which -ing is not a suffix but is rather part of the base itself.

nothing 74.5. NE 633.
something 74.6. NE 632.

Although nothing and something were primarily elicited as single-word responses to a direct question, e.g., "What is in my hand?" the high proportion of conversational replies—except from fws. H, P, and Wn—provides strong evidence for the usual informal pronunciation. Had even more conversation material been recorded, it is certain that a high-

er frequency of /ɪn/ would have appeared, since most of the free responses have that pronunciation. Even as it is, 21 infs. are reported as using both /nʌθɪŋ/ and /nʌθɪn/, and 13 infs. as having both /sʌmθɪŋ/ and /sʌmθɪn/ including the assimilated variant [sʌmpm̩].

Distribution of the principal variants is essentially social, not regional. It is clear that the variants with terminal /ɪn/ are not characteristic of cultivated speech, and that they consistently increase in frequency as the educational level drops. Although nearly all infs. use /ɪn/ at least occasionally, it is the Type I speakers who seem most likely to use /ɪn/ as the normal alternate form.

	Type I	Type II	Type III
/nʌθɪŋ/	77%	92%	94%
/nʌθɪn/	35%	17%	6%
/sʌmθɪŋ/	84%	88%	88%
/sʌmθɪn/	28%	20%	13%

	Mn.	Ia.	N.D.	S.D.	Nb.	Ave.
/nʌθɪŋ/	91%	78%	93%	76%	84%	86%
/nʌθɪn/	28%	27%	12%	29%	27%	24%
/sʌmθɪŋ/	80%	90%	96%	85%	84%	86%
/sʌmθɪn/	37%	12%	34%	31%	27%	23%

/nʌθɪŋ/ 1-5, c6-8, 9, c10, 11-12, c14-17, 18, c19, 20-21, c22-23, 24, c25, 26, 28, c29, 30, c32-33, 34, c36, 37, c39, 40-42, c43-48, 49, c50-53, 54-55, 57-58, c59-64, 65; 101-4, 106, c107, 108, 110-12, vr115, 116, c117, 119-28, 130-32, c133, 136-39, 141-42, 144-46, 149-50, 152; 201-3, c204, 205-8, 210-16, c217, 218-19, 221-24, cvr225; 301-2, 304-5, 307-8, 310, c311, 313, c315, 316-21, 323-26; 401-2, c403-5, 406, 408-12, cvr413, 414-16, 418-22, 424-28, 431-37.

/nʌθɪn/ c13, c19, c22, c25, c27, c31-32, c35, c38, †40, c46, c51, 52, c56, c59-61, c63, 64; c105, c109, 113-14, cvr115, 117, 129, 134-35, 140, 143, 145, 147-48; c209, c220, cvr225; c303, 306, 309, c311-12, c314, c317, c322; c405, c414, c416-17, 423, c429, 430.

/sʌmθɪŋ/ 1-2, c3, 4-5, c7, 8-12, c13, 14, 18-20, c21-22, 23, c25, 26-28, c29, c32, 33-34, 36-37, c39, 40-42, c43-45, c47-48, 49, c51-53, 54, c55, 58, c59-63, 64-65; 101-4, 106, c107, 108, c109, 110-13, vr115, c116-17, 119-27, 129-39, 141-46, 148-49, c150, 152; 201, c202-3, 204, c205, 206-12, c213-14, 215, c216, 217-19, c220-21, 222-24, c225; 301-5, 308, c309, 310, c311-12, 313, 316, c317, 318-20, c321-22, 323, c324, 325-26; 401-2, c403, 406, c407, c409, 410-12, cvr413, 414-15, c416-17, 418, c419, 420-22, c423, 424-28, c430-31, 432-47.

/sʌmθɪn/ c6, c13, c15-17, c24-25, c30-32, c35, c38-39, †40, c46, c50-52, c56-

57, c59-61, c63; 105, c114, c117, 128, 140, 147; c225; 303, c309, c311, c314-15, 317, c322; c404-5, c408, 415, c416, c419, c423, c429.

A footnote to the discussion of -ing is that for inf. 317 the city of Brookings, South Dakota, is /brukənz/.

/n/ - /ŋ/

onion 43.4. NE 257.

An unusual nasal alternation appears in the minor variant /ʌŋjɨn/ for onion. It is unusual because an already alveolar nasal /n/, which correlates with the palatal /j/, is replaced by a velar nasal with no apparent phonetic cause. The *Oxford English Dictionary* records forms with initial ing- and Scottish and dialectal variants perhaps close to the original French. Half a dozen examples of /ʌŋjɨn/ appear in the *Linguistic Atlas of New England*, and three turned up in the Wisconsin segment of the North Central survey.

Five UM infs. have /ʌŋjɨn/. Three Type I speakers are in Minnesota, and two Type II speakers are in North Dakota and Nebraska, respectively.

I 21, !23, 36. II 217; 412.

/m/ - /n/

mushroom 44.6. NE 279. PEAS 179; F177.

Persisting in English since the original borrowing of French mousseron in the 15th century, a variant of mushroom with final -n is common in southern England and in the eastern United States. Curiously ignored by commercial dictionaries, it is noticeably viable among folk speakers and it survives in the East as an older form in cultivated speech. In the North this variant occurs usually in a disyllabic form (see p. 303). But in Rhode Island, some areas of Upstate New York and northern Pennsylvania, and the Midland in general the trisyllabic form is more common.

In the UM use of mushroon or musheroon /ˈmʌšə̩run/ is strongest in Iowa and the Dakotas and among Type I infs., with whom its frequency is twice as great as among Type II's. Yet, since three college graduates have it also, it is only a relative, not an absolute, social marker.

	Type I	Type II	Type III
/m/	46%	75%	87%
/n/	55%	23%	20%

	Mn.	Ia.	N.D.	S.D.	Nb.	Ave.
/m/	71%	48%	56%	57%	71%	61%
/n/	28%	54%	48%	43%	26%	38%

/m/ 1-8, c10, 11, 14, 18-20, 23-24, 26, 29-30, 32-34, 36, 38-47, 49-54, 57-64; 102-3, 106, 108-12, 114, 116-17, 119-21, s122, 123, 125-26, 128, 131, 133, 137, 141, 147; 201, 203, 205-6, 208, 210, 213-15, 221, 224-26; 302, 304-5, 308-10, 312-13, 315, 318-19, 321, 323-24, 326, 328; 401, 406-8, 410-13, 416, 418-21, 424-28, 430-31, 433-37.

/n/ 9, 12-13, 15-17, 21-22, c23, 25, r27, 28, 31, 35, 37, †40, 48, 55-56, 65; 101, 104-5, 113, 115, c116, 118, c122, 124, 127, 129-30, 132, 134-36, 138-40, 142-46, 148-49; 202, 204, 207, 209, 211-12, 216-20, 222-23, c224; 301, 303, 306-7, 311, c314, 316-17, 320, 322, 325, 327; 402-5, 409, ¹414, 417, 422, 429, 432.

Comment:
"I guess it should be /rum/. It's spelled with m"—314; 402.

Stop/Fricative Alternation

[k] - [χ]

bucket 14.1. NE 129.

Although the velar fricative [χ] is not infrequent as a slow release from the velar stop [k], as in bucket [bʌkχɨt], [χ] is not usually listed as an independent consonant in English. Sixteen scattered UM infs., however, do have it as a clear allophone in bucket, and doubtless more instances would have appeared had the fws. H, P, and Wn not recorded /k/ only phonemically.

The inadequate size of the population with [bʌχɨt] does not warrant a general conclusion, but it may be observed that twice as many Type I's as Type II's have this variant, and that it is used by only one Type III inf.

I c6, 21, c41, 44, c48, 55; 216, 223; c322, 324.
II 33; 105; 203, 208; 315.
III 222.

Metathesis

Two infs., 23 and 209, both in Type I, have possible instances of metathesis in their unusual variant of skillet (item 14.4). Each insists that skittle [skɪtl̩] is the correct form.

CHAPTER 5

Miscellany

Several unrelated categories of phonetic phonomena recorded in the UM survey are put here simply because they do not easily fit into the preceding chapters on the vowels and the consonants.

THE COLLOQUIAL NASALS

The attitudes of UM infs. toward the colloquial nasals of affirmation and negation are like their attitudes toward UM weather. Some people are strongly negative, others are reluctantly resigned, but most are cheerfully accepting.

In view of the traditional insistence of elementary teachers and many parents upon Yes or No responses from children, instead of inarticulate grunts, it was hypothesized that the records would reveal a clear socioeducational contrast if not a regional pattern. No such contrast emerges. The only reflection of that insistence, as with other school-preserved injunctions that deny general usage, appears in the fact that, of the 19 infs. about whose negative attitude an overt comment is made, a disproportionate 12 are in Type I (7, 19, 21, 55, 65; 204, 207, 223, 225; 301, 314; 434); only six in Type II (54, 64; 210; 302, 313; 402); and only one in Type III (50). This last is a farmer somewhat insecure in his usage. Two Type I infs., 55 and 65, specifically condemn the nasals as "incorrect" and "improper." Yet all but one of the college graduates use them.

It was also hypothesized that the "open mouth" nasal with [x̃] rather than [m] would be largely limited to Type I speakers. This hypothesis likewise was not supported by the data, which reveal this variety to occur with all the inf. types.

The colloquial nasals are nonsyntactic units consisting of two nasal syllables.

The essential distinction between an affirmative unit and a negative unit is that the second syllable of the negative unit is preceded by a glottal stop. Otherwise, several variables yield a rather bewildering series of variants that correlate with such speaker attitudes as emphasis, concession, indifference, and surprise. The variables are chiefly obstruency, pitch, and stress.

No sound basis for even a rough statistical breakdown of the data can be found, since almost certainly any one inf. might on other occasions use variations not elicited or heard during the interview. The following treatment, then, must be limited to presentation of the noted variations, with only an inference as to relative frequency.

Affirmation

The affirmative units are sought by item 75.4 in the worksheets. They characteristically lack a medial glottal stop and occur both with and without complete oral obstruction, i.e., with nasal consonants and with nasalized vowels. Of the 167 responses with usable transcriptions 110 are with nasal consonants. Although [ŋ] is possible, it was not recorded, and it is not unlikely that some of the responses transcribed as a nasalized vowel [ə̃] actually were with the velar consonant. Five of the 110 have [n]—31, 34; c412, c423, c429; and 105 have [m]. All are treated below as having /m/.

Two main pitch patterns or intonation contours occur, one with a rise from low to high, and one with a fall from high to low. With each contour there are two main stress patterns, one with initial primary stress. An initial glottal stop was often recorded by fws. H, P, and Wr and sometimes by fw. A; it is omitted from the following listing. If the second syllabic in the unit is a nasal consonant, it is

334

preceded by a voiceless onset. If it is a nasalized vowel, it is preceded by [h] or a voiceless vowel. In the following transcription [ʌ] is subsumed under [ə].

⌐ m ⌐ˈm̥m c2-3, 9, c12-13, c16, 26, 32, c33, c59, 61-63; 102, 107-9, 111-13, 119, 121-22, 124, 133, 135, c146, 147, 149, c152; c202, 205, 208, 212, 216, c222, 226; c303-4, c309-10, 321, 325; 401, c404, c406, c408, c410-11, c413-14, c416-17, c424-25, 427-28, c430, 433, 435.

ˈm ⌐m̥m 31, c41-42, 50; 203-4, c220-21, c223, 224.

ə̃ ⌐ˈhə̃ 14; 101, 103-4, 110, 114-16; 218, c219; c327; c403, c405, c410, c413, c416, c423, 425-26, c428, c431, 432, c434, 435. With [ʊ̃] 23, 47; 213; 327. With [ɑ̃] c18; c431.

ˈə̃ ⌐hə̃ 23-24, 39-40, 49, 54; 101, 106, 120, 123, 134, 139; 211, 217; 402. With [ɛ̃] c150; c437.

⌐m ˈm̥m c4-5, c42.

ˈm ⌐m̥m 34, 36, 48, c49; 315, 320; 403, c418.

ˈə̃ ⌐hə̃ 34; 213; c303-4, 326, c327.

m ⌐m̥m 10, 20, c27, 64; 219; 323; 432.

ˈə̃ hə̃ 38; 224.

ˈm m̥m c408.

ˈə̃ hə̃ c404.

Fieldworkers did not always record both stress and pitch. Initial stress only is recorded for infs. c16-18, 22, 58; 210; final stress only for infs. 57; 120-21, 128, 142, 148, 150. Rising intonation only is recorded for infs. 125, f126, 127, 129, c130, 136-38, 140-41, 143-45; falling intonation only for infs. 117 and 432.

Negation

The negative colloquial nasal, queried by item 75.5 in the worksheets, is recorded from only 81 infs. That so few provide examples may be due both to a greater difficulty in eliciting it and to their general reluctance to use it. Several infs. express the opinion that, unlike the affirmative, the negative is impolite.

Besides the essential medial glottal stop, it is to be noted that in contrast with the affirmative unit the more common stress pattern is with initial primary stress and that the more common pitch

pattern is from high to low. The optional initial glottal stop has been ignored in the following transcriptions. Those with [n], 31, 63; 217, are included with [m].

ˈm ⌐ʔm̥m 22, c23; c423.

ˈə̃ ⌐ʔə̃ə̃ 20, 24, 27-28, 32, 39-41, 61; 101, 103-5, 108-10, 113, 115, 119, 138-39; 213, 224; c411, c414, c416-17, c423, 425, 428, c431, 432.

ˈm ⌐ʔm̥m 2, 4, 9, c10, 13, 23, 26, 31, 34, 36, 42, 49, 62-63; 102, c106, 111-12, 114, 133, 136-37; 203, 208, 217, 221; 311, 315, c320, 323, 325; 425, 428.

ə̃ ⌐ʔə̃ə̃ 107, 121; 203.

Those infs. for whom only initial stress is recorded are as follows: with [m]—13-14, c16-17, 18, 48, 56; with [ə̃]—15; 116, 120, 128, 132, 134, 148; 212; 316; 430. Those for whom only pitch is recorded are as follows: rising intonation—46, 52; c413, 433; falling intonation—122, 124-27, 129-31, 135, 140-41, 143-45; 306, 319, 328; 426, 432-33, 435.

SPELLING PRONUNCIATION

burial 59.6. NE 526.

Although a possible three or four instances of /bʊrɪəl/ instead of customary /bɛrɪəl/ are recorded in the *Linguistic Atlas of New England*, it seems likely that the two occurrences in Minnesota are examples of idiosyncratic spelling pronunciation. They are offered by infs. 7 and 57.

calm 57.5. NE 478.

Calm is a lexical variant offered by 97, nearly one-half, of the UM infs. (See Volume 1.) Since the mass of evidence in the UM files attests the close linguistic relationship of at least the northern portion of the UM to western New England, the great discrepancy with respect to the contrast between historical /kɑm/ and the spelling pronunciation /kɑlm/ almost surely gives evidence of the surprising rapid acceptance of the latter. Of the 416 infs. in New England only three were recorded with /kɑlm/ in the early 1930's. Twenty years later two of the 50 infs. in Wisconsin had /kɑlm/. But by the time of the UM survey more than one-third of the infs. in Northern speech territory had adopted the spelling pronunciation, as, indeed, had a similar proportion in the Midland area of Iowa and Nebraska. (See also <u>palm</u>, p. 20-21.)

	Type I	Type II	Type III
/kɑlm/	43%	31%	54%
/kɑm/	57%	69%	46%

	Mn.	Ia.	N.D.	S.D.	Nb.	Ave.
/kɑlm/	45%	18%	38%	43%	45%	38%
/kɑm/	55%	72%	62%	57%	55%	62%

/kɑlm/ 1, 4, s5, ¹7, 9-10, 17, 32, 34, 38, 40, 43-46, 51-52, s58, 60; 106, 121, 135, 150; 207, 211, 219; 315, 318, 320-21, 326, 328; 401, 403, 406, 435, 437.
/kɑm/ 2, 8, s13, 18, 20, 22, 26, 28-29, 31, 33, 39, 47, 50, 53-55, 57, 61-65; 101-3, 107-8, 110, 118-19, 123, 126-27, 130-31, 132, 137, 139, 144-45, 152; 205, 212-15, 226; 302, 305-7, 310, 312-13, 319; 412, 421, 426-28, 433.

clapboard 9.9. NE 350.

Common eastern <u>clapboard</u> has become only an uncommon lexical variant in the UM. (See Volume 1.) Its decline and decrease in familiarity accompanies a corresponding increase in the spelling pronunciation /klæpbɔrd/. Although this form occurs in New England, it is only a minor variant along with dominant form /klæbɚd/. In the UM, however, 13 of the 20 infs. volunteering the term have the spelling pronunciation. Only seven, 35%, retain the historic form.

/klæbɚd/ 118, 131; 222; 310; 413, 426, ¹433.
/klæpbɔrd/ 31; 101, 103, 112, 120, 146, 149, 152; 215, 219; 315; 402, 410.

diphtheria 60.4. NE 508.

By the time of the second edition of the Merriam-Webster *New International Dictionary* in 1934 the field research in New England had revealed that, except perhaps among cultured speakers, the dominant spoken form of <u>diphtheria</u> was the spelling pronunciation /dɪpθɪrjə/. Yet that great work and other commercial dictionaries still admitted only historical /dɪfθɪrjə/.

In 1961, however, Webster's *Third New International Dictionary* grudgingly admitted /dɪpθɪrjə/ with the admonition that some people consider it incorrect, and later commercial dictionaries have accepted it without overt comment.

The fieldwork in the UM, in the meantime, gathered data for describing the intervening situation, at mid-century.

In the UM /dɪpθɪrjə/ strongly dominates in all five states, with even greater strength in the western half. It is like-wise dominant among both Type I and Type II speakers, although one-half of the college group retain older /dɪfθɪrjə/. Incidentally, both of the UM infs. who are physicians have the spelling pronunciation with /dɪp/.

	Type I	Type II	Type III
/dɪf-/	5%	18%	50%
/dɪp-/	95%	82%	50%

	Mn.	Ia.	N.D.	S.D.	Nb.	Ave.
/dɪf-/	19%	14%	12%	8%	3%	12%
/dɪp-/	81%	86%	88%	92%	97%	88%

/dɪf-/ 18, 29, 34, 40-42, 46, r58, 61; 106, 110, 125-26, vr131, 144; 206, 210, 226; 313, 326; 411.
/dɪp-/ All others except 118; 307-8; 430.
Comment:
Inf. is proud of his /f/ and called attention of the fw. to it—61. "Few people say it correctly, /dɪfθɪrjə/"—404.

evening 3.6. NE 76.

Probably induced by the spelling or, less likely, by analogy with <u>even</u>, a trisyllabic pronunciation of <u>evening</u> with an epenthetic vowel, /ivənɪŋ/, is offered in the UM by 10 scattered infs.: six in Type I—c11, 117, 124, 140; 316; 415; and four in Type II—14, 17; 105; c414. None of the cultivated speakers has this pronunciation. That it may be a developing form is suggested by the fact that only one northern Vermont inf. has this variant in New England, and likewise one in the Wisconsin segment of the North Central survey.

mongrel 26.6. NE 212.

The gradual displacement of a historical pronunciation by an increasingly accepted spelling pronunciation appears clearly in the distribution of two variants of <u>mongrel</u>, the older with a mid-central stressed /ʌ/ and the newer with /ɑ/ or, rarely, /ɔ/.

In the UM the older original pronunciation occurs most frequently among the oldest and least educated speakers and least frequently within the college group. Some of the latter choose it because they are familiar with its designation as "correct."

All Canadian infs. have /mʌngrəl/.

	Type I	Type II	Type III
/ʌ/	43%	31%	18%
/ɑ/	57%	69%	82%

	Mn.	Ia.	N.D.	S.D.	Nb.	Ave.
/ʌ/	26%	23%	34%	50%	26%	35%
/ɑ/	74%	77%	66%	50%	74%	65%

/ʌ/ 1-3, 6, 16, 27, *41, 42, 44, s!48,
49-50, 55, 57, 61, 65; 101, s107, 113-15,
129, 151; 201-2, 206, 208, 226; 306, 308,
317-20, 324; c404, 410, 420, 427, 431.
/ɑ/ 9-12, 14, 18, 23, 28, 30, 33-34,
37-38, 40, 43, 45-47, 51, 54, 58-60, 62-
63; 102, 105-6, s107, 109-12, 116-17,
119-21, 123-24, 126, 128, 130-31, 137,
142, 148-49, 152; 205, 210, 213-14; 304,
310-11, 313, c325, 326-28; 401-2, 413,
418-19, 421-22, 424-26, 428, 433-34, 426.

The data for mongrel reveal also the
incidence of what is probably another
spelling pronunciation, the replacement
of /ŋ/ by /n/ in the historical /ŋg/
cluster, leaving the form /mʌngrəl/ or
/mɑngrəl/.

Although only 26 infs. offer this variant, its distribution suggests a possible
social contrast, since it is favored by a
higher proportion of better educated
speakers. Only 18% of the responding Type
I infs. have it—34, 46; 124, 126, 148;
306, 324; 413, 418; 24% of the Type II's—
43, 47, 54, 60, 63; 128, 130, 149; 308,
310, 318; 420, 433; and 36% of the Type
III's—11; 110, 131; 319.

Incidentally, mongrel apparently raises
difficulties with other speakers. What
may be another spelling pronunciation,
/mʌŋrəl/ with deletion of /g/, is offered
by three infs.: 201-2; 316. Three others,
16; 105, 114, delete the /r/ so as to
yield /mʌŋgəl/. Another inf., 316, deletes both /g/ and /r/ so as to produce
/mʌŋəl/, and the ultimate in deletion is
reached by inf. 138 with /mog+l/.

often 54.4. NE 711.

Although the spelling pronunciation
/ɔft+n/ has recently enjoyed the blessing
of presidential use, it is still a minority variant with only halfhearted recognition by some, but not all, commercial
dictionaries, and, at least in the UM, a
possible social preference by the less
well educated.

The historical and still general pronunciation /ɔf+n/ originated with the
gradual acceptance in the 17th century of
a phonological rule deleting medial /t/
following a voiceless fricative. (Queen
Elizabeth I wrote "offen.") That the
present restoration of /t/ in often has
shibboleth value is suggested by the fact
that its users do not similarly restore
/t/ to soften, listen, hasten, chasten,
and fasten.

Less than one-third of the UM infs. are
recorded with /ɔft+n/, with a slightly
higher proportion in Types I and II and
a slightly greater frequency in Northern

speech territory. Conversely, more than
three-fourths are recorded with /ɔf+n/,
evenly distributed by type but with a
slightly greater frequency in the Midland
speech territory. Twenty, about 10%, of
the infs. are reported as using both
forms, a situation suggesting perhaps a
feeling of insecurity with respect to the
pronunciation as well as a conscious de-
sire to use what is considered "correct"
on certain unordinary occasions. Eighteen
of the 20 first responded with one form
but in later conversation used the other.
One Nebraska Type III speaker, a school
official, commented that some people in
the community said /ɔft+n/ because of
their considering it as a badge of social
superiority. His own form is /ɔf+n/.

	Type I	Type II	Type III
/ɔf+n/	82%	79%	81%
/ɔft+n/	29%	30%	19%

	Mn.	Ia.	N.D.	S.D.	Nb.	Ave.
/ɔf+n/	78%	84%	73%	79%	89%	77%
/ɔft+n/	38%	22%	31%	29%	24%	29%

/ɔf+n/ 1, 5-11, c12-14, 15, c17, 18-19,
21-23, c24, 25-27, c28, 29, c31, 32-36,
39-43, c45, 46, c47, 49, c51, 52-55, 57-
60, c61-63, 65; 101-3, c104, 106, 108-14,
cvr115, 116-18, 120-29, vr131, c132, 133,
135-37, cvr140, c141, 142-46, 148-50,
152; c201, 202, 205, c209, 212, 214,
c221, 224; 301-7, 309-11, 313, 315-16,
318-20, 322, 324-28; 402, c403-4, 405-9,
c410-11, 412-13, c414, 415-16, c417-19,
420-21, 423-28, 431-35, c436-37.
/ɔft+n/ 2, c3, 4, 9, 12, c14, 15, c16,
18, 20, 24, 30, c31, 34, 37-38, c39, †40,
c44, c48-49, 50, c51, 56, 58, 60, c61-62,
c64; c103, 105, c107, 110, c113, 119,
130, 134, c138, 139, 141, 147; c201, 202,
205, c209, 212, 214, c221, 224; cvr305,
308, c312, c314, 319, c321-23; 401, c411,
c414, 417, c422, 426, 429-30, c436, 437.

palm 55.5. NE 490.

Although both calm (see p. 335) and
palm manifest the increasing acceptance
of a spelling pronunciation with /l/, it
is not being accepted at the same rate in
the two words, either socially or regionally. Palm, generally, is showing more
resistance to /pɑlm/ than calm is to
/kɑlm/.

In the UM about one-fourth of the Type
I and Type II infs. have adopted /pɑlm/,
but only one college graduate has this as
his normal form. Another Type III inf.,
Minnesota 58, first responded with his
usual /pɑm/ but then, asked to repeat,
shifted to /pɑlm/. Fieldworker variation
in transcription may account for the low

incidence of /pɑlm/ in Iowa, in view of the high proportion in Nebraska.

	Type I	Type II	Type III
/pɑlm/	25%	29%	7%
/pɑm/	75%	71%	93%

	Mn.	Ia.	N.D.	S.D.	Nb.	Ave.
/pɑlm/	43%	6%	23%	21%	35%	27%
/pɑm/	57%	94%	77%	79%	65%	73%

/pɑlm/ 1, 4, 7-9, 24, 30, 35, 41-44, 48, 51-53, r58, 59, 62-63; 128-29, 135; 201, 204, 209, 211, 216, 218; 303, 315-16, 320-21, 323; 402, 404, 406, 408, 417, 419, 422-23, 428, 435-37.

Further evidence of the lack of parallel development of calm and palm is that only 18 infs. have accepted a spelling pronunciation for both words: 1, 4, 7, 9, 43-44, 51-52, 60; 135, 211, 315, 320-21; 406, 435-37.

raspberries 48.6. NE 276.

Although not acknowledged in commercial dictionaries, a spelling pronunciation of raspberry with voiceless /s/ instead of accepted /z/ may be on the increase. In the New England survey of 1930-31 only 3% of the 416 infs. are recorded with [s] or [ᶎ]. These 14 examples are scattered thus: three in Maine, three in northern Vermont, and eight in Massachusetts. But in the Wisconsin sector of the North Central survey 16% of the infs. have /s/ and the UM survey reveals a similar contrast.

The spelling pronunciation with /s/ ([s, ᶎ]) is a clear UM social marker. It is most likely to occur in Type I speech and less likely in Type II. Not one in the college group has it. This variant, further, may be slightly more acceptable among Northern speakers. Eighteen of the 35 infs. with /s/ have the full spelling form with /sp/; 17 have only /s/ before -berry.

All the Canadian infs. have /s/.

	Type I	Type II	Type III
/s/	22%	13%	0

	Mn.	Ia.	N.D.	S.D.	Nb.	Ave.
/s/	17%	10%	38%	15%	14%	14%

/s/ 1-4, 7-8, 13, *19, 26, 36, *41; 116, 129, 143, 149, 152; 201, c202, 206, 209-10, 214-17, 223; c306, 307, 310, 323; 407, sn414, 417, 430, 435.

sumac 48.4. NE 250.

Both /s/ and /š/ are historical initial consonants for sumac, but the word may be conveniently treated here because the spelling is the reason offered by many persons for their /s/ pronunciation.

In the UM the distribution of the /s/ and /š/ variants is both social and regional. Although /šumæk/ easily is the dominant form, the proportion of Type III speakers with /'sumæk/ is more than twice as great as that of Type I speakers. Further, the frequency of the /s/ variant is much greater in the western half of the UM than in the eastern half. Both contrasts suggest the continued expansion of /s/ and the ultimate decline of /š/.

	Type I	Type II	Type III
/s/	24%	46%	56%
/š/	76%	56%	44%

	Mn.	Ia.	N.D.	S.D.	Nb.	Ave.
/s/	34%	30%	55%	60%	42%	39%
/š/	70%	70%	45%	40%	61%	62%

/s/ 1-3, 8-10, 18, 26, c28, 29-30, 33, 37, cr40, *41, 42, 45, 53, 56, 61; 103, 110-11, 117, 120, 126-27, 136, 144-45, 150, 152; 202, 204-5, 208, 210-11, 217, 219, 221-22; 304, 309-10, 314, 318-19, 324-25; 406, 409, 411-14, ¹416, 418-19, 422, 424, 428, 430-31, 433, 437.
/š/ 6, 11-13, 16, c19, 20-24, 27, 31-32, 34-36, 38-40, ¹42, 43-44, 46-52, 54-55, 57-60, 62, c63, 64-65; 102, 104-8, c109, 112, 114-16, 118-19, 121-25, 129-30, 132-35, 137-39, 141-42, 146-49; 207, 212-14, 218, 220, 225-26; 303, 311-13, 316-17, 320-21, 323, 326-28; 401-2, c403, 404-5, 407-8, 410, ¹411, 416-17, ¹418, 420-21, 423, †424, 425-27, 429, 432, †433, 434-35.

no response 1, 4-5, 7, 14-15, 17; 101, 113, 140, 143, 151; 201, 203, 206, 209, 215-16, 223-24; 301-2, 305-7, 315, 322; 415, 436.

Comment:
"I'd call it /šumæk/ up north, talking

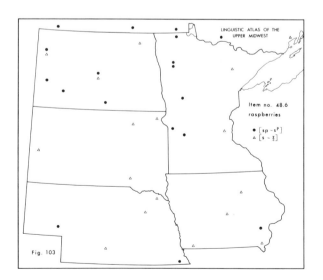

LINGUISTIC ATLAS OF THE UPPER MIDWEST

Item no. 48.6
raspberries

● [sp ~ sᵖ]
△ [s ~ ᶎ]

Fig. 103

to the natives"—37. "Some call it /šumæk/, but that's wrong"—418. Infs. called it /šumæk/ "when we were kids"— 424, 433.

<u>toward(s)</u> 25.8. NE 722.

This term may conveniently be treated in this category because for many speakers the preservation of one of the two chief variant types is due to the spelling. Without regard here to the genitival -<u>s</u> (for which see Volume 2, p. 69), these two types are the monosyllabic and the disyllabic. The first is represented by /tord/ and /tɔrd/; the second by the forms /ˌtuˈwɔrd/ and /təˈwɔrd/, with a reduced one-syllable subvariety that retains /w/, /twɔrd/.

Unfortunately, <u>toward</u> was added to the worksheets too late for full coverage of Minnesota. The available data, however, offer presumptive evidence that /tord/ and /tɔrd/ are in somewhat higher favor among Northern speakers and that the variants with /w/ are in higher favor among Midland speakers. It would appear also that the former are more acceptable to cultivated speakers and that /təwɔrd(z)/, etc., are more likely to be used outside the college group.

	Type I	Type II	Type III
/tord(z), tɔrd(z)/	67%	58%	82%
/təwɔrd(z)/ etc.	34%	59%	18%

	Mn.	Ia.	N.D.	S.D.	Nb.	Ave.
/tord(z), tɔrd(z)/	83%	63%	77%	67%	51%	64%
/təwɔrd(z)/ etc.	16%	38%	23%	33%	51%	37%

/tord(z), tɔrd(z)/ 16, c29-31, c35-36; 101-2, 104, 106-7, 109-10, 113-14, vr115, 116-20, 122-24, 126, 128-29, 131, 133-34, 137, 140-43, 148-50, 152; c201, 202-3, 205-6, 209-13, c214, 215, 217-19, 222, c223, 224-26; 301, 303-4, 307, 309, 311-13, 316-17, 319, c320, 322, c323, 325, 326-27, c328; 401-2, c403, 406, cvr407, 408, c409, 410-11, c413-14, 415, 419, 423-24, 428-31, 436.

/tuˈwɔrd(z), təˈwɔrd(z)/ 105, 132, 139, 145, 147, 151; 204, c208, 216, 220, c221; 302, 305-6, 310, c314, 315, 318, 321, c324; c404, 405, 407, 412, c414, 417-21, c422, 425-27, 432, 434-35, 437.

/twɔrd(z)/ c13; 103, 108, 111-13, 121, 125, 127, 130, 135-36, 138, 144, 146; 207; 416, 433.

<u>yolk</u> For the spelling pronunciation see p. 257.

FOREIGN SUBSTRATUM

The extent of the influence of foreign parentage upon first-generation pronunciation is described in Volume 1, pp. 138-39. The infs. exhibiting this influence are 4, 13, 19, 25, 41, 48; 149; 206, 224; 417, 421, 434.

BACK-FORMATION

Although back-formation is not a phonetic process, the resulting form may demand phonetic consideration, as when the historical plural <u>sheaves</u> (34.2) /šivz/, from <u>sheaf</u> /šif/, thus yields a new singular form <u>sheave</u> /šiv/, as pronounced by Type I infs. 52 and 56.

Two other instances of similar back-formation appear in incidental conversations: /lɪŋk/ as a new singular from <u>lynx</u> /lɪŋks/, used by Type I inf. 13, and /əpɛndɪk/ from <u>appendix</u> /əpɛndɪks/, used by Type II inf. 219. This occurrence of <u>link</u> may have a regional history, as the *Dictionary of Canadian English on Historical Principles*, with a citation for 1896, comments that this form was common among Northwest fur trappers.

MALAPROPISM AND OTHER ABERRATION

Certain malapropisms and other deviant forms recorded from free conversation are included here because of their social significance. Fifteen of the 18 infs. below are in Type I; three (17, 22; 121) are in Type II; none are in Type III.

<u>aluminum</u> /ælumɪjʌm/, 415.
<u>architect</u> /arčɪtɛkt/, 311.
<u>asphalt</u> /æšfɛlt/, 11.
<u>bronchial</u> /branɪkəl/, 220.
<u>creosoting</u> /ˈkriəˌsutɪŋ/, 15.
<u>culvert</u> /kʌlbɚt/, 109; 207.
<u>derivation</u> /dəˌrɪviˈešən/, 314.
<u>dilapidated</u> /dɪˈlæpɪˌletɨd/, 22.
<u>massacred</u> 'masqueraded' /ˌmæskəˈredɨd/, 407.
<u>mausoleum</u> /məˈsoljəm/, 121.
<u>modern</u> /madrən/, 216.
<u>modernizing</u> /ˈmadəˌraɪzɨn/, 35.
<u>perennial</u> /ˈpraɨntəl/, 17.
<u>proposition</u> /ˌprapəˈlɪšən/, 207.
<u>reciprocate</u> /riˈsɪpiˌet/, 204.
<u>stamina</u> /stæmiə/, 314.
<u>status</u> /stæčəs/, 220; 311.
<u>sumac</u> 'shoemate' /ˈšuˌmet/, 133, 146.
<u>tarpaulin</u> /tarˈpoljɨn/, 301.

Appendixes

Appendixes

Community Names

Inf.	City or Town		County or District	
			MINNESOTA	
1	Sprague	sp̥r̥e·g	Provencher	prə'vɑntʃ ι^
2	Fort Frances	ˌfo⁾ɚt 'frænsι⁾s	Rainy River	ˌrenι⁾ 'rιvɚ
3	Fort William	ˌfo⁾ɚt 'wι⁾ljəm	Papoonge	ˌpə'puⁿndʒ
4	Roseau	'ro ˌzoŏ^	Roseau	'ro ˌzoŏ^
5	International Falls	ιntɚˌnæʃənəl 'fɒɫz	Koochiching	'kuˇtʃ ι⁾tʃ ι⁾ŋ
6	Grand Marais	ˌgɹæn mə'ree^	Cook	kʊk
7	Gentilly	'dʒ εntlι^	Polk	poɫk
8	Fisher	'fιʃɚ	Polk	poɫk
9	Crookston	'krʊkstən	Polk	pok
10	Bemidji	bə'mιdʒ ι^	Beltrami	ˌbεl 'tɹæmiˇ
11	Grand Rapids	ˌgɹænd 'ræpɫ⁽dz	Itasca	a⁾ι^ 'tæskə
12	Grand Rapids	ˌgɹænd 'ræpι⁾dz	Itasca	a⁾ι^ 'tæskə
13	Virginia	vɚ'dʒ ιnjə	St. Louis	NR
14	Virginia	ɤɚ'dʒ ɫ⁽njə	St. Louis	'se·ⁿt ˌlʉ⁾·ε^s
15	Duluth	də'lʉˇ·ʉ^θ	St. Louis	'se·ⁿt ˌlʉˇ·u^ɫs
16	Oneota	ˌoˇʊ⁽nɫ⁽ 'ɐutə	St. Louis	NR
	Duluth	dlʉˇʉθ		
17	Duluth	NR	St. Louis	ˌsε·nt 'ɫʊŭɫ⁾ˇs
18	Duluth	də'lʉˇʉ⁾θ	St. Louis	'se·ⁿt lʉˇʉ·ɫ⁽s
19	Fergus Falls	ˌfɚgəs 'fɒ⁽ɫz	Otter Tail	'ɑtɚ ˌte⁽l
20	Fergus Falls	ˌfɚgəs 'fɔˇlz̧	Otter Tail	'ɑtɚ tee^⁾l
21	Brainerd	'bɹenɚd	Crow Wing	'kro ˌwι⁾ŋ
22	Deerwood	dι⁾ɚwʊd	Crow Wing	'kroι⁾ŋ
	Bay Lake Township	'be ˌle̥⁾k taˇʊ⁽nʃι⁾p		
23	Mora	'moˇrə	Kanabec	kə'nebι⁾k
24	Mora	'moˇrəˇ	Kanabec	kə'nebε̃⁾k
25	Graceville	'gresvι̃⁾l	Big Stone	'bιg ˌstoˇn
26	Graceville	'gresvι⁾l	Big Stone	'bιg 'stoo^n
27	Sauk Centre	sɔˇk sεntɚ	Stearns	stɚnz

343

28	Sauk Centre	sɒk sɛntɚ	Stearns	stɚnz
29	Clearwater	ˈlkɪˆɚˌwɒˁtɚ	Wright	raˆɪˆt
30	Clearwater	NR	Wright	NR
31	Minneapolis	NR	Hennepin	NR
32	Minneapolis	mɪniˇˈæpləˆs	Hennepin	ˈhɛnĭˀpɪn
33	Minneapolis	ˌmɪniˈæplɫs	Hennepin	ˈhɛn+ˇᵡɪˀn
34	Minneapolis	NR	Hennepin	NR
35	Minneapolis	NR	Hennepin	NR
36	Little Canada	ˌlɪtl ˈkæn+də		
	St. Paul	ˌseˇɔn ˈpɔˇ•ɫ	Ramsey	ˈræmziˇ
37	St. Paul	sentᵗ pɔˇɫ	Ramsey	ˈræmziˇ
38	St. Paul	seˇɔn ˈpɔɫ	Ramsey	ˈræmziˀ
39	Marine on St. Croix	mɚˈrin ɑn ˘sent ˈkrɔɪ	Washington	ˈwɔˇʃɪŋtɚn
40	Stillwater	ˈstɪlwɒˆɾɚ	Washington	ˈwɒʃɪˀŋtən
41	Montevideo	mɑntɪˇβɪdiˇoˁ	Chippewa	tʃɪp+ˇwɚˁeˀ
42	Montevideo	ˌmɑntɪˀˈvɪdjoˁ	Chippewa	NR
43	Hutchinson	ˈhʌtʃ+nsn	McLeod	məˈklaˀuˇd
44	Hutchinson	ˈhʌtʃɪˀŋsn	McLeod	mɪˈklaud
45	Hutchinson	ˈhʌtʃənsn	McLeod	məˈkləuˇd
46	Marshall	ˈmɑɚʃəɫ	Lyon	ˈlaɪˀ-ˌən
47	Minneota	ˈmɪniˈotə	Lyon	la+ˀ-ən
48	Faribault	NR	Rice	rɑˆ+s
49	Faribault	NR	Rice	NR
50	Faribault	ˈfærɪˀbo	Rice	NR
51	Mankato	ˌmænˈketoᵁ	Blue Earth	ˈbluˁ ˈɚθ
52	Mankato	ˌmænˈketoᵁ	Blue Earth	ˈbluˇᵁ ɚθ
53	Mapleton	ˈmep+tn	Blue Earth	ˈbluˇᵁ ɚθ
54	Red Wing	NR	Goodhue	NR
55	Red Wing	NR	Goodhue	NR
56	Winona	wɑiˀˈnonə/wəˆˈnonə	Winona	NR
57	Winona	w+ˈno•nə	Winona	NR
58	Winona	wəˈnonə	Winona	NR
59	Worthington	ˈwɚðɪˀŋtn	Nobles	ˈnoᵒˆb+lz
60	Worthington	ˈwɚðɪntn	Nobles	ˈnobəlz
61	Worthington	ˈwɚðɪntn	Nobles	ˈnoblz
62	Albert Lea	ˈælbɚt liˇⁱ	Freeborn	fribɚn
63	Clark's Grove	ˈklɑɚks ˈgroᵁv	Freeborn	ˈfriˇⁱ bɔɚn
64	Green Leafton	ˌgriˇⁱn ˈliˇⁱftən	Fillmore	ˈfɪlmoˇɚ
65	Spring Valley	ˌsprɪŋ ˈvæliˇ	Fillmore	ˈfɪlmoɚ

IOWA

| 101 | Rock Rapids | NR | Lyon | lɑɪˆ+n |
| 102 | Rock Rapids | NR | Lyon | lɑɪˆ+n |

103	Estherville	NR	Emmett	NR
104	Armstrong	NR	Emmett	NR
105	Mitchell	mɪtʃ ə^l	Mitchell	NR
106	St. Ansgar	seˡ^nt ˈænzgɚ	Mitchell	mɪtʃ əl
107	Decorah	dɪˈkɔrə	Winnishiek	ˈwɪn+ʃik
108	Decorah	ˌdiˈkɔrə	Winnishiek	ˈwɪnəˌʃɪk
109	Sioux City	NR	Woodbury	NR
110	Sioux City	NR	Woodbury	NR
111	Sioux City	NR	Woodbury	NR
112	Havelock	NR	Pocahontas	NR
113	Fonda	fɑndə	Pocahontas	NR
114	Blairsburg	ˈblɛɚzˌbɚg	Hamilton	hæm+ltn
115	Jewell	dʒuˇ+ˇl	Hamilton	NR
116	Janesville	ˈdʒeˡ^nzˌv+l	Bremer	brimɚ
117	Janesville	dʒeɩ^nzv+ᵊl	Bremer	briˇmɚ
118	Cedar Falls	NR	Black Hawk	NR
119	Epworth	NR	Dubuque	NR
120	Dubuque	dəbjuk	Dubuque	NR
121	Dubuque	dəbjuk	Dubuque	NR
122	Onowa	ãnəwɑ	Monona	mənouˇnə
123	Onowa	NR	Monona	mənou^nə
124	Crescent	krɛsənt	Pottawattamie	pɑtəwɑtəmiˇ
125	Crescent	krɛsənt	Pottawattamie	pɑɾəwɑɾəmiˇ
126	Elk Horn	ɛlk ɔɚn	Shelby	ʃɛlbiˇ
127	Audubon	ᴰɑdəbən	Audubon	NR
128	Des Moines	d+mɔɩn	Polk	pou^k
129	Des Moines	dɪ mɔɩ^n	Polk	pouk
130	Des Moines	dɪ mɔɩ^n	Polk	poᵒ^k
131	Des Moines	dɪ mɔɩn	Polk	pho•k
132	Laurel	lɔɚə^l	Marshall	ˈmɑɚʃ+l
133	Laurel	lɔɚə^l	Marshall	NR
134	Pella	pɛlə	Marion	mɛɚɩ^ən
135	Oskaloosa	ɒskəlᵾˢs+	Mahaska	məhæskiˇ
136	Oskaloosa	ɑskəlᵾˢə	Mahaska	məˈhæskə
137	West Branch	NR	Cedar	NR
138	Solon	ˈsoᵁl+ˇn	Johnson	NR
139	Maquoketa	məkoᵁkətə	Jackson	dʒæksən
140	Walcott	NR	Scott	NR
141	Princeton	NR	Scott	NR
142	Clarinda	klɹɚində	Page	pe^ɩ^dʒ
143	Clarinda	klərɪndə	Page	peɩ^dʒ
144	Lamoni	ləˈmounɑiˇ	Decatur	diˇkeɪɾɚ
145	Garden Grove	gɑɚdn grouˇv	Decatur	dɪkeɪɾɚ

146	Bloomfield	bluˇmfiəld	Davis	deˡvəs
147	Bloomfield	bluˇmfiˇəl	Davis	deˡvəs
148	West Point	wɛs pɔɪnt	Lee	li
149	Donnellson	dɑnlsn	Lee	li
150	Keokuk	ˡkɪˇə˒ˌkʌˋk	Lee	NR
151	Griswold	grɪzwə̆˒ɬd	Cass	kˋæːəs
152	Iowa City	ˡaɪˀəwə ˌsɪriˇ	Johnson	ˡdʒɑnsəˆn

NORTH DAKOTA

201	Estevan	ˡɛstɬˌvæn	Saskatchewan	səsˡkætʃ əˋˌwən
202	Killarney	kʌˆˡlɑˈniˇ	Manitoba	NR
203	Kenmare	ˡkɛnˌmɛˈ	Ward	wɔˈd
204	Rolla	ˡrɑˋlə	Rolette	ˌroˡlɛt
205	Rolla	rɑlə	Rolette	roˡlɛt
206	Akra	ˡækrə	Pembina	pɛmbəˆnə
207	Pembina	ˡpɛmbɬˇˌnĕ	Pembina	NR
208	Pembina	ˡpɛmbɬ̆nə	Pembina	NR
209	Williston	ˡwɪˀlɪˀsˌtən	Williams	wɪˀljəˆmz
210	Williston	ˡwɪˀɬsˌtən	Williams	wɪˀljɬmz̥
211	Harvey	hɑˈviˇ	Wells	wɛlʒ̥
212	Devils Lake	ˌdɛvlz̥ ˡleˇɪk	Ramsey	ræmziˇ
213	Devils Lake	ˡdɛvlz leˡkˋ	Ramsey	ˡræmziˇ
214	Medora	məˡdɔˇˈə	Billings	ˡbɪlɪˀŋz
215	Havelock	ˡhævəˌleˆk	Hettinger	ˡhɛɬɪˀndʒˈ
216	Bismarck	ˡbɪz̥ˌmɑˈk	Burleigh	ˡbˈlɪˆ
217	Bismarck	ˡbɪzmɑˈk	Burleigh	ˡbˈlɪˆ
218	Jamestown	ˡdʒemsˌtaʊn	Stutsman	ˡstʌtsmən
219	Jamestown	ˡdʒeˀ•mzˌtaʊn	Stutsman	ˡstʌtsmən
220	Fargo	ˡfɑˈgɔ	Cass	kæᵃˆs
221	Fargo	ˡfɑˈgo	Cass	kæᵃˆs
222	Fargo	ˡfɑˈgo	Cass	kæɛ̆ˆs
223	Westfield	ˡwɛstˌfiˇⁱld	Emmons	ˡɛmənz
224	Ellendale	ˡæˆləˆnˌdeɬl	Dickey	ˡdɪkiˇ
225	Fairmount	ˡfɛˈmɑˋʊⁿnt	Richland	ˡrɪtʃlənᵈ
226	Wahpeton	ˡwɑpɪˇtən	Richland	rɪtʃlənᵈ

SOUTH DAKOTA

301	Buffalo	ˡbʌfˑʌo	Harding	hɑˈdɪˀŋ
302	Faith	feə̆ˋˆθ	Meade	miˇⁱd
303	Selby	ˡsɛlbɪˀ	Walworth	NR
304	Selby	sɛlbiˇ	Walworth	NR
305	Aberdeen	NR	Brown	NR
306	Lincoln	NR	Brown	NR

307	Sisseton	NR	Roberts	NR
308	Sisseton	sɪsətən	Roberts	NR
309	Lead	ḻiˇⁱd	Lawrence	lɔænᵗs
310	Lead	ḻⁱd	Lawrence	lɑɾæˆnᵗs
311	Rapid City	ˌræp̆ɪˀd ˈsɪɾɪˆ	Pennington	pɛnɪˀŋtən
312	Rapid City	ræp̄ꜜd sɪɾiˇ	Pennington	pɛntŋtən
313	Philip	ˈfɪḻꜜp	Haakon	hɔˇkꜜn
314	Fort Pierre	pɪˀɚ	Stanley	stænliˇ
315	Pierre	pɪˀɚ	Hughes	hjuᵁz
316	Miller	NR	Hand	NR
317	Brookings	NR	Brookings	NR
318	Medary	məˈdɛri	Brookings	NR
319	Brookings	ˈbrukɪŋz	Brookings	NR
320	Hot Springs	ˈhɑˀt spꬵɪŋz	Fall River	fɔˇl rɪvɚ
321	Winner	wᶦˀnɚ	Tripp	tꬵɪp
322	Geddes	ˈgɛdiˇzꬵ	Charles Mix	NR
323	Lake Andes	leˇk ˈændiˇz	Charles Mix	tʃɑɚlz miks
324	Vermillion	vɚmɪljəˆn	Clay	kḻleᵛe
325	Vermillion	vꬵ̆mɪljəˆn	Clay	kḻle•
326	Rapid City	ˌræp̆ɪˀd ˈsɪɾiˇ	Pennington	ˈpɛntŋˌtən
327	Alexandria	ˌælɪˀkˈzændriᴶa	Hanson	hænsn
328	Alexandria	ˌælɪksændꭎɪˆᴶə	Hanson	ˈhæˆnsꬵn

NEBRASKA

401	Chadron	ˈʃædrən	Dawes	dɔˇz
402	Chadron	ˈʃædrən	Dawes	NR
403	Valentine	vælntaɪˆn	Cherry	tʃɛɾɪˆ
404	Valentine	ˈvælənˌtaˆɪˆn	Cherry	tʃɛriˇ
405	Bassett	ˈbæsꬵt	Rock	rɒk
406	Bassett	ˈbæsꬵt	Rock	rɑˀk
407	Hartington	hɑɚtɪˀŋtən	Cedar	siˇᵛⁱdɚ
408	Hartington	ˈhɑɚꬵɪˀŋˌtən	Cedar	ˈsidɚ
409	Scottsbluff	ˌskɑtsˈbḻʌf	Scottsbluff	NR
410	Scottsbluff	NR	Scottsbluff	NR
411	Scottsbluff	ˈskɑtsˈbḻʌᵊˆf	Scottsbluff	NR
412	Mullen	ˈmʌlə̆ˆn	Hooker	ˈhukɚ
413	Burwell	ˈbꭎwɛəl	Garfield	ˈgɑɚfɪⁱld
414	Burwell	ˈbꭎwəl	Garfield	gɑɚfɪⁱld
415	Norfolk	ˈnɔɚfɚk	Madison	ˈmædəsən
416	Norfolk	nɔɚfɔɚk	Madison	ˈmædəsən
417	Chappell	tʃæpḻ	Deuel	du•ɬ
418	North Platte	nɔɚθ pḻæᵋt	Lincoln	ˈlɪŋkəˆn
419	North Platte	ˈnɔɚθ ˈpḻæᵋˇt	Lincoln	ˈlɪŋkəˆn

420	Donnebrog	NR	Howard	NR
421	St. Paul	ˈseɪnt ˈpɔl	Howard	hɑꟳwɚd
422	Grand Island	ˌgrænd ˈɑˡlənd	Hall	hɔl
423	Doniphan	ˈdɑ·nəfən	Hall	ˈhɔ·ꟲl
424	Lincoln	ˈlɪɪˇŋkən	Lancaster	ˈlænˌkæstɚ
425	Lincoln	ˈlɪɪˇŋkən	Lancaster	ˈlænˈkæstɚ
426	Lincoln	ˈlɪɪˇŋkən	Lancaster	ˈlænˈkæstɚ
427	Valley	ˈvæᵊlɪⁱ	Douglas	ˈdʌɡləs
428	Omaha	ˈouməhɔ̠ˇ	Douglas	dʌɡləs
429	Benkelman	ˈbɛŋkəlˌmən	Dundy	ˈdʌndɪˆ
430	Holdrege	ˈhoᵒˆldɹ˖ʤ	Phelps	fɛᵊlps
431	Holdrege	ˈhoᵁldɹɪʤ	Phelps	fɛᵊlps
432	Hubbell	ˈhʌˇbəl	Thayer	θɛɚ·
433	Hebron	ˈhibrən/ c.~bɚn	Thayer	θɛɚ
434	Humboldt	ˈhɑmboult	Richardson	ˈrɪtʃədsən
435	Humboldt	hɑmboᵁlt	Richardson	r˖ˇtʃɚds˖n
436	Chappell	tʃæpꟁ	Deuel	duᵊˊꞀ
437	Benkelman	ˈbɛŋkəlˌmən	Dundy	dʌndɪˊ

Selected City and State Names

Worksheets in the several regional atlases include the names of selected cities and states in order to ascertain the regional pronunciation. Some in the UM worksheets are found also in those for New England and the North Central area; most have been added. A study of those names exhibiting regional variation is that of Harold B. Allen, "Distribution patterns of place-name pronunciations," *Names* 6(1958), 74-79.

Michigan 64.5a.

The typical pronunciation in the UM is /ˈmɪšəgən/, with nonsignificant allophonic variation from [ə] to [+] in the final syllable. In Minnesota four Type I infs. (7, 10, 21, 23) and two Type II infs. (24, 49) are recorded with the full vowel [æ]. One inf. (c206) has /č/ instead of /š/, and another (c17) has /ž/.

Illinois 64.5b.

The conspicuous variable in the pronunciation of Illinois is the final consonant, sometimes occurring because of the spelling. The historical pronunciation

without the consonant is most frequent among those UM infs. living closest to Illinois; that with the spelling pronunciation with final /z/ is most frequent in North Dakota.

This variant also produces a social contrast. Where the final /z/ occurs, it is clearly more likely to be used by a Type I speaker.

	Type I	Type II	Type III
/∅/	64%	86%	81%
/z/	37%	16%	19%

	Mn.	Ia.	N.D.	S.D.	Nb.	Ave
/∅/	68%	90%	62%	79%	75%	75%
/z/	37%	10%	38%	21%	25%	26%

A second but less obvious variable in the pronunciation of Illinois is that of the weak medial vowel, a variable with distinct regional contrast. The variant with medial schwa [ə] is Midland-oriented; those variants with [+] or [ɪ] are Northern-oriented. For several speakers, mostly Midland, the medial vowel has become so weak as to quite vanish and hence leave a two-syllable variant /ɪlnɔɪ(z)/. The several variants exhibit no marked social contrast, however.

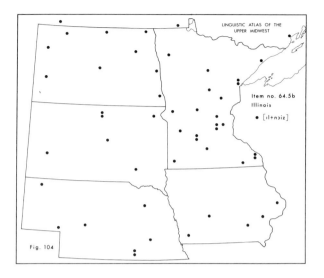

Fig. 104

	Mn.	Ia.	N.D.	S.D.	Nb.	Ave.
[ə]	35%	57%	31%	50%	100%	54%
[ɨ]	46%	33%	46%	46%	0	35%
[ɪ]	20%	4%	23%	4%	0	11%
[∅]	1%	8%	0	0	0	2%

Ohio 64.6a.

The pronunciation /oˈhai-o/ is used by nearly three-fourths of the UM infs. including the four with initial [ə]. A slight but consistent regional pattern is evident in the distribution of the initial and final vowels. For instance, the form /oˈhai-o/ seems to have a slight Midland weighting; /əˈhai-o/ is Northern. The variant /oˈhai-ə/, with final schwa, is apparently declining; it is rare in the more recently settled western half of the UM.

	Mn.	Ia.	N.D.	S.D.	Nb.	Ave.
/oˈhai-o/	68%	81%	63%	84%	89%	72%
/oˈhai-ə/	15%	16%	4%	0	5%	11%
/əˈhai-o/	17%	0	33%	9%	3%	12%
/əˈhai-ə/	0	2%	0	4%	3%	2%

Dakota 64.6b.

Because points on the articulatory range from a weakly aspirated [t'] to the almost negligible tap [ɾ] were not uniformly treated by the several fws., an adequate appraisal of the distribution of variants cannot be made. Fieldworkers P and Wr tend to write only [t] where the voice recordings clearly have [ɾ]; fw. M writes only [ṭ]. Fieldworker A's early records generally have [ṱ] for a consonant he later transcribes as [ɾ]. A fair generalization is that without regional contrast nearly all UM infs. have for poststress intervocalic /t/ in Dakota a

lenis rapidly articulated [ṱ] or [ɾ]. Only seven infs. are reported as having a clear [t]: 3; 46, 52, 64; 401, 404, 411.

Infrequent variation from the usual final /ə/ occurs for seven Midland-oriented speakers (113-14, 146-47; c225; c317, c322), who have the form /dəˈkoti/, and with two infs. (c44; c102), who have a distinct final [ɚ].

New York 64.7a. NE 11.

Lexical variants of this item appear in Volume 1.

Variations in the pronunciation of the vowels are essentially those described in this volume in the treatment of new (p. 306) and in the discussion of vowels followed by /r/. New typically is /nu/ and York is typically /jɔrk/ or /jɒrk/. Two Iowa infs. (115 with [ɚ] and c119 with [eˇ]) have an unround vowel. Unlike the situation in the eastern states there is only one instance of the absence of postvocalic /r/, [jɔək], in the speech of Iowa inf. 130.

The word York typically carries primary stress in each of the lexical variants: New York, New York State, State of New York, and York State, with only a few exceptions noted by the fws. In New York there is primary stress on New for infs. 56-58 and 419 and even stress on each word for infs. 32, 39, 43-45, and 52, but this transcription may be a fw.'s idiosyncrasy. In New York State the primary stress is on State for infs. 7, 29; 211, 217, 219, 221; 301, 328; 401, 425, 437, and on New for one inf., 48.

Pennsylvania 64.7b.

The noted variants in the pronunciation of Pennsylvania apparently have geographical contrast, although one or two of them may have been transcribed idiosyncratically by fws.

The vowel of -syl- is recorded as [ɨ] or, rarely, as [ɪˇ] by two-thirds of the UM infs. but with a markedly higher frequency in the Northern speech sector. Conversely, [ə] is more frequent in the Midland sector.

Fieldworker M records the medial syllable only as [sɪ]. Fieldworker G records five instances of metathesis as [slə] [slɨ], in the speech of infs. 16, 43-45, and 52. Three fws. record this syllable as [sə] or [s+] with omission of [ɪ] in the speech of the following: 32, 37, 39, 46-47, 55, 59, 62-63; 147; 218.

	Mn.	Ia.	N.D.	S.D.	Nb.	Ave.
/s+l/	74%	53%	96%	81%	56%	69%
/səl/	17%	48%	4%	19%	44%	28%

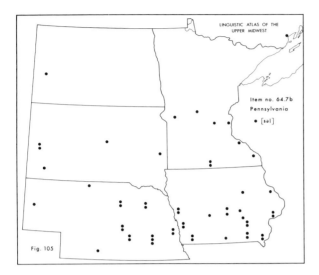

The final syllable is generally [jə], but it has two minor variants. For some speakers, mostly in Northern territory, it becomes two syllables, with [i‑ə] or [ijə]. They are infs. 4‑5, 7, 10, 24, 26‑27, 31, 45, 50, 53‑55, 65; 140‑41; 204, 207, 224; 301, 310, 316. For others, largely in Midland territory, it is either [ji] as with infs. 47 and 109 or, more frequently, simply [i], as with infs. 59; 113‑14, 135, 143, 146; c311, c322; 402, 422, 429.

Iowa 64.8a.

In addition to such typical variation in the initial diphthong as is considered in the treatment of /aɪ/ in Chapter 2, the pronunciation of Iowa exhibits special contrasts with respect to the two other vowels as well.

The medial /o/ ranges from a full [o] to [ə]. Although the regional average places [ə] in a slight majority, its frequency in Iowa itself is much higher, a frequency supported by the voice recordings. Nine infs.—four each in Minnesota and Iowa and one in South Dakota—have dropped the medial vowel completely in their pronunciation [aɪwə]. Retention of /o/ quality is strongest in Minnesota and Nebraska. There is no contrast among the three inf. types.

	Mn.	Ia.	N.D.	S.D.	Nb.	Ave.
/o/	68%	23%	31%	46%	56%	47%
/ə/	25%	70%	69%	54%	73%	54%

Although one-third of the UM infs. cling to the historical pronunciation of Iowa with final /e/ that bears secondary stress, this variant is clearly moving toward obsolescence, probably through the influence of the spelling. Had this Algonkian name first been transliterated as Ioway, the original vowel almost surely would have been preserved. Compare, for example, the replacement of /e/ by /ə/ in Chippewa but its retention in Ojibway, the Canadian version of the same word.

As it is, however, only one-half of the oldest infs. have this pronunciation, and only one-fifth of the middle-aged group. Not one of the Type III speakers keeps this form. It is somewhat curious that /ˈaɪəˌwe/ is actually most frequent in South Dakota and not in Iowa.

	Type I	Type II	Type III
/ˈaɪəˌwe/	51%	19%	0
/ˈaɪəwə/	52%	85%	100%

	Mn.	Ia.	N.D.	S.D.	Nb.	Ave.
/ˈaɪəˌwe/	23%	34%	36%	52%	34%	33%
/ˈaɪəwə/	78%	70%	64%	48%	69%	68%

Minnesota 64.8b.

The pronunciation of this atlas's home state is typically /ˌmɪnəˈsotɑ/, with three variables. One variable /t/ has essentially the same allophonic distribution of [t], [t̪], and [ɾ] as is described for the /t/ in Dakota above. A second variable, the weak medial vowel, occurs dominantly as schwa /ə/ in Midland-oriented areas but in Minnesota and North Dakota as a high-front vowel ranging from /ɪ/ to [i˔] or as lower high-central [ɨ].

This contrast is consistent with that discussed in the treatment of the reduction vowel, p. 290. No social contrasts appear.

	Mn.	Ia.	N.D.	S.D.	Nb.	Ave.
/ə/	32%	75%	40%	79%	94%	64%
/ɪ/	34%	6%	40%	4%	0	18%
/ɨ/	37%	18%	20%	18%	6%	22%

The third variable, the final vowel, is uniformly /ə/ except in the speech of five informants, four of whom are in Midland speech territory: 114, 135, 146; c225; 317. They have a final /i/.

Wisconsin 65.1a.

Wisconsin is typically pronounced as /wɪsˈkɑnsɪn/ without regionally or socially significant variation. The vowel of the first syllable ranges idiosyncratically from [ɪ] to [ɨ] and, less often, to [ə], with frequent slight rounding induced by the preceding /w/. The vowel of the second syllable is uniformly /ɑ/ except for the incidence of a low-back rounded /ɔ/ or /ɒ/ in the speech of the following infs.: 14, 56; 129, 143; 306, 308, 317. The vowel of the third syllable

ranges from the usual /ɨ/ to the less
common [ə].

Canada   65.1b.

Canada is typically pronounced as
/ˈkænədə/. Like the medial vowel in Illinois and Minnesota, that in Canada has a
raised allophonic variant, [ɨ], or, infrequently, [ɪˀ], likely to be heard in
Northern speech territory. One inf., 144,
has [ˈkæn:də].

	Mn.	Ia.	N.D.	S.D.	Nb.	Ave.
[ə]	67%	98%	81%	79%	97%	82%
[ɨ]	34%	2%	19%	21%	3%	18%

A minor variant of the final vowel is
/i/, which is chiefly restricted to the
speech of certain infs. with a Midland
background: 59; c107, 113-14, 132, 146;
220; 301, 303, 311, 316-17, 322; 429,
434.

Nebraska   65.1c.

Nebraska is almost uniformly pronounced
/nəˈbræskə/. The only distinctive variation is in the final syllable, where 10
Midland-oriented infs. have /i/: c114,
135, c138, 146, 148; 311, 322; 417, c429,
432. All but inf. 138 are in Type I. Some
nonsignificant variation occurs in the
initial syllable where the vowel is transcribed rarely as [uˤ] 148-49; [ɛˀ] 203-
4; 328; c402, c408, 417; [ɨ] 305-6, 316-
19, 327; 431; [ɪˀ] cvr413, 415, 420, 426,
432; and [ɜˤ] c419. Fieldworker A tends
to transcribe /r/ as the retroflex flap
[ɾ].

Missouri   65.1d. NE 17.

The two conspicuous pronunciations of
Missouri, /mɪˈzuri/ and /mɪˈzurə/, are
evenly matched for the UM as a whole but
reveal clear social and geographical contrast within the region. The variant with
final /i/ is somewhat preferred by the
more highly educated and by the infs. in
Northern speech territory and, as a
spelling pronunciation, is thus quite
different from the final /i/ used by some
Midland speakers in Iowa, Dakota, Canada,
and the like.

	Type I	Type II	Type III
/i/	47%	54%	64%
/ə/	54%	48%	36%

	Mn.	Ia.	N.D.	S.D.	Nb.	Ave.
/i/	83%	37%	79%	54%	45%	51%
/ə/	17%	65%	21%	46%	58%	50%

/i/ 29-31, 36, 38; 102, 105-6, 108-9,
c113, 114, 121, 126, 128, 131, 134-35,
c138, c140, 143-44, 146, 151; 202-11,

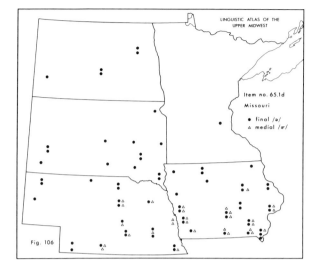

LINGUISTIC ATLAS OF THE
UPPER MIDWEST

Item no. 65.1d

Missouri

● final /ə/
△ medial /ɚ/

Fig. 106

c219, 220-26; 301, c302, 303-6, 308,
c309-10, 311, 315, c317, 319, c322, 326;
c404, 407-8, c410, 411-12, 415, 417-19,
421, c423, c425, c427, 428.
    /ə/ 35; 101, 103-4, c107, 110-12, 115-
17, 119-20, 122-25, 127, 129-30, vr131,
132, c133, 136-37, 139, c140, 141-42,
145, 147-50; 212-13, c214, c216, 217;
307, c312-14, 316, 318, c320, 321, 323-
25; c401-2, 403, 405-6, 409, 413-14, 416,
420, 422-24, 426, c429, 431, 434-35, 437.

An apparently significant minor variable is the vowel of the first syllable,
which is usually some variety of /ɪ/ or
/ɨ/ but which is an allophone of /ə/ for
30 infs. in southern Iowa, and five in
Nebraska but for only one speaker elsewhere, in North Dakota. This disparity
may be exaggerated by the practice of the
two fws., H and Wr, who tend to write
[ə].

Perhaps another significant variable is
the vowel of the stressed syllable, but
again the variation is suspect as the
transcription practice of fws. H and Wr,
who generally write [ɚ] for the usual
/ur/.

A once-taught spelling pronunciation
with medial /s/ survives in the speech of
Type II infs. 203 and 430 and perhaps, as
[ʒ], in the speech of Type I infs. 206
and 207. This is in sharp contrast with
the New England situation. There, this
state name, relatively unfamiliar, has
voiceless medial /s/ in the speech of
about 35% of all infs.

Chicago   65.2a.

There are two widespread pronunciations
of Chicago, one with a medial stressed
unround vowel occurring as [ɑ] or [ɔ] and

one with rounded [ɔ] or, more commonly,
[ɒ]. They exist in a 1:2 ratio in the UM,
with an apparent slight Northern weighting for the unround vowel. It seems also
to be more acceptable to Type III speakers.

	Type I	Type II	Type III
[a, ɑ˞]	32%	29%	56%
[ɔ, ɒ]	69%	71%	44%

	Mn.	Ia.	N.D.	S.D.	Nb.	Ave.
[a, ɑ˞]	45%	22%	35%	31%	28%	32%
[ɔ, ɒ]	58%	78%	65%	73%	72%	68%

The final syllable also provides a contrast. The general pattern with some allophones of /o/ is broken in the speech
of 14 infs. by the appearance of /ə/, all
but one of whom are in Midland speech
territory, principally Iowa and Nebraska:
109, 117, 126, 135, 139, 142, 148; 207;
317, 319; 416, 423-24, 434.

Another minor variable is evident in
the uncommon use of the affricate /č/ instead of /š/ as the initial consonant.
This pronunciation is offered by the following infs.: 8, 45, 52; 146; 415.

St. Paul 65.2b.

St. Paul is typically pronounced [ˌsɛ̃nt
ˈpɔɫ], with minor variants offered by
only a few infs.

An expected major contrast between
rounding and unrounding of the vowel in
Paul is prevented by the rounding effect
of the bilabial /p/. Only three infs. are
actually recorded as having an unround
[ɑ˞]—c29; 102, 104. More than two-thirds
of all the others have the fully rounded
/ɔ/, generally as [ɔˇ]; nearly all the
remainder have /ɒ/, often as [ɒˬ]. Three
have /ɑʊ/: infs. 48, 56-57.

	Mn.	Ia.	N.D.	S.D.	Nb.	Ave.
[ɔ]	66%	72%	65%	64%	79%	65%
[ɒ]	28%	24%	35%	36%	21%	32%

For twelve scattered infs. Saint, under
no more than secondary stress, lacks the
/t/, as in /ˌsɛn ˈpɔl/: 19, c36, 38; 129,
135, 142; 306-7, 316-17; 416, 425. For
three infs. Saint carries primary stress:
30, 52; 320; and fw. G records six infs.
with even stress on the two words: 39,
43, c44, 45-47. Three Iowans are recorded
with /sæn/ for Saint, and a Canadian has
a British variant in /sɪnt/. Fieldworker
Wr records several infs. with a glottal
stop instead of [t], as in the curious
[seɪŋ?], 426.

Des Moines 65.2c.

Des Moines, characteristically pro-

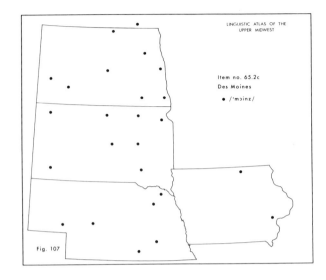

LINGUISTIC ATLAS OF THE
UPPER MIDWEST

Item no. 65.2c
Des Moines

• /ˈmɔɪnz/

Fig. 107

nounced /dɛ ˈmɔɪn/ by four out of five
UM speakers, has a spelling-induced variant, /dɛ ˈmɔɪnz/, fairly common among the
noncollege infs. in Minnesota and North
Dakota. Spelling exerts its full influence on one Canadian with his pronunciation /dɛs ˈmɔɪnz/.

	Type I	Type II	Type III
/dɛ ˈmɔɪn/	75%	79%	100%
/dɛ ˈmɔɪnz/	25%	19%	0

	Mn.	Ia.	N.D.	S.D.	Nb.	Ave.
/dɛ ˈmɔɪn/	33%	96%	61%	65%	83%	79%
/dɛ ˈmɔɪnz/	67%	4%	35%	32%	17%	20%

The data for Minnesota are inadequate,
however, since this item was not queried
there until near the end of the fieldwork.

The vowel of Des varies nonsignificant-
ly from [ɛ] to [ɪˇ] and [ɨ]. The stressed
vowel is typically [ɔɪˬ] or [ɒˬɪˬ].

/dɛ ˈmɔɪn/ 29, 38; 101-4, 106-17, 119-
36, 138-39, 141-50; 203, 205, 207-11,
216, 218-19, 221-23, 225; 302-3, 309-13,
317-19, 321-22, 324-26; 401-7, 409-14,
416, 419-24, 426-29, 431, 433-35, 437.

/dɛ ˈmɔɪnz/ 30-31, 35-36; 105, 137;
204, 213-15, 217, 220, 224; 301, 304,
306, 308, 315-16, 320, 323; 408, 415,
417-18, 425, 432.

Detroit 65.3a.

An anticipated major contrast in pronunciations of Detroit turned out to be
insignificant. All but eight of the UM
infs. stress the second syllable. Of
these eight, three Midland-oriented
speakers stress the first syllable:
/ˈdiˌtrɔɪt/ (121; 328; c404). Five Minne-

sota speakers are recorded with even stress (18, 47-48, 60, 62).

All but three infs. have a low-back beginning for the stressed diphthong, five out of six with allophones of [ɔɪ], and one-sixth with varieties of [ɒɪ]. Since most of the latter were transcribed by fw. A, the distinction may be idiosyncratic. Three infs., 14; 146; 308, have a mid-beginning with [oɪ].

All but five infs. have a distinctive vowel in the weakly stressed initial syllable ranging from [ɪ˙] to [ɪ] and, infrequently, centralized to [ɨ]. No social contrast appears, but a likely regional contrast is evident in the fact that of the 17 infs. with [ɨ] all except four in Minnesota are in Midland speech territory: 15-16, 36, 58; 106, 115, 130; 308, 320, 327; 416, 423-25, 427, 434-35. One inf., 220, has [ɛ˙]. The five with nondistinctive schwa, [ə], are all in Midland territory: 141, 143, 157; 305, 307. Clearly, centralizing is a Midland characteristic here.

In Detroit the consonant /r/ is usually a fricative [ɹ], often with a voiceless onset [ɹ̥], but this feature is not recorded by fws. H, P, and Wn, who write only /r/. No significant contrasts appear.

Duluth 65.3b.

The two principal variants of the pronunciation of Duluth exhibit a contrast between rounding and lack of rounding in the vowel of the first syllable, i.e., between /dʊˈluθ/ and /dəˈluθ/. The former is dominant in Minnesota, the latter elsewhere. A third variant, with raising or fronting of the vowel to /ɨ/, /ɪ/, or even a rare /i/, is widely distributed but is strongest in Iowa, possibly because of fw. variation. No social contrasts appear. Five infs. have quite lost the weak vowel with their pronunciation /dluθ/—16; 213; 322; 416, 435.

	Mn.	Ia.	N.D.	S.D.	Nb.	Ave.
/ɪ/	18%	51%	28%	19%	19%	28%
/ə/	26%	34%	44%	45%	41%	35%
/ʊ/	57%	14%	24%	33%	33%	33%

/ɪ/ [i] 45; s107, 119-20. [ɪ] 31, 46, 49; 101-2, 111, 113, 125, 132, 134-38, 142-43, 146; 204-5, 210-11, 218-19; 303, 309-11. [ɨ] 26, 48, 53, 56, 60; 109-10, 115-17, 123, 128, 145; 203; 304; 412-13, 424, 426, 431. [ɤ] 11-12.

/ə/ c6, c10, c13, 17-18, 21, 25, 30, c35, 38, 43, 49, 51-52, 54, 63; 103, 105, 112, 114, 120, 122, 124, 127, 129-30, 133, 140-41, 147-50; 208-9, 214-15, 217, 221-26; 301-2, 305, 307-8, 312, 316-17,

319, 323-25; 402, 409-10, 414, 417, 421-22, c423, 428-29, 434.

/ʊ/ [ʉ] 65; 121; 403. [ʊ] 1-3, c4, 5, 8, c9, c19, 20, 23-24, 27-29, 32-34, c36, 37, 40-42, 44, 50, 55, 59, 61-62, 64; 104, 106, 108, 144; 201, 206-7, 212, c216, 220; 306, 313-15, 320, 326, 328; 401, 404, 406, 408, 411, 418-19, 437. [ʉ] 14-15; 57; 126. [u] 7, 39, 58; 131; 321.

Omaha 65.3c.

Omaha occurs with a range of variables in the final syllable under secondary stress, ranging from /ˈoməha/, with no rounding, to /ˈoməhɔ/, with full rounding. More than two-thirds of the UM informants have some degree of rounding in the final vowel. They are about evenly divided between those with a variety of /ɒ/ (40%) and those with various allophones of /ɔ/ (30%). Minnesota has none with /ɔ/, however. The infs. with an unround vowel are split between those with /ɑ/ (16%) and those with /ɚ/ (13%).

	Type I	Type II	Type III
/ɒ - ɔ/	27%	29%	45%
/ɑ - ɚ/	72%	71%	55%

	Mn.	Ia.	N.D.	S.D.	Nb.	Ave.
/ɒ - ɔ/	33%	18%	33%	46%	31%	30%
/ɑ - ɚ/	67%	82%	67%	54%	69%	70%

Minneapolis 65.4a.

Two main pronunciations of Minneapolis occur, one with full five syllables /ˌmɪniˈæpəlɪs/ and one with only four /ˌmɪniˈæplɪs/. Even with an allowance for fw. variation, it seems clear that the former is Midland-oriented and the second is Northern-oriented.

	Mn.	Ia.	N.D.	S.D.	Nb.	Ave.
/-pəlɪs/	23%	53%	27%	39%	68%	41%
/-plɪs/	71%	43%	73%	61%	26%	55%

In the four-syllable form the /l/ of /plɪs/ generally has a voiceless onset and frequently occurs as a flap [ɺ]. A minor variation appears when the /l/ is lengthened so as to yield the impression of a syllabic [l̩] followed by a glide. Other minor and nonsignificant variations occur. Some speakers in the Midland area have a strong linking palatal glide [j] as in [ˌmɪniˈjæpəlɪs]. Three infs. (135; 429, 432) have /ɑ/ as the stressed vowel instead of /æ/. Rhetorical primary stress sometimes is placed on the primary syllable.

Washington 65.4b.

In the UM, Washington, the name of the nation's capital, is generally pronounced

/ˈwɔš+ŋtən/. There are, however, three minor variables—the extent of rounding of the first vowel, retroflexion in the initial syllable, and the medial nasal.

The situation with respect to rounding is much like that in wash (see p. 262), except that the unrounded /ɑ/ or /ɑ˞/ has a slightly greater spread with occurrences in North Dakota. But the rounded /ɔ/ or /ɒ/ is everywhere dominant in a ratio of approximately 7:1. For two Iowa infs. the unrounded vowel has a noticeable offglide—[weᶦʃ] 119 and [wɑ˞ᶦʃ] 132.

Although sometimes mildly ridiculed by persons esthetically insensitive to the acoustic charm of r-colored vowels, the pronunciation of Washington either with a strong /r/ following the vowel, e.g., [ɔr], or with a retroflex vowel, e.g., [ɔ˞], persists in the UM with a clear relationship to its incidence of occurrence in the eastern states. Sporadic in New York State in the word wash, retroflexion is common in western Pennsylvania.

Likewise in the UM retroflexion is sporadic in Minnesota but twice as frequent in Midland speech territory, i.e., in Iowa and Nebraska (see map). It continues also to be more likely to appear in the speech of the less educated: Type I 20%, II 15%, and III 6%.

A third variable, the medial nasal, offers a contrast between /ŋ/ and /n/. For at least five infs. the nasal has become assimilated to /n/ by the following /t/: 25, 32, 48, 63; 305.

	Mn.	Ia.	N.D.	S.D.	Nb.	Ave.
/ɑ - ɑ˞/	14%	12%	12%	11%	29%	14%
/ɔ - ɒ/	86%	88%	88%	89%	71%	86%

/ɑ - ɑ˞/ [ɑ] c10, 27, 29; c107, 119, vr131; 322-23; 411, 413, 421, 423, 428, 431, 433-34. [ɐ] 102, 119; 431. [ɑ˞] 1-2, 6, 30, 48, 58; 104, 147, 150; 202, 211, 214; 301; c419, 424.

/ɔ - ɒ/ [ɔ] c4, 5, 8-9, 11, 16, 19-26, 28, 31, 35-38, 40-41, 43-44, 49-50, 54, c59, 61, 64-65; 111, 113, 116-17, 120-22, 124-30, 134-36, 138-39, 141-42, 145-46, 148-49, c152; c201, 203-5, 218, 220-21, 223, 226; 302, 304-7, 309, c311, c313, c316, 317, 319-21, 325, 327-28; 401, c402, 403-4, 406, 409, 412, 416, 420, 422, 425, 432, 435. [ɒ] 12-13, 15, 17-18, 32-34, 39, 42, 45-47, 51-53, c55, 56-57, 60, 62-63; 101, 103, 105-6, 108-10, 112, 114, vr115, 123, 132-33, 137, 140, 143-44; 206-9, c210, 212-13, 215-16, c217, 219, c224, 225; 303, 308, 312, 314-15, 317, 324, 326; 405, 407-8, 410, 414-15, 417-18, 426-27, 429, 437. [β] 14.

	Type I	Type II	Type III
/ɔr/	20%	15%	6%

	Mn.	Ia.	N.D.	S.D.	Nb.	Ave.
/ɔr/	11%	22%	0	18%	31%	17%

/ɔr/ [ɔr - ɒr] c4, 19-22, 25, 64; 112-14, vr115, 116, 138-39; 306-7, 317, 319; 402, 408, 429. [ɔ˞ - ɒ˞] 101, 109, 111, 133; 325; 403, 405, 409, 415-16, 420, 433, 437.

Stream Names

After distinguishing semantic differences among stream, brook, creek, and river (24.5), each inf. was asked for the names of nearby streams. Of the many names recorded only those of special phonological or lexical interest can be given here. These include names of Indian origin and terms whose pronunciation might reflect a regional pattern. Such names as Cedar Creek, Long Creek, Mud Creek, Rapid Creek, Smith Creek, Spring Creek, and Willow Branch are not included. (B = brook; C = creek; R = river.)

When stress is indicated in the transcription, a primary stress symbol ['] is to be taken as implying that the absent generic brook, creek, or river has secondary stress. If only a secondary stress symbol [ˌ] appears in the specific name,

the implication is that the generic has primary stress. It is to be noted, however, that within the whole term, such as Roseau River, the stress pattern may sometimes be reversed by the demand of rhetorical emphasis.

Inf.
no.

Minnesota

2 Frog C [frɒg].

3 Six Mile C [sɪks maˀɫl].

4 Roseau R [ˈrozoˬ].

6 Cascade R [ˌkæˀsˈkeᵗˇd]; Devil's Track R [ˌdɛvəlz ˈtræ·ᵗk]; Pigeon R [ˈpɪdʒn̩]; Skadans C [skaˈdɑns].

7 Barnham C ['bɑrnhəm]; Gentilly C
   ['ʤɛntlɪ^]; Marais R [mə're>e^].

11 Ball Club C ['bɔl ˌklʌb].

12 Forest C ['fɔ^r+st]; Shoal B [ʃo·ɫ].

13 Burnside R ['bɜ^ən̩ˌsɑ·ɫd]; Harris C
   ['hɛ̥ˇr+s].

14 Mississippi R [ˌmɪ>sə'sɪp+]; Sand
   Lake C ['sæn ˌleˇ+k].

15 Talmadge C [ˌtælm+ʤ].

16 Coffee C ['kɒˤəf+ˤ]; Nemadgi C
   [nə'mɑ̯ədʒ+ˤ].

17 Cloquet R [kɫo̯ˤuˤˌkeˇ+]; Moosehorn R
   ['muˇu̯ˤs ˌhɔ^ən]; Otter C [ˌɑ>tə˞];
   St. Louis R ['seˇ+nt ˌɫ̯ʉ̯+s].

18 Coffee C ['kɒf+ɔ̂]; St. Louis R
   ['seˇ+nt ˌɫʉuˤ+s]

19 Otter Tail R [ɑ>tə˞ te+l].

21 Mayo B ['meoˤ].

22 Nokassippi C [ˌnokə'sɪpi>].

23 Snowshoe B ['snoʃuˇ].

24 Bogus B [bogəs]; Rice C [reˤɪs].

25 Pomme de Terre R [ˌpɑmdə 'tɛrɪ^].

26 Mastinka R [məs'tɪŋkə]; Pomme de
   Terre R ['pɑmədi> ˌtɛr]; Whetstone
   R ['hwɛtˌstoˤn].

28 Hoboken C ['hoˌbok+n].

29 Rum R [rʌm].

30 Clearwater R ['kɫ̯ɪ˞ˌwɑ>tə˞].

31 Minnehaha C [ˌmɪn+'hɑhə].

32 Minnehaha C [ˌmɪni>'hɑhə].

33 Minnehaha C [ˌmɪnɪ^hɑhɑ^].

41 Dry Weather C [dɹɑ>i> wɛð˞].

42 Dry Weather C [dɹɑɪ̂ wɛð˞]; Hawk C
   [hɔˇk].

47 Yellow Medicine R ['jɛlŏˤ
   ˌmɛd+sĭ>n].

48 Waterfall C ['wɑ̯t̯˞fɑl].

51 Minneopa C [mɪni>opə]; Winneshiek C
   ['wɪnɪ>ʃi>ik].

53 Cobb R ['kɑb]; Minneopa C
   ['mɪni-'opə].

54 Bullard's C [bʊlɚdz]; Trout B
   [trɑˤʊt].

56 Root R ['rut]; Whitewater R
   [hwɛɪtwɒt̯˞].

59 Des Moines R [dɛ̆>'mɔ+n].

60 Whiskey C ['hwɪskiˇ].

61 Kanaranzi C ['kænə'rænzi>].

62 Bancroft C ['bænkrɔft].

63 Bancroft C ['bænkrɔft].

64 Root R [rʊt].

65 Root R [ruˇᵘt].

Iowa

102 Kanaranzi C [ˌkænə'rænziˇ].

103 Des Moines R [dɪ^ 'mɔɪ^n].

104 Des Moines R [dɪ> 'mɔɪ^n].

107 Iowa R ['ɑɪ^oˌwiˇ].

108 Trout R [trɑɤt].

109 Broken Kettle ['broᵘk+n ˌkɛt+l];
    Missouri R [mə'zʊriˇ].

110 Missouri R [mɪ'zʊrə].

111 Missouri R [mɪ>'zʊrə].

112 Des Moines [də ˌmɔɪ^n].

113 Little Jesus C [ˌlɪt+l 'ʤiz+s].

118 Black Hawk C [blæ·k hɔˇ·k]; Iowa R
    ['ɑ+ˇə>wə].

120 Whitewater C [ʍwɑɪ^t wɑt˞].

124 Indian C ['ɪnʤ ən].

125 Boyer C ['bʊjɚ]. Inf. says outsiders
    call it ['bɔɪjɚ].

126 Indian C [ɪndɪ^ən].

131 Walnut C ['wɑlnʌt].

132 Iowa R [ɑˤɪ^-oweɪ^].

137 Wapsipinikin [ˌwɑpsɪ^pɪnɪ^k+n].

139 Maquoketa R [mə'koᵘkətə].

141 Mississippi R [mɪssəsɪpi].

142 Nodaway C [nʌdəweˤɪ].

146 Fox C [fɒks].

147 Wakanda [wə'kɑ^ndə].

148 Des Moines R [də mɔɪn]:

151 Baughman Branch [bɔˇ·fmən]; Nishna-
    botna R [nɪʃn+^'bɑᵓtn+]; Walnut C
    [wɒ^ɫnət].

152 Raulston C [rɒɫstən].

North Dakota

201 Souris R ['sʊrɪ>s].

202 Pembina R ['pɛmb+nə].

204 Souris R ['sʊrɪ>s].

206 Tongue R [tɐŋ].

207 Pembina R ['pɛmbɨnə]; Tongue R
    [tʌŋ].

208 Pembina R [ˈpɛmbɨnə]; Tongue R [tʌŋ].

209 Missouri R [mɪˈzuriˇ].

212 Sheyenne R [ˌʃaɪˢˈæˆn].

214 Wanigan C [ˈwɑnɪˀgən]; Little Missouri R [m+ˈzurə].

215 Chanta Peta C [ˈʃænt̮əˆ ˌpiˢdə].

218 Seven Mile Coulee [ˈsɛvn̩ meˇɪˀl ˌku·liˇ].

219 Pipestem R [ˈpaɪˀpstɛm].

220 Elm R [ɛlð̃ˆm]; Ottertail R [ˈɑtɚtel]; Sheyenne R [ˌʃaɪ-ˈæˇn].

222 Sheyenne R [ˌʃeˢɪˢ-ˈɛˢn]; Wild Rice R [waˀɪˀld räˀɪˢs].

225 Bois des Sioux R [bwɔˇ də suˢ]; Mustinka R [məˈstɪŋkə]; Whiskey C [hwɪskiˇ].

226 Bois des Sioux R [ˌbɔɪ də ˈsu:].

South Dakota

301 Big Nasty C [bɪg næstiˢ].

303 Missouri R [mɪˈzuriˢ].

305 Moccasin C [ˈmãkəsɪn].

306 Elm R [ɛlm]; Moccasin C [ˈmɔgəs+n].

309 Deadwood C [ˈdɛdwud]; Elk C [ɛlk]; Gold Run C [ˈgold ˌrʌn]; Spearfish C [ˈspɪˀrfɪʃ].

312 Blackhawk C [blækhɔˢk]; Dead Man's C [ˈdɛd ˌmænz]; Newton Fork [nutəˆn foˢərk].

313 Bad R [bæ·d]; Dead Man C [ˈdɛd ˌmæn]; Dirty Woman C [dɚtiˢ ˈwumən]; Mexican C [ˈmɛksɪˀkəˆn].

314 Missouri R [m+ˈzurəˆ]; Sheyenne R [ˈʃaɪˆ-æˆn].

315 Chappelle C [ʃəˈpɛl].

316 Missouri R [m+ˈzori].

317 College C [ˈkɔˢlɪʤ]; Medary C [mɛˈdɛri]; Sioux R [su·].

318 College C [ˈkɑlɪʤ]; Sioux R [su·].

319 College C [ˈkɑlɪʤ]; Sioux R [su·].

320 Alkali C [ˈælkəˌlaˀɪˢ]; Elm C [ɛlm]; Fall R [ˈfɔl].

321 Bad R [bæd]; Keyapaha R [ˈkiˇjəpəˌhʊ]; White R [ʰwaˢɪˆt].

323 Choteau C [ˈʃo̞t̮ə]; Missouri R [mɪˢzurə].

328 Rock C [rɑk].

Nebraska

401 Chadron C [ˈʃædrən]; Dead Horse C [ˈdɛd ˌhɔɚs]; White Clay C [ˈhwaˀɪˆt ˈkl̥eˇeˆ].

402 Niobrara R [naɪoˢbrɛrə].

403 Minichaduza [ˌmɛnɪˢkəˈduzə]; Niobrara [ˌnaɪˢəˈbrɛrə].

404 Middle Loup R [lup]; Minichaduza R [ˌmɪniˇkəˈduzə]; Niobrara R [ˌnaɪoˢ ˈbrɛˇrə]; Schlegel C [ˈʃl̥egəˆl].

405 Long Pine C [lɔŋ paˀɪˆn].

407 Bow Valley C [ˌbo ˈvæliˇ]; East Bow C [boºˢ].

409 Horse C [hɔɚs]; Kiowa C [ˈkaɪˆoˢwɡˢ]; Lodge Pole C [ˈlɑʤ pol]; Pumpkin [ˈpʌŋk+n]; Rawhide C [ˈrɔhaˀɪˆd]; Spotted Tail [ˌspɑt+d ˈte+l].

410 Pumpkin C [ˈpʌmpkɪˀn].

411 Nine Mile C [ˈnaˢɪˢn maɪˢl]; Squaw C [skwɔ].

412 Calf C [kæˢf]; Loup R [lup].

415 Norfolk C [ˌnɔɚfɔɚk].

417 Lodge Pole C [ˈlɑʤ poˢl].

418 White Horse C [ˈhwaˢɪˆt hɔˇɚs].

419 White Horse C [ˈhwaɪt ˌhɔɚs].

425 Antelope C [ˈæntəˌloup]; Haynes Branch [ˈheɪnz ˈbræntʃ]; Salt C [ˈsɔlt].

426 Haynes Branch [ˈheɪnz bræntʃ]; Salt C [sɔlt].

427 Rawhide C [rɔʰaɪd].

428 Little Papillion [ˈpæpˀoᵘ].

429 Indian C [ˌɪndj+n]; Rock C [rɑk]; South Fork [sɑˢoˢˆθ].

434 Porter Branch [ˈpɔɚtɚ]; Whiskey Run [ˈhwɪˢsk+ ˈrʌˆn].

436 Lodge Pole C [ˈlɑʤ pol]; Lost C [lɒ·st].

437 Burnt Wood C [ˈbɚntwud]; Indian C [ˈɪndĩjən]; Rock C [rɑk].

Indexes

To facilitate reference the index has been subdivided so as to set off from the usual index list of names and topics the two special phonetic and lexical categories.

Since in Volume 3 there is a running comparison of Upper Midwest data with the materials of the eastern surveys, there have been omitted from the names and topics index the numerous references and allusions to the model work, *The Pronunciation of English in the Atlantic States*, and to its authors, Hans Kurath and Raven I. McDavid, Jr., when cited as authors, and to the states and dialect regions treated in that work.

The list of phones and phonemes is not intended to be exhaustive. It includes the treatments of the various sounds and the principal variants of each considered vowel but it does not indicate all minor variants. Virgules and brackets are omitted.

An asterisk * by a page number in the word index signifies that the item is illustrated in the text by an accompanying map.

Indexes

Names and Topics

Phones and Phonemes

Words